BEYOND TOP SECRET

Other books by Timothy Good

Alien Liaison: The Ultimate Secret

Revised US Edition:
Alien Contact: Top-Secret UFO Files Revealed

Alien Update

The UFO Report

BEYOND
TOP SECRET

The Worldwide UFO Security Threat

With a Foreword by

Admiral of the Fleet

The Lord Hill-Norton GCB

Timothy Good

Sidgwick & Jackson

First published 1996 by Sidgwick & Jackson

an imprint of Macmillan Publishers Ltd
25 Eccleston Place, London SW1W 9NF
and Basingstoke

Associated companies throughout the world

ISBN 0 283 06245 2

3 5 7 9 8 6 4 2

A CIP catalogue record for this book is available from
the British Library

Photoset by Parker Typesetting Service, Leicester
Printed and bound in Great Britain by
Mackays of Chatham plc, Chatham, Kent

To Leonard Stringfield (1920–1994)

Contents

Contents

Part Three

The United States

Acknowledgements

IT WOULD BE impracticable to acknowledge here all those who have contributed either directly or indirectly to the production of this book, but I would like to record my thanks in particular to the following individuals and organizations:

Walter Andrus and the Mutual UFO Network; Shlomo Arnon; The Australian Department of Transport; Vicente-Juan Ballester Olmos; The Australian Centre for UFO Studies; Leslie Banks DFC, AFC; Juan José Benítez; John Berry; Graham and Mark Birdsall of Quest International; Tommy Blann; Bob Boyd and the Plymouth UFO Research Group; Joe Brill; Angus Brooks; Ty Brown; Grant Cameron; Glenn Campbell and *The Groom Lake Desert Rat*; The Canadian Department of Transport; Scott Carpenter; Jimmy Carter; Captain Bruce Cathie; Central Independent Television; The Central Intelligence Agency; Centro Italiano Studi Ufologici; Robert Chapman; Maurice Chatelain; The China UFO Research Organization; Citizens Against UFO Secrecy; The Civil Aviation Authority; Gordon Cooper; Timothy Cooper; Billy Cox; T. Scott Crain Jr; Leonard Cramp; Dr Robert Creegan; Denis Crowe; Stephen Darbishire; The Defense Intelligence Agency; Derek Dempster; Glenn Dennis; Robert Dorr; Hilary Evans and the Mary Evans Picture Library; Lucius Farish and the UFO Newsclipping Service; The Federal Aviation Administration; The Federal Bureau of Investigation; The Federal Counter-Intelligence Service (Russia); Raymond Fowler; The Fund for UFO Research; Marie Galbraith; Peter Gersten; Dr Jean Gille; Dr L. M. Gindilis; Barry Goldwater; Lee Graham; Patricia Grant; Selman Graves; Dr Pierre Guérin; Bill Gunston; Dr Richard Haines; Richard Hall; Colonel Charles Halt; *Hansard*; Dr James Harder; Harry Harris; HRH Prince Philip, the Duke of Edinburgh; Walter Haut; Her Majesty's Stationery Office; Michael Hesemann; The Trustees of the Imperial War Museum; Luciano Iorio; The Italian Air Force; The J. Allen Hynek Center for UFO Studies; Dr Robert Jacobs; Gregory Kanon; John Keel; Desmond Leslie; Ken Llewelyn; London Weekend Television; The *Los Angeles Times*; Dr Paul Lowman; James

McDivitt; Derek Mansell; Dr Jesse Marcel Jr; Victor Marchetti; The Ministry of Defence; Dr Edgar Mitchell; Lawrence Moore; The National Aeronautics & Space Administration; The National Military Command Center; The National Security Agency; Paul Norman and the Victorian UFO Research Society; The North American Aerospace Defense Command; Chuck Oldham; Paramount Pictures; Karl Pflock; Colin Phillips and UFO Research Queensland; Nick Pope; Popperfoto; André Previn; Colonel L. Fletcher Prouty; The Public Record Office; Kevin Randle & Donald Schmitt; Jenny Randles; Ron Regehr; Bruce Renton; Madeleine Rodeffer; The *Roswell Daily Record*; The Royal Air Force; The Royal Australian Air Force; The Royal New Zealand Air Force; Livia Russell; Roy and Pearl Russell; James Salandin; Eric Saunders; Congressman Steven Schiff; Captain Graham Sheppard; John Schuessler; William Sherwood; The Spanish Air Force; William Steinman; Clifford Stone; M. R. Sutton; Captain Kenju Terauchi; Robert Todd; Topham Picturepoint; Mollie Travis and the Trustees of the Broadlands Archives; Admiral Stansfield Turner; The US Departments of the Air Force, Army, Defense, Navy, and State; Guido Valentich; Jacques Vallée, Martine Castello, and Ballantine Books; Andreas von Rétyi; Fred Whiting, and F. H. C. Wimbledon.

I am especially indebted to Admiral of the Fleet The Lord Hill-Norton for his unswerving support, often in the face of ridicule from the press; William Armstrong of Sidgwick & Jackson, for accepting *Above Top Secret* (after it had been rejected by numerous publishers), and for commissioning *Beyond Top Secret*; Ray Boeche, for numerous documents he obtained from the Defense Intelligence Agency and for all his research material relating to the USAF Woodbridge/Bentwaters case; Arthur Bray, for Canadian Government documents and for material from his book, *The UFO Connection*; William Chalker, for numerous Australian reports; Ingrid Connell, until recently my editor at Sidgwick & Jackson, for her dedication and professionalism, as well as her patience in coping with my numerous amendments to the manuscript; Gordon Creighton, the indefatigable editor of *Flying Saucer Review*, for allowing me to take advantage of the wealth of information contained in this fine journal (established in 1955); Bob Davenport, for his excellent copy-editing; Paul Dong and Wendelle Stevens, for much information contained in their book, *UFOs Over Modern China*; Lawrence Fawcett and Barry Greenwood, for the use of much material from their ground-breaking book, *Clear Intent*; Stanton Friedman, for information published in his various papers and in his book, *Crash at Corona* (co-authored by Don Berliner); Nikolai Lebedev, for providing me with many reports he investigated in the former Soviet Union; Andrew Lownie, my agent, whose perspicacity led to the publication of *Above Top Secret*; William Moore, for sharing his vast knowledge with me over a long period, for providing me with numerous declassified intelligence documents, and for the use of information from his book, *The Roswell Incident* (co-authored by Charles Berlitz), and other publications; Ralph Noyes, for giving me so much of his time, providing me with a wealth of information about his experiences in the Ministry of Defence, trying unsuccessfully to interest various publishers in *Above Top Secret* – and also dealing with my word-processor problems; Nicholas Redfern, for several documents from the Defense Intelligence Agency and Public Records Office, and for additional information; Chris Rutkowski, for his articles on the Falcon Lake (Canada) case; Dr Berthold Schwarz, for generously allowing me to use the report given to him by an intelligence officer who was exposed to a recovered alien craft and bodies, published in his book, *UFO Dynamics*; Carey Smith, my current editor at Sidgwick & Jackson; Warren Smith, for lengthy extracts relating to CIA/UFO involvement contained in his book, *UFO Trek*; Dorothee Walter, for help with word-processing and translations; Larry Warren and Peter Robbins, for much co-operation on the USAF Woodbridge/Bentwaters case, and Todd Zechel, for a great deal of information relating to CIA/UFO involvement, published in various articles.

I am also indebted to those whose information is contained herein but who, since I wrote *Above Top Secret*, have passed on, especially Major Donald Keyhoe, to whom that book was dedicated; Coral and Jim Lorenzen of the former Aerial Phenomena Research Organization; Sid Padrick; and Leonard Stringfield, to whom this book is dedicated.

Finally, I must express my warmest gratitude to those who have helped but cannot be named.

Foreword

by Admiral of the Fleet
The Lord Hill-Norton GCB
Chief of the Defence Staff 1971–73
Chairman of the NATO Military Committee 1974–77

IN MY FOREWORD to Timothy Good's 1987 book *Above Top Secret*, I wrote '. . . Tim Good is one of the most thorough and best informed researchers into this arcane subject . . . and his book is based soundly upon fact, and a great deal of most convincing evidence . . .' The same can certainly be said for this, his latest offering. It is packed with a mass of new reports and evidence, emphasizing in a way which cannot be denied that the UFO phenomenon is a very real one, and one which now demands the closest attention.

I have frequently been asked why I am so keenly interested in UFOs, and there are several excellent reasons. The first is that the evidence is now so consistent and so overwhelming that no reasonably intelligent person can deny that something unexplained is going on in our atmosphere. I would like a serious attempt to be made to find out what it is. I am always amazed that people whose word on any other subject would be accepted without question – such as parsons, military officers, policemen, astronauts, airline pilots – are simply mocked when they speak of UFO experiences.

The second reason follows from the first. I am fed up with the knee-jerk reaction of the media (certainly in the UK) to the very word UFO: what might be called the 'little green men ha-ha-ha' syndrome. As Nick Pope, who handled UFO investigations in Britain's Ministry of Defence, has remarked to Tim Good, 'One mention of UFOs and people switch off.' This does not seem in the least sensible to me, and I have often wondered whether the ridicule heaped on the subject in British newspapers – though not, I am glad to say, by our television – is the reaction of ignorance, even fear of the unknown, by the third-rate journalists concerned, or whether, rather more dangerously, it has been inspired by some higher authority.

This gives rise to the third strand of my interest, which is the widespread cover-up of the results of official government investigations in most of the developed countries of the world. Tim Good removes any possible doubt that there is such a cover-up: in the United States on a massive scale, in Great Britain, and in several other countries.

Much in the world has changed since I suggested in 1987 some reasons for this cover-up; in particular, the end of the Cold War has fundamentally altered the mutual suspicion of possible military advantage jointly held by the USA and the former Soviet Union. I now suggest four reasons which have led governments to go to extraordinary lengths to conceal the results of their very urgent and detailed investigations, over a period of at least 50 years.

The first and most obvious reason is the overwhelming defence/ military advantage which would at once come to hand in the country which first discovered the secrets of these craft. The second is the military/ political embarrassment factor, which would follow an admission by any government that there were artefacts in our atmosphere which are not manmade, are vastly superior technically to anything we can deploy, and against which, if hostile, we would have no defence. The third follows the second: governments fear that their public might panic; they fear the possible collapse of our power structures, our legal system, and our religious beliefs, if they made this admission. There may even be serious doubts in some countries about who is actually dealing with these matters; in a sense it is an intra-government struggle for power. The commercial possibilities to be reaped by the first organization to crack this puzzle are so enormous, and the global dominance that would follow success so overwhelming, that governments must fear the intervention of powerful commercial/industrial cartels over their heads.

Each of these possibilities is reasonable, perhaps all of them are, and I know of one very high-powered outfit in the States which has no doubt that the last of these dangers is real. I do not, for my part, think our publics are in the least likely to panic. Either they would not believe it, or they would simply regard it as another nonsense perpetrated by their universally despised political leaders; they would be more likely simply to shrug their shoulders and get on with what in 1996 is the really difficult business of living, winning the lottery, coping with negative equity, planning their holidays, or doing all four.

However these possibilities may strike you, and there are obviously others, what must now be common ground is that there have been thousands, probably tens of thousands of sightings and encounters, perhaps even recoveries of crashed craft, which have been reported in detail, sometimes recorded on cameras or with instruments, from all over the world, and which can no longer be sensibly denied. There have been major investigations, some lasting fifty years, by the governments of the USA, France, Russia, Italy and Spain for certain, and probably that of the UK and other countries. At the end of it all we have no hard *official* information to weigh against some hundreds of books on the subject by private individuals or groups of people, and quite a number of television programmes mostly broadcast in recent years. I do not believe that it can any longer be plausibly denied that there is a government cover-up. What I must confess defeats me is a plausible reason for it.

For those of you who enjoyed *Above Top Secret*, here is a great deal of new and convincing evidence, and for new students a fascinating start to the study of what, for me at any rate, remains a baffling enigma.

HILL-NORTON

Introduction

ARE GOVERNMENTS OF the world withholding dramatic evidence – or even proof – that some unidentified flying objects present a serious threat to our security? This question has been asked repeatedly since 'flying saucers' made headline news throughout the world in 1947. Official denials have given rise to the suspicion that we are being told less than the truth, and that a wide-scale cover-up is in operation.

In October 1981, in response to an enquiry about the involvement of the intelligence community in the study of UFOs, I received the following reply from that well-known authority on the British security and secret services, Harry Chapman Pincher:

> There is no way I can help you with UFOs because I am convinced that they are entirely mythical. I can assure you that the 'world's secret services' are not wasting the smallest resource on keeping tabs on them. For many years I have had access to the highest levels of Defence Intelligence both in Britain and the U.S. There is not the slightest evidence there to support the existence of UFOs other than those explicable by normal means – meteorites, satellites, aircraft, etc.[1]

Chapman Pincher clearly has been misinformed. Documentary evidence made available in the US under provisions of the Freedom of Information Act, and increasingly available in other countries – much of which is presented in this book – proves conclusively that UFOs have continued to be the subject of intensive secret research by intelligence agencies since the Second World War.

Few governments deny the existence of unidentified flying objects *per se*. Lord Strabolgi, representing Her Majesty's Government in the historic House of Lords debate on the subject in January 1979, acknowledged this point: 'There are undoubtedly many strange phenomena in the skies, and it can be readily accepted that most UFO reports are made by calm and responsible people. However, there are generally straightforward explanations to account for the phenomena.'

Lord Strabolgi then went on to enumerate the many 'straightforward explanations' that account for the majority of reports. Few would disagree with him on this point. UFO researchers concur that up to 90 per cent of all sightings (a figure agreed by the Ministry of Defence) can be attributed to misidentifications, hallucinations, delusions and hoaxes. On the question of unexplainable sightings, which form the crux of the matter, Lord Strabolgi argued that in such cases 'the description is too vague or the evidence too remote, coupled with a coincidence of different phenomena and with exceptional conditions'. In some cases few would disagree, yet Lord Strabolgi overlooked the fact that several thousand sightings have been made by highly qualified observers whose descriptions are anything but vague, and whose evidence is compelling.

As to the suggestion of a cover-up, His Lordship was adamant:

> It has been suggested that our Government are involved in an alleged conspiracy of silence. I can assure your Lordships that the Government are not engaged in any such conspiracy . . . There is nothing to have a conspiracy of silence about . . . There is no cover-up and no security ban . . . There is nothing to suggest to Her Majesty's Government that such phenomena are alien spacecraft.[2]

A bona-fide UFO, however, does not necessarily imply an alien spacecraft. A wide range of hypotheses has been proposed to account for the unexplainable reports, of which the extraterrestrial hypothesis is but one. So the question really should be: Are there any unexplainable reports which represent something beyond our present knowledge, and are governments concealing what they have learned? And if the answer is positive, what exactly has been learned and why is there need for concealment? This book attempts to answer these and other questions relating to the many-faceted UFO phenomenon.

In this fully revised, updated and restructured edition of my original book *Above Top Secret*, I have deleted a number of cases that have turned out to have a conventional explanation, or which have proven to be either bogus or spurious, or which I have deemed superfluous. These are replaced by many important new cases from all over the world, with the emphasis, as before, on documented reports by qualified military and civilian witnesses (such as pilots – over 100 of which are included), as well as confirmation by defence chiefs in several countries proving that UFOs exist as a serious security threat. New information provided by military, scientific and technical intelligence specialists and others suggests that *some* UFOs are indeed alien spacecraft; furthermore, that in the United States a number of such craft, materials and occupants have been retrieved and studied by the scientific intelligence community. Together with documented data I have adduced showing a cover-up in the interests of national and international security, these cases augment the overwhelming body of evidence proving that the phenomenon continues to cause grave concern at high levels of many of the world's governments, despite their statements to the contrary.

Prologue

The Ghost Aircraft

OFFICIAL INVESTIGATIONS INTO unidentified flying objects in comparatively recent times began in 1933, when, according to contemporary newspaper reports, mysterious, conventionally shaped, unmarked aircraft appeared over Scandinavia and, to a lesser extent, the US and Britain. Often seen flying in hazardous weather conditions which would have grounded conventional biplanes of the period, the 'ghost aircraft', as they were called, frequently circled low, projecting powerful searchlights on to the ground. Another puzzling behaviour was that, although engine noises accompanied these sightings, the 'aircraft' sometimes described low-level manoeuvres in complete silence.

On 28 December 1933 the 4th Swedish Flying Corps began an investigation, and on 30 April 1934 Major-General Reuterswaerd, Commanding General of Upper Norrland, issued the following statement to the press:

> Comparisons of these reports show that there can be no doubt about illegal air traffic over our secret military areas. There are many reports from reliable people which describe close observation of the enigmatic flier. And in every case the same remark can be noted: No insignias or identifying marks were visible on the machines . . . The question is: Who or whom are they, and why have they been invading our air territory?[1]

To this day, those questions remain unanswered, though it is possible that some of the sightings could be explained in terms of German or Russian reconnaissance flights. There is no evidence of concealment in the Major-General's statement: rather, it was a frank admission by an official who was prepared to share his bewilderment with the press. Yet journalists did encounter official reluctance to discuss the matter, probably for the simple reason that the authorities were at a loss to explain how their airspace could be invaded by aircraft of unknown origin. One suggestion was that a Japanese aircraft was initially responsible for the sightings, as witness this report from Helsinki, Finland, in February 1934:

> Continued night flights over North Finland, Sweden and Norway, by so-called 'ghost aviators' which have caused much apprehension already as to prompt the General Staff to organize reconnoitering on a wide scale by Army planes, all over Northern Finland, still remain a deep mystery . . . As the authorities are extremely reticent, the newspapers have interviewed aviation experts, who state the mystery fliers show exceptional skill, undoubtedly superior to that of Northern European aviators. According to one expert's theory, the first of the ghost aviators was a Japanese, scouting the Arctic region, whose activities caused the Soviets to despatch aeroplanes to watch the Japanese. The Soviet authorities, however, refute this theory.[2]

Researcher John Keel has catalogued the 'ghost aircraft' sightings of this period, and believes that no nation on Earth had the resources to mount such an operation at that time, least of all Japan. He points to the similarity between sightings in Scandinavia and those reported from the US and Britain at the time. Keel cites some reports from London, one of which refers to an unidentified aircraft seen flying over central London on 1 February 1934 for a period of two hours. *The Times* reported the following day that from the sound of the engines the 'plane' was a large one, and that its altitude was sufficiently low for its course to be traced by its lights. The Air Ministry knew nothing about the aircraft, and enquiries at a number of civil airfields around London drew a blank. The sighting led to a question being asked in the House of Commons four days later, to which the Under-Secretary of State for Air, Sir Philip Sassoon, replied: 'The aircraft to which my hon. Friend evidently refers was a Royal Air Force aircraft carrying out a training exercise in co-operation with ground forces. Such training flights are arranged in the Royal Air Force without reference to the Air Ministry.'

Four months later two unidentified aircraft were seen and heard circling low over London late on the night of 11 June. According to *The Times* the following day, the Air Ministry stated that 'although night flying was frequently practised by RAF machines, and several were up last night, service pilots were forbidden by regulations to fly over London at less than 5,000 ft. The identity of the machines in question was not officially known.'

It is tempting to dismiss the ghost aircraft reports as conventional planes on illegal or secret flights but, as John Keel emphasizes, approximately 35 per cent of the Scandinavian sightings took place during severe weather conditions, including blizzards and fog, and the mystery planes often flew dangerously low over hazardous terrain. It is also a fact that the governments of Sweden, Norway and Finland took the hundreds of reports very seriously and launched massive investigations which never led to a satisfactory explanation.[3] However, there is no doubt that many reports from the ghost aircraft wave (which continued until 1937 in Scandinavia) were due to misperceptions of stars and planets, as well as of conventional aircraft, by an over-excited populace, as is evident from about 1,400 pages of archive material recently released by the Royal Norwegian Air Force and Defence Department.[4] Yet some reports remain puzzling – particularly those involving reliable sightings of various types of unidentified flying objects or lights (in addition to the ghost aircraft), similar to those reported in later years.

The Second World War

The Los Angeles Air Raid

On 25 February 1942, less than three months after the Japanese invasion of Pearl Harbor – and a day after an attack from the Santa Barbara Straits (north of Los Angeles) by a Japanese submarine – unidentified aircraft appeared over the city of Los Angeles, causing widespread alarm. Fourteen hundred and thirty rounds of anti-aircraft shells were fired in an attempt to bring down what were considered to be Japanese planes.

At least a million southern-California residents awoke to the wail of air-raid sirens as Los Angeles County cities blacked out at 02.25 hours. Twelve thousand air-raid wardens reported dutifully to their posts, most expecting nothing more than a dress rehearsal. At 03.16, however, the 37th Coast Artillery Brigade's anti-aircraft batteries began firing 12.8 lb shells at the targets as searchlight beams studded the sky. The shelling continued intermittently until 04.14. Three people were killed and three died of heart attacks directly attributable to the barrage; several homes and public buildings were severely damaged by unexploded shells. At 07.21 the blackout was lifted and the sirens sounded the all-clear. What about the Japanese invaders?

Aircraft of the 4th Interceptor Command had been warming up waiting for orders to intercept and engage the intruders, yet no such orders were given during the fifty-one-minute period between the first air-raid alert and the first military barrage. Allegedly, no enemy aircraft were involved in the 'invasion'. According to thousands of witnesses, a large unidentified flying object remained stationary while the anti-aircraft shells burst around it and against it (see plate section). A *Herald Express* staff writer said he was certain that many shells burst directly in the middle of the object and he could not believe that it had not been shot down. The object eventually proceeded at a leisurely pace over the coastal cities between Santa Monica and Long Beach, taking about twenty minutes of actual flight time to move 20 miles; it then disappeared.

An interesting eyewitness account of the phantom raid has been provided by Paul T. Collins, who had been working late at the Long Beach plant of the Douglas Aircraft Company and was returning home when he was stopped by an air-raid warden in Pasadena who told him to turn out the lights of his car and stay parked beside the road until the all-clear sounded. Pacing back and forth across the street trying to keep warm, Collins suddenly saw bright red spots of light low on the horizon to the south which were moving in a strange manner:

> They seemed to be 'functioning' or navigating mostly on a level plane at that moment – that is, not rising up from the ground in an arc, or trajectory, or in a straight line and then falling back to earth, but appearing from nowhere and then zigzagging from side to side. Some disappeared, not diminishing in brilliance at all, but just vanishing into the night. Others remained pretty much on the same level and we could only guess their elevation to be about ten thousand feet.

In less than five minutes at least half a dozen red flashes rent the sky among the strange spots of light, followed in about 100 seconds by the dull, cushioned thuds of the bursting shells. One of the anti-aircraft batteries around the Douglas Aircraft plant, at Dougherty Field, or the Signal Hill Oil Field, had fired a salvo into the moving spots of red light, according to Collins, whose position was about 20 miles from the aircraft factory:

> Taking into account our distance from Long Beach, the extensive pattern of firing from widely separated anti-aircraft batteries, and the movement of the unidentified red objects among *and around* the bursting shells in wide orbits, we estimated their top speed

conservatively to be five miles per second . . . We did not see the enormous UFO seen by thousands of observers closer to the coast. Very likely it was below our horizon and a few miles farther up the coast at that time.[5]

The military were thoroughly embarrassed and confused by the incident, but were obliged to come up with an explanation. In Washington, US Navy Secretary Frank Knox announced that there had been no planes over Los Angeles and that the barrage of anti-aircraft fire had been triggered by a false alarm and jittery war nerves. This statement incensed the press, who called attention to the loss of life and implied that the raid was a propaganda exercise by government officials who wanted to move vital industries inland.[6]

Although Knox stated that no planes were in the sky over Los Angeles, there is evidence that an aircraft was shot down during the anti-aircraft barrage. According to John E. Seidel, a carrier for the *Los Angeles Times* at the time, the first edition of the newspaper was delayed so that a first-page supplement could be added. The article stated that 'foreign' aircraft had been in the air and that: 'At 5 a.m., the sheriff's office announced that an airplane has been shot down near 185th Street and Vermont Avenue. Earlier, the Fourth Air Force in San Francisco said that at least one plane had been downed in the raid.' The supplement did not appear with later editions of the *Times*, nor was there any reference to the previously reported downed plane in these editions. Seidel learned from a colleague that, according to an aunt of his who lived near 185th and Vermont, a plane had crashed near her house but the Army quickly removed the wreckage and cleaned up the area. Years later, Seidel was told by an Air Force officer that there *were* planes in the air over Los Angeles on the morning in question, but they were American, not foreign.[7] If one of these planes was accidentally shot down, it provides another understandable reason for military embarrassment regarding the incident.

After reading my book *Above Top Secret*, aviation authority Jack Carpenter, a native of Long Beach, wrote to me as follows:

I well remember that night of 25 Feb. 42. After being awakened, I saw what we then thought to be aircraft – quite a few of them – visible in the light of the searchlights overhead. As I recall, they were travelling SSE. The next day when in an elevator at Buffum's (the local department store) I saw part of a shell fragment – shrapnel – being shown off by a local resident. This has, until today, been one of the enigmas of my life. Now it appears to make sense.[8]

The Los Angeles story, as with so many other UFO reports, reads like something straight out of science fiction, yet it happened. A hitherto 'secret' memorandum released in 1974 under provisions of the Freedom of Information Act (though following the incident it was published with almost identical details in the *Los Angeles Examiner* as a statement from Henry L. Stimpson, Secretary of War[9]) leaves little room for doubt that something extraordinary occurred that night. The memorandum was written by General George C. Marshall, Chief of Staff, and sent to President Franklin Roosevelt on 26 February 1942:

> The following is the information we have from GHQ at this moment regarding the air alarm over Los Angeles of yesterday morning:
> From details available at this hour:
> 1. Unidentified airplanes, other than American Army or Navy planes, were probably over Los Angeles, and were fired on by elements of the 37th CA [Coast Artillery] Brigade (AA) between 3:12 and 4:15 AM. These units expended 1430 rounds of ammunition.
> 2. As many as fifteen airplanes may have been involved, flying at various speeds from what is reported as being 'very slow' to as much as 200 MPH and at elevations from 9000 to 18000 feet.
> 3. No bombs were dropped.
> 4. No casualties among our troops.
> 5. No planes were shot down.
> 6. No American Army or Navy planes were in action.
> Investigation continuing. It seems reasonable to conclude that if unidentified airplanes were involved they may have been from commercial sources, operated by enemy agents for purposes of spreading alarm, disclosing locations of antiaircraft positions, and slowing production through blackout. Such conclusion is supported by varying speed of operation and the fact that no bombs were dropped.

Though General Marshall concluded that conventional aircraft were involved, he must have been baffled by the claim that none was shot down, despite the intensive barrage of shells.

~~SECRET~~

OCS 21347-86

February 26, 1942.

MEMORANDUM FOR THE PRESIDENT:

The following is the information we have from GHQ at this moment regarding the air alarm over Los Angeles of yesterday morning:

"From details available at this hour:

"1. Unidentified airplanes, other than American Army or Navy planes, were probably over Los Angeles, and were fired on by elements of the 37th CA Brigade (AA) between 3:12 and 4:15 AM. These units expended 1430 rounds of ammunition.

"2. As many as fifteen airplanes may have been involved, flying at various speeds from what is officially reported as being 'very slow' to as much as 200 MPH and at elevations from 9000 to 18000 feet.

"3. No bombs were dropped.

"4. No casualties among our troops.

"5. No planes were shot down.

"6. No American Army or Navy planes were in action.

"Investigation continuing. It seems reasonable to conclude that if unidentified airplanes were involved they may have been from commercial sources, operated by enemy agents for purposes of spreading alarm, disclosing location of antiaircraft positions, and slowing production through blackout. Such conclusion is supported by varying speed of operation and the fact that no bombs were dropped."

(Sgd) G. C. MARSHALL

Chief of Staff.

DECLASSIFIED
E.O. 11652, Sec. 3(E) and 5(D) or (E)
OSD letter, May 3, 1972
By_____ NARS Date 4-9-74

mkn

~~SECRET~~

A memorandum from General George Marshall to President Roosevelt giving details of the Los Angeles air alarm in February 1942. (*US Army*)

The 'officially reported' speeds of up to 200 m.p.h. come nowhere near Paul Collins's estimate of up to 'five miles per second'. Either Collins was off the mark or the official estimates were. There also is the possibility that none of the military observers was in a position to make an accurate assessment, or that they simply could not bring themselves to report such fantastic speeds and manoeuvres.

The evidence points to a cover-up by those in the military who were in a position to know what really happened, even if they were at a loss to explain the incident.

Formations of Unidentified Aircraft

On the morning of 12 August 1942 formations of unidentified aircraft were seen by Sergeant Stephen J. Brickner of the 1st Paratroop Brigade, 1st Marine Division, US Marine Corps, above Tulagi in the Solomon Islands. The following is extracted from his personal account:

> . . . suddenly the air raid warning sounded. There had been no 'Condition Red' . . . I heard the formation before I saw it. Even then, I was puzzled by the sound. It was a mighty roar that seemed to echo in the heavens. It didn't sound at all like the high-pitched 'sewing machine' drone of the Jap formations . . . the formation was huge; I would say over 150 objects were in it. Instead of the usual tight 'V' of 25 planes, this formation was in straight lines of 10 or 12 objects, one behind the other. The speed was a little faster than Jap planes, and they were soon out of sight.
>
> A few other things puzzled me: I couldn't seem to make out any wings or tails. They seemed to wobble slightly, and every time they wobbled they would shimmer brightly from the sun. Their color was like highly polished silver. No bombs were dropped, of course. All in all, it was the most awe-inspiring and yet frightening spectacle I have seen in my life.[10]

A sceptic might argue that Sergeant Brickner was suffering from combat fatigue, and that the aircraft were conventional, yet the reference to the 'wobbling motion' of the objects is typical of many postwar reports of unidentified flying objects, and the incident seems to have left the witness profoundly impressed.

The Foo-Fighters

In 1943 many Allied and enemy airmen began to report sightings of small, apparently remote-controlled objects which followed and sometimes buzzed aircraft during missions. Among American forces, rumours spread that the Germans had introduced a new weapon designed to interfere with the ignition systems of bombers' engines, but, since the 'foo-fighters' (as they were nicknamed by pilots of the 415th Night Fighter Squadron) never engaged in hostile action, many flight crews became convinced that the objects were some type of psychological-warfare device.

The US 8th Army ordered a thorough investigation into the sightings but was unable to arrive at a satisfactory solution. Explanations were proposed, of course, including 'St Elmo's fire', ball lightning, and combat fatigue, but it is improbable that these account for *all* the reports, especially those involving scores of objects observed simultaneously by different aircrews.

In late 1943, Staff Sergeant Louis Kiss was a tail gunner on the *Phyllis Marie*, a B-17 Flying Fortress bomber of the 390th Bombardment Group, 3rd Division, 8th Air Force, when a foo-fighter was encountered over central Germany. Kiss observed an odd-looking sphere approach the aircraft from the rear. Described as about the size of a basketball and of a shimmery gold colour, the sphere approached the aircraft slowly and hovered just above one wing, then passed over the top of the aircraft and hovered over the other wing. Sergeant Kiss was tempted to fire at the device, but decided against the idea. The sphere then moved to the rear again and disappeared rapidly into the remainder of the B-17 formation.[11]

Reports of foo-fighters were not restricted to the European theatre of operations. An interesting sighting took place in Sumatra on 10 August 1944, for example, witnessed by the crew of an American B-29 bomber commanded by Captain Alvah M. Reida of the 486th Bomb Group, 792nd Squadron, 20th Bomber Command, based at Kharagapur, India:

I was on a mission from Ceylon, bombing Palembang, Sumatra . . . shortly before midnight. There were 50 planes on the strike going in on the target at about 2 or 3 minute intervals. My plane was last in on the target and the arrangement was for us to bomb, then drop photo flash bombs, attached to parachutes; make a few runs over the target area, photographing damage from preceding planes . . . Our altitude was 14000 feet and indicated airspeed about 210 mph. While in the general target area we were exposed to sporadic flak fire, but immediately after leaving this area it ceased.

At about 20 or 30 minutes later the right gunner and co-pilot reported a strange object pacing us about 500 yards off our starboard wing. At that distance it appeared as a spherical object, probably 5 or 6 feet in diameter, of a very bright and intense red or orange in color ... My gunner reported it coming in from about 5 o'clock position at our level. It seemed to throb or vibrate constantly. Assuming it was some kind of radio-controlled object sent to pace us, I went into evasive action, changing direction constantly as much as 90° and altitude at about 2000 feet. It followed our every maneuver for about 8 minutes, always holding a position 500 yards out and about 2 o'clock in relation to the plane. When it left, it made an abrupt 90° turn, and accelerated rapidly, disappearing in the overcast ... during the strike evaluation and interrogation following the mission, I made a detailed report to Intelligence thinking it was some new type of radio-controlled missile or weapon.[12]

Sightings of the so-called foo-fighters abated to a certain extent in 1945 (though similarly described objects have been reported worldwide since then). In 1952, Lieutenant Colonel W. W. Ottinger of the US Air Force Directorate of Intelligence's Evaluation Division, stated that an evaluation of foo-fighter reports was made at the end of the war. The evaluation concluded that there was nothing to the phenomenon at all. To this day, the study has not been made public.[13]

UFOs Endanger Aircraft

On 28 August 1945, US Air Force intelligence officer Leonard Stringfield was one of twelve 5th Air Force specialists aboard a transport aircraft flying from Ie-shima to Tokyo via Iwo Jima when an alarming incident occurred, which led to his lifelong interest in the UFO phenomenon. Approaching Iwo Jima at about 10,000 feet in a sunlit sky, Stringfield was startled to see three teardrop-shaped objects from his starboard-side window:

... They were brilliantly white, like burning magnesium, and closing in on a parallel course to our C-46. Suddenly our left engine feathered, and I was later to learn that the magnetic navigation-instrument needles went wild. As the C-46 lost altitude, with oil spurting from the troubled engine, the pilot sounded an alert; crew and passengers were told to prepare for a ditch! I do not recall my thoughts or actions during the next, horrifying moments, but my last glimpse of the three bogies placed them about 20 degrees above the level of our transport. Flying in the same, tight formation, they faded into a cloud bank. Instantly our craft's engine revved up, and we picked up altitude and flew a steady course to land safely on Iwo Jima.[14]

Many similar incidents involving serious effects on aircraft instruments are discussed throughout this book.

The Ghost Rockets

In 1946 over 2,000 reports of 'ghost rockets' and other unidentified flying objects were reported by witnesses in Finland, Norway, Sweden and Denmark, followed by reports from Portugal, Morocco, Italy, Greece and India. The ghost rockets – so called because they often looked like rocket-shaped objects with fiery trails – sometimes performed fantastic manoeuvres, crossing the sky at tremendous velocity, diving and climbing, but at other times proceeded in a leisurely manner.[15] There also were reports of landings and crashes.

The overwhelming majority of the reports came from Sweden, causing consternation not only in official circles in that country but also at the US Embassy in Stockholm. A confidential Department of State telegram from the Embassy, dated 11 July 1946, provides a dramatic example of the situation at that time:

For some weeks there have been numerous reports of strange rocket-like missiles being seen in Swedish and Finnish skies. During past few days reports of such objects being seen have greatly increased. Member of Legation saw one Tuesday afternoon. One landed on beach near Stockholm same afternoon without causing any damage and according to press fragments are now being studied by military authorities. Local scientist on first inspection stated it contained organic substance resembling carbide. Defense staff last night issued communiqué listing various places where missiles had been observed and urging public report all mysterious sound and light phenomena. Press this afternoon announces one such missile fell in Stockholm suburb 2:30 this afternoon. Missile observed by member Legation made no sound and seemed to be falling rapidly to earth when observed. No sound of explosion followed however.

Military Attaché is investigating through Swedish channels and has been promised results Swedish observations. Swedes profess ignorance as to origin, character or purpose of missiles but state definitely they are not launched by Swedes. Eyewitness reports state missiles came in from southerly direction proceeding to northwest. Six units Atlantic Fleet under Admiral Hewitt arrived Stockholm this morning. If missiles are of Soviet origin as generally believed (some reports say they are launched from Estonia), purpose might be political to intimidate Swedes in connection with Soviet pressure on Sweden being built up in connection with current loan negotiations or to offset supposed increase in our military pressure on Sweden resulting from the naval visit and recent Bikini [Atoll] tests or both.

On 13 August 1946 the *New York Times* reported that 'the Swedish General Staff today described the situation as "extremely dangerous", and it is obvious that Sweden no longer is going to tolerate such violations'. The violations continued, however, and it is perhaps revealing that Sweden continued to tolerate them.

A sighting reported in a hitherto secret US Air Force publication describes an encounter by a Swedish Air Force pilot on 14 August 1946:

. . . at 1600 hours, he was flying at 650 feet over central Sweden when he saw a dark, cigar-shaped flying object about 50 feet long and 3 feet in diameter flying 200 feet above and approximately 6,500 feet away from him at an estimated speed of 400 m.p.h. The missile had no visible wings, rudder, or other projecting part; and there was no indication of any flame or light as has been reported in the majority of other sightings. His report states that the missile was maintaining a constant altitude over the ground and, consequently, was following the large features of the terrain . . .

The writer of the article speculated that the object was most probably a Soviet guided missile of the V-1 type.[16]

Speculations also centred on the theory that the Russians were testing rockets of the V-2 type with the aid of captured German scientists and engineers, and the Swedish General Staff summoned urgent assistance from the United States and Great Britain. Lieutenant General James Doolittle, a US Army Air Force intelligence expert with specialized knowledge of long-distance bombing techniques, arrived in Stockholm together with General David Sarnoff, an intelligence expert in aerial warfare, and the two men were consulted by Colonel C. R. Kempf, the Chief of Swedish Defence. Sarnoff was later quoted as saying that the objects reported were neither mythological nor meteorological but were 'real missiles'.[17] But then came the cover-up. On 22 August 1946 the *Daily Telegraph* stated:

> The discussion of the flight of rockets over Scandinavia has been dropped in the Norwegian newspapers since Wednesday. On that day the Norwegian General Staff issued a memorandum to the press asking it not to make any mention of the appearance of rockets over Norwegian territory but to pass on all reports to the Intelligence Department of the High Command . . . In Sweden the ban is limited to any mention of where the rockets have been seen to land or explode.

The reasons for press censorship being introduced at this time are perfectly understandable. Firstly, it was an established practice during the V-1 and V-2 bombardments of the London area in the Second World War not to reveal where the rocket-bombs had fallen, so that the enemy would remain in ignorance of the degree of accuracy of his targeting. Secondly, the ghost rockets were causing considerable public concern and, because they had been unable to come up with an explanation for the sightings, the authorities wanted to play down the situation.

On 23 August 1946 the British Foreign Office stated that English radar experts, having returned from Sweden, had 'submitted secret reports to the British Government on the origin of the rockets'.[18] One of the scientists to examine the reports was R. V. Jones, Director of Intelligence on Britain's Air Staff at the time, as well as scientific adviser to Section IV of MI6, the Secret Intelligence Service. Professor Jones remained unimpressed by the reports he examined, attributing them to initial sightings of 'two unusually bright meteors, which were clearly visible in daylight. One of these led to many reports almost simultaneously, from a wide area of Sweden.' The subsequent wave of sightings was caused simply by overenthusiastic observers in the prevalent Cold War climate, he believed. He totally dismissed the possibility that the sightings could have had anything to do with Soviet missiles:

The Russians were supposedly cruising their flying bombs at more than twice the range that the Germans had achieved, and it was unlikely that they were so advanced technologically as to achieve a substantially greater reliability at 200 miles than the Germans had reached at 100 miles. Even, therefore, if they were only trying to frighten the Swedes, they could hardly help it if some of their missiles crashed on Swedish territory. The alleged sightings over Sweden were now so many that, even giving the Russians the greatest possible credit for reliability, there ought to be at least 10 missiles crashed in Sweden. I would therefore only believe the story if someone brought me in a piece of a missile.

Although no crashed missiles were ever found, one observer claimed to have seen objects fall from one of the ghost rockets and had collected the pieces. These were passed by the Swedish General Staff to the other Director of Intelligence in the Air Staff, and were eventually analysed at the Royal Aircraft Establishment, Farnborough. In great excitement, the scientists reported that one of the fragments contained over 98 per cent of an unknown element. Jones asked the head of the chemical department at the RAE if they had tested for carbon. 'There was something of an explosion at the other end of the telephone,' said Jones. 'Carbon would not have shown up in any of the standard tests, but one had only to look at the material, as Charles Frank and I had done, to see that it was a lump of coke.'[19]

Professor Jones may have been justified in his scepticism about the sample as well as the purported origin of the missiles, but he evidently was mistaken in his outright rejection of the reports, which continued to cause grave concern. The US State Department upgraded the security classification of some of its communications with the American Embassy, Stockholm, such as the following 'Top Secret' telegram from Stockholm, dated 29 August 1946:

While over 800 reports have been received and new reports come daily, Swedes still have no tangible evidence. Full details of reports thus far received have been forwarded to Washington by our Military and Naval Attachés. My own source personally convinced some foreign power is actually experimenting over Sweden and he guesses it is Russia. He has promised to notify me before anyone else if anything tangible should be discovered.

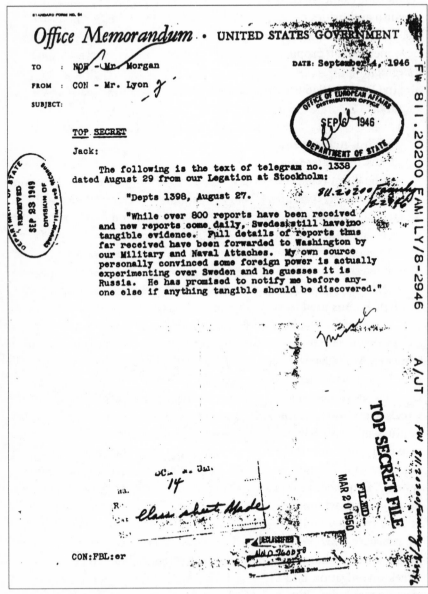

A 'Top Secret' Department of State memorandum relating to the 'ghost rocket' wave of 1946. (*US State Department*)

On 6 September 1946 the *Daily Telegraph* published a photograph of one of the missiles, taken near Stockholm by Erik Reuterswaerd, who reported it to the Swedish General Staff. Together with Allied experts, the Swedish authorities came to the conclusion that the 'projectile' was within the 'flame' or trail, rather than ahead of it. 'This supports the theory that a new method of propulsion is being used in these weapons,' stated the *Telegraph*.

In October 1946 the Swedish Government announced the results of its inquiry:

> Swedish military authorities said today that they had been unable to discover after four months of investigation the origin or nature of the ghost rockets that have been flying over Sweden since May.
>
> A special communiqué declared that 80 per cent of 1,000 reports on the rockets could be attributed to 'celestial phenomena' but that radar had detected some [200] objects 'which cannot be the phenomena of nature or products of the imagination, nor can be referred to as Swedish airplanes'.
>
> The report added, however, that the objects were not the V-type bombs used by the Germans in the closing days of the war.[20]

In an interview in London on 5 September 1946 the Greek Prime Minister, M. Tsaldaris, said that on 1 September a number of projectiles had been seen over Macedonia and Salonika.[21] The following year Greece's leading scientist, Professor Paul Santorini, was supplied by the Greek Army with a team of engineers to investigate what were believed to be Russian missiles flying over Greece. Santorini's credentials include the proximity fuse for the Hiroshima atomic bomb, two patents for the guidance system used in US Nike missiles, and a centrimetric radar system. Educated at Zurich, where his physics professor was Albert Einstein (with whom he played violin duets), Santorini retired as Director of the Experimental Physics Laboratory of Athens Polytechnic in 1964. On 24 February 1967 he gave a lecture to the Greek Astronautical Society, broadcast on Athens Radio, during which he revealed the results of the Greek investigation into the ghost rockets: 'We soon established that they were not missiles. But, before we could do any more, the Army, after conferring with foreign officials, ordered the investigation stopped. Foreign scientists flew to Greece for secret talks with me.'[22] This statement was personally verified by the respected American researcher Raymond Fowler, who had written to Santorini to check on the accuracy of the newspaper quotes attributed to him following the broadcast.[23] The professor also confirmed that a 'world blanket of secrecy' surrounded the UFO question because, among other reasons, the authorities were unwilling to admit the existence of a force against which we had 'no possibility of defence'.[24]

Part One

The United Kingdom

Defence Intelligence

To GAIN A proper perspective on the official UK attitude towards unidentified flying objects, it is essential to examine some reports from the early 1950s – a period when there was less secrecy than now about the subject. Where possible I have used original sources, including official documentation, some of which has not been available previously.

The Ministry of Defence consistently has maintained that all UFO reports held by the MoD before 1962 have been destroyed. In 1980, for instance, I was told: 'The earliest records held by the MoD prior to 1962 have been destroyed. All the records held before that date were destroyed some years ago. If there had been any evidence of important papers the records would have been retained.'[1] It came as a pleasant surprise, therefore, to discover that a number of pre-1962 UFO reports have been retained at the Public Record Office in Kew, London. One of these relates to a 1952 enquiry by the Prime Minister.

In July 1952, following the dramatic wave of UFO sightings over Washington, DC, which resulted in worldwide news coverage (see Chapter 14), Prime Minister Sir Winston Churchill felt sufficiently concerned to write the following personal minute to the Secretary of State for Air, and to Lord Cherwell (Frederick A. Lindemann, Churchill's scientific adviser): 'What does all this stuff about flying saucers amount to? What can it mean? What is the truth? Let me have a report at your convenience.'[2]

Back came the reply from the Air Ministry two weeks later:

The various reports about unidentified flying objects, described by the Press as 'flying saucers', were the subject of a full Intelligence study in 1951. The conclusions reached . . . were that all the incidents reported could be explained by one or other of the following causes:–
(a) Known astronomical or meteorological phenomena.
(b) Mistaken identification of conventional aircraft, balloons, birds, etc.

(c) Optical illusions and psychological delusions.

(d) Deliberate hoaxes.

2. The Americans, who carried out a similar investigation in 1948/9, reached a similar conclusion.

3. Nothing has happened since 1951 to make the Air Staff change their opinion, and, to judge from recent Press statements, the same is true in America . . .[3]

A copy of this report was sent to Lord Cherwell, who wrote to the Prime Minister on 14 August 1952, stating that 'I have seen the Secretary of State's minute to you on flying saucers and agree entirely with his conclusions.'

The Prime Minister was misinformed. Firstly, the Air Staff was unable to explain all the incidents. The Deputy Director of Intelligence at the Air Ministry from 1950 to 1953 has confirmed that 10 per cent of reports came from well-qualified witnesses, where there was corroboration, and where no explanation could be found (see pp. 8–9). Secondly, the Americans had *not* 'reached a similar conclusion' that all the incidents could be explained. An Air Intelligence Report, once classified Top Secret, concluded in 1948: 'The frequency of reported sightings, the similarity in many of the characteristics attributed to the observed objects and the quality of observers considered as a whole, support the contention that some type of flying object has been observed . . . The origin of the devices is not ascertainable.'[4]

As early as 1947 the US Air Matériel Command concluded, in a 'Secret' memorandum, that 'the phenomenon reported is something real and not visionary or fictitious . . . There are objects probably approximating the shape of a disc, of such appreciable size as to appear to be as large as man-made aircraft.'[5] By the end of July 1952, the time of Churchill's enquiry, US authorities were in a state of near panic, and a CIA memorandum confirms that 'since 1947, ATIC [Air Technical Intelligence Center] has received approximately 1500 official reports of sightings . . . During 1952 alone, official reports totaled 250. Of the 1500 reports, Air Force carries 20 percent as unexplained and of those received from January through July 1952 it carries 28 percent unexplained.'[6] (See Chapter 14.)

One must assume, therefore, that either the Air Staff had not been given these facts by their American colleagues or – less likely – that they withheld them from the Prime Minister.

RAF Topcliffe

On 19 September 1952, during NATO's 'Operation Mainbrace' exercise, two RAF officers and three aircrew at RAF Topcliffe observed a UFO following a Meteor jet, which was approaching RAF Dishforth, Yorkshire. The sighting took place at 10.53 hours as the Meteor was descending in a clear sky, reported Flight Lieutenant John Kilburn:

> The Meteor was crossing from east to west when I noticed the white object in the sky . . . silver and circular in shape, about 10,000 ft up some five miles astern of the aircraft. It appeared to be travelling at a lower speed than the Meteor but was on the same course.
>
> I said: 'What the hell's that?' and the chaps looked to where I was pointing. Somebody shouted that it might be the engine cowling of the Meteor falling out of the sky. Then we thought it might be a parachute. But as we watched the disc maintained a slow forward speed for a few seconds before starting to descend. While descending it was swinging in a pendulum fashion from left to right.
>
> As the Meteor turned to start its landing run the object appeared to be following it. But after a few seconds it stopped its descent and hung in the air rotating as if on its own axis. Then it accelerated at an incredible speed to the west, turned south-east and then disappeared.
>
> It is difficult to estimate the object's speed. The incident happened within a matter of 15 to 20 seconds. During the few seconds that it rotated we could see it flashing in the sunshine. It appeared to be about the size of a Vampire jet aircraft at a similar height.
>
> We are all convinced that it was some solid object. We realized very quickly that it could not be a broken cowling or parachute. There was not the slightest possibility that the object we saw was a smoke ring, or was caused by vapour trail from the Meteor or from any jet aircraft . . .
>
> We are also quite certain that it was not a weather observation balloon. The speed at which it moved away discounts this altogether. It was not a small object which appeared bigger in the conditions of light. Our combined opinion is that . . . it was something we had never seen before in a long experience of air observation.

Other witnesses were Flight Lieutenant Marian Cybulski, Master Signaller Albert Thomson, Sergeant Flight Engineer Thomas Deweys, Flight Lieutenant R. Paris, and Leading Aircraftsman George Grime.[7]

Copies of the official report on the incident (reproduced on p. 7) were sent to the Commander-in-Chief, Air/East Atlantic (a NATO command post), the Secretary of State for Air, Chief of the Air Staff, Assistant Chief of the Air Staff (Intelligence), Assistant Chief of the Air Staff (Operations), as well as to the Air Ministry's Scientific Intelligence Branch.

Captain Edward Ruppelt, once head of the US Air Force Air Technical Intelligence Center's 'Project Blue Book' UFO investigation, relates that an RAF intelligence officer at the Pentagon told him that the Topcliffe incident was one of a number in 1952 (including another report by RAF pilots during 'Operation Mainbrace') 'that caused the RAF to officially recognize the UFO'.[8] Ruppelt also relates that during his tenure as head of Blue Book at ATIC, based at Wright-Patterson Air Force Base, 'two RAF intelligence officers who were in the US on a classified mission brought six single-spaced typed pages of questions they and their friends wanted answered'.[9]

The Deputy Directorate of Intelligence

A week after the Topcliffe story was published, the *Sunday Dispatch* ran an article which claimed that the RAF had secretly been investigating flying-saucer reports since 1947:

> A staff of technical experts – mostly commissioned officers under the direction of a wing commander – are analysing every report of a flying saucer over British territory. Though the exact location of the flying saucer investigation bureau – known as the DDI [Deputy Directorate of Intelligence] (Technical) – is secret, I can reveal it occupies rooms in a building, formerly an hotel, not five minutes' walk from the Air Ministry in Whitehall. The building is closely guarded.

The *Sunday Dispatch* reporter added that intelligence officers at RAF Topcliffe had interrogated the officers and aircrew who witnessed the sighting. 'Till the experts have made a thorough investigation,' an Air Ministry spokesman was quoted as saying, 'it is impossible to do more than guess. Our experts will examine this report in the same way as they

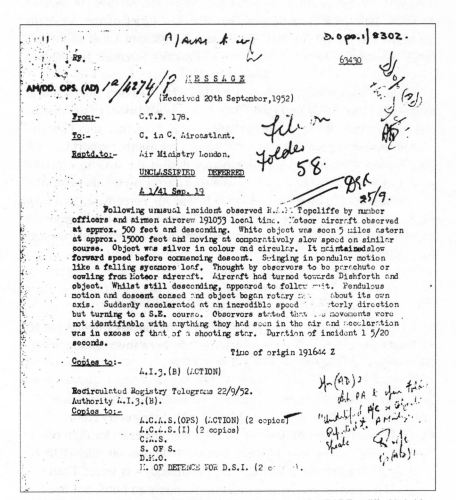

MESSAGE

(Received 20th September,1952)

From:- C.T.F. 178.

To:- C. in C. Aircastlant.

Reptd.to:- Air Ministry London.

UNCLASSIFIED DEFERRED

A 1/41 Sep. 19

Following unusual incident observed R.A.F. Topcliffe by number
officers and airmen aircrew 191053 local time. Meteor aircraft observed
at approx. 500 feet and descending. White object was seen 5 miles astern
at approx. 15000 feet and moving at comparatively slow speed on similar
course. Object was silver in colour and circular. It maintained slow
forward speed before commencing descent. Swinging in pendular motion
like a falling sycamore leaf. Thought by observers to be parachute or
cowling from Meteor aircraft. Aircraft had turned towards Dishforth and
object. Whilst still descending, appeared to follow suit. Pendulous
motion and descent ceased and object began rotary motion about its own
axis. Suddenly accelerated at an incredible speed ... terly direction
but turning to a S.E. course. Observers stated that ... movements were
not identifiable with anything they had seen in the air and acceleration
was in excess of that of a shooting star. Duration of incident 1 5/20
seconds.

Time of origin 191644 Z

Copies to:-

A.I.3.(B) (ACTION)

Recirculated Registry Telegrams 22/9/52.
Authority A.I.3.(B).
Copies to:-

A.C.A.S.(OPS) (ACTION) (2 copies)
A.C.A.S.(I) (2 copies)
C.A.S.
S. OF S.
D.M.O.
M. OF DEFENCE FOR D.S.I. (2 c....).

An Air Ministry report giving details of the sighting by personnel at RAF Topcliffe, Yorkshire,
in September 1952. (*Crown Copyright*)

have been examining every similar report of objects seen in the sky which are not aircraft and which are generally referred to as flying saucers.'[10] The Air Ministry eventually admitted that they were unable to explain the sighting, after eleven weeks of inquiry, and a spokesman added: 'The special branch which has been dealing with this is keeping an open mind on the subject and all reports received are still being studied.'[11]

Details of the secret investigation bureau are given in the following chapter. Here it is worth noting that during a meeting with an official at DDI (Tech.) in 1954, investigator Ronald R. Russell was told that the directorate had 15,000 reports on file from 1947 to 1954, and that these were stored in three drawers with Yale locks, doubly secured by a hinged plate locked in turn with a large padlock.[12]

One wonders why so few of those reports have been made available to the public. If the figure of 15,000 reports is even nearly accurate, and one assumes that 10 per cent were unexplainable, it is difficult to believe that they have all been disposed of. While it is true that at least 95 per cent of documents are periodically 'weeded' by the MoD reviewers, some can be withheld for up to 100 years if it is felt that national security would be compromised or the Government embarrassed by their release. Indeed, the Public Record Office (PRO) has acknowledged that many records of the Defence Ministry's Scientific Intelligence Branch (not necessarily UFO-related) will be under extended closure for 50, 75 or 100 years.[13]

That 10 per cent of sightings are unexplainable has frequently been misrepresented by the MoD in misleading statements to Parliament and the general public since 1955, by referring to these sightings as 'unexplained due to insufficient information'. Quite the opposite is the case.

The Deputy Director of Intelligence at the Air Ministry during 1950–53 was Group Captain Harold B. Collins. In a letter to former Ministry of Defence official Ralph Noyes, Collins summarized the results of Air Ministry findings at that time:

> If my memory serves, we prepared a paper which divided the more recent reports into four classifications:
>
> (1) Some 35% that could be immediately discounted.
>
> (2) Some 25% for which we were able to find a definite or probable explanation.
>
> (3) Some 30% where there was no corroboration or there were doubts about the reporter and for which we could find no explanation.

(4) Some 10% where the reporter was well qualified, i.e. Farnborough test pilot, etc. where there was corroboration and where the report itself carried conviction; but where we could find no explanation.[14]

It is unfortunate that Group Captain Collins did not elaborate on the fourth category, but it serves well to emphasize that 10 per cent of 15,000 reports represents a significant number of sightings by well-qualified witnesses for which there was no explanation. This is at variance with official statements over the past thirty-five years or so.

Although not connected to the Deputy Directorate of Intelligence (Technical), Ralph Noyes was private secretary to the late Air Chief Marshal Sir Ralph Cochrane, Vice-Chief of the Air Staff from 1950 to 1952. Noyes recalls an occasion at the Air Ministry in 1952 when Cochrane chatted about the subject with Sir Robert Cockburn, Chief Scientific Adviser to the Ministry. Cochrane referred to the alarming wave of sightings over Washington, DC, in July that year, and mentioned that the US Chief of Staff, General Hoyt Vandenberg, whom Cochrane knew personally, 'didn't think there was much in it'. Cockburn was asked to look into the flying-saucer suggestion, because the Washington sightings had caused alarm at the Air Ministry. Cochrane was very much inclined to take Vandenberg's view, Noyes told me. Although Vandenberg had dismissed a 'Top Secret' *Estimate of the Situation* which concluded that UFOs were interplanetary in origin – a report delivered to him by Air Technical Intelligence Center in August 1948 – he nevertheless ordered that it should be destroyed, because he feared it might cause panic, and felt there was insufficient proof to support its conclusions.[15]

The West Malling and Lee Green Incidents

On 3 November 1953, at 10.00 hours, Royal Air Force Flying Officer T. S. Johnson and his navigator, Flying Officer G. Smythe, were flying a two-seat Vampire jet night-fighter on a sector reconnaissance at 20,000 feet near their base at RAF West Malling in Kent, when they saw a stationary object at a much higher altitude. Suddenly it moved towards their aircraft at tremendous speed before disappearing. Circular in shape, the object emitted a very bright light around the periphery. This sighting lasted thirty seconds.

Expecting derision when they reported the incident to their station commander, Group Captain P. Hamley, the airmen were surprised when

their report was immediately forwarded to Fighter Command Headquarters. Later, two RAF intelligence officers interrogated the men for an
hour and a half.

On 11 November the War Office announced that at 14.30 on 3
November an Army radar set being tested at the Anti-Aircraft Command
barracks at Lee Green, Kent, had picked up a large echo on a south-east
bearing at an angle of 42° and a sound range of 17 miles. It was tracked on
radar from 14.45 to 15.10 by a number of Army technicians, including
Sergeant H. Waller, who commented that the object could not possibly
have been a balloon. To obtain the sort of signal received, the object must
have been metallic; in fact, the signal was much stronger than those
obtained from conventional aircraft, he said – 'three or four times larger
than the largest airliner'.

On 12 November the War Office, which controlled inland radar at
that time, claimed that the object was merely a meteorological balloon
released from Crawley, Sussex, at 14.00, and added that the object seen by
the Vampire crew was another balloon that had been released that
morning. A radio-sonde balloon of that period, however, was only 75 feet
across, and according to Sergeant Waller the object he tracked was 350–
450 feet in diameter.[16]

The West Malling and Lee Green incidents provoked questions in the
House of Commons. On 24 November 1953, Nigel Birch, Parliamentary
Secretary, Ministry of Defence, replying to Lieutenant Colonel Wentworth
Schofield MP and Frederick Bellenger MP, who asked about the sightings,
replied: 'Two experimental meteorological balloons were observed at
different times on November 3rd . . . There was nothing peculiar about
either of the occurrences.' (Laughter)

Birch added in answer to further questions that the balloons were
fitted with a special device to produce as large an echo on a radar screen as
an aircraft, and that they had been released at unusual times. He hoped
there would not be any more trouble. George Isaacs MP then asked: 'Will
the Minister agree that this story of flying saucers is all ballooney?' (Loud
laughter), to which Mr Birch responded that Mr Isaacs' appreciation was
'very nearly correct'. (Laughter)[17]

Air Force Concern

Behind the scenes, the Royal Air Force was not so amused. On 16
December 1953, a directive issued by Fighter Command, classified
'Restricted', stated that sightings of aerial phenomena by RAF personnel

were in future to be reported immediately in writing by officers commanding units to the Deputy Directorate of Intelligence (Technical) at the Air Ministry, with copies to Group and Command Headquarters. Additionally, any reports received from civilians were also to be sent to the Ministry.

The directive continues:

> It will be appreciated that the public attach more credence to reports by Royal Air Force personnel than to those by members of the public. It is essential that the information should be examined at Air Ministry and that its release should be controlled officially. All reports are, therefore, to be classified 'Restricted' and personnel are to be warned that they are not to communicate to anyone other than official persons any information about phenomena they have observed, unless officially authorised to do so . . .[18]

RAF Pilot's Close Encounter over Southend

Nearly a year later another sighting was reported by an RAF pilot which has never been satisfactorily explained, and, like the West Malling incident, is not yet available in the Air Ministry file at the Public Record Office.

On 14 October 1954, Flight Lieutenant James Salandin, of No. 604 County of Middlesex Squadron, Royal Auxiliary Air Force, took off at 16.15 from his base at RAF North Weald in Essex, in a Meteor Mk 8. Weather was clear. As he later told me:

> When I was at about 16,000 feet I saw a lot of contrails – possibly at 30–40,000 feet – over the North Foreland. Through the middle of the trails I saw three objects which I thought were aeroplanes, but they weren't trailing. They came down through the middle of that towards Southend and then headed towards me.
>
> When they got to within a certain distance two of them went off to my port side – one gold and one silver – and the third object came straight towards me and closed to within a few hundred yards, almost filling the windscreen, then it went off towards my port side. I tried to turn round to follow, but it had gone.
>
> It was saucer-shaped with a bun on top and a bun underneath, and was silvery and metallic. There were no portholes, flames, or anything.

Salandin immediately reported the sighting to North Weald. After landing, he related further details to Derek Dempster, 604 Squadron's intelligence officer, who fortuitously was to become the first editor of *Flying Saucer Review* in 1955. The report was sent to the Air Ministry, but nothing further was heard about it. Had it not been for Dempster, the story might never have come to light. He told me that he is absolutely convinced of Salandin's sincerity, having known him well as a fellow pilot in 604 Squadron.

'Jimmy' Salandin's only regret is that there was insufficient time to trigger the gun-camera button. But his memory of the sighting remains vivid. 'I haven't found a satisfactory explanation for what I saw,' he told me, 'but I know what I saw.'[19]

Mystery Aerial Formations Baffle the War Office

Three weeks after Flight Lieutenant Salandin's sighting, the War Office admitted that it was completely baffled by strange formations of 'blips' tracked on radar, moving from east to west. A thorough check revealed that they could not have been caused by aircraft. From late October to early November 1954 there were six sightings of the unidentified targets, which appeared from nowhere, usually at midday, flying at a height of 12,000 feet. First seen by a civilian radar scientist, they were subsequently plotted by all radar sets in the (unspecified) area, on both fine and cloudy mornings. A War Office spokesman described the incidents as follows:

> We cannot say what they are. They first appear in a 'U', or badly shaped hairpin, formation. After a time they converge into two parallel lines and then take up a 'Z' formation before disappearing. They are invisible to the human eye, but on the radar screen they appear as lots and lots of dots formed by between 40 and 50 echoes. They cover an area in the sky miles long and miles wide.
>
> Every time they have been seen they followed the same pattern. It was always around midday. We have checked and found that our [radar] sets are not faulty. We are still maintaining a watch. All our sets in the area have picked them up.

The location of the radar trackings was not identified, and one witness said that they had been given very high-level orders to maintain the utmost secrecy. 'And even if I did know what they are,' he added, 'I am too worried myself to say anything.'

The Air Ministry seemed anxious to play down the incidents, pointing out that there were many objects such as meteorological balloons, experimental aircraft, carrier pigeons with metal rings on their legs, and even toy kites, which could generate an image on radar. But the trained radar specialists said that none of these objects would produce such regular, repeated patterns.[20]

HRH Prince Philip, Duke of Edinburgh

In February 1954, young Stephen Darbishire, together with his cousin, Adrian Myers, took two photographs (see plate section) of a flying saucer near Coniston, Cumbria. The object was identical to those photographed by the controversial UFO 'contactee' George Adamski. The Duke of Edinburgh was sufficiently impressed to invite Stephen to Buckingham Palace just over a month later, so that the full details could be related to one of his aides. A full report of the interview was then sent to the Duke, who was in Australia at the time.[21]

Via Major the Honourable Andrew Wigram, Prince Philip has confirmed this report for me and graciously has allowed me to use the following brief comment, which he made at a dinner party in 1962. 'There are many reasons to believe that they [UFOs] do exist: there is so much evidence from reliable witnesses . . .'[22]

Defence Chiefs Admit Interest

By 1954 defence chiefs in Britain were convinced that a problem existed, even if few were prepared to admit as much in public. The following statement, for example, was made by the Defence Minister of the time, Earl Alexander of Tunis: 'This problem has intrigued me for a long time . . . There are of course many phenomena in this world which are not explained and . . . the orthodox scientist is the last person to accept that something new (or old) may exist which cannot be explained in accordance with his understanding of natural laws.'[23]

Air Chief Marshal Lord Dowding, Commander-in-Chief of RAF Fighter Command during the Battle of Britain in 1940, was enormously interested in the subject of UFOs and on a number of occasions made some courageous statements, such as the following, published in an article he wrote in 1954:

More than 10,000 sightings have been reported, the majority of
which cannot be accounted for by any 'scientific' explanation, e.g.
that they are hallucinations, the effects of light refraction, meteors,
wheels falling from aeroplanes, and the like . . . They have been
tracked on radar screens . . . and the observed speeds have been as
great as 9,000 miles an hour . . . I am convinced that these objects
do exist and that they are not manufactured by any nation on
earth. I can therefore see no alternative to accepting the theory
that they come from some extraterrestrial source . . .

I think that we must resist the tendency to assume that they all
come from the same planet, or that they are actuated by similar
motives. It might be that the visitors from one planet wished to
help us in our evolution from the basis of a higher level to which
they had attained.

Another planet might send an expedition to ascertain what have
been these terrible explosions which they have observed, and to
prevent us from discommoding other people beside ourselves by
the new toys with which we are so light-heartedly playing.

Other visitors might have come bent solely on scientific
discovery and might regard us with the dispassionate aloofness
with which we might regard insects found beneath an upturned
stone.[24]

Admiral of the Fleet the Earl Mountbatten of Burma, Supreme Allied
Commander in South-East Asia during the Second World War and Chief
of the Defence Staff from 1958 to 1965, showed considerable interest in
the UFO subject for a number of years. His biographer, Philip Ziegler,
writes that Mountbatten once tried to persuade the *Sunday Dispatch* to put
a team on to the more promising cases, and in a private letter to the editor
he also propounded his hypothesis that the UFOs were themselves the
inhabitants of other planets, rather than actual machines. 'I know this
sounds ridiculous,' he wrote, 'and I am relying on you . . . not to make
capital out of the fact that I have put forward such a far-fetched
explanation.'[25]

The Landing at Broadlands

One wonders if Lord Mountbatten felt inclined to modify his hypothesis
when, in February 1955, a flying saucer complete with occupant was
alleged to have landed on his estate at Broadlands, near Romsey,

Hampshire. The story was related to me many years ago by Desmond Leslie, who had investigated it personally and later published an account,[26] following Mountbatten's tragic murder by Irish terrorists in 1979. Thanks to Philip Ziegler, Mollie Travis (Mountbatten's private secretary at the time) and the trustees of the Broadlands Archives, photocopies of the original statements made immediately after the incident were made available to me.

The first statement is by the witness, Frederick Briggs, with an appended drawing, and the second is by Mountbatten himself (pp. 16–17), with an endorsement by Ronald Heath, his electrician. Briggs's statement is as follows:

> I am at present employed at Broadlands as a bricklayer and was cycling to my work from Romsey on the morning of Wednesday, the 23rd February 1955. When I was about half way between the Palmerston or Romsey Lodge and the house, just by where the drive forks off to the Middlebridge Lodge, I suddenly saw an object hovering stationary over the field between the end of the gardens and Middlebridge Drive, and just on the house side of the little stream.
>
> The object was shaped like a child's huge humming-top and half way between 20ft. or 30ft. in diameter.
>
> Its colour was like dull aluminium, rather like a kitchen saucepan. It was shaped like the sketch which I have endeavoured to make, and had portholes all round the middle, rather like a steamer has.
>
> The time was just after 8.30 a.m. with an overcast sky and light snow on the ground.
>
> I turned off the drive at the fork and rode over the grass for rather less than 100 yards. I then dismounted, and holding my bicycle in my right hand, watched.
>
> While I was watching a column, about the thickness of a man, descended from the centre of the Saucer and I suddenly noticed on it, what appeared to be a man, presumably standing on a small platform on the end. He did not appear to be holding on to anything. He seemed to be dressed in a dark suit of overalls, and was wearing a close fitting hat or helmet.
>
> At the time the Saucer was certainly less than 100 yards from me, and not more than 60ft. over the level where I was standing, although the meadow has a steep bank at this point, so that the

Saucer would have been about 80ft. over the lower level of the meadow.

As I stood there watching, I suddenly saw a curious light come on in one of the portholes. It was a bluish light, rather like a mercury vapour light. Although it was quite bright, it did not appear to be directed straight at me, nor did it dazzle me, but simultaneously with the light coming on I suddenly seemed to be pushed over, and I fell down in the snow with my bicycle on top of me. What is more, I could not get up again. Although the bicycle only weighs a few lbs. it seemed as though an unseen force was holding me down.

Whilst lying on the ground I could see the tube withdrawn quickly into the Saucer, which then rose vertically, quite as fast as the fastest Jet aircraft I have seen, or faster.

There had been no noise whatever until the Saucer started to move, and even then the noise was no louder than that of an ordinary small rocket let off by a child on Guy Fawkes Night.

It disappeared out of sight into the clouds almost instantaneously, and as it went, I found myself able to get up. Although I seemed to be lying a long time on the ground I do not suppose, in reality, it was more than a few seconds.

I felt rather dizzy, as though I had received a near knockout blow on the point of the chin, but of course there was no physical hurt of any sort, merely a feeling of dizziness.

I picked up my bicycle, mounted it and rode straight on to Broadlands where I met Heath standing by the garage.

I was feeling very shaky and felt I must regain my confidence by discussing what I had seen. I said to him: 'Look, Ron, have you known me long enough to know that I am sane and sober at this hour of the morning?' He laughed and made some remark like, 'Well, of course.' Then I told him what I had seen.

Heath and I went back along the road where I showed him the tracks of my bicycle. I then went back to work, where I saw my foreman, Mr. Hudson, and told him what I had seen.

Lord Mountbatten's statement reads:

The attached statement was dictated by Mr. Briggs to Mrs. Travis on the morning of the 23rd February 1955 at my request.

My own electrician, Heath, reported his conversation and I

subsequently interviewed Mr. Briggs, with my wife and younger daughter, and as a result of his account, Heath and I accompanied him to the place from which he saw the Flying Saucer.

We followed the marks of his bicycle in the snow very easily, and exactly at the spot which he described the tracks came to an end, and foot marks appeared beside it. Next to the foot marks there were the marks of a body having fallen in the snow, and then the marks of a bicycle having been picked up again, there being a clear gap of 3ft. between where the front wheel marks originally ended and then started again. The rear wheel marks were continuous but blurred. From then on the bicycle tracks led back to the drive.

The bicycle tracks absolutely confirm Mr. Briggs' story, so far as his own movements are concerned.

He, Heath and I searched the area over the spot where the Flying Saucer was estimated to have been, but candidly we could see no unusual signs.

The snow at the bottom of the meadow had melted much more than at the top, and it would have been difficult to see any marks.

This statement has been dictated in the presence of Heath and Mr. Briggs, and Heath and I have carefully read Mr. Briggs' statement, and we both attest that this is the exact story which he told us.

Mr. Briggs was still dazed when I first saw him, and was worried that no one would believe his story. Indeed, he made a point of saying that he had never believed in Flying Saucer stories before, and been absolutely amazed at what he had seen.

He did not give me the impression of being the sort of man who would be subject to hallucinations, or would in any way invent such a story. I am sure from the sincere way he gave his account that he, himself, is completely convinced of the truth of his own statement.

He has offered to swear to the truth of this statement on oath on the Bible if needed, but I saw no point in asking him to do this.

At the bottom of Mountbatten's signed statement is an endorsement by Ronald Heath.

Philip Ziegler makes short shrift of the episode, and comments that by 1957 Mountbatten had become disillusioned with the amount of rubbish published on the subject, and, although he never rejected the possibility

The attached statement was dictated by Mr. Briggs to Mrs. Travis on the morning of the 23rd February 1955 at my request.

My own electrician, Heath, reported his conversation and I subsequently interviewed Mr. Briggs, with my wife and younger daughter, and as a result of his account, Heath and I accompanied him to the place from which he saw the Flying Saucer.

We followed the marks of his bicycle in the snow very easily, and exactly at the spot which he described the tracks came to an end, and foot marks appeared beside it. Next to the foot marks there were the marks of a body having fallen in the snow, and then the marks of a bicycle having been picked up again, there being a clear gap of 3ft. between where the front wheel marks originally ended and then started again. The rear wheel marks were continuous but blurred. From then on the bicycle tracks led back to the drive.

The bicycle tracks absolutely confirm Mr. Briggs' story, so far as his own movements are concerned.

He, Heath and I searched the area over the spot where the Flying Saucer was estimated to have been, but candidly we could see no unusual signs.

The snow at the bottom of the meadow had melted much more than that at the top, and it would have been difficult to see any marks.

This statement has been dictated in the presence of Heath and Mr. Briggs, and Heath and I have carefully read Mr. Briggs' statement, and we both attest that this is the exact story which he told us.

Mr. Briggs was still dazed when I first saw him, and was worried that no one would believe his story. Indeed, he made a point of saying that he had never believed in Flying Saucer stories before, and had been absolutely amazed at what he had seen.

He did not give me the impression of being the sort of man who would be subject to hallucinations, or would in any way invent such a story. I am sure from the sincere way he gave his account that he, himself, is completely convinced of the truth of his own statement.

He has offered to swear to the truth of this statement on oath on the Bible if needed, but I saw no point in asking him to do this.

Mountbatten of Burma

I confirm that I have read and agree with the above statement.

R K Heath

A statement by Lord Mountbatten relating to the reported landing of an unknown craft at his estate in Hampshire in 1955. (*Broadlands Archives*)

that such objects existed, he felt they must be susceptible to rational explanation. Ziegler also cites an interesting observation made by Mountbatten, before his interest waned, in 1950:

> The fact that they can hover and accelerate away from the earth's gravity again and even revolve round a V2 in America (as reported by their head scientist) shows they are far ahead of us. If they really come over in a big way that may settle the capitalist–communist war. If the human race wishes to survive they may have to band together.[27]

Flying Saucers – Top Secret

In APRIL 1955 the Air Ministry announced that the report of a five-year investigation into flying saucers by the Royal Air Force had been submitted to high-ranking officers but that it was never to be revealed to the public for security reasons. In view of the Ministry's oft-repeated statement that UFOs do not constitute a threat to the nation's security, this was a curious announcement, and it provoked Major Patrick Wall MP to ask the Under-Secretary of State for Air, George Ward, to confirm whether he proposed to publish a report. Ward's reply failed to address the question:

> Reports of flying saucers, as well as other abnormal objects in the sky, are investigated as they come in, but there has been no formal enquiry. About 90% of the reports have been found to relate to meteors, balloons, flares and many other objects. The fact that the other 10% are unexplained need be attributed to nothing more sinister than lack of data.[1]

The reference to 10 per cent of cases that might have been explained if it had not been for 'lack of data' is without foundation, as discussed in the previous chapter.

The Kilgallen Story

On 22 May 1955, Dorothy Kilgallen, the well-known American journalist, cabled the following International News Service syndicated report from London:

> I can report today on a story which is positively spooky, not to mention chilling. British scientists and airmen, after examining the wreckage of one mysterious flying ship, are convinced these strange aerial objects are not optical illusions or Soviet inventions, but are flying saucers which originate on another planet.

The source of my information is a British official of Cabinet rank who prefers to remain unidentified. 'We believe, on the basis of our inquiry thus far, that the saucers were staffed by small men – probably under four feet tall. It's frightening, but there is no denying the flying saucers come from another planet.'

This official quoted scientists as saying a flying ship of this type could not have possibly been constructed on Earth. The British Government, I learned, is withholding an official report on the 'flying saucer' examination at this time, possibly because it does not wish to frighten the public.

When my husband [Richard Kollmer, Broadway producer and radio commentator] and I arrived here for a brief vacation, I had no premonition that I would be catapulting myself into the controversy over whether flying saucers are real or imaginary . . .[2]

The story has been discounted as a hoax, and investigators have never been able to authenticate it. Gordon Creighton, the former diplomat, intelligence officer, and long-time editor of *Flying Saucer Review*, told me that the crash was alleged to have taken place during the Second World War, and the story was related to Dorothy Kilgallen during a cocktail party given by Lord Mountbatten in May 1955, but I have been unable to substantiate this with his former private secretary.

Creighton was unsuccessful in obtaining a reply to a letter he addressed to Kilgallen, as was the Swedish researcher K. Gösta Rehn, who, like many others, reasoned that the story was simply a newspaper gimmick for which the journalist had been reprimanded. British authorities were said to have issued a sharp denial of Kilgallen's report. Had the journalist simply been teased, Gösta Rehn wondered. 'This suggestion does not accord with the objective tone of the report. Why should the Englishman have told her about it if he were not deeply interested in the secret, relied on her confidence and his own anonymity? And why should Dorothy Kilgallen risk her reputation as one of the USA's star journalists by propagating an untrue story?'[3] To the best of my knowledge, Kilgallen never denied the story. Furthermore, a number of similar stories from reliable sources have surfaced over the years (see Part Three), not all of which can be discounted, however absurd they may seem.

RAF Bentwaters/Lakenheath

An impressive sighting by RAF and US Air Force personnel took place on the night of 13/14 August 1956, when at least one UFO was tracked simultaneously by three different ground-based radars at RAF/USAF Bentwaters and Lakenheath, Suffolk, as well as on airborne radar, and the objects were also seen from the ground and in the air. This is the account by F. H. C. Wimbledon, RAF fighter controller on duty at RAF Neatishead, Norfolk, at the time:

> I was Chief Controller on duty at the main RAF Radar Station in East Anglia on the night in question. My duties were to monitor the Radar picture and to scramble the Battle Flight, who were on duty 24 hours a day, to intercept any intruder of British airspace not positively identified in my sector of responsibility . . .
>
> I remember Lakenheath USAF base telephoning to say there was something 'buzzing' their aircraft circuit. I scrambled a Venom night fighter from the Battle Flight through Sector and my controller in the Interception Cabin took over control of it. The Interception Control team would consist of one Fighter Controller (an Officer), a Corporal, a tracker and a height reader. That is, four highly trained personnel in addition to myself could now clearly see the object on our radar scopes . . .
>
> After being vectored onto the trail of the object by my Interception Controller, the pilot called out, 'Contact', then a short time later, 'Judy', which meant the Navigator had the target fairly and squarely on his own radar screen and needed no further help from the ground. He continued to close on the target but after a few seconds, and in the space of one or two sweeps of our scopes, the object appeared behind our fighter. Our pilot called out, 'Lost Contact, more help', and he was told the target was now behind him and he was given fresh instructions.
>
> I then scrambled a second Venom which was vectored towards the area but before it arrived on the scene the target had disappeared from our scopes and although we continued to keep a careful watch was not seen by us.
>
> . . . the fact remains that at least nine RAF ground personnel and two RAF aircrew were conscious of an object sufficiently 'solid' to give returns on radar. Naturally, all this was reported and a Senior Officer from the Air Ministry came down and interrogated us.[4]

In a letter to the *Sunday Times*, Mr Wimbledon revealed that the Headquarters, Fighter Command, was fully informed, and that the strictest secrecy was imposed.[5] The case was taken off the secret list in January 1969 when the USAF-sponsored scientific study of UFOs, headed by Dr Edward Condon, published its findings (see Chapter 16). The investigation team concluded that 'this is the most puzzling and unusual case in the radar-visual files. The apparently rational, intelligent behaviour of the UFO suggests a mechanical device of unknown origin as the most probable explanation.'[6]

During a televised public meeting at Banbury Town Hall on 26 January 1972, a member of the audience asked Ministry of Defence spokesman Anthony Davies what the Ministry had to say about the Bentwaters/Lakenheath case. Mr Davies replied that he could say nothing because the papers had been destroyed.[7] I asked former MoD official Ralph Noyes if he was aware of this. He pointed out that as head of Defence Secretariat 8 (DS8), which, among other tasks, handled UFO reports from the public, he saw only a small proportion of the UFO material during his tenure with DS8 (1969–72), because the bulk of reports was handled by S4, another MoD department.

'I think it is *very* surprising if those papers were destroyed,' he added:

> There is every indication that at the time of the incident the Air Ministry, as it then was, was exceedingly interested, if not positively uneasy. If the papers have been destroyed this does look like a thoroughly improper step to have taken. There is no doubt that something important took place at Bentwaters/ Lakenheath, even if it was only a very extraordinary misperception by radar operators and pilots, and that should surely have remained on record.

Ralph Noyes, who retired from the Ministry of Defence in the grade of Under-Secretary of State in 1977, revealed to me that gun-camera film had been taken by one of the Venom pilots, and that he was shown this at Whitehall, together with a number of other film clips taken by RAF aircrew. The films were shown at a briefing arranged by the head of S4, attended by the Director of Air Defence, some Air Staff personnel, and a representative from the Meteorological Office. 'The briefing was intended to inform those few of us who had a concern with these matters what the phenomena might be about,' he explained. 'The flavour of the discussion was that it *might* be something obscure meteorologically. The film clips were very brief, rather fuzzy and not particularly spectacular. But they existed!'[8]

Nicholas Pope, formerly with the MoD's Secretariat (Air Staff) 2a – the successor to DS8 – made extensive enquiries on our behalf to locate these film clips, but nothing has been found. 'I am afraid that this suggests that such material was destroyed, either because it was not judged to be of sufficient interest or significance, or (in the case of old films) because it had deteriorated beyond the point at which it might have been saved,' he wrote to me.[9]

RAF West Freugh

On 4 April 1957 up to five unidentified targets were tracked on radar in Scotland, and radar stations throughout Britain were ordered by RAF Intelligence to keep a twenty-four-hour watch.

'I have been ordered by the Air Ministry to say nothing about the object,' Wing Commander Walter Whitworth, Commanding Officer at RAF West Freugh, was quoted as saying. 'I am not allowed to reveal its position, course and speed. From the moment of picking it up, it was well within our area. It was an object of some substance – quite definitely not a freak. No mistake could have been made by the [Ministry of Supply] civilians operating the sets. They are fully qualified and experienced officers.'[10]

Wing Commander Whitworth said later that the matter had been taken extremely seriously by the Air Ministry, where a spokesman said that no detailed statement would be issued until experts had a full report. Documents relating to this incident were released thirty years later under provisions of the Official Secrets Act. The Deputy Directorate of Intelligence (Technical) investigators confirmed that a stationary object was first tracked by radar at Balscalloch at heights varying from 50,000 to 70,000 feet and that another radar station 20 miles away also locked on to the target. Later, four more targets, moving in line astern, were plotted by both radar stations. The sizes of the radar echoes were considerably larger than would be expected from normal aircraft. Indeed, the radar operators considered that the size was nearer that of a ship's echo. Even if balloons had been in the area, the report concluded, 'these would not account for the sudden change of direction and the movement at high speed against the prevailing wind . . . It is concluded that the incident was due to the presence of five reflecting objects of unidentified type and origin.'[11]

Room 801 – Top Secret

Nine weeks after the West Freugh report, *Reynolds News*, like the *Sunday Dispatch* in 1952, claimed that the Air Ministry conducted top secret research into the UFO phenomenon at one of its offices on Northumberland Avenue, London. The report stated that on the ninth floor of what was formerly the Hotel Metropole a top-secret room existed, Room 801, where all reports of UFOs were collected and studied by experts.

In the ten years during which the Air Ministry had been analysing the reports (1947–57), a Ministry spokesman was quoted as saying, they had 'something like 10,000 sightings' on file and, although many reports had been 'cleared up', there were some which could not be explained. 'Nobody in the know', he admitted, 'is prepared to say that all reports about these mystery objects are nonsense.'

It appeared that the interior of Room 801 was never seen by unauthorized persons. A large map of the British Isles hung on one wall, the report continued, and on it were literally thousands of coloured pins, with the heaviest concentration appearing to be over the Norwich area. At airfields all over Britain fighter planes were kept ready to intercept and if necessary to engage any UFO within combat range.[12]

Gordon Creighton had been an intelligence officer at Northumberland Avenue during the period in question, so I asked him if he could substantiate the story in any way, although he was not involved with the Air Ministry. 'I was on the next floor to the department that dealt with UFOs,' he replied. 'There was only one floor above us: that floor was DDI (Tech.), so everybody that went up in the lift above us was from that department. There weren't any other departments on that floor. But I and one or two other people in my department used to have fun when we were going up or down in the lift with a bunch of these chaps, talking about UFOs!'

Creighton learned that the Deputy Directorate of Intelligence (Technical) employed full-time researchers into the UFO subject – a fact consistently denied by the MoD – and that there was close liaison with the Americans. 'What I thought was fascinating', he told me, 'was that in those early days I met quite a number of US Air Force intelligence people, *and* CIA, who of course were deeply interested – always pretended they weren't – and we had *long* discussions about it.'[13]

FLYING SAUCERS ARE NO LONGER A JOKE

THE SECRET OF ROOM 801

REYNOLDS NEWS REPORTER

IN Room 801 of what was once the Hotel Metropole, Britain's Air Ministry is investigating Flying Saucers—and that's official. After years of speculation it can now be revealed that Defence Chiefs are taking the Flying Saucer SERIOUSLY.

Not only is there this special department for following up all "Saucer" reports but there is action, too.

At airfields all over Britain, fighter planes are kept ready to intercept, and if necessary engage, any unidentified flying object within combat range.

The heart of all this activity—Room 801—was once an attic on the ninth floor of the former hotel building in London's Northumberland Avenue, off Trafalgar Square.

Its existence was admitted last night by an Air Ministry spokesman. He disclosed that it has been investigating Flying Saucer reports since 1947. "We have something like 10,000 on our files," he said.

Mystery remains

Many of these had been "cleared up." But there were some that could not be explained.

"This is why nobody in the know is prepared to say that ALL reports about these mystery objects are nonsense," he added.

Earlier, I spoke to a man who has been inside Room 801. Its secrets are well guarded. But hanging over three padlocked filing cabinets is a map of the British Isles covered with thousands of coloured pins.

"The heaviest concentration of pins," he said, "appears to be over the Norwich area."

Again I talked to Mr. R. R. Russell, a Board of Trade technician, who has reported flying saucer sightings to the Ministry. He showed me some special forms on which these reports have to be made.

The Ministry, he said always insisted on the greatest secrecy.

An article from *Reynolds News* (London, 16 June 1957) revealing details of some of the Air Ministry's top-secret investigations. (*Gordon Creighton*)

Airliner Communications Interference

On 31 May 1957 at 07.17 hours a British airliner was flying over Kent, just south of Rochester, when both the captain and the first officer sighted a UFO which simultaneously cut out all radio communications. The following is a personal account by the captain, whose name has been withheld by request:

I was in command of a scheduled airline service from Croydon Airport to Holland. As we got to a position two nautical miles south of Rochester my First Officer and myself became aware of a brilliant object bearing 110° (T) from north and elevated about 10° above the haze level. We were flying at 5,000 feet above sea level, heading 082° magnetic 074° (T). The UFO was about two-thirds the size of a sixpence in the windscreen at first. It then appeared to come towards us. When it was about the size of a sixpence the object became oval in shape and turned away. Then it became as before and reduced in size to about half the size of a sixpence. Then to our astonishment the UFO disappeared completely as we watched it. We did not see the UFO go, but became aware that we were looking at an empty sky.

We were unable to contact London Radar due to a complete radio failure in the aircraft, nor were we able to report to London Airways, nor to London Flight Information. Radio failure, especially complete radio failure, is rare these days, and in our case was due to our circuit breakers not keeping 'In'. A radio circuit breaker 'breaks circuit' when the system is overloaded by an extra source of electrical or thermal energy. On this occasion we were not using all our equipment, so there was no cause for overloading. However, our radio equipment became fully service-able after the UFO had gone, and all circuit breakers stayed 'In'.

Is it too much to ask if the UFO was able, through overloading our electrical system, to prevent our reporting it or asking for radar confirmation? When we returned to the UK a similar report to [this one] was made to both the Ministry of Transport and Civil Aviation, and to the Air Ministry.[14]

RAF Gaydon

On 21 October 1957 Flying Officer D. W. Sweeney, flying a Meteor jet on a training exercise from RAF North Luffenham, nearly collided with an unidentified flying object over RAF Gaydon, Warwickshire. The incident occurred at 21.18 at an altitude of 28,000 feet. After taking evasive action Sweeney tried to approach the object, whereupon its six lights went out and it disappeared. The pilot's report was confirmed by radar a few minutes earlier at RAF Langtoft, when the object was tracked over Gaydon at about 28,000 feet. A check on military and civilian aircraft movements showed that the Meteor was the only plane in the area at the time.[15]

Questions in the House of Commons

On 19 April 1958 aircraft were scrambled at RAF Lakenheath to intercept unidentified targets which had been plotted on radar within 10 miles of the base. These targets subsequently were explained by the US Air Force as freak weather conditions. Nevertheless, the incident led to a question in the House of Commons on 10 June by George Chetwynd MP: 'How many instances of unidentified flying objects have been reported on by the defence services of the United Kingdom during the past twelve months, and what steps were taken to co-ordinate such observations?'

Charles Orr-Ewing, the Under-Secretary of State for Air, replied: 'Reports of 54 unidentified flying objects have been received in the last twelve months. Such co-ordination as is necessary is undertaken by the Air Ministry. Most of the objects turn out to be meteors, balloons or aircraft. Satellites have also accounted for a number of recent reports.'[16]

This was the last time the Government released figures of specifically military reports, and even in this guarded reply there is careful avoidance of the words 'by the defence services'. I have been unable to extract such figures from the Ministry of Defence. 'It is not possible to say how many "UFO" reports have been made by military personnel since 1947,' I was told in 1984.[17]

On 30 July 1958 George Chetwynd pressed further questions in the House of Commons. He began by asking the Secretary of State for Air, George Ward, what action was being taken to ascertain the identity of UFOs which had not been recognized as meteors, balloons, aircraft or satellites. Replied Ward: 'We investigate all reports of UFOs as fully as the details allow, but I am afraid there will always be some which remain unexplained because the reports are not sufficiently precise.'

Mr Chetwynd then asked if the 'Right Honourable Gentleman' was aware that a number of scientific societies were conducting research to establish the existence of flying saucers. Could he say whether his department had any information which would back up this claim and, if so, whether he would be prepared to give it to these societies? George Ward repeated that the bulk of the reports was explained, and only a very small proportion was not, adding: 'We think that the reason why these are not explained, too, is that the data we have about them is not sufficient.' Mr Chetwynd persisted: 'Is there any evidence to back up the claims that there are flying saucers?' The Minister did not reply.[18]

On 5 November 1958 Roy Mason MP, who later became Minister of Defence, asked the Air Minister to what extent official records were kept of sightings; what departments within the Air Ministry existed solely to collate information on this question; and to what extent this information suggested that some of the unidentified phenomena might not originate on this planet. In a written reply, Air Minister George Ward said: 'If a report on an unidentified flying object has a bearing on the air defence of this country it is investigated and the results recorded. No staff are employed whole-time on the task. Although some of the objects have not been identified for lack of data, nothing suggests that they are other than mundane.'[19]

This was clearly an unsatisfactory reply for Roy Mason, and on 21 January 1959 he asked the Air Minister another question in the Commons: What specific instructions had been sent to the commanders of Royal Air Force stations to collect reports from air crews having allegedly sighted unidentified flying objects; what inquiries had been held following such sightings; and to what extent was there collaboration between the department and the respective departments in Canada and the United States on this problem? Ward replied that RAF units had standing instructions to report unusual flying objects when they could not be readily explained. Reports which might have a bearing on air defence were investigated, he added, and no special collaboration with Canada or the United States was required.[20]

A sighting by officials at London Airport one month later led to further questions in the Commons. The Times of 26 February 1959 reported that RAF Fighter Command Headquarters had described the object as 'a bright yellow light varying in intensity some 200 feet from the ground. It stayed in one position for about 20 minutes, then climbed away at high speed.' Police, air traffic controllers and others examined the UFO through binoculars. In a written reply on 11 March, Air Minister Ward stated:

A pale yellow light was seen by officials at London Airport above one of the runways from 7.25 to 7.45 on the evening of February 25. There was no corresponding response on the airport radars or on air defence radars. The light was not identified . . . There was insufficient evidence to determine what the cause of this light could have been.[21]

The Air Minister Admits to a Cover-Up

Desmond Leslie, the co-author with George Adamski of *Flying Saucers Have Landed*, is a second cousin to the late Sir Winston Churchill. Dubbed the 'Saucerer Royal' because he was well acquainted with British royalty and various VIPs in the Government during the 1950s, he also had served in the Royal Air Force as a fighter pilot during the Second World War. He was thus ideally placed to assess the true attitude of officialdom to the subject, and that of George Ward in particular.

Ward was Parliamentary Under-Secretary of State for Air when Leslie first met him in 1953 and presented him with a copy of his book. I quote from part of the letter that Ward subsequently wrote to Leslie, dated 18 January 1954:

Dear Saucerer Royal,

Thank you so much for sending me your book . . . I was delighted to have it. I read every word during the weekend. It is even more fascinating than I expected.

I can well understand why you got so absorbed in the subject. My head has been full of thoughts about it for two days . . . I was lost in admiration at the immense amount of research you had done . . .

Let's meet again as soon as possible. There is a mass of things I want to ask you . . .

I spent the morning with old Handley Page at his [aircraft] works. I couldn't escape from the horrible thought that all our efforts to fly higher and faster and further are simply brute force. God, I wish we knew how to build a [flying saucer]! Let's damn well find out . . .

It is evident that George Ward had become very interested in the subject before his debunking statements in the House of Commons. When the Air Ministry 'explained' the sighting in 1953 by Flying Officers

Johnson and Smythe near RAF West Malling as 'balloons', Desmond
Leslie telephoned the Air Minister and politely hinted that he was a fibber.
Ward laughed and replied: 'What am I to say? *I* know it wasn't a balloon.
You know it wasn't a balloon. But until I've got a saucer on the ground in
Hyde Park and can charge the public sixpence a go to enter, it must be
balloons, otherwise the Government would fall and I'd lose my job.'

Ward went on to explain the difficult position he found himself in,
along with other members of Her Majesty's Government, and said that if
he admitted the existence of flying saucers without evidence that the
general public could actually touch, the public would consider that the
Government had gone barmy and lose their faith in it.

Leslie also challenged George Ward about the near collision with an
unknown craft reported by Flight Lieutenant Salandin over the Thames
Estuary in 1954 (Chapter 1), when, after the story was published, RAF
North Weald had its switchboard jammed with enquiries, and asked why
the Air Minister had issued an order forbidding pilots to report such
sightings to the public or press.[22] 'Look,' replied Ward, 'I'm trying to run
an air force. When a story like this breaks, the poor [Commanding
Officer] is driven frantic. His telephone is jammed with calls and he is
unable to get on with the business of running an efficient airfield.'[23]

These statements are conclusive proof of a cover-up by Her Majesty's
Government, though for what seem legitimate, understandable reasons.
However, in so far as George Ward's reason citing the lack of tangible
proof is concerned, there are grounds for sustaining the belief that such
proof does exist, even if it has not always been made available to successive
Government ministers.

A Matter of National Security

Press Censorship?

OVER THE NEXT few years the number of UFO sightings in the United Kingdom declined considerably, and newspaper reports became correspondingly less frequent, leading to a suspicion in some quarters that they were being censored by officialdom. Journalist Roger Muirfield, for example, wrote in 1960: 'Although I cannot explain why the truth is being suppressed, I am certain it is merely a rearguard action that is being fought, consciously or subsconsciously, by those who are responsible for the moulding of public opinion. Somewhere, I am certain, the penny has dropped, but the public must not be told.'[1]

Waveney Girvan, editor of *Flying Saucer Review* at the time, was convinced that there was no press censorship as such; rather, the media had become bored with a subject which for many had become ridiculous and no longer newsworthy.[2] These sentiments were echoed in 1962 by Robert Chapman, science correspondent of the *Sunday Express* and author of *Unidentified Flying Objects*. He has assured me that he has found no evidence of a D-notice being brought to bear on reports of UFOs; other journalists and editors have confirmed this for me.

The D-Notice and the Official Secrets Act

A D-notice is a formal letter of request circulated confidentially to newspaper editors, warning them that an item of news, which may be protected under the Official Secrets Act, is regarded by the defence authorities as a secret affecting national security. A D-notice has no legal authority and can only be regarded as a letter of advice or request, but it warns that 'whether or not any legal sanction would attach to the act of publication, publication is considered to be contrary to the national interest'.[3]

The Official Secrets Act prohibits all forms of espionage and bars government officials from divulging secrets and unauthorized persons from receiving them. The Act is invariably linked to the D-notice system and, since a D-notice warns an editor that publication of a given news item may violate the Act, the effect is one of censorship. Is there any evidence that some news items on UFOs have been subject to censorship, *per se*? Freelance journalist Tony Gray told me that a colleague of his was once warned off a UFO story by 'someone in the Government'. This is only one of several rumours that have reached me indicating that pressure has been applied to editors and journalists. If such pressure had ever been *widely* applied, this would in itself constitute a sensational story that Fleet Street would have lost little time capitalizing on – a counterproductive move in so far as the Ministry of Defence would be concerned, since the Ministry, in my view, is anxious to avoid any suggestion of a cover-up. Debunking is a more effective measure. Yet in one case, at least, the Official Secrets Act *was* invoked to prevent further newspaper coverage of an important UFO event.

In 1989 the editor of the *Heywood Advertiser* revealed that, following investigations into a 1957 sighting in Wardle, Lancashire, which led to follow-up articles in his newspaper and a question in the House of Commons (described in *Above Top Secret*[4]), his newspaper was effectively silenced. 'We went into [the case] very thoroughly indeed and no matter what continued to report the pros and cons of the debate for several weeks,' wrote Alan Fitzsimmons, a young reporter at the time. 'That all came to an end when the very top man from the Ministry of Defence called at our office personally, took us into a private back room and read the Official Secrets Act to us, with the warning to discontinue reporting further on that strange occurrence.'[5]

The New Ministry of Defence

In 1964 the Air Ministry, Admiralty and War Office were unified into the new Ministry of Defence, largely at the instigation of Lord Mountbatten, Chief of the Defence Staff at the time. The Air Ministry became the Air Force Department, within which was a secretariat called S4 (Air) that had, among other jobs, the task of handling complaints from the public about alleged low-flying infringements as well as dealing with reports of UFO sightings by members of the public. Another department within the Central Staffs – Defence Secretariat 8 (DS8) – handled similar tasks at this time.

The newly formed DS8 took over the responsibilities of Secretariat 6. 'The significant change was that instead of belonging to the Air Force Department it now belonged to the Secretary of State,' the former head of DS8, Ralph Noyes, explained to me during an interview in 1985:

It gave it a certain authority, and was one of Denis Healey's means of trying to get all information about all three services collated at the Central Staffs. The old S6, the old S4, had had the same uneasy division between them about these reports from the public that the new DS8 and the new S4 (Air) had, and that persisted. It was very frustrating to me, and the head of that other division. We would sometimes say to each other in the corridor: 'We've got something here. Is it yours? Is it mine?' And if it looked very clearly like a low-flying complaint – something that suddenly frightened a lot of sheep in a valley in Wales, and was pretty clearly a Lightning [interceptor jet] or something – then it was for S4 to deal with, and I used to sigh with relief and let S4 get on with it, and find out from the unit if a Lightning had been outside the designated low-flying area.

But often enough stuff came to DS8 because S4 – very often having received it as the main point of entry – said, 'Nothing to do with us. This isn't low-flying. This wasn't an exercise. There's nothing here that we've got any responsibility to the public for. Over to you.' So DS8 tended to get a lot of UFO reports, quite often through S4, sometimes directly from the public.

The prime task of dealing with UFO reports and replying to the public, however, lay with S4 at that time, as Ralph Noyes has confirmed. 'Does this mean,' I asked him, 'that you didn't necessarily see the best material?' 'It certainly does,' replied Noyes. 'If by "best" material you mean close encounters on the ground – I wouldn't.' Nor would he necessarily have been privy to military reports. For example, following a review of official UFO reporting procedures, an Air Ministry memorandum, dated 14 November 1962, reveals that 'Reports from civilian sources and replies thereto are dealt with by S6, and reports from service sources, including unidentified radar responses, are dealt with by A.I. (Tech) 5(b).' Researcher Nicholas Redfern was informed by the Ministry of Defence that files relating to reports received by this specialist military division (Air Intelligence, Technical Branch 5b) in the early 1960s were destroyed.[6]

Questions to Ministers

In July 1964 Mr A. Henderson MP asked the Secretary of State for Defence, Hugh Fraser: 'To what extent is there co-operation between the

Royal Air Force and the United States Air Force with a view to ascertaining the facts relating to flying saucers or other unidentified flying objects; and what information is now available to his department on this matter?' Replied Mr Fraser: 'We are generally aware of the experience of the United States Air Force. Some 90 per cent of the sightings investigated by my Department have had a perfectly rational explanation. In the remaining 10 per cent of cases, the information available was insufficient to support an adequate enquiry. We have discovered no evidence for the existence of so-called flying saucers.'[7] Once again, the House of Commons was deliberately or inadvertently misinformed about the true nature of the 10 per cent of sightings.

On 19 July 1966 Sir John Langford-Holt MP asked Prime Minister Harold Wilson in the House of Commons whether, since the Defence Secretary was responsible only for the air-defence implications associated with reports of unidentified flying objects, he would allocate to a department the assessment of their wider implications. The Prime Minister replied that he would not. Sir John then added that an enormous number of reports were coming in to the Government from people who were not all cranks. It would be proper, he said, for someone in the Government to take a serious interest in them. The Prime Minister answered that they were taken seriously when there was adequate information. Many reports were of natural phenomena, and those that were not were balloons, and so on.[8]

In 1984 I wrote to the former Prime Minister (Lord Wilson of Rievaulx, who died in 1995) asking to what extent he was aware of secret studies being conducted on the subject in the UK and USA, citing certain documentary evidence in my possession that I was prepared to send him if necessary. I received the following reply: 'I am afraid I have no knowledge of the matters to which you refer, and I am sorry that I cannot therefore be of any help to you with regard to the queries you raise.'[9]

I wrote a letter in similar vein to former Prime Minister Edward Heath in 1982, and received much the same response. 'As far as UFOs are concerned,' he replied, 'I am afraid I cannot comment as I have no knowledge of the subject.'[10] A letter I wrote in 1985 to Prime Minister Margaret Thatcher was referred to the Ministry of Defence, who replied in traditional vein.

Asked at a public meeting in 1963 why the Government was trying to 'hush-up the sightings of flying saucers', the former Minister of Defence (1959–62) Harold Watkinson, without actually answering the question, returned an intriguing reply: 'Before I left the Ministry I had to sign a large number of papers promising never to reveal certain facts I had learned as Minister of Defence. The subject of flying saucers may be included.'[11]

The 1967 Wave of Sightings

Nineteen sixty-seven was one of the busiest years for sightings ever recorded in the United Kingdom and many other countries, and the Ministry of Defence was inundated with reports. One sighting not reported is the following, which took place outside British airspace on the night of 22 March 1967, observed by the crew of a 135-seat, four-engine turboprop Vickers Vanguard airliner, operated by British European Airways (later British Airways). First Officer Graham Sheppard related the encounter to me:

> Halfway home on a Gibraltar–London sector, we were well clear of the north coast of Spain over the Bay of Biscay. The sky was clear and cloudless, the stars brilliant in the night sky. Thus far the flight for us three crew had been routine and uneventful.
>
> At some point our attention was drawn to an exceptionally bright star straight ahead in our 12 o'clock position and at an elevation of about 20°. The other co-pilot who was occupying the centre seat attempted to identify the star by use of a rotating plastic star chart which, on alignment to the month [March] and sky quadrant, yielded nothing.
>
> We observed this star for several minutes when quite abruptly it started to move to our left, descending as it did so to about a 10 o'clock position at an elevation of about 10° – i.e. a little above the horizon. As it moved, its colour changed from bright white through red, blue, green iridescence, then when in the new position it commenced high-speed aerobatics of such angular accelerations that conventional aerodynamics could not account for it.
>
> After a short display of zipping around the sky it was suddenly joined by another, as if from nowhere. Both UFOs then engaged in a dazzling display of high-speed aerobatics, all the while gradually drifting away to our 9 o'clock position – i.e. our left wing-tip.
>
> We asked Bordeaux Radar controlling that sector if they had any traffic. They replied, 'Unidentified traffic 10 miles west of you', which I would say was exactly where the UFOs were.

The Captain, a World War II veteran, advised us not to report the sighting as it would have adverse career implications . . .[12]

Another Observation by Airliner Crew

In mid-1967 (exact date not recorded), three crew members of a Vanguard operated by British European Airways encountered a disc-shaped aircraft in the vicinity of Manchester. First Officer Graham Sheppard, co-pilot on the flight, was to witness his second sighting that year, and described the encounter to me as follows:

> We were flying airway Amber 1 from Scotland to London, in the cruise at about 24,000 feet near Manchester, when the incident occurred. The weather was sunny and fine; smooth conditions with fair weather cumulus below us, providing excellent depth reference in respect of other craft.
>
> Preston Radar, the controlling authority, alerted us: 'You have fast-moving, opposite-direction traffic on the Airway, in your 12 o'clock [straight ahead], height unknown.' Almost immediately into view came a disc-shaped craft heading slightly to our right side on a reciprocal track. As P2 [co-pilot, in the right-hand seat] on this sector I was operating the radio and confirmed to Preston Radar: 'We have contact. It is in our 1 o'clock – 2 o'clock – 3 o'clock . . .' as it sped by. It then disappeared behind us.
>
> I had a clear view of the UFO shining in the sunlight with its clearly reflective surface, like metal. It was shaped like a hub-cap or a discus, with a diameter of at least 30 feet. Its distance from us was about a quarter-mile to our right – i.e. to the west – and several hundred feet below us. Its speed was much higher than a contemporary Trident or BAC 1-11 jet airliner, and I emphasize that relative speeds of other aeroplanes in close proximity were routine and normal judgements.

Sheppard told me that, although short in duration, the sighting was of immense interest. 'No report was made. No note was made in my logbook and I can only assume that the admonition by the captain after the Bay of Biscay sighting was enough to discourage me from writing anything anywhere.'[13]

In 1993 Sheppard, then a British Airways captain flying Boeing 757s and 767s, went public with these reports (although I had published one of them the previous year[14]), leading to media attention. There were serious repercussions. In a letter from a British Airways chief pilot, Sheppard was warned that an overlap existed between his status as a BA captain and any statements which he made on all matters relating to aviation, including UFO phenomena. Sheppard was warned about the possible media reaction, particularly the ridiculing of his views and subsequent damage to his image as a BA captain, and he was left in no doubt of the likely repercussions in the event of a breach of rules. The chief pilot emphasized that Sheppard was not being singled out in this respect, since these rules apply to every employee of BA.

It must be stressed that the implied threat of Graham Sheppard's suspension from his duties has little to do with an official cover-up (though it can have the same effect). Evidently British Airways was merely reinforcing the regulations concerning its employees' relations with the media, and in this particular case fear of company ridicule was the principal motive behind the warning. Sometimes there is a fine line between fear of ridicule and concern about national security! (In late 1994 Sheppard took early retirement from BA; currently he flies Boeing 767s for another major international airline.)

Air Force Encounters

On the afternoon of 27 October 1967, thirteen-year-old Timothy Robinson and his family were startled by the roar of jet aircraft overhead. Timothy – a keen aircraft spotter – dashed to the back garden of his home in Winchester, Hampshire. 'I saw [two] Lightnings go over at about four times the height of the house,' he told Robert Chapman, science correspondent of the *Daily Express*. Ahead of the aircraft, Timothy saw a black mushroom-shaped object streaking away in the sky. 'It was hanging tail down, not spinning, but going at a tremendous speed,' said Timothy. 'It was going west, then abruptly changed direction to north-west and disappeared into a cloud, climbing steeply. It looked as if the aircraft were banking to follow it but were outmanoeuvred.' The Ministry of Defence denied that it had any Lightnings over Winchester at the time, and was unable to explain the presence of any other type of aircraft.[15]

In response to my enquiry as to how many sightings had been reported to the Ministry of Defence by RAF pilots in 1967, I was informed that there was only one.[16] Eventually the MoD revealed that the sighting was made by the pilot of an RAF Victor aircraft on 13 July, but it was unwilling to provide me with further details.[17] It is clear, at any rate, that that sighting does not relate to the report cited here.

The Moigne Downs Incident

One of the most remarkable sightings of the 1967 wave was that by J. B. W. (Angus) Brooks, a former RAF intelligence officer and British Airways flight administration officer. While walking his dogs on the morning of 26 October and taking a brief respite from a force-8 gale at Moigne Downs, near Ringstead Bay, Dorset, Brooks noticed an object which descended at lightning speed, decelerated abruptly, then levelled out to a point about a quarter of a mile from his position at roughly 200–300 feet altitude. In his own highly detailed report, Brooks describes the shape of the craft before levelling:

> . . . a central circular chamber with a leading fuselage in the front and three separate fuselages together at the rear. On slowing to 'hover' position, the two outer fuselages at the rear moved to position at side of 'craft' to form four fuselages at equidistant position around centre chamber. There were no visible power units and no noise of applied power for reverse thrust, movement of fuselages, or for 'hovering'. On attaining 'hover' the 'craft' rotated 90° clockwise and then remained motionless, unaffected by very strong wind.

The object remained motionless for the next twenty-two minutes while Brooks noted further details. The craft appeared to be constructed of a translucent material: the central chamber was about 25 feet in diameter and the 'fuselages' or appendages about 75 feet in length, making a total length of 175 feet (see p. 40). 'At 11.47 a.m.,' he wrote, 'two of the fuselages moved around to line up with a centre third fuselage and the "craft" climbed with speed increasing' then disappeared.[18]

The object was hovering equidistant between Winfreth Atomic Power Station, the Admiralty Underwater Weapons Establishment at Portland and the US Air Force Communications Unit at Ringstead Bay. Neither the USAF nor the Atomic Energy Authority was able to confirm any unusual activity at the time in question. One of Brooks's dogs, an Alsatian, seemed very distraught throughout the encounter, frantically pawing at him and refusing to obey orders to 'sit', although she remained beside him. Brooks speculatively attributed this to VHF sounds emanating from the object

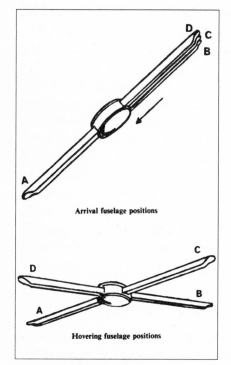

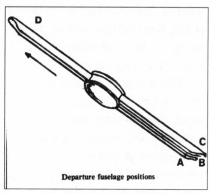

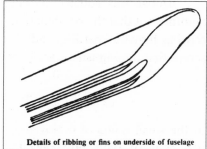

An unknown aerial vehicle observed by Angus Brooks, a former RAF intelligence officer and British Airways flight administration officer, at Moigne Downs, Dorset, in October 1967. Its length was estimated to be 175 feet. (*J. B. W. Brooks/FSR Publications Ltd*)

which might have disturbed her, but on subsequent visits to the area the dog clearly was anxious. The other dog, a Dalmatian, was unaffected by the object, and wandered off to hunt. Six weeks later the twelve-year-old Alsatian died of cystitis, which may be merely coincidental.

In February 1968 Angus Brooks was interviewed by a team from the Ministry of Defence, comprising Dr John Dickison, a scientist from the Royal Aircraft Establishment at Farnborough, Alec Cassie, an RAF psychologist, and Leslie Akhurst from the MoD's S4 unit. In a lengthy letter to Mr Brooks following their investigation, the team offered its opinion that what had really been seen was a 'vitreous floater' or dead cell in the fluid of the eyeball, which assumed more dramatic proportions owing to the probability that Brooks 'fell asleep or entered a near sleep state', dreaming the rest.

While it is true that Brooks had undergone a corneal transplant some years before the Moigne Downs sighting, which might have engendered larger than normal floaters in the vitreous humour of the eyeball, he argued in his answering letter that 'muscae volantes [vitreous floaters] move upwards and downwards and, as the craft entered the vision circle at 030 deg., moved across descending to centre of vision, hovered for twenty-two minutes, then exited vision circle at 320 deg., this hardly conforms . . .' Brooks was equally unimpressed with the MoD's dream theory, pointing out that the combination of a howling gale and his dog painfully clawing him was hardly conducive to 'dropping off'.[19] It is difficult to accept that the Ministry actually believed in these fatuous theories, either.

Landing Traces Covered up by the Authorities

In the small hours of 6 November 1967, on a section of the then A338 road between Avon and Sopley, Hampshire, driver Karl Farlow found that the lights of his diesel truck had suddenly and unaccountably failed. As he pulled up he observed a glowing, 15-feet-wide egg-shaped UFO, which moved slowly across the road from the right, moved slowly to the left, then accelerated and disappeared. The object made a sound like a refrigerator and gave off a smell like a drill boring through wood.

Before the object disappeared, a Jaguar car came from the opposite direction, and its lights and engine stalled. 'Our vehicles were stationary 25 to 30 yards from each other,' Farlow reported. 'The object was in between us. It glowed in the most beautiful green colour I have ever seen. It was like nothing on earth . . . I sat in the cab petrified. I don't want ever to experience anything like that again. This was no hallucination.'

Perhaps because it was a diesel, the engine of the truck was unaffected by the encounter. After the object left, the driver of the Jaguar, a veterinary surgeon, suggested to Farlow that they phone the police from a nearby call-box (also with its lights out). The police arrived shortly afterwards. 'Mr Farlow was very frightened,' said Constable Roy Nineham, who was in the patrol car. 'The most startling part of his report is that his lights failed and came on again when the object he saw disappeared.' The witnesses noticed that there were marks on the ground beside the road, and that the road surface appeared to have melted. The police took Farlow and the vet to Bournemouth police station, where they were interviewed separately until 04.30. The vet's girl passenger was taken to hospital suffering from shock.

The following day both men were taken to Christchurch police station and interviewed by a man from the Ministry of Defence. Later that day Farlow was driven back to the site by the police to collect his belongings from the truck, and noticed a group of people investigating the site with instruments, a bulldozer levelling the ground, and a man repainting the telephone booth. A week later Farlow observed that a 200-foot stretch of the road had been completely resurfaced, as if to cover all traces of evidence.[20,21]

Further Questions in the House of Commons

The wave of sightings over Britain in 1967 peaked in October, when hundreds of reports were made, including the famous sighting of a 'flying cross' which was chased by two policemen in Devon on 24 October and led to questions in the House of Commons on 8 November. Peter Mills, MP for Torrington, Devon, asked first about sightings in his own county, and received assurances from Merlyn Rees, Under-Secretary of State for Defence:

> The objects . . . had been proved on investigation to be either aircraft or lights. Of the lights, the majority were the planet Venus, but the source of a few lights has not been positively identified. I can say, however, that none of these unidentified lights was an alien object. There are standing arrangements for RAF stations to report unusual objects and for the investigation of such reports. I do not think that any further action is necessary.

Mills pressed further questions, and asked Rees if he could give assurance that the Ministry of Defence consulted scientists for advice about UFO sightings. Replied Rees: 'I can give that assurance. This is not just an air defence matter. We have access to scientists of high repute – they have been consulted on all these matters – and also to psychologists.'[22]

Two weeks later, on 22 November, Major Patrick Wall MP asked the Secretary of State for Defence what exchange of information or other co-operation was taking place between his department and the official American and Russian investigations into the subject of UFOs. Rees answered: 'We are in touch with the Americans on this subject but not with the Russians. I understand the conclusions which the Americans have reached coincide with ours.'[23]

While it is true that the British Government was not in touch with the Russians on the subject at that time, only two weeks later the British Embassy in Moscow was directed by London 'to further investigate the subject with a view to co-operating with the Russians in observation teams for UFOs', according to a US Defense Intelligence Agency document released in 1985 (see pp. 239–40).

In early 1968 Edward Taylor MP asked the Secretary of State for Defence 'how many reports of unidentified flying objects were received in 1967; how many of these reports were subsequently shown to have a natural explanation; and if he will make a statement'. In a written reply on 22 January, Merlyn Rees stated:

The total number of reports received in 1967 reflects a wave of public interest in UFOs, reaching a peak towards the end of the year. The analysis of the reports published below shows that, as in previous years, the vast majority were found to have mundane explanations; the remainder of the reports contained insufficient information for conclusive investigation but nothing to suggest that they related to incidents materially different in kind from those that were explained.[24]

The MoD had supplied Rees with a list of statistics from 1 January 1959 to 31 December 1967. Out of 362 reports for 1967, only 46 were categorized as 'unexplained' owing to 'insufficient information'. This nonsense has been trotted out regularly in the House of Commons and seldom has been challenged. A glance at the reports I have cited will show that, far from lacking sufficient information, they are highly detailed and clearly anomalous, no matter what the definitive explanation may be. For the year 1963 only *two* reports out of a total of fifty-one reported to the

MoD were listed in the 'unexplained' or 'insufficient information' category. Was there really insufficient information in the Moigne Downs and Avon incidents, for example, or was the Ministry baffled and alarmed by these reports, preferring to state that there was 'nothing to suggest that they related to incidents materially different in kind from those that were explained'?

On 11 June 1968 Sir John Langford-Holt asked Prime Minister Harold Wilson 'whether he is aware that under the present arrangements some reports of unidentified flying objects are made to the Ministry of Defence and police reports are made to the Board of Trade; and whether he will arrange that all such reports are made to one department'. Replied the Prime Minister: 'No, I am not so aware. Reports from any source, including any received by the Board of Trade, are passed on to the Ministry of Defence.'[25] The Prime Minister was correctly informed: all reports on UFOs made by the police are sent to the Ministry of Defence in the first instance, though some reports also are sent to other government departments from time to time.

In May 1968 a Wing Commander from RAF Fylingdales early-warning station stated that much time had been wasted by the Royal Air Force in investigating so-called UFO reports, all of which had proved to be absolutely fruitless.[26] Yet behind the scenes the Ministry of Defence – and the RAF in particular – continued to take sighting reports seriously.

Ministry of Defence Collaboration

A number of UFO researchers have approached the Ministry of Defence directly with a view to establishing a degree of collaboration. On 29 September 1967, for example, Antony Pace and Roger Stanway of the British UFO Research Association (BUFORA) visited the MoD main building in Whitehall, London, where they were granted an interview with Mr Cassells of S4.

Stanway and Pace related details of sightings that they had personally investigated in the Staffordshire area during the preceding two months, which subsequently formed the basis for their book on the subject.[27] Cassells began by explaining the Ministry's position on the subject, assuring the researchers that all UFO reports were treated seriously by the MoD, but that its interest was limited solely to aspects relating to defence; consequently there was no department, scientist or other person in the

MoD exclusively devoted to the UFO question. He added that no person from the Ministry ever made on-the-spot inquiries or field investigations when UFOs were reported, owing to lack of manpower and financial resources.[28]

Following publication of their book, which they had sent to Leslie Akhurst at S4, Stanway and Pace again visited Whitehall on 20 June 1968. The interview took place in an office on the sixth floor, and Mr Akhurst was joined by Dr John Dickison and Alec Cassie. (This was the same team which had investigated the Moigne Downs sighting in February. Evidently the MoD's manpower and financial resources had been extended since the first visit.) The meeting lasted over an hour, and 'all three gentlemen were without exception friendly, helpful and as frank as I think they could have possibly been under the circumstance'. Stanway was particularly struck by the fact that Alec Cassie was able to recall instantly the exact page number in the book at which a certain case report started.

Nothing particularly significant emerged from the meeting. The following month Leslie Akhurst summed up the Ministry's attitude in a letter to Roger Stanway which reiterated the MoD's standard policy and praised the two researchers for their book, though adding that it contained 'no evidence of air defence implications or of craft under extraterrestrial control . . . [nor] any new scientific evidence'.[29]

Instances of the Ministry of Defence requesting collaboration from civilian researchers were rare during this period, but in 1972 the MoD approached Derek Mansell, director of data research for Contact (UK), a leading UFO organization, asking if he would be prepared to send his best cases to S4 (Air) at Whitehall. Mansell readily agreed, and was provided with 500 printed envelopes to mail the reports, which were not to be more than a month old, he was advised. The men from the Ministry, Anthony Davies and Leslie Akhurst, suggested that Contact's report forms should be modified to bring them more in line with their own pro-formas. Derek Mansell told me that an informal 'investigation' of Contact was carried out by the two men. 'We never hid anything,' he said. 'I told them all our sources, including the Russians and the police.'

Official Pressure?

There have been a number of cases where Ministry of Defence personnel are alleged to have warned witnesses and investigators not to publicize their sightings or to pursue investigations. Though in the majority of cases evidence that the MoD was actually responsible is far from conclusive, some government department or departments seem to have been involved.

Following a UFO sighting that was reported in a local newspaper in the late summer of 1974, three of the four witnesses were visited one evening by 'a man from the Government' who asked them to sign a printed form agreeing not to discuss the incident with the national media. 'The man just turned up at my house, showed his identification and asked to come in,' the principal witness told me in 1986. There were three of us that had the sighting, and my little girl. He was not interested in her – just myself, my ex-wife, and [a] friend.' The interviews lasted a total of about two hours.

> We were interviewed at length separately [and] were shown different drawings of various types of UFOs . . . all the paper work was printed and not type-written . . . the papers certainly had codes which didn't mean anything to either of us.
>
> We were then told we had seen a UFO, but should not tell or inform the [national] media. He then produced three documents and we each signed saying that we would not. He then put his papers into a black case . . . I would prefer if my name was left out of it, as I fear reprisal after signing the document.[30]

Together with Mark Birdsall, one of the UK's leading investigators, I interviewed the witness in his home. Birdsall and I are satisfied that the witness was telling the truth.

I asked the MoD's Secretariat (Air Staff) 2a (which succeeded Defence Secretariat 8) for an opinion. 'That's absolute nonsense,' David Ross, of Sec(AS)2a, told me. 'To whom else did he report the sighting? It certainly wouldn't come from the MoD . . . I mean, we do on occasion visit [witnesses] and ask if they can describe what they've seen . . . On no account has *anyone* in the Ministry of Defence the authorization to say, "Don't discuss it with anyone else." '[31]

'Is it possible', I asked Mr Ross a few months later, 'that there are other departments involved that you wouldn't be aware of?' 'I would say categorically to that: no,' he answered, 'because this is the focal point within the United Kingdom for UFO reports so therefore it would have to come through this office. That's why we've always been able to say there is no such thing as a cover-up because everything comes through this office and we know everything that goes on.' 'Even if the security services were involved?' I suggested. 'The security services wouldn't be involved,' Mr Ross replied. 'There's no reason for them to be involved.'[32]

Despite David Ross's assurances, I do not accept that the MoD Secretariat knows everything that goes on. I doubt very much that it receives military sighting reports of any significance; Ralph Noyes certainly did not when he headed the unit. Nor would Sec(AS)2a necessarily be aware of clandestine investigations possibly carried out by the police Special Branch (which liaises closely with MI5) or even the Defence Intelligence Staff: compartmentation of intelligence would take care of that. The now proven involvement in UFO investigations of America's Central Intelligence Agency, National Security Agency and Defense Intelligence Agency as well as other official bodies (some of which liaise with their British counterparts) leads me to suspect that covert inquiries might be carried out in Britain, with few being aware of the fact. If I am mistaken, the only alternative is that civilian investigators are using false identification cards and documents to gain access to witnesses' homes, persuade them that they represent the Government, and discourage further dissemination of their reports.

Maureen Hall, a former policewoman, related to me an occasion in October 1978 when she was visited by a man from the MoD who politely advised her to drop an investigation she was carrying out for BUFORA at the time. The case involved the sighting of a hexagonal-shaped object over Chingford, Essex, on 20 September 1978. The man produced an ID card and said that he lived in the Belvedere, south-east London, area, but unfortunately Hall, new to UFO investigations at the time, misplaced the man's name and address.

Charles Bowen, ex-editor of *Flying Saucer Review*, once spoke to a senior captain of British Airways who informed him that UFO sightings by aircrews should be reported only to the Ministry of Defence, and that there should be no communication of information to the public or the media. The captain confided his own encounter with an unknown flying object and added that many of his colleagues had also had sightings. An RAF test pilot – who was a neighbour of Bowen's in the mid-1960s – volunteered a similar disclosure, admitting that his interest in the subject stemmed from his own experience.[33]

In 1981 I interviewed a man who claimed to have been working at Heathrow Air Traffic Control in September 1966 when a UFO was observed during the small hours. All personnel in the control tower saw the object hovering at low altitude above the airport, at a time when there were no aircraft movements. The UFO was tracked on radar, and its speed at departure was clocked at 3,000 m.p.h. The Ministry of Defence was notified, and investigators allegedly arrived on the scene and told the witnesses that they had 'seen nothing', threatening them with charges under the Official Secrets Act if they revealed the sighting publicly. In response to an enquiry to the MoD, I received the following statement: 'As you are no doubt aware, the Official Secrets Act applies to the release of information obtained in the course of official duty. However, our records show no occasions on which the Official Secrets Act has been specifically applied to the handling of UFO reports.'[34]

Secrecy also surrounded the sighting of an unidentified object by air traffic controllers at Gatwick Airport on 16 August 1978. 'The controllers definitely saw something,' an airport spokesman was quoted as saying, 'but they have clammed up over exactly what it was.'[35]

That year, 1978, was one of the busiest years for sightings ever recorded in the UK, many of which can almost certainly be attributed to the film *Close Encounters of the Third Kind*, first shown in March. In any event, many witnesses must have felt encouraged to come forward, whereas hitherto they might have been inhibited by fear of ridicule. The Ministry of Defence received a total of 750 reports – more than twice as many as in 1967. Hints of an official cover-up persisted. Questioned by a reporter about some sightings near Heathrow Airport in September, a spokesman for the Civil Aviation Authority denied that any UFOs had been tracked on Heathrow radar, but added: 'It's in the interest of national security that not too much fuss is made about this sort of thing.'[36]

The Meanwood Landing

Perhaps national security was involved in the report of a landed UFO seen by two fourteen-year-old girls at Meanwood, a suburb of Leeds, on 22 February 1979. That evening, as the girls were tobogganing down the slopes that surround their housing estate, they were startled by an aerial object which made a loud whining sound as it began to descend. On landing, the noise changed to a hum which then faded as the object rested on the snow. It was grey, egg-shaped, with two 'fins' on either side, and the size of a small car. Frightened, the girls made their way back up the slope then ran, pausing near the top to take another look at the object. It rested on the ground for about three minutes, then, humming again, rose into the air and came in the girls' direction, landing once again on a steeper part of the slopes about 80 feet away. After a few minutes the object wobbled and took off.

The girls, Lynsey Tebbs and Susan Pearson, ran home and were immediately separated by adults and asked to draw the object. Their sketches were practically identical. Investigators Graham and Mark Birdsall of the Yorkshire UFO Society (now Quest International) visited the landing site three days later and found, in two places, strange indentations in the still settled snow which were apparently consistent with the witnesses' testimony. Soil samples evinced no radiation.[37] The same or a similar UFO was seen in the early hours of the following morning by ambulance drivers Michael Duke and Leslie Evans at the South Kirkby ambulance station near Hemsworth, 20 miles from Meanwood.[38]

Shortly after the story appeared in the press two days later,[39] the girls were visited by 'an official from the Government' who interviewed them separately in private for twenty minutes and investigated the landing-site. The man produced an identity card, Lynsey's father told me, but he cannot recall the name or any details on it. 'After he'd finished speaking to them he turned round to me and said, "Well, do you believe it?" And I said, "I don't know – I'm a bit sceptical." And he said, "I can assure you that they have seen something, that is definite, because the questions I asked them they would not be able to answer unless it happened." He wouldn't tell us what he asked them, and the girls couldn't remember when they came out – they were only young at the time,' Mr Tebbs told me in 1986. 'My wife and I were not allowed in the room while the interview took place.'

The official, who said that he was from a Government department that 'kept a record of everything' on the subject, advised the girls not to discuss the incident further.[40]

The First House of Lords Debate

On 18 January 1979 a historic debate on UFOs took place in the House of Lords, the first time in its 700-year history that this controversial subject had been considered there. The debate was instigated by the Earl of Clancarty, the author Brinsley Le Poer Trench, who died in 1995. Of the many peers who supported his charge of a Government cover-up, the Earl of Kimberley, former Liberal spokesman on aerospace, was one of the most vociferous:

> I think the general public should be encouraged to come forward
> with evidence. Many do not, for fear of being ridiculed. Let them
> be open; let them be honest; let them badger their Member of

Parliament and the Government to be open with them and to cease what I am convinced is a cover-up here. The people of Britain have a right to know all that the Governments, not only of this country but others throughout the world, know about UFOs.

Also supporting the charge was Lord Rankeillour, who stressed that each year there were many sightings of UFOs, and that the effect on the witnesses was always one of concern; yet this very point was ignored or ridiculed by most governments around the world. As far as the United Kingdom was concerned, he added:

> . . . those who report seeing UFOs are taken to be misinformed, misguided and rather below par in intelligence. If this is so, why has some of my information on this subject been given to me by the Ministry of Technology? Why should this Ministry waste its time gathering false information? Of course, it is not false information: it is data reported by civil and Air Force pilots, policemen, sailors and members of the general public who have all had personal experience which has intrigued and/or frightened them . . .
>
> I suspect that the British Government do have a Department studying UFO sightings, for why else should they bother to publicly debunk reported ones if they are of no interest to them? Quite apart from the fact that the Government have not admitted to the existence of UFOs, these machines are potentially dangerous . . .

Lord Rankeillour's statement that he received some of his information on the subject from the Ministry of Technology is indeed interesting: his suspicion that the Government has a special department studying the phenomenon, apart from a publicly acknowledged secretariat in Whitehall, is not without foundation. For too many years Members of Parliament and the public have been led to believe that only a small office handles UFO reports, and that this office is merely located in a department which among other duties handles low-flying complaints, thus conveying the impression that the Ministry attaches a very low priority to the problem.

Lord Strabolgi, representing Her Majesty's Government, insisted at the conclusion of the debate that there had been nothing to convince the Government that any UFO reports showed evidence of visits by alien spacecraft, and went on: 'It has been suggested in this debate that our Government are involved in an alleged conspiracy of silence. I can assure your Lordships that the Government are not engaged in any such conspiracy . . . There is nothing to have a conspiracy of silence about.'[41]

Was Lord Strabolgi covering up for the Government, or was he expressing his own personal opinions? It is my contention that he was not given all the facts by those who briefed him in the Ministry of Defence, and that what information he was given tended to support his own convictions, thus his endorsement of the official line was coincidental.

Although the Earl of Clancarty's motion was defeated, enormous interest in the debate was shown both by peers and by members of the public, and all copies of the relevant *Hansard* were sold out. The House of Lords All-Party UFO Study Group was formed by the Earl of Clancarty shortly afterwards, comprising about thirty peers: its first meeting was held in June 1979. Guest speakers at its monthly meetings since then have included prominent ufologists from all over the world, and I had the honour of addressing the group on 24 June 1980. Regrettably, it no longer meets. But Admiral of the Fleet the Lord Hill-Norton, a former Chief of the Defence Staff and member of the Lords' group, became steadfast in his resolve to pressurize the Government into admitting that UFOs pose a threat to national security.

No Defence Significance?

RAF Neatishead Tracks Uncorrelated Target

In late october or early November 1980 an unidentified object was tracked at RAF Neatishead radar station, Norfolk, during night-flying exercises 50 miles away in the Wash area, involving two Royal Air Force F-4 Phantom jets.

According to radar operator Malcolm Scurrah, the incident began shortly after 20.00 hours, when an uncorrelated stationary 'target' at 5,000 feet appeared on the radar screen he was monitoring. Checks with Eastern Radar controllers revealed that no aircraft should have been in the vicinity. Furthermore, the unknown target did not emit an IFF (Identification Friend or Foe) signal, normally transmitted by transponders on aircraft.

Suddenly the target was seen to 'jump' up several thousand feet on the radarscope. As the radar operators watched, the object climbed in a series of 'jumps' to over 90,000 feet in the space of fifteen minutes before disappearing off the screens.

Scurrah learned shortly afterwards that the unknown target had been tracked on the main radar screens and was seen to perform manoeuvres which outstripped those of any conventional aircraft. The night-flying exercise was postponed and one of the F-4 pilots was instructed to investigate. 'The fighter controller and his assistant, and the supervising officers as well, were all listening in on the frequency of this aircraft, and guiding the pilot in so he could get a radar fix himself, because he was flying "blind" at that time,' Scurrah told Graham Birdsall, editor of *UFO Magazine*. 'So they started guiding him towards this thing, and that's where I came in. I was asked for heights on this object, but at the time I thought I was giving heights on the other jet because I thought they were into the night-flying exercise. I didn't know it was hovering because on the height-finding radar you can't see movement as such; all you can see is altitude.'

The F-4 approached to within half a mile of a 'very bright light' in front of him. 'Suddenly, from being stationary, this thing just zoomed off, very, very fast,' said Scurrah.

Interestingly, Scurrah also learned that the following day two senior RAF controllers, who were responsible for all Section Operations Centre (SOC) activities the previous night, had been interviewed separately by unfamiliar high-ranking Air Force officers from London. 'Things were said to them, and thereafter they didn't talk about it,' said Scurrah. Subsequently other senior RAF personnel arrived at Neatishead and took away all radar tapes of the encounter.[1]

Aerial Display over North-West Kent

Walking back to my flat in the London Borough of Bromley area on 15 December 1980, my attention was drawn to a motionless, bright star-like object in the cloudless sky. The time was 16.07. Realizing that the object was in the wrong position for Venus, I considered the probability that it might have been a balloon or an aircraft reflecting the last rays of the Sun, but naturally wondered if it might have been a UFO. I dashed the remaining distance back home, intending to observe the object through my telescope and take photographs and movie film if necessary. But there was no sign of anything apart from a few distant airliners. The time was now 16.15.

The following day Russell Bowie, a reporter from the *Kentish Times*, phoned to ask if I had had any reports of an unusual aerial object the previous day. I told him I had not, but volunteered my own brief sighting. Bowie then told me that for one and a quarter hours about forty witnesses at the Orpington Hospital redevelopment site had watched a UFO which alternately hovered, moved slowly, shot across the sky, then finally 'divided' and disappeared vertically – at 16.15.

I contacted Peter McSherry, clerk of works for Lovell (Southern) Ltd, who was a principal witness. The object was first seen at 15.00 directly above the site, he told me, and was apparently motionless. Shortly afterwards an aircraft was seen passing below the object, and the UFO proceeded to move across the sky and stop. After a while it emitted a puff of vapour and began to move slowly towards the east, where it again remained stationary. McSherry fetched his 20× binoculars and then was able to observe that the object was of an elongated triangular shape, with a reddish-orange nose, silvery body and diamond-blue rear section. He estimated the object's altitude to be 50,000 feet, which can only be very approximate since its size was not known.

The aerial device then turned over on its axis and pointed its 'nose' towards the west. Another puff of vapour appeared and in seconds it had traversed the sky and returned to its original position directly above the redevelopment site. At 15.20 it turned over on its axis again and moved slowly across the sky. By this time at least forty people, including hospital engineers as well as workmen from Lovell's, were observing the object, which remained stationary in the west.

At 15.35 it turned on its axis yet again and shot off towards the Moon at fantastic speed. Eventually it returned to the east, where it remained until 16.00, at which time it turned on its axis and, emitting a puff of vapour from its 'tail' section, accelerated at 'thousands of miles per hour' and returned to its original position above the site. At 16.15 the nose was pointing towards the west, but it then turned upwards and seemed to divide into two distinct objects which took off vertically, leaving vapour trails for a moment before disappearing.

On 17 December a short extract from a thirty-minute video film taken of the UFO was shown on Thames Television News. The film had been made in the presence of witnesses at Seal Chart, near Sevenoaks, Kent, and, although it shows only a point of light in a cloudless sky, it nevertheless corroborated the sighting. I visited the family who took the film and studied it. Their recorded commentary as they described the object's movements provides valuable testimony.

Shortly after the family set up their video camera at about 15.00, the aerial device appeared to divide into approximately three sections, disappeared vertically, then presumably regrouped and reappeared as a single object. A few minutes before departure the object split up into at least three sections (Peter McSherry reported only two) which moved around each other, disappeared again, regrouped, then divided and disappeared vertically. This does not show on the film, due to the limitations of video technology at the time.

Surely the objects seen on the afternoon of 15 December 1980 must have been tracked on radar, or reported by one or more of the numerous airliners and other aircraft flying in the vicinity at the time? My enquiries at the London Weather Centre and the Civil Aviation Authority at Heathrow Airport drew a blank: no unusual sightings had been reported to them during the period in question. (In the *Manual of Air Traffic Services*, air traffic controllers are issued with official instructions for the reporting of UFO sightings:[2] details are to be telephoned immediately to the Aeronautical Information Service (Military), based at the London Air Traffic Control Centre, and a written report, based on Ministry of Defence questions, is to be sent by the originating air traffic service unit to the MoD's Secretariat (Air Staff) 2 – see p. 55.)

3   UNIDENTIFIED FLYING OBJECTS

A controller receiving a report about an unidentified flying object must obtain as much as possible of the information required to complete a report in the format shown below.

Report of Unidentified Flying Object

A   Date, Time and Duration of Sighting
Local times to be quoted.

B   Description of Object
Number of objects, size, shape, colours, brightness, sound, smell, etc.

C   Exact Position of Observer
Geographical location, indoors or outdoors, stationary or moving.

D   How Observed
Naked eye, binoculars, other optical device, still or movie camera.

E   Direction in which Object was First Seen
A landmark may be more useful than a badly estimated bearing.

F   Angular Elevation of Object
Estimated heights are unreliable.

G   Distance of Object from Observer
By reference to a known landmark wherever possible.

H   Movements of Object
Changes in E, F and G may be of more use than estimates of course and speed.

J   Meteorological Conditions During Observations
Moving clouds, haze, mist, etc.

K   Nearby Objects
Telephone or high-voltage lines; reservoir, lake or dam; swamp or marsh; river; high buildings, tall chimneys, steeples, spires, TV or radio masts; airfields, generating plant; factories; pits or other sites with floodlights or other lighting.

L   To Whom Reported
Police, military organisations, the press, etc.

M   Name and Address of Informant

N   Any Background Information on the Informant that may be Volunteered

O   Other Witnesses

P   Date and Time of Receipt of Report

The details are to be telephoned immediately to AIS (Military), LATCC.

The completed report is to be sent by the originating air traffic service unit to the Ministry of Defence Sec (AS).

A LIST OF TELEPHONE NUMBERS AND LOCATIONS IS SHOWN IN THE
DIRECTORY AT APPENDIX 'H'

Instructions to air traffic controllers by the Ministry of Defence for the reporting of UFO sightings (1991). (*M. R. Sutton, Editor,* Manual of Air Traffic Services *Part I/Civil Aviation Authority*)

In January 1981 I had a meeting with my Member of Parliament, Sir Philip Goodhart, who was Army Minister at the time, and related details of the sighting to him. Sir Philip and I had corresponded in the past, and, although he had never been able to find evidence that UFOs were treated seriously by the Government, he liked to be kept informed about sightings in his own constituency.

Not long afterwards I sent a full report on the incident to the MoD. 'Whilst it is not normally Ministry of Defence policy to comment on the identity of UFOs,' it replied, 'the diagram and description of the object are indicative of the temperature gradient associated with a meteorite or similar body entering the Earth's atmosphere.'[3]

In a follow-up letter I pointed out that a meteorite or similar body entering the Earth's atmosphere is always a fast-moving object. The object I had seen for a few minutes was stationary, and other witnesses reported that it remained so for periods before moving to another part of the sky. The Ministry sensibly refrained from commenting on this inconsistency in its reply.

As far as I am concerned, the sightings of 15 December 1980 remain unexplainable in terms of balloons, meteorites, satellites, rockets, flares or even terrestrial unmanned aerial vehicles (UAVs – used for reconnaissance). Both the Civil Aviation Authority and the MoD claim there were no unusual sightings reported from any source, so we are asked to believe that while UFOs were manoeuvring over south-east London for one and a quarter hours, not a single report was made by civilian or military pilots flying in the area. The objects should have been tracked on radar, unless they were able to screen themselves – not an impossible feat in view of the advanced state of 'Stealth' technology incorporated in the design of several American military aircraft, enabling them to reflect a very low radar profile, to say nothing of numerous occasions when UFOs have been observed visually yet have not appeared on radar screens (and vice versa).

The sightings over the London area, and perhaps the RAF radar/visual contact reported from Norfolk in November, assume greater significance when we examine the extraordinary series of incidents which took place just outside two NATO bases in eastern England in late December 1980.

Close Encounters outside RAF Woodbridge/Bentwaters

Less than two weeks after the London sighting, one of the most sensational UFO events ever reported by military personnel occurred in Rendlesham Forest, just outside the perimeter of the twin US Air Force 81st Tactical

Fighter Wing bases of RAF Woodbridge and RAF Bentwaters, near Ipswich, Suffolk (closed in 1993). The following is an official report to the Ministry of Defence from Lieutenant Colonel (later Colonel) Charles Halt, US Air Force deputy base commander at the time, dated 13 January 1981:

Subject: Unexplained Lights
To: RAF/CC
1. Early in the morning of 27 Dec 80 (approximately 0300L), two USAF security police patrolmen saw unusual lights outside the back gate at RAF Woodbridge. Thinking an aircraft might have crashed or been forced down, they called for permission to go outside the gate to investigate. The on-duty flight chief responded and allowed three patrolmen to proceed on foot. The individuals reported seeing a strange glowing object in the forest. The object was described as being metalic in appearance and triangular in shape, approximately two to three meters across the base and approximately two meters high. It illuminated the entire forest with a white light. The object itself had a pulsing red light on top and a bank(s) of blue lights underneath. The object was hovering or on legs. As the patrolmen approached the object, it maneuvered through the trees and disappeared. At this time the animals on a nearby farm went into a frenzy. The object was briefly sighted approximately an hour later near the back gate.
2. The next day, three depressions 1½" deep and 7" in diameter were found where the object had been sighted on the ground. The following night (29 Dec 80) the area was checked for radiation. Beta/gamma readings of 0.1 milliroentgens were recorded with peak readings in the three depressions near the center of the triangle formed by the depressions. A nearby tree had moderate (.05–.07) readings on the side of the tree toward the depressions.
3. Later in the night a red sun-like light was seen through the trees. It moved about and pulsed. At one point it appeared to throw off glowing particles and then broke into five separate white objects and then disappeared. Immediately thereafter, three star-like objects were noticed in the sky, two objects to the north and one to the south, all of which were about 10° off the horizon. The objects moved rapidly in sharp angular movements and displayed red, green and blue lights. The objects to the north appeared to be elliptical through an 8–12 power lens. They then turned to full circles. The objects to the north remained in the sky for an hour

DEPARTMENT OF THE AIR FORCE
HEADQUARTERS 81ST COMBAT SUPPORT GROUP (USAFE)
APO NEW YORK 09755

REPLY TO
ATTN OF: CD   13 Jan 81

SUBJECT: Unexplained Lights

TO: RAF/CC

1. Early in the morning of 27 Dec 80 (approximately 0300L), two USAF
security police patrolmen saw unusual lights outside the back gate at
RAF Woodbridge. Thinking an aircraft might have crashed or been forced
down, they called for permission to go outside the gate to investigate.
The on-duty flight chief responded and allowed three patrolmen to proceed on foot. The individuals reported seeing a strange glowing object
in the forest. The object was described as being metalic in appearance
and triangular in shape, approximately two to three meters across the
base and approximately two meters high. It illuminated the entire forest
with a white light. The object itself had a pulsing red light on top and
a bank(s) of blue lights underneath. The object was hovering or on legs.
As the patrolmen approached the object, it maneuvered through the trees
and disappeared. At this time the animals on a nearby farm went into a
frenzy. The object was briefly sighted approximately an hour later near
the back gate.

2. The next day, three depressions 1 1/2" deep and 7" in diameter were
found where the object had been sighted on the ground. The following
night (29 Dec 80) the area was checked for radiation. Beta/gamma readings
of 0.1 milliroentgens were recorded with peak readings in the three depressions and near the center of the triangle formed by the depressions.
A nearby tree had moderate (.05-.07) readings on the side of the tree
toward the depressions.

3. Later in the night a red sun-like light was seen through the trees.
It moved about and pulsed. At one point it appeared to throw off glowing
particles and then broke into five separate white objects and then disappeared. Immediately thereafter, three star-like objects were noticed
in the sky, two objects to the north and one to the south, all of which
were about 10° off the horizon. The objects moved rapidly in sharp angular
movements and displayed red, green and blue lights. The objects to the
north appeared to be elliptical through an 8-12 power lens. They then
turned to full circles. The objects to the north remained in the sky for
an hour or more. The object to the south was visible for two or three
hours and beamed down a stream of light from time to time. Numerous individuals, including the undersigned, witnessed the activities in paragraphs
2 and 3.

CHARLES I. HALT, Lt Col, USAF
Deputy Base Commander

The memorandum from Colonel Charles Halt to the Ministry of Defence describing some of
the sensational events reported outside RAF/USAF Woodbridge in December 1980.
(US Air Force)

or more. The object to the south was visible for two or three hours and beamed down a stream of light from time to time. Numerous individuals, including the undersigned, witnessed the activities in paragraphs 2 and 3.

The document was released in 1983 to Robert Todd of the Citizens Against UFO Secrecy (CAUS) group in the United States, under provisions of the Freedom of Information Act, and thanks to information provided to CAUS by Airman Larry Warren, the first witness to go public. According to the letter of release, '. . . the Air Force file copy has been properly disposed of in accordance with Air Force regulations. Fortunately, through diligent enquiry and the gracious consent of Her Majesty's Government, the British Minister of Defence and the Royal Air Force, the US Air Force has provided a copy for you.'[4]

Squadron Leader Donald Moreland, British commander at the adjoining RAF/USAF base at Bentwaters, had been responsible for securing the document from Colonel Halt, and sent it to the Ministry of Defence. Yet in February 1981 Dot Street and Brenda Butler (co-authors with Jenny Randles of *Sky Crash*, a book which deals with the case) were told during a private meeting with Moreland that he knew nothing about the incident,[5] and the MoD refused to be drawn until two years later, when Mrs Titchmarsh of Defence Secretariat 8 wrote to Jenny Randles: '. . . turning now to your interest in the sighting at RAF Woodbridge in December 1980. I can now confirm that USAF personnel did see unusual lights outside the boundary fence early in the morning of 27 December 1980; no explanation for the occurrence was ever forthcoming.'[6]

Colonel Halt's report, it should be noted, mentions a good deal more than 'unexplained lights' being seen outside the base, so Randles subsequently wrote several more letters to the MoD requesting further information about the case, but these were never answered. Nor could Martin Bailey of the *Observer* elicit any more details from the MoD. He was told that permission to release files on the case had not been received.

Squadron Leader Moreland eventually admitted that there had been a 'minor incident' outside the Woodbridge base, but this involved only 'a few lights flipping among the trees'.[7] He was more forthcoming in an interview with journalist Keith Beabey in September 1983: 'I put the events the Colonel related to me down to an inexplicable phenomenon. Whatever it was, it was able to perform feats in the air which no known aircraft is capable of doing.'[8] These feats included the ability of the object to split into five sections, as witnessed by Colonel Halt on 29 December. It is worth recalling that the UFO seen over London also divided into at least three separate parts on occasions.

News of the Woodbridge incident first leaked out in January 1981, when Brenda Butler was approached by a US Air Force security policeman (the first of several who spoke with the authors of *Sky Crash*). Given the pseudonym of 'Steve Roberts', he confided that a UFO had 'crash-landed' in Rendlesham Forest on the night of 27 December, and that he himself had witnessed its three small silver-suited occupants carrying out repairs while suspended in a shaft of light. The craft had remained on the ground for several hours, he claimed, during which time Colonel (later Brigadier General) Gordon Williams, overall base commander at the time, had supposedly communicated with the 'aliens'! Many military personnel were present, and films and photos were taken which were immediately confiscated by senior officers when the craft had taken off.[9] Although Roberts's story seems improbable, and a sketch he made of the landed craft does not tally with descriptions provided by other witnesses, some aspects of his version of events have been corroborated.

A few weeks later another investigator, Paul Begg, was informed by a radar operator at RAF Watton in Norfolk that an 'uncorrelated target' had been picked up on its radar sets on the night of 27 December, but had been lost about 50 miles south in the vicinity of Rendlesham Forest. The Air Defence Radar Centre at West Drayton, Middlesex, was advised of the incident, and it was learned that the object had been tracked elsewhere, including RAF/USAF Bentwaters. A few days later USAF intelligence officers turned up at Watton and told the radar men that it was possible they had tracked an unknown-structured object that had crash-landed in a forest near Ipswich. Military personnel who went to investigate found the engine and lights of their jeep failing as they approached the landing-site, and had to proceed on foot. They allegedly encountered an unidentified object on the ground, and Colonel Williams was said to have communicated with its occupants.[10]

Regardless of whether the latter part of the story is disinformation (and it seems improbable to me that the story of aliens – if true – would have been disclosed to the British radar operators), it supposedly was the reason given by the USAF intelligence officers for confiscating RAF Watton's radar tapes. In a letter to researcher Nicholas Redfern, RAF Watton (Eastern Radar) did at least acknowledge that a UFO incident had been recorded in its log early on the morning of 28 December. Timed at 03.25, the log states: 'Bentwaters Command Post contacted Eastern Radar and requested information of aircraft in the area – UA37 [Upper Air

Route Amber 37] traffic southbound FL370 [Flight Level 37,000 feet] – UFO sightings at Bentwaters. They are taking reporting action.' Redfern was also informed that all tape recordings from the period – both sound and radar – had been routinely disposed of.[11]

Not surprisingly, the claim of aliens being present has been refuted by General Williams, though he has confirmed that the details in Colonel Halt's memorandum are essentially correct. If this is so, then *something* must have landed outside Woodbridge/Bentwaters in late December 1980. The following accounts are by some of the US Air Force 81st Security Police Squadron personnel involved in what appear to have been several separate incidents – more than are referred to in Halt's memorandum. Although his memorandum implies that the first incident occurred in the early hours of 27 December, he now confirms that the unusual events around Bentwaters/Woodbridge began on the night of 25/26 December.[12]

In her book on the Rendlesham Forest affair, *From Out of the Blue*, Jenny Randles relates how, at about 00.00 hours, Gordon Levett, a civilian witness who lived in the village of Sudbourne, four miles east of the Bentwaters base, sighted an extraordinarily bright unknown flying vehicle which passed low over his house, hovered briefly, then drifted away in the direction of RAF Woodbridge. Shortly after 02.00, two security policemen at the East Gate of Woodbridge reported a brilliant glowing light which appeared to crash into the forest. The men were ordered to stay on site until relief guards arrived.[13]

Airman John Burroughs

The relief team arrived at the East Gate to investigate the area of the 'crash' site. One of these men was Airman (First Class) John Burroughs, who in his official deposition wrote as follows:

> On the night of Dec. 25–26 at around 03:00 while on patrol down at East Gate, myself and my partner saw lights coming from the woods due east of the gate [close to Tangham Wood]. The lights were red and blue, the red one above the blue one and they were flashing on and off.
>
> . . . we crossed a small open field that led into the trees where the lights were coming from and as we were coming into the trees there were strange noises, like a woman screaming, also the woods lit up and you could hear the farm animals making a lot of noise and there was a lot of movement in the woods. All three of us hit

the ground and whatever it was started moving back towards the
open field. After a minute or two we got up and moved into the
trees and the lights moved out into the open field . . .[14]

In an interview with journalist Antonio Huneeus, Burroughs explained
that the UFO looked like 'a bank of [differently coloured] lights that threw
off an image of like a craft. I never saw anything metallic or hard'. He also
reported an odd sensation. 'Everything seemed like it was different when
we were in that clearing. The sky didn't seem the same . . . it was . . . like
everything seemed slower than you were actually doing; and all of a sudden
when the object was gone, everything was like normal again . . .'[15]

Sergeant Jim Penniston

Sergeant Penniston confirms that during the time of the first reported
incidents, an unidentified 'bogey' had been tracked by Eastern Radar and
Heathrow Airport, London, and that contact with it was lost about 5 miles
from the Bentwaters base. He then received a call from Central Security
Control requesting him to proceed to the East Gate at the Woodbridge
base and contact Airman Burroughs. Arriving at the area of the first
sighting and meeting with Burroughs and another security policeman,
who were gazing in awe at the illuminated phenomenon, he began to see
an object with a defined shape as he approached for a closer look. This
proved to be difficult: it took a great deal of effort to walk, as if an invisible
barrier had been encountered.

'The air was filled with electricity; you could feel it on your skin as we
approached the object,' Penniston related on *Strange But True?*, a London
Weekend Television series. 'It was about the size of a tank [and] was
triangular in shape. Underneath the craft was high-intensity white light
emanating out of it, and it was bordered by red and blue lighting,
alternating . . . On the upper left side of the craft was an inscription that
measured 6 inches high, er, of symbols. They looked familiar, but I
couldn't ascertain why.'

The surface of the object appeared to be moulded in a black, smoky
glass-like material, with no sharp edges. The security men continued to
watch the spectacle for about twenty minutes. 'Slowly it started moving
back, weaving in around the trees,' said Penniston. 'It got about 40 feet
away then it raised up into the air [and] shot off as fast as you could
blink.'[16,17]

During a lecture in Leeds in 1994, organized by Harry Harris and

Quest International, Colonel Halt reported that the security men were so close to the object that they started to walk around it, and that at one point, according to Penniston, Burroughs tried to climb on it! As they went around one side, the craft became almost invisible on that side. The object was resting on a tripod-type undercarriage, with the legs extending outwards, said Halt.[18]

Sergeant Adrian Bustinza

Sergeant Adrian Bustinza, security police acting shift supervisor for 'C' Flight at Woodbridge at the time, related his version of events to American investigators Ray Boeche and Scott Colborn in 1984, and Boeche kindly provided me with a copy of the recorded interview.

Boeche began by reading Colonel Halt's memorandum to Bustinza, asking him if it was accurate. Bustinza confirmed: 'That's about right, because I remember the animals very clearly, because I bumped into the animals myself . . . For a while there we sort of tried to forget everything, and joked around about the animals . . . but I was kind of glad I bumped into the animals!' He continued:

We were in the alert area, and I was on my way over to RAF Woodbridge base [at around] midnight [date not specified]. While we were over there one of my patrols sighted an object of some sort – he didn't describe it, he just said it was like a fire in the forest area. I notified my acting commander, who was Lieutenant Englund, and he went ahead and called the commander that night, Colonel Halt, and he told Lieutenant Englund to check out the situation. We proceeded to check out the situation; myself and Lieutenant Englund and Sergeant Ball.

What I remember clearly was that when we got there [Colonel Halt] pointed to the individuals he wanted to go with him. So we went back to Bentwaters base, grabbed two light-alls [floodlights] and had a patrol refuel them, and once we refuelled them we took them out there to see if we could light up the area to see if there was anything out there. In the process of trying to check the light-alls, everything was malfunctioning. When we got to Point A – the sighting of the object – we had trouble turning the light-alls on. Our truck wouldn't run, either. It was kind of like all the energy had been drained out of both light-all units . . .

We started to search . . . One individual had said he had

spotted the object – like sitting on the ground. We proceeded to look and in the process found kind of like triangular tripods . . . burned into the [ground] at three different standpoints . . . They were like it was a heavy object. They took radiation readings of the holes, and they got a radiation reading as I recall. Then I recall we were walking through the woods and we came upon the lights again. And that's when I first saw the object . . .

We got – I think it was the flight chief [Sergeant Ball], and I believe another individual officer. We kept searching the area, kind of like trying to follow the object. And it was moving through the trees. And in the process we came upon a yellow mist, about 2 or 3 feet off the ground. It was like dew but it was yellow . . . like nothing I've ever seen before . . . We kind of, like, ignored it. We were worried about the [other] object . . . to see if we could locate it again, or catch up to it again . . .

We did see the object again. It was hovering low, like moving up and down anywhere from 10 to 20 feet, back up, back down, back up. There was a red light on top and there were several blue lights on the bottom, but there was also like [a prism] . . . rainbow lights on top [and] several other colours of light . . . It was a tremendous size. It even surprised me that it was able to fit into the clearing – a tremendous size, and I use the word 'tremendous' carefully. It was a round, circular shape; I hate to say like a plate, but it was thicker at the centre than it was at the edge.

Bustinza and the other witnesses were ordered to form a perimeter around the object at roughly 15-feet intervals. After observing the object for about thirty minutes, Bustinza says it took off suddenly. 'It was gone in a flash,' he said, 'almost like it just disappeared. When it left, we were hit by a cold blast of wind which blew towards us for 5 or 10 seconds . . . It was a really scary feeling . . . I was just frozen in place at first: my life actually passed in front of my eyes.'

Bustinza neither denies nor confirms the alleged presence of alien beings. But he does claim that at some stage Colonel Gordon Williams arrived at the site (a claim which has been dismissed by several other witnesses). He also claims that photographs and film were taken by both American *and* British personnel:

There were two bobbies there . . . Colonel Halt approached myself and Larry [Warren] . . . Was it Larry? I'm trying to remember – I'm not too sure of the other guy's name. [Halt] told us to approach the individuals, who at the time were standing in the grass area . . . they had some very sophisticated camera equipment, which wasn't unusual for the British . . . [Halt] told us to confiscate the material from the British nationals. Well, we confiscated the film and we turned it over to Colonel Halt and [he] put it into a plastic bag and Colonel Halt said it would be dealt with at a higher level of command. He didn't say exactly at what level or anything. I would assume it went to the photography department on base at the time. It could easily have been the intelligence department as well.[19]

The allegation that British police were present at this incident has been refuted, but Chuck de Caro of Cable News Network (CNN) saw a policeman's notebook at Woodbridge Police Station which shows that on the night of 25/26 December Airman Armald from the Woodbridge base law-enforcement desk called out the Woodbridge police concerning 'lights in the woods'. On the morning of 26 December the police apparently returned to the site and were shown 'landing-marks' by Air Force personnel, who told them that an object had landed there. In 1994 Colonel Halt also confirmed that the British police were called, but they failed to arrive due to another incident. Called out again, they did eventually take a cursory look at the landing-site and commented that the traces must have been caused by 'hens nesting or rabbits burrowing'.[20]

Adrian Bustinza further claims that two American law-enforcement officers had taken photographs, but he cannot recall their names. In support of this claim, Ray Boeche was told by a highly placed USAF records-management official at the Pentagon in March 1985 that photos were taken 'and that some of them, but not all, were fogged. However, our records here do not show the existence of any photographs at all.' In addition, Colonel Halt confirmed to Boeche that a movie film was taken which was immediately flown to the USAF European Headquarters at Ramstein Air Force Base, Germany.[21]

Airman Lawrence Warren

Yet another USAF security policeman claims to have witnessed the landed UFO: Airman (First Class) Lawrence Warren, who was stationed at Bentwaters at the time. Initially expressing fears for his life, Warren was the first witness to go public, and the first to name others involved in the incidents. His version of events differs in some important respects from those of the other personnel, but in my view it is equally deserving of consideration. Warren has taken me to the site of the incident on 28/29 December, at Capel Green, a field about half a mile from the East Gate at RAF/USAF Woodbridge, and gives a convincing impression that he is telling the truth about his involvement therein.

'What I first saw was a fog or a misty kind of self-illuminated object on the ground,' he told me, describing his initial encounter following the truck drive from Bentwaters to the Woodbridge base East Gate and beyond, during which he saw deer running as if in a panic. He continued:

> It looked kind of transparent and it came up to about a foot in height. It was just fog, but it had a 50-foot diameter. There were cameras in that field filming it: they were being manned by personnel from the base – they weren't security police – there were still photographs being taken by two cops from the town of Woodbridge or the Suffolk Constabulary.
>
> A red light came in [from] the opposite direction to the Orford Ness lighthouse. It came in over the trees [and] did an arc over the fields and stopped over this illuminated stuff on the ground . . . at about 25 feet in height. It was the size of a basketball. It 'exploded' – it was a silent explosion, and it was so bright that my eyes just whited out. When my eyesight returned, not only had a majority of people standing around me run away, there were many people 'frozen' in place. A lot of people had gone off in the woods and there were some senior people – lieutenants and that sort – who were all hiding in pine trees in the forest. It sounds funny, but they were gone and we were wide open.
>
> And then I know it's hard to believe because I don't believe it either, but I tell you there was a triangular object [that] was distorted like a prism. It had multi-colours on it. I never saw this device actually fly; it was just there . . . It had a lot of raised surfaces and a delta appendage on both sides and one coming from the front, and it concaved: it went to a red light on top . . . and a mother-of-pearl effect for the most part all over, and blue lights at the bottom – much like the [Halt] document describes.
>
> I went to check my watch at one point. I had a cheap Timex watch, and everything was half-speed, even voices seemed half-speed . . . We moved towards this thing. We cast shadows on [it] . . . A light came around one of the sides of this delta-type

appendage on one side – it was about a foot off the ground. Sergeant Bustinza knocked me on the arm and said: 'Do you see it?' And I'm looking at this thing in a half dream state, and it started to fade, and what you could see were literally faces inside it. It faded out and this one ball containing whatever this is inside it split into three . . . I clearly saw the faces – mainly the eyes, these large eyes . . . You could see the upper extremities rather clearly. At times these things seemed transparent. They were bluish-gold in colour and it looked like they were wearing silver clothing. But I couldn't see hands clearly . . .

One of the most contentious of Larry Warren's claims is that Colonel Gordon Williams came into the field at this point – a claim supported by Adrian Bustinza but discounted by several other witnesses. Yet Warren stands by his claim. Moving towards the stationary apparition, Williams then appeared as if he was trying to communicate with the beings, in the sense that he held his arms out in a questioning manner, Warren explained to me. A sharp noise was heard, like the branch of a tree snapping, and the entities' arms seemed to come up as if for protection, then 'a protective membrane went over the eye part, and they got real bright'.

Sergeant Robert Ball then began to dismiss the security police from the site, according to rank, Warren continued. 'There were a lot of people in that field. This involved no less than eighty people at that one site.'

Warren told me he was physically and psychologically traumatized by the experience, as were some of the others involved (one committed suicide). His eyes suffered damage to the retinas, and less than six hours afterwards he found himself with a shock of grey hair. He also revealed that, during a debriefing following the incident, he and other security policemen were shown a fifteen-minute film of UFOs taken by US military personnel during the Second World War, the Korean War and Vietnam, and some film taken by astronauts during the Apollo programme (including unknown objects on the Moon). The purpose of the film show was to impress upon the men the reason for maximum security concerning the UFO situation.[22]

In 1994, when Warren applied for a new passport, he was informed that the old one he posted had arrived 'altered or mutilated', and as such was 'voided'. Subsequently he learned from the US Department of State that the real reason for confiscating the old passport was that he was in violation of the National Security Act (1947) for speaking about 'sensitive defense issues' in a public forum. Most probably, this relates to the fact that on several public occasions Warren has spoken about the tactical nuclear weapons previously kept at RAF Bentwaters (at the time, according to Warren, the largest NATO nuclear weapons storage dump). For many months, all records pertaining to him disappeared off State Department computers: effectively, he did not exist. It was nearly a year before Warren received a new passport, with the help of former US Attorney General Ramsey Clark.

There is a great deal more to Larry Warren's story – and the Rendlesham Forest affair in general – which is described at length in a book he has written with Peter Robbins.[23]

Official and Unofficial Denials

The Rendlesham Forest story was first briefly publicized in *Flying Saucer Review* in 1981,[24] and an expanded account appeared in the same journal in the following year,[25] but negligible interest was shown by the media. Then in October 1983, following release of the Halt memorandum, the story made headline news in an article by Keith Beabey in the *News of the World*.[26] Partly because the story appeared in a newspaper with a reputation for publishing sensational (and salacious) items, the more serious papers lost no time in debunking it. For example, Adrian Berry, science correspondent of the *Daily Telegraph*, commented:

> All that had happened was that a United States Air Force Colonel at RAF Woodbridge had seen an unexplained light in the surrounding woods. That was all. The newspaper ran its ridiculous story, and two days later a ranger from the Forestry Commission showed how the strange light could only have been the rotating beam of the Orford Ness Lighthouse five miles away.[27]

Berry evidently had decided that the story should be debunked at all costs, ignoring practically every statement contained in Halt's memorandum, in particular the description of a landed, metallic, triangular-shaped object. My letter to Berry pointing out this disgraceful misrepresentation went unacknowledged.

On 24 October 1983 Major Sir Patrick Wall MP addressed some questions on the incident to Defence Minister John Stanley in the House of Commons, asking 'if he has seen the United States Air Force memo dated 13 January 1981 concerning unexplained lights near RAF Woodbridge' and 'whether in view of the fact that the [memo] on the incident . . . has been released under the Freedom of Information Act, he will now release reports and documents concerning similar incidents in the United Kingdom', and, finally, 'how many unexplained sightings or radar intercepts have taken place since 1980'. Replied the Defence Minister:

> I have seen the memorandum of 13 January 1981 to which my Honourable Friend refers. Since 1980 the Department has received 1400 reports of sightings of flying objects which the observers have been unable to identify. There were no corresponding radar contacts. Subject to normal security restraints, I am ready to give information about any such reported sightings that are found to be a matter of concern from a defence standpoint, but there have been none to date.[28]

The Woodbridge case is thus dismissed in one sentence. It is regrettable that Sir Patrick failed to press further questions, but MPs are understandably loath to become too involved in such a controversial and ridicule-prone subject, especially without a clear mandate from the electorate. The subject is of little or no relevance to the vast majority of citizens, and little progress will be made until such time as large numbers of those who are interested or have had sightings start lobbying their MPs. And the UFO movement, lacking as it does any effectively co-ordinated lobby in the UK, has not helped matters.

Ralph Noyes, former head of Defence Secretariat 8, wrote in November 1983 to the then head of DS8, Brian Webster, requesting further information about the case. Nearly four months later, following several reminders, he received a reply that stated in part:

> The Department satisfied itself at the time that there was no reason to consider that the alleged sighting had any defence significance. That is not to say, however, that Colonel Halt and the other personnel mentioned in the report were, as you suggest, suffering from hallucinations . . . What the true explanation is, I do not know . . . I can assure you, however, that there is no evidence of anything having intruded into British airspace and 'landing' near RAF Woodbridge.[29]

So what was Colonel Halt referring to when he wrote about an apparently landed, metallic, unidentified flying object, which had evidently intruded into British airspace? The Ministry simply avoided directly answering that question.

In February 1985 Noyes wrote to Webster again, asking seven specific questions relating to the incident, of which I quote three:

> Is the MoD aware of the tape recording which Col. Halt claims to have made on 29 December 1980 (and of which alleged copies are now in the hands of several members of the public)? Is the MoD aware of the ciné film allegedly made on site on 29 December? In the light of the answers to these questions does the MoD adhere to its view that nothing unknown or untoward ventured into British airspace?

A reply was received nearly three months later from Peter Hucker, of the newly formed Defence Secretariat (Air Staff) 2a, which replaced DS8 in January 1985, pointing out that Brian Webster was no longer its head. The questions posed by Noyes were answered as follows: 'I can assure you that no unidentified flying object was seen on radar recordings during the period in question, and that the MoD has no knowledge of the tape-recording or ciné-film you mention . . . there has been nothing to alter the view that there was no defence significance to the incident.'[30]

The Halt Tape

In spite of the Ministry's denial of knowledge regarding a tape-recording made by Colonel Halt, an edited copy was released to solicitor and UFO investigator Harry Harris in 1984 by Colonel Sam Morgan, former base commander at Woodbridge. The tape describes some of the events that occurred on the night of 29/30 December when Halt and others were investigating the landing-area and taking radiation readings.

The duration of the complete tape is nearly eighteen minutes, although it is evident from the extracts quoted that over two hours had elapsed. I have omitted the first half of the tape, which relates to the radiation readings taken at the landing-site. Several voices share the commentary, including Lieutenant Bruce Englund, already mentioned by Sergeant Bustinza; Major Malcolm Zickler, chief of base security; and Sergeant Nevells, a non-commissioned officer assigned to the Disaster Preparedness Operations, who was, according to Colonel Morgan, handling the Geiger counter.

A transcript has been made by science journalist Ian Ridpath and Harry Harris, from which I quote the relevant passages:

VOICE: . . . 1.48 We're hearing very strange sounds out of the farmer's barnyard animals. They're very, very active, making an awful lot of noise . . . You just saw a light? (garbled) Slow down. Where?

VOICE: Right on this position. Here, straight ahead in between the trees – there it is again. Watch – straight ahead off my flashlight, sir. There it is.

HALT: I see it too. What is it?

VOICE: We don't know, sir.

HALT: It's a strange, small red light. Looks to be maybe a quarter to half a mile, maybe further, out. I'm gonna switch off. The light is gone now. It was approximately 120 degrees from our site. Is it back again?

VOICE: Yes, sir.

VOICE: Well, douse flashlights then. Let's go back to the edge of the clearing so we can get a better look at it. See if you can get the starscope on it. The light's still there and all the barnyard animals have gone quiet now. We're heading about 110, 120 degrees from the site out through to the clearing now, still getting a reading on the meter . . . We're about 150 or 200 yards from the site. Everywhere else is just deathly calm. There is no doubt about it – there's some type of strange flashing red light ahead.

VOICE: Sir, it's yellow.

HALT: I saw a yellow tinge in it too. Weird. It appears to be maybe moving a little bit this way. It's brighter than it has been. It's coming this way. It is definitely coming this way! Pieces of it are shooting off. There is no doubt about it! This is weird!

VOICE: Two lights! One to the right and one light to the left!

HALT: Keep your flashlights off. There's something very, very strange. Keep the headset on; see if it gets any . . . Pieces are falling off it again!

VOICE: It just moved to the right.

VOICE: Yeah! . . . Strange! . . . Let's approach to the edge of the wood up there . . . OK, we're looking at the thing. We're probably about two to three hundred yards away. It looks like an eye winking at you. Still moving from side to side. And when you put the starscope on it, it's like this thing has a hollow centre, a dark centre, like the pupil of an eye looking at you, winking. And it flashes so bright in the starscope that it almost burns your eye . . . We've passed the farmer's house and across into the next field and now we have multiple sightings of up to five lights with a similar shape and all, but they seem to be steady now rather than a pulsating or glow with a red flash. We've just crossed a creek and we're getting what kind of readings now? We're getting three good clicks on the meter and we're seeing strange lights in the sky.

HALT: 2.44. We're at the far side of the second farmer's field and made sighting again about 110 degrees. This looks like it's clear off to the coast. It's right on the horizon. Moves about a bit and flashes from time to time. Still steady or red in colour. Also after negative readings in the centre of the field we're picking up slight readings – four or five clicks now, on the meter.

HALT: 3.05. We see strange strobe-like flashes to the er . . . well, they're sporadic, but there's definitely some kind of phenomenon. 3.05. At about 10 degrees, horizon, directly north, we've got two strange objects, er, half-moon shape, dancing about with coloured lights on 'em. That, er, guess to be about 5 to 10 miles out, maybe less. The half-moons are now turning to full circles, as though there was an eclipse or something there, for a minute or two . . . 03.15. Now we've got an object about 10 degrees directly south, 10 degrees off the horizon. And the ones to the north are moving. One's moving away from us.

VOICE: It's moving out fast!

VOICE: This one on the right's heading away too!

VOICE: They're both heading north. OK, here he comes from the south; he's coming toward us now. Now we're observing what appears to be a beam coming down to the ground. This is unreal!

HALT: 03.30. And the objects are still in the sky although the one to the south looks like it's losing a little bit of altitude. We're going around and heading back toward the house. The object to the south is still beaming down lights to the ground.

HALT: 04.00 hours. One object still hovering over Woodbridge base at about 5 to 10 degrees off the horizon. Still moving erratic, and similar lights and beaming down as earlier . . .[31]

Is the tape a fake? Journalist John Grant traced Colonel Morgan to the US Space Command headquarters at Peterson USAF base in Colorado and asked him this question via telephone. 'I do not think it is a hoax,' Morgan replied:

I think the men really were out there that night and they saw something which frightened them. You can hear their excited conversations and references to frightening strange lights. The only opinion I have is that, based on the evidence available, those guys definitely saw something which cannot be explained. As for them fabricating it all and putting on an act, I do not think they could have pulled it off.[32]

Cover-Up

In October 1985 I met the American investigator Ray Boeche, who did a great deal of research into this case in the United States. He told me that he had had many discussions on the matter with Senator Jim Exon (Democrat, Nebraska), a member of the Senate Armed Services Committee who, according to Boeche, had spent much time looking into the Woodbridge affair. Results of Senator Exon's inquiries suggest a cover-up.

Boeche telephoned Colonel Halt to ask him if he would agree to discuss the Rendlesham incidents with the Senator and provide corroborative evidence. Halt agreed, saying: 'I've got a soil sample right here, and I can put my hands on plaster casts. Halt also stated that he would be prepared to confirm that a certain captain drove General Gordon Williams, overall base commander at the time, from the Rendlesham landing site to a fighter plane at Bentwaters with what Williams told the captain was a canister of motion-picture film of the UFO. The film was flown quickly to the USAF European Headquarters at Ramstein Air Force Base, Germany, and has not been heard of since. The Air Force specifically denies that any photographs or films were taken of the event.

According to the Senator's defence aid, Exon did speak with Halt, but Boeche has been unable to obtain any information about the meeting other than a 'No comment'. When, eventually, he managed to speak directly with the Senator he was given extremely evasive answers. 'Has he found out something that's disturbed him?' Boeche asked me. 'Or has he been told to back off?'

During the course of many conversations and letters about the Woodbridge case, former Ministry of Defence official Ralph Noyes has left me in no doubt that there has been an official cover-up. In view of his long career with the MoD, which he joined after his Second World War service as a navigator on operational missions in Beaufighter aircraft in the Middle East and South-East Asia, his opinion cannot be lightly dismissed.

In the afterword of his science-fiction book on UFOs, *A Secret Property*, he sums up his feelings about the Woodbridge case:

> The Ministry of Defence may well have good reasons for withholding information about the Rendlesham incidents. As a former Defence official, I would not wish to press questions on any matter touching national security; and in those circumstances I would not be surprised if questions pressed by others were met with a refusal to reply. But I cannot help feeling that it is something of a lapse from the usual standards of a government department to issue a direct misstatement. Concealment is one thing (and is often justified), false denial is another.
>
> The RAF Woodbridge case of December 1980 strikes me as one of the most interesting and important of recent years, anyway in this country.[33]

Admiral of the Fleet the Lord Hill-Norton, former Chief of the Defence Staff from 1971 to 1973 and former Chairman of the NATO Military Committee, is also convinced that there has been a cover-up on this extraordinary case. In May 1985 he wrote to the Secretary of State for Defence (then Michael Heseltine), asking pertinent questions. Nearly two months went by before he received a reply from Lord Trefgarne, on behalf of the Minister:

> You wrote to Michael Heseltine on 1 May 1985 about the sighting of an unidentified flying object near RAF Woodbridge in December 1980. Michael has asked me to reply as UFO questions fall within my responsibilities.
>
> I do understand your concern and I am grateful to you for having taken the trouble to write. I do not believe, however, that there are any grounds for changing our view, formed at the time, that the events to which you refer were of no defence significance.[34]

Lord Trefgarne was Parliamentary Under-Secretary of State for the Armed Forces at the time, and Lord Hill-Norton responded to his letter as follows:

> . . . I am astounded that a serious letter to a Minister from a member of the House of Lords was allowed to remain unanswered for seven weeks.

I am sorry that you take the view that the sort of uproar which occurred in Suffolk in December 1980 is of 'no defence significance', because I have no doubt from my rather longer experience that you are mistaken. Unless Lt. Col. Halt was out of his mind, there is clear evidence in his report that British airspace – and probably territory – were intruded upon by an unidentified vehicle in that month, and that no bar to such intrusion was effective. If Halt's report is not believed, there is equally clear evidence of a serious misjudgement of events by members of the USAF at an important base in the UK. Either way the events can hardly be without defence significance.[35]

Lord Trefgarne's reply was more conciliatory this time, assuring the Fleet Admiral that the Ministry 'does take the subject seriously', and he invited Lord Hill-Norton to a private meeting. A date was arranged in September 1985, but in the meantime Lord Trefgarne was promoted to the position of Minister of State for Defence, and official duties necessitated a postponement of the meeting to 9 October.

Both Ralph Noyes and myself had briefed Lord Hill-Norton about the subject in general, and Woodbridge in particular. Trefgarne personally flew down to Hampshire for the meeting in his private plane, together with a representative from the Ministry's Defence Secretariat (Air Staff) 2. The Minister was helpful and courteous, Lord Hill-Norton told us, but did not give the impression of having been briefed in great depth about the Woodbridge case. He was aware, he said, that reports had been made of unidentified events in British airspace and that some had remained unexplained, but he was convinced that none of them had ever been shown to have defence significance, including two reports from defence establishments made that year. In response to further questions, Lord Trefgarne admitted that traces of unidentified events certainly occurred from time to time on radar and were recorded on radar tapes. None had ever been considered to be of defence importance after proper study, and no tape was retained for long: they were costly, and the practice was to recycle them for operational use after a short while. Similarly, Lord Trefgarne said that he saw no defence significance in the Woodbridge case, and only after sustained questioning by the Admiral did he agree that it might be of defence significance if responsible Americans had had serious misperceptions at an important NATO base on British territory.

Colonel Charles Halt

In October 1986 I spoke with Colonel Charles Halt, who was based at the time with the 485th Tactical Missile Wing in Belgium. My first question dealt with the authenticity and accuracy of his document to the Ministry of Defence. 'As far as you're concerned, Colonel Halt, your memorandum is legitimate?' I asked. 'It certainly is,' he affirmed. He denied that any movie film was taken of the UFO, or that he had ordered Adrian Bustinza to confiscate photographs taken by British policemen. 'That's not true,' he said. 'I suspect time has clouded his memory. I confiscated nothing from anyone – I had no authority to. We were guests in your country. I can tell you that your bobbies wouldn't have probably given them to me if I'd asked.'

I then asked Colonel Halt if the radar tapes at RAF Watton had been confiscated by USAF intelligence officers. 'Well, I don't know that they were confiscated,' he answered. 'I do know that they were used at a later date because I was questioned specifically on times and areas of the sky and so on . . . It's your Government's business, not mine!'

And the story of aliens? Had this been thrown in to confuse the issue? I wanted to know. 'There's only one individual who talks about that [Larry Warren], and I can't speak for him,' said the Colonel (though in fact several others made the same claim). 'I can't disprove what he says, but I can't corroborate it either . . . There are a lot of things that are not in my memo, but there was no response from the Ministry of Defence so I didn't go any further with them.'[36]

In his 1994 interview for a *Strange But True?* London Weekend Television documentary, Halt said that he was baffled by the MoD's lack of response. 'To this day I'm very puzzled why nobody ever came back and asked for additional information, asked questions, or even interviewed me. It doesn't really add up.' He also pointed out that he knew the individuals who had reported the original event, and 'they were very credible people'. During the events he witnessed on the night of 29/30 December, he confirms that the floodlights, or 'light-alls' – set up to illuminate the pine-forest during the investigation of the landing traces – malfunctioned. 'In addition,' he reported, 'we had problems with our radios: all three frequencies we were using were intermittent and did not work properly that night.' He also commented that he was glad that a tape-recording had been made. 'If we hadn't made the tape, even I would have trouble believing what happened that night,' he said.[37]

During his lecture in Leeds in 1994, Charles Halt (now retired from the US Air Force) provided further information about the Rendlesham Forest affair. Following the incident, for instance, a C-141 StarLifter transport aircraft made an unscheduled landing at Bentwaters with a 'special group' of personnel on board who went straight to the East Gate area, though Halt claims that no one knew what they did nor what were the results of their investigation. (Larry Warren told me that the aircraft was in fact a C-130 Hercules with a US Air Force Special Response Team from Germany, sent to check on the nuclear weapons. During the incidents, according to several witnesses, beams of light from the UFOs were directed on the hardened bunkers containing the weapons, possibly affecting them in some way.)[38]

Halt produced a plaster cast (one of several made by Jim Penniston) of one of the craft's tripod landing-legs. The cast was about 10–12 inches long and about 8 inches wide. 'There appeared to be a definite smooth surface to the underside, giving the impression of a shallow dome shape,' reported Mark Birdsall of Quest International. 'I believe that Halt mentioned something in the region of two tons would have created the hole.'[39]

Highly Classified Findings

Clifford Stone, a former US Army staff sergeant who was working for a branch of military intelligence at the time of the incidents, learned that there was a total blackout of information on the case. Even senior officials were not informed about the purpose of the various unscheduled visits by military aircraft to the twin bases (such as the one reported by Colonel Halt). During an interview for the London Weekend Television documentary in 1994, Stone revealed that these flights contained teams of specialists who gathered specific data in their fields of expertise. The information was then sent to Washington, DC, where it was assessed then accumulated in a final, highly classified report.

'That finalized report concluded that real objects were seen; that these objects were a result of a highly evolved advanced technology; the technology was so advanced that we cannot to this day replicate it; that there was an intelligence involved, and that that intelligence did not originate on Earth.'[40]

The Security Threat

Close Encounters Reported by Police

AS MANY POLICE OFFICERS are out on patrol during the small hours, it is hardly surprising that several hundred UFO sightings have been reported by the police. Although the majority of these sightings are of odd lights in the sky, a substantial number include close encounters. In such cases, either the witnesses are lying or they have seen a genuinely unexplainable object at close quarters.

Report by a Woman Police Constable

Independent investigator Patricia Grant has interviewed a woman police constable who claims to have seen a UFO in Isfield, near Lewes, Sussex, on a bright day in the early autumn of 1977. The witness prefers to remain anonymous, partly due to official pressure, she claims. At about 17.20 on the day in question the policewoman noticed a curious, silent object, estimated to be as large as a 4-inch plate held at arm's length, at no more than 300 feet altitude. A conventional plane was immediately ruled out by the witness, who had been trained in aircraft recognition in the Royal Observer Corps. She felt no fear. On impulse she waved at the object, which came closer. It seemed to be of light greenish-grey metal with a moderately reflective surface. On top of the dome protruded a blue-green light, and underneath the object could be seen a very dense black circular section (see plate section). At its closest approach the object was estimated to be no further than 50 feet away.

The witness had been waiting at a bus-stop during the encounter, and when the bus eventually arrived she experienced a numbness, stiffness and lack of co-ordination in her limbs. Stumbling to the top deck, from which she hoped to obtain a better view, she discovered that the object was nowhere in sight. Almost immediately after taking her seat she developed an acute headache that persisted until the following morning. Other symptoms developed, including thirst and conjunctivitis: her eyes burned and watered for a week afterwards, and she suffered recurrent gastric disturbances. (The witness is also a qualified nurse, holding a general nursing certificate.) Even more peculiar was the sense of 'timelessness' she experienced during the encounter: about twenty minutes seem to have been unaccounted for while she waited at the bus-stop.

Pat Grant, with whom I have discussed the case at length, is totally convinced of the witness's sincerity. Regrettably, no one else saw the object, it seems, and, as for so many others, this was the most frustrating aspect of the incident for the witness. Perhaps the most positive development is that subsequently she seldom became upset or angry, having admitted to a short temper before the incident.[1]

Structured UFO Encountered by Three Police Officers

On a January night in 1978, Sergeant Tony Dodd and Police Constable Alan Dale were driving in the vicinity of Cononley, near Skipton, Yorkshire, in their official line of duty, when a strange aerial machine came into view. 'We were going down a country lane,' Dodd told me, 'and you know what it's like up there – it was *dark* – and the only light you've got is your headlights. Suddenly the road in front of us lit up. Of course, the immediate reaction is: Where's the light coming from? But it was coming from above. We stopped the car, looked up, and there was this thing coming from our right to our left.'

The object was about 100 feet away, moving at less than 40 m.p.h. 'It was glowing – like a bright white incandescent glow – and it came right over our heads,' the former police sergeant recalled in 1986:

> The whole unit was glowing. It was as if the metal of what this thing was made of was white hot. And there were these three great spheres underneath, like huge ball-bearings – three of them equally placed around it. There was a hollow area underneath and like a skirting around the bottom, but these things protruded below that.
>
> It was absolutely awe-inspiring . . . I don't know how to explain it to you – it was such a beautiful-looking thing. It seemed to have portholes round the dome – an elongated domed area. And what stood out more than anything else was the coloured lights dancing round on the outside of the skirt at the bottom . . . which gave the visual impression that it was rotating. Now whether the thing *was* going round and giving that impression, I don't know. I would say it was lights that were going round, because when you were looking

at the portholes they didn't seem to be going round in a circle as
you would have expected. The object was completely soundless.

'When the thing had passed over our heads it sort of went into the
distance then suddenly appeared to come down: there's a big wood to our
left, right on a distant hillside, and it *appeared* to go down in that wood,'
said Dodd, who added that a third police officer had seen the object.

'We carried on along this road, and as we got towards the village we
could see these lights coming towards us from the other direction – it was
another police car. We stopped, and he said: "I've just been watching this
damn great UFO, and it seems to have come right down somewhere over
here!" '2

The fact that a highly unusual and silent aerial machine was witnessed
by three police officers must surely count as compelling evidence in the
search for proof that our airspace is regularly penetrated by craft of
unknown origin and purpose.

Police Officer Abducted?

Another close-encounter case which has impressed me favourably is that
of PC Alan Godfrey, whom I met in September 1986 following a Central
Television programme on which we both appeared. Godfrey's experience
occurred on 29 November 1980 shortly after 05.00 in the morning in the
town of Todmorden, Yorkshire. Other police officers reported a UFO in
the vicinity around the same time. This is how Godfrey described his
encounter on television:

> I was driving a police car at the time, and in the early hours of the
> morning I came across what I thought at that time was a bus that
> had slid across the road sideways. And when I approached the
> object – I got within about 20 yards of it – and immediately I came
> across what I now would describe as a UFO.
>
> It was about 20 feet wide and 14 feet high [and] diamond-
> shaped. It had a bank of windows in and the bottom half was
> rotating. The police blue beacon was bouncing back off it, as were
> my headlights. It was hovering off the ground about 5 feet. And it
> was very frightening – very frightening.

Author and investigator Jenny Randles reports that Godfrey noticed
the bushes and trees beside the road shaking, which he presumed to be

caused by the object. Attempts to contact base by radio, using both VHF and UHF, failed, so the policeman sketched the object on his clipboard. Then a strange thing happened: the next minute he found himself 100 yards further down the road and there was no sign of the UFO.

PC Godfrey drove back to the centre of town, where he picked up a colleague, gave him some brief details, then took him to the site, where both policemen noticed that the road above which the object had hovered was dry in patches, although soaked with rain elsewhere. Returning to the police station, Godfrey saw that the time was 05.30. This he found puzzling, since it had seemed to him that less time had elapsed. Later it transpired that he had experienced a peculiar time-lapse, and during several hypnotic regression sessions he came out with a bizarre story of apparently having been taken on board the craft.[3] Solicitor Harry Harris has made video recordings of these sessions, and while the abduction story may be woven with strands of fantasy from his subconscious mind – Godfrey himself told me that he remains uncertain as to what actually happened to him during the missing time period – there is no doubting the very real fear that he relived when regressed to the time of the encounter.

Alan Godfrey was asked on television what had happened in the police as a result of the story becoming known. 'Nothing happened at all for about twelve months,' he replied, 'and then, due to publicity at that time being aroused around the case, a lot of pressure was put on me not to say anything. I was made to sign documents, I had to visit certain places . . . I had to dissociate myself from any person that was interested in UFOs.'

'Did you feel that you were maybe the victim of some kind of a cover-up?' Godfrey was asked. 'Well,' he began cautiously, 'that's Catch 22!' 'Well, yes or no?' persisted the interviewer. 'Er . . . yes,' the former policeman reluctantly admitted.[4]

A Home Office Directive

In 1982 I interviewed a retired police inspector, who has asked not to be identified, in an effort to find out what official instructions the police had for reporting sightings on UFOs. 'What I can say to you', my informant volunteered, 'is that the subject itself was the subject of a Home Office directive. The Home Office sends out directives to the Chief Constable, or they send a letter, laying down certain procedures to be followed in the event of UFOs being sighted.'

These directives – which sound similar if not identical to the instructions given to air traffic controllers (p. 55) – were then incorporated in the Force Policy Manual, he explained.

> I saw one of these directives. There were certain specified telephone numbers . . . monitoring stations in relation to aircraft [the UK Warning and Monitoring Service, part of Britain's Civil Defence network] . . . We had a set procedure, because it would be out of range of a tracking-station . . . they were Air Force stations, which would also have been contacted in the event of, say, if you saw an aircraft in distress. So it was obviously radar that they were relying on there, and also somebody that they were relying on who had control of aircraft in the area.

Injury Caused by Unknown Craft

At 03.00 on 11 September 1981 Bob Boyd, Chairman of the Plymouth (Devon) UFO Research Group (PUFORG), received a phone call from John Greenwell, who had just finished work as a disc jockey at a local radio station and had gone to collect his girlfriend from her mother's house. On arrival he was told that his girlfriend's sister, Denise Bishop, had experienced a UFO encounter three and three-quarter hours earlier at Weston Mill, Plymouth. Greenwell had immediately telephoned the nearest police station and was told that they had no procedure for handling UFO reports, but was given Boyd's phone number. Boyd, who happened to live in the vicinity of the alleged encounter, decided to investigate there and then, despite the late hour.

Bishop, a twenty-three-year-old accounts clerk at the time, previously had given no consideration to the UFO question; neither had she read any books on the subject. This is her story, as related to Bob Boyd only hours after the encounter on 10 September 1981:

> I was coming into my house at approximately 11.15 p.m., and as I approached the corner of the bungalow I thought I saw some lights behind the house. As I got to the back door and could see up the hill behind our house, I saw an enormous UFO hovering above the houses on top of the hill.
>
> The object was unlit and a dark metallic grey, but coming from underneath the object and shining down on the rooftops beneath it were six or seven shafts of light. These were lovely pastel shades of pink and purple and also white. I saw all this in an instant and I

was terrified. I hurriedly reached for the door but as I put my hand on the handle, from the unlit side of the ship a lime-green pencil beam of light came down and hit the back of my hand. As soon as it hit my hand I couldn't move. I was stopped dead in my tracks. The beam stayed on my hand for at least thirty seconds, in which time I could only stand and watch the UFO.

I was very frightened, although the UFO was a fantastic sight to see. It was huge and silent. In fact the whole area seemed very quiet. The green beam, which didn't give off any illumination and was rather like a rod of light, then switched off and I continued to open the door. It was as if a film had been stopped then started again. I had been stopped in mid-stride and when the beam went off continued the same movement. I opened the door and rushed in the house. As I did so the UFO lifted into the sky slightly and moved away and out of my sight.

Rubbing my hand, I ran in and told my sister. We went back outside but there was nothing to be seen. Coming in again my sister examined my hand but there was nothing there. I went and sat down, and a few minutes later my sister's dog sniffed my hand, making it sting. On looking at it I noticed spots of blood, and after washing it saw it was a burn. At 2.30 a.m. my sister's boyfriend came in and said we must report it to the police. He phoned the police but they couldn't help except to give us Bob Boyd's number.

On arrival at Bishop's house, Boyd took a couple of black and white photographs of the burn mark, which appeared as a patch of shiny skin with spots of blood and bruising. 'It looked as if a patch of skin had been removed, exposing the shiny, new skin beneath,' he reported. He tried to persuade Bishop to go to the casualty ward at the local hospital, but she refused. Because the wound was hurting, Boyd suggested that she immerse her hand in cold water, but that only made it worse. Antiseptic cream, however, afforded some relief.

On the following morning Bob Boyd, accompanied by Des Weeks, Secretary of the Plymouth group, and a nurse, visited Bishop, who now appeared to be in a state of shock. The burn mark was worse. The nurse examined it and tried unsuccessfully to persuade Bishop to see a doctor. On 14 and 15 September Boyd phoned RAF Mount Batten to ensure that the Ministry of Defence was notified about the incident and to impress upon them the rarity and importance of the case. Wing Commander J. S.

Fosh took further details and explained that, although RAF Mount Batten did not investigate UFO sightings, he felt sure that when the report was passed on to the Ministry of Defence in London they would probably want to interview the witness. To date there has been no interview.

Convincing Witness

When I met Denise Bishop in July 1982, I found her convincing and level-headed, and can see no reason why she should have concocted such a story. She had shunned publicity, having turned down a Westward Television interview, although she did eventually concede to allowing local reporter Roger Malone to write up her story in October 1981.[5]

Derek Mansell of Contact UK became intrigued with the case and offered his assistance. In December 1981 he wrote to Bob Boyd enclosing a report from a consultant orthopaedic surgeon at a leading London hospital (who unfortunately but understandably prefers to remain anonymous). The surgeon stated his opinion that the burn mark had the characteristics of a laser burn, and that there was normally 'a 48-hour delay in the commencement of the healing process'. This was confirmed by Boyd and his group, who on 15 September noted the formation of a scab, which eventually disappeared, leaving Bishop with a scar which faded gradually, though reappearing in cold weather.[6] Though faint, the scar was still visible when I visited Bishop ten months after the incident.

The pencil-thin beam of light that causes temporary paralysis has been reported by other witnesses, and it is not beyond the realms of possibility that Bishop could at some time have read about this in a newspaper or magazine article and then stored it in her subconscious memory. Yet she appears to have no predisposed belief in either UFOs or the paranormal – a prerequisite if we are to suggest that a strong 'wish to believe' psychosomatically induced the scar (a speculation put forward to account for stigmata, for example).

It is unfortunate that no one else saw the object, as far as we know, although the Plymouth group was able to locate people whose pets had behaved in a peculiar manner at the precise location over which it hovered.

Does this incident constitute a threat to the defence of the United Kingdom? Or a potential threat? If so, was the Ministry of Defence avoiding its responsibilities by not investigating further?

House of Lords, 1982

On 4 March 1982 the Earl of Clancarty asked in the House of Lords: 'How many reports have been received by the Ministry of Defence on unidentified flying objects in each of the last four years, and what action had been taken in each case?' Viscount Long, representing the Government, replied: 'My Lords, in 1978 there were 750 sightings; in 1979 there were 550 sightings; in 1980, 350 sightings; and in 1981, 600 sightings. All UFO reports are passed to operations staff who examine them solely for possible defence implications.'

The Earl of Clancarty was not satisfied with these figures and stated that he believed the number to be far higher, but Viscount Long pointed out – quite correctly – that not all reports reached the MoD: 'If the noble Earl is suspicious that the Ministry of Defence is covering up in any way, I can assure him that there is no reason why we should cover up the figures which he has mentioned if they are true,' he said.

The Earl of Kimberley, former Liberal spokesman on aerospace and a member of the House of Lords UFO Study Group, then asked Viscount Long how many of the 600 sightings reported to the MoD in 1981 'still remain unidentified and were not subject to security, or were Russian aeroplanes, or anything like that'. Long's reply was as amusing as it was unconvincing: 'My Lords, I do not have those figures. They disappeared into the unknown before we got them.'

Replying to a question from Lord Strabolgi, who had represented the Government in the 1979 House of Lords debate, Viscount Long stressed that most sightings can be 'accounted for in one way or another, but nobody has got a really constructive answer for all of them'. Another member of the Lords UFO Study Group, Admiral of the Fleet Lord Hill-Norton, then asked 'whether it is true that all sighting reports received by the Ministry of Defence before 1962 were destroyed because they were deemed to be "of no defence interest". And if it is true, who was it decided that they were of no interest?'

'My Lords,' responded Long, 'my reply to the noble and gallant Lord – I was wondering whether he was going to say that the Royal Navy had many times seen the Loch Ness monster – is that since 1967 all UFO reports have been preserved. Before that time they were generally destroyed.'[7] The Admiral chose not to pick up the gauntlet, but he might have wondered why only part of his first question was answered and the second one ignored altogether.

During an interview on BBC Television transmitted a week after the

Lords debate, Lord Hill-Norton was asked: 'As a former Chief of the Defence Staff [1971–3], wouldn't you have known if there was information available which hadn't been released to the public?'

'I think I *ought* to have known,' he replied, 'but I certainly didn't, and, had I known, I would not, of course, be allowed on an interview like this to say so. So that in itself seems significant. What I *do* believe is that information has come to the Ministry of Defence – probably over a period of twenty years or even longer – which is not available to the public, and was not available to me while I was in office.'[8]

On 7 April 1982 another question was raised in the House of Lords, and I attended the debate, at the invitation of the Earl of Clancarty. The Earl of Cork and Orrery asked: 'How many of the 2,250 sightings of UFOs reported to the Ministry of Defence in the years 1978–81 were, and still are, classified for reasons of security?' Viscount Long, again replying for the Government, jumped up and stated enthusiastically: 'None, my Lords.' The Earl then asked two supplementary questions, one of which enquired into the possibility of the Ministry of Defence releasing reports to interested individuals and organizations. Long said that there was 'no reason why he should not come and see the reports. Not many of them come in because not many people actually report sightings. There is no cover-up in that respect.'

The Earl of Kimberley challenged Viscount Long on his reply to a supplementary question he had asked at the previous debate. 'Why,' he enquired, 'had he said that the figures had got lost on the way to the Ministry, whereas today he says that they are there and available for anyone to see? Can he therefore place them in the Library for all of us to see?' Long replied that he would look into the possibility and added: 'I should like all of your Lordships to see them in the Library, if possible.'

Lord Shinwell asked if it was possible 'that all the information is well-known to the Ministry of Defence, but that for diplomatic and other reasons it is not prepared to make an announcement'. Long replied that the Ministry was not prepared to do so 'because it has not got the facts to make an announcement with authority behind it'.

Lord Beswick pointed out that the question on the order paper referred to 2,250 sightings, yet 'the noble Viscount says that there are very few sightings reported to the Ministry of Defence. Does this mean that the figure in the Question is incorrect?' Long explained that the contradiction was due to the original assumption that there were probably many sightings that were not reported to the Ministry, but after another question by Lord Beswick he confirmed that the figure of 2,250 sightings was correct.

An amusing exchange followed:

VISCOUNT ST DAVIDS: My Lords, has anybody yet found an empty beer can marked, 'Made in Centaurus', or any similar object? Until they have, will the Ministry deal with these matters with very considerable scepticism, please?

VISCOUNT LONG: My Lords, I am not the Minister for conservation, if it is a question of beer cans.

LORD MORRIS: My Lords, if something is said to be unidentified, how can it possibly be said to exist?

VISCOUNT LONG: A very good question, my Lords.

LORD LEATHERLAND: My Lords, can the Minister tell us whether any of the unidentified flying objects are Ministers who are fleeing from the Cabinet just now?

VISCOUNT LONG: No, my Lords.[9]

Abduction in Aldershot

The remarkable story of Alfred Burtoo's close encounter beside the Basingstoke Canal in Aldershot, Hampshire, during the small hours of 12 August 1983, is a fisherman's tale with a difference: the one that got away was a flying saucer – complete with little 'green' men. If the witness was not lying – and I for one am convinced he was not – we are presented with an important, highly detailed account which may teach us a great deal about the UFO phenomenon, irrespective of what interpretation we choose to place on it. We may also come to understand more of the reasons why the authorities are anxious to play down the subject.

Background

Because of its many military establishments, Aldershot is known as 'The Home of the British Army'. Alfred Burtoo himself had an Army background, having served in the Queen's Royal Regiment in 1924 and the Hampshire Regiment during the Second World War. Well-known as a local historian, he had in his time worked as a farmer and gardener, and, while living in the Canadian outback, had hunted bears and fought wolves. Burtoo told me that he was afraid of nothing, and regarding his encounter, which would have terrified most people, said: 'What did I have to fear? I'm seventy-eight now and haven't got much to lose.' Before his experience he had read no books or magazines on the UFO subject, which held no interest for him.

Mr Burtoo was a keen and experienced fisherman, and since the weather report for 11/12 August predicted a warm, fine night he set off from his home in North Town, Aldershot, at 00.15 hours, accompanied by his dog, Tiny. On reaching Government Road he encountered a Ministry of Defence policeman on his beat, and after a brief chat headed towards his selected fishing-site, about 115 yards north of the Gasworks Bridge on Government Road. He undid his fishing-rod holdall and took out the bottom joint of his fishing-umbrella, pushed it into the soil, and tied the dog to it. While unpacking his tackle box he heard the gong at Buller Barracks strike one o'clock. He set up the rod rests, cast out his tackle, and then sat down watching the water for fish movements.

The Encounter

'After about fifteen minutes,' Mr Burtoo told me, 'I decided to have a cup of tea, which I poured from my thermos. I stood up to ease my legs and was putting the cup to my mouth when I saw a vivid light coming towards me from the south, which is over North Town. It wavered over the railway line and then came on again, then settled down. The vivid light went out, though I could still see a light through the boughs of the trees. I thought: Well that can't be an aeroplane; it's too low – because it was at about 300 feet.

'During this time I had set the cup down on the tackle box and lit a cigarette, and while smoking it my dog began to growl. It was then that I saw two "forms" coming towards me, and when they were within 5 feet of me they just stopped and looked at me, and I at them, for a good ten or fifteen seconds.' Tiny, an obedient dog, had stopped growling by this time, on her master's command.

'They were about 4 feet high, dressed in pale-green coveralls from head to foot, and they had helmets of the same colour with a visor that was blacked out,' Burtoo said. 'Then the one on the right beckoned me with his right forearm and turned away, still waving its arm. I took it that he wished me to follow, which I did. He moved off and I fell in behind him, and the chap that was on the left fell in behind me. We walked along the towpath until we got to the railing by the canal bridge. The "form" in front of me went [under] the railing, while I went over the top, and we crossed Government Road then went down on the footpath.'

The Craft

'Going around a slight left-hand bend I saw a large object, about 40 to 45 feet across, standing on the towpath, with about 10 to 15 feet of it over the bank on the left of the path. And I thought: Christ, what the hell's that? – didn't think about UFOs at the time. When we got down there this "form" in front of me went up the steps and I followed. The steps were off-line to the towpath, and we had to step on the grass to go up them.' Portholes were set in the hull, and the object rested on two ski-type runners [see plate section].

'Going in the door, the corners weren't sharp, they were rounded off. We went into this octagonal room. The "form" in front of me crossed over the room, and I heard a sound as if a sliding door was being opened and closed. I stood in the room to the right of the door, and the "form" that had walked behind me stood just inside, between me and the door. I don't know whether it was to stop me going out or not . . .

'I stood there a good ten minutes, taking in everything I could see. The walls, the floor and the ceiling were all black, and looked to me like unfinished metal, whereas the outside looked like burnished aluminium. I did not see any sign of nuts or bolts, nor did I see any seams where the object had been put together. What did interest me most of all was a shaft that rose up from the floor to the ceiling.[10] The shaft was about 4 feet in circumference, and on the right-hand side of it was a Z-shaped handle. On either side of that stood two "forms" similar to those that walked along the towpath with me.

'All of a sudden a voice said to me: "*Come and stand under the amber light.*" I could not see any amber light until I took a step to my right, and there it was way up on the wall just under the ceiling. I stood there for about five minutes, then a voice said: "*What is your age?*" I said: "I shall be seventy-eight next birthday." And after a while I was asked to turn around, which I did, facing the wall. After about five minutes he said to me: "*You can go. You are too old and infirm for our purpose.*"

'I left the object, and while walking down the steps I used the handrail and found it had two joints in it, so I came to the conclusion it was telescopic. I walked along the towpath to about halfway between the object and the canal bridge, stopped and looked back, and noticed that the dome of the object looked very much like an oversized chimney cowl, and that it was revolving anticlockwise.

'I then walked on to the spot where I had left my dog and fishing-tackle, and the first thing I did when I got there was to pick up my cold cup of tea and drink it. And then I heard this whining noise, just as if an electric generator was starting up, and this thing lifted off and the bright light came on again. It was so bright that I could see my fishing-float in the water 6 feet away from the opposite bank of the canal, and the thin iron bars on the canal bridge. The object took off at a very high speed, out over the military cemetery in the west, and then a little later I saw the light going over the Hog's Back and out of sight. This was around 2.00 a.m.'

Mr Burtoo settled down to wait for dawn, which came at 03.30, and then, he told me, 'I got into what I had come out for – the fishing!' Incredible though it may seem, he did not feel inclined to report his experience to anyone at the time. He sat there fishing until 10 o'clock in the morning, at which time two Ministry of Defence mounted policemen rode up to him. 'Any luck, mate?' one of them asked. 'Yes,' replied Burtoo. 'I've had three roach, five rudd, a tench of $2\frac{1}{2}$ lb, and lost a big carp which took me into the weeds.' He then started to tell the policemen about the UFO, and one of them said: 'Yes, I dare say you did see that UFO. I expect they were checking on our military installations.'

Was this just a tongue-in-cheek comment to placate the old boy? At that moment, anyway, a man from the canal lock yard came along and told the MoD policemen that horses were not allowed on the towpath, and so the conversation was cut short. Mr Burtoo continued fishing until 12.30, and returned home half an hour later. He told his wife and a friend of hers that he had seen a UFO, but refrained from telling them that he had been taken on board. 'I knew the wife would say: "No more fishing for you, old man!"'

No Witnesses

Alfred Burtoo did not return to the landing-site until two days later, when he noticed that the foliage between the canal and the towpath was in disarray. Unfortunately, no photos or soil samples were taken. He felt that someone in the guard hut of the nearby Royal Electrical and Mechanical Engineers workshops must have seen or heard something, but checks by investigator Omar Fowler drew a blank. Fowler was also unable to trace the two mounted policemen. And the occupants of a bungalow near the canal lock beside Gasworks Bridge were away at the time.

Throughout his experience Burtoo was hoping that a train would cross the railway bridge (Aldershot to London, main line) which is about 100 yards to the south of the landing-site, but there was none – at least, not while he was outside the craft. But even if a train had gone by it is doubtful if anyone would have noticed the object except at those times when it was at its most brilliant, i.e. during landing and take-off. No cars were seen on either Government Road or Camp Farm Road, which runs beside the Basingstoke Canal at the spot where Burtoo was fishing, nor have any witnesses come forward.

Publicity

The story of Alfred Burtoo's encounter made headline news in the local paper two months later, as a result of his having written to the *Aldershot News* initially enquiring if anyone had reported an unusual light at the time of the incident.[11] The paper then notified Omar Fowler of the Surrey Investigation Group on Aerial Phenomena (SIGAP), who subsequently interviewed Mr Burtoo in October 1983.[12] My first recorded interview with the witness took place the following month, in the presence of local reporter Debbie Collins. The *Aldershot News* published our positive findings,[13] and this attracted the attention of the American tabloid the *National Enquirer*, which ran a story in 1984.[14]

Further Details of the Encounter

Mr Burtoo told me that the shape of the central room in the craft was octagonal and the ceiling was very low. The floor appeared to be covered with a soft material of some kind, because he was unable to hear his footsteps. The internal lighting did not appear to emanate from any particular source, with the exception of the beam of amber light underneath which he was asked to stand. The lighting in general was rather dim. There were no dials, controls, seats, or other objects visible, apart from the central column with its Z-shaped handle.

He said that the temperature inside the craft was a little warmer than outside, which would make it about 65 °F. He noticed a faint smell similar to that of 'decaying meat'.

The occupants moved like human beings, although they walked with a rather stiff gait, Burtoo explained to me. No facial features could be discerned, since these were covered by the visors. The pale-green one-piece suits also covered the hands and feet, and appeared to be moulded on to their thin bodies 'like plastic'. He did not notice if the gloves covered fingers. There were no belts, zippers, buttons or fasteners. All four beings were of the same size and unusually thin shape.

The beings spoke in a kind of 'sing-song' accent, similar to 'a mixture of Chinese and Russian'. Burtoo, in fact, was convinced that they originated here on Earth. 'I myself do not think they come from outer space,' he said, 'for we are told by scientists that this planet is the only one with water. If that is the case, how can they survive?'

I asked Mr Burtoo why on earth he refrained from asking any questions: surely that would be the first thing to do in such a situation. He explained that he simply did not feel it was the right thing to do, as he was anxious to avoid causing offence. As to his 'rejection', which he found mildly disappointing, he attributed this to his bronchial and arterial problems, and thought that the scanning device (if that is what it was) detected the plastic replacement(s) following an operation for arteriosclerosis.

Aftermath

Alfred Burtoo suffered none of the side-effects sometimes reported by close-encounter witnesses, such as temporary paralysis, nausea, diarrhoea, skin disorders, eye irritation, and so on; nor was he aware of any amnesia or time-lapse, but he told me that he did feel 'different' after the experience. He ate little for a while, resulting in some loss of weight, and felt less inclined to go out. He also found difficulty getting to sleep, due to continually turning the events over in his mind. He had few regrets about his extraordinary experience, which in my opinion ranks as one of the most convincing close-encounter cases I have investigated.

'Until I had this encounter with the UFO,' Mr Burtoo told me, 'I always took the talk about them with a pinch of salt, but now I know they are a fact. During the time I was with them I felt no fear, only curiosity, nor were they hostile towards me nor I to them. My only regret about the whole affair is that I did not have another person along with me to see and experience something that I did not believe until it happened to me, and I think myself lucky that I am here today to speak about it, for I am sure that these men were out to abduct some person, and that person could have been me. But at the same time I will say that it was the greatest experience of my life.'

Alfred Burtoo died on 31 August 1986, aged eighty. Mindful of the possibility that he had finally confessed the story to be a hoax, I wrote to his wife, Marjorie, some months later, and asked if this was so. 'It was not a hoax,' she replied:

What Alf told you was the absolute truth. My friend who was with me when Alf came home can verify what he said. He looked absolutely shaken and he told both of us about his experience that he had with the UFO. He was just like a man who had seen a miracle happen and we knew he was telling the truth because no one could believe otherwise if they had heard him and saw him that morning. My husband was not a man who believed in fantasies or had hallucinations. He was down to earth, and you can take it from me that Alf never changed his mind on the story of what he had seen and experienced.

No Defence Threat

When my investigation into the case was completed, I sent a report to the Ministry of Defence. 'I was interested to see the report of Mr Burtoo's alleged encounter,' replied Peter Hucker of Secretariat (Air Staff) 2a:

We have no record of corresponding reports which might support this story. There was certainly no report submitted to us by the MoD police concerning the incident . . . MoD interest in the subject is limited to those sightings which are directly relevant to the air defence of the UK . . . the majority of reports received here are often weeks old, and we simply cannot devote public funds to the detailed investigation of such sightings when no threat to national defence has been demonstrated.[15]

Yet how does one define a defence threat in this context? We already have a multitude of reports involving interference with communications and power systems, temporary paralysis and injury (such as the Denise Bishop case) and, in the case of Alfred Burtoo, an abduction close to an important military base. Do these not constitute a defence threat?

Further Questions in the Commons

On 9 March 1984 Sir Patrick Wall MP asked the Secretary of State for Defence 'how many alleged landings by unidentified flying objects have been made in 1980, 1981, 1982 and 1983, respectively; and how many have been investigated by his Department's personnel; how many unexplained sightings there have been in 1980, 1981, 1982 and 1983, respectively, and which of these had been traced by radar and with what result.'[16] John Lee, Defence Under-Secretary for Procurement, replied five days later in the House of Commons:

For the years in question, the Ministry of Defence received the following numbers of reports of sightings of flying objects which the observer could not identify: 350, 600, 250, and 390. Reports of alleged landings are not separately identified. The Department was satisfied that none of these reports was of any defence significance and, in such cases, does not maintain records of the extent of its investigations.[17]

John Lee ignored the question of radar traces, but six weeks later Sir Patrick Wall focused on this issue when he asked the Secretary of State for Defence whether there had been any unusual radar traces of airborne objects in the Rossendale Valley (Lancashire) area. 'No, sir,' came the written reply. Junior Transport Minister David Mitchell was even more abrupt. He answered a mere 'No!' to Sir Patrick's written request for information on 'whether he has received any reports of unauthorised landings from the air in the area of the Rossendale Valley'.[18]

The UK Intelligence Community

The United Kingdom has three intelligence and security services, known collectively as 'the Agencies'. These are the Security Service (MI5), the UK's domestic intelligence agency, which serves to protect the state against threats of terrorism, espionage and subversion; the Secret Intelligence Service (SIS or MI6), the principal function of which is the production of secret intelligence in support of HM Government's security, defence, foreign and economic policies; and Government Communications Headquarters (GCHQ), which provides government and military commands with signals intelligence (SIGINT) by monitoring a variety of communications and other signals, such as radar.

The MoD's Defence Intelligence Staff (DIS) also forms a vital part of Britain's intelligence machinery. It was created in 1964 by the amalgamation of all three service intelligence staffs (i.e. those of the Air Force, Army and Navy) and the civilian Joint Intelligence Bureau to serve the MoD, the Armed Forces and other government departments,[19] although each service maintains responsibility for its own intelligence-gathering and security. The DIS includes nearly ninety individual departments, at least one of which receives certain UFO reports from Secretariat (Air Staff) 2a (see p. 98).

The main body for advising on intelligence-gathering priorities and for their assessment is the Joint Intelligence Committee (JIC). The JIC is served by Current Intelligence Groups (CIGs) for daily analysis and an Assessments Staff for co-ordinating papers to be prepared for discussion. Its members include senior officials in the Foreign and Commonwealth Office, the Ministry of Defence, the Treasury, the heads of the three Agencies, the JIC's Intelligence Co-ordinator, and the Chief of the Assessments Staff. Subject to ministerial approval, the JIC is responsible for setting the UK's intelligence requirements as well as for producing a weekly survey on matters of intelligence concern.[20]

A former Director and Deputy Chief of the SIS has informed me that the SIS – Britain's equivalent of the CIA, with whom it liaises closely – did not have any interest in the UFO subject while he was in office. 'It simply wasn't what we call a "target of opportunity,"' he explained, and suggested that 'perhaps we leave it to the Americans'. That the SIS is not involved in UFO matters has been corroborated for me by other intelligence experts, including Donald McCormick and Nigel West.

I also have found no evidence – thus far – for the involvement of MI5 or GCHQ, although it is difficult to disregard the probability that GCHQ has been involved in view of its inseparable link with America's National Security Agency (NSA), an organization that has been involved in UFO investigations since its inception in 1952. Based in two locations in Cheltenham, but with globally dispersed listening-posts, GCHQ specializes in intercepting and decoding communications on a worldwide basis, notably diplomatic traffic, military communications, radar intelligence (RADINT) and broadcasts. According to the late James Rusbridger, the Foreign Office, through the joint GCHQ/NSA agreement, can intercept and monitor any telephone call entering or leaving Britain. These are automatically monitored, he claimed, 'because the computers that operate this system are programmed to search every international circuit for particularly sensitive names and numbers'.[21]

Per Ardua Ad Astra*

Rumours of secret Ministry of Defence research into UFOs have occasionally surfaced over the years, but until recently nothing of substance had emerged since 1957, when it was reliably reported that top-secret studies were being conducted by the Air Ministry in Northumberland Avenue, London (where the Defence Intelligence Staff still carry out intelligence evaluation). This was corroborated by Gordon

*'Through hardship to the stars' – the RAF motto.

Creighton, a former intelligence officer who served with the Joint Intelligence Bureau among others, who told me that RAF intelligence officers regularly liaised with their American counterparts as well as the CIA on the UFO problem (Chapter 2).

In 1985 I learned that a Birmingham witness who had telephoned the MoD in Whitehall one night to report a UFO incident was referred to another telephone number. The witness, George Dyer, told me that he had phoned the MoD at about 20.00 hours in the summer of 1984 and was advised to phone another number 'in the West Country' (which he has since forgotten). 'Well, I won't ring tonight; there won't be anybody there,' Mr Dyer told the MoD. 'On the contrary,' came the response; 'it's manned all the time.'[22]

I contacted the MoD in Whitehall and asked about this number. 'The only twenty-four-hour number is the number here,' I was told, 'although often people will report sightings to RAF stations or the police . . . I'm not aware of any official research centre.'[23] So George Dyer was misinformed. Or was he?

Shortly afterwards I learned from two completely independent sources – one of them a scientist – that top-secret investigations into UFOs were carried out (at least, in the late 1970s) by the RAF at a certain establishment in pastoral Wiltshire. The name of that establishment is RAF Rudloe Manor. Situated exactly 100 miles from London, Rudloe Manor was officially listed as a headquarters of the former RAF Support Command, as well as the headquarters of the Provost and Security Services (UK), located in separate facilities. In addition to its normal policing duties, the Provost and Security Services is the branch of the RAF that is involved in counter-intelligence, such as investigating breaches of security.

Perhaps the most relevant function of Rudloe Manor in the UFO context is the Flying Complaints Flight, formerly based in Whitehall as part of the old S4 unit but now based at the Provost and Security Service headquarters (although the MoD's Secretariat (Air Staff) 2b also deals with low-flying complaints). As ex-MoD official Ralph Noyes has confirmed, S4 handled complaints about low-flying infringements, as well as dealing with reports of UFO sightings by members of the public. I therefore assume that the Flying Complaints Flight at Rudloe Manor is used as a cover for the 'lodger unit' (a unit housed within another unit) wherein secret research into UFOs is (or was) conducted. The distinction between low-flying complaints and UFO reports appears to be academic.

The UFO research centre allegedly comprised no more than thirty personnel, I am told, and was manned permanently. Finding further evidence for Rudloe Manor's secret research has been frustrating, even risky. In April 1985 I was questioned by vigilant MoD police while walking around the perimeter of a Royal Navy facility which adjoined the Manor. Evidently dissatisfied with my less than truthful answers, to say nothing of the spurious identity I showed (I had come prepared), the two policemen arrived several hours later while I was in the middle of a meal at the Rudloe Park Hotel, where I was staying. Afterwards I accompanied the officers for further questioning at HMS Copenacre, one of the Navy's two facilities in the area. Because by this time it was clear that I was in trouble, I felt bound to give the true reasons for my visit during the half-hour interrogation that ensued. It was obvious that the MoD personnel were far from convinced about my quest for evidence of UFO research, however, and reasonably suspected me of being a subversive.

I was brought back to the hotel, and after spiritual consolation at the bar retired to my room. At around midnight there came a knock on the door. This time it was the civil police. Following further questioning and a thorough search of my belongings I was driven to Chippenham police station, where, after a most enjoyable discussion about flying saucers with the bemused officers, I was interrogated by a detective constable who had come from Swindon. Computer checks having established that I had no police record, and having been assured that I had not actually committed an offence of any kind, I was let off with a friendly warning to exercise greater precaution when walking around military bases in future. I volunteered the films from my cameras, and these were developed, printed and returned free of charge to my door by the police some months later, nothing of any sensitivity having been found. By the time I arrived back at the hotel it was 03.30. It was a salutary experience.

Ralph Noyes was totally sceptical when I first told him about Rudloe Manor and its alleged clandestine research into UFOs. It was the first time such a rumour had surfaced as far as he was concerned: not once while he was head of DS8 in Whitehall had he heard the place mentioned in connection with UFOs. But supposing the lodger unit was only installed in or after 1972, the year Noyes left the MoD? Or had he simply been kept in the dark? After all, my informants had made it clear that very few people were in the know. We decided to try to find out more.

Late one night in May 1985, in my presence, Noyes telephoned Rudloe Manor, giving his name and a few details of his background in the MoD to the duty officer. He then explained that he had a perplexing UFO sighting to report that had occurred earlier that night in Hertfordshire (in fact it had occurred weeks earlier in London), but that before proceeding he needed to be absolutely certain that he was phoning the right place. 'Surely I should be phoning Whitehall?' he asked. 'No, sir,' replied the duty officer, 'you've reached the right place.' When Ralph had finished relating his sighting and put down the phone, his astonishment was palpable. Maybe UFO reports *were* studied at Rudloe Manor, after all, he pronounced.

Lord Hill-Norton was equally baffled. Certainly no one had ever told him anything about secret research into UFOs at Rudloe Manor when he was Chief of the Defence Staff. He questioned Lord Trefgarne, Minister of State for Defence, on the matter, but was informed that the Flying Complaints Flight dealt only with public complaints about low-flying and had nothing whatsoever to do with the study of unidentified aerial events, which Secretariat (Air Staff) 2a alone was responsible for handling at Whitehall. The MoD has consistently denied that any other unit is involved in UFO investigations, although in late 1986 it admitted to me that DI55 (a department of the Defence Intelligence Staff) co-operated with Sec(AS)2. Details of DI55's functions are not available[24] (although it is known that DI55 SIG, for example, deals with signals intelligence).

Ralph Noyes has pointed out to me that *if* there was a secret lodger unit monitoring UFO reports at Rudloe Manor (or any other establishment), the personnel and equipment used would have needed to be virtually indistinguishable from those used at the parent establishment and would have been parented for 'housekeeping' by the larger establishment to assist in burying its costs; operationally controlled by its own local director, who would report to some higher authority; and commanded by this separate authority, which would have been firmly screened from having to give any account of itself either to the parenting establishment or to its command channels. Although there are precedents for making this type of arrangement (the research into radar in the late 1930s being one example), Noyes remains sceptical.

'You can't just smuggle a lodger unit with special tasks on to an existing establishment without clear instructions being issued down the command channels,' he explained to me:

> This means issuing a few documents (though they can be brief, cryptic and highly classified), and it also needs clear understandings among at least a few senior officers (e.g. at least the Chief of Air Staff, the [then] Vice-Chief of Air Staff and the C. in C. Strike Command or Support Command) so that the inevitable administrative problems can be swiftly sorted out with minimum risk of breaching security.[25]

That Rudloe Manor has been involved in UFO investigations to some extent seems borne out by the fact that it functioned as a twenty-four-hour receiving station for reports from members of the public, although this is denied by the MoD. As Nick Pope of Sec(AS)2a (1991–4) has emphasized to me, *all* RAF stations will accept UFO reports from members of the public: he has no knowledge of a specific UFO investigations unit either at Rudloe Manor or anywhere else. That Rudloe Manor is (or was) the main receiving-point is partly proven to my satisfaction by the fact that Ralph Noyes was advised by the duty officer there to address a letter giving further details of his sighting to the Flying Complaints Flight, RAF Rudloe Manor, rather than to Whitehall. The most Lord Hill-Norton has been able to uncover so far about the matter is that reports received by Whitehall are 'referred elsewhere'. They certainly are.

I believe that reports of particular interest are forwarded to the US Defense Intelligence Agency's London liaison office (DIALL) at the MoD, for example, since US defence attachés worldwide are mandated to collect such reports. The DIA also forwards some of its UFO reports to the MoD's Defence Intelligence Staff, as is evident from the distribution list on a 1992 unclassified DIA document. I am equally sure that a similar reciprocal arrangement exists between the US National Security Agency and the GCHQ.

Researcher Nicholas Redfern has learned that, in addition to the Defence Intelligence Staff's DI55 office, reports received by Sec(AS)2a are routinely forwarded to the Airborne Early Warning (AEW) squadron at RAF Waddington in Lincolnshire (where currently seven Boeing Sentry AEW1 aircraft and three Nimrod R1P reconnaissance aircraft are based) and the Ground Environment division at RAF Bentley Priory, Middlesex. More significantly, an RAF source has informed Redfern that military reports of UFO sightings are channelled first to the squadron commander, then to the station commander, and finally to the Provost and Security Services at Rudloe Manor. Redfern also has obtained an officially released report relating to a UFO sighting witnessed by a civilian in 1962 which was investigated by the Provost and Security Services Special Investigation Section.[26]

As mentioned in Chapter 4, the *Manual of Air Traffic Services* gives precise instructions to air traffic controllers in the United Kingdom for the reporting of UFOs and states that the details are to be telephoned immediately to the Aeronautical Information Service (AIS), London Air Traffic Control Centre. The completed form is then sent by the originating air traffic service unit to the MoD at Whitehall. The AIS unit, originally based at RAF West Drayton, receives the input of all military and civil radar, together with all military and civil flight plans (with a few exceptions), so that a continuous and complete picture of all activity in British airspace is maintained. It is also to the AIS that the civil police are (or were) requested to send reports of UFOs. The editor of the 1991 *Manual of Air Traffic Services* has informed me that the list of telephone numbers contained in the appendix does not include that of Rudloe Manor.[27] And, as far as Nick Pope is aware, Sec(AS)2a is the central repository for such reports (though few military ones, in my opinion).

Interestingly, researcher Chris Fowler was informed by Kerry Philpott of Sec(AS)2a in December 1995 that: 'In the past, Rudloe Manor was indeed the RAF coordination point for reports of "unexplained" aerial sightings . . . once received, they were simply forwarded to Sec(AS)2 for appropriate action.' I wrote to Miss Philpott asking for more details. 'I have spoken to staff at RAF Rudloe Manor,' she replied, 'and although they cannot be precise about the date when Rudloe Manor ceased to be the RAF coordination point for reports of "unexplained" aerial sightings, from corporate memory they believe it was in the early part of 1992.'[28]

In *Alien Liaison* I give further details of the research reportedly carried out at Rudloe Manor and in London, including the experience of a former senior non-commissioned officer who served as an investigator with the Provost and Security Services. He confirmed that, before Rudloe Manor, the Flying Complaints Flight was headquartered at Government Buildings, Acton, London, and that while in charge of personnel security there (1963–5) he became aware of a small but highly secret branch of the Flying Complaints Flight (sometimes referred to as the low-flying section). 'I had access to every top-secret file there was, except low flying,' he revealed, 'because they dealt with UFOs. We could get in anywhere, but not in that department. I remember they used to have an Air Ministry guard in the passage; you couldn't get past them. We could see the Provost Marshal's top-secret files, yet I couldn't get into the place dealing with UFOs.'[29]

Ministry of Defence Co-operation

In 1991 Nick Pope took over from Owen Hartop as the executive officer manning the 'UFO desk' at Secretariat (Air Staff) 2a. Sec(AS)2, comprising about fifteen personnel, is divided between Sec(AS)2a, which among other tasks handles UFO reports from members of the public (and, ostensibly, those from the military), and, across the corridor, Sec(AS)2b, which deals partly with low-flying complaints. Sec(AS)2a itself comprises only three people, headed by a higher executive officer, with one executive officer and one administrative officer.

Pope explained to me that, to facilitate handling public enquiries, he made a point of studying the subject in depth, unlike most of his predecessors, who apparently showed little interest. And, in a move that was frowned upon by some of his fellow civil servants in the division, he initiated meetings with several leading researchers, such as John Spencer and myself. Although these initiatives had nothing to do with official policy, an era of unprecedented co-operation ensued, which in turn helped solve many cases which at first had seemed puzzling. In one such case, involving an 'illuminated spaceship' reported around the London area in November 1993, Pope and I shared the task of contacting various civilian authorities to try to identify the object. The 'spaceship' turned out to be an illuminated airship, flown by Virgin Lightships.

Alas, Nick Pope's successor at Sec(AS)2a, who took over the desk in 1994, is less than enthusiastic about the subject, so for the time being the era of co-operation has come to an end. A true pioneer, Pope has written a book about his experiences as 'UFO desk officer' at the MoD. With the title of *Open Skies, Closed Minds*, this ground-breaking book takes an in-depth look at the official attitude, and highlights some intriguing UFO cases which convinced Pope that a serious problem exists. Furthermore, he has no doubts that we are confronted by an alien intelligence.[30]

'One mention of the phrase "UFO" and people switch off,' Pope remarked to me in 1995:

> But I've studied the phenomenon for three years and I'm convinced that it's real. It doesn't require any leap of faith; all it requires is that we look at what we already have. The evidence is here now.
>
> The role of the UK Government in UFO research is to evaluate whether there is or is not a threat to the defence of the UK. If, as the evidence suggests, structured craft of unknown origin routinely penetrate the UK Air Defence Region, then it seems to me that, at the very least, this must constitute a potential threat. How can we say there's no threat when we do not know what these objects are, where they come from, or what they want?[31]

British Airways Jet in Near Miss

Returning from Milan on 6 January 1995, two BA pilots, Captain Roger Wills and First Officer Mark Stuart, flying a Boeing 737 with sixty passengers on board, reported a near miss with an unknown structured craft on their approach to Manchester's Ringway Airport at 18.48. Excerpts from the official summary of the incident follow:

> The B737 pilot reports that he was over the Pennines about 8 or 9 NM SE of Manchester Airport at 4000 ft, while being radar vectored by Manchester radar . . . Although it was dark, visibility was just over 10 km . . . While flying just above the tops of some ragged [cloud] both he and the first officer saw a lighted object fly down the RH [right hand] side of the ac [aircraft] at high speed from the opposite direction. He was able to track the object through the RH windscreen and side window, having it in sight for a total of about 2 seconds. There was no apparent sound or wake. The first officer instinctively 'ducked' as it went by.
>
> The first officer . . . looked up in time to see a dark object pass down the right hand side of the ac at high speed; it was wedge-shaped with what could have been a black stripe down the side . . . It made no attempt to deviate from its course . . . He felt certain that what he saw was a solid object – not a bird, balloon or kite . . . There was no known traffic in the vicinity at the time and no radar contacts were seen . . .

In its report, the civil Aviation Authority's Joint Airmiss Working Group (JAWG) concluded that: 'Despite exhaustive investigations the reported object remains untraced . . . The Group were anxious to emphasise that this report, submitted by two responsible airline pilots, was considered seriously and they wished to commend the pilots for their courage in submitting it . . . Such reports as these are often the object of derision, but the Group hopes that this example will encourage pilots who experience unusual sightings to report them without fear of ridicule . . .'[32]

It is largely thanks to former British Airways Captain Graham Sheppard, I feel, that the Joint Airmiss Working Group has now encouraged pilots to come forward with such reports 'without fear of ridicule'. In briefing-notes on the safety implications of UFO close approaches prepared for the JAWG in February 1995, Sheppard (whose encounters with unknown flying objects are described in Chapter 3) commented:

> It is to Captain Wills' credit that he has decided to report his UFO encounter of January 6th. He is the latest of a long list of pilots who have experienced the unmentionable. Fortunately he did not take the evasive action which may well have resulted in disaster. It would not be surprising to discover that, in the past, unexplained aeroplane losses have been caused by instinctive manoeuvring to avoid a conflicting UFO. Mature and informed discussion of the above is long overdue. I feel that the commercial sensibilities of the airlines should now be set aside along with the media's inability to give serious treatment to the subject. Otherwise this discrete and notifiable hazard to aircraft safety will continue to be concealed and thus gratuitously omitted from the briefing syllabus.[33]

UK Policy Influenced by the US

In the 1970s Dr Robert Creegan, Professor of Philosophy at the State University of New York, made a number of research trips to Britain and on an informal basis discussed the question of an official cover-up with various involved parties. 'I did get the impression', he told me, 'that "pressure" applied by officials in the United States was a cause (or one of the causes) for a British policy of giving so little information vis-à-vis the UFO problem.'[34]

Dr Creegan was more forthcoming in an article for an American periodical:

> It was made evident to me that the British at that time desired to please the US establishment. And it was strongly hinted that US officials seemed rather excitable about UFO problems and were making frantic efforts to suppress public interest . . . that a panicky US attitude was the reason for British silence . . . the Ministry had to appease the American military-industrial complex and so could not assist one in a search for truth.
>
> UFOs alarm the establishment because, whatever theory is correct, a major loss of control is apprehended, associated with reports of objects which affect mechanisms of control and which deeply puzzle and confuse both the public and many of its would-be leaders . . .[35]

Part Two

Around the World

France

I must say that if your listeners could see for themselves the mass of reports coming in from the airborne gendarmerie, from the mobile gendarmerie, and from the gendarmerie charged with the job of conducting investigations, all of which reports are being forwarded by us to the National Centre for Space Studies, then they would see that it is all pretty disturbing.

THUS SPOKE FRANCE's Minister of Defence, Monsieur Robert Galley, in an interview with Jean-Claude Bourret, broadcast on France-Inter on 21 February 1974, following a wave of sightings in the latter part of 1973 and early 1974.

France, with its independent defence policy, has pursued an equally independent policy on *objets volants non identifiés* (OVNI) – or *soucoupes volantes* (flying saucers) – since the early 1950s. In July 1952 a government research committee was set up, replaced by a General Staff Committee in 1954. M. Catroux, Secretary of State for Air, was asked by parliamentary member Jean Nocher to set up a commission 'to study this phenomenon objectively by extracting the truth from among the mistakes and possible hoaxes'.[1]

In his 1974 broadcast, Robert Galley stated that a department had been established in 1954 in the Ministère des Armées (Ministry of Defence) for the purpose of collecting and studying the many reports that were flooding in during the great global wave of sightings that year. That department was based at the headquarters of the French Air Force's Department for Research. Galley confirmed that there were 'sighting reports from pilots, from the commanding personnel of various Air Force centres, with quite a lot of details, all of which agree in quite a disturbing manner – all in the course of the year 1954'.[2]

A curious sequel to the French Minister's interview was that tapes of interviews with eminent ufologists (including Gordon Creighton) which were to have been broadcast as part of the series were stolen from Jean-

Claude Bourret's office. Had the Minister's positive statements gone too far?

Police and Security Services Alerted by Landing

During the 1954 UFO wave in France (and elsewhere) there were many reports of landed craft complete with occupants, and one of the most impressive cases is that of Marius Dewilde, of which I shall give only brief details, as related by the great pioneer Aimé Michel. On 10 September at about 22.30 hours Dewilde was alerted by the sound of his dog howling and trying to get inside his house outside the village of Quarouble, near Valenciennes. Taking his torch, he went outside.

'Two creatures such as I had never seen before were not more than three or four yards from me,' he reported:

> The one in front turned toward me. The beam of my light caught a reflection from glass or metal where his face should have been. I had the distinct impression that his head was enclosed in a diver's helmet. In fact, both creatures were dressed in one-piece outfits like the suits divers wear. They were very short, probably less than three and a half feet tall, but very wide in the shoulders, and the helmets protecting their 'heads' looked enormous. I could see their legs, small in proportion to their height, it seemed to me, but on the other hand I couldn't see any arms. I don't know whether they had any.

Dewilde tried to get hold of the entities, but when he was 6 feet away he was blinded by an extremely powerful light emitting from a sort of square opening in a dark object resting on the nearby railway tracks. 'I closed my eyes and tried to yell, but I couldn't,' he continued. 'It was just as if I had been paralyzed. I tried to move, but my legs wouldn't obey me.' Finally the beam of light went out and Dewilde found himself able to move again and ran toward the railway track. The object was rising from the ground and hovering, and a 'thick dark steam was coming out of the bottom with a low whistling sound'. The craft went up vertically and eventually disappeared.

Awakening his wife and a neighbour, Dewilde then ran to the nearest police station, about a mile away. As Michel reports, the witness was in such a state of agitation that the police took him for a lunatic and dismissed him. He then ran to the police commissioner's office, where his report was taken more seriously.[3]

The investigation which followed involved the airborne gendarmerie, the mobile gendarmerie, and the Direction de la Surveillance du Territoire, or DST – France's equivalent of the British MI5 or the American FBI. Many years later Aimé Michel revealed to Gordon Creighton that the DST had calculated that the indentations made by the object indicated that it must have weighed [at rest] at least 35 tons.[4]

Huge UFO Observed over Paris

At 22.50 on 19 February 1956 air traffic controllers at Orly Airport, Paris, were astonished to see a 'blip' appear on their radar screens that was twice the size of a conventional aircraft. It appeared to cruise around, hover, then accelerate at fantastic speeds, and was tracked for a total of four hours. Shortly after it first showed up on radar, the unknown object was directly over Gometz-le-Châtel (Seine et Oise), then thirty seconds later it was 30 kilometres away, having moved at a speed of 3,600 k.p.h. (nearly 2,500 m.p.h.).

A second but smaller blip then appeared, identified as an Air France DC-3 Dakota flying over the military base at Les Mureaux at 4,500 feet – 800 feet lower than the UFO. Orly radioed the pilot immediately and advised him that unidentified traffic was on his approximate path. Radio Officer Beaupertuis caught sight of the object through a window. It was on the starboard side – enormous in size, rather indistinct in outline, and lit in some areas with a red glow. Reporting to the French Ministry of Civil Aviation later, Captain Desavoi confirmed the sighting and provided further details:

> For a full thirty seconds we watched the object without being able to decide exactly on its size or precise shape. In flight it is virtually impossible to estimate distances and dimensions. But of one thing we are certain. It was no civil airliner. For it carried none of the navigation lights regulations stipulate are a must. I was then warned by Orly that the object had moved to my port side, so I turned towards it. But they called to say it had left us and was speeding toward Le Bourget. About ten minutes later control called again to say the object was several miles above us. But we couldn't see it, nor did we see it again.[5]

French Air Force Commanding General Confirms UFO Reality

Neither the DST nor the DGSE (Directorate-General of State Security) have released any documents on their UFO research, to the best of my knowledge, but a few statements by concerned military officers have added weight to the growing body of testimony in favour of UFO reality.

General Lionel Max Chassin (1902–70), who rose to the rank of Commanding General of the French Air Forces and served as General Air Defence Co-ordinator, Allied Air Forces, Central Europe (NATO), first became interested in UFOs in 1949, when he began receiving reports from pilots. From 1964 until his death in 1970 he acted as President of the Groupement d'Étude de Phénomènes Aériens (GEPA). In 1958 he wrote an important preface to Aimé Michel's book *Flying Saucers and the Straight-Line Mystery*, which began by referring to the various types of human response to extraordinary phenomena. Of the sceptics, Chassin wrote:

> Obsessed with the notion of his own omniscience, it enrages him to be confronted by phenomena that do not agree with this conviction. Finding in his limited armoury no explanation that satisfies him, he . . . rejects the most obvious facts in order to avoid putting his faith to the test. The mistaken pride and anthropocentrism that supposedly went out with Copernicus and Galileo make him a peril to science, as history abundantly proves . . .
>
> That strange things have been seen is now beyond question, and the 'psychological' explanations seem to have misfired. The number of thoughtful, intelligent, educated people in full possession of their faculties who have 'seen something' and described it grows every day. Doubting Thomases among astronomers, engineers, and officials who used to laugh at 'saucers' have seen and repented. To reject out of hand testimony such as theirs becomes more and more presumptuous . . .
>
> If we persist in refusing to recognize the existence of these unidentified objects, we will end up, one fine day, by mistaking them for the guided missiles of an enemy; and the worst will be upon us.[6]

That the world's defence forces have taken measures to deal with this contingency since 1958 (and earlier, in some countries), when Chassin wrote these words, I am certain.

Secret Service Officer Confirms Worldwide Collaboration

In 1965 George Langelaan, novelist, journalist and former officer of the French secret service (known at that time as the SDECE – Service de Documentation Extérieur et de Contre-Espionnage), gave a lecture at Mourenx, Landes, during which the subject of UFOs cropped up. Langelaan declared that the Russian and American secret services had collaborated on the problem, and had arrived at the conclusion that 'The flying saucers exist, their source is extraterrestrial, and the future – relatively quite soon – should permit confirmation of this statement.'[7] No such confirmation has been forthcoming at an official level, though in later chapters I shall cite some evidence suggesting international collaboration dating back to 1955.

The Valensole Case

No résumé of the French scene, however brief, would be complete without mentioning one of the most thoroughly investigated close encounters on record: the famous Valensole case of 1965.

At about 05.45 on 1 July 1965, farmer Maurice Masse was in his lavender field near Valensole, Basses Alpes, when he heard a strange whistling sound. Stepping out from behind a heap of stones, he saw an object shaped like a rugby football with a cupola on top, about the size of a Renault Dauphine car. It was standing on six legs, with a central pivot. Through an open doorway he could see two seats, back to back.

Masse at first thought the object was a helicopter or an experimental craft, but was then surprised to notice what he took to be two eight-year-old boys stealing his lavender plants, some of which had been missing. The 'boys' were less than 4 feet tall, clad in fairly dark grey-green one-piece suits. On seeing Masse approaching them they straightened up, and one of them levelled a 'tube' at the farmer, and he was immobilized.

Masse noticed that the two humanoids had large hairless heads, smooth white skin, high fleshy cheeks, large eyes that slanted away, pointed chins, and mouths without lips. They made a strange gurgling ('*gargouillement*') sound from deep within their throats as they communicated with each other. 'They were looking at me, and must have been making fun of me,' Masse said in an unofficial statement to Maître Chautard, a local magistrate. 'Nevertheless their facial expressions were not ill-natured, but very much the reverse.' Masse said that in fact he felt a great sense of peace exuding from the beings.

Shortly afterwards the humanoids returned to their craft via a sliding 'door'. The legs whirled and retracted, and the machine took off. It was a quarter of an hour before Masse recovered his mobility. The ground where the craft had rested was soaked with moisture, although it had not been raining, and investigators found strange, geometrically spaced indentations. More remarkable was the fact that no lavender plants would grow at the landing-site until ten years later.

Four days after the incident Masse suddenly collapsed, seized with an irresistible urge to sleep, and would have done so for twenty-four hours had not his wife and father woken him up. Rather than his usual five to six hours' sleep, Masse found he needed at least ten or twelve, for a period of several months.

All those who investigated the case, including the gendarmerie headed by Lieutenant-Colonel Valnet, Maître Chautard, and the mayor and parish priest of Valensole, concluded unanimously that Maurice Masse was telling the truth.[8,9,10]

UFOs and the Gendarmerie Nationale

As Dr Jean Gille points out, the French gendarmerie are part of the French Armed Forces and as such are accountable exclusively to the highly centralized executive powers: the Attorney-General or (in some cases) the President.[11] In an internal journal, not generally available to members of the public, gendarmerie Captain Kervendal and the journalist/researcher Charles Garreau gave a résumé of the UFO phenomenon, including the following significant statement:

> What can we of the Gendarmerie do about this business? By virtue of the Gendarmerie's presence throughout the whole national territory of France, by virtue of its knowledge of places and, above all, of people; by virtue of the integrity and the intellectual honesty that are characteristic of its personnel, and also by virtue of the rapidity with which the Gendarmerie can be on the spot, they are well placed indeed to serve as a valuable auxiliary in the search for truth about the UFOs . . . Something is going on in the skies . . . something that we do not understand. If all the airline pilots and Air Force pilots who have seen UFOs – and sometimes chased them – have been the victims of hallucinations, then an awful lot of pilots should be taken off and forbidden to fly.

In Section II of a questionnaire that indicates which aspects of the phenomenon the gendarmerie should concentrate on, Kervendal and Garreau emphasize that close attention should be paid to the shape of UFOs, effects felt by the witnesses, such as tingling sensations, and the behaviour of animals in the vicinity. In those cases where an animal has died in unusual circumstances following a sighting, an autopsy and blood analysis should be made, as well as tests for traces of radiation.

Landing cases are thoroughly dealt with in Section III: traces left by the craft are to be closely examined, and samples of soil, vegetation and roots should be submitted to the nearest agricultural research centre. The level of radioactivity is to be measured and recorded at the landing-site and compared with readings 100 metres away. Great importance is attached to aerial photography of the site by helicopter, using infra-red film.[12]

GEPAN

In 1977 the Groupe d'Études Phénomènes Aerospatiaux Non Identifiés (GEPAN) was established under the auspices of the Centre National d'Études Spatiales (CNES) – France's equivalent of the American space agency NASA. GEPAN had a committee of seven scientists, headed by Dr Claude Poher, director of the Sounding Rockets Division of the CNES. The group was to collaborate with the gendarmerie, and was given access to laboratories and scientific centres all over France, as well as other agencies around the world. President Giscard d'Estaing took a close personal interest in the project.

It all looked very promising at first. For example, in an analysis of eleven cases studied in 1978, GEPAN concluded that in as many as nine cases a physical phenomenon existed whose origin, propulsion and *modus operandi* were beyond human knowledge.[13] But later that year Dr Gille, *Chargé de Recherche* at the National Centre for Scientific Research (CNRS), attended a GEPAN meeting for private investigation groups at the CNES headquarters in Toulouse. He was told during the seven-hour meeting that the scientific attachés at GEPAN could devote only 10 per cent of their time to those cases that were given to them by the gendarmerie. More significantly, Dr Gille discovered that those cases that GEPAN did receive had been screened by the highest authority in the Gendarmerie Nationale.

'Those with the very highest "strangeness/probability" index', he learned, 'do not go to GEPAN at all, but go to certain other bodies which

are, if we might so term it, of a far less "obtrusive" nature than GEPAN.'
In short, Dr Gille believed that GEPAN was no more than a Government-
monitored public-relations agency. The real, fundamental, research on
UFOs was done elsewhere.

Dr Gille is convinced that the meeting presaged the demise of GEPAN
as an effective group. Commented Gordon Creighton: 'It seems that
France's Socio-Communists have indeed just attempted to kill off GEPAN,
since, being sensible chaps, they all know that UFOs don't exist anyway,
and they are indeed convinced that the whole idea of the Centre was
simply a silly private fad of Giscard d'Estaing's.'[14] GEPAN has on several
occasions appeared to be on the brink of collapse: at the meeting attended
by Dr Gille, for instance, Dr Poher announced his resignation and took off
on a long cruise around the world. However, his place was taken by Alain
Esterle, and investigations continued into those cases passed on to GEPAN
by the military.

The Masters of Silence

Fernand Lagarde, one of France's most effective researchers, also expressed
serious misgivings about the state of official research, believing that the
'Open-door policy' seemingly initiated with the establishment of GEPAN
had come to an end. Lagarde found that his requests for information and
documents from official sources were blocked at every stage, just as
elsewhere in the world. 'We have now to face the fact that a lid . . . marked
secret, has come down on all official research,' he wrote in 1981. 'Sighting
reports likely to be of interest to us no longer find their way to us.' The
'Masters of Silence', as he called them, had taken over once more.[15]

Another distinguished French researcher who shares this view is the
astrophysicist Dr Pierre Guérin of the French Institute of Astrophysics and
a senior research officer in the CNRS. In 1984 I met Dr Guérin in Paris,
and over lunch we discussed the cover-up. The demise – or apparent
demise – of GEPAN was first on the agenda. 'It's now limited to only *two*
people,' said Dr Guérin, 'Monsieur Velasco, the head – he's not even a
scientist, he's an engineer – and his secretary. That is all!' GEPAN, he
confirmed, was under the aegis of the CNES, which itself was under the
direction of a scientific committee which was not well-disposed towards
the subject.

One of the main problems, Dr Guérin explained to me, is that the
majority of scientists reject UFOs because they simply do not fit into a
current scientific framework:

In science there is no proof of any phenomenon if no scientific model for it exists. The *observation* of the facts is not the actual fact! We have the testimonial proof, but not the scientific proof. Scientists are not only embarrassed by UFOs: they're furious because they don't understand them. There is no possibility of explaining them in three-dimensional space-time physics.

'What about the more reliable reports of actual recovered UFOs?' I asked, knowing that Dr Guérin had published some positive statements on this controversial aspect of the phenomenon. 'Even if there are crashes,' he replied carefully, 'scientists wouldn't understand the propulsion system. The idea that a scientific secret exists is false, I'm certain. I don't believe that a small group has material *proof*, but they do have evidence. If they had proof, other countries would have learned about it. I am completely convinced that nobody has the fundamental explanation.'

I then asked him what hypothesis for the origin of UFOs best explained the facts. He replied that the extraterrestrial hypothesis, though not proven, is the most economic explanation, considering that the evolution of life in the universe can lead to other advanced forms of life.

As Dr Guérin tucked into his steak, I raised the question of the horrific animal mutilations that have proliferated in the United States and elsewhere (including France) since 1967. In these disturbing incidents – and there have been thousands – carcasses of animals, usually cattle, have been found in remote areas with vital organs missing: eyes, tongues, udders, sexual organs and rectal area removed with surgical precision. In many cases blood is completely drained from the animal, with no traces on the surrounding ground. While satanic cults and natural predators might have been responsible for some of these mutilations, there have been numerous occasions when mysterious helicopters, lights and UFOs have been observed at the scene, whose source has never been identified see my book *Alien Liaison*). 'The testimonial facts are always doubtful,' Dr Guérin answered, 'but the material facts, independent of the witnesses – in the case of the mutilations – are of a superior degree than testimonial evidence.'[16]

Dr Guérin was somewhat guarded in his answers to my questions. Scientists are mindful of their reputations, especially when the subject of UFOs crops up, and I am sure he was bothered about being misquoted. But in published articles he has been more forthcoming – courageously so.

'Unless you are in the know,' he wrote in 1982, 'and are privy at the very highest level to the secrets of the military intelligence services or to

the secrets of the heads of State to whom those miltary intelligences report
. . . nobody is capable of knowing for certain whether, yes or no, there do
exist material, concrete (and therefore irrefutable) proofs of UFOs *as
such*.' Dr Guérin went on to admit that the stories of recovered UFOs
'have the ring of truth about them . . . But the material proofs alleged to
exist remain concealed by the authorities, who are the sole possessors of
them.'

As to material proof for UFOs, Dr Guérin is certain that the
mutilation cases provide such proof. Dismissing official explanations and
pointing out the worldwide nature of the incidents, Dr Guérin notes that
the incisions and excisions of organs on the animals' carcasses prove the
existence of an ultra-sophisticated surgical skill, surpassing present-day
capabilities – a fact confirmed by those private veterinarians who have
examined the carcasses. He concludes:

> Rather than invoking I know not what imaginary and gratuitous
> 'paranormal' manifestation to explain these facts (as certainly all
> too many ufologists of the 'New Wave' will want to do . . .), I
> prefer, for my part, to apply *Occam's Law* in the interpretation of
> what we observe, and, consequently, to conclude that the animal
> mutilations, associated as they are with the passage overhead of
> flights of silent machines coming from the skies and impossible as
> they are for us to perform in the present state of our surgical
> techniques, cannot be anything else but a manifestation of the
> activities of extraterrestrial visitors.

The astrophysicist, in referring to the official FBI report which
attributes all the mutilations to natural predators (such as coyotes), is
unequivocal in his indictment: 'Here we have . . . an indubitable proof of
the wilful and conscious intention of the American authorities to deceive
public opinion over UFO phenomena,' he states. 'The US Government
agents who are talking about coyote bites to account for the animal
mutilations are lying and are lying knowingly, in obedience obviously to
orders received from above.'

In discussing the reasons for the cover-up, Dr Guérin offers the
following hypothesis:

> To the extent that the discovery of the presence of a hypersoph-
> isticated non-human technological activity within our Terrestrial
> Space could not possibly be regarded with indifference by those

who have the task of governing the world, these latter will attempt to exploit, each party for themselves, any data that is in their possession, while at the same time publicly denying that they have such data, [and] publicly suffocating all ufological research in a haze of 'psychological' interpretations! That is not to say that the 'Invaders' may not be engaged in a pretty bit of suffocation of the subject themselves . . .[17]

A Landing Case yields impressive Scientific Evidence

Despite rumours of GEPAN's demise the organization continued, albeit on a limited scale. In 1983 the Minister of Defence, Charles Hernu, decided that GEPAN's research should continue, under the direction of two engineers of the CNES. Some of the results have been highly significant, as Dr Guérin concedes.

A sixty-six-page internal memorandum submitted by GEPAN to the CNES in March 1983 deals with a UFO landing case that occurred near the village of Trans-en-Provence, Var, on 8 January 1981. Physical traces were collected by the gendarmerie within twenty-four hours and were later analysed in several Government laboratories. The incident must surely rank as one of the most convincing physical trace cases ever studied.

The witness was Renato Nicolai, a fifty-five-year-old farmer, on whose property the object had landed briefly. Believing the object to be an experimental military device, Nicolai notified the gendarmerie. His testimony follows:

My attention was drawn to a small noise, a kind of whistling. I turned around and I saw, in the air, a ship which was at just about the height of a pine tree at the edge of my property . . . descending towards the ground . . . I saw no flames, neither underneath nor around the ship.

While the ship was continuing to descend, I went closer to it, heading towards a little cabin . . . From there I saw the ship standing on the ground. At that moment, the ship began to emit another whistling, a constant, consistent whistling. Then it took off and once it was at the height of the trees, it took off rapidly . . . As the ship began to lift off, I saw beneath it four openings from which neither smoke nor flames were emitting. The ship picked up a little dust when it left the ground.

I was at that time about 30 metres from the landing site. I

thereafter walked towards the spot and I noticed a circle about 2 metres in diameter. At certain spots on the curve of the circle, there were two traces.

The ship was in the form of two saucers upside down, one against the other. It must have been about 1.5 metres high. It was the colour of lead. The ship had a border or type of brace around its circumference. Underneath the brace, as it took off, I saw two kinds of round pieces which could have been landing-gear or feet. There were also two circles which looked like trap-doors. The two feet, or landing-gear, extended about 20 centimetres beneath the body of the whole ship.[18]

Soil samples and wild alfalfa, as well as control samples, were collected at the landing site and were subjected to analyses by various laboratories. These tests included physico-chemical analysis, electron diffraction, mass spectrometry by ion bombardment, and biochemical analysis of the vegetable samples.[19] Some of the results of these analyses revealed the following: that there had been a strong mechanical pressure forced on the surface, probably the result of a heavy weight; a thermatic heating of the soil, not exceeding 600°C, and chlorophyll pigment in the leaf samples was weakened from 30 to 50 per cent.

The GEPAN report stated that attempts to duplicate these changes were unsuccessful, and added:

The action of nuclear irradiation does not seem to be analogous with the energy source implied in the observed phenomenon; on the other hand, a specific intensification of the transformation of chlorophylls . . . could be tied to the action of a type of electric energy field. On the biochemical level, the analysis was made on the entirety of the factors of photosynthesis, lipids, sugars and amino acids. There were many differences between those samples from the spot of the landing and those that were closer to the spot.

It was possible to qualitatively show the occurrence of an important event which brought with it deformations of the terrain caused by mass, mechanics, a heating effect, and perhaps certain transformations and deposits of mineral traces . . .[20]

Among the most puzzling results of the analysis was the state of the alfalfa leaves at the landing-site. As Michel Bounias of the National Institute of Agronomy Research (INRA), who made the discovery, explained: 'From an anatomical and physiological point, they had all the characteristics of their age, but they presented the biochemical character- istics of leaves of an advanced age – old leaves! And that doesn't resemble anything that we know on our planet.'[21]

Concluded Jean-Jacques Velasco of GEPAN: 'The laboratory conclu- sion that seems to best cover the effects observed and analysed is that of a powerful emission of electromagnetic fields, pulsed or not, in the microwave frequency range.'[22] Alain Esterle of GEPAN was equally impressed. 'We are in the presence of traces for which there is no satisfactory explanation and we can find no reason to suspect that the witness is deliberately lying,' he concluded. 'For the first time, we found a combination of factors which leads us to accept that something similar to what the eyewitness described actually did happen.'[23]

Doubts about GEPAN

In spite of these encouraging developments, doubts have continued to be raised about GEPAN's true function. In 1983 physicist Dr Jean-Pierre Petit of the CNRS was told by the head of GEPAN, Jean-Jacques Velasco: 'We are collecting UFO reports, but we don't know what to do with them. Once a case has been investigated, we publish a note on it, and that is that. We have no scientific structure behind GEPAN.'

Dr Petit went on to say that during a meeting in Paris, organized by France-Inter on 12 June 1984, with GEPAN representatives as well as fifty- five journalists present, the CNES public relations officer Monsieur Metzle made a curious admission. 'In 1977,' he is reported to have said, 'it was necessary to tranquillize public opinion concerning the UFO phenom- enon. And it was in that spirit that GEPAN was created.'[24]

In 1985, Jean-Jacques Velasco announced that GEPAN had collabo- rated closely with the gendarmerie to log about 1,600 UFO reports (up to 1985). While the majority have been explained as natural phenomena or aircraft, Velasco emphasized that as many as 38 per cent did not fall into this category – a high percentage of unknowns by any standards.[25]

SEPRA

In 1988 GEPAN was renamed SEPRA (Service d'Expertise des Phénom- ènes de Rentrées Atmosphériques – Service for the Evaluation of Atmospheric Re-Entry Phenomena), the UFO section of which is still run by Jean-Jacques Velasco. SEPRA has yet to publish any research

reports, however, and researchers retain misgivings about the organization. 'Velasco sits on a fence between officialdom, which ties his hands,
and his own profound belief in extraterrestrials,' says Perry Petrakis of the
French UFO group SOS OVNI.[26] 'Although Velasco never refuses
appearances in the media, he carefully avoids annoying questions by
keeping a low profile in French ufology.'[27]

In January 1991 the European Parliament's Committee on Energy,
Research and Technology put forward a proposal to set up a European
UFO evaluation centre within SEPRA, the details of which are discussed in
the next chapter.

Further Official and Unofficial Reactions

What is France's official position on unexplained sightings, and is there
any evidence that some UFOs are extraterrestrial in origin? Answers to
these questions were given to me in 1986 by the Air Attaché at the French
Embassy in London. 'Despite the [fact that] UFO flights are still forbidden
over France,' he explained facetiously, 'the trespassers are generally
reported to the Gendarmerie. As mentioned by Mr Galley, our previous
Minister of Defence, all enquiries are then centralized in a department of
the Centre National d'Études Spatiales for study.'[28]

What about the unexplained sightings? I insisted. Does the Air Force
believe, like the air forces of some smaller countries such as Zimbabwe,
that these relate to extraterrestrial civilizations? The attaché was
unimpressed. 'So far,' he told me, 'the French Air Force is not concerned
by this problem and no Air Staff generals are named for quotations about
it. Perhaps the French sky is more cloudy than Zimbabwe's.'[29]

Evidently the attaché was unaware that, according to a French military
source I spoke with, Air Force pilots are subject to strict rules for the
reporting of UFO sightings, and can lose their jobs if they discuss them
publicly. The attaché seemed equally unaware that General Chassin,
former Commanding General of the French Air Force, had made a
number of positive statements on the subject back in the 1950s, and had
written the following in 1961:

> . . . We must become dedicated, then, in our zeal that the
> conspiracy of silence may not suppress news of phenomena of the
> highest importance, with consequences which may be incalculable
> for the whole human race . . . Undoubtedly the day will come,
> whatever we do, when the truth will break in upon us. But we risk

being taken by surprise . . . We should begin a great crusade of common sense in order to avoid what could be very dangerous. We invite all earthmen to join in who will not allow themselves to be blinded by orthodoxy and who desire above everything to see the truth triumphant.[30]

Italy

UFO Fleets over Rome

CRITICS WHO WONDER why UFOs never appear over large cities in full view of thousands of witnesses would do well to consider the events that took place over Rome in November 1954, following a wave of sightings in Italy and in many other countries.

Diplomat Dr Alberto Perego was among a crowd of about 100 people near the church of Santa Maria Maggiore on 30 October who stood and gazed upwards in astonishment as two 'white dots' moved around the sky in complete silence at a height of about 2,000 metres. Was this some new kind of aircraft, Dr Perego wondered?

On 6 November Dr Perego was in the Tuscolano district when the 'white dots' appeared again, but this time there were dozens of them. He noted at the time that:

> Today, between 11.00 a.m. and 1.00 p.m., the sky of Rome has been crossed by several dozens of flying machines travelling at a height of around 7,000 or 8,000 metres. They were moving at variable speeds, which at times seemed to be as high as 1,200 or 1,400 km per hour. The machines appeared like 'white dots', sometimes with a short white trail.
>
> At first I calculated that there were about fifty of them, but later I realized that there were at least one hundred. Sometimes they were isolated, sometimes in pairs, or in threes or fours or sevens or twelves. Frequently they were in diamond or 'lozenge' formations of four, or in 'V' formations of seven.

At noon, Perego reported, a large formation of twenty objects appeared from the east, followed by another twenty coming from the opposite direction. 'The two "V"-shaped squadrons converged rapidly until the vertices of the two "V"s met, thus forming a perfect "St Andrew's Cross" of forty machines, with ten to each bar.' The convergence seemed to occur at a height of about 7,000 or 8,000 metres over the Trastevere–

Monte Mario district of Rome – right over the Vatican City. The entire 'cross' then performed a three-quarter turn on its axis, becoming more of an 'X' shape, then broke off into two separate curves which moved off in opposite directions. The performance had lasted about three minutes, Dr Perego noted. But the show was not over:

> As I watched, I saw what appeared like a large bluish shadow forming in the sky ten minutes later and realized that it was a fresh concentration building up as, in formations and squadrons of four and seven and twelve, they began to reappear. This time I was able to make a better count, and could see that they totalled at least one hundred. This time the concentration was in another part of the sky, and not directly above the Vatican.

Dr Perego then noticed what appeared to be a shining filament-type material coming out of the sky – the substance that subsequently has been nicknamed 'angel hair', reported by witnesses throughout the world.

> I was able to seize a handful of it, [he said]. It looked like the fine twigs and filaments of a Christmas tree, but thinner, and very long. It was not like the filaments used in the last war by the US bombers to disturb the enemy radar [chaff]. It was not tinfoil, but rather a 'glassy' sort of substance, which evaporated completely in a few hours.

The following day, 7 November, not a word appeared in the newspapers. Perego's enquiries at the Ministry of Foreign Affairs drew a blank: they knew nothing about the sightings. At 11.30 hours, returning to the Tuscolano district, Perego was astonished to see further formations of objects, totalling about fifty, which remained in the sky for two and a half hours. 'The squadrons would always arrive from different directions,' he recalled, 'and always in regular formations . . . They would fly away over the country around Rome, and return in formation ten minutes later for the next "concentration".'

Yet again, the strange 'angel hair' descended over Rome, which thousands of people must have witnessed, but there was still no word from the press apart from a report in *Il Messagero* that in England RAF radar had detected squadrons of mysterious objects on 6 November (see pp. 12–13). 'At the British War Office, they are concerned,' concluded the report. Not, it seems, in the Italian War Office.

The next day, Dr Perego called on Air Force General Pezzi, Chief of the Cabinet of the Ministry of Defence. 'He received me very courteously,' said Perego, 'but he said he knew nothing whatever about the events I described. I read my notes to him, and asked him to report the matter to the Minister of Defence.'

On 10 November Dr Perego was received by the Principal Secretary of Foreign Affairs, but drew a blank once more: the official knew nothing about the matter and was surprised that the military authorities had made no report to him. The reason became apparent the following day, when Perego visited General de Vincenti, commander of the Italian Air Force, who explained that, since radar operated over certain fixed zones, at certain times, and only up to 6–7,000 metres, nothing had been tracked.

When the mysterious objects made yet another appearance over Rome, on 12 November, again in the morning, Dr Perego immediately contacted General de Vincenti at Air Defence Headquarters, who said that orders had been issued for observations to be made. Although no official confirmation from military sources was forthcoming, Perego paid a visit to the Vatican Observatory at Castel Gandolfo near Rome and learned that a Brazilian priest on duty at about 11.00 had seen some strange objects pass twice over the Observatory, very low, at terrific speed and in complete silence.

It was two years before Dr Perego came to accept the fact that what he and thousands of others witnessed over Rome could only have been the manifestation of an extraterrestrial intelligence, a revelation that inspired him to become a leading champion of the *dischi volanti* (flying saucers).[1]

Landing at Istrana Air Base?

Istrana Air Base, 30 kilometres north-west of Venice, allegedly was the scene of a UFO landing, complete with occupants, on an evening in mid-November 1973. According to a newspaper account, two sentries on the perimeter of the base saw two 'beings' dressed in white, about 1.5 metres tall. A little further away could be seen an unidentified craft.

After the occupants went into the craft, the sentries immediately reported the incident. *Veneto Notte* claimed that marks were found at the landing-site, and commented: 'The authorities in charge of the Istrana military air base have classified the matter as top secret, and nobody is at present prepared to admit that it occurred.'[2]

The story is lacking in details, but I have included it because so many similar incidents have taken place at military bases throughout the world – incidents invariably shrouded in a cloak of secrecy.

UFO Blacks Out NATO Base at Aviano

The important NATO base at Aviano, north-east Italy, was the scene of a dramatic UFO sighting in the small hours of 1 July 1977. At 03.00, an American soldier, James Blake, noticed a peculiar large bright light hovering at a height of about 100 metres in the 'Victor Alert Zone' where two military aircraft were kept. According to Antonio Chiumiento, who learned of the incident from a number of sources, including an Italian Air Force NCO, the object was seen by many military personnel. About 50 metres in diameter it resembled a spinning top revolving on its own axis, with a dome on top, changing colours from white to green then red. A noise like a swarm of bees in flight could be heard. The object remained over the base for about an hour, causing a major power blackout.

One of the independent witnesses was Benito Manfré, a nightwatchman living at Castello d'Aviano, 1.5 kilometres away. Alerted by the incessant barking of his dog in the middle of the night, he went out on to the veranda and noticed that the NATO base was in total darkness – something that he had never observed before. 'What particularly aroused my attention,' he said, 'was the presence of a "mass" of stationary light low down over a certain spot on the base itself.'

Signor Manfré tried to persuade his wife to come and join him, but she was too tired, so he remained alone, transfixed by the object, which he described as a 'glowing disc'. After five minutes or so the object slowly moved away from the Victor Alert Zone then noiselessly climbed away beyond the mountains near Aviano. 'Ten seconds or so after the mysterious object had left the base,' said the nightwatchman, 'the base's lights came on again. I must add that my dog only stopped barking when the luminous "disc" had left the area . . . about half an hour later I was able to note a certain amount of movement of vehicles of the American military police.'

Although nothing about the episode was made public, it was the subject of intense speculation in Aviano. Predictably, the story was debunked by the military: the official explanation was that 'the phenomenon must be attributed to a reflection of the Moon on some low clouds'. How the Moon could descend to an altitude of 100 metres, appear to have a diameter of 50 metres and cause a major security alert (NATO's Brussels headquarters was informed) as it blacked out the entire base was, of course, left unexplained. As Antonio Chiumiento emphasized, the minimum temperature in the particular area was too high in relation to the percentage of humidity to allow for cloud formation at that altitude, nor was the Moon in the right place.[3]

Ministry of Defence Releases File

In March 1978 the Italian Ministry of Defence released a file containing details of six unclassified UFO reports by military personnel in 1977. One of the cases involved the sighting by two pilots of a 'luminous circle' on 27 October over the military airfield at Cagliari, Sardinia, which had been tracked by other witnesses, including personnel at the control tower at Elmas. A jet sent up to investigate was unable to intercept the object.

The principal witnesses were Major Francesco Zoppi, chief pilot of the *Orsa Maggiore* Squadron of the Italian Army Light Aircraft Corps (ALE) 21st Helicopter Group, together with his co-pilot, Lieutenant Riccardelli. In a statement published before the ministry released the file on the case, the pilots described their experience:

> We had taken off in the helicopters for a normal training flight when, at a distance of about 300 metres, I saw, in front of me, an extremely bright orange-coloured circle . . . we at once contacted the control tower [who] replied that nothing was visible from the ground. Meanwhile, the fiery circle continued to be there, right in front of us, and moving at a speed almost identical to our own. Then I asked the other two helicopters of our squadron whether they could see it. One said they could, and that they were seeing the same thing as we were, while the third helicopter, piloted by Captain Romolo Romani, replied that they saw nothing.
>
> The luminous circle then vanished at a speed impossible for any aircraft of this world to equal. I called the control tower again, and was informed that in the meantime other people had seen it and had been following it with binoculars. But the radar had detected nothing.[4]

On 5 January 1978 the Ministry of Defence explained that what had been seen was nothing other than 'an aircraft operating out of Sardinia in the course of an ordinary flight mission' which the pilots failed to recognize 'owing to particular weather conditions during twilight'.

Another case released by the Ministry, which had not received any publicity beforehand, also occurred in the vicinity of the Elmas air base. On 2 November 1977 Italian Air Force pilots and the pilots of two German

Air Force F-104G Starfighters, as well as personnel at the Elmas control tower, observed a similar circular or elliptical 'ball of fire' flying at tremendous speed. These reports were included in the file released to the Italian National UFO Research Centre and another group. Inadvertently a copy was sent to a group consisting of two teenagers, who handed it over to the press, creating considerable embarrassment for the Ministry, which was obliged, once again, to discredit the Elmas sightings.[5]

Close Encounter near Mount Etna

Close encounter cases involving reports of UFO occupants seen by a group of people rather than by a single witness are comparatively rare and, although that does not automatically rule out hoax or mass delusion, such cases obviously connote greater credibility.

At about 22.30 on the night of 4 July 1978, two Italian Air Force sergeants, Franco Padellero and Attilio di Salvatore, together with Maurizio Esposito, an Italian Navy officer, and Signora Antonina di Pietro, were off duty near Mount Etna, Sicily, when they noticed a triangle of three bright red lights in the sky which seemed to be pulsating. Suddenly one of the lights detached itself, headed towards the group, then disappeared down a slope about 1,000 feet away.

The group decided to investigate and drove in di Salvatore's car to where the light seemed to have landed. As they rounded a bend, they noticed a dazzling light coming from a dip at the side of the road. Stopping the car, they went and looked over the edge. Resting near a rocky precipice on the slope below was a saucer-shaped object about 40 feet across, with a brilliant yellow (illuminated) dome. The rest of the object was of a reddish hue with blue and red lights on top. By the side of the craft were five or six very tall beings, according to the report, with black overall-type tight-fitting suits and blond hair. Their features were described as human and 'beautiful'.

Two of the beings began climbing up the slope towards the witnesses, who by now found themselves immobilized by an unknown force. The beings smiled as they came to within about 15 feet of the group, then one of them nodded towards the saucer and they both climbed back down the slope. The saucer now began to glow with multicoloured tiny points of light – yellow, red and blue predominating. When a car went by, all the lights went out, brightening again when the car had passed. The witnesses recovered their mobility shortly afterwards then drove away without waiting to see the object depart. All four felt drained of energy for some time after the incident.[6]

Such stories do not provide proof of extraterrestrial visitors, yet there are intriguing aspects of the case that have been corroborated elsewhere. Also, such witnesses have little to gain by hoaxing – particularly if they are themselves military people.

Italian Air Force Pilot's Encounter

On 18 June 1979 at around 11.30, Italian Air Force senior warrant officer Giancarlo Cecconi of the 14th Jet Fighter Group (Wing No. 2) was returning to base in a Fiat G-91R following a photo-reconnaissance flight over the Apennine mountains in northern Italy when he received a radio message from San Angelo di Treviso military airbase to contact the radar crew at Istrana airfield, because it had detected an unidentified target moving at low altitude.

The Istrana base gave Cecconi details of the UFO, which was manoeuvring in a strange manner and appearing intermittently on the radarscope above Quinto in Treviso province. As the pilot headed for the area, he observed a large black spot standing out clearly against the blue sky. On closer approach, it looked like a long, opaque, black object shaped like an aircraft's extra fuel tank. Passing by it at a distance of about 80 metres he took his first sequence of film. (The G-91R is equipped with three, special, high-speed cameras.) In all, Cecconi took about eighty frames of the object, which seemed to be about 8 metres long and 3 metres wide. A small white transparent dome was visible on the upper part.

Meanwhile, staff on duty at San Angelo di Treviso airbase continued to observe and follow the object with binoculars, while maintaining radio contact with Cecconi. They informed the pilot that the object appeared to be leaving an azure-bluish trail. As Cecconi made one more turn to approach the object, it disappeared instantly: this was confirmed by both the ground observers and radar.

The film prints yielded a sequence of sharp images of the object, one of which was later shown to researcher Antonio Chiumiento and other investigators from the National UFO Research Centre (CUN) during one of several meetings with Cecconi.

In November 1984, following a request by Chiumiento for official documentation on the case, including photographs, the Ministry of Defence stated in their reply that 'The object in question, which was detected immediately, was photographed with the cameras aboard the aircraft, and was unequivocally identified by photo-interpretation personnel as a cylindrical balloon constructed from black plastic bags.'

This explanation is less than satisfactory, particularly in view of some comments made by the pilot to Antonio Chiumiento. 'It is inconceivable that any flying object of ours could behave in such a way as that thing did,' Cecconi insisted. 'No state on Earth could construct anything like it. On the basis of our knowledge of physics, it would never have been able to be airborne.'

If the Ministry's 'plastic balloon' is to be believed, it is puzzling that the photographs were not released. Although the magazine *Epoca* published three of the alleged photos, provided by the Ministry of Defence in 1985,[7] Chiumiento pointed out that these were remarkably different from the photo shown him by Cecconi. Still more puzzling is the fact that in its summary of UFO sightings from March 1979 to April 1985, put out by the General Staff of the Italian Air Force, the Cecconi case is listed as 'Unidentified'.[8]

Air Force General Staff Statistical Survey

In Italy, sightings of UFOs (*oggetti volanti non identificati* – OVNI) are dealt with officially by the Ministry of Defence; specifically, the Air Force General Staff (2nd Department), which is entrusted by the Defence General Staff with the task of collecting, within the scope of defence, all data concerning such reports, with the collaboration of the Army, Navy and Carabinieri General Staffs. The Air Force General Staff shares its interest in the phenomenon with the Inspectorate of the Board of Telecommunications and Flight Assistance (Telecommunicazione ed Assistenza al Volo) and with all regional operations centres, and periodically sends an updated summary of sightings to the Ministry of Defence.

In its statistical survey of sightings from 1979 to 1990, the Air Force General Staff noted that 111 reports were received, with a peak of thirty-two in 1980. A slight majority of sightings occurred in the central region of Italy, particularly along the coasts of the Adriatic and Tyrrhenian seas (a statistic disputed by Italy's foremost research group, the Centro Italiano Studi Ufologici (CISU).[9] According to the Air Force survey, the most reliable reports include the following:

On the evening of 17 August 1988, several sightings of UFOs were confirmed by the control towers of Venezia, Linate, Malpensa, Torino and Genova airports. On the night of 7 March 1990, a surgeon from Catania (Sicilia) observed a very shiny, oval-shaped object, rotating on its axis, for about an hour above Giarre. On 24 April 1990 at 08.15, during a training flight near Catania, two military pilots (instructor and trainee) noticed a spherical-shaped flying object which climbed rapidly to the altitude of their plane (2,000 metres). All attempts to approach the object proved useless, since it kept its distance with sudden accelerations. After about five minutes, the UFO disappeared in a tremendous burst of speed.[10]

In its appraisal of the Air Force General Staff's survey, CISU comments on the small number of reports officially received and filed, which they say is below a twentieth of the reports collected by their own organization. 'The official statistical data given by the Ministry, therefore, must be accepted for what they are: a summary report of information collected over eleven years, without any pretence of analysis or evaluation.'[11]

Italian Airliner Encounters Unknown Missile over Britain

Although the following case *may* relate to a conventional guided missile, it is included here because the origin of the missile was never determined, and the sighting officially is listed as of an unidentified flying object.

At 21.00 hours on 21 April 1991, Captain Achille Zaghetti, piloting an Alitalia MD80 jet airliner with fifty-seven passengers, *en route* from Milan to London, descending into Heathrow over Lydd, Kent, was alarmed to see what appeared to be a guided missile, less than 1,000 feet above the aircraft. 'I was crossing 22,100 feet, and we were heading 321 [degrees] when I saw something coming, heading 110–120 . . . It was coming from the left to right,' he reported later to investigator Clas Svahn. 'I used the word "missile" because of the shape, not because I saw a missile. It was *like* a missile . . . about 10 feet long, light brown colour, and I said to my co-pilot, "Look out! Look out!" . . . and he saw what I saw.'[12]

Captain Zaghetti immediately reported the near miss to London Air Traffic Control Centre, which confirmed a faint radar trace 10 nautical miles behind the Alitalia airliner, but reported that no other aircraft were in the vicinity. Although the sighting had occurred almost directly over the Lydd Ranges, a Ministry of Defence firing-range, the MoD denied there were any military operations in the area at the time. Duncan Lennox, editor of *Jane's Strategic Weapons Systems*, said the description fitted that of a target missile or drone used for artillery and air-defence practice. Target missiles typically are 3.5 metres long, turbojet-powered and fly at about 400 m.p.h.[13] The MoD was adamant in its denial. 'Whatever he might have seen might have been something that was flying, but was certainly not anything that was fired,' an MoD spokesman stated:

(3A)

NEAR COLLISION - AIR TRAFFIC INCIDENT REPORT FORM

NOTE 1°) To be filled in printed characters and in english language.
2°) Shaded boxes contain items to be included in an initial report by radio.
3°) Items marked this # must be deleted as appropriate.

SECTION 1 - GENERAL INFORMATION

TYPE OF INCIDENT	A	INCIDENT (NEAR COLLISION) PROCEDURAL 'FACILITY #
NAME OF PILOT-IN-COMMAND	B	ZAGHETTI
OPERATOR	C	ALITALIA
IDENTIFICATION MARKINGS OF AIRCRAFT	D	I - DAWC
AIRCRAFT TYPE	E	MD 80
RADIO CALL SIGN - IN COMMUNICATION WITH - FREQUENCY AT TIME OF INCIDENT	F	AZ 284 - LON 124.1 - AT ~ 2000
AERODROME OF DEPARTURE	G	MILAN - LINATE
AERODROME OF FIRST INTENDED LANDING AND DESTINATION, IF DIFFERENT	H	LONDON - HEATHROW
TYPE OF FLIGHT PLAN	I	IFR
POSITION AT TIME OF INCIDENT - HEADING OR ROUTE - TRUE AIRSPEED	J	~ 30 NM SOUTH BIGGIN VOR - HEADING 320° TAS 380
FL, ALTITUDE OR HEIGHT - ALTIMETER SETTING - ATTITUDE	K	LEVEL FLIGHT CLIMBING (DESCENDING) TURNING # FL 222 - ALT 1013 - RATE 2000
FLIGHT WEATHER CONDITIONS AT TIME OF INCIDENT	L	IMC VMC — Distance above below cloud fog haze `VMC` — 30 Km (NM#) — Distance horizontally from cloud / Between cloud layers / In cloud rain snow sleet/fog haze / Flying into out of sun / Reported estimated flight visibility — 30 Km (NM#)
DATE AND TIME OF INCIDENT IN GMT	M	REPORTED BY RADIO TO LON 127.1 AFIS TWR APP (ACC) FIC # AT 04/21/91 ~ 2000 date - time

SECTION 2 - DETAILED INFORMATION

DESCRIPTION OF OTHER AIRCRAFT, IF RELEVANT — Type, high low wing, N. of engines — Radio call sign, registration — Markings, colour, lighting — Other available details	N	OBJECT SIMILAR MISSILE - WITHOUT EXHAUST FLAME - UNKNOWN — LIGHT BROWN - SIMILAR DESERT COLOUR — ABOUT 3 METERS LENGTH - ROUND SHAPE -
DESCRIPTION OF INCIDENT — If desired add comment or suggestion, including your opinion on the probable cause of the incident. (In case of near-collision give information on respective flight paths, estimated vertical and horizontal sighting and miss distances between aircraft and avoiding action taken by either or both	O	DURING DESCENT, AT FL 222 I SAW FOR ABOUT 3-4 SECONDS A FLYING OBJECT, VERY SIMILAR TO A MISSILE, LIGHT BROWN COLOURED, WITH A TRACK OPPOSITE THEN MINE WHICH WAS 320° - IT WAS HIGHER THAN US ABOUT 1000 ft.

AT ONCE I SAID " LOOK OUT. LOOK OUT TO MY COPILOT WHO LOOKED OUT AND SAW WHAT I HAD SEEN - AS SOON AS THE OBJECT CROSSED US I ASKED TO THE ACC/OPERATOR IF HE SAW SOMETHING.. ON HIS SCREEN AND HE ANSWERED " I SEE AN UNKNOWN TARGET 10 N.M. BEHIND YOU -

DATE 04/22/91 TIME 8 P.M.	FUNCTION AND SIGNATURE CPT	FUNCTION AND SIGNATURE
PLACE LONDON	OF PERSON SUBMITTING ZAGHETTI	OF PERSON RECEIVING
OF COMPLETION OF FORM	REPORT	REPORT

SECTION 3 - SUPPLEMENTARY INFORMATION
by ATS unit concerned (not for pilot's use)

HOW REPORT RECEIVED	P	RADIO TELEPHONE / TELEPRINTER # AT ARO AFIS/TWR APP ACC/FIC #
DETAILS OF ATS ACTION — Clearance, incident observed on radar, warning given, result of local enquiry, etc	Q	

Delete as appropriate

SIGNATURE OF ATS OFFICER   DATE TIME GMT

ICAO - PANS RAC / DOC 4444 - RAC 501/10

The official report by Captain Achille Zaghetti of Alitalia, describing the object encountered over Kent in April 1991. (*Civil Aviation Authority, obtained by L. Williams-Davies*)

It was a Sunday. The only ranges we have in the Kent area are
Lydd and Hythe, and they are concerned with small arms only . . .
It's absolutely in the middle of the busiest traffic area. People just
don't fire missiles there, but of course, we do have quite a few
UFO reports and often people who see these things describe them
as missile- or cigar-shaped . . .[14]

The MoD added that, although remotely piloted vehicles were
sometimes used as targets for test firings, they never went as high as
22,200 feet.[15] In a letter to a researcher dated 25 July 1991, the Civil
Aviation Authority stated:

After extensive civil and military investigations . . . the Air
Defence Department has not been able to confirm the identity of
the object but the possibility of a missile from an army firing
range has been ruled out. In addition, the Ministry of Defence had
no report of any space related activity that can provide an
explanation. The description also did not correspond with that
expected had the object been a meteorological balloon. We have
therefore closed the investigation and listed the sighting as an
Unidentified Flying Object.

Nevertherless, consideration must be given to the possibility that the
object sighted may have been either a stray target drone or a misguided
cruise missile, launched by Britain or one of its NATO partners, which
embarrassed officials were obliged to categorize as a UFO.

Alien Encounters

On 29 June 1993, Guiseppe Zitella, a forty-nine-year-old, former non-
commissioned officer of the Italian Air Force, claims to have
encountered a strange creature in a wheat field at Pettorano sul Gizio,
near Sulmona, in central Italy. Zitella and his wife first observed
something like a balloon in the sky, which landed. Zitella approached the
object, at which point he realized that the 'balloon' was in fact some kind
of creature.
    'It was 80 centimetres high,' Zitella reported, with 'brown legs
attached to the round head. It seemed to be all covered by black plastic,
and on the legs I saw a V-like sign. It didn't say anything. It hopped and
looked me in the face. I have no doubt it was alive.' The creature made two

or three leaps as it moved away from Zitella, then, as if propelled by a mysterious energy, it rose perpendicularly and departed.

Police and scientists, some reportedly from the Consiglio Nazionale delle Ricerche, investigated and found a circular burned area, 1 metre in diameter, in the wheat field.[16]

I might have paid little heed to this story were it not for the fact that a similar creature was seen over a period of several months, beginning in May 1993, by witnesses in Ascoli Piceno, Abruzzo, a town 100 kilometres north-north-east of Pettorano sul Gizio. One of the principal witnesses was twenty-three-year-old Filiberto Caponi, who on various dates exposed a number of clear, Polaroid, colour photographs of the creature. The photos were shown on the Italian TV station RAI-DUE in November 1993, when members of the Caponi family – Filiberto, his grandmother and his father, who had all seen the creature – were interviewed.[17]

In February 1994 I went to Italy specifically to interview Filiberto Caponi, together with his father. I was immediately impressed by the sincerity of the witnesses, as were all those present, including a journalist friend who had alerted me to the case.

The story is too lengthy and complex to include here in detail, but it should be noted well that when first observed and photographed by Caponi, just outside his home in May 1993, the creature appeared to be enclosed in some kind of small 'sack' or 'bag', which leaped 2 or 3 metres into the air when Caponi touched it with his foot. Subsequent photos taken over several months reveal a simian-like creature of unknown species, apparently in two stages of growth, with undeveloped arms and legs, rough brownish skin, and almond-shaped eyes. On numerous occasions the creature gave out piercing screams, heard by the local populace. Caponi keeps an open mind about the creature's origin. For many months he was convinced that it was a mutated animal, the result perhaps of a genetic experiment.

In late 1993 Caponi was visited by four members of the carabinieri, armed with a search warrant, who asked him to hand over the original photographic prints (which have yet to be returned). Later he was taken to the barracks for a four-hour interview in the presence of the district attorney. He was strongly advised to drop the whole matter and was asked to sign a form stating that he had faked the photos with models, using his skills as a self-employed ceramics artisan, and was charged with 'creating panic, public disturbance, and spreading false rumours'. Fortunately this charge was dropped at the court hearing.[18]

In addition to being favourably impressed with the photos, I was struck by the fact that Caponi seemed to have retained his sense of shock and wonder following the experiences, as well as a fear of reprisal from the authorities if he continued to discuss the case. I advised him nevertheless to write a book, and offered my assistance with finding a publisher.

European Parliamentary Interest

Following a resolution proposed by Belgian deputy Elio Di Rupo to the European Parliament in 1991, in the wake of the extraordinary wave of sightings over Belgium in 1989–90, the Committee on Energy, Research and Technology (CERT) held numerous meetings, chaired by Tullio Regge, an Italian independent MEP and physicist. Di Rupo's intention was to establish an all-European agency, run by the Commission of the European Communities and with a standing committee of experts from the member states, which would collate and analyse UFO reports from the military, scientific organizations and the general public.[19]

In a report tabled in December 1993 and accepted unanimously by the Committee, Regge proposed that the French governmental organization SEPRA (see Chapter 6) be given a statute enabling it to carry out inquiries throughout the Communities' territory. The proposal to establish what might have become known as the European UFO Observation Centre attracted a great deal of ridicule in the media, and the motion was defeated in early 1994.

The 1993 report expresses scepticism about the majority of UFO sightings. '. . . the few remaining inexplicable sightings (about 4%), must for the time being be regarded as UFOs in the literal sense of the term,' it states (yet earlier in the same report, in referring to statistics supplied by SEPRA, Regge says that 'Considerable uncertainties persist in the remaining 40% of [unexplainable] cases'). 'The lack, perhaps temporary or accidental, of an explanation in no way allows us to regard a sighting as certain proof or even an indication that aliens exist with technologies vastly superior to our own. However, scientists still have a duty to continue researching into these events in order to arrive at a satisfactory explanation.'

After writing to the air forces of all member states, Tullio Regge received a number of replies, including a detailed response from the Italian Air Force staff, which sent an unclassified summary of all sightings recorded in the last decade (discussed earlier). Regge claims to have interviewed personally 'hundreds' of civil aviation pilots, but reported that 'there was only one Alitalia steward who described an encounter with a

UFO on a flight from Rome to Venice,' when during a violent downpour which forced the airliner to fly on to Ronchi airport, 'three green spheres of light, probably about 100 metres away, came into view alongside it. The spheres also left traces on the ground radar and were seen by passengers.' Regge postulated that 'a rare meteorological phenomenon . . . might be a possible explanation . . .'

Professor Regge continued:

> More recently, the Spanish Air Force . . . released a list of sightings, including one which bears some resemblance to the Alitalia case mentioned above. For years air forces in all countries kept UFO sightings secret because they were afraid – a fear which has subsequently proved completely groundless – that the UFOs were caused by secret weapons deployed by the USSR, while the USSR in turn, for similar but opposite reasons, kept its own data secret.[20]

In an interview published in the Italian magazine *UFO*, Regge emphasized that the proposal by the CERT had focused on the creation of a European evaluation centre within SEPRA, rather than a study of the phenomenon *per se*, but thanks to ridicule in the media – particularly in the UK – this point was ignored by the critics. 'I was attacked by two British Labour Euro-MPs who probably hadn't even read the report,' said Regge:

> I was accused of asking for money to do research into Father Christmas, and things of this kind. They put obstacles in my path, and this developed into a strong attack in the British press. I believe that the Labour MEPs decided to attack this report for political reasons, just to make a fuss . . . I must say that my appreciation of the British political scene is now very low!

Owing to the ensuing ridicule, the President of the European Parliament decided to omit the debate from the EP's agenda on 21 January 1994. Regge therefore proposed a new text, again unanimously approved by CERT, but because the EP was approaching the end of the session, owing to the election on 12 June 1994, there was insufficient time to bring this proposal before the full session of Parliament.[21]

It remains to be seen if this controversial and ridicule-prone subject will be debated in future sessions of the European Parliament.

Portugal and Spain

Portuguese Air Force Jets in Forty-Minute Encounter

ON THE NIGHT of 4 September 1957 a flight of four US-built, Portuguese Air Force F-84 Thunderjets took off from Ota Air Base, Portugal, on a routine, navigation training mission. It was a clear night with an almost full moon. Air-to-ground visibility reported in flight was greater than 50 statute miles. The pilots were Captain José Lemos Ferreira (flight commander) and Sergeants Alberto Gomes Covas, Mañuel Neves Marcelino and Salvador Alberto Oliveira. Captain Ferreira takes up the story:

> After we reached Granada, at 2006 hours, and started a port turn to change course to Portalegre, I noticed on my left and above the horizon a very unusual source of light . . . after three or four minutes I decided to report it to the other pilots. At that time the pilot flying on my right wing told me he had already noticed it. The other two pilots flying on my left wing had not yet seen it. Together we started exchanging comments over the radio about our discovery and we tried several solutions but none seemed to be a reasonable explanation . . . The thing looked like a very bright star, unusually big and scintillating, with a coloured nucleus which changed colour constantly, going from deep green to blue to passing through yellowish and reddish colorations . . .
>
> All of a sudden the thing grew very rapidly, assuming five or six times its initial volume, becoming quite a spectacle to see [then as] fast as it had grown, [it] decided to shrink, almost disappearing on the horizon, becoming a just visible, small, yellow point. These expansions and contractions happened several times, but without becoming periodic and always having a pause, longer or shorter, before modifying volume. The relative position between us and the thing was still the same, that is about 40° on our left, and we could not determine if the changing dimensions were due to very fast approaches and retreats on the same vector or if the

modifying took place stationary . . . After about seven or eight minutes of this the thing had been gradually getting down below the horizon and dislocated itself for a position about 90° to our left . . . At 2038 hours I decided to abandon the mission and to make a port turn in the general direction of Coruche since nobody was paying any attention to the exercise. We turned about 50° to port but still the thing maintained its position of 90° to our left, which could not be possible with a stationary object.

By now the phenomenon was well below our level of 25,000 feet and apparently quite near, presenting a bright red and looking like a curved shell of beans at an arm's length. After several minutes on our new course we discovered a small circle of yellow light apparently coming out of the thing, and before our surprise elapsed we detected three other identical circles on the right of the thing. [They were all] moving with their relative positions changing constantly and sometimes very rapidly. Still we could not estimate the distance between us and them, although they were below us and apparently very near. In any case, the big 'thing' looked ten to fifteen times greater than the yellow circles and apparently was the director of operations since the others were moving around it.

As we [neared] Coruche the 'big thing' suddenly and very rapidly made what looked like a dive, followed up by a climb in our direction. Then everybody went wild and almost broke formation in the process of crossing over and ahead of the UFO. We were all very excited and I had a hard time to calm things down. As soon as we crossed over, everything disappeared in a few seconds, and later we landed without further incident. From the first moment we detected the UFO to the final show, a registered time of forty minutes had elapsed, and during it we had ample opportunity to verify every possible explanation for the phenomenon. We came to no conclusions, except that after this do not give us the old routine of Venus, balloons, aircraft and the like, which has been given as a general panacea for almost every case of UFOs.

At the same time that the pilots had their encounter, the Coimbra Meteorological Observatory registered extraordinary localized variations in the Earth's magnetic field, as proven by charts at that establishment.[1]

Near Collision with an Airliner

On 17 September 1968 at 23.00 hours, a Fokker F-27 of the Spantax company, piloted by Captain Julián Rodríguez Bustamente, flying near Gran Canária, one of the Canary Islands, encountered a point of light which headed in his aircraft's direction at high speed on a collision course. Suddenly, without deceleration, the object halted, taking up position about 20 or 30 metres from the aircraft's port wing. The crew reported that the bright spherical object was about 3 metres in diameter and glowed with an intense green glow that penetrated the entire area of the flight-deck and cabin. The UFO turned and dropped to a lower altitude, but returned to wing level before departing at an incredible speed.

Among the passengers were the U.D. Las Palmas football team, who had a clear view of the object for about three minutes. The crew reported the sighting to air traffic control in the Canary Islands, who were unable to offer an explanation. An official report was also sent to the Air Ministry, which forbade the crew to make public statements about the encounter.[2]

Defense Intelligence Agency Interest

Since its founding in 1961, America's Defense Intelligence Agency (DIA) has required its defence attachés around the world to collect intelligence about all foreign UFO events. This collection requirement is obvious just from reviewing the numerous UFO intelligence reports released, under provisions of the Freedom of Information Act, that actually pre-date the DIA by over a decade and continue into the current decade. A wave of sightings in Spain in 1973–4 was summarized in twenty-nine reports (translated from local newspapers) then forwarded to the Pentagon. Captain Richard Fox, Acting Defense Attaché, pointed out that the reports had not been checked for their validity but that the data were being forwarded 'strictly for information of those parties interested'.

One of the sightings was witnessed on 23 March 1974 by the chauffeur of the President of Cádiz Provincial Commission on a highway near Sanlúcar do Barrameda. A luminous, metallic object 'moved up with great brilliancy. As observer approached object, he felt a strange sensation. His car finally practically came to a stop, wavering back and forth like a feather.'

On 27 March 1974 another interesting observation was made by a truck driver at Valdehijaderos, who reportedly saw:

. . . three silver ships parked on the highway with light similar to floodlight. Observer stopped motor of his car and some figures approached him. He ran, frightened, and they followed him. He threw himself into a gutter. His pursuers passed within two 2 metres and he saw them. They were about 2 metres tall, had arms and legs but he did not see their faces. After they passed he returned to the truck. The beings returned to observe him again, then they entered their ships and left. Next day the Guardia Civil made an investigation. They found a hole in the ground, which the driver said he had not made.

Captain Fox commented: 'It is of interest to note that in April of this year teams of extra sensory perception specialists held a meeting in Malaga for the purpose of scientifically studying the UFOs seen in that vicinity. Results of this meeting unknown.'[3]

Landing at an Air Force Target Range

On the night of 2 January 1975 six military personnel at the Spanish Air Force bombing and gunnery range at Las Bárdenas Reales near the Zaragoza Air Base saw two unidentified objects, one of which apparently landed or hovered low over the ground, between 23.00 and 23.25.

According to the official report (see p. 140), the principal witness (name deleted) observed the second object through binoculars and described it as 'shaped like an inverted cup' with white lights on the upper and lower parts and intermittent white and amber lights on its sides. He was unable to estimate the size, but thought it was about that of a truck. When it took off, a powerful light on its underside illuminated the entire area. No sound could be heard.[4]

Spanish military authorities of the Third Air Force Region appointed an investigating judge to inquire into the incident.[5] The official explanation given at the time was that the soldiers reporting the landing had experienced an optical illusion. The following year, the Air Ministry released some documents on the case which show that explanation to have been a false one. Concluded the Air Force: 'All the witnesses were questioned one by one and separately; no contradictions were found; all coincided exactly in their descriptions. From their reports could be established the fact that . . . unidentified flying objects flew . . . at a low altitude and low speed over the ground [then] rapidly ascended and, gaining high speed, disappeared in a NW direction.'

CONFIDENCIAL

INFORUE QUE FOR ULA EL COJANDANTE DEL AREA DE AVIACION (S.V.)
.... SOBRE LA NOTICIA DE APARICION
DE OBJETOS VOLADORES NO IDENTIFICADOS EN EL POLIGONO DE TIRO
DE LAS BARDENAS REALES EL DIA 2 DE ENERO DE 1.975,

En el Polígono de Tiro de Las Bardenas Reales a 8 de Enero de 1.975.

Testigos presenciales

Soldado .... (Mecánico)
Cabo .... (Estudiante)
Soldado .... (Agricultor)
Soldado .... (Agricultor)
Soldado .... (Agricultor)
Sargento 1ª

Se adjunta fotocopia de las declaraciones de estos testigos e informe del Comandante del Destacamento, así como un croquis de las evoluciones que según dichas declaraciones, efectuaron dos objetos voladores no identificados sobre dicho Polígono.

Circunstancias que concurrieron en la observación.

El Sargento 1ª observó el segundo de los objetos voladores con unos prismáticos.
La observación del Cabo y los Soldados que estaban de guardia en la Torre Principal, fue a simple vista.
Las condiciones meteorológicas en el momento de la observación eran:
Despejado y con claridad suficiente para percibir los perfiles de los montes cercanos, había bruma por el horizonte.
Los medios de apreciación de distancia y alturas se realizaron por medio de referencias sobre el terreno.
Durante todo el tiempo de la observación no se ofreció ningún ruido extraño.

CONCLUSIONES

Tomada declaración a todos los testigos presenciales, uno por uno, y por separado, no hubo ninguna contradicción, todos coincidieron exactamente en sus manifestaciones.
De sus informes se desprende, que el día 2 de Enero sobre las 23,00 horas un objeto volador no identificado, sobrevoló el Campo de Tiro de Bardenas Reales, inicialmente a escasa altura sobre el terreno y a poca velocidad hasta el momento en que llegó a la altura de la Torre Principal, lugar de la observación, en el que se elevó rápidamente adquiriendo gran velocidad y desapareció en dirección N.U.

CONFIDENCIAL

The official report of the sighting by military personnel at Las Bárdenas Reales, near Zaragoza Air Base, Spain, January 1975. (*Spanish Air Force*)

Spanish Air Ministry Releases UFO Files

In October 1976 Juan José Benítez, a reporter for *La Gaceta del Norte*, was invited to the Air Ministry in Madrid where, in the office of an Air Force lieutenant general and chief of staff, he was handed a file containing documentation by the Spanish Government on twelve of their most outstanding cases. The documents were backed up with photographic evidence, including gun-camera film taken by Air Force pilots.

Although it was made clear to Señor Benítez that release of the documents was not on an official basis, he was, nevertheless, given a go-ahead to publish the reports.[6] 'The first twelve files were handed to me in person on October 20 1976, in the old Air Ministry building in Madrid,' said Benítez:

The other two files came to me in the closing weeks of 1978 and also from the hands of the senior general . . . When you read and analyse these files, which total almost 300 folio pages, it becomes definitely and categorically clear that the UFOs exist and, quite evidently, are a matter of the deepest concern to governments of the whole planet.[7]

Spanish Air Force General Confirms UFO Reality

In June 1976 General Castro, divisional general commanding the air zone of the Canary Islands at the time, granted an interview with *La Gaceta del Norte* during which he announced that UFOs were taken extremely seriously at a high level. 'As a General, my opinion is the same as the Air Ministry,' he said, 'but in my own personal capacity, as Carlos Castro Cavero, I have for some time held the view that UFOs are extraterrestrial craft.'

The General said that he had personally witnessed a UFO for more than an hour over the town of Sadaba, near Zaragoza. 'It was an extremely bright object,' he recalled, 'which remained there stationary for that length of time and then shot off towards Egea de los Caballeros, covering the distance of twenty kilometres in less than two seconds. No human device is capable of such a speed.'

General Castro revealed that the Spanish Air Ministry possessed about twenty cases that had been investigated thoroughly by experts and found to be completely unexplainable in conventional terms. He added that pilots had flown alongside UFOs in aircraft, but when they tried to close in the objects moved off at speeds far higher than anything made by man.[8]

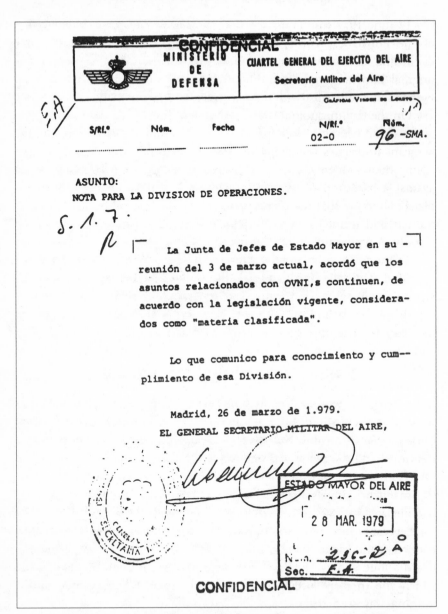

CONFIDENCIAL

| | MINISTERIO DE DEFENSA | CUARTEL GENERAL DEL EJERCITO DEL AIRE |
| | | Secretaría Militar del Aire |

Gráficas Vicente de Loarte

| S/Rf.° | Núm. | Fecha | N/Rf.° 02-0 | Núm. 96 -SMA. |

ASUNTO:
NOTA PARA LA DIVISION DE OPERACIONES.

> La Junta de Jefes de Estado Mayor en su reunión del 3 de marzo actual, acordó que los asuntos relacionados con OVNI,s continuen, de acuerdo con la legislación vigente, considerados como "materia clasificada".
>
> Lo que comunico para conocimiento y cumplimiento de esa División.
>
> Madrid, 26 de marzo de 1.979.
> EL GENERAL SECRETARIO MILITAR DEL AIRE,

ESTADO MAYOR DEL AIRE

2 8 MAR. 1979

N....... 290-2

Sec. E.A.

CONFIDENCIAL

The UFO subject confirmed by the Joint Chiefs of Staff in Spain in 1979 as a 'classified matter'. (*Spanish Ministry of Defence/Vicente-Juan Ballester Olmos*)

Portuguese Air Force Pilot's Alarming Encounter

On 17 June 1977 José Francisco Rodrigues, a twenty-three-year-old pilot of the Portuguese Air Force 31st Squadron, based at Tancos, had a disturbing encounter with a UFO in his Dornier 27 light aircraft. The original information on this important story was supplied by Joaquim Fernandes, a journalist with the *Journal de Noticias*.

On the day in question the weather was poor, with intermittent rain and a cloud ceiling of less than 3,000 feet. Visibility was about 5 miles. Sergeant Rodrigues was flying over the Castelo de Bode dam at around noon when suddenly, emerging from the clouds, he saw a dark object against a backdrop of white stratocumulus, slightly to the right of his plane. Thinking that the object was perhaps a cargo plane, he banked to the left and immediately radioed to ask if there was any traffic in the vicinity. A reply came in the negative.

As the pilot completed a turn to port, the unknown object suddenly appeared at his eleven o'clock position 'no more than 6 metres away'. It was definitely not a cargo plane. The upper section, partially concealed by cloud, was black, and on the lower section there appeared to be four or five 'panels'. The object was approximately 13 to 15 metres in diameter. Suddenly it accelerated and vanished from what the pilot believes was an initial stationary position.

The Dornier began to vibrate violently and went into an uncontrolled dive. Struggling to regain control, Rodrigues pushed the control column forward. Air speed increased to 140 knots, then 180 knots as the ground came nearer. Control was fortunately regained when almost 'touching the tree tops' and the plane was landed in one piece – with a badly shaken pilot. During the encounter the directional electric gyroscope (connected to a magnetic compass) rotated wildly, and by the time the plane landed it had deviated by 180° relative to the magnetic compass.

Sergeant José Vicente Saldanha, the duty controller that day, confirmed Rodrigues's radio call and said that about a minute later he heard a loud shout. The base is about 5 kilometres from the dam above which the incident occurred, but, owing to hills and poor visibility, nothing was seen from the tower. However, the pilot spoke with two witnesses (presumably from another area of the base) who saw the plane descend in a 'falling leaf' pattern, then disappear. They also heard the engine roaring as the pilot regained control.

Such was Sergeant Rodrigues's state of shock when he landed that he had difficulty speaking. An examination by the base doctor revealed no obvious medical cause that would account for his condition, and the duty controller felt certain that a simple engine problem would not have upset the pilot to such a degree. Moreover, fault could not be found with the engine.

The Portuguese Air Force's Chief of Staff eventually (and reluctantly) allowed veteran researchers José Garrido and Vitor Santos to interview both the pilot and the controller. The researchers noted that:

> As Sergeant Rodrigues completed his 315° turn . . . with a large radius, the object reappeared to his left 'at 11 o'clock' and very close. It is hard to decide . . . whether the object moved or not during the forty seconds that the plane took to complete the turn, although the original [report] conveys that idea. At any rate, during his second glimpse Sergeant Rodrigues thought that the object was motionless, or practically so, and then accelerated and departed. In either case this implies a series of manoeuvres by the object, including an anomalous acceleration which . . . rules out a balloon or a conventional machine.

No official explanation for the incident was offered by the Air Force,[9] though I did receive an official report on this and some other incidents from the Portuguese Embassy in London. 'The position of our government is of cautious alert,' I was informed. 'Pilots of the Portuguese Air Force are instructed to register details of any non-identified objects which they might see while flying.'[10]

Another Near Collision

One of Spain's most dramatic airline encounters with UFOs happened on 11 November 1979, when Comandante Francisco Lerdo de Tejada, flying a Super Caravelle of the Spanish Air Transport (TAE) company from Salzburg in Austria to Tenerife, took evasive action to avoid colliding with an unknown object in the vicinity of Ibiza. The airliner had 109 passengers on board, most of whom were German and Austrian tourists. Captain Tejada described the incident in an interview with Juan José Benítez:

> A few minutes before 11.00 p.m. we got a call from Air Control Barcelona. They asked us to switch over to 121.5 megacycles, which is an emergency frequency . . . So we switched to that frequency, and imagined that there might perhaps be a ship or

aircraft in difficulties. But then, when we made contact, all we got was the noise of a transmitter, though we were unable to identify what it was all about. It was at that moment, or a few seconds later, that we saw the red lights . . . Two very red, powerful lights.

They were heading towards us at 9 o'clock of our position . . . The two lights seemed to be set at the two extremities. All of the movements of the two lights were perfectly co-ordinated, just as if it were one single device we were dealing with . . . The speed at which they came at us was staggering. I have never seen anything like that speed . . . The two lights, in line, came up to us on a bearing of 250° . . . When we saw them first, they were at about 10 miles. Then they made towards us, and then were literally 'playing with us' at not much under half a mile or so . . .

The object was moving upwards and downwards at will, all round us, and performing movements that it would be quite impossible for any conventional machine to execute . . . What sort of aircraft flies at that sort of speed? What sort of aircraft takes up a position at less than half a mile from my jet liner and then sets about 'playing games' with me?

Captain Tejada said that the object's size was 'approximately the same as a jumbo jet', and that its approach speed was such that he was obliged to make a 'break' – turning the aircraft sharply to avoid collision. According to one news report, an elderly male passenger collapsed when he saw the objects zigzagging across the night sky towards the plane. 'The situation finally got so serious', said the captain, 'that we decided to call Manises and request permission to make an emergency landing.'

The plane touched down at Manises Airport, Valencia, shortly before midnight, with the UFO still visible over the airport buildings, seen by the airport director, Señor Morlán, together with his air traffic controller and a number of ground personnel. Captain Tejada and his flight crew were interrogated by the Air Force shortly after landing. 'As is usual in all cases of this sort,' reported Benítez, 'the Spanish Air Force . . . initiates an extensive investigation and appoints an official with the title of *Juez-Informador* to preside over it. He is generally a high-ranking Air Force officer.'[11]

Although the Air Force has overall responsibility, all the armed forces, as well as the police and various civilian authorities in Spain, take a serious and active interest in the UFO phenomenon. As researcher J. Plana Crivillén points out, the General Civil Aviation Administration, for example, is responsible for the collection (via the Commission on Air Traffic Incidents) of all UFO sighting reports originating from airports, air traffic controllers, and the airlines. Following a sighting by commercial pilots, air traffic control centres are obliged to ensure that the chief of the service room records the details in the station logbook. In addition, since conversations between air traffic controllers and pilots are automatically recorded in the event of a near miss or accident, any data relating to aerial phenomena are transcribed and made available to various interested parties.[12]

Cat and Mouse

Following the near collision reported by Captain Tejada on 11 November 1979, Air Defence Command at Torrejón Air Force Base (Madrid) scrambled a Mirage F-1CE jet from Los Llanos AFB (Albacete), flown by Captain-Pilot Fernando Cámara, to intercept unknown targets. 'Pegaso' Operations Centre (at Torrejón) informed the pilot that the radar staff at Manises Airport (which is also an Air Force Base) were seeing stationary aerial lights; one above the runway and another over the port of Valencia. Cámara was ordered to identify the lights and to prepare his weaponry.

According to Benítez, the Mirage arrived over Valencia at about 02.20 [12 November] at an altitude of 7,500 metres, but the pilot was unable to locate any targets and none showed on his radar. However, as the Mirage passed over Valencia, a powerful noise of unknown origin 'like a siren' broke in on all the radio channels. It was then that Cámara caught sight of a strange light towards the south and, ordered to chase it, he set off in pursuit. But the light would not let him get near it and still nothing showed on the radarscope. The 'siren' noise stopped once the jet left Valencia. Cámara decided to turn back when he was over the Mediterranean and out of Spanish airspace; furthermore, the light now seemed to be over the coast of North Africa.

Pegaso Operations Centre then redirected Cámara to Valencia, where another aerial light was visible. At a distance of 26 kilometres from the city, the pilot observed a three-coloured, stationary light at about 6,000 metres altitude, which failed to register on his radar. Once again the siren sound could be heard. When Cámara tried to approach the object, it suddenly accelerated instantly to the same speed as the Mirage (1,100 k.p.h.), maintaining a certain distance from the aircraft. Cámara attempted to film the object, but his onboard camera jammed. Other instruments seemed to be affected, too.

Because the chase was proving futile, Pegaso Operations Centre ordered the pilot to head for Sagunto (Valencia) as there was yet another unidentified light in the sky. Over Castellón, the siren noise started up again, and Cámara saw a very bright white stationary disc over the Mediterranean, near the Columbretes Islands, though yet again it did not register on his radar. The 'cat and mouse' game once again ensued, the UFO always keeping the same distance from the Mirage. Finally, at about 03.30, over Menorca, the Mirage began to run short of fuel and Cámara headed back to his base at Los Llanos. Even on the approach to base, Benítez reported, the object continued tracking the jet and jamming its electronic equipment.[13]

Vicente-Juan Ballester Olmos, one of Spain's leading investigators, believes that the data provided in this report are not reliable, however. He told me that the Air Force had recently (in 1995) declassified its file on the incident, and that a more thorough evaluation was necessary before an accurate assessment of the case could be made.[14] But interestingly, another such incident occurred less than a week later, Ballester Olmos confirms.

A declassified Air Force report states that at 17.20 on 17 November, Pegaso Operations Centre detected an unknown track some 40 kilometres south of Morril (Granada), where a radar facility operates. The uncorrelated target remained outside Spanish airspace for fifteen minutes, then headed towards the Spanish coast. At 17.45 a Mirage F-1 took off from Los Llanos Air Force Base to intercept the target. As the aircraft approached, the radar echo faded intermittently. At 18.07 the Mirage arrived in the vicinity of the target, but at 18.12 Pegaso Operations Centre reported having lost the trace altogether. Just before it vanished, the unknown target was positioned above the radar site at Morril. At 18.16 the Mirage pilot gave up and began to return to Los Llanos, but minutes later he saw three powerful red-yellow lights in the shape of a triangle, apparently 19 kilometres away and on a flight level of 9,100 metres. The pilot headed towards the lights and directed his 70-kilometre-range onboard radar at them. Nothing was detected. Furthermore, in spite of a speed of 1,160 k.p.h., the Mirage could get no closer to the lights, which were seen in the direction of Algeria.

After ten minutes of fruitless pursuit, the Mirage pilot decided to return to base. During his descent, something curious happened. Some childish, laughing voices broke in on the UHF-11 channel which linked the pilot to the Pegaso Operations Centre. 'Hello, how are you? Hello, hello,' they said in Spanish. The interference lasted for thirty seconds but was not heard at the Operations Centre.[15]

Further Air Force Files Released

It is thanks to the efforts of researcher Vicente-Juan Ballester Olmos, together with his colleague Joan Plana, that the Spanish Air Force has now declassified so many additional UFO reports. This could not have taken place without the co-operation of several high-ranking personnel, especially Lieutenant General Ramón Fernández Sequeiros, Chief of the Air Force Staff (JEMA), and Lieutenant General Alfredo Chamorro Chapinal, Commander-in-Chief of Air Operations Command (MOA).

In December 1991, the Cabinet of the Chief of the Air Staff proposed to the Minister of Defence its plan for the declassification of UFO reports. In January 1992, documents as well as the responsibility for handling all UFO matters were transferred to the Intelligence Section of the MOA. The latter was instructed to analyse the information and to prepare corresponding management procedures for classification and declassification of the files. In April 1992, Lieutenant General Sequeiros attended a meeting of the Joint Chiefs of Staff (JUJEM) and requested that UFO files be declassified. The Joint Chiefs agreed to downgrade the classification level of such reports to the equivalent of 'Confidential', although each report was to be analysed by intelligence officers to determine if its release might threaten national security; if not, its complete declassification would be decided by the Chief of the Air Force Staff: previously, such decisions required consensus of the Joint Chiefs.[16]

Scientific Symposium in Portugal

On 23 October 1993 the first scientific UFO symposium to be held at a Portuguese university was hosted by the Comissão Nacional de Investigação do Fenomeno Ovni (CNIFO) at Porto's Faculty of Arts, moderated by leading researcher Joaquim Fernandes. Among those in attendance were representatives from the Meteorological Institute, the National Defence Institute, and the Portuguese Air Force. Conceição de Silva, former General-in-Chief of the Air Force, contributed to the workshop discussions.

Among the goals of the symposium were the initiation and development of co-operation with government agencies, in particular the Air Force Information Division, and to gain access to UFO reports in the files of the Portuguese Joint Staff of the Armed Forces Intelligence Division in Lisbon. Distinguished scientists from the Porto, Lisbon and Vila Real universities signed a document establishing a protocol which

ANEXO

EXPEDIENTES CASOS OVNIs

Date	Place	Type	Info	
6 AGO 62	San Javier	Luz	inf	
17 MAY 57	Lérida	OVNI	inf	
3 JUN 67	Torrejón-Talavera	OVNI	INF.I.	*
14 MAR 68	Canarias-Sahara	Luz	INF.L	
15 MAY 68	Diversos puntos Peninsula	Luz	inf	
6 SEP 68	Madrid y otros puntos	OVNI (sonda?)	int	
17 SEP 68	Tenerife-Las Palmas	Luz	inf	
13 OCT 68	Algeciras	OVNI	inf	
4 NOV 68	Vuelo Valencia-Sagunto	Luces	int	
6 NOV 68	Castellbilbal (Barcelona)	Circulo lumnin.	--	
NOV.DIC 68	Puente de Almuhey (León)	Disco luminoso	inf	
DIC 68	Palenc.Madrid.Almeria.Vizcay	Varios	--	
19 DIC 68	Madrid	OVNIs	inf	*
24 ENE 69	Madrid	Luz parpad.	inf	
8 FEB 69	Sacedón (Guadalajara)	Bola roja	inf	
25 FEB 69	Sagunto (Valencia) vuelo	OVNI destell.	INF.M	*
2 ABR 69	Bocerra (Lugo)	Nave	--	
13 MAY 69	BA de Reus	OVNI	INF.L	
26 SEP 69	Gerona	OVNI	INF.L	*
16 JUN 70	Burgos	OVNI	inf	
23 FEB 71	Varios puntos. Vuelos	Luces	INF.M	*
14 MAR 71	Majadahonda (Madrid)	OVNI	inf	
26 SEP 73	Valencia	OVNI luminoso	INF.L	*
20 MAR 74	Aznalcollar (Sevilla)	OVNIs	INF.M	*
24 NOV 74	Tenerife-Gran Canaria	Luces	INF.M	*
1 ENE 75	Burgos	OVNI	INF.L	*
2 ENE 75	Poligono Bardenas	OVNI	INF.L	*
10 ENE 75	Burgos	OVNI	INF.L	copia
14 ENE 75	BA Talavera	Ecos GCA	int	*
23/24MAR 75	Madrid	OVNI	INF.I.	
3,4,5AGO 75	Pozuelo (Madrid)	Peonza lum.	inf	
22 JUN 76	Gran Canaria	Luz	INF.E	*
19 NOV 76	Fuerteventura y G.Canaria	Efecto óptico	INF.E	+\
19 NOV 76	Aeropuerto de Málaga	Cúpula brill.	--	
ENE 77	BA Talavera la Real	Extraterr. ??	--	
13 FEB 77	Gallarta (Vizcaya)	Platillo.Seres	INF.E	
meses 78	Alcorcón (Madrid)	Luz móvil	--	fotos
4 JUL 78	Barcelona	OVNI	--	
24 OCT 78	Menorca	OVNIs	INF.I.	
14 FEB 79	Andraitx (Mallorca)	Luz desde avión	--	
5 MAR 79	Gran Canaria	Luz	INF.E	diaposit.
13 MAR 79	Mediterraneo-Valencia	Extraña traza	inf	
11/12NOV 79	Palma-Manises (Sóller)	Diversas luces	INF.E	
17 NOV 79	Sur-Este peninsular	Traza. Luces	INF.I. fotocopia	
28 NOV 79	Madrid	Eco radar.luces	INF.L fotocopia	
29-31MAR 80	Zaragoza	Ecos y luces	INF.L	
22 MAY 80	Gran Canaria. Sur	OVNI luminoso	INF.M	
8 DIC 80	Atlantico altura Rif	Acc.aéreo?	--	
JUN 81	Valencia (carta)	OVNIs	--	
19 AGO 82	Blanes (Gerona)	Disco	--	
12 JUL 83	Benicasim (CS). Torrejón	OVNI luminoso	inf	
11 ENE 84	Villanubla	Sonda?	--	
12 FEB 85	Lanzarote	OVNI luminoso	--	
23 DIC 85	Atlántico (Barco)	Luces	--	
1 MAY 88	Burlada (Navarra)	OVNI	-	

---- CLAVES DE REFEREN

The first listing of the official Spanish Air Force intelligence files on fifty-five UFO reports (1962–88), included in a 1991 information note from Flight Safety to the Air Force's Chief of Staff. (*Spanish Air Force/Vicente-Juan Ballester Olmos*)

stressed the importance of the data contained in aeronautical and military UFO reports, similar to the breakthrough achieved in Spain by Vicente-Juan Ballester Olmos.[17]

The Official Dilemma

'I believe in the existence of UFOs,' said Spanish Air Force General Castro in 1976, and he went on to give his own carefully reasoned thoughts on the cover-up. 'The position is that it is as difficult for official quarters to admit that something exists as it is for the Church to affirm that this or that is a miracle.'

General Castro believes that the reason governments do not publicly acknowledge this reality is due not to fear on their part, but rather to a sense of misgiving in the face of an intangible fact on which they are being asked to venture an opinion. Many countries collaborated on research into the subject, he said, and when definite conclusions had been arrived at it might then be possible to inform the world.[18]

Australia and New Zealand

RESPONSIBILITY FOR MONITORING Unidentified or Unusual Aerial Sightings (UAS), as they are officially designated in Australia, rested solely with the Royal Australian Air Force (RAAF), I was informed by the Department of Defence in 1982. At each RAAF base specific officers were appointed to investigate sightings, investigation being restricted to those instances formally reported to the RAAF. When required, assistance was sought from other government departments such as Aviation, Meteorology, Science and Technology (for satellite predictions), plus observatories. 'No Australian Secret Service participates in the investigations,' I was assured.[1]

The Air Force Office of the Department of Defence also sent me a copy of their *Summaries of Unusual Aerial Sightings 1976–1980*. The percentage breakdown of RAAF investigations, it was pointed out, closely matched those of the Royal Air Force and US Air Force investigations, and only about 3 per cent of the reports were attributable to 'unknown causes'. In all its investigations to date, which averaged about 100 per year, the RAAF 'have found no tangible evidence of life from other planets'.[2]

Early Official Investigations

Official Australian investigation into unidentified flying objects goes back as far as 1920, according to researcher Paul Norman, when the SS *Amelia J.* disappeared at a time when strange unexplained lights were being reported around the entrance to Bass Strait. A search aircraft sent to investigate the lights also disappeared and never returned.[3]

The Bass Strait area has featured in a number of mysterious cases, most notably the disappearance of the young pilot Frederick Valentich in 1978 (discussed later in this chapter).

In 1930 the RAAF sent a squadron leader to Warrnambool, Victoria, on the north shore of Bass Strait, where witnesses had reported sightings of unidentified 'aircraft'. No evidence could be found that the aircraft were either Australian or foreign; nor could they even be positively identified as normal aircraft.

The squadron leader who conducted the investigation subsequently became Air Marshal Sir George Jones, Chief of the Air Staff (1942–52).[4] Sir George had his own sighting of a UFO from his home in Mentone, Melbourne, on 16 October 1957, when together with Lady Jones he observed a balloon-like object travelling at the speed of a Sabre jet at about 1,000–1,500 feet altitude.[5] He maintained a serious interest in the subject, and on retirement became a member of the Victorian UFO Research Society.[6]

Bill Chalker of the Australian Centre for UFO Studies has unearthed two interesting RAAF reports dating back to the Second World War. The first refers to an incident during the summer of 1942, when an RAAF pilot was on flying patrol, off the Tasman Peninsula late one afternoon, following reports by fishermen of strange lights on the sea at night in Bass Strait. At 17.50 hours an unidentified object came out of a cloud bank; the pilot described it as 'a singular airfoil of glistening bronze colour', about 150 feet in length and 50 feet in diameter, with a dome on top that reflected sunlight. The UFO flew alongside the plane for a few minutes, then suddenly turned away at 'a hell of a pace'. It made another turn then dived straight into the ocean, throwing up 'a regular whirlpool of waves'.

The second sighting took place one night in February 1944, when at around 02.30 a Beaufort bomber flying at 4,500 feet over Bass Strait was joined by an unidentified object, described as a 'dark shadow' with a flickering light and flame coming out of the rear. The object appeared to be only 100–150 feet away, and stayed with the plane for 18–20 minutes, during which time both radio and direction-finding instruments failed. Eventually the object shot off at about three times the speed of the bomber (235 m.p.h. at that time).

Chalker reports that no enemy action was ever confirmed in Bass Strait, although a total of seventeen aircraft went missing in that area during the Second World War.[7]

In 1952 officers of the Department of Civil Aviation sought to establish a special bureau to collate facts about UFOs. From the Cabinet itself, however, came instructions that the subject was more properly a matter for the Security Service to investigate, and accordingly a security spokesman confirmed shortly afterwards that they had investigators working on reports with the aid of scientists from the radio-physics division of the Commonwealth Scientific and Industrial Research Organization (CSIRO).[8]

Missing Film

On 23 August 1953 the Deputy Director of Civil Aviation in New Guinea, Tom Drury, took an 8mm movie film (using a telephoto lens) of a UFO over Port Moresby. The object was elongated like a bullet and shot out of a cloud travelling at a speed estimated to be at least five times faster than a jet flying at the speed of sound.

> It never slackened speed or changed direction [said Drury], but simply faded into the blue sky while its vapour trail faded after it. The vapour trail was very clear-cut . . . This is visible in the remaining section of the film in my possession . . . I was absolutely certain of its reality. It was filmed, my wife and children saw it. If anyone in the Territory had qualifications to identify an unknown aircraft, I had. It is my business to know what is in the air. I know all types of aircraft and have flown thirty-two of them.

Drury refers to the 'remaining section of the film' in his possession. What became of the rest? He had sent the original film, consisting of ninety-four frames, to the Minister for Air (William McMahon), who in turn sent it to the US Air Force at the Pentagon. The film was returned about nine months later – minus the most important frames showing the actual object.[9,10,11]

Bill Chalker eventually discovered five negatives of photographs of some individual frames from the film in a 1973 Directorate of Air Force Intelligence file, but the actual film showing the UFO was not returned to its owner. Chalker has confirmed that it was examined by the CIA's National Photographic Interpretation Center in Washington, DC,[12] and a former employee of the National Security Agency, Todd Zechel, charges that the film was retained by the CIA's Office of Scientific Intelligence.[13]

Navy Pilot's Sighting

In his book *Flight into the Ages*, RAAF senior public relations officer Ken Llewelyn describes an interesting sighting reported by a Royal Australian Navy pilot in 1954. Lieutenant Shamus O'Farrell, flying a British-built Hawker Sea Fury piston-engined fighter from Nowra Naval Air Station, encountered unknown aircraft during a night-navigation exercise, in the vicinity of Goulburn, near Canberra, at an altitude of just over 12,000 feet.

The incident occurred in fine weather and good visibility at about 20.00 hours.

'I was surprised when I spotted two aircraft, one on either side of me, each with a single bright light above it, but with no navigation lights,' reported O'Farrell. 'I thought about it for some time to make sure I wasn't seeing things that weren't there. But sure enough, I could see two dark, cigar-shaped objects – not very long, about the size of a Dakota – but their central bright lights made the outlines quite distinct. I could see no other detail . . .'

Reluctant to report the sighting, O'Farrell called his base at Nowra and merely asked if they could see him on radar. Petty Officer Jessop confirmed that *three* aircraft were visible on the radarscope, and asked O'Farrell to identify himself by flying a 180° turn. The Sea Fury was then identified as the central of three aircraft. O'Farrell finished with another 180° turn because he lagged behind the other two aircraft, which had continued to move ahead. 'Then, when I came back up, they settled back in formation with me. I still believed they could be aircraft without their lights on.'

The Nowra base was concerned because no other aircraft should have been airborne on the east coast at that time. The unknown objects paced the Sea Fury for about ten minutes in all, always in immaculate formation. 'Then suddenly,' O'Farrell reported, 'they left me and headed off to the north-east, going very fast. I was about to press the transmit button and report to base when Nowra radar contacted me and said, "Those other two contacts are leaving the screen fast to the north-east" . . . I felt very relieved that they had gone.'

The departing objects – whose speed was estimated to be around 1,000 m.p.h. – were also sighted by two ground observers, one of whom was an air traffic controller at Sydney's Mascot Airport.

On landing, O'Farrell was met by Nowra's medical officer and given an examination. Ken Llewelyn reports that the pilot's room also was searched for evidence of excessive alcohol consumption, but O'Farrell drank very little. Several interrogations by RAAF intelligence officers ensued to try to establish the identity of the unknown objects, but the case remains unexplained. O'Farrell became one of the Navy's most experienced fighter pilots, with more than 4,500 hours flying time to his credit, and retired with the rank of Commodore after a posting to Washington, DC, as Australian Naval Attaché.[14]

The O'Farrell sighting reportedly was classified Top Secret, though details leaked to the media. That same year (1954) the Minister for Air,

William McMahon, formally charged the RAAF to investigate UFO reports.[15]

Aircraft Shadowed by Huge Disc over New Zealand

'[New Zealand's] Ministry of Defence is not specifically charged with any formal responsibility for investigating UFOs,' I was informed in 1985, 'and neither is any other government department. The Ministry does however take an active interest in all such reports and within the limitations of its resources conducts investigations as necessary.'[16]

The Ministry kindly sent me results of its investigation into the famous UFO sightings tracked on radar and filmed over the east coast of South Island on 20/21 and 30/31 December 1978. But I would prefer to cite an important case that was not acknowledged by the MoD as having taken place but which was related to me by a witness.

Derek Mansell served in Britain's Royal Air Force from 1950 to 1955 before spending five years in the Royal New Zealand Air Force as a ground-crew airman. Sometime in June of 1956 or 1957 (regrettably he cannot recall the exact date), Mansell told me, a Bristol 170 Mark 31M Freighter in which he was flying on a weekly run from Dunedin to Auckland encountered a UFO over Wellington, though no one on board actually saw the object.

Suddenly, the aircraft seemed to have flown into a violent squall, with the usual turbulence. 'We were enveloped in a shadow, like a cloud,' Mansell said. 'The engines started to run badly and the dials didn't function correctly. The compass spun like mad, and all communications to ground and other aircraft failed.' After about twenty-five minutes everything returned to normal.

When the Freighter landed at Ohakea the pilot of a Douglas C-47 Dakota, which also had just landed and had been following the Freighter, asked if the latter had seen a huge metallic disc, about 250 feet in diameter, with a blue light on top and a red one on the bottom, which apparently had been just above the Freighter. The Freighter crew replied in the negative, but mentioned the sudden turbulence and interference with instruments and communications. The Dakota pilot reported that he was unable to contact the Freighter at this time, and said that the UFO had shadowed the other plane for twenty-five minutes. According to Mansell, photographs of the object were taken by the Dakota crew which have never been released.

The air movements officer asked the commanding officer of Ohakea

Air Force Base to attend the subsequent debriefing, which lasted two hours. Crews of both the Freighter and the Dakota were forbidden to leave the room while the CO asked the adjutant to bring in forms which they were obliged to sign. Reminded of their obligations under the Official Secrets Act, they were warned not to discuss the matter with anyone.

The Maralinga Case

An extraordinary eyewitness account of a UFO seen hovering over the former British nuclear test site at Maralinga, South Australia, was given to the British researcher Jenny Randles by a Royal Air Force corporal stationed there at the time. Following nuclear detonations in September and October 1957, an unidentified object was seen hovering over the airfield by the corporal and some colleagues. Described as a 'magnificent sight', the craft was of a silver-blue colour, with a metallic lustre. The corporal said that the object had a line of 'windows' or 'portholes' along its edge, and that it was seen so distinctly that metallic plating could be made out on its surface.

An air traffic control officer is also alleged to have seen the object, and checks with Alice Springs and Edinburgh airfields revealed that there were no aircraft in the vicinity at the time. No photographs were taken, the RAF corporal said, because the top security status of the base area meant that all cameras had to be locked away. The UFO departed swiftly and silently after about fifteen minutes. 'I swear to you as a practising Christian this was no dream, no illusion, no fairy story – but a solid craft of metallic construction,' the witness told Randles.[17]

The Australian Security and Intelligence Organization

The Australian Security and Intelligence Organization (ASIO), developed from the Allied Intelligence Bureau with the co-operation of the British in 1948, is divided into two main branches: one for intelligence-gathering and the other responsible for counter-intelligence. In their 1982 letter to me, the RAAF stated that there had been no participation by either the ASIO or the ASIS (Australian Secret Intelligence Service) in UFO investigations. Yet there is some evidence for involvement of the former.

In 1959 Stan Seers, former president of the Queensland Flying Saucer Research Bureau (QFSRB – now UFO Research Queensland), received a phone call from a man requesting a meeting in a large car park in Brisbane, hinting that Seers might learn something to his advantage about

UFOs. Suspecting a hoax, Seers let the man make a few additional calls before agreeing to a meeting. At no time did the caller identify himself or his business until Seers met him at the appointed meeting-place, where he produced an identity card and introduced himself as D. D. (Dudley Doherty, I have since learned) of the Australian Security and Intelligence Organization. Mr D insisted that the conversation should take place in his own car (probably because it was bugged), and, since he seemed courteous and genuine, Seers agreed.

Mr D began the conversation with a résumé, covering quite a number of years, of the background of not only Seers but also two close friends in the QFSRB, then came to the point. 'He asked would I personally "play ball" (to use his expression) with his department,' Seers reported:

> In return they would assist us in the field of UFO research wherever and whenever they could, all of which was to be strictly between him and me. The crux of the suggested agreement was the understanding that in the event of any really 'hot' UFO information – landings, contacts, etc. – he would if necessary put me into direct telephone communication with Prime Minister Bob Menzies.

Stan Seers understandably had difficulty in believing any of this, but nevertheless agreed to meet Mr D at a later date. To test the man's credentials, Seers asked him if he could obtain the return of a letter on loan to the RAAF from the QFSRB. The letter was returned within forty-eight hours. 'Mr D was obviously of some standing in his own department,' related Seers. 'Further proof of this was the unlisted phone number he gave me for use in emergencies only: I recall how easy it was to remember – 22222.'

After conferring with other members of the QFSRB committee, Seers called the number and was promptly answered by a well-educated female voice who 'having enquired my name and business (all without answering my query regarding the "firm" she represented) swiftly put me through to friend D'. A further meeting was arranged, at which Seers informed Mr D that the committee had decided unanimously to co-operate with the ASIO. This provoked an angry response from Mr D, who was furious that the other committee members had been told, but, as Seers pointed out, at no time had he consented to the request for secrecy, having merely indicated that he required time to consider the proposal.

Seers informed Mr D that all UFO information would be made

available to his department on a reciprocal basis, and agreed to refrain from publicity. 'Needless to say,' said Seers, 'we had never at any time considered it to be any other than a one-way arrangement – in their direction only.' In the weeks that followed, Mr D personally interviewed all twelve members of the QFSRB committee, informing them that, with regard to the first meeting, Stan Seers had 'twisted the truth'.

Mr D subsequently attended numerous meetings of the QFSRB and became an ardent UFO enthusiast himself, remaining in close contact with the group for a total of eleven years before his death in 1970.[18] Colin Phillips, a committee member at the time, takes a less sinister view of Dudley Doherty's involvement than Stan Seers. He told me that, although Doherty attended the meetings in his professional capacity, the Australian Government was very sensitive about Communists in 1950–60, and 'people with new and different ideas who talked about peace, etc. were suspect. It was therefore quite natural that ASIO should send someone along to our meetings to keep an eye on us – I would not be very impressed with the operation of ASIO if they had not.'[19] Quite so. But in my view the ASIO would also have had an interest in monitoring those UFO reports that were not made available to it through military channels.

The Directorate of Scientific and Technical Intelligence

ASIO is not the only Australian Intelligence agency alleged to have been involved in studying the UFO problem. Bill Chalker confirms that a scientist attached to the Directorate of Scientific and Technical Intelligence, which was part of the Joint Intelligence Bureau, co-operated with other defence intelligence scientists in 1968–9 in organizing a proposal for a 'rapid-intervention team' to investigate those UFO incidents involving physical evidence. However, as a result of criticizing the Air Force's handling of UFO reports, he was denied access to them, and plans for the rapid-intervention team were shelved. The former JIB scientist affirmed that, although the Directorate of Air Force Intelligence files on UFOs are the most substantial, there are other such files held by the Department of Defence that are unlikely to see the light of day. This owes more, however, to the sensitive methods by which the reports were acquired than to the actual content.[20]

USAF Pilot's Sighting

Bill Chalker has found many interesting reports among the files released by the RAAF Directorate of Air Force Intelligence. On 15 November 1960,

This damaged and retouched photograph by a *Los Angeles Times* reporter shows searchlight beams converging on a mysterious aerial intruder over the Culver City area of Los Angeles early in the morning of 25 February 1942. The small blobs of light are bursts of anti-aircraft shells.

(*Los Angeles Times Photo*)

'The evidence is now so consistent and so overwhelming that no reasonably intelligent person can deny that something unexplained is going on in our atmosphere.' Admiral of the Fleet The Lord Hill-Norton. (*Author*)

'More than 10,000 sightings have been reported, the majority of which cannot be accounted for by any "scientific" explanation . . . I am convinced these objects do exist and that they are not manufactured by any nation on earth.' Air Chief Marshal Lord Dowding, Commander-in-Chief of RAF Fighter Command during the Battle of Britain, in 1954. (*Imperial War Museum*)

Left: James Salandin, the former Royal Auxiliary Air Force pilot who encountered three unknown aerial craft while flying a Meteor Mk 8 jet over Southend in October 1954. (*Author*)

Below: A Gloster Meteor Mk 8, of the type Salandin was flying when the incident occurred. (*James Salandin*)

Graham Sheppard at the controls of a Boeing 757. In 1967 Captain Sheppard had two radar-confirmed UFO sightings, witnessed from the flight deck of Vanguard airliners. (*Author*)

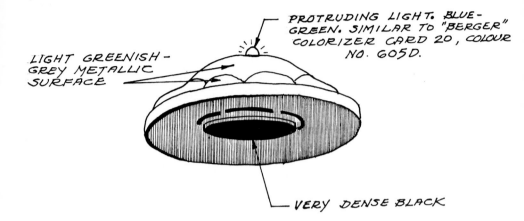

LIGHT GREENISH - GREY METALLIC SURFACE

PROTRUDING LIGHT. BLUE-GREEN. SIMILAR TO "BERGER" COLORIZER CARD 20, COLOUR NO. 605D.

VERY DENSE BLACK

The craft reported by a woman police constable and former Royal Observer Corps member at Isfield, near Lewes, Sussex, in 1977. (*Patricia Grant*)

RAF Rudloe Manor in Wiltshire where, according to information from several sources, secret investigations into the UFO phenomenon have been conducted for many years. (*Author*)

Right: Ralph Noyes, former head of the Ministry of Defence's Secretariat 8, which dealt with UFO reports from members of the public. While with DS8 Noyes was shown gun-camera films of UFOs taken by RAF pilots. (*Author*)

Below: Former US Airman Larry Warren, who witnessed some of the extraordinary events near RAF/USAF Woodbridge, Suffolk, in December 1980. Warren is shown at the site where a craft of unknown origin landed in full view of military personnel. (*Author*)

Denise Bishop, who was struck on the hand and immobilized by a beam of light from a UFO outside her home in Weston Mill, Plymouth, in September 1981. (*Author*)

The scar on Denise's hand, as it appeared the next day. (*Bob Boyd*)

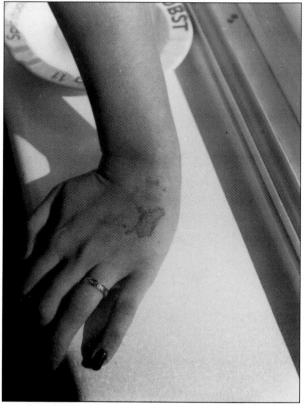

Alfred Burtoo near the site of his abduction by alien beings, beside the
Basingstoke Canal, Aldershot, in August 1983. The craft landed on the towpath
to the left of the canal, shown in the distant background. (*Author*)

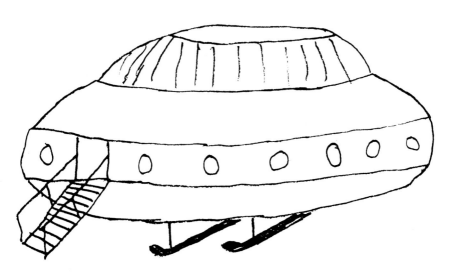

Sketch by Alfred Burtoo of the craft on which he was taken aboard.

'If, as the evidence suggests, structured craft of unknown origin routinely penetrate the UK Air Defence Region, then it seems to me that, at the very least, this must constitute a potential threat.' Nick Pope, UFO desk officer for the Ministry of Defence's Secretariat (Air Staff) 2a from 1991 to 1994. (*Author*)

A UFO photographed by a US Marine Air Group pilot over the North-east China Sea during the Korean War. While the sharply delineated straight line in the middle and the black lower half suggest photographic trickery, similar bizarre effects have been noted in other cases. (*W. Gordon Allen*)

Right: An unknown aerial craft projecting beams of light, photographed by a doctor on 23 March 1974, near Tavernes, Var, during a wave of sightings in France.

Below: 'If listeners could see for themselves the mass of reports coming in from the airborne gendarmerie, from the mobile gendarmerie, and from the gendarmerie charged with the job of conducting investigations . . . then they would see it is all pretty disturbing.' Robert Galley (right), French Minister of Defence, interviewed by Jean-Claude Bourret on France-Inter radio, in February 1974. (*Jacques Vainstain*)

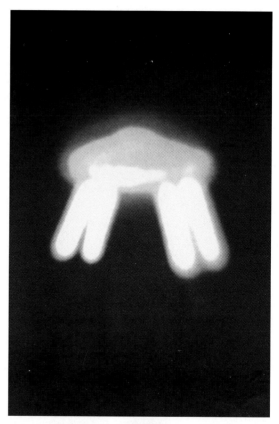

Left: Frederick Valentich, who disappeared with his aircraft after reporting an unknown aerial craft which hovered above him during a flight from Melbourne to Tasmania in October 1978. (*Guido Valentich*)

Right: An unknown aerial craft which was observed at close quarters by the pilots of two Portuguese Air Force training aircraft, north-west of Lisbon, on 2 November 1982. The object, about 2 metres in diameter, at one stage flew in wide circles around one of the planes at an estimated speed of over 2,500 k.p.h. (*Flying Saucer Review*)

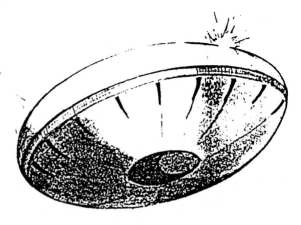

Dr Vannevar Bush, the presidential scientific adviser who in 1947 was appointed head of a top-secret group to investigate the retrievals of alien craft and bodies. (*Popperfoto*)

'The matter is the most highly classified subject in the United States Government, rating higher even than the H-bomb. Flying saucers exist.' Wilbert Smith, in a 1950 Top Secret Canadian Government memorandum. (*Van's Studio Ltd*)

Stephen Michalak, who encountered a landed craft of unknown origin near Falcon Lake, Manitoba, Canada, in May 1967. The burn marks on Michalak's body, seen when he was in hospital, match the 'ventilation or exhaust' on the craft, from which a blast of hot air struck and burnt him. (Photo: *Mary Evans Picture Library*; sketch: *Canadian UFO Report*)

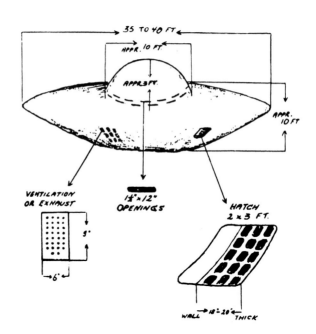

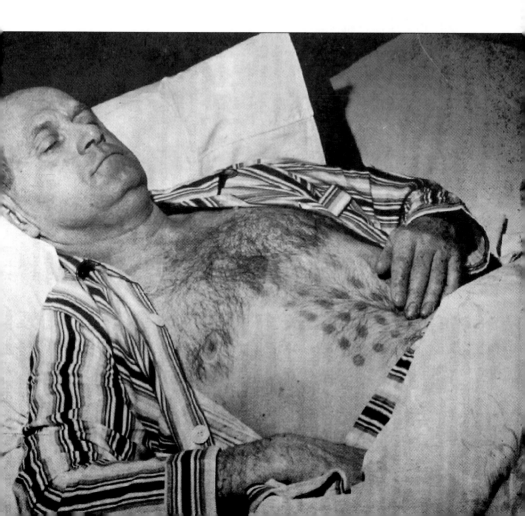

'Unidentified flying objects are a very serious subject which we must study fully. This is a serious challenge to science and we need the help of all Soviet citizens.' Professor Felix Zigel of the Moscow Aviation Institute, Moscow Central Television, November 1967. (*Henry Gris*)

Colonel Boris Sokolov, Soviet Air Force, who confirms that a huge state-funded UFO research project was initiated in 1977, lasting ten years and involving the co-operation of the Ministry of Defence and the USSR Academy of Sciences. (*Lawrence Moore*)

for example, about 50 kilometres from Cressy, Tasmania, a US Air Force RB-57 aircraft operating out of RAAF East Sale encountered a UFO, and the following is the pilot's official report:

> Approximately 1040 LCL while flying on a mission track 15 miles north of Launceston, my navigator called out an aircraft approaching to our left and slightly lower. Our altitude at this time was 40,000 feet, TAS of 350 knots, heading of 340 degrees.
>
> I spotted the object and immediately commented to [the navigator] that it was not an aircraft, but looked more like a balloon. We judged its altitude to be approximately 35,000 feet, heading 140 degrees and its speed extremely high.
>
> From a previous experience I would say its closing rate would have been in excess of 800 knots. We observed this object for five or seven seconds before it disappeared under the left wing.
>
> Since it was unusual in appearance, I immediately banked to the left for another look, but neither of us could locate it.
>
> The colour of the object was nearly translucent somewhat like that of a 'poached egg'. There were no sharp edges but rather fuzzy and undefined. The size was approximately 70 feet in diameter and it did not appear to have any depth.[21]

Official Controversy

In 1963 Senator J. L. Cavanagh asked that the Federal Government dossier on UFOs should be made public, but the Minister for Air refused, stating that no single dossier containing all the facts was available, and, although 3–4 per cent of sightings remained unexplained, the vast majority of reports could be explained in terms of balloons, aircraft, and astronomical objects.[22]

Others, however, were convinced that a cover-up was in operation, including Dr Harry Messel, Professor of Physics at Sydney University, who in 1965 reportedly stated: 'The facts about saucers were long tracked down and results have long been known in top secret defence circles of more countries than one. Whatever the truth, it might be regarded as inadvisable to give people at large no clue about the true nature of these things.'[23]

But is the cover-up due more to confusion in high places than to a deliberate policy to withhold sensational information? Two minute papers dating back to 1966 provide evidence against a cover-up. The first was part of a submission by the Directorate of Public Relations in the Department of Air to the Directorate of Air Force Intelligence, and argues for a change in RAAF policy. '. . . by continuing with the old policy of playing our UFO cards close to the chest,' the minute states, 'we only foster the incorrect (but nevertheless widely held) belief that we have much vital information to hide'. The other minute paper comments on the current RAAF files as follows: 'It would . . . appear that there is some need for rationalisation of our files on this subject. There are at least four different files which contain a confusion of policy, reported sightings and requests for information. Three of these files are classified, two of which are secret although there appears to be nothing in the files consistent with this classification.'[24]

These minutes would seem to argue against a deliberate cover-up policy, yet we should bear in mind that those who wrote the submission probably were not cleared for access to information about UFOs that had been classified as Top Secret or beyond (i.e. further compartmentalized). From my own investigations into the British Ministry of Defence's UFO investigations, I know that only relatively few people are cleared for access to the sort of information that is held in the highest security classifications, and I see no reason for believing that the official position in Australia is any different.

Ansett-ANA Sighting

At about 03.25 on 28 May 1965 an Ansett-ANA DC-6b airliner (registration VH-INH) was paced by an unidentified flying object during a flight from Brisbane to Port Moresby, New Guinea. Captain John Barker described the object as oblate in shape with exhaust gases emanating from it, and related that it paced the airliner for ten to fifteen minutes, witnessed by the co-pilot and a stewardess.

The sighting took place in the vicinity of Bougainville Reef, off the Queensland coast, and Captain Barker radioed details to Townsville Ground Control, adding that he was taking photographs of the object. On landing at Port Moresby, Barker was informed that he was not to have the film processed in New Guinea but was to return with it to Australia. When he eventually arrived at Brisbane, Barker was flown directly to Canberra, where both the film and the flight recorder were confiscated.

The source for this story is William Orr, duty officer of the Department of Civil Aviation at Townsville, who was in radio contact with Barker when he relayed details of the sighting. Orr passed on the information to John Meskell, a detective with the Criminal Investigation Branch who had been on duty at the Townsville Control Tower at the time. Meskell stated that Orr had been forbidden to discuss the incident, but added:

> This latter part is only hearsay and came from Orr [who] then told me that the Chief of DCA [Department of Civil Aviation] came to Townsville and took the twelve-hour tapes from the DCA Control Tower with the full conversation between Orr and the pilot, and Orr was told to 'shut his mouth' about the whole thing, under threat of his job.[25]

The Directorate of Air Force Intelligence in Canberra denied in a letter to Peter Norris that any such incident had taken place:

> This is the first information we have received of the reported sightings and therefore have no record of the incident. Perhaps you may care to follow the matter up with the Department of Civil Aviation, but as it is normal practice for that Department to refer all sightings to the RAAF it seems most unlikely that they had it reported.[26]

Peter Norris accordingly wrote to the DCA and received the following reply:

> . . . we asked our Brisbane office to check whether Air Traffic Control personnel at Townsville had any knowledge of the reported sightings on 28th May. No persons on duty that day have any recollection of unusual communications and we have not received any formal incident report by any Airline Captain operating in the vicinity of Townsville that day. Unfortunately, our communications recording tapes are re-used after a holding period of 90 days and we therefore cannot use this source to confirm belief that there were no unusual communications through Departmental facilities.[27]

According to Stan Seers, a former investigator for the USAF Project Blue Book UFO inquiry, Dr J. Allen Hynek, obtained a copy of Captain Barker's official statement to the Australian authorities from the US Air Force, via the Australian Department of Air;[28] it states in part: 'I had always scoffed at these reports, but I saw it. We all saw it. It was under intelligent control, and it was certainly no known aircraft.'[29]

There is no reference to this remarkable sighting in the RAAF *Summary of Unidentified Aerial Sightings Reported to the Department of Air (1960–1965)* – a revealing omission indeed.

US Air Force UFO Film

An example of a report that probably never found its way into the RAAF files, but purportedly ended up with the CIA, has been provided by the well-known researcher and author Budd Hopkins. A US Air Force sergeant with a Top Secret security clearance, known to Hopkins, states that at a CIA screening in Texas in 1967 he was shown a movie film of a UFO which had been taken from a RAAF aircraft during a photo-mapping flight over central Australia in about 1965. The short film extract allegedly showed 'a huge, hovering, windowed craft' with three smaller UFOs attached to it 'as a kind of tail'. A door on the largest object opened – two vertical panels and two horizontally aligned ones sliding apart – and the three smaller UFOs flew inside. The panels closed, the large object canted at an angle, then disappeared in seconds. According to Hopkins's informant, the filmed image of the UFOs was extraordinarily large and clear, filling the entire movie screen.[30]

Captain Cathie and the Defense Intelligence Agency

America's Defense Intelligence Agency showed considerable interest in the controversial theories of Captain Bruce Cathie, a New Zealand airline pilot who claims to have discovered evidence for a worldwide 'grid system' used by UFOs. Cathie's meetings with US defence attachés in Wellington, as well as his correspondence with them, are documented in a number of released DIA documents.

Cathie first approached the US Embassy in Wellington in the mid-1960s, since which time the DIA kept a file on him. The earliest documented memo is from Colonel John Burnett, US Air Attaché, to the Foreign Technology Division (FTD) at Wright-Patterson Air Force Base, dated 26 August 1965, which states in part: 'Captain Cathie visited with me for about one half hour. I observed this New Zealander to be not only rational but intelligent and convinced that certain UFOs he and others have seen are from outer space . . .'

The Foreign Technology Division responded by sending Colonel Burnett a brochure outlining the Air Force findings on UFOs, adding: 'Since no evidence exists that these objects represent interstellar travel there is no basis for Captain Cathie's beliefs.' Despite the FTD's evident scepticism, Burnett continued to send them details of Cathie's findings for at least another year. The reason for this is simply that Burnett, in company with US defence attachés worldwide, was 'task-ordered' by the DIA to collect and report on all UFO matters which came to his attention.

Bruce Cathie told me that it was Colonel Burnett who revealed that intensive research allegedly was carried out at Wright-Patterson AFB,[31] referred to in Cathie's second book. 'The scientific laboratory there, set up for the purpose, was described as a complex of buildings covering a large area and staffed by many of the world's top scientists,' claimed Cathie. 'Experimental work was carried out twenty-four hours a day, 365 days a year. At one stage the official [Burnett] asked me if I would consider a trip to America to visit the base. Naturally I said I would – any time they cared to put out an invitation. Perhaps the idea was vetoed in the States, for I heard no more of this.'[32]

By 1967 Colonel Burnett was relieved by Colonel Lewis Walker, who seems to have been less impressed with Cathie's theories than his predecessor, but, since he was formally bound by the DIA remit to collect all UFO-related information, Walker forwarded Cathie's material to the Pentagon. An Intelligence Information Report dated 8 February 1968 states:

Captain Cathie is still employed as an aircraft F-27 Friendship pilot by National Airways Corporation . . . His superiors know of his interest and activity in UFO's and his forthcoming book 'Harmonic 33'. He has been checked for security reasons and no adverse reports are known . . . He admits that many people consider him some kind of nut but he persists in his theory. On [deleted] January 1968 he came to my office and reported that four UFO's had been detected by the Auckland Air Traffic Control radarscope on [deleted] January 1968 at 2335 hours local time . . . Three objects were 15 miles apart in line, with the fourth object in line 30 miles behind the three. Relative speed was extremely high. In addition, two UFO's – disc-shaped – appeared east of Auckland Airport on the same track as first four. Captain Cathie was asked if official reports were submitted on these sightings, and he said no, that Civil Aviation personnel had been warned not to report any more of these observations. Captain Cathie was advised to submit any additional information that he might have . . .

By May 1968, however, Colonel Walker seems to have tired of Cathie. A report to the DIA dated 1 May indicates that, although Cathie was not considered a 'nut', on the last three occasions that he called at the Defense Attaché's office to discuss his latest findings, 'These conversations were ignored'. Cathie had complained that he had been put under surveillance and that in Invercargill in April he had been accosted by three Americans who had asked him to accompany them, which he refused to do. Cathie believed these men came from a US Navy ship, but according to Colonel Walker the only US ship that was south of Auckland at the time was the USS *Eltanin*, which was in the Antarctic. The report concludes:

> Capt. Cathie said that he had been cleared by the NZ government to pursue his research and that he had a letter to this effect signed by the Prime Minister. He stated that the Member of Parliament from his area, Dr. Findley, had interceded for him and obtained government approval for his work. He then asked the DATT [defense attaché] to 'call your agents off. I have official approval to continue my work. I don't want them tailing me'.
>
> The DATT made no reply to this request. This man is obsessed with his theory and no amount of argument can convince him that he has not stumbled on a highly complicated system which he says leads directly to the existence of UFOs.

I sent copies of these documents to Captain Cathie and asked him to comment. '[Walker] is only saying that in his opinion I am obsessed with my research,' he replied, 'and that there is no way they can talk me out of it. Which is fairly correct, except for the word obsessed. My research is my hobby and I find it most interesting. The evidence which I now have will prove without doubt that my unified equations are correct.'[33]

RAAF East Sale

Stan Deyo, a former US Air Force pilot, claims that in 1972, during a meeting with Dr Tom Keeble, Director of the Mechanical Engineering Division of the Department of Defence Aeronautical Research Laboratory in Melbourne, Keeble disclosed that the RAAF have extensive movie-film libraries of UFOs. Deyo claims that these films and other classified material on UFOs are kept at RAAF East Sale, Victoria.[34] I wrote to Dr Keeble to check the veracity of this story, but received no reply. Certainly, if such films exist in RAAF archives – and I am confident they do – East

Sale would be the logical repository, since it is a centre for military photographic interpretation.

Aircraft Communications Interference During Multiple UFO Sighting

A sighting by Captains Walter Gardin and Gordon Smith during a flight from Adelaide to Perth on 22 August 1968, involving temporary loss of communications between their aircraft and ground control, contains some striking parallels with the famous observation by Captain James Howard and his crew over Labrador, Newfoundland, in 1954 (see Chapter 10). The following report was made by the co-pilot, Captain Gordon W. Smith of Murchison Air Services/Southern Airlines of Western Australia. The aircraft, an eight-seat Piper Navajo, registration VH-RTO, was returning empty from Adelaide and cruising at 8,000 feet, with an air speed of 190–195 knots and tracking 270° magnetic, and Smith was asleep in the cabin when the sighting first occurred:

> At 0940 (1740 WST) Walter abruptly wakened me in great excitement and asked me to come into the cockpit quickly. I did so, and he asked me if I could see what he was looking at. At first I didn't because I was still suffering from the effect of sleep. However, after about thirty seconds I could see what he was excited about.
>
> Some distance ahead at the same level, and about 50° to my right (I was in the right seat), I saw a formation of aircraft. In the middle was a large aircraft, and formated to the right and left and above were four or five smaller aircraft. We were on a track of 270° and these aircraft appeared to be maintaining station with us.
>
> As we had not been notified of this traffic, I radioed Kalgoorlie DCA [Department of Civil Aviation] communications centre asking them what traffic they or RAAF had in our area. The answer was none. So I then notified Kalgoorlie that we had this formation in sight and they, in turn, notified some east-bound traffic of the danger of unidentified traffic 130 nautical miles east of Kalgoorlie.
>
> At about this time we lost communications with Kalgoorlie on all frequencies. We were receiving Kalgoorlie carrier wave with no voice propagation, only a hash and static. In the next ten minutes I transmitted about seven times and I believe Walter did about five times with no results.

Also at about this time we noticed that the main ship split into two sections still maintaining the same level, and the smaller aircraft then flew out left and right but staying in the same level and coming back to the two main halves of the bigger ship. At this time there appeared to be about six smaller aircraft taking turns of going out and coming back and formating on the two halves.

Sometimes the two halves joined and split, and the whole cycle continued for ten minutes. The shape of the main ship seemed to have the ability to change, not drastically, but from, say spheroid to a slightly elongated form with the colour maintaining a constant dark grey to black.

However, the smaller craft had a constant cigar shape and were of a very dark colour. Their travel out and back had a peculiarity not associated with normal aircraft in that they appeared to travel out and come back without actually turning like a normal aeroplane would have to do.

At 0950 GMT the whole formation joined together as if at a single command, then departed at a tremendous speed. It did not disappear as, say, gas would, but it departed in about three or four seconds diminishing in size till out of sight.

Captain Smith reported that radio communications were restored immediately following the departure of the UFOs (as in many other cases reported by pilots and others worldwide). Distance of the objects was impossible to estimate, since their size was unknown, but for comparative size the main craft compared with a Boeing 707 as seen from 10 miles away. Neither Gardin nor Smith 'had the presence of mind to check if any deviation existed in our magnetic compass or Automatic Direction Finder whilst in the presence of the UFOs', they said. Explanations in terms of balloons, conventional aircraft, tricks of light, gases, etc. were ruled out by the pilots. 'We conclude that the UFOs were in fact aircraft with the solidity of aircraft, except perhaps for the fact of the ability of the larger UFO to split and change shape slightly.'[35]

When the American atmospheric physicist Dr James McDonald attempted to make further enquiries about the incident, the pilots refused to respond. Years later, a pilot member of the Victorian UFO Research Society who was personally acquainted with Gardin and Smith confirmed that the pilots had been ordered not to discuss the encounter.[36]

Parliamentary Statement

On 20 October 1969 the Minister for Air, the Honourable F. M. Osborne, made a statement in Parliament summarizing the Defence Department's analysis of Unusual Aerial Sightings to date. He concluded: 'Nothing that has arisen from that 3 or 4 per cent of unexplained cases gives any firm support for the belief that interlopers from other places in this world or outside it have been visiting us.'[37]

Australia seems to have the lowest percentage of unexplained sightings in the world, if the Minister for Air and his department are to be taken at their word. Whatever the percentage, the highly detailed and convincing reports by qualified observers described in this chapter render official explanations totally invalid. It should be obvious to all but the most bone-headed sceptic that intelligently controlled objects are intruding into our airspace, even should their origin and agenda remain undetermined for now.

Incident at North West Cape

On 25 October 1973 two US Navy personnel observed a UFO hovering near the restricted US Naval Communication Station at North West Cape, Western Australia, which is used by the National Security Agency (in conjunction with Australia's Defence Signals Directorate). The Department of Defence (RAAF) report relating to the incident was acquired a few years later by Bill Chalker, who was surprised that such a report was made available to a civilian researcher.

At about 19.15 hours that day, Lieutenant Commander M (US Navy) sighted a 'large black, airborne object' approximately 8 kilometres to the west at an estimated altitude of 600 metres. 'After about 20–25 seconds the craft accelerated at unbelievable speed and disappeared to the north,' he reported. There was no noise or exhaust. The second witness, civilian Fire Captain Bill L, described the sighting as follows:

At 1920 hours, I was called by the [petty officer of the watch] to close the Officers' club. I proceeded towards the club in the Fire Department's pick-up 488, when my attention was drawn to a large black object, which at first I took to be a small cloud formation, due west of Area B [the location of the station's high-frequency transmitter] . . . On alighting from pick-up 488, I stood for several minutes and watched this black sphere hovering. The sky was clear and pale green-blue. No clouds were about whatsoever. The object was completely stationary except for a halo around the centre, which appeared to be either revolving or pulsating. After I had stood watching it for approx. 4 minutes, it suddenly took off at tremendous speed and disappeared in a northerly direction, in a few seconds. I consider this object to have been approx. 10 metres in diameter, hovering at 300 metres over the hills due west to the Base. It was black, maybe due to my looking in the direction of the setting sun. No lights appeared on it at any time.[38]

The Disappearance of Delta Sierra Juliet

Of all cases reported in Australia none has generated so much worldwide attention than that of Frederick Valentich, a twenty-year-old flying instructor who disappeared in his Cessna 182 aircraft shortly after reporting a UFO sighting over the Bass Strait near Cape Otway, on a flight from Moorabbin, Victoria, to King Island, Tasmania, on 21 October 1978.

Forty-seven minutes after taking off from Moorabbin Airport, Melbourne, at 18.19 hours, Valentich reported sighting an unidentified aircraft to the Melbourne Flight Service Unit controller, Steve Robey. The official transcript of the recorded transmissions between the Cessna (registration VH-DSJ) and Melbourne Flight Service Unit (FSU) has been provided for me by Bill Chalker. The following communications between the aircraft and Melbourne FSU were recorded from 19.06 hours. The word/words in brackets are open to other interpretations:

TIME	FROM	TEXT
1906:14	VH-DSJ	MELBOURNE this is DELTA SIERRA JULIET is there any known traffic below five thousand
:23	FSU	DELTA SIERRA JULIET no known traffic
:26	VH-DSJ	DELTA SIERRA JULIET I am seems (to) be a large aircraft below five thousand
:46	FSU	D D DELTA SIERRA JULIET what type of aircraft is it
:50	VH-DSJ	DELTA SIERRA JULIET I cannot affirm it is four bright it seems to me like landing lights
1907:04	FSU	DELTA SIERRA JULIET
:32	VH-DSJ	MELBOURNE this (is) DELTA SIERRA JULIET the aircraft has just passed over me at least a thousand feet above
:43	FSU	DELTA SIERRA JULIET roger and it is a large aircraft confirm
:47	VH-DSJ	er unknown due to the speed it's traveling is there any air force aircraft in the vicinity

:57	FSU	DELTA SIERRA JULIET no known aircraft in the vicinity
1908:18	VH-DSJ	MELBOURNE it's approaching now from due east towards me
:28	FSU	DELTA SIERRA JULIET
:42		// open microphone for two seconds //
:49	VH-DSJ	DELTA SIERRA JULIET it seems to me that he's playing some sort of game he's flying over me two to three times at a time at speeds I could not identify
1909:02	FSU	DELTA SIERRA JULIET roger what is your actual level
:06	VH-DSJ	my level is four and a half thousand four five zero zero
:11	FSU	DELTA SIERRA JULIET and confirm that you cannot identify the aircraft
:14	VH-DSJ	affirmative
:18	FSU	DELTA SIERRA JULIET roger standby
:28	VH-DSJ	MELBOURNE DELTA SIERRA JULIET it's not an aircraft it is // open microphone for two seconds //
:46	FSU	DELTA SIERRA JULIET can you describe the er aircraft
:52	VH-DSJ	DELTA SIERRA JULIET as it's flying past it's a long shape // open microphone for three seconds // (cannot) identify more than (that it has such speed) // open microphone for three seconds // before me right now Melbourne
1910:07	FSU	DELTA SIERRA JULIET roger and how large would the er object be
:20	VH-DSJ	DELTA SIERRA JULIET MELBOURNE it seems like it's stationary what I'm doing right now is orbiting and the thing is just orbiting on top of me also it's got a green light and sort of metallic (like) it's all shiny (on) the outside
:43	FSU	DELTA SIERRA JULIET
:48	VH-DSJ	DELTA SIERRA JULIET // open microphone for five seconds // it's just vanished
:57	FSU	DELTA SIERRA JULIET
1911:03	VH-DSJ	MELBOURNE would you know what kind of aircraft I've got is it (a type) military aircraft
:08	FSU	DELTA SIERRA JULIET confirm the er aircraft just vanished
:14	VH-DSJ	say again
:17	FSU	DELTA SIERRA JULIET is the aircraft still with you
:23	VH-DSJ	DELTA SIERRA JULIET (it's ah nor) // open microphone for two seconds // (now) approaching from the southwest
:37	FSU	DELTA SIERRA JULIET
:52	VH-DSJ	DELTA SIERRA JULIET the engine is rough idling I've got it set at twenty three twenty four and the thing is (coughing)
1912:04	FSU	DELTA SIERRA JULIET roger what are your intentions
:09	VH-DSJ	my intentions are ah to go to King Island ah Melbourne that strange aircraft is hovering on top of me again // two seconds open microphone // it is hovering and it's not an aircraft
:22	FSU	DELTA SIERRA JULIET
:28	VH-DSJ	DELTA SIERRA JULIET MELBOURNE // 17 seconds open

microphone //
:49   FSU   DELTA SIERRA JULIET MELBOURNE

There is no record of any further transmissions from the aircraft.
   The weather in the Cape Otway area was clear with a trace of
stratocumulus cloud at 5000 to 7000 feet, scattered cirrus cloud at 30,000 feet,
excellent visibility and light winds. The end of daylight at Cape Otway was at
1918 hours.
   The Alert Phase of SAR [Search and Rescue] procedures was declared at
1912 hours and, at 1933 hours when the aircraft did not arrive at King Island,
the Distress Phase was declared and search action commenced. An intensive
air, sea and land search was continued until 25 October 1978, but no trace of
the aircraft was found.[39]

The search and rescue operation was headed by an RAAF Lockheed
P-3 Orion maritime reconnaissance aircraft assisted by some light aircraft.
Although an oil slick was found about 18 miles north of King Island on 22
October, it was not established as having any connection with Valentich's
plane. The Cessna was equipped with a radio survival beacon, but nothing
was heard from it.[40]

Paul Norman learned that pilots were requested to report sightings of
UFOs and lights in the sky, and those who were flying at the same time
and using the same radio frequency were instructed not to divulge any
details of their communications. Attempts were made to make it look as
though Valentich's plane was not in the location that he reported.[41]

One month later the outline of a submerged aircraft was allegedly
sighted about 48 miles north of King Island by the pilot of a Cessna 337
from Hawk Flying Service, who was unable to confirm the observation on
a second pass over the area. Aviation officials apparently dismissed the
sighting because the seas were too rough and the water too deep for
anything to have been seen on the seabed from the air.

Steve Robey, the Melbourne Flight Service Unit controller, was
absolutely convinced that Valentich was not perpetrating a hoax. 'Towards
the end I think he was definitely concerned for his safety,' he said. 'I
considered that he would have had to have been a good actor to have put it
all together the way he did . . . It was a kind of rushed communication . . .
as if he was startled.'[42]

The Tape

Frederick Valentich's father, Guido, told me that he was given a copy of
the recorded communications of his son by the Department of Transport,
with Robey's voice deleted.[43] Bill Chalker has heard part of the complete

COMMONWEALTH OF AUSTRALIA DEPARTMENT OF TRANSPORT	Reference No.
AIRCRAFT ACCIDENT INVESTIGATION SUMMARY REPORT	V116/783/1047

Publication of this report is authorised by the Secretary under the provisions of Air Navigation Regulations 283 (1)

1. LOCATION OF OCCURRENCE

	Height a.m.s.l.	Date	Time (Local)	Zone
Not known	-	21.10.78	Not known	EST

2. THE AIRCRAFT

Make and Model	Registration	Certificate of Airworthiness
Cessna 182L	VH-DSJ	Valid from 14 February 1968

Certificate of Registration issued to	Operator	Degree of damage to aircraft
Cephus Day, 33 Reserve Road, Beaumauris. Victoria	SAS Southern Air Services, Northern Avenue, Moorabbin Airport, Victoria	Not known
		Other property damaged —

Defects discovered

—

3. THE FLIGHT

Last or intended departure point	Time of departure	Next point of intended landing	Purpose of flight	Class of operation
Moorabbin	1819 hours	King Island	Travel	Private

4. THE CREW

Name	Status	Age	Class of licence	Hours on type	Total hours	Degree of injury
Frederick VALENTICH	Pilot	20	Private	Not known	150 (Approx.)	Presumed Fatal

5. OTHER PERSONS (All passengers and persons injured on ground)

Name	Status	Degree of injury	Name	Status	Degree of injury

6. RELEVANT EVENTS

The pilot obtained a Class Four instrument rating on 11 May 1978 and he was therefore authorised to operate at night in visual meteorological conditions (VMC). On the afternoon of 21 October 1978 he attended the Moorabbin Briefing Office, obtained a meteorological briefing and, at 1723 hours, submitted a flight plan for a night VMC flight from Moorabbin to King Island and return. The cruising altitude nominated in the flight plan was below 5000 feet, with estimated time intervals of 41 minutes to Cape Otway and 28 minutes from Cape Otway to King Island. The total fuel endurance was shown as 300 minutes. The pilot made no arrangements for aerodrome lighting to be illuminated for his arrival at King Island. He advised the briefing officer and the operator's representative that he was uplifting friends at King Island and took four life jackets in the aircraft with him.

The aircraft was refuelled to capacity at 1810 hours and departed Moorabbin at 1819 hours. After departure the pilot established two-way radio communications with Melbourne Flight Service Unit (FSU).

The pilot reported Cape Otway at 1900 hours and the next transmission received from the aircraft was at 1906:14 hours. The following communications between the aircraft and Melbourne FSU were recorded from this time: (Note: The word/words in brackets are open to other interpretations.)

TIME	FROM	TEXT
1906:14	VH-DSJ	MELBOURNE this is DELTA SIERRA JULIET is there any known traffic below five thousand
:23	FSU	DELTA SIERRA JULIET no known traffic
:26	VH-DSJ	DELTA SIERRA JULIET I am seems (to) be a large aircraft below five thousand

The official report on the case of Frederick Valentich, who disappeared with his aircraft after reporting an unknown aerial craft which hovered above him during a flight in October 1978.

(Australian Department of Transport)

RELEVANT EVENTS (cont'd)

TIME	FROM	TEXT
:46	FSU	D D DELTA SIERRA JULIET what type of aircraft is it
:50	VH-DSJ	DELTA SIERRA JULIET I cannot affirm it is four bright it seems to me like landing lights
1907:04	FSU	DELTA SIERRA JULIET
:32	VH-DSJ	MELBOURNE this (is) DELTA SIERRA JULIET the aircraft has just passed over over me at least a thousand feet above
:43	FSU	DELTA SIERRA JULIET roger and it it is a large aircraft confirm
:47	VH-DSJ	er unknown due to the speed it's travelling is there any airforce aircraft in the vicinity
:57	FSU	DELTA SIERRA JULIET no known aircraft in the vicinity
1908:18	VH-DSJ	MELBOURNE it's approaching now from due east towards me
:28	FSU	DELTA SIERRA JULIET
:42		// open microphone for two seconds //
:49	VH-DSJ	DELTA SIERRA JULIET it seems to me that he's playing some sort of game he's flying over me two three times at a time at speeds I could not identify
1909:02	FSU	DELTA SIERRA JULIET roger what is your actual level
:06	VH-DSJ	my level is four and a half thousand four five zero zero
:11	FSU	DELTA SIERRA JULIET and confirm you cannot identify the aircraft
:14	VH-DSJ	affirmative
:18	FSU	DELTA SIERRA JULIET roger standby
:28	VH-DSJ	MELBOURNE DELTA SIERRA JULIET it's not an aircraft it is // open microphone for two seconds //
:46	FSU	DELTA SIERRA JULIET MELBOURNE can you describe the er aircraft
1909:52	VH-DSJ	DELTA SIERRA JULIET as it's flying past it's a long shape // open microphone for three seconds // (cannot) identify more than (that it has such speed) // open microphone for 3 seconds // before me right now Melbourne
1910:07	FSU	DELTA SIERRA JULIET roger and how large would the er object be
:20	VH-DSJ	DELTA SIERRA JULIET MELBOURNE it seems like it's stationary what I'm doing right now is orbiting and the thing is just orbiting on top of me also it's got a green light and sort of metallic (like) it's all shiny (on) the outside
:43	FSU	DELTA SIERRA JULIET

RELEVANT EVENTS (cont'd)

TIME	FROM	TEXT
:48	VH-DSJ	DELTA SIERRA JULIET // open microphone for 5 seconds // it's just vanished
:57	FSU	DELTA SIERRA JULIET
1911:03	VH-DSJ	MELBOURNE would you know what kind of aircraft I've got is it (a type) military aircraft
:08	FSU	DELTA SIERRA JULIET confirm the er aircraft just vanished
:14	VH-DSJ	SAY AGAIN
:17	FSU	DELTA SIERRA JULIET is the aircraft still with you
:23	VH-DSJ	DELTA SIERRA JULIET (it's ah nor) // open microphone 2 seconds // (now) approaching from the southwest
:37	FSU	DELTA SIERRA JULIET
:52	VH-DSJ	DELTA SIERRA JULIET the engine is is rough idling I've got it set at twenty three twenty four and the thing is (coughing)
1912:04	FSU	DELTA SIERRA JULIET roger what are your intentions
:09	VH-DSJ	my intentions are ah to go to King Island ah Melbourne that strange aircraft is hovering on top of me again // two seconds open microphone // it is hovering and it's not an aircraft
:22	FSU	DELTA SIERRA JULIET
:28	VH-DSJ	DELTA SIERRA JULIET MELBOURNE // 17 seconds open microphone //
:49	FSU	DELTA SIERRA JULIET MELBOURNE

There is no record of any further transmissions from the aircraft.

The weather in the Cape Otway area was clear with a trace of stratocumulus cloud at 5000 to 7000 feet, scattered cirrus cloud at 30000 feet, excellent visibility and light winds. The end of daylight at Cape Otway was at 1918 hours.

The Alert Phase of SAR procedures was declared at 1912 hours and, at 1933 hours when the aircraft did not arrive at King Island, the Distress Phase was declared and search action was commenced. An intensive air, sea and land search was continued until 25 October 1978, but no trace of the aircraft was found.

7. OPINION AS TO CAUSE

The reason for the disappearance of the aircraft has not been determined.

Approved for publication	*(signature)*	(A. R. Woodward) Delegate of the Secretary	Date 27.4.1982

tape which is in the possession of Dr Richard Haines, a former NASA-contracted research scientist.[44] Haines's preliminary findings concluded that a strange seventeen-second burst of metallic noise which followed Valentich's last transmission contained '36 separate bursts with fairly constant start and stop pulses bounding each one: there are no discernible patterns in time or frequency'. The effect, Haines said, was similar to rapid keying of the microphone, but control tests were noticeably different from the original sound.[45] Further findings by Dr Haines are published in his definitive work, *Melbourne Episode: Case Study of a Missing Pilot*.[46]

As to the original tape, Chalker told me that the Department of Aviation erased it, or so he was informed by the Assistant Secretary of Air Safety Investigation, A. R. Woodward, who also claimed that no more copies existed.

The Official Verdict

In May 1982 the Bureau of Air Safety Investigation (Australian Department of Aviation) released its official findings 'to parties having a bona fide interest in the occurrence'. The Aircraft Accident Investigation Summary Report concludes:

Location of occurrence:	Not known
Time:	Not known
Degree of injury:	Presumed fatal
Opinion as to cause:	The reason for the disappearance of the aircraft has not been determined.

Bill Chalker was highly dissatisfied with this conclusion. He tried to extract further information from G. V. Hughes, then Assistant Secretary of Air Safety Investigation. Chalker asked if there had been any further official investigation of a possible UFO connection with the disappearance. Hughes replied: 'The RAAF is responsible for the investigation of reports concerning "UFO" sightings, and liaison was established with the RAAF on these aspects of the investigation. The decision as to whether or not the "UFO" report is to be investigated rests with the RAAF and not this Department.'

In 1982 Chalker was given officially sanctioned direct access to the RAAF UFO files, held by the Directorate of Air Force Intelligence in Canberra, but the file on the Valentich case was conspicuous by its absence. 'The Intelligence Liaison Officer explained to me that the RAAF did not investigate the affair because they were not asked to by the Department of Aviation!' said Chalker. The RAAF saw the report as more appropriately in the domain of an air accident/safety inquiry, he was told.

In November 1982 Chalker was finally given permission to examine the Department of Aviation UFO files in Melbourne, but specifically was denied access to the Valentich file(s) on the grounds that they were air accident investigation files and not UFO files. Mr G. V. Hughes explained the reason for this:

> The file concerning this occurrence is no more or less restricted than any other accident investigation file. As a signatory to the International Convention on Civil Aviation, we subscribe to the Standards and Recommended Practices contained in Annex 13 to the Convention, in respect of aircraft accident investigation specifically, when it is considered that the disclosure of records, for purposes other than accident prevention, might have an adverse effect on the availability of information in that or any future investigation, such records are considered privileged.[47]

The Cessna Found?

In December 1982 Ron Cameron, an independent film producer working on a documentary about the Valentich case, told Bill Chalker that two divers had told him they had located the missing Cessna on the seabed off Cape Otway. The divers claimed to have taken sixteen photographs of the plane, and offered them to Cameron (together with details of the plane's position) for $10,000. Cameron understandably refused the offer in the absence of verification, but the divers did show him five photographs purporting to show the Cessna – mostly intact, and with the correct registration marks. There was no body inside the aircraft, he was told.

A salvage operation was considered, involving the Department of Aviation, but the latter dropped the idea on the grounds that it would lead to unwelcome publicity. Cameron then lost track of the divers, one of whom supposedly joined the US Coast Guard in California. In 1983 he was still considering the possibility of a salvage operation, but nothing further seems to have been done, and the claim is regarded as dubious.[48]

What Happened to Valentich?

Many guesses have been advanced to account for the mysterious disappearance of Delta Sierra Juliet and its young pilot – some feasible, others bizarre. Had Valentich staged the whole incident, for example? There is no evidence at all for this, other than an unsubstantiated rumour that he was seen alive and well and working at a petrol service station in Tasmania.[49] Valentich had good reasons for completing the flight: to log up more night-flying experience, to pick up some crayfish in Tasmania for the officers of the Air Training Corps (of which he was an instructor), and to join his family and friends in a reunion back in Melbourne at 22.00 that night. Also we have the testimony of Steve Robey, the Flight Service Unit controller, who was convinced by the tone of Valentich's voice that he was genuinely alarmed.

Guido Valentich told me that his son was a keen student of the UFO subject from the age of fifteen. 'As he grew older and joined the Air Training Corps and going to various RAAF bases, he became more and more convinced of UFO existence and in other words he also convinced us . . . that he would like perhaps to come to a closer encounter.' Guido added that his son had learned a lot about the subject from the RAAF. 'I learned that he met a few Air Force pilots, especially last time when he was at one base for fifteen days in August–September 1978, when he came home more positive than ever on UFO existence.' Had the RAAF or the Government given Guido any explanation as to what had actually happened to his son? I asked. 'No. The Department of Transport gave me a briefing on the search and how it was conducted for four days after my son went missing, and that was all,' he said. 'I have asked for the result of the analysis of the tape (air to ground) but they have not been able to give me any satisfactory answer of any kind.'

Unofficially, the chief co-ordinator of the search and rescue team, Mr Eddie, told Guido Valentich that he thought the Cessna had simply ditched in the water and disappeared within a minute, taking the pilot with it. As Guido pointed out, however, the Cessna 182 is constructed of modular units which should have floated on impact for some period of time. Secondly, VHF radio transmissions from an altitude below 1,000 feet should not normally be receivable 90 miles from the aircraft's position, but Valentich's communications with the Flight Service Unit at Melbourne were loud and clear to the last word, as was the seventeen-second burst of 'metallic' noise which followed. This presupposes that he was still at or above 1,000 feet, and Guido is convinced that his son was still at 4,500 feet when contact was lost.[50] (In principle, the radio horizon for any line-of-sight radio transmitter located above the Earth's surface generally is given by the square root of twice the altitude of the transmitter. Accordingly and in theory then, the Cessna would have been at an altitude of above 1,130 feet at the time of transmission.)

Sightings on the Same Day

Many people reported seeing UFOs on the same day and during the night of Valentich's disappearance, and fifteen of these reports have survived rigorous investigation, according to Bill Chalker. These sightings all took place between midday and 21.00; six were in Victoria, one on King Island, and the rest further afield. Roy Manifold, who was vacationing at Crayfish Bay, Cape Otway, inadvertently took two photographs of peculiar objects just twenty minutes before Valentich reported his sighting. Of Manifold's six photos of the sunset, the fourth shows a 'dense black lump' apparently stirring up the sea, while the sixth shows a strange mass situated in the sky directly above the anomaly in the fourth picture, taken some forty seconds earlier, which appears to show an object accompanied by a trail of small, bright blue shapes.

Film faults and processing defects were ruled out by Kodak. The RAAF dismissed the sixth photo as showing nothing more than a cumulus cloud breaking up, but, as Bill Chalker argues, this would require the cloud to have suddenly moved into a view at over 200 m.p.h., since it does not appear in any of the other frames.[51]

In 1990 Paul Norman spoke to a man who, together with three other witnesses, claims to have seen an unusual green light flying just above an aircraft at the time of the incident (Valentich's aircraft was the only one in the area). The observations took place from a hill 2 kilometres west of Apollo Bay (Cape Otway). 'One of the ladies noted a green light to the south-west and called to the others to look,' Norman reports. 'Her uncle looked up and saw the lights of an aircraft and thought she was referring to those lights. She said, "No, look above the aircraft." The uncle then saw the green light flying above. He estimated both the aircraft and the green light were about ten to twelve miles distant.' The witnesses were reluctant to report the sighting at the time for fear of ridicule.[52]

We may never know exactly what happened to Frederick Valentich, but the evidence strongly suggests that he encountered an unidentified aerial object which was in some way responsible for his disappearance. If so, the Australian Government would have a good reason for playing down the incident – and the UFO subject in general.

On 2 May 1984 the RAAF curtailed its lengthy public association with the UFO controversy when the Minister of Defence, Gordon Scholes, stated: 'The vast majority of reports submitted by the public have proved not to have a national security significance.'[53] This is obviously the case. But what about the small residue of unexplained sightings by the public, to say nothing of military reports? It is self-evident that these are of enormous significance, and clearly affect national security. Yet the public must not be told the truth.

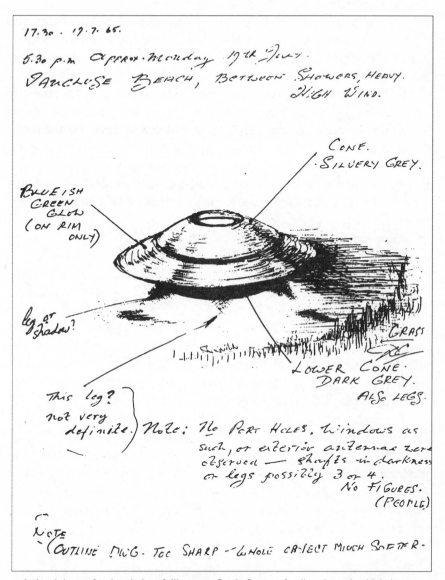

A sketch by professional aircraft illustrator Denis Crowe of a disc-shaped vehicle he saw taking off from Vaucluse Beach, Sydney, on 19 July 1965. (*Denis Crowe*)

Canada

'. . . THE MATTER IS the most highly classified subject in the United States Government, rating higher even than the H-bomb . . . Flying Saucers exist . . . Their modus operandi is unknown but concentrated effort is being made by a small group headed by Doctor Vannevar Bush . . . The entire matter is considered by the United States authorities to be of tremendous significance.'

These sensational comments are included in one of the most important official documents on UFOs ever to be released (see pp. 181–3): a hitherto Top Secret memorandum by Wilbert Brockhouse Smith, a former senior radio engineer who worked on secret defence projects for the Canadian Government's Department of Transport, and who held a master's degree in electrical engineering and several patents. Smith had obtained this information by making 'discreet enquiries through the Canadian Embassy staff in Washington', who were able to put him in touch with Dr Robert Sarbacher, an American scientist and former consultant to the US Research and Development Board.

The memo, dated 21 November 1950, was sent to the Controller of Telecommunications, and recommended that a research project be set up to study the subject. 'We believe that we are on the track of something which may well prove to be the introduction of a new technology,' Smith wrote. 'The existence of a different technology is borne out by the investigations which are being carried on at the present time in relation to flying saucers.'

Project Magnet

The Department of Transport was not slow in accepting Smith's recommendation, and on 2 December 1950 Project Magnet was established by Commander C. P. Edwards, then Deputy Minister of Transport for Air Services. Smith was appointed Engineer-in-Charge, with another two engineers and two technicians working part-time. The

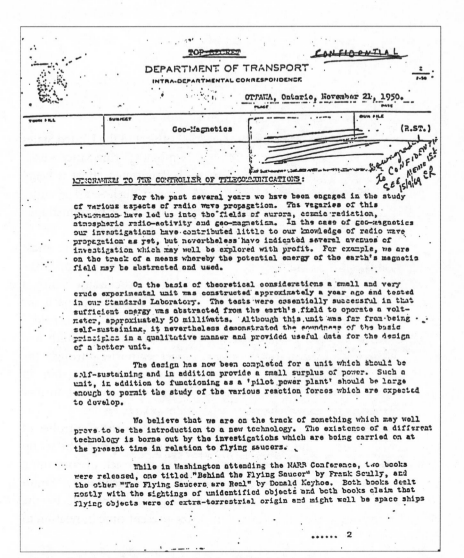

TOP ~~SECRET~~   ~~CONFIDENTIAL~~

DEPARTMENT OF TRANSPORT
INTRA-DEPARTMENTAL CORRESPONDENCE

OTTAWA, Ontario, November 21, 1950.

YOUR FILE	SUBJECT		OUR FILE
	Geo-Magnetics		(R.ST.)

MEMORANDUM TO THE CONTROLLER OF TELECOMMUNICATIONS:

For the past several years we have been engaged in the study of various aspects of radio wave propagation. The vagaries of this phenomenon have led us into the fields of aurora, cosmic radiation, atmospheric radio-activity and geo-magnetism. In the case of geo-magnetics our investigations have contributed little to our knowledge of radio wave propagation as yet, but nevertheless have indicated several avenues of investigation which may well be explored with profit. For example, we are on the track of a means whereby the potential energy of the earth's magnetic field may be abstracted and used.

On the basis of theoretical considerations a small and very crude experimental unit was constructed approximately a year ago and tested in our Standards Laboratory. The tests were essentially successful in that sufficient energy was abstracted from the earth's field to operate a volt-meter, approximately 50 millivolts. Although this unit was far from being self-sustaining, it nevertheless demonstrated the soundness of the basic principles in a qualitative manner and provided useful data for the design of a better unit.

The design has now been completed for a unit which should be self-sustaining and in addition provide a small surplus of power. Such a unit, in addition to functioning as a 'pilot power plant' should be large enough to permit the study of the various reaction forces which are expected to develop.

We believe that we are on the track of something which may well prove to be the introduction to a new technology. The existence of a different technology is borne out by the investigations which are being carried on at the present time in relation to flying saucers.

While in Washington attending the NARB Conference, two books were released, one titled "Behind the Flying Saucer" by Frank Scully, and the other "The Flying Saucers are Real" by Donald Keyhoe. Both books dealt mostly with the sightings of unidentified objects and both books claim that flying objects were of extra-terrestrial origin and might well be space ships

...... 2

A previously Top Secret memorandum from Wilbert Smith of the Canadian Government's Department of Transport, 1950, in which 'flying saucers' are revealed to be 'the most highly classified matter in the United States Government, rating higher even than the H-bomb'.
(*Department of Transport, Canada*)

from another planet. Scully claimed that the preliminary studies of
one saucer which fell into the hands of the United States Government
indicated that they operated on some hitherto unknown magnetic
principles. It appeared to me that our own work in geo-magnetics
might well be the linkage between our technology and the technology
by which the saucers are designed and operated. If it is assumed that
our geo-magnetic investigations are in the right direction, the theory
of operation of the saucers becomes quite straightforward, with all
observed features explained qualitatively and quantitatively.

I made discreet enquiries through the Canadian Embassy
staff in Washington who were able to obtain for me the following
information:

a. The matter is the most highly classified subject in the United
   States Government, rating higher even than the H-bomb.

b. Flying saucers exist.

c. Their modus operandi is unknown but concentrated effort is being
   made by a small group headed by Doctor Vannevar Bush.

d. The entire matter is considered by the United States authorities
   to be of tremendous significance.

I was further informed that the United States authorities are investigating
along quite a number of lines which might possibly be related to the saucers
such as mental phenomena and I gather that they are not doing too well since
they indicated that if Canada is doing anything at all in geo-magnetics they
would welcome a discussion with suitably accredited Canadians.

While I am not yet in a position to say that we have solved
even the first problems in geo-magnetic energy release, I feel that the
correlation between our basic theory and the available information on
saucers checks too closely to be mere coincidence. It is my honest opinion
that we are on the right track and are fairly close to at least some of the
answers.

Mr. Wright, Defence Research Board liaison officer at the
Canadian Embassy in Washington, was extremely anxious for me to get in touch
with Doctor Solandt, Chairman of the Defence Research Board, to discuss with
him future investigations along the line of geo-magnetic energy release.

.... 3

- 3 -

I do not feel that we have as yet sufficient data to place before Defence Research Board which would enable a program to be initiated within that organization, but I do feel that further research is necessary and I would prefer to see it done within the frame work of our own organization with, of course, full co-operation and exchange of information with other interested bodies.

I discussed this matter fully with Doctor Solandt, Chairman of Defence Research Board, on November 20th and placed before him as much information as I have been able to gather to date. Doctor Solandt agreed that work on geo-magnetic energy should go forward as rapidly as possible and offered full co-operation of his Board in providing laboratory facilities, acquisition of necessary items of equipment, and specialized personnel for incidental work in the project. I indicated to Doctor Solandt that we would prefer to keep the project within the Department of Transport for the time being until we have obtained sufficient information to permit a complete assessment of the value of the work.

It is therefore recommended that a PROJECT be set up within the frame work of this Section to study this problem and that the work be carried on a part time basis until such time as sufficient tangible results can be seen to warrant more definitive action. Cost of the program in its initial stages are expected to be less than a few hundred dollars and can be carried by our Radio Standards Lab appropriation.

Attached hereto is a draft of terms of reference for such a project which, if authorized, will enable us to proceed with this research work within our own organization.

(W.B. Smith)
Senior Radio Engineer

WBS/cc

broadcast and measurement section of the Telecommunications Division was given a directive to carry out the project with whatever assistance could be obtained from sources such as the Defence Research Board and the National Research Council. Dr O. M. Solandt, Chairman of the Defence Research Board, offered his full co-operation.[1]

The Canadian Government has continually tried to play down the work of Wilbert Smith and Project Magnet. In 1964, for example, the Department of Transport informed an enquirer:

> . . . we would reiterate that at no time has this Department carried out research into the field of unidentified flying objects. As stated by Mr. Depuis in Hansard on December 4, 1963, a small program of investigation in the field of geomagnetics was carried out by the Telecommunications Division of this Department between 1950 and 1954. This minor investigation was for the purpose of studying magnetic phenomena, particularly those phenomena resulting from unusual boundary conditions in the basic electro-magnetic theory . . . This personal project was at no expense to the Department, nor did it have any Departmental sponsorship.[2]

That the Government was being less than honest has now been established with the release of official Project Magnet documents, obtained by Arthur Bray, a former RCAF and Navy pilot. One of these is the *Summary of Sightings Reported to and Analysed by Department of Transport During 1952*, containing twenty-five UFO reports, from which I would like to cite two sightings by qualified observers. The first took place at Halifax, Nova Scotia:

> On June 15 at 8.32 a.m., A.S.T., a meteorological assistant on reserve army manoeuvers, noticed what seemed to be a large silver disc in the sky south-east of Halifax. It moved south-west for about 30 seconds at an estimated altitude of 5,000 to 8,000 feet and then ascended vertically and in 2 to 5 seconds merged in altocumulus clouds at 11,000 to 12,000 feet. If the altitude estimates are correct, from the bearing and elevation data obtained from this observer, the diameter of the disc works out at about 100 feet. A large standard aircraft was in the sky at the time and the object seemed to move much more rapidly than the plane. The object's speed was estimated to be at least 800 miles per hour.[3]

TOP SECRET

Mr. Edwards should write to the Dept of National Defence Ottawa

requesting that clearance may be obtained for Mr. W. B. Smith to visit

the appropiate Service in the United States to discuss the use of
terrestial magnetic forces in relation to . . . aerodynamic problems
associated with saucer shaped objects .

In the covering request, the Department of Transport should relate in as

much detail as possible the objects of this study and also detail the

work which has been carried out in the geophysical field in Canada.

Information unofficial- obtained from Dr. Robert I Sarbacher , dean of

the Graduate school, Georgia University.

A Top Secret memorandum relating to the information acquired by Wilbert Smith from Dr
Robert Sarbacher. (*Department of Transport, Canada*)

The second sighting occurred at MacDonald Airport, Manitoba, on 27 August 1952:

> A disc-shaped object with shadows on it as if it had an irregular surface was seen by two meteorological officers at 4.45 a.m., C.S.T. at MacDonald Airport. The object made two turns about the field and when struck by the light from the rotating beacon made off toward the north-east and was out of sight within a second. There was no sound whatsoever. The object glinted like shiny aluminium when the beacon light struck it.[4]

In an interim report on Project Magnet dated 25 June 1952, Wilbert Smith stated:

> If, as appears evident, the Flying Saucers are emissaries from some other civilization, and actually do operate on magnetic principles, we have before us the Fact that we have missed something in magnetic theory but have a good indication of the direction in which to look for the missing quantities. It is therefore strongly recommended that the work of Project Magnet be continued and expanded to include experts in each of the various fields involved in these studies.[5]

On 10 August 1953 Smith filed another report on Project Magnet, which contained some extraordinary conclusions:

> It appears then, that we are faced with a substantial probability of the real existence of extra-terrestrial vehicles, regardless of whether they fit into our scheme of things. Such vehicles of necessity must use a technology considerably in advance of what we have. It is therefore submitted that the next step in this investigation should be a substantial effort towards the acquisition of as much as possible of this technology, which would without doubt be of great value to us.[6]

The Canadian Government has denied that Smith's conclusions are in any way representative of 'officialdom', and Smith himself disclaimed official status for the report, emphasizing that it simply represented his own views and those of his small research group. It was neither endorsed nor rejected by the Government, yet Smith's credentials and integrity are beyond dispute, and for years afterwards he continued to represent his department before the House of Commons Broadcasting Committee.[7]

In December 1953 Smith set up a UFO detecting station at Shirleys Bay, outside Ottawa, with registering devices including a gamma-ray counter, a magnetometer, a radio receiver and a recording gravimeter. But so intent were government scientists to avoid being associated with such a controversial project that even on the day the station went into operation Dr Solandt was quoted as saying that reports of its establishment were completely untrue. In fact, the building housing the detecting equipment was loaned to Smith by the Defence Research Board, of which Dr Solandt was Chairman!

A definitely anomalous disturbance was recorded on 8 August 1954, but heavy fog prevented Smith and his associates from seeing anything in the sky. Perhaps coincidentally, the Department of Transport announced two days later that it was closing down the station, although the actual decision to do so had been made in June that year. Smith explained that the reason for discontinuing Project Magnet was that it had become an embarrassment to the Government due to unwelcome publicity. But Smith himself was given the go-ahead to continue with the project on an unofficial basis in his own free time. As researcher Arthur Bray comments, a cover-up is indicated by the fact that the public was led to believe that the Government was no longer interested in flying saucers.[8]

Project Second Storey

In April 1952 another secret government committee, separate from Project Magnet but also involving Wilbert Smith, was established by Dr O. M. Solandt, Chairman of the Defence Research Board. With the code-name of Project Second Storey, the committee comprised the following members: Flight Lieutenant V. L. Bradley, Defence Research Board; Group Captain D. M. Edwards, Directorate of Air Intelligence; Dr Peter Millman (Chairman), Dominion Observatory; H. C. Oatway (Secretary), Defence Research Board; Commander J. C. Pratt, Directorate of Naval Intelligence; Wilbert B. Smith, Department of Transport.

According to the minutes made available to Arthur Bray by the National Research Council, only five meetings took place, although it is known that there were more. The minutes of the first meeting, on 21 April 1952, refer to a Royal Canadian Air Force report relating to the US Air Force Project Blue Book UFO investigation. This report was not made available, but Bray eventually was able to acquire a copy from a private source. Hitherto classified Secret, the RCAF document noted that there were certain patterns of sightings over major US port areas and atomic-energy establishments, and that 5 per cent of the reports came from scientists at the White Sands (missile) Proving Grounds, New Mexico. The report concluded with hopes that an official exchange of data could take place between Canada and the United States.

At the fifth meeting, on 9 March 1953, it was pointed out that, although the evidence to date did not warrant a full-scale investigation by the Canadian Armed Forces, reports should continue to be collected at a central point, namely, the Directorate of Scientific Intelligence, Defence Research Board. The minutes make it clear that Project Second Storey should continue to hold meetings at the discretion of the Chairman, yet no further minutes have been made officially available since they are probably still classified. Among them are almost certainly the minutes of a meeting to discuss Wilbert Smith's extraordinary Project Magnet report dated 10 August 1953, wherein he concluded that 'we are faced with the substantial probability of the real existence of extra-terrestrial vehicles'. Arthur Bray was informed by a reliable source that this report went as high as Prime Minister Louis St Laurent, who held it for three months.

Dr Allen McNamara of the National Research Council admitted in a letter to Arthur Bray that the Project Magnet report *was* submitted to the Project Second Storey Committee in 1953, but that 'Mr Smith's conclusions were not supported by his own Department or the Second Storey Committee'.[9] Why, then, are the minutes of this and other meetings still classified? A clue to the degree of sensitivity over the UFO projects is contained in a Canadian Government memorandum in my possession, dated 15 September 1969, which states in part:

> Dr P. M. Millman, National Research Council, has advised me that the documents reporting the results of the Second Story [*sic*] studies in project 'Magnet' be declassified . . . Since the question of flying saucers is still attracting public attention and since this file covers documents relating to the studies behind project 'Magnet' and, indeed, records much of the discussion in the Department of Transport surrounding project 'Magnet' which is confidential in nature, it is recommended that this file be down classified at least to the confidential level. At no time should it be made available to the public.

Eventually, as we have seen, certain Project Magnet and Second Storey documents were released to bona-fide researchers, but there is no doubt that some of the material remains classified. Arthur Bray subsequently acquired a copy of the minutes of another Project Second Storey meeting from a private source. The government transmittal slip is dated 15 March 1954, and it is assumed that the meeting was held no earlier than a few weeks before that date. The minutes contain nothing really interesting, however, apart from some comments by Wilbert Smith on the experiments being conducted at the Shirley Bay detecting station:

> Whether the phenomenae [*sic*] be due to natural magnetic causes, or alien vehicles, there would probably be associated with a sighting some magnetic or radio noise disturbance. Also, there is a possibility of gamma radiation being associated with such phenomenae. It has been suggested by some mathematicians that gravity waves may exist in reality . . . While we know practically nothing of such waves in nature, nevertheless, if the possibility exists, flying saucer phenomenae, being largely an unknown field, might be a good place to look for such waves.[10]

Physical Evidence

During a recorded interview with C. W. Fitch and George Popovitch in November 1961, Wilbert Smith admitted that a number of fragments from UFOs had been recovered and analysed by his research group, including one that had been shot from a UFO near Washington, DC, in July 1952. 'I was informed that the disc was glowing and was about two feet in diameter,' said Smith.

> A glowing chunk flew off and the pilot saw it glowing all the way to the ground. He radioed his report and a ground party hurried to the scene. The thing was still glowing when they found it an hour later. The entire piece weighed about a pound. The segment that was loaned to me was about one third of that. It had been sawed off . . . There was iron rust – the thing was in reality a matrix of magnesium orthosilicate. The matrix had great numbers – thousands – of 15-micron spheres scattered through it.

Smith was asked if he had returned the piece to the US Air Force when he had completed his analysis. 'Not the Air Force. Much higher than that,' he replied. 'The Central Intelligence Agency?' asked the interviewers. 'I'm sorry, gentlemen, but I don't care to go beyond that point,' said Smith, but added: 'I can say to you that it went to the hands of a highly classified group. You will have to solve that problem – their identity – for yourselves.'[11] Almost certainly, the group was the same one which Smith alluded to in his Top Secret 1950 memorandum.

Wilbert Smith also confirmed that a mass of unidentified metal was recovered by his group in July 1960 in Canada. 'There is about three thousand pounds of it,' he told Fitch and Popovitch during the same interview.

> We have done a tremendous amount of detective work on this metal . . . We have something that was not brought to this Earth by plane nor by boat nor by any helicopter. We are speculating that what we have is a portion of a very large device which came into this solar system – we don't know when – but it had been in space a long time before it came to Earth; we can tell that by the micrometeorites embedded in the surface . . . We have it but we don't know what it is![12]

Naturally, all such documentation on these cases, which simply must have been discussed by the Project Second Storey Committee, remains classified to this day. And how curious that, in an interview in 1969, Dr Peter Millman, former Chairman of the committee, should say that meteorites are the 'only proven thing that comes from outer space that we can examine. After all, we've never had a piece of a flying saucer.'[13]

UFOs Follow British Airliner over Labrador

Although the following case is cited frequently in the literature, I have included it here because the principal witness's own account is less well-known and is more detailed than are previous versions.

Captain James Howard was in command of a British Overseas Airways Corporation (now British Airways) Boeing Stratocruiser, G-ALSC, flight 510–196 from New York to London via Goose Bay, on 29 June 1954, which left New York at 21.03 GMT. About thirty minutes later, nearing the boundary of New York Air Traffic Center, Boston informed Captain Howard to hold a position somewhere near the coast of Rhode Island. No reason for the hold was given, but Howard assumed that there was conflicting traffic ahead. After about ten to twelve minutes he pointed out to Boston that his fuel reserves were not limitless, and requested onward clearance. Control then said he could proceed providing that he accepted a detour via Cape Cod, rejoining the original track well north of Boston.

About three hours later, crossing the St Lawrence estuary near Seven Islands, Quebec, flying at 19,000 feet above broken cloud at about 14,000 feet, Captain Howard saw some strange objects:

> They were moving at about the same speed as we were (230 knots approx) on a parallel course, maybe 3 or 4 miles to the north-west of us (we were heading NE). They were below the cloud at this time, at a guess at 8,000 ft. Soon after crossing the coast into Labrador, the cloud layer was left behind and the objects were now clearly in view, seeming to have climbed more nearly to our altitude. At this time the sun was low to the north-west, sky clear, visibility unlimited.

Captain Howard and the crew had ample time to study and sketch the objects, as they accompanied the airliner for twenty minutes. Some passengers had also seen the objects and were staring out of the windows on the port side. 'There was one large object and six smaller globular things,' Howard reported:

> The small ones were strung out in a line, sometimes three ahead and three behind the large one, sometimes two ahead and four behind, and so on, but always at the same level. The large object was continually, slowly, changing shape, in the way that a swarm of bees might alter its appearance. They appeared to be opaque and hard-edged, grey in colour, no lights or flames visible.

After watching the UFOs for ten minutes or so, Captain Howard judged that he was now within VHF radio range of Goose Bay, Labrador, so he asked his co-pilot, Lee Boyd, to request information from control.

> They asked us to describe what we were seeing, and told us that they had an F-94 on patrol and would vector him towards us. (The F-94 was a radar-equipped two-seat fighter.) A little later Goose Bay asked us to change frequency and talk direct to the fighter. On doing so we learned that he had us in radio contact – no mention of anything else visible. I gave him a bearing of the objects from us, and as I did so I noticed that the small objects had

disappeared. (My Navigator who was watching them closely at this time said that they appeared to converge on, and enter, the large one.)

As the F-94 approached, the large object dwindled in size, still on the same relative bearing as the Stratocruiser, and after a few seconds disappeared. Captain Howard then started his descent into Goose Bay for the refuelling stop, and landed at 01.45 GMT. 'We were questioned at length by USAF Intelligence at Goose Bay (who, incidentally, seemed totally unsurprised at the sighting – they told us there had been several others in the Labrador area recently),' said Howard. 'We left Goose Bay at 03.14 GMT for London, arriving at 12.27 on the 30th.'

Captain Howard subsequently learned that a doctor and his wife, who were on holiday in Massachusetts, had seen a number of objects flying overhead in a north-easterly direction at about the time the Stratocruiser was being held near the coast of Rhode Island. Unfortunately, Goose Bay had only short-range airfield control radar at the time, and the F-94 did not report having tracked the objects on its radar equipment. Since the Stratocruiser left for London before the fighter returned, Captain Howard had no opportunity to question the crew. But if the hold *was* caused by unidentified traffic in the Boston control area, Howard surmised, the objects were presumably tracked on radar there.[14]

More Official Contradictions

In a classified Canadian Government memorandum of December 1957, the contents of which were later forwarded by the Department of External Affairs to the High Commissioner's Office in London in response to an enquiry, it was stated that 'The RCAF has no official policy concerning the subject. There is no office within the National Defence Headquarters commissioned to deal with the reports of these phenomena . . . There has never been a serious investigation of any report on file at AFHQ [Air Force Headquarters].'[15]

That the Royal Canadian Air Force was seriously concerned with the UFO subject has been established with the release of the hitherto secret RCAF report, dating back to 1952, referred to earlier, in which the hope was expressed that there would be future co-operation between the RCAF and the US Air Force. Also, two of the committee members of the secret Project Second Storey group were Flight Lieutenant Bradley (Defence Research Board) and Group Captain Edwards (Directorate of Air

Intelligence), so the statement that 'there has never been a serious investigation of any report on file at AFHQ' is nonsense.

In February 1959 the Department of National Defence instituted a series of *Communications Instructions for Reporting Vital Intelligence Sightings*,[16] in line with the US Joint Chiefs of Staff JANAP 146 procedure orders of the same title. Later, co-operation between the United States and Canada in the reporting of UFOs was laid down in, for example, the *Canadian–United States Communications Instructions for Reporting Vital Intelligence Sightings*, (CIRVIS/MERINT) JANAP 146 (E), issued in March 1966 by the Joint Chiefs of Staff as well as the Canadian Defence Staff. This publication lists instructions for the reporting of 'information of vital importance to the security of the United States of America and Canada and their forces, which in the opinion of the observer, requires very urgent defensive and/or investigative action by the US and/or Canadian Armed Forces'. Sightings within the scope of JANAP 146 include 'Unidentified flying objects' as distinct from 'Hostile or unidentified single aircraft or formations of aircraft', and there are lengthy and elaborate instructions for reporting UFOs.[17]

Further proof for the serious involvement of the Canadian Armed Forces – and the RCAF in particular – is contained in a memorandum dated 24 November 1967 from Wing Commander D. F. Robertson, together with other documents. In 1967 it was decided to transfer the RCAF's UFO files to the National Research Council. 'If NRC accepts the responsibility of investigating UFOs, and they work with the University of Toronto in co-operation with DND [Department of National Defence], in my opinion we are on the right track,' wrote Robertson nine days after he had prepared a lengthy brief on UFOs in the hope that the NRC would undertake responsibility for continuing investigations. Robertson's file contained several reports which he had hoped would convince the NRC that extraterrestrial activity was behind some of the sightings in Canada.

Why then was the RCAF apparently no longer interested in UFO research? An unsigned assessment of Wing Commander Robertson's brief stated: 'The marked increase in the air section administrative work load which is directed towards actioning UFO reports is reaching a stage which is considered detrimental to the primary operational responsibilities and duties of the section,' and blamed high administrative costs during the previous year and 'over-zealousness' on the part of its research team. Another, and more significant, reason was given for the DND opting out of UFO research: 'The primary interest of UFOs lies in the field of science and, to a lesser degree, to one that is associated with national security.'[18]

In February 1968 the NRC agreed to become the Government's official archive for all existing and subsequent UFO reports, and the files were kept in an office of the Council's Upper Atmosphere Section (Astrophysics Branch) in Ottawa. Apparently this was only a custodial function: the NRC neither solicited nor investigated UFO reports. 'We do not feel, in general, that there's any point in us spending any time and energy chasing all over after such vague reports. I think we have better things to do,' said Dr Allen G. McNamara, Head of the Upper Atmosphere Section.[19] 'No scientific evidence indicates that any of these objects are of extraterrestrial origins.'[20] But there was one dissenting voice, at least. Professor Rupert Macneill, a geologist on the NRC's Associate Committee on Meteorites, commented: 'I may be wrong . . . But my opinion is that there are definitely things that are being seen that we know nothing about, and as far as I'm concerned, they're definitely real. They've got to be! Now if we don't know what these things are, and if we can find out, we should do so.'[21]

Although supposedly the NRC undertook only custodial duties regarding UFO reports, a letter from the Department of National Defence in my possession, dated 1972, states that since the beginning of 1968 'UFO reports received by the Canadian Forces are passed to the National Research Council. The branch examines reports for scientific reasons warranting further investigation. The Department of National Defence and other Federal Government agencies may be called upon to carry out these investigations for NRC.' So, the NRC was definitely involved in investigations, despite statements to the contrary.

The DND letter goes on to state its official position on the subject: 'We neither agree with nor deny the existence of UFOs. Investigations to date indicate that there is no evidence to suggest that UFOs present a threat to the world, however, certain reports suggest that they exhibit a unique scientific or advanced technology that could possibly contribute to scientific or technical research.'

The 1972 letter confirms that before 1968 all sightings of UFOs reported to Canadian Forces Headquarters were investigated by the Director of Operations, but that 'it has not been the practice to allow the general public to study these files'.[22]

Having written a letter to Prime Minister Pierre Trudeau in 1971, Arthur Bray was referred to the Department of External Affairs, from which he received the following interesting comment on the official attitude: 'The Canadian Government does not underestimate the seriousness of the question of UFOs and this matter is being kept under consideration and study in a number of departments and agencies.'[23]

One of these departments was the Institute for Aerospace Studies at the University of Toronto, which began a study into UFOs in late 1967, headed by Dr Gordon Patterson. In October 1968 the press reported that this study group was on the verge of collapse 'owing to a lack of something to investigate'.[24] Arthur Bray failed to obtain any information from the Institute, however, and nor was any report forthcoming from scientists at the IAS, despite the fact that it is normal procedure for such reports to be made public.[25]

Cover-Up

In 1964 an enormous circular object, spewing flame-coloured exhaust, passed slowly over a car occupied by Bert Gammie and his mother and daughter in Cariboo Valley, British Columbia. After he telephoned the RCAF in Vancouver, Gammie was visited by a senior officer who carried a briefcase full of UFO photographs to make comparisons. The officer, whom Gammie knew, emphasized that, despite their acquaintanceship, he would deny having been there if the visit received any publicity.[26]

The Royal Canadian Mounted Police also takes UFO sightings very seriously, and has received hundreds of reports over the years. Former RCMP officer John Pushie confirms that he has spoken to people who have served in military radar stations, as well as people in general, who had apparently seen something but had been afraid to say anything about it. 'I realize that many government agencies take UFO sightings seriously, the RCMP being one,' he admitted in 1980. 'Policy in the past has been to report all investigations concerning sightings on "Secret" letterhead. I can personally vouch for this as I served with the RCMP for five years.'

Pushie relates a sighting that took place near his home in Sydney, Nova Scotia, in July 1968. A man driving his car around Blacketts Lake Road noticed a saucer-shaped object descending below the tree line near the lake. He parked his car and ran towards the object along a trail through the woods. When he was about 75 feet from the object, which was now hovering about 6 feet above the ground in a clearing adjacent to the lake, it suddenly took off. The RCMP were called and, while carrying out their investigation, blocked off both access roads to the lake. 'The incident received very little media coverage,' said Pushie. 'No further facts were made available.'[27]

Bill Toffan, a young RCMP constable, sighted a UFO on Highway 16 about 60 miles east of Prince Rupert, British Columbia, in April 1976. As he drew closer to it there was a blinding flash and he nearly lost control of his car. After a brief press report appeared, Toffan was ordered not to discuss the incident. But RCMP subdivision head Edward Trefry denied that there was a cover-up. 'We're not trying to hide anything,' he said. 'It's simply policy which has been laid down throughout this subdivision that all press releases are made by senior personnel at each detachment instead of by the individual officer.'[28]

Researcher Henry McKay has experienced difficulties in dealing with the National Research Council which have contributed to suspicions of a cover-up. In 1969 he submitted his field notes on a particular case to the NRC. A year later, when he went back to determine the results of its investigation, the NRC claimed they had no information on the case, but after McKay pointed out that he had submitted certain data to a specific individual and office the file was suddenly discovered. Bureaucracy rather than secrecy, one wonders? On another occasion some substance from an alleged UFO landing-site discovered by a farmer in southern Ontario was submitted to the NRC by the Ontario Provisional Police. 'The substance was turned over to the Ontario Government forensic lab and to this date they haven't released the results of their analysis,' McKay reports. 'The only official answer I got was that it was a police matter and didn't concern me.'[29]

The Falcon Lake Incident

One of the most evidential cases ever to have been reported in Canada is that of Stephen Michalak, a mechanic, who encountered a landed UFO near Falcon Lake, on the boundary between Manitoba and Ontario, on 20 May 1967. For the following summary I am indebted to Chris Rutkowski's thorough description.

At 12.15 that day Michalak, who was engaged in some amateur prospecting, was startled to see two cigar-shaped objects with 'bumps' on them, glowing red, and descending. The objects appeared more oval and disc-shaped as they came closer. Suddenly, the object furthest away stopped in mid-air as the other came nearer and then landed about 160 feet away. The object in the air hovered for a short period then departed silently, changing colour from red to orange to grey, then back to orange as it disappeared behind clouds. The craft on the ground also changed colour, from red to grey and finally 'hot stainless steel', surrounded by a goldenish glow. It was about 35 feet in diameter and 12 feet high.

Michalak knelt on a rock as he observed the object through welding goggles that he normally wore to protect his eyes from chips of rock. A dazzling purple light flooded out of openings in the upper part of the object. The witness sat on the rock for the next half-hour, sketching the object and noting as many details as possible. Waves of warm air and a smell of sulphur radiated from the craft, and there were noises like the whirring of an electric motor as well as a hissing sound.

A door then opened in the side of the craft, with lights coming from the inside. Michalak decided to approach closer, and when he was 60 feet away he heard two human-like voices, one higher pitched than the other. Convinced by now that the device was a new experimental American aircraft, he asked the occupants if they were having trouble. There was no response, although the voices had subsided, so he asked in Russian: 'Do you speak Russian?' There was still no response, even when he tried German, Italian, French and Ukrainian, then English again.

Michalak approached even closer – so close that the light from it became unbearable, so he pushed down the tinted green lenses on his goggles and peered inside the opening. He saw a 'maze' of lights on a panel, and beams of light in horizontal and diagonal patterns, as well as a group of lights flashing in a random sequence. He then stepped back and awaited a reaction.

Suddenly, three panels closed completely over the opening, so Michalak began to examine the side of the craft with his gloved hand. He could see no indications of welding or joints, and the surface was highly polished, appearing like coloured glass reflecting light. When he pulled his hand back he found that the glove had burned and melted, as had his hat. The craft – or at least the rim – then seemed to change position, for he found himself facing a grid-type 'exhaust vent' which he had noticed earlier to the left of the opening. A blast of hot air then struck his chest, setting his shirt and vest alight, causing severe pain. He ripped these off and looked up to see the craft taking off like the first object, and felt a rush of air.

A strong smell similar to burned electrical circuits combined with sulphur pervaded the air. Michalak's burning clothes set some moss on fire, so he stamped on the ground to extinguish the flames and then walked back to where he had left his things. He noticed that his compass was behaving erratically, though after a while it returned to normal. Returning to the landing-site, which looked as though it had been swept clean apart from a 15-feet circle of pine needles, dirt and leaves, Michalak began to suffer from a pounding headache as well as from nausea. He headed back to his motel, vomiting frequently on the way.

On reaching the highway, Michalak realized that he was now about a mile from where he had originally entered the woods, so he set off in the correct direction. A passing RCMP officer stopped in his car, listened to Michalak's story, and then left, explaining that he had other duties to perform. The witness eventually made it back to the motel, but, believing he was 'contaminated', decided to remain outside. At 16.00, however, he went into the motel coffee-shop and asked for a doctor, but as the nearest was 45 miles away he decided to catch the next bus home to Winnipeg. While waiting, he telephoned the *Winnipeg Tribune*. 'The pain was unbearable . . . I was afraid that I had ruined my health and visualized the resulting hell should I become disabled,' he said. 'There had to be some way of getting medical help . . . I thought of the press . . . I did not want to alarm my wife, or cause a panic in the family. I phoned her as a last resort, telling her that I had been in an accident.' When he arrived home his son took him to Misericordia Hospital, where he stayed overnight.

Physiological Effects

On arrival at the hospital Michalak refrained from telling the examining physician the full story, preferring to say only that he had been burned by 'exhaust coming out of an aeroplane'. He was treated for first-degree burns and released. Two days later he was examined by his family doctor, who prescribed painkillers and sea-sickness tablets. Tests a week later by the Whiteshell Nuclear Research Establishment showed no radiation above the normal background level.

For several days after the incident Michalak was unable to keep his food down and lost 22 lb. His blood lymphocyte count was down from 25 to 16 per cent, returning to normal after four weeks. Medical reports also showed that he had skin infections, 'having hive-like areas with impetiginous centres'. He suffered from diarrhoea and 'generalized urticaria' (hives), and periodically felt weak, dizzy and nauseous. He also experienced numbness and chronic swelling of the joints. An 'awful stench' seemed to come from inside his body at times.

A haematologist's report indicated that Michalak's blood had 'some atypical lymphoid cells in the marrow plus a moderate increase in the number of plasma cells'. The witness also complained of a burning sensation around his neck and chest, and occasions when his body 'turned violet', his hands swelled 'like a balloon', his vision failed, and he lapsed into unconsciousness.

In August 1968 Michalak spent two weeks at the Mayo Clinic in Rochester, Minnesota, USA, at his own expense. He was found to be in good health, apart from neurological dermatitis, and simple syncope (fainting spells due to sudden cerebral blood-pressure loss) attributed to hyperventilation or impaired cardiac input (Michalak had been suffering from heart problems for a number of years). Psychiatric tests showed no evidence of delusions, hallucinations or other emotional disorders.[30] A peculiar geometric pattern of burn marks which appeared on Michalak's chest and abdomen was diagnosed as being thermal in origin. The marks matched the 'exhaust grill' of the UFO, which had about thirty small openings (see plate section).

Altogether, Michalak was examined by a total of twenty-seven doctors, and none was able fully to explain the cause of his symptoms.[31] Investigations were carried out by the departments of Health and Social Welfare and National Defence, the National Research Council, the University of Colorado, the Canadian Aerial Phenomena Research Organization, the RCMP and the RCAF, as well as the Whiteshell Nuclear Research Establishment. Dr Horace Dudley, former chief of the Radio-isotope Laboratory, US Naval Hospital, New York, believes that the symptoms of nausea and vomiting, followed by diarrhoea, loss of weight and the drop in lymphocyte count, 'is a classical picture of severe whole body [exposure to] radiation with X or gamma rays'.

'I would guess,' said Dr Dudley, 'that Mr Michalak received in the order of 100–200 roentgens. It is very fortunate that this dose of radiation only lasted a very short time or he would certainly have received a lethal dose . . .'[32]

Findings at the Landing-Site

Stewart Hunt, an investigator for the Department of Health and Social Welfare, found a small contaminated area at the landing-site, no larger than 100 square inches, that showed a 'significant' level of radium 226, for which no satisfactory explanation could be found. Tests conducted by the Whiteshell Nuclear Research Establishment, however, apparently revealed nothing abnormal, and in June 1979 a re-analysis confirmed that all the energies detected could be adequately explained in terms of the decay of natural uranium. Despite these findings, the radiation found by Hunt was of sufficient quantity for the Radiation Protection Division to consider restricting entry to the forest area in 1967.

A year after the encounter, Michalak returned to the landing-site with a friend and, using a Geiger counter, discovered two 'W-shaped' silver bars, four and a half inches in length, as well as some other chunks of the same material, under some lichen above which the UFO was alleged to have hovered. In spite of doubts raised by the University of Colorado UFO Project investigator Roy Craig, researcher Brian Cannon found that the silver concentration was 'much higher than would normally be found in native silver such as sterling or coinage', though the amount of copper, at 1 or 2 per cent, was consistent with commercial silver, if less than many specimens. The metal showed signs of heating, bending *and* radioactivity, and was imbedded on the outside with fine quartz crystals as well as small crystals of a uranium silicate material and pitchblende, and feldspar and haematite. Yet why, asks Chris Rutkowski, was this silver missed earlier by other investigators?

Official Reactions

Squadron Leader P. Bissky, representing the Royal Canadian Air Force, concluded that the entire case was a hoax, yet a statement in the National Research Council's Non-Meteoritic (i.e. UFO) Sightings File (Department of National Defence, DND 222), reads: 'Neither the DND, nor the RCMP investigation teams were able to provide evidence which could dispute Mr Michalak's story.' And the RCMP forensic analysis was 'unable to reach any conclusion as to what may have caused the burn damage' to Michalak's clothing.

In June 1967 it was reported that MP Ed Schreyer had asked in the Canadian House of Commons about UFO investigations, with the Michalak case in mind. The Speaker of the House 'cut off the subject without government reply'. On 6 November 1967 Defence Minister Leo Cadieux, replying to requests by several Cabinet members to obtain information on the Michalak case, stated that 'it is not the intention of the Department of National Defence to make public the report of the alleged sighting'. On 11 November 1967 Ed Schreyer (who subsequently became Governor-General) formally placed a written question on the Commons order paper seeking information on UFOs.

On 14 October 1968 – seventeen months after the incident – House Leader Donald MacDonald refused MP Barry Mather access to reports on the Michalak case. But on 6 February 1969 Mather was given permission by a member of the Privy Council to examine their file on UFOs, 'from which a few pages have simply been removed'. Significantly, it was stated that outright release of the file 'would not be in the public's interest and [would] create a dangerous precedent that would not contribute to the good administration of the country's business'.[33]

Although most of the government report on the Michalak case was eventually made available to enquirers at the National Research Council, the complete file has never been released. In 1982, when the Canadian Government passed the Freedom of Information Act (FOIA), researcher Graham Conway filed a FOIA request for the Michalak file, which an authoritative document listed as being the most complete and extensive among the UFO reports, containing between 125 and 150 pages. He received only 113 pages.[34]

Further Sightings by Pilots

Less than six weeks after the Falcon Lake incident, three air traffic controllers and two technicians monitoring an east-bound Air Canada flight suddenly noticed an unknown object on the radarscope, heading at high speed toward Kenora, Ontario. The date was 7 July 1967, and later that evening the same or a similar object was detected on the Kenora Airport radarscope, heading north-east. For a total of three hours the object described a series of manoeuvres, executing 180-degree turns and chasing two Air Canada flights before resuming its original north-east heading and finally disappearing from the radarscope.[35]

On 15 November 1967 the crew of Quebec Air flight 650 sighted a very bright object at the end of the runway at Sept Iles, Quebec. It was larger than a star, stationary, and at an unknown altitude.

In July 1974 a Scandinavian Airlines captain flying 35 to 40 miles south-east of Quebec City reported a triangular-shaped object moving in a south-westerly direction. During the sighting, Bagotville Airport experienced radio-frequency interference.[36]

On 10 October 1974 John Breen, a Canadian Armed Forces pilot, was paced by a UFO over Newfoundland, *en route* from Deer Lake to Gander. A passenger flying with him first noticed a strange light following the plane when they were about 50 miles from Gander. Every time Breen looked at the light it seemed to turn off, but finally he got a better view of it. 'It seemed to be a sort of triangle- or delta-shaped, luminescent greenish light following us,' Breen told investigator Gregory Kanon. 'It was on for, say, two or three or four seconds and then turned off for a bit and on again. It was fairly regular. And then, as it carried on, it became pretty well a steady light.'

About 25 to 30 miles from Gander, Breen radioed the airport and asked if they had any other traffic in the vicinity. They replied in the negative. 'Then I said, we've definitely got an aircraft or something here with us,' Breen reported. The object was not a reflection of his Cessna 150's lights, and about 14 miles north of the airport, where the Gander River opens out into Gander Lake, the object could clearly be seen reflected in the water.

'I started a right turn and then cut hard left,' Breen said. 'Gander then picked up the object for two or three sweeps, which would have been about 10 to 12 seconds. When we turned around, I just saw it going off the other way and then I lost it because of the back of the aeroplane.'[37]

Less than ten hours later, at approximately 04.15 on 11 October 1974, an unidentified object was sighted by the captain and crew of a Capital Airlines DC-8 airliner, *en route* to Gander Airport at 7,500 feet. The object drew alongside the plane, flashing red and white lights, maintaining a parallel course until finally disappearing in cloud cover about 5 miles from Gander. The airliner was flying at approximately 290 m.p.h. at the time, and the object maintained the same speed but occasionally accelerated a little ahead of the jet, then resumed its position alongside. Both the captain and the first officer stated that the object was not an aircraft, and Gander Air Traffic Control confirmed that no other aircraft were in the vicinity.[38]

The following week, the pilot of a small private plane nearly collided with a gigantic, apparently metallic object which shot across a runway at Saint Anthony, Newfoundland.[39]

Researcher Arthur Bray contacted Transport Canada, the department responsible for civil air safety in Canada, and enquired about official studies and regulations regarding sightings of UFOs reported by pilots. 'No studies on UFOs have been carried out by Transport Canada,' a senior officer informed him, 'nor does Transport Canada have any regulations regarding UFOs.'[40]

Radar/Visual Case at Falconbridge

In October and November 1975 a spate of low-level UFO sightings over Strategic Air Command bases in Maine, Michigan, Montana and North Dakota caused widespread official concern, particularly since some of the unknown objects exhibited a 'clear intent' over nuclear-missile sites. A log extract from the Alert Center Branch of the US Air Force Aerospace Intelligence Division, on 31 October, mentions sightings near the Canadian border: 'CONTACTED CIA OPS CENTER AND INFORMED THEM OF U/I FLIGHT ACTIVITY OVER TWO SAC BASES NEAR CANADIAN BORDER. CIA INDICATED APPRECIATION AND REQUESTED THEY BE INFORMED OF ANY FOLLOW UP ACTIVITY.'

Why, I wonder, did this USAF current-intelligence organization feel compelled or motivated to notify CIA Operations Center in 'real time' – unless they were well aware of the potential UFO threat?

Then, on 11 November, a UFO was reported visually and tracked on radar at the Canadian Forces radar site at Falconbridge, Ontario. The following message from the Commander-in-Charge of North American Aerospace Defense Command (NORAD) was relayed to NORAD units in North America:

> THIS MORNING, 11 NOV 75, CFS FALCONBRIDGE REPORTED SEARCH AND HEIGHT FINDER RADAR PAINTS ON AN OBJECT UP TO 30 NAUTICAL MILES SOUTH OF THE SITE RANGING IN ALTITUDE FROM 25,000 FT TO 72,000 FT. THE SITE COMMANDER AND OTHER PERSONNEL SAY THE OBJECT APPEARED AS A BRIGHT STAR BUT MUCH CLOSER. WITH BINOCULARS THE OBJECT APPEARED AS A 100 FT DIAMETER SPHERE AND APPEARED TO HAVE CRATERS AROUND THE OUTSIDE.

On 13 November NORAD informed the media in Sudbury, Ontario, that the sighting had occurred at 04.05 and that two F-106 jets of the USAF Air National Guard's Fighter Interceptor Squadron at Selfridge Air Force Base, Michigan, were scrambled, but the pilots reported no contact with the object.

In the 11 November message, the NORAD Commander-in-Charge confirmed that 'reliable military personnel' had reported the sightings in the US and at Falconbridge, and concluded:

> BE ASSURED THAT THIS COMMAND IS DOING EVERYTHING POSSIBLE TO IDENTIFY AND PROVIDE SOLID FACTUAL INFORMATION ON THESE SIGHTINGS. I HAVE ALSO EXPRESSED MY CONCERN TO SAFOI [Secretary of the Air Force Office of Information] THAT WE COME UP SOONEST WITH A PROPOSED ANSWER TO QUERIES FROM THE PRESS TO PREVENT OVER REACTION BY THE PUBLIC TO REPORTS IN THE MEDIA THAT MAY BE BLOWN OUT OF PROPORTION. TO DATE EFFORTS BY AIR GUARD HELICOPTERS, SAC HELICOPTERS AND NORAD F-106S HAVE FAILED TO PRODUCE POSITIVE ID.

The USAF was anxious to play down these disturbing incidents. An Air Force document of the same date advised that 'unless there is evidence

C O N F I D E N T I A L
SUBJ: SUSPICIOUS UNKNOWN AIR ACTIVITY
THIS MESSAGE IN FIVE PARTS,
PART I. SINCE 28 OCT 75 NUMEROUS REPORTS OF SUSPICIOUS
ORJECTS HAVE BEEN RECEIVED AT THE NORAD COC, RELIABLE
MILITARY PERSONNEL AT LORING AFB MAINE, WURTSMITH AFB,
MICHIGAN, MALMSTROM AFB MT, MINOT AFB ND, AND CANADIAN
FORCES STATION FALCONBRIDGE ONTARIO, CANADA, HAVE
VISUALLY SIGHTED SUSPICIOUS OBJECTS, PART II, OBJECTS
AT LORING AND WURTSMITH WERE CHARACTERIZED TO BE
HELICOPTERS, MISSILE SITE PERSONNEL, SECURITY ALERT
TEAMS AND AIR DEFENSE PERSONNEL AT MALMSTROM MONTANA
REPORT AN OBJECT WHICH SOUNDED LIKE A JET AIRCRAFT,

PAGE 2 RUWRNLA5489 C O N F I D E N T I A L
FAA ADVISED THERE WERE NO JET AIRCRAFT IN THE
VICINITY. MALMSTROM SEARCH AND HEIGHT FINDER RADARS
CARRIED THE OBJECT BETWEEN 9500 FT AND 15,600 FT AT
A SPEED OF SEVEN KNOTS, THERE WAS INTERMITTENT
RADAR CONTACT WITH THE OBJECT FROM 0807532 THRU 09002
NOV 75. F-106S SCRAMBLED FROM MALMSTROM COULD NOT
MAKE CONTACT DUE TO DARKNESS AND LOW ALTITUDE, SITE
PERSONNEL REPORTED THE OBJECT AS LOW AS 200 FT AND
SAID THAT AS THE INTERCEPTORS APPROACHED THE LIGHTS
WENT OUT, AFTER THE INTERCEPTORS HAD PASSED THE
LIGHTS CAME ON AGAIN, ONE HOUR AFTER THE F106S

PAGE 3   C O N F I D E N T I A L

A North American Aerospace Defense Command (NORAD) document relating to sightings of unknown objects over nuclear-missile bases in 1975. (*Stanton Friedman*)

TURNED TO BASE MISSILE SITE PERSONNEL REPORTED
E OBJECT INCREASED TO A HIGH SPEED, RAISED IN
TITUDE AND COULD NOT BE DISCERNED FROM THE STARS.
RT III. MINOT AFB ON 10 NOV-REPORTED THAT THE
TE WAS BUZZED BY A BRIGHT OBJECT THE SIZE OF A
R AT AN ALTITUDE OF 1000 TO 2000 FT, THERE WAS
I NOISE EMITTED BY THE VEHICLE. PART IV, THIS
IRNING, 11 NOV 75, CFS FALCONBRIDGE REPORTED
ARCH AND HEIGHT FINDER RADAR PAINTS ON AN OBJECT

GE 3 RUWRNLB5489 C O N F I D E N T I A L
I TO 30 NAUTICAL MILES SOUTH OF THE SITE RANGING
I ALTITUDE FROM 25,000 FT TO 72,000 FT, THE SITE
IMMANDER AND OTHER PERSONNEL SAY THE OBJECT
IPEARED AS A BRIGHT STAR BUT MUCH CLOSER. WITH
INOCULARS THE OBJECT APPEARED AS A 100 FT DIAMETER
IHEPE AND APPEARED TO HAVE CRATERS AROUND THE
ITSIDE. PART V. BE ASSURED THAT THIS COMMAND IS
JING EVERYTHING POSSIBLE TO IDENTIFY AND PROVIDE
ILID-FACTUAL INFORMATION ON THESE SITINGS, I
IVE ALSO EXPRESSED MY CONCERN TO SAFOI THAT WE
IHE UP SOONEST WITH A PROPOSED ANSWER TO QUERIES
ROM THE PRESS TO PREVENT OVER REACTION BY THE
IBLIC TO REPORTS BY THE MEDIA THAT MAY BE BLOWN
IT OF PROPORTION. TO DATE EFFORTS BY AIR GUARD
ILICOPTERS, SAC HELICOPTERS AND NORAD F106S HAVE
AILED TO PRODUCE POSITIVE ID.
IDS-2.
I
5489
INOTES
J

which links sightings, queries can best be handled individually at the source and as questions arise. Responses should be direct, forthright and emphasize that the action taken was in response to an isolated or specific incident. IOS should keep all levels and appropriate Majcoms informed of questions asked, media affiliations and responses given.'

Official Reticence

Wilbert Smith, whose untimely death of cancer in 1962 robbed not only Canada but the world of one of the most intelligent and original minds in the field of UFO research, was well qualified to assess the various reasons behind the official cover-up, having headed Canada's first secret investigation into the subject.

To most people, Smith pointed out, the Government is the final authority on all matters. Government, however, comprises a large number of individuals who, although experts in their own fields, are very much laymen in other areas. If a new situation – such as UFOs – develops, and there is no suitable bureau for it, he said, it was unfair to expect early answers from the Government. 'The best that a government can do', he explained, 'is to make use of a "backdoor" arrangement with which we are all familiar, namely, the "classified project". But even this is a gamble in that it is predicated on the project yielding positive results with the answers all tied up in a neat little bundle, otherwise the project flops and slips into oblivion.'

Smith affirmed that the United States authorities were well aware that UFOs were of alien origin, and that 'it was soon apparent that these objects did not constitute any particular menace to humanity and there was practically nothing which we could do about it if they did'. The aliens were in complete control of the situation, while we were mere observers.

In as much as various classified US Air Force projects were aimed largely at debunking UFO reports, Smith said, the Air Force had painted itself into an awkward corner:

> What solid information that did come out of these projects was most disturbing indeed, striking at the very roots of our conventional science. But there wasn't enough of this information on which to base any substantial reform in scientific thinking: just enough to produce an uneasy feeling that all was not well. So naturally, the least said about this the better, until more was known . . . Meanwhile, since they do not have enough answers for

the questions that are now being raised, they most certainly are not going to invite a deluge of further questions by admitting anything.

Smith reasoned that the reluctance of politicians to speak out on the subject was largely due to lack of public support. 'Furthermore,' he said, 'because of the type of publicity from which the whole matter of flying saucers has suffered, politicians, who are naturally very sensitive to public reaction, are reluctant to stick their necks out.'

Smith believed that we could not expect any significant statement on UFOs by any government agency, and the nearest we would come to any sort of official statement would be from those few researchers in the government service who (like Smith, although he did not say as much) were personally satisfied of their findings and who were willing to risk the censure of their colleagues and the prestige of their positions. 'More often than not,' he said, 'these people must wait until they retire from government service before they feel free to make any statements at all.'[41]

Wilbert Smith was right. However, the UFO situation has become increasingly more complex since he expressed these opinions in the late 1950s. There is a lot of evidence since then that UFOs are not always harmless, as the Falcon Lake incident exemplifies. Even if hostility was unprovable, there is no doubt in my mind that the Canadian Government was reluctant to release its conclusion on the case for fear of arousing public over-reaction. Indeed, as already mentioned, the Government stated categorically that outright release of its UFO files 'would not be in the public's interest' and 'would create a dangerous precedent'. So this is one aspect of national security that undoubtedly heads the list of reasons for official reticence on the matter, and I fully sympathize with the Government's dilemma in this respect.

Another aspect was cited by Smith himself in a 1953 secret Project Magnet report: that the UFOs exhibited a technology considerably in advance of ours, leading him to propose that the next stage in official investigations should be a 'substantial effort towards the acquisition of as much as possible of this technology'. If the military has now acquired new technology as a result of top-secret research into UFOs – and I support this hypothesis – it would be yet another perfectly understandable reason for withholding information on UFOs in the interests of national security.

Smith made no secret of his unofficially expressed opinion that actual contact had been established with the occupants of some UFOs, and that he had acquired a great deal of information as a result of investigating such contacts. 'But it soon became apparent', he wrote in an article in 1958, 'that there was a very real and quite large gap between this alien science and the science in which I had been trained. Certain crucial experiments were suggested and carried out, and in each case the results confirmed the validity of the alien science. Beyond this point the alien science just seemed to be incomprehensible.'

Smith was convinced that Earth had been colonized many times by the people from elsewhere (or 'The Boys Topside', as he liked to call them). 'To orthodox thinkers this may seem strange,' he said, 'but not nearly so strange as our orthodox ideas on evolution!'[42] But if Smith was personally convinced about such controversial matters, to what extent were the authorities aware that extraterrestrial contact had been established at this time? An illuminating answer is provided in a letter that Wilbert Smith wrote to a friend of mine in 1959: 'For your information every nation on this planet has been officially informed of the existence of the space craft and their occupants from elsewhere, and as nations they must accept responsibility for any lack of action or for any official position which they may take.'[43]

China

SINCE THE MODERN ERA of UFO sightings began, in the Second World War, practically no information has been available from the country with the largest population in the world – the People's Republic of China. In 1978 China's leading newspaper, the *People's Daily*, published the first article on UFOs (*Fei Die*) to appear in that country, written by Heng Sheng-Yen of the Chinese Academy of Social Sciences.[1] Further articles were published in the *Guang Ming Daily* during the following two years, and in 1980 a Chinese UFO researcher, Paul Dong (Moon Wai), a resident of California, wrote an article featuring reports by pilots, scientists and other reliable observers throughout the world.[2]

Tremendous interest in a hitherto forbidden subject was now aroused throughout China. The journal *Aerospace Knowledge*, for example, received several hundred letters requesting the Chinese Government to launch an investigation into the phenomenon. In May 1980 the Chinese UFO Studies Association was established under the auspices of Wuhan University in central China, with branches in Beijing, Shanghai and in the provinces of Guangdong, Sichuan, Shanxi, Hubei and Guangxi. The association, headed by Cha Leping, a student of astrophysics, subsequently became incorporated into the China UFO Research Organization as an official branch of the Chinese Academy of Social Sciences. (It is also worth noting here that Britain's *Flying Saucer Review* has for many years been subscribed to by the Chinese Academy of Sciences.)

The China UFO Research Organization's first issue of the *Journal of UFO Research* sold 300,000 copies on the news stands. Paul Dong – former editor-in-chief of the journal – lectured on the subject all over China in 1981, creating something of a sensation, speaking to packed audiences at the Peking Ching Hua University Students Union, the Peking Planetarium, the Guangchou Science Museum and Canton Jinan University, for example, and during his one-month tour he collected hundreds of UFO cases from the period 1978–81. Since that time hundreds more cases – some dating back to 1940 and even earlier – have been gathered and published in the journal. Many of these reports have been compiled by Paul Dong and published privately in a valuable book, *UFOs over Modern China*. I am indebted to him and to his publisher, Wendelle Stevens, for allowing me to cite some of these reports, which have been translated by the Foreign Language Bureau in Beijing. I am also grateful to Dong for allowing me to use material from his Chinese-published book, *Questions and Answers on UFOs*.

Why did the Chinese wait so long to take the UFO problem seriously? According to Paul Dong, three specific factors prompted the Chinese Government to recognize the phenomenon. On a summer evening in 1965 two bright, disc-shaped objects violated Beijing's airspace. Two years later a similar incident occurred near the outskirts of Beijing, when a bright, globe-shaped object was observed by thousands of witnesses as it streaked across the night sky at fantastic speeds, stopped and hovered, then disappeared over the horizon. Speculation among the masses that Taiwan or another hostile country had developed a secret weapon that might threaten China's national security led to the sanctioning of the academic research group. The third factor leading to official recognition was the frequency of reports received by the authorities from the provinces in the late 1970s.[3] Official recognition is now beyond dispute.

The first sighting to be published in postwar China described an 'enormous [flying] platter [which] emanated luminous rays in all directions . . . and dazzled all who saw it'.[4] The date was July 1947, weeks after pilot Kenneth Arnold's famous sighting in the USA, and the report was released by the Chinese Palace of State. It was the only first-hand Chinese report to be made public before the communist victory in the Chinese Revolution isolated China from the West as far as UFO reports (and much else!) was concerned. In the new People's Republic of China under Mao Zedong nothing was spoken or written about the subject until the period of the Cultural Revolution, when UFO reports began to filter out through underground channels. Officially the subject was considered to be 'counter-revolutionary'.[5] Under China's new regime, however, hundreds of reports from this period – and beyond – have now been published.

Airliner Chased by UFOs

On an unspecified day in October 1963, a Li-2 airliner (a Soviet-built version of the Douglas DC-3 Dakota) on the Kuangtung to Wuhan air route was chased by three luminous unidentified flying objects for fifteen minutes. The pilots gave a minute-by-minute report by radio to the Chinese Civil Aeronautics Administration, and on landing the crew were debriefed by air traffic control. The passengers were interviewed by the authorities and were ordered not to discuss the incident with anyone.[6]

Jet Fighters Scrambled

On 1 January 1964 many citizens in Shanghai observed a huge cigar-shaped aerial object flying slowly towards the south-west. MiG fighters were scrambled in pursuit but failed to force the UFO down. The official explanation was that the object was an American missile.[7]

'Combat Stations'

In early 1968 four coastguard artillerymen of the Navy garrison at Luda, Liaoning province, in north China, saw a gold, luminous, oval-shaped object which flew alongside, leaving a thin trail in the air. It climbed steeply at great speed and disappeared.

At the moment when the object began to climb, all communications and radar systems failed, almost causing an accident in the fleet. The naval patrol went on alert and the fleet commander ordered his men to prepare for combat. Half an hour later communications and radar returned to normal. A two-man coastguard patrol reportedly saw the UFO land on the south coast and fired at it with automatic rifles and machine-guns, but soldiers sent to investigate found no trace of the object.[8]

A Landing in the Gobi Desert

In mid-April 1968 Gu Ying (later an interpreter for the New China Agency) was sent to a military construction regiment in the north Gobi Desert, where he worked on an irrigation project. Quite late one day a comrade drew the battalion's attention to a strange phenomenon. This is the first-hand account:

> I saw a great disc of light trailing flames as it slowly descended to the Gobi's sands. It was a luminous red-orange in colour and had an apparent diameter of three metres before it landed. It passed alongside at a slight inclination above the horizon. We could see a separate more luminous point of light flashing in the mass of light. As it was less than a kilometer from us when it passed by, we

could see the detail clearly. It landed suddenly and the commander of the company telephoned the headquarters of the regiment, who dispatched a team of motorcycle troops to approach it.

Without doubt the arrival of the motorcycle troops was detected by the disc, because it suddenly ascended like an arrow and disappeared in the sky above. As the northern frontier [with the USSR] passes through this region, most witnesses felt that this was a new reconnaissance machine from the enemy to the north inspecting the progress of work on the canal. We did not know anything about UFOs at that time.

The object left traces of its landing in the form of a seared cross on the ground. As we knew nothing of these objects we did not study the mark . . . We only thought in political terms and believed that this signified some kind of preparation for an eventual enemy attack from the north. The soldiers long stationed in the Gobi had seen these things before, and the great fireballs in the sky were not so unusual to them. The landing and take-off were a new twist.[9]

Owing to the prevalence of UFO reports in the border area, a special military UFO study group was formed to keep track of sightings.[10] In my opinion, it is probable that a sizeable proportion of sightings reported in the Gobi Desert area were due to rocket launches from the Shuang-Chengzi missile test centre.

Multiple-Witness Sightings

Multiple-witness UFO sightings have been reported in China just as in other countries. One of the most spectacular took place at 20.30 on 7 July 1977, at Zhangpo county in Fujian province. Nearly 3,000 people were watching an open-air showing of the Romanian film *Alert on the Danube Delta* when some of the audience suddenly saw two oblate, orange-coloured, luminous objects descending towards the crowd. The objects passed so low over the spectators that the objects almost touched the ground, emitting a vivid glow, flying only a few metres apart. Heat could be felt, and a humming sound was heard.

Panic spread; people threw themselves to the ground. In the ensuing stampede, two children were trampled to death and 200 more were injured. The UFOs ascended rapidly and disappeared in seconds. Lin

Bing-Xiang, a doctor at the county hospital, and Chen Caife, an officer of the County Public Security Bureau, and another official have corroborated this sensational incident. The authorities, suspecting an optical illusion related to the film, re-ran it, but nothing unusual showed up.[11,12]

Not the least extraordinary fact to emerge from the Chinese UFO reports is the number of multiple-witness military cases; these rival and occasionally surpass those so far made available in the West. Whether this trend continues remains to be seen, but the following report is an outstanding example of a UFO witnessed by several hundred personnel.

On 23 October 1978 a large luminous unidentified object appeared in the sky directly above Lintiao Air Base in Gansu province. This is Air Force pilot Zhou Quingtong's eyewitness account:

> The pilots of our brigade and several hundred other persons in the airfield district were watching a cinema film in an open-air theatre. Several minutes after the show had begun, that is at four minutes past the 20th hour, there was a flurry of disturbance in the audience and we all looked up at the sky, which was cloudless and full of stars . . .
>
> I saw a huge object flying from east to west. It first appeared in the eastern sky at an angle of 60 degrees above the horizon, then flew over our heads and was cut off from our view by [a] row of buildings . . . The object had a very peculiar appearance. It was an immense oblong object but was not clearly visible. It had two large lamps, like searchlights, in front, shooting out white light forward, and a luminous trail issued from the rear. Both the front and rear light beams were changing in length and brightness at times, illuminating the space around the object like a mass of smoke or mist.
>
> The speed was not very great, and it progressed in a straight line. It was of a huge size, occupying about 20 to 35 degrees of arc of vision. It was in sight for two or three minutes. It was clearly not a meteor, nor a swarm of locusts or birds, nor an airplane. As we are all fighter pilots we could say this with some certainty. It was not very high above the ground.
>
> After many days we were still talking about it. Someone said, Alas! If we only had a camera and had taken a photograph, the question could be solved.[13]

Chinese researchers speculated that because there were similarities in the description of the objects observed, there could be a connection with the sighting, over the Bass Strait, Australia, two days earlier, by pilot Frederick Valentich, who disappeared together with his plane immediately afterwards (see Chapter 9).

Power Failure and a Close Encounter

The wave of sightings continued into 1979, producing interesting reports. One such was an incident that took place at 20.45 hours on 12 September 1979, when witnesses in Xuginglong and Huaihua City in Hunan province experienced a complete power failure in their area. Fifteen minutes later a bright flying object appeared overhead, emitting a vertical stream of white rays. The object flew upwards at an angle and vanished soundlessly a minute later, leaving two masses of semi-spherical luminous clouds about 100 metres across.[14]

Perhaps because of their controversial (and anti-Marxist?) nature, close encounters with UFO occupants have not received much attention in China. Yet a few cases have come to light since the easing of restrictions in 1980.

On 13 December 1979 at 04.00 near Longwangmiao on the Lanxi–Xin'angiang highway, two truck-drivers in separate vehicles observed an extraordinary sight. Wang Dingyuan (of the Weihus Steel Construction Plant) was driving in the front truck when he noticed a powerful vertical beam of light and two 'unusual human beings' standing beneath it on the highway. Both drivers came to an abrupt halt and the apparition vanished.

The men discussed the incident, although the second driver, Wang Jianming (of the Jinhus Chemical Works), had seen nothing, so it was decided that they should swap positions, with Wang Jianming driving in front. After 5 or 6 kilometres the front driver noticed a beam of light and figures standing beside the highway about 200 metres ahead. The figures were 1.5 metres tall and wore helmets on their heads and 'space apparel' with something like a thermos bottle slung across their shoulders and a square pack on their backs. Each was apparently holding what looked like a 'short cudgel' in his left hand, and a red light emitted from the top of the helmets.

Wang Jianming stopped his truck, turned off the headlights, and then turned them back on. The figures were still there, even when he repeated the procedure. Wang then dismounted with a crowbar in his hand, and at that moment both the light-beam and the figures vanished.[15]

Tientsin Airport Tracks UFO

The year 1980 produced a bumper harvest of UFO sightings in China, when altogether ninety-eight reports were received by the China UFO Research Organization, although it is believed that many others were not reported. The editor of *Aerospace Knowledge*, Xie Chu, wrote: 'We no longer can ignore the existence of UFOs because of the great number of sightings reported in our country.'[16]

In early August 1980 hundreds of thousands of witnesses saw UFOs for several days running in the skies over Tientsin and the Gulf of Zhili (now called Bo Hai). On the evening of 16 October 1980 at Tientsin Airport, radar officers and technicians of the Tientsin Civil Aviation Bureau were observing the movements of Flight 402 on their radar screens when suddenly an unexplained echo showed up. When the airliner was about 2 kilometres from the runway, the plane's bright dot of light on the screen veered out of control for seven seconds or so.

The radar operators had presumed they were watching Flight 402, but when the controller contacted the aircraft and asked for its position they realized that the echo on the screen did not relate to the plane – Flight 402 had taken off from Beijing, and its flight path would have taken it across Tientsin, crossing the airfield from east to west. Another anomaly was that the radar azimuth was 20 degrees, but at the time the unexplained blip showed up on the radarscope Flight 402 was bearing about 80 degrees, north of the runway and out of range of the directional radar.

At 21.53 hours, when Flight 402 had crossed the airfield to a point 13 kilometres from the runway on its final approach, the unexplained echo showed up again in the same position on the radarscope, moving from west to east. It was visible simultaneously on the screen together with the aircraft. Seconds later it vanished.

Three minutes later the strange echo reappeared. A second aircraft, Flight 404, was also above Tientsin, at an altitude of 1,500 metres, but its position was at variance with the echo, and moving in the opposite direction. As Flight 404 was on its final approach, two echoes – instead of one – again appeared on the radarscope. The UFO, from its original position north of the runway, was doing about 250 kilometres per hour. According to the captain of Flight 404, the automatic direction finder (ADF) on his instrument panel registered an anomaly: the indicator needle appeared to lock on to a transmitting source not known on the chart. The captain assumed his instrument was faulty, and asked the radio officer to use his earphones to pick up the radio beacon's audio signal. This was in order, and two minutes later the ADF returned to normal.

Just before touchdown, when Flight 404 was a few hundred metres from the runway, the assistant controller in the tower heard some interference on the radio and assumed it was either the aircraft or the radio room tuning in. 'Who's tuning in to the tower?' he asked. 'We're working flat out – don't call us!' The aircraft crew experienced the voice-radio and radar interference, though the source could not be identified by ordinary means.[17]

Extraordinary Parallels with Events in the UK

Chapter 4 refers to the sighting on 15 December 1980 of a UFO over south-east London and north-west Kent, seen by many witnesses for over an hour and by me for a few minutes. According to those who watched it through binoculars, the object was cone-shaped, with a red nose, a silvery centre and a sparkling diamond-blue rear section. While studying the Chinese UFO Research Organization's reports I came across extraordinary parallels with this case. An identical object was seen in Beijing four months later, for instance, when at 07.00 on 25 April 1981 Du Shengyuan observed a curious object circling in the sky. Immediately he tried to telephone the *Beijing Evening News* as well as the Beijing and Central television stations but he was unable to get an answer as it was too early in the morning. He went back outside and continued to observe the strange object, which by that time was directly overhead at more than 2,000 metres altitude:

> With the aid of binoculars I made it out to be ellipsoid in shape, but more like a bullet. Its middle part was white, like the moon in daytime but brighter. The bottom was luminous green, like the rays from the launch of a rocket . . . The whole thing was strangely luminous. I continued my observation until it went out of sight at 07.25. It flew in a changeable way, now fast, now very slowly, now stopping altogether before speeding forward. It was watched by all the twenty-odd residents in the courtyard.[18]

This is precisely the same description given by Peter McSherry of the December 1980 sighting, with the insignificant exception of the rear section of the object, which he described as being 'sparkling diamond-blue' rather than 'luminous green'.

A similar object also may have been seen in China within thirty hours of the British sighting. On 14 December 1980 at 17.35 four witnesses saw an object 'like a cone, smaller at the top and larger at the base' which 'jumped up' from the top of a mountain west of Xiangshan and gave out 'light blue rays'. The object alternately disappeared and reappeared, just as the UFO in London had done.[19]

Peter McSherry and other witnesses said that the UFO they saw occasionally split up into two, three and even more sections which shot away and then regrouped. On 5 June 1981, at 22.00, Ding Shiliang and other students at Xi'an University, Shanxi province, observed a luminous flying object which 'split from the middle into two parts, then three, then even four. In another moment two of the units on either side vanished, leaving the two other segments still in position, one above the other'. After performing further astonishing separations and disappearances, 'another appeared and the two objects approached each other and merged into one . . . Later it split into two again, diminished in size and finally vanished at 22.20, not to return.'[20]

Because details of the British sighting in December 1980 were published for the first time in *Above Top Secret* in 1987, it is impossible for the Chinese to have been aware of these facts. Neither could they have known about the events later in December 1980 at Rendlesham Forest, outside the RAF/USAF bases of Woodbridge and Bentwaters, when a landed UFO was seen by a number of military personnel, and when Lieutenant Colonel Charles Halt reported sighting an object which at one point 'appeared to throw off glowing particles and then broke into five separate white objects and then disappeared', as described in his official memorandum to the Ministry of Defence (see Chapter 4).

Air Force Jets Affected by UFOs

In the middle of June 1982, UFO activity increased suddenly in northern China, and on 18 June in particular there were many sightings reported from Heilongjiang province, between 21.10 and 22.53 hours. One of the most interesting cases is that reported by five Chinese Air Force pilots on patrol over north China's military frontier.

At about 21.57 the jet fighters' electrical power systems malfunctioned; communications and navigation systems failed. Suddenly the pilots encountered an unidentified flying object of a milky yellowish-green luminous colour, about the size of the full moon. The object grew larger and picked up speed, at which point it looked 'as big as a mountain of mist'. Then black spots were seen in the interior of the phenomenon.

'When I first saw the object,' one pilot stated in his report, 'it flew toward me at a high rate of speed as it whirled rapidly. While it was rotating it generated rings of light. In the centre of the light ring was fire. In ten seconds the centre of the ring exploded, then the body of the object expanded rapidly.'

The planes were forced to return to base because of the equipment failures. The other four pilots also prepared reports, which were subsequently published in the first issue of the *Journal of UFO Research*, together with their sketches.[21] It is not known if gun-camera film was taken.

UFO Paces Airliner

On 11 June 1985 a Chinese Civil Aviation Administration Boeing 747 encountered a UFO on the Peking to Paris flight that almost forced the captain to make an emergency landing. Flight CA 933 was over Lanzhou, the capital of Gansu province, when the object was observed by Captain Wang Shuting and his crew at 22.40. The UFO, located at 39 degrees 30 minutes North and 103 degrees 30 minutes East, flew across the path of the airliner at its altitude of 33,000 feet at a very high speed. The object reportedly illuminated an area of 25 to 30 miles and had a huge diameter. It was elliptical in shape and had an extremely bright spot in the centre, with three horizontal rows of bluish-white lights on the perimeter. The official news release, which attracted worldwide attention, stated that no passengers reported the two-minute sighting.[22]

I am reminded of a similar but much longer sighting witnessed by the crew and passengers of a Soviet Aeroflot airliner flying from Tbilisi to Tallin in 1984, when the object (or rather 'cloud') was said to be enormous in length (see pp. 248–50). And in August 1985 the pilot of an Olympic Airways flight from Zurich to Athens reported that he had a near collision with a mystery object near the Italian/Swiss border. More UFOs were seen that same month by the crew and forty-five journalists aboard a Boeing 737 *en route* to Buenos Aires.[23] So the crew of the Chinese jumbo jet were not alone in reporting a dramatic aerial encounter with the ubiquitous UFOs in 1985.

Air Force Pilot Chases UFO

On the evening of 27 August 1987, Chinese Air Force pilot Mao Xuecheng chased an unknown aerial object in the Shanghai vicinity, and described his encounter to reporters as follows:

I had orders to fly at 19.35 on the 27th, and to return to base after completing air patrol duty. As I was approaching the airspace above the Yangtze river, I suddenly observed that ahead of me to the right, above Jaiding county, was a very bright, dazzling flying object. I immediately hit the throttle hard and pursued it closely from an angle of 110 degrees at a rate of 900 k.p.h. At that time, the clock was showing a little past 19.57.

I observed carefully and noticed that the unidentified object was descending, the focus of light was an orange spot, and the spiral tail it was trailing was also orange. At 19.59 it went from descending to ascending, and its speed was now much faster than when it had been descending. After forty-five more seconds I was unable to keep up with it, so I requested permission to land.[24]

Numerous ground observers in Shanghai and other areas reported sighting a similar object that day. According to one account, the Shengsi county electric generator suddenly cut off when the object flew over: the island was thrown into darkness. Interestingly, many people also reported that their wristwatches stopped.[25]

Army Personnel Chased by a Disc

At 21.10 on 10 January 1990, two soldiers from a unit of the People's Liberation Army were speeding along in a jeep 5 miles outside Taiyuan City, Shanxi province, when one of them became aware of an object that seemed to follow them. Looking up, he saw a black, disc-shaped object. The men increased speed, hoping to shake off their pursuer, but after fifteen minutes the object was still just above and pacing them.

Overcome with fright, the driver, Cao Yongnian, recalled that there were things called UFOs which could out-fly jets, so he realized it would be pointless to run away. Instead, he slowed down to 50 m.p.h., but after about fifteen minutes the black object was still above them. The soldiers decided to stop. The object stopped as well, rising to about twice its previous height and beginning to give off constantly changing colours of light – blue, green, yellow and red. After a while the men became less frightened and even considered taking a shot, but instead they decided to try shouting at it. Moving to the side of the road, they waved and shouted: 'Come down, let's have a talk!' The UFO responded by flying around in a circle then zooming off![26]

Encounters with Airliners

At 18.05 on 18 March 1991, Flight 5556 (airline not specified) took off from Shanghai's Hongqiao Airport bound for Jinan, the capital of Shandong province, some 800 kilometres to the north. At 18.13 Jin Xing, a controller from the Hongqiao Airport control centre, observed an elliptical ring of 'apricot-pink' light at an altitude of about 3,000 metres, near the airliner, and radioed the captain.

After Captain Zhu reported he had the object in sight, he informed the control centre that the object was spurting a bright red blaze of light from its tail, and that it was moving very quickly within the ring of light. Zhu, piloting a British-built twin-turboprop Shorts 360-300 with thirty-six passengers on board, decided to give chase. As the airliner flew over Kunshan, a small city about 60 kilometres from Shanghai, the colour of the ring changed from orange to black, and two smaller objects separated from the ring. One of these objects was circular, the other rectangular. The two flew to and fro, maintaining a distance of about 300 metres from each other.

Forty kilometres further on, the objects suddenly turned toward the plane at high speed. Frightened, Zhu asked the control centre for emergency help, at which point the objects joined together and flew rapidly up and away.

This chase lasted nine minutes. Captain Zhu, an experienced pilot, reported that the sky was cloudless and visibility excellent. The oval or circular object was larger than his plane, he said. No other aircraft were in the vicinity at the time of this alarming experience.[27]

According to a newspaper account, Southwest Airlines Flight 2408, *en route* from Cheng Du, Sichuan province, to Sha Men, Fujian province, encountered an unknown object above Ji Yong City, about 260 miles from Cheng Du, on 17 May 1991. At about 20.00 the crew of the Boeing 707 suddenly noticed a large, round, silver-coloured object to the right of the plane. As a safety precaution, the pilot tried to evade the object by descending and turning off all lights. Four minutes later the object went up into the clouds and disappeared. The UFO was also witnessed by the crew of Flight 154 (position unknown).[28]

Officialdom and the Scientific and Industrial Community

Having tried for several years to ascertain the official Chinese Government attitude to the UFO question, I finally succeeded in 1986 when Zhang

Laigui, Air Attaché at the Chinese Embassy in London, sent me an interesting article on the subject that had appeared in the *China Daily* in 1985, together with a translation. Zhang stated in his accompanying letter that he regarded the article as 'an official statement and viewpoint of the Chinese Government'.[29]

The article, headed 'UFO Conference Held in Darlian', reports that several dozen Chinese scientists had gathered in that city in August 1985 to exchange views on UFO research for the first time. Some forty papers were presented, seventeen of which were selected for a collected work. Subjects included viewpoints and methods of the Chinese regarding UFO research, theoretical works on the UFO phenomenon, and the relationship between UFOs and human body sciences.

The article mentions the degree of interest in the UFO subject in China, referring to the establishment of the China UFO Research Organization (identified in the article as the China Society of UFO Research, or CSUR), with a total membership of 20,000. Chairman of the CSUR, Professor Liang Renglin of Guangzhou Jinan University, said that more than 600 UFO reports had been made during the previous five years in China.

'UFOs are an unresolved mystery with profound influence in the world,' the article concludes. 'Some people believe in their existence, while the opponents think it's a matter of fiction or illusion . . . Various kinds of organizations have been established in the world, including USA, USSR, UK, Japan, and Central and South American nations, to try to unveil the UFO mystery.'[30]

At a scientific conference held in Beijing in May 1992, which dealt mostly with ball-lightning phenomena, superconductivity and space propulsion technology, the China UFO Research Organization (CURO) announced that it would like to host a major international UFO conference in the near future. This semi-official organization is a member of the China Association for Science and Technology (largely supported by the government), and has 3,600 formal members as well as 40,000 research associates. UFO researchers from the Chinese Academy of Sciences and other institutes were present at the conference. Wang Changting, a senior engineer and acting chairman of CURO, pointed out that interest in the subject in China is more extensive than in any other country, and claimed that hosting such a conference would lead to new scientific developments as well as greater social stability.[31]

In 1995 it was reported in London's *Independent* newspaper that the China UFO Research Organization, though described by Wang Changting as an 'independent, unofficial, civil, academic body', is currently housed at the Military Weapons Industry Academic Department of the state China North Industries Group in western Beijing. The group has collected over 5,000 reports of UFO sightings in Chinese airspace. 'We also study the application of UFO phenomena to the national economy,' Wang revealed, 'such as new materials and new technologies.'[32]

The Soviet Union

IN 1967 AN EXTRAORDINARY article appeared in the Russian magazine *Smena* (Change) of which I have an original copy: Dr Felix Yurevich Zigel, Doctor of Science and Assistant Professor of Cosmology at the Moscow Aviation Institute, a respected scientist who had been awarded the prestigious Order of Lenin, announced that UFOs were worthy of scientific study. He referred to research done in the United States by Dr J. Allen Hynek, Dr Jacques Vallée and Professor Frank Salisbury, commenting that Dr Donald Menzel's debunking theories, propounded in his book *Flying Saucers*[1] (translated into Russian in 1962), could no longer be considered valid.

Zigel also gave an interesting résumé of sightings by Soviet scientists since 1960, including that of Assistant Professor V. Zaitsev, who, during a flight between Leningrad and Moscow on 12 July 1964, saw what he described as 'a huge disc which appeared suddenly below the airliner's fuselage, flew a parallel course for a while then turned aside with a burst of speed'.[2] The article caused something of a sensation in a country where previously only debunking statements and articles (as well as Menzel's book) had appeared on the subject. In fact the USSR Government had been as deeply concerned as others by sightings dating back to the early 1940s.

Stalin's Concern

In July 1947 Sergei P. Korolyev, then one of the Soviet Union's leading rocket scientists, was invited to the Ministry of State Security (MGB – later KGB) headquarters in Moscow, where he was informed by the MGB chief that the invitation was at the behest of Josef Stalin. Korolyev was taken to a special apartment and given many foreign documents dealing with flying saucers (reportedly including descriptions of the celebrated Roswell, New Mexico, incident), together with a team of translators, and told that he had three days to come up with an opinion.

Three days later Korolyev was summoned to a meeting with Stalin, who asked him whether these mysterious objects posed a threat to the state. Korolyev replied that UFOs did not appear to be weapons of a potential enemy, but that the phenomenon was real nevertheless. According to Korolyev, Stalin also consulted other leading scientists, who came up with the same conclusion.[3]

Close Encounters of a Soviet Test Pilot

Arkadii Ivanovich Apraksin was a highly decorated Soviet Air Force pilot, having gained in the Second World War the awards of Red Star, Red Banner and Patriotic War First Class, as well as medals for the defence of Stalingrad and the capture of Berlin. Apraksin was interviewed in September 1951 by Yuri Fomin, docent (lecturer) of Voronezh University, and one of Russia's pioneering UFO researchers, who later passed the story to Dr Zigel. The latter incorporated the following account (which I have abridged) in one of his manuscripts, which has been translated by the researcher Joe Brill.

On 16 June 1948, while Apraksin was testing a new Soviet jet aircraft, he encountered a 'cucumber-shaped' aerial phenomenon flying on a cross course to his. Cones of light beams radiated from the object, which appeared to be descending. Apraksin reported the sighting to his base at Kapustin Yar, Basunchak, and received confirmation that the object had been tracked on radar and had not acknowledged instructions to land. The test pilot was ordered to close with the UFO, and if it refused to land he was to open fire.

When Apraksin closed to within about 10 kilometres the light beams 'opened up in a fan' and reportedly struck his aircraft, temporarily blinding him. He discovered simultaneously that the entire electrical control systems as well as the engine were inoperable. He managed to glide the plane to a safe landing, however, the UFO having disappeared into a cloud layer.

A detailed statement was prepared, and an expert arrived from Moscow who examined the aircraft in detail, cross-examined Apraksin, and checked the completed testimony for contradictions. The pilot was given a forty-five-day leave, but ten days before its expiry he was summoned to the Air Force Directorate of the Ministry of Defence in Moscow. Apraksin was sent then to an airfield in the European sector of the Arctic, where he was subjected to another interrogation. After spending three months at this airfield, where he test-flew another aircraft, Apraksin was recalled to the air base at Kapustin Yar.

On 6 May 1949 Apraksin is said to have taken yet another new plane for a test flight. At its maximum ceiling of 15,000 metres he encountered another unidentified object, similar to the previous one. The 'flying cucumber' once again directed cones of light at his aircraft from a distance of about 10 to 12 kilometres, causing effects as before, but also damaging part of the perspex cockpit canopy, resulting in loss of air pressure. Unable to communicate with base, Apraksin managed to land the plane on the banks of the Volga, 49 kilometres from Saratov. He then passed out.

On regaining consciousness Apraksin found himself in a hospital at Saratov. A detailed statement was taken from him again, and after two and a half months he apparently was ordered to appear before a special medical board in Moscow, which then sent him to a psycho-neurological institute. During his six months' stay at this 'institute' Apraksin allegedly was subjected to psychotherapy and shock therapy. Taped interviews were compared with recordings of his previous report in an effort to uncover inconsistencies. In January 1950 Apraksin appeared before a medical board which judged him 'Group One Disabled', effectively barring him from active service. Later that year, and in 1951, he went to the Defence Ministry in Moscow and was received by a deputy minister, but his application for return to duty was refused.

'He assures me that he is in perfect health,' wrote Fomin, and 'that everything which he saw occurred in fact; that they do not want to consider him normal for reasons he cannot understand, and that the failure to believe his story will bring harm to the Motherland.'[4]

I have so far been unable to trace a reference to Apraksin in recognized books on Soviet aviation. He is not mentioned in Bill Gunston's definitive book *Aircraft of the Soviet Union*,[5] and the author told me that he has not come across the name. I then wrote to the Director of the M. V. Frunze Central House of Aviation and Space in Moscow, and eventually received the following reply: 'The Central House of Aviation and Space . . . has no information about test flight activities of A. I. Apraksin. He is not a Hero of the Soviet Union.'[6]

I began to suspect that the story had been concocted, but my confidence in the case was restored when I discovered a reference to it in an official statistical analysis of sightings in the Soviet Union published by the USSR Academy of Sciences.[7] The name of the pilot was not given, so I wrote to Dr L. M. Gindilis of the Sternberg Astronomical Institute in Moscow, one of the authors of the report, requesting further details. In his reply, Dr Gindilis confirmed that the Apraksin case was indeed included in the statistical analysis, and that the report had been written by

Yuri Fomin, who was Apraksin's chance co-traveller in a train on 25 September 1951.

Dr Gindilis went to the trouble of asking Fomin if he knew of Apraksin's whereabouts. 'My one-time acquaintance with Arkadii Ivanovich Apraksin is still exciting me,' replied Fomin, but he added that 'at present I have no information about [him], though till the early 1970s I did make some [attempts] to find him.'[8]

It is unfortunate that there is so far no official trace of Apraksin, yet Fomin confirms his existence and was evidently impressed with the story. The Soviets were skilful in removing names from the history books when occasion demanded, and perhaps Apraksin, having committed what at that time must have been considered a blasphemy, fell victim to the system.

CIA Concern

Under the US Freedom of Information Act a number of documents released by the CIA clearly indicate concern with the Soviet Union's attitude towards the UFO problem. A hitherto 'Secret' memorandum from the Assistant Director of Operations, George Carey, to the Deputy Director of Intelligence, Allen Dulles, dated 22 August 1952, states that 'a search of Foreign Documents Division files has so far produced no factual evidence that the subject has been mentioned in the Soviet satellite press within the past two years', but refers to a broadcast from Moscow on 10 June 1951 in which it was stated that the Chief of Nuclear Physics in the US Naval Research Bureau had explained UFOs as being 'used for stratospheric studies. US Government circles knew all along of the harmless nature of these objects, but if they refrained from denying "false reports, the purpose behind such tactics was to fan war hysteria in the country".'

On 11 September 1952 the CIA's Assistant Director of Scientific Intelligence, H. Marshall Chadwell, sent a secret memorandum to the CIA Director, General Walter Bedell Smith, which stated:

Intelligence problems include:
(1) The present level of Russian knowledge regarding these phenomena.
(2) Possible Soviet intentions and capabilities to utilize these phenomena to the detriment of US security interests.
(3) The reasons for silence in the Soviet press regarding flying saucers.

US Officials Witness Flying Discs

A fascinating air intelligence report of three US officials travelling by train in Russia in 1955 was declassified thirty years later under provisions of the Freedom of Information Act. Originally classified Top Secret, it was downgraded to Secret in 1959. The witnesses were Senator Richard Russell, Lieutenant Colonel E. U. Hathaway, a US Army staff officer assigned to the Senate Armed Forces Committee, and Ruben Efron, committee consultant. I quote from part of the once Top Secret cable cited in the report, which was sent to US Air Force Headquarters on 13 October 1955 by the US Air Attaché at the American Embassy in Prague, Lieutenant Colonel Thomas Ryan, who had debriefed the witnesses:

> On 4 Oct. 55 at 1910 hours between Atjaty and Adzhijabul in Trans-Caucasus region, two round and circular unconventional aircraft resembling discs or flying saucers were seen taking off almost vertically one minute apart. Disc aircraft ascended near dusk with outer surface revolving slowly to right and with two lights stationary on top near middle part. Sparks or flame seen coming from aircraft. No protrusions seen on aircraft which passed over observers' train. Both flying disc aircraft ascended relatively slowly to about 6000 feet, then speed increased sharply in horizontal flight both on northerly heading. Flying attitude of disc remained same during ascent as in cruise, like a discus in flight. Two operating searchlights pointing almost vertical seen near takeoff area located about 1–2 miles south RR [railroad] line. After sighting Soviet trainmen became excited and lowered curtains and refused permission to look out windows. US observers firmly believe these unconventional aircraft were genuine saucer or disc aircraft.

'We've been told for years that there isn't such a thing,' commented Lieutenant Colonel Hathaway to the Air Attaché, 'but all of us saw it.'[9] A full report was also sent to the CIA.

Researcher Loren Gross notes that there are three somewhat differing official US versions of this event: (1) Senator Russell's statements to Herbert Scoville, the CIA's Assistant Director of Scientific Intelligence (27 October 1955); (2) a CIA report written before the Scoville interview; (3) the Air Intelligence Information Report by Lieutenant Colonel Ryan based on an interview with Lieutenant Colonel Hathaway (13 October 1955 –

the version I have used). Gross has documented numerous instances where the descriptions differ from one another. The most important difference relates to the description of the objects seen: in the CIA report (2), a witness (possibly Senator Russell) is quoted as having seen only the second object, which was described as triangular in shape, with three lights 'one on each point of the triangle . . . As we watched, it was ejected from its launching site, making not less than three and not more than seven fast spirals in the air, after which it climbed extremely fast . . . We watched it climb and saw it reach a high altitude, the search [light] followed it all the way.'

Such differences among the three versions can perhaps be attributed to misreporting, though Loren Gross believes that the facts may have been altered to suit particular theories espoused by the source agencies: the Ryan version supports an unexplained disc-shaped vehicle, while the CIA report favours a high-performance Soviet aircraft,[10] perhaps delta-shaped. Organizational predilections and bureaucratic rivalries notwithstanding, these inconsistencies cannot be brushed aside. Yet clearly some kind of unusual aerial craft was observed.

The searchlight beams suggest that the discs were observed in the vicinity of a military base, and it is not inconceivable that the Russians were testing a secret disc-shaped aircraft, possibly designed with the aid of German scientists who are known to have been working on such aircraft during the Second World War.[11] Rumours abound that both the Americans and Russians, as well as the Canadians, have successfully developed such discs, but with the exception of a few circular craft such as John Frost's Avro-Car – which despite the extravagant claims made for it was capable only of limited hovering – there seems little evidence for this.[12] The unlikelihood of Soviet-built discs was emphasized in a CIA memorandum from W. E. Lexow, Chief of the Applied Science Division, Office of Scientific Intelligence, dated 19 October 1955:

> The objects reportedly sighted . . . are described to be similar to Project 'Y' which is in the research stage at Avro Aircraft Ltd, Canada . . . Project 'Y' is being directed by John Frost [who] is reported to have obtained his original idea for the flying machine from a group of Germans just after World War II. The Soviets may also have obtained information from this German group.
>
> Since two objects were reportedly seen in operation at one time in an area where it is most unlikely that experimental flying would be conducted, it is likely that these objects were in service. This

would indicate very rapid progress in this development for the Soviets. It does, however, seem inconsistent that the Soviets, if they have such an object in service, would continue their large development and production programs on conventional type aircraft . . .

Encounter over Greenland

Valentin Akkuratov, the well-known Soviet chief navigator of Soviet polar aviation, described an encounter with an unidentified aerial object as follows:

In 1956, engaged in strategic ice reconnaissance in a [Tupolev] Tu-4 plane in the area of Cape Jesup (Greenland), we dropped down from the clouds to fair weather and suddenly noticed an unknown flying craft moving on our portside parallel to our course. It looked very much like a large pearl-coloured lens with wavy, pulsating edges. At first we thought it was an American aircraft of an unknown design, and since we did not want to encounter it we went into the clouds again.

After we had flown for 40 minutes toward Bear Island, the cloud cover ended abruptly; it cleared ahead and on our portside we saw once again that same unknown craft. Making up our minds to see it at close quarters, we changed our course abruptly and began the approach movement, informing our base at Amderma of the manoeuvre. When we changed our course, the unknown flying machine followed suit and moved parallel at our speed.

After 15 to 18 minutes of flight the unknown craft sharply altered its course, sped ahead of us and rose quickly until it disappeared in the blue sky. We spotted no aerials, super-structure, wings or portholes on that disc. Nor did we see any exhaust gases or condensation trail. It flew at what seemed to us an impossible speed.

Sceptics argue that sightings of this sort, where no solid superstructure is evident, are merely optical phenomena of the mirage, rainbow or halo type. Dr Felix Zigel, who cited this report, discounted such interpretations in most cases. He also countered the explanation that ball lightning is the cause of many UFO reports:

The appearance of UFOs is almost always accompanied by a luminescence of air and the formation of an atmospheric plasma. This fact is the basis for the 'plasma' hypothesis of UFOs as accumulations of atmospheric plasma of the ball-lightning type. But this explanation does not hold up either. Ball-lightning is always a thunderstorm product, and the appearance of UFOs has no relation to weather. Ball-lightning diameters as a rule run four to five inches, no larger; the diameter of flying discs are tens and even hundreds of times that size.[13]

Sensational Encounters

By the 1960s some extraordinary stories – largely unsubstantiated – reached the Western media. According to science writer Alberto Fenoglio, for example, in an article in an Italian journal devoted to missile and space research[14] (subsequently condensed and translated by researcher Roberto Pinotti), Soviet Air Defence personnel observed UFOs circling and hovering for over twenty-four hours above Sverdlovsk, headquarters of a tactical missile organization, in spring 1959. Fighter aircraft sent to intercept reported that the UFOs easily outmanoeuvred them and zigzagged to avoid their machine-gun fire.[15]

Fenoglio, who claimed to have obtained his information from Soviet sources in the West, including a well-known diplomat, also described other sensational sightings during this period. In the summer of 1961 near Rybinsk, 150 kilometres from Moscow, new surface-to-air missile batteries were being set up as part of Moscow's air-defence network. A huge, disc-shaped object allegedly appeared at an estimated altitude of 20,000 metres, surrounded by a number of smaller objects. 'A nervous battery commander panicked and gave – unauthorized – the order to fire a salvo at the giant disc,' reported Fenoglio:

The missiles were fired. All exploded when at an estimated distance of some two kilometres from the target, creating a fantastic spectacle in the sky. A second salvo followed, with the same result. The third salvo was never fired, for at this point the smaller 'saucers' went into action and stalled the electrical apparatus of the whole missile base. When the smaller discoidal UFOs had withdrawn and joined the larger craft, the electrical apparatus was again found to be in working order.[16]

What are we to make of such sensational stories? In translating Fenoglio's original article, Roberto Pinotti noted that sceptics would point to the anonymity of Fenoglio's informants and conclude that the reports are fabricated. Yet, it seems unlikely that a respected journal would have published Fenoglio's material unless there was seen to be some substance to it.

At least one UFO report in 1961 seems to have been given some credence by the prestigious USSR Academy of Sciences Institute of Space Research. On 31 August several cars were stalled on a highway 30 miles from Moscow when a UFO reportedly hovered on top of an overpass for a few minutes. The cars were unable to start their engines until the UFO left the area.[17]

Passengers and Crew Disappear from Aircraft

The following story was obtained directly from the Soviet Embassy in London by the British researcher Derek Mansell in January 1965. The report originated with the Moscow Aviation Institute, and a brief account was first published in the West by Alberto Fenoglio in 1962.[18] Mansell's version contains some additional details. The incident is said to have taken place on an unknown date in 1961.

According to the report, an Antonov An-2P mail-plane took off from an airfield at or near Sverdlovsk, bound for Kurgan, with seven people on board. About 128 to 160 kilometres from Sverdlovsk, just after the pilot had communicated with ground control, the aircraft disappeared from the radar screen. Ground control tried unsuccessfully to regain communications. A search was launched, involving several helicopters and a large detachment of troops. Because the captain had radioed a position during his last communication, it did not take too long to recover the plane.

The aircraft was found intact in a small clearing in dense forest. There was no way it could have landed there. Authorities stated that it looked as if the plane had been put down gently from above. Most puzzling was the fact that there was no sign of anyone on board. All the mail was intact, and when the engine was started it ran on the first try.

The Moscow Aviation Institute report claims that an unidentified object was tracked on radar and that strange radio signals were heard at the time of disappearance. No marks or footprints were found at the site. According to Fenoglio's version of events, a well-defined 30-metre circle of scorched grass and depressed earth was found at a distance of 100 metres from the aircraft.

Night Encounter over Yalta

During a training flight on the night of 13 August 1967, Fighter Pilot (1st Class) Lieutenant Colonel Lev Vyatkin encountered an unknown flying machine beside his aircraft. The incident occurred sometime after 23.00 hours. Conditions were good, and the lights of the Black Sea resort of Yalta could be seen clearly below.

'I saw the object when I looked up from the instruments,' reported Vyatkin years later. 'It was a very large oval-shaped object which was somehow fixed to the port of my plane.' Concerned, the pilot radioed the flight commander, Major Musatov, and asked what other aircraft were in the zone. A reply came in the negative.

Vyatkin banked his plane to the right, trying not to lose sight of the strange object though avoiding a too close approach. 'I tried to determine in what direction it was moving. However, several seconds later its lights went gradually down as if a rheostat switch had been turned off inside.' Meanwhile, Vyatkin made a complete right turn, returning to his original course.

I considered my next move and then decided to make the left turn I had planned, trying to be as careful as possible. Hardly had I banked the plane to the left and adjusted the speed and thrust when I saw a flash of bright light from above, straight on the course of my plane. Then a slanting milky-white ray appeared in front . . . closing in on the plane. Had I not levelled out, I would have run into the ray with the fuselage or, to be more exact, with the cockpit. All the same I hit the ray with the left wing . . . approaching [it] at very high speed, not taking my eyes off it, so I had time to notice and feel something very strange. No sooner had the wing touched the ray than the latter broke into a myriad of tiny sparkles like those you see in a spent firework. The plane shook violently and the instruments read off the scale.

Is the ray solid? I thought instinctively, with my eyes still on the strange sparkling pillar which stretched downwards. Soon the light above and the ray below disappeared. Flying back to the airfield I kept searching the starry skies above for more surprises, but everything was quiet. My night flight ended safely. For many days afterwards the surface of the wing which had come into contact with the strange ray shone at nights, as if to remind me of the phenomenon.[19]

Further CIA Interest

An unevaluated CIA report dated 18 August 1967, with the subject heading 'Report on Conversations with Soviet Scientists on Subject of Unidentified Flying Objects in the USSR', yields valuable information on the conflicting attitudes of the Soviet scientific community to the problem at the time. The name of the CIA (or CIA-sponsored) scientists involved are deleted, together with the date(s) of the interviews. It is worth recording that from 22 to 31 August 1967, a week after the CIA report was written, Dr Robert J. Low, co-ordinator of the University of Colorado UFO Project at the time, attended the International Astronomy Union conference in Prague to represent the project and to report on the UFO situation in Iron Curtain countries. Also in attendance was Franklin D. Roach, principal investigator of the Colorado University project. Both men's expenses were paid by the US Government, but not through the UFO project.[20] It is not unlikely that either Low or Roach could have interviewed the Soviet scientists in Russia before the Prague visit: Low visited a number of European countries on project business during the month of August that year.

The first scientist referred to in the CIA report, a radio astronomer, 'emphatically stated that he knew of no sightings of UFOs in the USSR and added with a laugh that if they were only seen in the US, they must be of Soviet origin'. Another unnamed Soviet scientist, who was 'very interested in the problem . . . had read Menzel's book (which has been translated into Russian) but did not accept his conclusions. [He] knew of some sightings in the northern part of the USSR, but said that reports of such sightings are not printed in Soviet newspapers because they are not regarded as scientific observations.' The CIA report commented: 'This is interesting in view of the readiness of Soviet newspapers to print rather fantastic reports of hypotheses and "observations" suggested by the more imaginative members of the scientific community. Apparently some official sanction is needed.' The CIA commentator added that the anonymous scientist 'has been interested in US reports of UFOs and readily accepts their reality. In fact, it is his personal opinion that the UFOs may originate on Venus.'

The report refers to a stellar spectroscopist who was 'also dissatisfied with Menzel's book and felt that there was definitely an opportunity for additional research'. The CIA report concluded:

The general feeling one gets is that no official treatment of the UFO problem has been given in the USSR . . . At the same time,

there is almost universal awareness of the history and characteristics of the phenomenon often associated with considerable
interest. The result is that a demonstration of the inadequacy of
US Official explanations coupled with some proof of the reality of
the observations might excite enthusiasm more rapidly among
Soviet astronomers than among their US counterparts who are
more strongly influenced by the official ridicule associated with
UFOs in the US.

Although the CIA report (which has several paragraphs blacked out
by a censor) states that there seems to have been 'no official treatment of
the UFO problem' in the USSR, a research committee was established in
the Ministry of Defence as early as 1955.[21] And during that year, it is
rumoured, leaders of the secret services of the USSR, USA, France and
Britain met in Geneva, where they unanimously agreed on a policy of
secrecy on the UFO problem as far as the public was concerned. I have
been unable to substantiate this story, however, although the reliable
American journalist Dorothy Kilgallen did mention it in her syndicated
column on 15 February 1954: 'Flying saucers are regarded as of such vital
importance that they will be the subject of a special hush-hush meeting of
the world military heads next summer.' As far as Britain's involvement is
concerned, a former Deputy Chief of MI6 has convinced me that it is
pure fabrication. Yet, as we learned in Chapter 6, George Langelaan, an
ex-officer of the French Secret Service, stated in 1965 that the Russian and
American secret services (if not the British and French) *had* collaborated
on the problem, and had concluded that the flying saucers were of
extraterrestrial origin.

In this connection, it is worth mentioning the comments of Victor
Marchetti, former executive assistant to the Deputy Director of the CIA:

If it were concluded that UFOs were not of terrestrial origin but,
rather, vehicles from outer space, the CIA and US Government,
aware that the phenomenon was of a worldwide nature, would
seek cooperation in the investigation from the Earth's other
technically advanced nations, such as the United Kingdom,
France, Germany, and even the USSR. The CIA would function
as the US Government's agent, just as the KGB would be the
USSR's, MI6 would be the UK's, and so on. These agencies . . . are
quite accustomed to cooperating with each other on matters of
mutual interest. Co-operation in the intelligence business is not

restricted to allies. There are times when the CIA and KGB have found it advantageous to work together.[22]

The Stolyarov Committee

On 18 October 1967 the first meeting of the UFO Section of the All-Union Committee on Cosmonautics of the DOSAAF (All-Union Voluntary Society for Co-operation with Army, Navy, and Air Force) took place, attended by 400 people. Retired Soviet Air Force Major-General Porfiri Stolyarov was elected Chairman, and Dr Felix Zigel agreed to be Deputy Chairman of the semi-official group. Members included a cosmonaut and eighteen scientists and astronomers, as well as 200 qualified observers stationed throughout the country.[23]

Stolyarov, on learning of the existence of a mass of top-secret official reports, asked the Soviet Air Ministry whether his group could have access to them. 'Yes,' he was told. 'First set up your group, and then you can have the UFO reports'. Nevertheless, Stolyarov was denied access to the reports. When he asked the reason for this he was reportedly told: 'Because this is too big a matter and you are too small.'[24]

On 10 November 1967 both Major General Stolyarov and Dr Felix Zigel appeared on Moscow Central Television to announce the formation of the committee, at the conclusion of which Dr Zigel made an extraordinarily outspoken appeal to his fellow countrymen:

> Unidentified Flying Objects are a very serious subject which we must study fully. We appeal to all viewers to send us details of any observations of strange flying craft seen over the territories of the Soviet Union. This is a serious challenge to science, and we need the help of all Soviet citizens. Please write to us at the following address in Moscow . . .

The committee was inundated with letters from the public. Within a few days Stolyarov and the committee had over 200 good reports, and the press was not slow in publishing viewers' sightings.[25]

Cover-Up

Perhaps the authorities had not anticipated such an enthusiastic response from the public. By the end of November 1967 the DOSAAF Central Section of the All-Union Committee of Cosmonautics, chaired by Army

General A. L. Getman, adopted and passed a resolution on the dissolution
of the UFO Section. None of the members of the UFO Section was invited
to the meeting, nor were they ever informed as to the reason for this
decision.[26]

John Miller, a correspondent of the *Daily Telegraph*, relates an
interesting account of his attempt to secure an interview with Stolyarov at
the time. Miller managed to track down the UFO Section headquarters to
an office in the Central House of Aviation and Cosmonautics (Krasnoar-
meiskaya Street, Moscow A-167), near the Soviet Air Force Academy. A
secretary said the General was out, so an appointment was made for the
following day. When Miller returned, there was no general, no secretary
and the office was completely bare! He questioned a Soviet official working
in the building about the Stolyarov Committee and asked what had
happened to it. The man shrugged and replied: 'You are imagining things,
comrade. Everybody knows that UFOs do not exist.'[27]

A US Defense Intelligence Agency document adds that a Reuters
correspondent went to see Major-General Stolyarov a few days after the
TV programme.

> The General was very polite [the report states], confirmed the
> information about the commission, the 18 astronomers and SAF
> [Soviet Air Force] officers and the 200 observers. In addition, he
> said five positive sightings had been made. Approximately a week
> later the Reuters correspondent went back to see General
> Stolyarov. However, this time the correspondent could not get
> past the General's secretary; was politely but firmly told the
> General was no longer available for interview.[28]

Further Reactions

Reactions to the formation of the Stolyarov Committee, and what it
implied, were worldwide. The *New York Times*, for example, referred to it
as an 'official' study group, on a parallel with the University of Colorado
UFO Project commissioned by the US Air Force, and this, according to
researchers Ion Hobana and Julien Weverbergh, particularly incensed
some of Russia's more conservative scientists. The USSR Academy of
Sciences held an extraordinary general meeting during which Dr L. A.
Artsimovitch invoked the honour of Soviet scientists in severely
reprimanding all UFO protagonists, 'who were making themselves look
ridiculous in the eyes of their Western colleagues . . . Even before the

Academy had officially pronounced upon the matter Vladimir Lechkout-sov, secretary of the National Committee of Russian Physicists, had granted an interview to a Canadian newspaper in which he denied the existence of any Russian organization for the solving of the UFO problem.'[29]

In the *New York Times* article, Dr Felix Zigel appealed for international scientific co-operation on the matter. 'Unfortunately, certain scientists both in the Soviet Union and the United States deny the very existence of the problem instead of trying to solve it,' he said. 'International scientific co-operation as the solution of this problem would long have become a reality had not sensationalism and irresponsible antiscientific assertions as regards "flying saucers" interfered . . . The UFO problem is a challenge to mankind. It is the duty of scientists to take up this challenge, to disclose the nature of the UFO and to establish the scientific truth.'[30]

Apparently, the British Government was first to take up the challenge. According to a Defense Intelligence Agency attaché's report, on 12 December 1967, two days after Zigel's appeal was published, the British Embassy was directed by London to investigate the possibility of collaborating with the Soviets:

> The Scientific Counselor of the British Embassy went to the State Committee for Science and Technology and inquired about the UFO Commission and the possibility of British–Russian cooperation in observation of UFOs. The British Counselor was politely received and the commission was freely discussed. The British were told they would receive a reply to their request about cooperation.
>
> The British did not receive an answer and did not pursue the subject. However, on [ ] January 1968 . . . the British Scientific Counselor was told the following: The commission for investigating UFOs had been set up in response to a public demand. The commission had met twice, but since there was insufficient information to sustain it the commission would be disbanded after the next meeting.
>
> The British Scientific Counselor believes the original announcement of the commission on TV was an oversight on the part of the censors because the commission has not been reported on or referred to anywhere else. Mr [deleted] believes the commission has not been disbanded, but will continue under cover . . . The

preceding information was given to RO [reporting officer] by source. RO also read confidential British files on this subject.[31]

On 20 February 1968 the US Embassy in Moscow sent an unclassified airgram to the US Department of State in Washington DC, drawing attention to the February issue of *Soviet Life*, in which an article by Zigel referred in detail to the Stolyarov Committee and concluded that international co-operation in studying UFOs was vital. The hypothesis that UFOs originate on other worlds, and that they are flying craft from planets other than Earth, Zigel was quoted as having said, 'merits the most serious examination'.

The existence or non-existence of the Stolyarov Committee continued to plague Soviet academicians. Even Arkadii Tykhonov, Secretary of the committee, wrote a letter to the editor of the French journal *Phénomènes Spatiaux* stating that the information published therein about the establishment of a UFO committee in the USSR was 'incorrect'.[32]

What seems particularly farcical is that anyone could deny the existence of the Stolyarov Committee after its establishment had been announced on Moscow Central Television. The authorities seemed determined to stamp out serious interest in the subject. In February 1968 *Pravda* (Truth) published the official view in an article signed by E. Mustel, Chairman of the Soviet Astronomical Services, D. Marynov, President of the All-Union Astronomical and Geodetic Society, and V. Leshkovtsev, Secretary of the National Committee of Soviet Physicists. Not a single object had been sighted over Russian soil which could not be explained, the article said, and people who reported such things were either deceitful or lacking in scientific training. UFOs were 'anti-Soviet products of decadent capitalistic warmongering . . . They are not seen by astronomers who attentively study the skies day and night. They are not encountered by scientists who study the state and conditions of earth's atmosphere. They have not been observed by the Air Defence Service of this country.'[33] These statements are patently absurd in view of the relatively high incidence of reports by scientists, astronomers and pilots in the Soviet Union, as officially published eleven years later in a statistical analysis by the Institute of Space Research of the USSR Academy of Sciences.[34]

Dr Zigel was ordered to terminate his research and was expressly forbidden to have any contact with Western journalists.[35] This is corroborated by the fact that Dr Edward Condon, head of the University of Colorado UFO Project, never received a reply to a letter he sent Zigel.

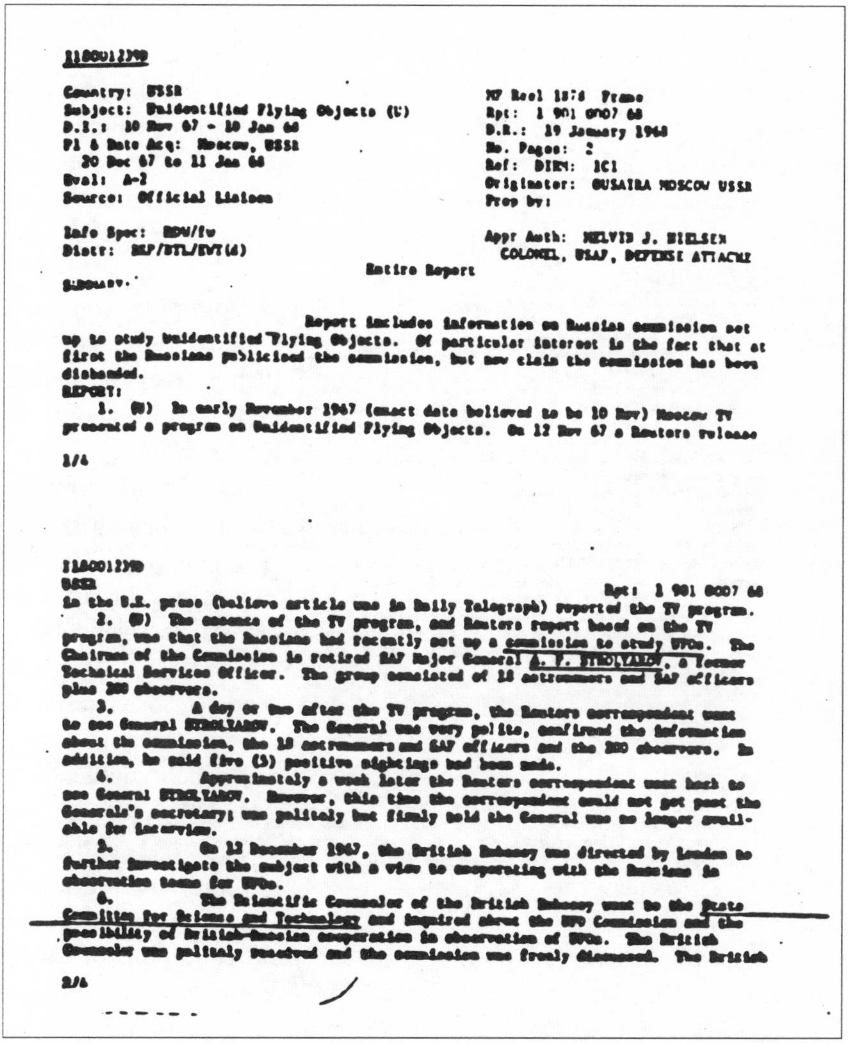

[illegible]

Country: USSR
Subject: Unidentified Flying Objects (U)
D.I.: 10 Nov 67 - 10 Jan 68
Pl & Date Acq: Moscow, USSR
20 Dec 67 to 11 Jan 68
Eval: A-2
Source: Official Liaison

Info Spec: [illegible]
Distr: [illegible]

NT Reel 1878 Frame
Rpt: 1 901 0007 68
D.R.: 19 January 1968
No. Pages: 2
Ref: DIRM: 1C1
Originator: USDAO MOSCOW USSR
Prep by:

Appr Auth: MELVIN J. NIELSEN
COLONEL, USAF, DEFENSE ATTACHE

Entire Report

SUMMARY:

Report includes information on Russian commission set up to study Unidentified Flying Objects. Of particular interest is the fact that at first the Russians publicised the commission, but now claim the commission has been disbanded.

REPORT:

1. (U) In early November 1967 (exact date believed to be 10 Nov) Moscow TV presented a program on Unidentified Flying Objects. On 12 Nov 67 a Reuters release

1/4

[illegible]
USSR
Rpt: 1 901 0007 68

in the U.K. press (believe article was in Daily Telegraph) reported the TV program.

2. (U) The essence of the TV program, and Reuters report based on the TV program, was that the Russians had recently set up a commission to study UFOs. The Chairman of the Commission is retired SAF Major General A. F. STOLYAROV, a former Technical Services Officer. The group consisted of 18 astronomers and SAF officers plus 200 observers.

3. A day or two after the TV program, the Reuters correspondent went to see General STOLYAROV. The General was very polite, confirmed the information about the commission, the 18 astronomers and SAF officers and the 200 observers. In addition, he said five (5) positive sightings had been made.

4. Approximately a week later the Reuters correspondent went back to see General STOLYAROV. However, this time the correspondent could not get past the General's secretary; was politely but firmly told the General was no longer available for interview.

5. On 12 December 1967, the British Embassy was directed by London to further investigate the subject with a view to cooperating with the Russians in observation teams for UFOs.

6. The Scientific Counselor of the British Embassy went to the State Committee for Science and Technology and inquired about the UFO Commission and the possibility of British-Russian cooperation in observation of UFOs. The British Counselor was politely received and the commission was freely discussed. The British

2/4

'. . . On 12 December 1967, the British Embassy was directed by London to further investigate the subject with a view to cooperating with the Russians in observation teams for UFOs . . .' A Defense Intelligence Agency attaché report relating to the announcement on Moscow Television in November 1967 of a Soviet commission to study UFOs. Note the reference to 'confidential British files on this subject'. (*DIA*)

1:600:2:49
USSR   Rpt: 1 941 1917 66
were told they would receive a reply to their request about cooperation.
        7.   The British did not receive an answer and did not pursue the subject.
However, on 8 January 1968 while on a routine visit to the Soviet State Committee
for Science and Technology, the British Scientific Counselor was told the following:
The commission for investigating UFOs had been set up in response to a popular demand.
The commission had met twice, but since there was insufficient information to sustain
it the commission would be disbanded after the next meeting.
        8.   The British Scientific Counselor believes the original announcement
of the work of the commission on TV was an oversight on the part of the censors
because the commission has not been reported or referred to anywhere else. He
believes the commission has not been disbanded, but will continue under cover. This
information was sent to London.
COMMENT:
        1.   The preceding information was given to RO by source. RO also read
confidential British files on this subject. RO did not approach Reuters correspondent because of delicate position of source. RO was unable to find anyone in Moscow
who saw TV program or read article in UK press.
        2.   On 10 or 11 November 1967 the U.S. Science Attache received a telephone
call from the Reuters correspondent and was asked if he had seen the TV program. When
the Science Attache replied that he had not seen the program, the correspondent
described it and asked the Science Attache if he thought the information was worth

1180012390
USSR   Rpt: 1 901 0007 68
reporting. The Science Attache said yes. The Science Attache, like the RO, has
not seen the UK press report. The U.S. Science Attache will receive two copies of
this report and will forward one copy to the appropriate S & T Agency in Washington.

Dr Robert Low, project coordinator, made one attempt at seeking collaboration with the Stolyarov Committee via the Soviet Embassy in Washington, but no further contacts were initiated in view of the lack of a response from Dr Zigel.[36]

Although forbidden from carrying out his 'dissident' research, Zigel nevertheless began privately to compile a manuscript of the mass of about 250 reports that had accumulated as a result of the television broadcast.[37] Paradoxically, despite public censure, Zigel (together with Yuri Fomin) was invited to give classified lectures on the subject to government and military officials – including the KGB – and was to re-emerge at the forefront of public Soviet UFO research eleven years later.

The Military Launches a Huge Investigation

At about 04.00 on 20 September 1977, over 170 witnesses, including border guards and militia, observed a large glowing object – described by many as cigar-shaped – raining down beams of light. It hovered over a town for some fifteen minutes before moving off towards the Finnish border.

In 1994, during an interview in Moscow for a British Central Television documentary, retired Soviet Air Force Colonel Boris Sokolov, who had headed the Ministry of Defence's investigation into the case, revealed that the object had been seen over a wide area for at least four hours before the above-mentioned incident. He told producers Lawrence Moore and Livia Russell:

> Later, having read the report, I found that a large group of military men had witnessed the event about several hundred kilometres away from Petrosavodsk, in one of the border regions. When they tried to report it, using their usual field communications – they had telephones and cable lines, radio and short-wave – none of them had worked. After the incident, which had lasted for several hours over Petrosavodsk, and a little shorter period of time over the border area, all communications were suddenly restored.

The military was so concerned about such a potential security threat that, for the first time in the USSR, a unique, state-funded, military and scientific research project was initiated, involving the co-operation of the USSR Academy of Sciences and the Ministry of Defence.

The most important thing [Sokolov continued] was the fact that the Ministry of Defence issued an order which named special officers in military units and regions who were given the responsibility of carrying out the duty of watching out for abnormal phenomena . . . over six million participated in the experiment, and during this period the rank-and-file personnel changed three times. It was a huge number; an experiment which will never be repeated. It lasted ten years, and the whole of the Soviet Union was involved.[38]

According to American journalists George Knapp and Bryan Gresh, who filmed an interview with Colonel Sokolov in Moscow in 1993, the Soviet Air Force had forty cases where pilots encountered UFOs during this ten-year period. 'Initially, they were commanded to chase, then shoot, the UFO,' Sokolov reportedly stated. 'But when our pilots would engage, the UFO would speed up. The pilot would give chase, lose control and crash.' This happened on three occasions. 'After that,' said Sokolov, 'the pilots received another order: when they see a UFO they should change course – and get out.'[39]

When queried by the Central Television team, the retired colonel claimed that his comments had been exaggerated. But George Knapp, whose company purchased 400 of the most interesting UFO reports compiled by Sokolov, assures me that these remarkable statements are recorded on videotape.

Naval Intelligence

In 1977 Dr Vladimir Azhazha, then a Soviet Navy submarine officer specializing in hydroacoustics, was asked by Vice Admiral Y. V. Ivanov, head of Naval Intelligence, to carry out research into 'hydrospheric aspects of the UFO issue'.

'We started with the appearance of UFOs over the sea, and their influence on the work of marine technology,' Dr Azhazha related to Lawrence Moore and Livia Russell during an interview in Moscow in 1994:

At the end, our working group wrote an instruction [manual] on observing UFOs . . . This was a small brochure which was introduced [in 1978] on hydrographic vessels and then on military vessels . . . Our group carried out this unpaid work and collected data where we could; from private individuals, from meteorologists, from letters which were sent to radio and television, and the Navy, which gave us data from all log-books.

Azhazha described an interesting naval case which took place on 7 October 1977, when the *Volga*, a 'floating base' ship for submarine maintenance, encountered UFOs 200 miles from the Kola Peninsula in the Barents Sea:

The captain of this ship, Tarankin, had a report about an approaching group of helicopters. Tarankin was surprised to hear this, as the ship was far from shore and land-based helicopters were never used. He also ruled out the possibility of other ships carrying helicopters at sea, because the intelligence services would obviously have known about it.

But when they approached, everyone suddenly realized that these were UFOs. They were flying around the masts; there were nine in all, and for eighteen minutes while they were flying around the *Volga* all radio communications were blacked out, and Tarankin was unable to contact the main base to report the event. When they left, the radio contact was restored. A plane from the intelligence service arrived, but time was lost and that was the end of it.[40]

During a conversation with Jacques Vallée and Martine Castello in Moscow in 1990, Dr Azhazha discussed this incident, one of many reported during the ten-year study. He added that, like other Navy reports, it was classified 'Top Secret'. Apparently, the captain ordered his men to observe the objects carefully. 'I want you to take pictures and to draw it,' he said, 'so that when we return to the Soviet Union no one will be able to say that your captain was drunk or crazy!'

Clearly the former Soviet Navy took the UFO subject seriously. 'We had to,' explained Azhazha:

There were too many incidents which could not be denied. It all began when we tried to understand the nature of certain underwater objects that followed our submarines. At times they even anticipated our maneuvers! Initially, we thought they were American devices. One day such an object came to the surface in a rather spectacular fashion. One of our ice-breakers was working its way in the Arctic Ocean when a brilliant spherical craft suddenly broke through the ice and flew up vertically, showering the vessel with fragments of ice. All the sailors on deck and the officers on the bridge saw it. And it was hard to deny the hole in the ice![41]

Rival Factions

In 1979 a group within the USSR Academy of Sciences Institute for the Study of Terrestrial Magnetism and Radioactivity was established – presumably as part of the ten-year military/scientific investigation referred to by Colonel Sokolov – to study 'anomalous atmospheric phenomena'. In *Nedelya* (The Week), scientists Vladimir Migulin and Yuri Platov, leaders of the new group, stated that UFOs were unquestionably 'natural phenomena' but conceded that 'there are a number of phenomena that are resistant to a trivial explanation'. The article contained severe criticisms of UFO enthusiasts, who, by their inept investigations and popularization of the UFO problem, served to hinder the new group from arriving at a complete solution to the phenomena 'within a few months'(!). The scientists urged witnesses to send reports of their sightings to the Academy of Sciences.[42]

In late 1978 another group was established by Dr Vladimir Azhazha, then Deputy Director of the Underwater Research Section of the USSR Academy of Sciences, and Nikita Schnee. The group was to be an official civilian UFO study section under the auspices of the A. S. Popov Scientific and Technical Society for Radio, Electronics and Communications, and called itself BPVTS (Search for Extraterrestrial Civilizations in the Neighbourhood of Earth by means of Radio-Electronics).

Members of the section included prominent figures such as Vice-Admiral M. M. Krylov, Chief of Communications in the Soviet Navy; Y. G. Nazarov, Deputy Head of the Soviet Control Centre for Space Flights; and E. V. Khrunov, pilot and cosmonaut. In an interview published in *Tekhnika Molodezhi* (Technical Youth), Khrunov stated: 'The UFO problem exists, and it is extremely serious. Thousands of people have seen UFOs, and up till now it is still not clear what they are. We are going to have to make a thorough investigation of this question. It is entirely possible that, concealed behind this question, there lies the problem of communication with extraterrestrial civilizations.'[43]

Nikita Schnee, Scientific Secretary of the new section, claimed that attempts to establish similar groups in other cities of the USSR had been thwarted by officialdom, although a group had been successfully set up in Estonia. At its inaugural seminar in November 1978 at Moscow University some unknown individuals stormed into the auditorium and disrupted the meeting. Later, the Vice-Principal of the university appeared and ordered the section to leave the hall, because, he said, it had already been booked for another meeting. To emphasize the point, he had brought along a number of rather bewildered-looking students, evidently gathered hastily from a nearby auditorium.

According to Schnee, none other than Dr Felix Zigel was responsible for the interruption, and confirmed as much in a telephone conversation afterwards. Learning of the impending seminar, Zigel had tipped off the Moscow City Committee of the Soviet Communist Party, as well as the KGB, and asked them to break up the meeting. Rather than being a deliberate attempt by the authorities to discourage UFO research, this interference with the BPVTS group was interpreted by Schnee as a ploy by the jealous Zigel to thwart the activities of other ufologists in the USSR.

In November 1979 the Moscow headquarters of the A. S. Popov Society ordered the UFO section to change its title to the more innocuous 'Section for the Investigation of Anomalous Atmospheric Phenomena'. In December 1979 the Moscow City Committee of the Soviet Communist Party forbade all operations of the section, although the group seems to have continued functioning.[44]

By any comparison, except perhaps with that of an American UFO 'exploitation' programme, the Soviet UFO research and investigation programme of 1976 until probably 1990 was extraordinary in breadth and scope, consuming state resources and having the highest level of prioritization because of the Cold War strategic implications – notably for anti-submarine warfare reasons. The reactions of Western intelligence agencies to this then major Soviet UFO investigation, in terms of intelligence data and reports, have yet to be revealed.

More Statements from Dr Felix Zigel

We have seen these UFOs over the USSR; craft of every possible shape: small, big, flattened, spherical. They are able to remain stationary in the atmosphere or to shoot along at 100,000 kilometres per hour. They move without producing the slightest sound, by creating around themselves a pneumatic vacuum that protects them from the hazard of burning up in our stratosphere. Their craft also have the mysterious capacity to vanish and reappear at will. They are also able to affect our power resources, halting our electricity-generating plants, our radio stations, and our engines, without however leaving any permanent damage. So refined a technology can only be the fruit of an intelligence that is indeed far superior to man.

These significant comments were made to the Latvian-born American journalist Henry Gris during an interview in 1981. Zigel further claimed that he had 50,000 UFO reports on file in the computer of the Moscow Aviation Institute, adding that from materials in his own archives he had compiled eight volumes. Only one had been published, he said, because the others, if released to the Soviet public, would trigger off an enormous wave of fear and unrest throughout the entire country.

Zigel went on to claim that at least seven landings of extraterrestrial spacecraft had occurred in the vicinity of Moscow between June 1977 and September 1979. He believed that there are three basic categories of UFO occupant: *spacemen*, the least frequently observed, who are very tall beings, 3 metres or so in height; *humanoids*, who are in general so similar to us in height and in many other respects that they could most probably mingle here undetected; and what Zigel called *aliens*, who are around 1 metre in height and, although resembling us in some respects, possess relatively large heads with no trace of hair, protruding eyes set far apart, wrinkled faces, and a pair of large nostrils by way of a nose.

In addition to these categories of what he termed 'flesh-and-blood extraterrestrials' Zigel stated that the spacecraft carry crews of robots or androids which possess the ability to disappear and reappear at will and, not being subject to the physical laws of our planet, seem to be 'deliberately constructed in order to confound all our notions of space, matter, time and dimensions'.[45]

My own findings, from over thirty-five years' research worldwide, correspond with those of Zigel.

Dramatic Events at Baikonur

According to Henry Gris, scientists Dr Alexei Zolotov and Dr Vladimir Azhazha told him that two UFOs hovered over the Baikonur Space Centre, Kazakhstan, for fourteen seconds on 1 June 1982, one directly above launch pad no. 1. The following day bolts and rivets were found which allegedly had been 'sucked out' of the support towers, causing welded sections to come apart. The other UFO reportedly hovered over a housing complex, knocking out thousands of panes of glass, or making fine holes in them. As a consequence, the entire cosmodrome was said to have been put out of action for at least two weeks.

This story was confirmed to Gordon Creighton by Henry Gris, who added that even UFO sceptic James Oberg of NASA had admitted to him that the base had indeed been out of commission during the period in question, and apparently could find no explanation for it.[46]

Commission for the Investigation of Anomalous Atmospheric Phenomena

By the beginning of 1983 the Russians were once again admitting that UFOs were a serious subject. An article in *Sovietskaya Kultura* of 6 January stated that the existence of UFOs should not be ruled out, and revealed that a Soviet Air Force pilot had had an encounter with one in 1981. The article said that there were still many unexplained phenomena behind the reports, and urged scientists to collate as much information as possible.[47]

In February 1984 the Commission for the Investigation of Anomalous Atmospheric Phenomena was established in Moscow, although its official announcement in the West was delayed until May. Affiliated to the Committee for the Protection of Natural Environment of the All-Union Council of Scientific Technical Societies, the new commission was headed by the distinguished former cosmonaut Pavel Popovich. Popovich told the trade-union newspaper *Trud* (Labour) that there had been hundreds of UFO reports each year in the Soviet Union, and that most could be explained away. But scientists had been disturbed by events in Gorky, 250 miles from Moscow, the previous year, which defied rational analysis.

On the evening of 27 March 1983 air traffic controllers at Gorky Airport had observed a steel-grey cigar-shaped object flying towards them which failed to respond to radio contact. It was about the size of a conventional aircraft but lacked wings, tail or fin, and was flying at an altitude of 3,000 feet at a speed of up to 125 m.p.h. The object behaved erratically, flying 45 miles to the south-east of Gorky before turning to head back to the airport, finally vanishing 25 miles to the north of the city. Popovich added that the new commission was taking this report very seriously, since the sighting had been made by reliable and well-trained aviation experts who had given precise and scientific observations, and who had tracked the UFO on radar for forty minutes.

The *Trud* article stated that other sightings witnessed by less well-trained observers would not be accepted by the commission,[48] although in July 1984 *Sovietskaya Rossiya* gave a box number at Moscow's main post office where citizens could send their UFO reports.

According to Dr Lev Chulkov, a graduate of the Moscow Aviation Institute, ufologists failed to gain access to the commission's officially sponsored research, nor did reporters get the right to cover the matter in newspapers. 'At the same time,' reported Chulkov, 'experts from the USSR Academy of Sciences were authorized to become censors. All manuscripts concerning UFOs were to be submitted to them. No editor-in-chief could publish a ufological article without their clearance. The General Censorship, known both in this country and outside it as *Glavlit*, enforced this order vigilantly.'[49]

Aeroflot Flight 8352 Escorted by UFO

On 30 January 1985 the official Soviet news agency Tass gave worldwide circulation to a dramatic UFO report, which first appeared in an article by V. Vostrukhin in *Trud* on that date. According to the report – which seems to have been overlooked by the censors – a Tu-134 airliner, Aeroflot flight 8352 from Tbilisi to Tallin via Rostov, encountered an unidentified object at 04.10 on an unspecified date (but later established as 7 September 1984), 120 kilometres from Minsk. The aircraft was operated by an aircrew from the Estonian Administration of the USSR Ministry of Civil Aviation, commanded by Captain Igor Cherkashin.

Second Pilot Gennadi Lazurin first noticed a yellow star-like object above and to starboard. Suddenly a thin shaft of light shot down from the object towards the ground, at which point Lazurin alerted the other crew members. The shaft of light then vanished and changed into a vivid cone of light, wider but paler than the first, followed by a third cone, wide and intensely bright. All four crew members on the flight deck reported that the unknown object was at a height of 40 to 50 kilometres above the Earth.

Lazurin began to make a quick sketch of this remarkable sight. On the area of ground illuminated by the cone-shaped beam, everything, including buildings, was distinctly visible. The searchlight beam then rose from the ground and centred on the aircraft, and the crew observed a blinding white point of light surrounded by concentric coloured circles.

Captain Cherkashin was hesitant about reporting the sighting, but then something happened that dispelled his doubts. The white point of light flared up and changed into a 'green cloud', and it seemed to him that the object was now approaching the airliner at an immense speed and was on the point of crossing his course at an acute angle. Cherkashin ordered Navigator Igor Ognev to radio Minsk Air Traffic Control. Just as details were being transmitted, the object came to a halt. The Minsk controller replied that the anomalous target was not visible on his radar.

The 'green cloud' then suddenly dropped down to the altitude of the airliner, ascended vertically, and began to swing from left to right, then down and up once again. Finally it took up a position beside the airliner and flew alongside at their altitude of 10,000 metres and speed of 800 k.p.h. Inside the cloud the crew could see a 'play of lights' flashing on and off, and then performing fiery zigzag manoeuvres. The Minsk traffic controller confirmed that he could see flashes on the horizon, in the vicinity of the airliner.

The 'cloud' continued to change shape, developing a 'tail' shaped like a waterspout, wide at the top and narrow at the bottom. Then the 'tail' started to rise and changed from its elliptical shape to a square, then to a sharp-nosed wingless 'cloud-aircraft', shining with a yellow and green glow.

At this point the flight attendant came to the flight-deck and said that the passengers wanted to know what the strange object was flying beside them. 'Tell them it's a cloud!' replied the captain. 'Yellow clouds – lights of cities reflecting from below. Green clouds – tell them it's the Aurora Borealis!'

Another Tu-134, passing through the Minsk Air Traffic Control Zone *en route* from Leningrad to Tbilisi, also observed the 'cloud-aircraft'.

Captain Cherkashin contacted the air traffic controllers at Riga and Vilna, who picked up both his aircraft and the UFO, which continued following the airliner until Tallin, Estonia. After landing there the crew was given some curious details by the air traffic controller: on the radarscope, behind the Tu-134, could be seen two other moving 'blips' the whole time, yet the blip of the airliner kept vanishing and reappearing. 'I would have understood it all right had you been "blinking" on the landing radarscope,' said the controller, 'but on the sky-scanning radar, that never happens – simply *can't* happen.'

The *Trud* article included a commentary by Dr Nikolai Zheltukhin, Vice-Chairman of the Commission for Anomalous Phenomena. 'It is particularly valuable,' he concluded, 'that we now possess a consistent and detailed picture of the transformation in the appearance of unidentified flying objects.'[50]

It is tempting to try to explain the sighting in terms of a bizarre meteorological phenomenon, a barium-cloud experiment, or a strategic air defence test; yet the facts as reported do not support such hypotheses.

Shortly after publication of the article, Dr Lev Chulkov reports, author V. Vostrukhin and the *Trud*'s science editor were sacked, followed by the editor-in-chief. In addition, Chulkov reports that crew members of the other Tu-134 airliner (*en route* from Leningrad to Tbilisi) were severely affected by their encounter with the 'cloud-aircraft'. When Captain V. Gotsiridze noticed the object, he decided to approach it for a closer look. The UFO reportedly shot a beam of light which struck both him and Second Pilot Kabachnikov. Several days afterwards Gotsiridze was taken to hospital, where he later died of a disease that resembled myeloma, i.e. malignancy of the bone marrow. A similar disease made Kabachnikov an invalid for life.[51] In 1989 journalist S. Omelchenko spoke to Flight Engineer Murman Gvenetadze, another crew member, who confirmed this disturbing incident with the unknown aircraft. 'It manoeuvred easily, changed its course and speed or hovered,' recalled Gvenetadze. 'We did not think of danger at all. It was just interesting. Now I would be scared after what happened to my friends.'[52]

The Soviet military paper *Krasnaya Zvezda* (Red Star) debunked the Aeroflot incidents as science fiction. Flying saucers and UFOs are not due to extraterrestrials, it said, but are more likely apparitions caused by temperature inversions, refracted light or radio waves, discarded booster rockets, decaying satellites and so on. The mystery surrounding the Aeroflot sightings could thus be explained as 'refracted light beams striking floating space garbage, or as bits of discarded rockets showering down through the atmosphere'.[53]

The KGB Releases Some UFO Files

The former KGB (Komitet Gosudarstvennoi Bezopastnosti – Committee for State Security), which following the dissolution of the Soviet empire was transformed in 1991 into the Federal Counter-Intelligence Service (FSK), the Foreign Intelligence Service (SVR) and the Federal Agency for Government Communications and Information, arguably once was (and still may be) the world's largest intelligence service.

In 1992 several anonymous, high-ranking, former Soviet Ground Forces officers, through independent UFO journals, informed the general public that information on UFOs had secretly been collected.[54] In April of that year it was reported that two Hollywood producers had bought the rights to aspects of the KGB's study of UFOs.[55] In 1992, as well, the editorial board of the Russian magazine *Aura-Z* received a package of KGB reports, previously classified 'Secret', detailing sightings by military and civilian personnel. Entitled 'Cases of Observations of Anomalous Occurrences in the Territory of the USSR, 1982–1990', the 124-page KGB document covers reports from a total of seventeen regions.

Multiple-Witness Sightings at an Army Weapons Depot

One of the most interesting cases from the KGB files occurred at an Army weapons depot in the district of Kapustin Yar, Astrakhan region, on the night of 28–29 July 1989. Depositions of seven military witnesses are included in the report: two junior officers, a corporal and four privates; as well as illustrations by the observers and a brief case summary by an unnamed KGB officer. Military personnel of the signals centre reported sightings of three UFOs, beginning at 22.12 hours on 28 July. A nearby military base also reported sighting a UFO from 23.30 on 28 July until 01.30 on 29 July. The report continues:

> After questioning the witnesses, it was determined that the reported characteristics of the observed UFOs are: disc 4–5 m. diameter, with a half-sphere on top, which is lit brightly. It moved sometimes abruptly, but noiselessly, at times coming down and hovering over the ground at an altitude of 20–60 m. The command of [censored] called for a fighter [from the base at Akhtubinsk] but it was not able to see it in detail, because the UFO did not let the aircraft come near it . . . .

Another witness, Private Bashev, reported that, as the object flew towards him and others, it 'divided itself in three shining points and took the shape of a triangle'. There are interesting parallels here with the sightings over south-east London in 1980 (see Chapter 4) and in Shanxi province, China, in 1981 (Chapter 11).

The most detailed description of one of the objects was provided by Ensign Valery N. Voloshin, communications officer-on-duty, whose observation (together with Private Tishchayev) lasted for two hours:

> One could clearly see a powerful blinking signal which resembled a camera flash in the night sky. The object flew over the unit's logistics yard and moved in the direction of the rocket weapons

depot, 300 metres away. It hovered over the depot at a height of 20
metres. The UFO's hull shone with a dim green light which
looked like phosphorous. It was a disc, 4 or 5 m. in diameter, with
a semispherical top.

While the object was hovering over the depot, a bright beam
appeared from the bottom of the disc, where the flash had been
before, and made two or three circles, lighting the corner of one of
the buildings . . . The movement of the beam lasted for several
seconds, then the beam disappeared and the object, still flashing,
moved in the direction of the railway station. After that, I
observed the object hovering over the logistics yard, railway
station and cement factory. Then it returned to the rocket
weapons depot, and hovered over it at an altitude of 60–70 m.
The object was observed from that time on, by the first guard-shift
and its commander. At 01.30 hrs., the object flew in the direction
of the city of Akhtubinsk and disappeared from sight.[56]

This is but one of many interesting reports released by the FSK.
Clearly, the UFO subject is taken seriously in the former Soviet Union. I
have been informed that the FSK maintains firm control over the
dissemination of information on the subject, principally through its
directorate which deals with military counter-intelligence.

The Voronezh Landings

During the last two weeks of September 1989, thousands of people
observed unidentified flying objects in Voronezh, Russia, and over thirty
people witnessed landings (on at least four occasions) of an unknown
craft, together with a giant, silver-suited humanoid and a 'robot'. One of
these landings occurred in the city's South Park. This sensational story
attracted worldwide media coverage – most of it inaccurate and ridiculous.
Jacques Vallée reports that investigations by various engineers and
authorities established that an unknown object, leaving impressions in
the ground indicating an approximate weight of 11 tons, had indeed
landed; moreover, several experts, including the head of the local Criminal
Expertise Department, testified to an increase in background radiation at
the landing-site.[57]

'Such things mustn't be taken too lightly,' commented a spokesman
for the local KGB administration. 'We must accumulate information on
any abnormal phenomena, wherever they take place, and carefully study

them. This is primarily a task for scientists . . . We are here to take steps –
if necessary – to ensure the citizens' safety.'[58]

Pilot Affected by an Encounter

During meetings with Russian scientists and witnesses in 1991, former
NASA contract research scientist Dr Richard Haines interviewed Vladimir
Kuzmin, an Air Force jet-pilot instructor who encountered a UFO on 24
or 25 December 1989. The unknown object was observed while Kuzmin
was making various aerobatic manoeuvres in an L-29 jet trainer at an
altitude of 8,000 metres, about 48 kilometres south of Chelyabinsk.

A yellow-white cigar-shaped object appeared to the north of Kuzmin's
position at an estimated distance of 18–25 kilometres and an altitude of
7,500 metres. It subtended an angle of about 5° of arc and remained
horizontal and stationary. By the time Kuzmin had performed a vertical
loop to gain a better view, the object had disappeared. Kuzmin radioed to
the air controller at the local airfield, but nothing could be seen on radar
except his own plane.

'Our careful reconstruction of the event established that Kuzmin
looked at the object for a total of about four minutes,' reports Dr
Haines:

> Some time after he landed he noticed that his exposed facial
> region was covered with a thick red crust which was sensitive (but
> not painful) to the touch. It was similar to a skin scald and was
> red. This gradually subsided and was gone after about ten to
> twelve days. No nausea, dizziness or other physiological effects
> were noted after the sighting. He did not report the incident to the
> authorities.

Dr Haines pointed out that the aircraft's plexiglass canopy blocks a
very large percentage of ultraviolet (UV) radiation. UV wavelengths are
those which are known to cause sunburn, so either the UFO emitted a very
high level of UV radiation or Kuzmin's encrusted facial skin was due to an
entirely different physiological response mechanism. It was probably not
microwave radiation, since no permanent tissue damage nor pain was
experienced.[59]

Official Recognition

In 1990 more military cases came to light. Officials seemed more prepared to acknowledge the reality of intrusions by unknown aerial craft. General Igor Maltsev, Chief of the Air Defence Forces, for example, admitted in April that year that over 100 observations of UFOs had been reported to him on 21 March. According to eyewitness accounts, he said, the UFOs were disc-shaped, with a diameter of from 100 to 200 metres.

In referring to one of the several Soviet Air Defence Force encounters (described in detail in my book *Alien Liaison*[60]), General Maltsev commented that 'The movement of the UFO was not accompanied by sound of any kind and was distinguished by its startling manoeuvrability. It seemed that the UFO was completely devoid of inertia. In other words, they had somehow "come to terms" with gravity. At the present time, terrestrial machines hardly have any such capability.'[61]

Asked if the Air Defence Forces regarded these intrusions as a 'violation of the sovereignty of the USSR', General Ivan Tretiak, then Deputy Defence Minister, replied that it was premature to regard the UFOs as a threat, because, although the reports by pilots indicated that the UFOs appeared to be of artificial origin, their real nature had yet to be determined. Even if it is proven that some UFOs are 'a product of a highly organized intelligence from a significantly more developed civilization than our own . . . any fight with such objects and their crews – before a clarification of their intentions – would be futile.'[62]

On 26 April 1990, President Mikhail Gorbachev was questioned about the UFO phenomenon during a meeting with workers in the Urals. 'The phenomenon of UFOs is real,' he reportedly replied, 'and we should approach it seriously and study it.'[63] Gorbachev was also quoted as having said: 'I know that there are scientific organizations which study this problem.'[64]

Radar Complex Attacked by a UFO

Shortly after midnight on 13 September 1990, at a radar tracking-station near Kuybyshev, 800 kilometres east-south-east of Moscow, Major A. Duplin observed a large target on the long-range radar screen. 'The brightness of this blip was comparable to that of a strategic bomber approaching us,' he said, 'and the distance was no more than 100 kilometres. Following my order, enquiries were made via the automatic identification system, but I was informed by Senior Sergeant Miketenok that this system had gone out of operation. At this moment, the "strategic bomber" target scattered, and changed into what looked like a flock of birds on the radar screen.'

An explanation that the multiple targets were the products of reflections caused by parts (such as boosters) from a rocket launch was soon discounted, since at a distance of 42 kilometres the radar screen showed a strong signal from the main target, representing an isosceles triangle. Another explanation was birds, but this was soon discounted. 'To glow on the screen at such a distance, these "birds" must have had a plumage of steel with cobalt!' remarked Major Duplin. (Later, the military correspondent who reported this story, Captain D. Rudzit, obtained permission via Air Defence Command to see a videotape of the radar recordings.)

As the target came closer, the underground command post ordered a team to investigate, headed by Captain P. Lazeiko. 'An unknown object passed over our heads as we came out of the underground bunker. Its height was no more than about ten metres,' reported Lazeiko.

> We could see it clearly, since the perimeter of the base is always lit by searchlights. The bottom of the object was smooth, but not mirror-like: it was like a thick layer of soot. We did not notice any openings, portholes or landing gear, but we saw three whitish-blue beams of light. The corners of the object were slightly rounded.

According to Senior Sergeant B. Gorin, commander of the guard, who was in the guardroom just after relief of the guard, Corporal A. Blazhis, a sentry, could not be contacted at post no. 4. At 00.20 Gorin sent two soldiers to find out what had happened. In his report, Sergeant A. Romanov, one of the soldiers, explained that all the telephone equipment at the post was in perfect working order but there was no sign of Blazhis. On learning this, Gorin gave the order 'To arms!' and organized a search for Blazhis. Half an hour later it was reported that Blazhis had disappeared, together with another sentry, A. Varenitsa.

'After the report,' said Major Duplin, 'I decided to scan the unidentified object, which had apparently landed near the fence by the short-range radar post [no. 12]. I had time to notice on the radar screen that just after the triangular object disappeared, sources of [radar] radiation could still be seen at the ends of where the triangle had been.'

Captain Lazeiko reported that as he ran up to post no. 12 he saw a flash, and the aerials appeared to be on fire, 'as if made of wood'. The military correspondent said that although he was not permitted to take photos at the site, he was shown the remains of the aerial.

Another witness to the landing, Corporal S. Dudnik, described the event as follows:

> I was standing on sentry duty at post no. 6 and saw the arrival of a large, black, triangular flying object, each side about fifteen metres in length. It landed from above – not too quickly – with a soft rustling sound. The thickness of the triangle was about three metres. The flash, which knocked down the aerial behind me, came from the centre of the side of the object. There were no openings that I could see, but it seemed to be aiming at the target, and I was directly in the firing line! Strangely, I did not come to any harm . . .

P. Beshmetov (rank-and-file) ran up to Dudnik when the fire started. 'He was standing near the barbed wire barrier with his tommy-gun directed to the large triangle, which was 100 metres from the barbed wire. I prepared to shoot, too,' said Beshmetov. His report continues:

> The triangle took off after one and a half hours, and the commander of the guard ordered all the soldiers back to their posts and to check the barrier. The colour of the radar truck before the flash was dark green, but afterwards its paint became black and blistered. Some parts of the truck had melted. The upper aerial had broken away and was lying on the ground, three metres away from the truck. All its steel parts had melted, with the exception of the aluminium dish itself. The officers told Captain Rudzit that the steel parts burned as if in a stream of oxygen, and they could not understand what sort of energy could have caused steel to burn from such a distance [143.5 metres from the UFO to radar post no. 12].
>
> When I came up to the storehouse, out came Corporal Blazhis. He was very surprised to see me walking along his post. I asked him where he had been for such a long time. He began to laugh, and said that as he was going to the phone to report to Sergeant Romanov, he suddenly lost his memory . . . Simultaneously, A. Varenitsa, the other missing sentry, also appeared at his post. He too remembered nothing, and is convinced that all the time he

remained at his post. In his opinion, it was as if we all appeared to them in an instantaneous film – suddenly soldiers appeared with tommy-guns.

The watches of corporals Blazhis and Varenitsa were one hour and fifty-seven minutes slow and one hour and forty minutes slow, respectively. In addition, the serial numbers of Blazhis' tommy-gun and bayonet were completely wiped out.

The ground looked as if it had been subjected to an explosion. According to witnesses, the object did not actually land, but hovered just above the ground. In his report to the commander of the radar complex, the head of the economic managerial platoon, Boris Voronkov, demanded punishment of the two sentries for burning the aerial and destroying a vegetable patch above which the UFO had hovered. The commander of the radar complex said that a special commission from the Ministry of Defence was due to visit to the site on 18 September 1990, five days after the incident.

Official Denial

These extraordinary events were reported in the main newspapers, as well as in the military newspaper *Za Rodinu* (Red Star), and the article was reprinted in full in Irkutsk by the local *Sovietskaya Molodezhi* (Soviet Youth).[65] On 23 September 1990 *Rabochaya Tribuna* (Workers Tribune) published a story explaining that the deputy chief of *Za Rodinu* was ordered to visit the headquarters of the military district commander, General Makashov, and that the military correspondent Rudzit and his chief now denied the incident. The following month *Trud* published information from the headquarters of the military district that the story of a UFO landing at the radar complex was an invention by the military correspondent of *Za Rodinu*.[66]

Finally, all serious interest in the story was killed when General Ivan Tretiak, Deputy Minister of Defence and Commander-in-Chief of the Air Defence Forces, debunked the incident:

Recently a report appeared in *Rabochaya Tribuna* that some kind of flying vehicle appeared in the Kuybyshev district and, what is more, it destroyed our radar station. Naturally, we were perplexed – why was there no report? A destroyed radar station is a major incident. Even if it had been hit by lightning, it would have been necessary to report this immediately. And here we have an attack by a flying vehicle. But it can be explained. *Rabochaya Tribuna* took these reports from the district [military] newspaper, *Za Rodinu*. It turns out that the hoax was thought up by a staff member of the newspaper in order to attract readers . . .[67]

Nikolai Lebedev, an engineer and journalist, one of Russia's leading UFO investigators, believes the report to be genuine, however. He told me that:

At the end of November 1990 I spoke with Emil Bachurin, a leader of the UFO research group in Perm. He told me that his close friend, a colonel, was invited to the radar complex not long after the visit from the Ministry of Defence commission on 18 September. The colonel was informed that the upper aerial of radar post no. 12 and its instruments were taken away by the commission, to be studied by the Scientific Research Department of the Ministry of Defence. The colonel personally was shown videotapes from the radar screen and the site where the incident had taken place. After having spoken with all the witnesses, he concluded that the incident did indeed happen as reported.[68]

Giant Sphere Reported by Cosmonaut

Two weeks after the Kuybyshev incident, cosmonauts on board the *Mir* space station, G. M. Manakov and G. M. Strekalov, were asked by journalist Leonid Lazarevich about 'the most interesting natural phenomena' to be seen on Earth from space. The interview took place on 28 September 1990. Manakov responded to the question as follows:

Yesterday, for example, I saw, if one may call it that, an unidentified flying object . . . It was a great, silvery sphere, it was iridescent . . . this was at 22.50 . . . There was an absolutely clean, clear sky. It is difficult to determine, but the object was at a great altitude over the Earth – perhaps 20–30 kilometres. It was much larger than a huge ship . . . This object had a regular shape, but what it was I don't know; perhaps an enormous, experimental sphere, or something else[69] . . . I was observing it for about six or seven seconds, then it disappeared . . . It simply was hovering over the Earth.[70]

A Common Security Threat

According to an account by H. G. Wells, a fascinating conversation took place between him and V. I. Lenin in 1920:

> . . . I said to Lenin that the development of human technology might some day change the world situation. The Marxist conception itself would then become meaningless. Lenin looked at me and he said:
>
> 'You are right. I understood this myself when I read your novel *The Time Machine*. All human conceptions are on a scale of our planet. They are based on the pretension that the technical potential, although it will develop, will never exceed the "terrestrial limit". If we succeed in establishing interplanetary communication, all our philosophical, moral and social views will have to be revised. In this case, the technical potential, become limitless, would impose the end of the role of violence as a means and method of progress.'[71]

There is no denying the possibility that, once it is established beyond doubt that extraterrestrials are visiting Earth, the social, philosophical, scientific and economic repercussions would have a profound effect on us all, irrespective of differing nationalities. Should the 'visitors' pose threats to humanity, the likelihood is that this will lead to an unprecedented degree of unity between the nation-states.

During the Geneva summit conference of November 1985, US President Ronald Reagan made that point to Soviet leader Mikhail Gorbachev when he told him 'how much easier his task and mine might be in these meetings that we held if suddenly there was a threat to this world from another species from another planet outside in the universe. We'd forget all the little local differences that we have between our countries, and we would find out once and for all that we really are all human beings here on this Earth together.'[72]

In referring to this discussion during a speech given at the Kremlin in 1987, Gorbachev added that 'The US President said that if the Earth faced an invasion by extraterrestrials, the United States and the Soviet Union would join forces to repel such an invasion. I shall not dispute the hypothesis, though I think it's early yet to worry about such an intrusion . . .'[73]

Defence Intelligence around the World

Germany

THE UNITED STATES' intelligence community has sustained a long-standing interest in the UFO subject, and under provisions of the Freedom of Information Act numerous reports of sightings and related information from all over the world, dating back to the 1940s, have been released. Many of these originate from 'open sources' such as foreign newspapers, journals (literature intelligence – LITINT) or broadcasts. The following such report, translated from a Greek newspaper by the Central Intelligence Agency, describes a UFO landing in East Germany, witnessed by Oscar Linke and his daughter near Hasselbach in July 1952:

> Furnished with the sworn testimony of an eyewitness, Oscar Linke, a 48-year-old German and former mayor of Gleimershausen, West Berlin, intelligence officers have begun investigating a most unusual 'flying saucer' story. According to this story, an object 'resembling a huge frying pan' and having a diameter of about 15 meters landed in a forest clearing in the Soviet Zone of Germany. Linke recently escaped from the Soviet Zone along with his wife and six children.
>
> Linke and his 11-year-old daughter, Gabriella, made the following sworn statement last week before a judge: 'While I was returning to my home with Gabriella, a tire of my motorcycle blew out near the town of Hasselbach. While we were walking along toward Hasselbach, Gabriella pointed out something which lay at a distance of about 140 meters from us. Since it was twilight, I thought that she was pointing at a young deer.
>
> 'I left my motorcycle near a tree and walked toward the spot which Gabriella had pointed out. When, however, I reached a spot about 55 meters from the object, I realized that my first impression had been wrong. What I had seen were two men who were now about 40 meters away from me. They seemed to be

dressed in some shiny metallic clothing. They were stooped over and were looking at something lying on the ground.

'I approached until I was only about 10 meters from them. I looked over a small fence and then I noticed a large object whose diameter I estimated to be between 13 and 15 meters. It looked like a huge frying pan. There were two rows of holes on its periphery, about 30 centimeters in circumference. The space between the two rows was about 0.45 meters. On the top of this metal object was a black conical tower about 3 meters high.

'At that moment, my daughter, who had remained a short distance behind me, called me. The two men must have heard my daughter's voice because they immediately jumped on the conical tower and disappeared inside. I had previously noted that one of the men had a lamp on the front part of his body which lit up at regular intervals.

'Now, the side of the object on which the holes had been opened began to glitter. Its color seemed green but later turned to red. At the same time I began to hear a slight hum. While the brightness and hum increased, the conical tower began to slide down into the center of the object. The whole object then began to rise slowly from the ground and rotate like a top. It seemed to me as if it were supported by the cylindrical plant which had gone down from the top of the object, through the center, and had now appeared from its bottom on the ground.

'The object, surrounded by a ring of flames, was now a certain number of feet above the ground. I then noted that the whole object had risen slowly from the ground. The cylinder on which it was supported had now disappeared within its center and had reappeared on the top of the object. The rate of climb had now become greater. At the same time my daughter and I heard a whistling sound similar to that heard when a bomb falls. The object rose to a horizontal position, turned toward a neighboring town, and then, gaining altitude, it disappeared over the heights and forests in the direction of Stockheim.'

Many other persons who live in the same area as Linke later related that they saw an object which they thought to be a comet . . . After submitting his testimony to the judge, Linke made the following statement: 'I would have thought that both my daughter and I were dreaming if it were not for the following element involved: When the object had disappeared, I went to the place where it had been. I found a circular opening in the ground and it was quite evident that it was freshly dug. It was exactly the same shape as the conical tower. I was then convinced that I was not dreaming.'

Linke continued, 'I had never heard of the term "flying saucer" before I escaped from the Soviet Zone into West Berlin. When I saw this object, I immediately thought it was a new Soviet military machine. I confess that I was seized with fright because the Soviets do not want anyone to know about their work . . .'[1]

The Defense Intelligence Agency

Established in 1961 by Robert McNamara – President Kennedy's Defense Secretary at the time – the Defense Intelligence Agency's mandate was to co-ordinate all US military intelligence services. The DIA Director works for the Secretary of Defense and for the Joint Chiefs of Staff directly, and the agency is staffed by both military officers and civilians. In addition to processing and analysing 'raw' intelligence gathered from military sources, which is then turned into finished intelligence reports that are circulated within the Pentagon and the intelligence community, the DIA prepares daily and weekly intelligence digests as well as its own estimates of enemy capabilities.[2] Along with other US national intelligence agencies' activities, those of the DIA are inter-agency, co-ordinated by the office of the Director of Central Intelligence, who also is Director of the CIA.

In 1980 I spoke with Peter Gersten, a New York lawyer representing Citizens Against UFO Secrecy (CAUS). He explained that in 1979 the DIA had submitted a motion to the US Attorney indicating that it had searched its complete record systems and had no documents on UFOs other than three it had found and released. One involved a Peruvian incident in 1980 (see pp. 267–8), while another, which was in the process of being translated, related to some sightings in the Soviet Union. The DIA had released the other document, which deals with the now well-known case of UFOs reported by an Imperial Iranian Air Force pilot (see pp. 283–9), in 1977.

In view of the DIA's denials that it had any further material on UFOs, it is interesting that in December 1985, under provisions of the Freedom of Information Act, the Agency released a total of thirty-seven UFO-related documents – amounting to 139 pages – to researcher Ray Boeche, who forwarded copies to me. In a covering letter to Boeche the DIA explained that 'it has been determined that there are 53 documents responsive to your request. Of these 53 documents, portions of 15 are properly classified and are not releasable.'

Some of the released documents, stamped 'Best Copy Available', are barely legible or totally illegible, either because the DIA considered them so insignificant that they were not deemed to be worth preserving in legible form, or because they were deliberately rendered illegible owing to the sensitive material contained therein.

British and Australian reports are not included among the released documents, and it is my assumption that there is an agreement between the DIA and British as well as Australian defence chiefs not to include such documentation in the released Freedom of Information cases. As mentioned in Chapter 5, there is close liaison between the DIA and the Ministry of Defence via the Defense Intelligence Agency Liaison, London (DIALL), which has its office in the MoD's main building in Whitehall. In view of Britain's 'special relationship' with the DIA, the CIA and the National Security Agency (NSA), it seems logical to me that UFO reports of interest would be passed on to the DIA by the MoD's Defence Intelligence Staff (DIS), since it is known that the DIA has forwarded information on the subject to the DIS as well as to Australian defence intelligence staff in Canberra.

Chile

In September 1965 the US Air Attaché in Santiago forwarded a news report to the DIA of a UFO sighting by the crew of Chilean National Airlines Flight LAN 904 on the 6th of that month, at about 21.30 hours. The captain of the DC-6B was Marcelo Cisternas, Chief of Flight Operations for the airline, who described the incident as follows:

> It was something mechanical – zigzagging – its movements were not precise – suddenly it changed direction and came directly towards us . . . During the 13 to 14 minutes this strange object followed us, it gave me the impression that when it located us it tried to identify us. At once we requested information from the Flight Control Tower in Arica and Iquque. We were informed that no other flights had been scheduled in that zone . . .
>
> I have never had a similar experience . . . It was not an optical vision due to atmospherical reflections. I am sure it was a mechanical apparatus. [Our] plane was flying at an altitude of 8,500 feet . . . the co-pilot, the engineer, hostess and steward also

saw it. It emitted a light of an intense color, then changed and
turned to radiant white. It was suspended at a distance of about
3 kms from us, in a straight line . . . Suddenly the same way it
appeared it withdrew at an incredible speed . . .[3]

In the summer of 1965 I happened to be touring throughout South
America (including Chile) with the Philharmonia Orchestra, and recall
that UFO reports appeared on the front pages of many newspapers on an
almost daily basis.

Argentina

In the 1960s, the Argentine Navy was charged with the official investiga-
tions into UFO sightings, especially those observed by its own personnel.
A 1965 official report prepared by Captain Sanchez Moreno from the
Naval Air Station Comandante Espora in Bahia Blanca revealed that:

> Between 1950 and 1965, personnel of Argentina's Navy alone
> made 22 sightings of unidentified flying objects that were not
> airplanes, satellites, weather balloons or any type of known
> (aerial) vehicles. These 22 cases served as precedents for
> intensifying that investigation of the subject by the Navy. In the
> past two years, nine incidents have been recorded that are being
> studied by Captain Pagani and a team of military and civilian
> scientists and collaborators. Likewise, a meticulous questionnaire
> was . . . distributed to different bases. In a short time, the Service
> of Naval Intelligence was in possession of a stack of highly
> significant reports . . .

Following a series of sightings at Argentine and Chilean meteorological stations on Deception Island, Antarctica, in June and July 1965,
Captain Engineer Omar Pagani disclosed at a press conference that 'The
unidentified flying objects do exist. Their presence and intelligent
displacement in Argentine airspace is proven. Their nature and origin are
unknown and no judgement is made about them'.[4]

Defense Intelligence Agency Interest

DIA attaché reports routinely include information from the local media
on a variety of intelligence-collection topics – including UFOs – and a

wave of sightings in Argentina from June to August 1968 led to the Defense Attaché in Buenos Aires, Colonel Charles Greffet, forwarding to the Pentagon twenty-three news clippings on UFO reports, of which I cite the following summaries:

1. La Razon (Buenos Aires) 8 Jun 68 – Describes how two experienced pilots, 22 and 13 years with Aerolineas Argentinas, saw a UFO while flying over Punta Arenas . . .

3. Los Principlos (Cordoba) 5 July 68 – Outlines details on the invention of a geomagnetic and light detector to warn of the presence of UFOs. Second article, same source, quotes Argentine Commander-in-Chief of Navy as suggesting that Argentine armed forces are participating in an investigation of UFOs . . .

5. Diario del Pueblo (Tandil) 13 July 68 – Describes landing of a UFO at the Air Force Base at Tandil . . .

13. La Razon (Buenos Aires) 26 July 68 – Describes attempt by five policemen in Olivarria to capture and later shoot three crew members of UFO . . .

16. La Razon (Buenos Aires) 27 July 68 – Relates new sighting near La Pastora, Alvear, and Tapalque. The latter describes the crew and inability of machine-gun bullets to affect them . . .

'It is significant to note,' commented Colonel Greffet, 'that a state of concern exists [among] the population in many parts of Argentina.'[5]

Reference 3 mentions the suggestion that the Argentine armed forces were participating in an investigation. Back in 1964, in fact, the volume of sightings had grown so huge that the Argentine Air Force set up its own UFO department, known as Division OVNI.[6] And in 1978 the Argentinine gendarmeria released official police reports of sightings (many having occurred in 1968) to the lawyer Antonio Baragiola.[7]

UFO Endangers Airliner

On the night of 31 July 1995, everything seemed normal as Aerolineas Argentinas Flight 734, with three crew and 102 passengers aboard, approached for landing at San Carlos de Bariloche, Rio Negro Province. Suddenly, at 20.10, Captain Jorge Polanco was forced to make a sharp manoeuvre to avoid colliding with an unknown flying object.

'As I was making the final approach,' reported Captain Polanco, 'I suddenly saw in front of the plane a white light which was bearing right down on us really fast before it halted about 100 metres away.' As Polanco frantically manoeuvred his plane, the UFO made a bizarre turn then flew parallel to the right of the Boeing 727. 'My plane performed normally, but the flying saucer – the size of an airliner – changed colours, with two green lights at each end and a flashing orange light in the middle. As I came in to land on my final approach, the lights of the runway and airport suddenly went out. I had to climb to 3,000 metres, always accompanied by the OVNI [*objeto volante no identificado*]. I couldn't believe my eyes and I was very concerned, as were my other two crew members.'

Without mentioning the UFO, Captain Polanco explained to the passengers that a power blackout had affected the supply of electricity to the airport (as he learned from the control tower) and that he would have to circle until authorized to land. He asked the tower if there was any other traffic in the area and was told that the only other plane was a Gendarmeria aircraft (a Piper PA-31-310) flying 600 metres above the airliner. Rubén Cipazuk, the Gendarmeria pilot, informed Polanco that he too could see the unknown object, and that it was following the airliner.

'When the lights came back on the ground and I recommenced my descent, the OVNI then disappeared at tremendous speed in the direction of Mount Otto,' said Polanco. The plane landed an hour late, and Polanco spent some time on the flight deck recovering from the experience. 'What we saw was not a plane; it was nothing that responded to the physical laws as we know them,' he reported. 'We saw something similar to the image of an inverted flying saucer, as large as a Boeing 727, and with a very powerful illumination that was blinding us.'

None of the passengers – among whom were some members of the National Commission on Atomic Energy and a reporter from *La Nación* newspaper – actually saw the object as described, but airport officials confirmed the incident. Major Jorge Oviedo, the airport chief, affirmed that the airliner was prevented from landing on its first attempt due to the sudden appearance of a strange object in its path, just at the moment when the airport was blacked out. Furthermore, instruments in the control tower were affected. 'All the airport's radio support was suddenly cut off, and there was a blackout in the whole city,' said Oviedo.[8,9]

Peru

Captain Oswaldo Sanviti has provided the following report of his airliner's encounter with two unknown objects in 1967:

. . . I was flying my plane, a Douglas DC-4 of the Compañia de Aviación 'Faucett' S.A. of Lima, Peru, from Chiclayo to Lima on Feb. 2, 1967, altitude 7,000 feet, and at 24:30 GMT . . . we saw at the W of our plane a very luminous object which we confused initially with a star or planet, but, after we were very sure that the apparent movement of the object was NOT the effect of our plane, we could see that [the] object was coming fast closer to our plane; we estimated the distance about 8 nautical miles. At this time it was really a spectacle, it had so much light that all the passengers of our plane saw [it] and started to be very nervous and exclaimed, 'There is an OVNI.'

After a while the OVNI passed over my plane and stopped right over us. At this moment we noticed a 15° left oscillation on our radio compass and later a 20° right [oscillation] without stopping, [and] all the lights in the main cabin started to reduce [in] intensity, the same as our fluorescent lights of the cockpit and all radios (reception) [went] out, [and] a bit of static noise. (After the flight we were informed that our transmission was 5 × 5 OK.)

The OVNI, from the 90° position over our plane, moved over to the E of our plane, increasing its light [by] about 50% into a bluish light and disappeared with a fantastic speed . . . After 5 minutes the OVNI returned with another one and situated itself [at] a close distance [from] our tail section and in this formation we flew [for] 5 minutes before landing at the Lima International Airfield.[10]

Air Force Jet Attacks a UFO

Two sightings reported by Peruvian Air Force personnel in May 1980, including the interception and attempted destruction of a UFO, are cited in a DIA document prepared by the US Air Attaché in Lima. The source was a Peruvian Air Force officer who, according to the Attaché, 'observed the event and is in a position to be party to conversation concerning the event. Source had reported reliably in the past.' The details are as follows:

SOURCE TOLD RO [reporting officer] ABOUT THE SPOTTING OF AN UNIDENTIFIED FLYING OBJECT IN THE VICINITY OF MARIANO MELGAR AIR BASE, LA JOYA, (PERU 16805S, 0715306W). SOURCE STATED THAT THE VEHICLE WAS

```
                        DEPARTMENT OF DEFENSE
                        JOINT CHIEFS OF STAFF        RECEIVED
                        MESSAGE CENTER
                                                JUN -3 1980
VZCZCHLT565                              7YUW
MULT                                        DIA LIS-20              18134
ACTION
      DTA!                                                          √
DISTR
      IADR(A1) J5(A2) J3INMCC NIDS SECDEF(07) SECDEF: USDP(15)
      ATSDIAE(01) ASDIPA&E(A1) ISDIA(20) NMIC
   -  CMC CC WASHINGTON DC
   -  CSAF WASHINGTON DC
   -  CNO WASHINGTON DC
   -  CSA WASHINGTON DC
   -  CIA WASHINGTON DC
   :  SFCSTATE WASHINGTON DC
   -  NSA WASH DC
      FILF
 (047)


TRANSIT/1542115/1542207/ABP152TOR1542204
DE RUESLMA #4888 1542115
7NY CCCCC
R 0220527 JUN 80
FM USDAO LIMA PERU
TO RUEKJCS/DIA WASHDC
INFO RULPALJ/USCINCSO QUARRY HTS PN
RULPAFA/USAFSO HOWARD AFB PN
BT
SUBJ: IR 6 876 0146 80 (U)
THIS IS AN INFO REPORT, NOT FINALLY EVAL INTEL
1. (U) CTRY: PERU (PE)
2. TITLE (U) UFO SIGHTED IN PERU (U)
3. (U) DATE OF INFO: 800510
4. (U)   ORIG: USDAO AIR LIMA PERU
5. (U) REQ REFS: Z-D13-PE050
6. (U) SOURCE: 6 876 0138. OFFICER IN THE PERUVIAN AIR FORCE
WHO OBSERVED THE EVENT AND IS IN A POSITION TO BE PARTY
TO CONVERSATION CONCERNING THE EVENT. SOURCE HAS REPORTED
RELIABLY IN THE PAST.

7.         SUMMARY: SOURCE REPORTED THAT A UFO WAS SPOTTED
ON TWO DIFFERENT OCCASIONS NEAR PERUVIAN AIR FORCE (FAP) BASE
IN SOUTHERN PERU. THE FAP TRIED TO INTERCEPT AND DESTROY THE
UFO, BUT WITHOUT SUCCESS.

PAGE  1                                                  AP191111
```

A Defense Intelligence Agency report on the interceptions of an unknown aerial vehicle by Peruvian Air Force pilots in May 1980. The distribution list includes the CIA and the National Security Agency. (*DIA*)

DEPARTMENT OF DEFENSE
JOINT CHIEFS OF STAFF
MESSAGE CENTER

PAGE 2   18134
8A.   DETAILS: SOURCE TOLD RO ABOUT THE SPOTTING OF AN
UNIDENTIFIED FLYING OBJECT IN THE VICINITY OF MARIANO MELGAR AIR
BASE, LA JOYA, PERU (16805S, 07153P6W). SOURCE STATED THAT THE
VEHICLE WAS SPOTTED ON TWO DIFFERENT OCCASIONS. THE FIRST WAS
DURING THE MORNING HOURS OF 9 MAY 80, AND THE SECOND DURING
THE EARLY EVENING HOURS OF 10 MAY 80.
               SOURCE STATED THAT ON 9 MAY, WHILE A GROUP OF FAP
OFFICERS WERE IN FORMATION AT MARIANO MALGAR, THEY SPOTTED A
UFO THAT WAS ROUND IN SHAPE, HOVERING NEAR THE AIRFIELD. THE
AIR COMMANDER SCRAMBLED AN SU-22 AIRCRAFT TO MAKE AN
INTERCEPT. THE PILOT, ACCORDING TO A THIRD PARTY, INTERCEPTED
THE VEHICLE AND FIRED UPON IT AT VERY CLOSE RANGE WITHOUT
CAUSING ANY APPARENT DAMAGE. THE PILOT TRIED TO MAKE A
SECOND PASS ON THE VEHICLE, BUT THE UFO OUT-RAN THE SU-22.
               THE SECOND SIGHTING WAS DURING HOURS OF DARKNESS.
THE VEHICLE WAS LIGHTED. AGAIN AN SU-22 WAS SCRAMBLED, BUT THE
VEHICLE OUT-RAN THE AIRCRAFT.
8B.   ORTG CMTS: RO HAS HEARD DISCUSSION ABOUT THE
SIGHTING FROM OTHER SOURCES. APPARENTLY SOME VEHICLE WAS
SPOTTED, BUT ITS ORIGIN REMAINS UNKNOWN.
9. (U) PROJ NO: N/A
10. (U) COLL MGMT CODES: AB
11. (U) SPEC INST: NONE. DIRC: NO.
12. (U) PREP BY: NORMAN H. RUNGE, COL, AIRA
13. (U) APP BY: VAUGHN E. WILSON, CAPT, DATT, ALUSNA
14. (U) REG EVAL: NO REL TO: NONE
15. (U) ENCL: N/A
16. (U) DIST BY ORIG: N/A

RT
#4880
ANNOTES
JAL 117

PAGE 2   PP101111

NNNN
8222087

SPOTTED ON TWO DIFFERENT OCCASIONS. THE FIRST WAS DURING THE MORNING HOURS OF 9 MAY 80, AND THE SECOND DURING THE EARLY EVENING HOURS OF 10 MAY 80.

SOURCE STATED THAT ON 9 MAY, WHILE A GROUP OF FAP [Peruvian Air Force] OFFICERS WERE IN FORMATION AT MARIANO MALGAR [sic], THEY SPOTTED A UFO THAT WAS ROUND IN SHAPE, HOVERING NEAR THE AIRFIELD. THE AIR COMMANDER SCRAMBLED AN SU-22 [Sukhoi] AIRCRAFT TO MAKE AN INTERCEPT. THE PILOT, ACCORDING TO A THIRD PARTY, INTERCEPTED THE VEHICLE AND FIRED UPON IT AT VERY CLOSE RANGE WITHOUT CAUSING ANY APPARENT DAMAGE. THE PILOT TRIED TO MAKE A SECOND PASS ON THE VEHICLE, BUT THE UFO OUT-RAN THE SU-22.

THE SECOND SIGHTING WAS DURING THE HOURS OF DARKNESS. THE VEHICLE WAS LIGHTED. AGAIN AN SU-22 WAS SCRAMBLED, BUT THE VEHICLE OUT-RAN THE AIR-CRAFT . . .

RO HAS HEARD DISCUSSION ABOUT THE SIGHTING FROM OTHER SOURCES. APPARENTLY SOME VEHICLE WAS SPOTTED, BUT ITS ORIGIN REMAINS UNKNOWN.[11]

Brazil

'The problem of "flying discs" has polarized the attention of the whole world, but it's serious and it deserves to be taken seriously,' said Colonel João A. Oliveira, during a briefing to the Army War College in Rio de Janeiro on 2 November 1954. 'Almost all the governments of the great powers are interested in it, dealing with it in a serious and confidential manner, due to its military interest.'[12]

As Chief of the Air Force General Staff Information Service, Colonel Oliveira had headed Brazil's first official military inquiry into UFOs in the mid-1950s. Later promoted to the rank of Brigadier General, he was interviewed about the subject by the Brazilian press in 1958. 'The flying saucer is not a ghost from another dimension or a mysterious dragon,' he declared. 'It is a *fact* confirmed by material evidence. There are thousands of documents, photos, and sighting reports demonstrating its existence . . .'[13]

Official research into UFOs has long been conducted by the Brazilian Air Force (Força Aérea Brasileira – FAB). In 1969 the IV Aerial Zone in

São Paulo (changed in 1973 to the IV Regional Air Command, IV COMAR) established a special UFO bureau called SIOANI (System of Investigation of Unidentified Aerial Objects) under Major Gilberto Zani.[14] That year an FAB directive, issued to local officials, stated: 'You will not under any circumstances give any information on UFO activity to any press, radio, or television reporter or representative. This is a matter of national security, and all press releases will be made by the Brazilian Air Force Public Relations Department.'[15] And a 1973 São Paulo State directive, entitled *Institutional Act No. 5 (State Security)*, warned: 'It is forbidden for TV, radio, newspapers, and other news media to divulge UFO reports without the prior censorship of the Brazilian Air Force.'[16]

The Brazilian Navy also has been deeply involved in UFO investigations. For example, following the extraordinarily well documented sighting over the island of Trindade off the Brazilian coast on 16 January 1958, when a sequence of photographs of a UFO was taken by a professional civilian photographer on board a Brazilian Navy training ship, the Navy at first kept the matter secret, but the photos were eventually given to the press by the President of Brazil, Juscelino Kubitscheck.[17]

Dr Olavo Fontes, one of Brazil's pioneering investigators, established contacts with naval intelligence sources in the late 1950s who left him in no doubt about the high priority attached to the subject. In a letter to the American researcher Coral Lorenzen of the Aerial Phenomena Research Organization, Dr Fontes provided some revealing information:

> The Brazilian Navy, for example, receives monthly classified reports from the US Navy and sends back to them any information available here . . . In Brazil only the persons who work on the problem know the real situation: intelligence officers in the Army, Navy and Air Force; some high-ranking officers in the High Command; the National Security Council and a few scientists whose activities are connected with it; and a few members of certain civilian organizations doing research for military projects.
>
> All information about the UFO subject from the military is not only classified or reserved for official uses, it is *top secret*. Civilian authorities and military officers in general are not entitled to know. Even our President is not informed of the whole truth.
>
> Military authorities throughout the world agree that the people are not entitled to know anything about the problem. Some

military groups believe that such a knowledge would be a tremendous shock – enough to paralyze the life in our country for many years in the future.[18]

Aerial Encounters

An interesting Brazilian Air Force report was obtained from official sources by the US Air Attaché in Rio de Janeiro, describing an encounter with an unknown object by the crew of a Brazilian Air Force C-47 and the crew of a Cruzeiro do Sul photo-mapping aircraft, in the vicinity of Porto Alegre, Rio Grande do Sul, on 27 March 1967. The Defense Intelligence Agency report continues:

> The object was initially sighted by the BAF crew who described it as a reddish colored full moon that appeared to be flying in circles. The BAF C-47 advised Salgado Filho Tower of the sighting, and the tower asked the Cruzeiro do Sul aircraft to intercept and identify the object. The Cruzeiro do Sul aircraft made contact with the object and pursued it for 15 minutes before it finally disappeared. No pictures were taken . . .
>
> In addition to the reported sightings by the aircraft crews, the object was also reportedly seen by ground observers in the Porto Alegre area . . . As yet the Air Ministry has not issued any official comment on these sightings and is presently studying the statements of the aircraft crews and ground observers.[19]

In May 1986, when UFOs saturated radar screens and were seen by the pilots of seven aircraft, the incidents were publicly confirmed by the Air Minister and reported worldwide – a clear indication that the military authorities had become more open with the public.

The first incident occurred at 21.10 hours on 19 May, when Colonel Ozires Silva, formerly President of the Embraer aircraft firm and head of the Petrobras oil company, together with Commander Alcir Pereira da Silva, were alerted by São Paulo radar to the presence of unidentified traffic in their vicinity. The pilots – flying an Embraer Xingu – saw a 'dancing' point of light in the sky which, when they flew closer, appeared as a bright red-orange light which came on for 10–15 seconds, then off, reappearing in a different location. This went on for about 30 minutes.

The Integrated Air Defence and Air Traffic Control Centre (CINDACTA) went on full alert as radar screens in the area became saturated with unknown targets, causing disruption to air traffic. Three Air Force F-5E Tiger jets were scrambled from Santa Cruz Air Base near São Paulo, followed by three Mirage III jets from Anápolis.

One of the F-5 pilots, Lieutenant Kleber Caldas Marinho, was vectored to a target but saw nothing at first. Ground and airborne radar confirmed that an object was 35 miles away, and when Marinho caught sight of it he reported an intense reddish light that changed colour to white, green, and back to red. Marinho's attempts to close on the target were futile. It was, he said, 'like attempting to reach a point at infinity'.

Captain Marcio Jordão, another F-5 pilot, managed to reduce the distance from the target to 12 miles, but it then moved out to sea beyond the 200-mile limit from Santa Cruz.

One of the Mirage pilots, Captain Armindo Souza Viriato de Freitas, provided further details:

> . . . I was warned by ground control that there were several targets ahead of me, at a distance of 20 miles and ranging in number from 10 to 13. I was also advised that the targets were approaching my plane, and finally that they were following me at a distance of 2 miles. I had to lower my plane, as the lights had descended, but from then on they climbed vertically. This was my only visual contact, but I could see them in my radar at a distance of 12 miles.

The Anápolis radar controller advised Captain Viriato that he had thirteen targets behind his plane at one stage – seven to one side and six to the other. The objects made incredible 180° turns on the plane's radarscope, although Viriato was unable to spot them in the air. 'No plane I know can make turns like that at 1,000 kilometres an hour,' he said. The speed of the objects at other times varied from 150 to 800 k.p.h. Lieutenant Valdecir Fernando Coelho, one of the air traffic controllers, was equally at a loss to explain the incidents, which lasted for over three hours: 'In my fourteen years of experience as a radar operator, I never saw anything like this.'

Air Minister Brigadier Otávio Júlio Moreira Lima later informed the President of Brazil, José Sarney, about the intrusions. At the press conference the Air Minister declared that 'radar is not subject to optical illusions. Radar echoes are due to solid objects, or massive clouds, which were not present that night.'

According to one report, the President of Brazil authorized the decision to release the story publicly.[20]

Indonesia

'UFOs sighted in Indonesia are identical with those sighted in other countries,' stated Air Marshal Roesmin Nurjadin, Commander-in-Chief of the Indonesian Air Force, in 1967. 'Sometimes they pose a problem for our air defence and once we were obliged to open fire on them.'[21]

The most active periods for UFO reports in Indonesia were 1953–4 and 1964–5, according to Air Commodore J. Salutun, former Member of Parliament and Secretary of the National Aerospace Council of the Republic of Indonesia. Salutun has confirmed the incident referred to by Air Marshal Nurjadin: 'The most spectacular UFO incident in Indonesia occurred when, during the height of President Sukarno's confrontation against Malaysia, UFOs penetrated a well-defended area in Java for two weeks at a stretch, and each time were welcomed with perhaps the heaviest anti-aircraft barrage in history.' He added:

I am convinced that we must study the UFO problem seriously for reasons of sociology, technology and security. The study of UFOs may lead to new and revolutionary concepts in propulsion and space technology in general, from which our present state-of-the-art may benefit. The study of UFOs is a necessity for the sake of world security in the event we have to prepare for the worst in the space age, irrespective of whether we become the Columbus or the Indians.[22]

Cuba

Nuclear physicist Stanton Friedman, one of America's leading UFO researchers, has obtained details of an alarming incident which included a statement by a security specialist attached to a unit of the US Air Force Security Service, based with the 6947th Security Squadron, whose mission was the monitoring of all Cuban military communications:

In March of 1967 . . . Cuban radar installations reported a bogey approaching the Cuban land mass from the northeast. 2 MiG-21 interceptors were scrambled when the bogey crossed Cuban air space at an altitude of approximately 10,000 meters and at a speed approaching Mach [1]. The interceptors were directed to the bogey by Cuban Ground Control Intercept and were guided to within 5 kilometers of the object.

The wing leader reported the object was a bright metallic sphere with no visible markings or appendages. After a futile attempt to contact the object for identification, Cuban Air Defense headquarters ordered the wing leader to arm his weapons and destroy the object. The wing leader reported his missiles armed and his radar locked-on.

Seconds later the wing man began screaming to the ground controller that the wing leader's aircraft had exploded. After regaining his composure he further reported that there was no smoke or flame; the aircraft had disintegrated. Cuban radar reported the object quickly accelerated and climbed beyond 30,000 meters and at last report was heading south-southeast toward South America.

A spot report was sent to National Security Agency headquarters, which is standard procedure in any case involving aircraft loss by an enemy country. NSA is required to acknowledge receipt of such a report, however they didn't and therefore we sent a follow-up report. Within hours we received orders to ship all tapes and pertinent intelligence to the Agency and were told to list the incident in the squadron files as aircraft loss due to equipment malfunction.[23]

Brad Sparks, an expert on intelligence matters pertaining to the UFO question, pointed out that data sent to the National Security Agency would have included direction-finding measurements which the NSA could later combine with other listening-sites' data in order to triangulate the location and altitude of the MiG-21 flight paths. 'If the [Air Force Security Service] equipment in Florida [Key West Naval Air Station] was sensitive enough,' commented Sparks, 'the UFO could have been tracked by its reflection of the Cuban ground and airborne radars.'

As a result of filing Freedom of Information requests on the incident to the NSA, CIA, Air Force, and Navy, researcher Robert Todd was interrogated by the FBI – partly because he was on the point of taking up the CIA's suggestion of checking with the Cuban Government for further details! One of the FBI agents explained to Todd that the Bureau had been asked to investigate the matter by the NSA, as NSA has no law-enforcement responsibilities. The agents began intimidating Todd by reading out the espionage laws, reminding him that these carried a penalty of life imprisonment or even death in some cases. No charges were brought against him, however.[24]

A Landing Case Investigated by Intelligence Specialists

The following year another disturbing encounter, reported by a reservist with the Cuban Army, led Fidel Castro to ask Soviet intelligence specialists to conduct extensive investigations. Reported in detail by Jacques Vallée in his book *UFO Chronicles of the Soviet Union*, the following is a synopsis of this extraordinary case.

Shortly after midnight on 14 June 1968, several bursts of machine-gun fire were heard coming from a location in the vicinity of Cabañas, where Isidro Puentes Ventura was on guard duty. At dawn, Puentes was found unconscious by an Army patrol and taken to a hospital in Pinar del Río, where he remained in shock and unable to speak for six days. Removed to the neurological ward at the Naval Hospital in Havana, Puentes was diagnosed to be suffering from emotional trauma, remaining in shock for another week.

At the site where Puentes had been posted, Cuban and Soviet intelligence investigators found forty-eight spent cartridges and fourteen bullets apparently flattened by impact, as well as equally spaced indentations in the ground, indicating that a heavy device had landed. Tests revealed that the soil had been exposed to a high degree of heat.

When Puentes recovered consciousness, he reported that he had come to within 150 feet of a brilliant round object on the ground, with a dome and several 'antennas' on top. Convinced that the device was an American helicopter, Puentes fired about forty rounds at it. The craft turned orange and emitted a strong whistling sound – Puentes' last recollection before losing consciousness.

Soviet intelligence specialists subjected Puentes to a fifty-hour interrogation, after which he was examined by a team of psychiatrists and put through fifteen hypnosis sessions. As Vallée reports, no contradictions were found in his story.[25]

South Africa

Like other air forces around the world, the South African Air Force takes UFOs seriously. In 1953 a Defence Headquarters spokesman in Pretoria revealed that there had been some reliable sightings by SAAF officers, and added: 'There is now a regular exchange of information between our Air Force and the Royal Air Force. Reports have also been referred to military intelligence.'[26] In 1955 the Air Chief of Staff admitted that the South

African Department of Defence classified official information on the subject as 'Top Secret – Not to be Divulged'.[27]

During a visit to South Africa in 1981, I learned from a defence source about a tragic case, felt to be UFO-related, which involved the disappearance of two SAAF pilots and their aircraft. On 18 June 1977 the two pilots, both with fifteen years and 7,000 hours flying experience, disappeared 40 miles north-west of Ludoritz, together with their French-built Mirage F1CZ jets. The last radio contact was at 10.48 hours, and at about 11.15 the planes simply vanished from the radar screens. It was evident that the pilots were frantically trying to communicate with base: the radio call button was being pressed but no transmission could be heard.

A simple accident – perhaps a collision? Both planes were equipped with standard life gear. A Navy ship was in the area within an hour, and a helicopter within two hours. Weather conditions were good; 3/8ths altocumulus at 25,000 feet and high cirrus at 45–50,000 feet – the altitude at which the planes were flying. No trace was ever found of either the pilots or the aircraft.

Zimbabwe

At 17.45 on 22 July 1985 two Hawk jets of the Air Force of Zimbabwe were scrambled from Thornhill Air Base, following sightings of an unidentified aerial object from Bulawayo and five other urban centres in the western province of Matabeleland South. The object was seen from the control tower at Bulawayo Airport and tracked on radar. 'This was no ordinary UFO,' said Air Marshal Azim Daudpota. 'Scores of people saw it. It was no illusion, no deception, no imagination.'

The object was described by trained observers at Bulawayo Airport as rounded, with a short cone above it. It shone very brightly in the afternoon sky and was difficult to see distinctly. The British-built Hawks arrived above Bulawayo to find the UFO hovering at about 7,000 feet, but it suddenly accelerated to a height of 70,000 feet in less than a minute. The Hawks levelled off at 31,000 feet then returned to Thornhill, where the object was seen for a few moments before disappearing horizontally at high speed.[28,29]

Air Commodore David Thorne, Director General of Operations, told me that the UFO appeared to follow the Hawks back to base. Unfortunately no gun-camera footage was taken, as the jets were not carrying film at the time, he explained. 'This is the first sighting in

Zimbabwe where airborne pilots have tried to intercept a UFO,' he said. Although the Air Commodore was unable to comment on behalf of the Zimbabwe Government, he nevertheless stated that: 'As far as my Air Staff is concerned, we believe implicitly that the unexplained UFOs are from some civilization beyond our planet.'[30]

Japan

I shall never forget the overwhelming hospitality accorded me by Japanese ufologists during my first visit to that country (with the London Symphony Orchestra) in 1964. While discussions focused on more general aspects of the subject, I was unable to acquire any information on the official line at that time, and a response years later from the Embassy of Japan in London shed no further light on the matter. 'Although there is considerable interest in UFOs in the private sector,' I was told, 'the Japanese government has not yet set up any research institute or department for them.'[31] Yet there is evidence for official concern in Japan.

In 1967 General Kanshi Ishikawa, Chief of Air Staff of the Japan Air Self-Defence Force (JASDF), made the following interesting statement:

> If UFOs are flying objects hovering in the sky, they should be caught by radar. Much evidence tells us they have been tracked on radar; so, UFOs are real and they may come from outer space . . . I can imagine that there are two types of UFOs; small ones for scouting and large ships for interstellar travel, utilizing electro-magnetic fields.
>
> The dream of our pilots is to acquire the technique of gravity-control, capable of perfectly free manoeuvrability. I believe the saucer-shape is the best design from the point of view of hydrodynamics . . . UFO photographs and various materials show scientifically that there are more advanced people piloting the saucers and motherships.[32]

'UFOs are impossible to deny,' said Colonel Fujio Hayashi, Commander of the Air Transport Wing, Irima Air Squadron, in the late 1960s. 'When we pilots scramble we have to identify the object clearly, whether it is an enemy or not . . . Though it is said that these unknown objects might be the secret weapons of some powers, it is very strange that we have never been able to find out the source for over two decades.'[33]

In September 1977 Lieutenant General Akira Hirano, Chief of Staff of the JASDF, admitted: 'We frequently see unidentified objects in the skies. We are quietly investigating them.' The following day, however, it was explained that the general had made a mistake: Hirano's staff denied that he had mentioned official investigations. 'If they're hostile, we want to have a full explanation before we upset the general populace,' an official admitted later, on condition that his name was not published.

Major Shiro Kubota claims to have had an alarming encounter with a UFO which led to the death of Lieutenant Colonel Toshio Nakamura, who was flying with him in an F-4EJ Phantom jet on 9 June 1974, when the incident is alleged to have occurred. Kubota told a reporter:

> We thought at first we were going to intercept a Soviet bomber, of the type which sometimes tests our northern air defences. After Toshio got us airborne, our Ground Control Intercept (GCI) explained to us that we were going upstairs to check out a bright-coloured light reported by dozens of observers and showing on radar. Several minutes later, we broke out of the clouds and levelled off at 30,000 feet on a clear, moonless night. That was when we spotted the light a few miles ahead.
>
> Even at first, I felt that this disc-like, red-orange object was a flying craft, made and flown by intelligent beings. It appeared to be about 10 meters in diameter, with square-shaped marks around its side which may have been windows or propulsion outlets. Toshio aimed us straight toward it and, as it grew larger in our gun sight, it dipped into a shallow turn, as if sensing our presence . . .
>
> Toshio armed our 20mm cannon and closed in on the UFO. Suddenly the object reversed direction and shot straight at us . . . Toshio threw the stick to the left and forced us into a sudden, violent dive. The glowing red UFO shot past – missing us by inches. Then it made a sharp turn and came at us again . . . The UFO began making rapid, high-speed passes at us, drawing closer and closer. Several times, the strange object narrowly missed us.

And then – if the report is to be believed – the UFO struck the Phantom jet. Both pilots ejected, but Nakamura's parachute caught fire and he fell to his death. The UFO either disappeared or disintegrated.

Japanese Air Defence authorities conducted a lengthy investigation into the incident, but no findings have been released to date, beyond an admission that the Phantom – serial number 17-8307 – crashed, killing

Nakamura, following a collision with 'an aircraft or object unknown'. Rather than remain silent about the incident, Kubota retired from active service.

Major General Hideki Komura, an adviser to Japan's top intelligence agency, the Naicho (Cabinet Research Office), has admitted that investigations into UFOs are carried out at top level. At first, he explained, the JASDF openly solicited reports from the public. 'This was in the late 1950s and we were, frankly, imitating your own Project Blue Book,' he told an American reporter. 'But we were deluged. Interest was so great, and so many reports poured in, that we were unable to separate the "good" reports from the *garakuda* [rubbish]. We had to give up. It simply was not working.'

General Komura was reluctant to disclose details of investigations then (1977) being conducted by defence and intelligence agencies, but revealed:

> We co-operate very closely with your [US] government. Remember how we invited your Foreign Technology Division officials here to examine the MiG-25 jet we received from a defecting Soviet pilot? The Foreign Technology Division is the outfit under which Project Blue Book once operated. We have co-operated many times on other issues, and visitors from another planet would certainly be a legitimate subject for inquiry.[34]

UFOs Pace a Japan Air Lines Jumbo

Of the many reports of sightings by Japanese airline pilots, the most interesting is that of the crew of a Japan Air Lines cargo flight on the night of 17 November 1986. Flight JAL 1628, *en route* to Anchorage, Alaska, from Reykjavik, Iceland, the middle leg of a Europe-to-Tokyo flight, was entering US airspace at 39,000 feet and Captain Kenju Terauchi and his crew were making final preparations before descending to Anchorage Airport. Suddenly they noticed some unusual lights accompanying their Boeing 747. 'They were flying parallel and then suddenly approached very close,' said Terauchi. He caught a brief glimpse of the main object's walnut-shaped silhouette and judged it to be 'two times bigger than an aircraft carrier' (see p. 282).

The pilot was instructed by air traffic control to descend to 4,000 feet and make turns, but the objects continued to follow the plane for thirty-two minutes before vanishing. US Federal Aviation Administration authorities admitted that the objects were tracked on radar but had not registered on the radar tapes.

The FAA investigated the incident and found the crew to be 'normal, professional, and rational'. Captain Terauchi, a pilot for twenty-nine years, said that he was unable to explain the phenomenon in conventional terms and speculated that it may have been extraterrestrial in origin since the objects moved and stopped so quickly and suddenly. 'We were carrying Beaujolais from France to Japan,' he commented. 'Maybe they wanted to drink it.'[35,36,37]

The following is extracted from one of the several interviews with the JAL crew carried out by FAA personnel; this by FAA agent Ronald E. Mickle:

> . . . Myself and [manager] Jim Derry interviewed the crew of JAL Flight 1628, which reported the unidentified air traffic. The flight crew consisted of the Captain, Kenju Terauchi, First Officer Takanori Tamefuji, and Flight Engineer Yoshio Tsukuda . . . Captain Terauchi stated he first sighted (visually) the unidentified air traffic (UAT) in the vicinity of Potat intersection and the ADIZ [Air Defense Identification Zone]. The aircraft he was piloting (B747) was at flight level 390, airspeed 0.84 Mach . . . the UAT was in front of his aircraft at a distance of approximately seven to eight nautical miles for approximately 12 minutes . . . the distance was indicated by the onboard Bendix color radar. Captain Terauchi stated that while he had a visual on the UAT, he spotted yellow, amber and green lights, and a rotating beacon, but no red lights . . . there were two distinct sets of lights, but appeared to be joined together (as fixed to one object). Captain Terauchi ascertained through visual sighting and radar, that the UAT was equal in size to a B747, possibly larger.
>
> Captain Terauchi stated that during the visual sighting, the lights of the UAT changed from a horizontal position to a vertical position and had positioned itself from in front of the B747 to port side. The UAT stayed on the port side for approximately 35 minutes.
>
> . . . The Captain stated he requested, and received, permission to perform a 360 degree turn while in the vicinity of Fairbanks, Alaska, which he had a visual on . . . the UAT maintained its position on the port side during the turn . . . visual sight was lost approximately 40 nautical miles north of Talkeetna, while continuing on to Anchorage.

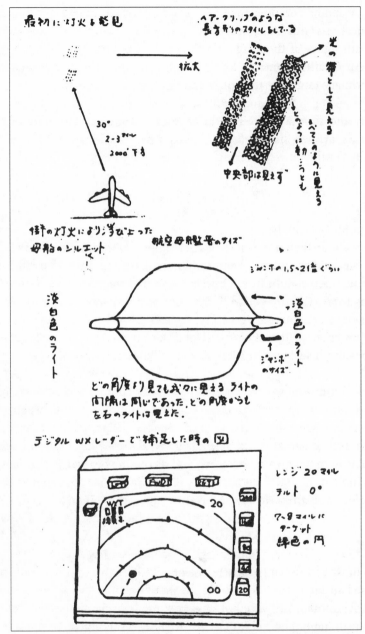

Drawings by Captain Kenju Terauchi of unidentified traffic encountered by his Boeing 747 of Japan Air Lines over Alaska in November 1986. *Top*: The UFO lights almost in front of the plane and a close-up of the lights. *Middle*: How the UFO appeared when glimpsed in silhouette: the JAL jumbo jet is dwarfed by the huge object. *Bottom*: where the UFO first appeared on the aircraft's radar screen. (*Kenju Terauchi/MUFON UFO Journal*)

Captain Terauchi stated there was static during VHF communications with [Anchorage] . . . [and] there was erratic movement with lights of the UAT during the visual contact . . . FAA ATC [Air Traffic Control] had indicated to him the presence of a primary target in addition to his aircraft.[38]

By the time a United Airlines flight (UA69) and a military C-130 Hercules arrived in the JAL 747's vicinity, having been requested to visually confirm the sighting, the object had disappeared.

Former Prime Minister's Interest

Few politicians in Japan – as in other countries – have dared to speak openly about their interest in this ridicule-prone subject. But in 1989 it was revealed that former Prime Minister Toshiki Kaifu, who has a long-standing interest, admitted that he had searched unsuccessfully for UFOs during trips to Australia, the South Pole, and Switzerland. 'I'll live on with hopes of . . . encountering a UFO some day,' he wrote in 1983.[39]

In a letter to the Mayor of Hakui City, endorsing a space and UFO symposium held there in 1990, Kaifu wrote:

> . . . I told a magazine this past January that, as an underdeveloped country with regards to the UFO problem, Japan had to take into account what should be done about the UFO question, and that we had to spend more time on these matters. In addition, I said that someone with far reaching vision had to solve the UFO problem . . . Secondly, I believe it is a reasonable time to take the UFO problem seriously as a reality.[40]

Iran

One of the most important Defense Intelligence Agency documents released so far is that describing the sensational sighting by the crew of Imperial Iranian Air Force F-4 Phantom jets who encountered a UFO over Tehran in September 1976. One of the pilots attempted to fire a guided missile at another object which came out of the UFO. The report was sent by the Defense Attaché at the US Embassy in Tehran to the DIA. The distribution list included the White House, the Secretary of State, the National Security Agency and the CIA:

A. AT ABOUT 1230 A.M. ON 19 SEP 76 THE IMPERIAL IRANIAN AIR FORCE (IIAF) COMMAND POST RECEIVED FOUR TELEPHONE CALLS FROM CITIZENS LIVING IN THE SHEMIRAN AREA OF TEHRAN SAYING THAT THEY HAD SEEN STRANGE OBJECTS IN THE SKY. SOME REPORTED A KIND OF BIRD-LIKE OBJECT WHILE OTHERS REPORTED A HELICOPTER WITH A LIGHT ON. THERE WERE NO HELICOPTERS AIRBORNE AT THAT TIME. THE COMMAND POST CALLED BG YOUSEFI, ASSISTANT DEPUTY COMMANDER OF OPERATIONS. AFTER HE TOLD THE CITIZEN IT WAS ONLY STARS AND HAD TALKED TO MEHRABAD TOWER HE DECIDED TO LOOK FOR HIMSELF. HE NOTICED AN OBJECT IN THE SKY SIMILAR TO A STAR BIGGER AND BRIGHTER. HE DECIDED TO SCRAMBLE AN F-4 FROM SHAHROKHI AFB TO INVESTIGATE.

B. AT 0130 HRS ON THE 19TH THE F-4 TOOK OFF AND PROCEEDED TO A POINT ABOUT 40 NM NORTH OF TEHRAN. DUE TO ITS BRILLIANCE THE OBJECT WAS EASILY VISIBLE FROM 70 MILES AWAY. AS THE F-4 APPROACHED A RANGE OF 25 NM HE LOST ALL INSTRUMENTATION AND COMMUNICATIONS (UHF AND INTERCOM). HE BROKE OFF THE INTERCEPT AND HEADED BACK TO SHAHROKHI. WHEN THE F-4 TURNED AWAY FROM THE OBJECT AND APPARENTLY WAS NO LONGER A THREAT TO IT THE AIRCRAFT REGAINED ALL INSTRUMENTATION AND COMMUNICATIONS. AT 0140 HRS A SECOND F-4 WAS LAUNCHED. THE BACK-SEATER ACQUIRED A RADAR LOCK ON AT 27 NM, 12 O'CLOCK HIGH POSITION WITH THE VC (RATE OF CLOSURE) AT 150 NMPH. AS THE RANGE DECREASED TO 25 NM THE OBJECT MOVED AWAY AT A SPEED THAT WAS VISIBLE ON THE RADARSCOPE AND STAYED AT 25 NM.

C. THE SIZE OF THE RADAR RETURN WAS COMPARABLE TO THAT OF A 707 TANKER. THE VISUAL SIZE OF THE OBJECT WAS DIFFICULT TO DISCERN BECAUSE OF ITS INTENSE BRILLIANCE. THE LIGHT THAT IT GAVE OFF WAS THAT OF FLASHING STROBE LIGHTS ARRANGED IN A RECTANGULAR PATTERN AND ALTERNATING BLUE, GREEN, RED AND ORANGE IN COLOUR. THE SEQUENCE OF THE LIGHTS WAS SO FAST THAT ALL THE COLORS COULD BE SEEN AT ONCE. THE OBJECT AND THE PURSUING F-4 CONTINUED ON A COURSE TO THE SOUTH OF TEHRAN WHEN ANOTHER BRIGHTLY LIGHTED

OBJECT, ESTIMATED TO BE ONE HALF TO ONE THIRD THE APPARENT SIZE OF THE MOON, CAME OUT OF THE ORIGINAL OBJECT. THIS SECOND OBJECT HEADED STRAIGHT TOWARD THE F-4 AT A VERY FAST RATE OF SPEED. THE PILOT ATTEMPTED TO FIRE AN AIM-9 MISSILE AT THE OBJECT BUT AT THAT INSTANT HIS WEAPONS CONTROL PANEL WENT OFF AND HE LOST ALL COMMUNICATIONS (UHF AND INTER-PHONE). AT THIS POINT THE PILOT INITIATED A TURN AND NEGATIVE G DIVE TO GET AWAY. AS HE TURNED THE OBJECT FELL IN TRAIL AT WHAT APPEARED TO BE ABOUT 3–4 NM. AS HE CONTINUED IN HIS TURN AWAY FROM THE PRIMARY OBJECT THE SECOND OBJECT WENT TO THE INSIDE OF HIS TURN THEN RETURNED TO THE PRIMARY OBJECT FOR A PERFECT REJOIN.

D. SHORTLY AFTER THE SECOND OBJECT JOINED UP WITH THE PRIMARY OBJECT ANOTHER OBJECT APPEARED TO COME OUT OF THE OTHER SIDE OF THE PRIMARY OBJECT GOING STRAIGHT DOWN, AT A GREAT RATE OF SPEED. THE F-4 CREW HAD REGAINED COMMUNICATIONS AND THE WEAPONS CON-TROL PANEL AND WATCHED THE OBJECT APPROACH THE GROUND ANTICIPATING A LARGE EXPLOSION. THIS OBJECT APPEARED TO COME TO REST GENTLY ON THE EARTH AND CAST A VERY BRIGHT LIGHT OVER AN AREA OF ABOUT 2–3 KILOMETERS. THE CREW DESCENDED FROM THEIR ALTITUDE OF 26M TO 15M AND CONTINUED TO OBSERVE AND MARK THE OBJECT'S POSITION. THEY HAD SOME DIFFICULTY IN ADJUST-ING THEIR NIGHT VISIBILITY FOR LANDING SO AFTER ORBITING MEHRABAD A FEW TIMES THEY WENT OUT FOR A STRAIGHT IN LANDING. THERE WAS A LOT OF INTERFERENCE ON THE UHF AND EACH TIME THEY PASSED THROUGH A MAG. BEARING OF 150 DEGREE FROM MEHRABAD THEY LOST THEIR COMMUNICATIONS (UHF AND INTERPHONE) AND THE INS FLUCTUATED FROM 30 DEGREES–50 DEGREES. THE ONE CIVIL AIRLINER THAT WAS APPROACHING MEHRABAD DURING THIS SAME TIME EXPERIENCED COMMUNICATIONS FAILURE IN THE SAME VICINITY (KILO ZULU) BUT DID NOT REPORT SEEING ANYTHING. WHILE THE F-4 WAS ON A LONG FINAL APPROACH THE CREW NOTICED ANOTHER CYLINDER SHAPED OBJECT (ABOUT THE SIZE OF A T-BIRD AT 10M) WITH BRIGHT STEADY LIGHTS ON EACH END AND A FLASHER IN THE

MIDDLE. WHEN QUERIED THE TOWER STATED THERE WAS NO OTHER KNOWN TRAFFIC IN THE AREA. DURING THE TIME THE OBJECT PASSED OVER THE F-4 THE TOWER DID NOT HAVE A VISUAL ON IT BUT PICKED IT UP AFTER THE PILOT TOLD THEM TO LOOK BETWEEN THE MOUNTAINS AND THE REFINERY.

E. DURING DAYLIGHT THE F-4 CREW WAS TAKEN OUT TO THE AREA IN A HELICOPTER WHERE THE OBJECT APPARENTLY HAD LANDED. NOTHING WAS NOTICED AT THE SPOT WHERE THEY THOUGHT THE OBJECT LANDED (A DRY LAKE BED) BUT AS THEY CIRCLED OFF TO THE WEST OF THE AREA THEY PICKED UP A VERY NOTICEABLE BEEPER SIGNAL. AT THE POINT WHERE THE RETURN WAS THE LOUDEST WAS A SMALL HOUSE WITH A GARDEN. THEY LANDED AND ASKED THE PEOPLE WITHIN IF THEY HAD NOTICED ANYTHING STRANGE LAST NIGHT. THE PEOPLE TALKED ABOUT A LOUD NOISE AND A VERY BRIGHT LIGHT LIKE LIGHTNING. THE AIRCRAFT AND AREA WHERE THE OBJECT IS BELIEVED TO HAVE LANDED ARE BEING CHECKED FOR POSSIBLE RADIATION. RO COMMENTS: (C) ACTUAL INFORMATION CONTAINED IN THIS REPORT WAS OBTAINED FROM SOURCE IN CONVERSATION WITH A SUB-SOURCE, AND IIAF PILOT OF ONE OF THE F-4S. MORE INFORMATION WILL BE FORWARDED WHEN IT BECOMES AVAILABLE.

This exceptional report was originally released to Charles Huffer in 1977, although initially he had been denied the document. Attached to it was a DIA Defense Information Report Evaluation – a rarity among documents released by the Agency. The concluding comments are remarkable:

An outstanding report. This case is a classic which meets all the criteria necessary for a valid study of the UFO phenomenon:
  a) The object was seen by multiple witnesses from different locations. (i.e. Shamiran, Mehrabad, and the dry lake bed) and viewpoints (both airborne and from the ground).
  b) The credibility of many of the witnesses was high (an Air Force general, qualified aircrews, and experienced tower operators).
  c) Visual sightings were confirmed by radar.

SECRET

NOW YOU SEE IT, NOW YOU DON'T! (U)

Captain Henry S. Shields, HQ USAFE/INOMP

(S) Sometime in his career, each pilot can expect to encounter strange, unusual happenings which will never be adequately or entirely explained by logic or subsequent investigation. The following article recounts just such an episode as reported by two F-4 Phantom crews of the Imperial Iranian Air Force during late 1976. No additional information or explanation of the strange events has been forthcoming; the story will be filed away and probably forgotten, but it makes interesting, and possibly disturbing, reading.

*   *   *   *   *

(S) Until 0030 on a clear autumn morning, it had been an entirely routine night watch for the Imperial Iranian Air Force's command post in the Tehran area. In quick succession, four calls arrived from one of the city's suburbs reporting a series of strange airborne objects. These Unidentified Flying Objects (UFOs) were described as 'bird-like', or as brightly-lit helicopters (although none were airborne at the time). Unable to convince the callers that they were only seeing stars, a senior officer went outside to see for himself. Observing an object to the north like a star, only larger and brighter, he immediately scrambled an IIAF F-4 to investigate.

(S) Approaching the city, the F-4 pilot reported that the brilliant object was easily visible 70 miles away. When approximately 25 NM distant, the interceptor lost all instrumentation and UHF/Intercom communications. Upon breaking off the intercept and turning towards his home base, all systems returned to normal, as if the strange object no longer regarded the aircraft as a threat.

SECRET

A US Air Force Security Service article about the encounter by pilots of the Imperial Iranian Air Force in September 1976, published in *Miji Quarterly*, Airforce Electronic Warfare Center, October 1978. (*US Air Force*)

SECRET

(S) A second F-4 was scrambled ten minutes after the first. The backseater reported radar-lock on the UFO at 27 NM/12 o'clock high position, and a rate of closure of 150 knots. Upon reaching the 25 NM point, the object began rapidly moving away to maintain a constant separation distance while still visible on the radar scope. While the size of the radar return was comparable to that of a KC-135, its intense brilliance made estimation of actual size impossible. Visually, it resembled flashing strobe lights arranged in a rectangular pattern and alternating blue, green, red, and orange. Their sequence was so fast that all colors could be seen at once.

(S) As the F-4 continued pursuit south of Tehran, a second brightly-lit object (about one-half to one-third the size of the moon) detached from the original UFO and headed straight for the F-4 at a high rate of speed. The pilot attempted to fire an AIM-9 missile at the new object but was prevented by a sudden power loss in his weapons control panel. UHF and internal communications were simultaneously lost. The pilot promptly initiated a turn and negative-G dive to escape, but the object fell in behind the F-4 at 3-4 NM distance. Continuing the turn, the pilot observed the second object turn inside of him and then away, subsequently returning to the primary UFO for a perfect rendezvous.

(S) The two UFOs had hardly rejoined when a second object detached and headed straight down toward the ground at high speed. Having regained weapons and communications systems, the aircrew watched the third object, anticipating a large explosion when it struck the ground. However, it landed gently and cast a bright light over a two-three kilometer area. The pilot flew as low over the area as possible, fixing the object's exact location.

(S) Upon return to home base, both crewmen had difficulty in

SECRET

33

SECRET

adjusting their night vision devices for landing. The landing was further complicated by excessive interference on UHF and a further complete loss of all communications when passing through a 150 degree magnetic bearing from the home base. The inertial navigation system simultaneously fluctuated from 30 to 50 degrees. A civil airliner approaching the area also experienced a similar communications failure, but reported no unusual sightings.

(S) While on a long final approach, the F-4 crew noted a further UFO. This was described as a cylinder-shaped object (about the size of a T-33 trainer) with bright steady lights on each end and a flasher in the middle. It quickly approached and passed directly over the F-4. In answer to the pilot's query, the control tower reported no other air traffic in the area, although they subsequently obtained a visual sighting of the object when specifically directed where to look.

(S) The following day, the F-4 crew was flown by helicopter to the location where they believed the object had landed. This turned out to be a dry lake bed, but nothing unusual was noticed. As the helicopter circled off to the west, however, a very noticeable beeper signal was received, and eventually traced to a nearby house. They immediately landed and asked the inhabitants if anything strange or unusual had occurred the previous night. Yes, they replied, there had been loud noises and a very bright light, like lightning. The helicopter returned to base and arrangements were made to conduct various tests, such as radiation checks, in the vicinity of the house. Unfortunately, the results of such tests have not been reported.   (XS03 2)

SECRET

d) Similar electromagnetic effects (EME) were reported by three separate aircraft.

e) There were physiological effects on some crew members (i.e. loss of night vision due to brightness of the object).

f) An inordinate amount of maneuverability was displayed by the UFOs.[41]

In 1994 further information came to light when interviews with some of the military personnel involved in the incident were shown on a *Sightings* television documentary. It was revealed, for example, that following the abortive attempt by the crew of the second F-4 (commanded by Iran's 'top-gun' pilot, Major Hussan Jafori) to fire a guided missile at the object, they feared for their lives and tried to eject from the plane, but the eject button malfunctioned. And as the F-4 approached for landing at Mehrabad Air Force Base the larger UFO followed it then described a low-altitude fly-by over the runway, causing a power failure for several seconds at the base. Twenty-five minutes after the UFO disappeared, it was observed by the pilot of an Egyptian Air Force jet over the Mediterranean Sea, then later by the crew and passengers of KLM Flight 241 in the Lisbon area. Ron Regehr, an analyst of the US Defense Support Program (DSP) satellite systems, has revealed that a DSP (nuclear event monitoring) satellite picked up signals from an 'unidentifiable technology' over Iran on the night in question.

General Mahmoud Sabahat, former Vice-Commander of the 2nd Tactical Fighter Base, said that on the day after the incident he attended a top-secret meeting between the head of the Iranian Air Force and Major-General Richard Secord, chief of the US Air Force section in Iran, and other personnel. 'When they heard our report and the report of the pilot[s],' said Hossein Pirouzi, air traffic supervisor at Mehrabad Air Force Base, 'they concluded that no country is able to have such a technology, and all of them believed it [must] be [an] object from outer space.'[42]

Further Sightings

In 1978, further sightings in Iran were brought to the attention of the Defense Intelligence Agency. The following case, though not acquired through official sources, merits inclusion here. The report was sent by the US Defense Attaché's office to the Joint Chiefs of Staff in the Pentagon – part of the normal routing for foreign intelligence reports. As with the previous case, the distribution list included the Secretary of State, the

National Security Agency and the CIA. The report was quoted from the Iranian English-language newspaper *Tehran Journal*, dated 18 July 1978:

> An unidentified flying object was seen by a number of people in the northern part of the city on Sunday night. Officials from the control tower at Mehrabad Airport and a Lufthansa aircrew also reported unusual readings on their instruments.
>
> Residents in northern Tehran were the first to spot the strange glowing object floating towards Saveh. They had been sleeping on the terraces of their houses, and immediately informed the control tower at Mehrabad Airport and the National Radio Network. The control tower confirmed the existence of the object but would give no further details. Soon afterward, the Lufthansa plane sent in its report.
>
> A similar flying object was seen last April by a local airline pilot, who claimed that he had photographed the object, but could not release photographs until the security division of the civil aviation authorities gave their permission. He claimed that while flying between Ahvaz and Tehran at 24,000 feet, he and his co-pilot had sighted a glittering object and had managed to photograph it. A Mehrabad radar control official said that on that occasion they had detected an object some 20 times the size of a jumbo jet on their screens.
>
> Civil Aviation Organization chief has . . . called for an investigation but the results of this enquiry have not yet been made public.
>
> An eye witness said yesterday that he was alone on his balcony on Sunday night when suddenly he saw the object emerge in the sky and hover directly above him. 'I was so upset that I wanted to scream, but could not do so,' he said. He added that he felt better once he realized that his neighbors had also seen it.[43]

Turkey

Cat and Mouse over Ankara

Between 24 and 27 October 1969, a remarkable series of sightings of an unknown flying object reported over Ankara caused great excitement among the local population. Although the military claimed the object was merely a weather balloon, this explanation was ruled out by the

AF FORM 112—PART I
APPROVED 1 JUNE 1948

RESTRICTED
(CLASSIFICATION)

COUNTRY	REPORT NO.	(LEAVE BLANK)
USA-MATS	IR-248-52	457032

AIR INTELLIGENCE INFORMATION REPORT

SUBJECT
Unidentified Flying Object over Paphos, Cyprus

AREA REPORTED ON
Cyprus

FROM (Agency) Intelligence Division, Hq MATS, Andrews AF Base, Washington 25, D. C.

DATE OF REPORT	DATE OF INFORMATION	EVALUATION
4 June 1952	10 May 1952	B-2

PREPARED BY (Officer)
Charles J. Powley, Captain, USAF

SOURCE Group of persons including British Scientist

REFERENCES (Control number, directive, previous report, etc., as applicable)

SUMMARY: (Give concise summary of report. Give significance in final one-sentence paragraph. List enclosures at lower left. Begin text of report on AF Form 112—Part II)

The following information was extracted from the Semi-monthly Intelligence Report #9 dated 15 May 1952 prepared by the MATS Liaison Officer, 1603-2 ATW Detachment, Atlantic Division, MATS, Nicosia, Cyprus.

At approximately 2030 hours on 10 May, in the city of Paphos, Southwest Cyprus, a group of persons including a noted British Scientist sighted an unidentified object which appeared to rise sharply from the level of the sea and disappeared into the sky. The object appeared to the observers to be of a circular shape and emitted a luminous light. It appeared to waver back and forth for a brief interval before fading out of sight directly overhead. At the time of the incident the sky was clear and there was no air traffic in the vicinity of Cyprus.

APPROVED:

J. L. Loomis
Lt Col USAF
for WILLIAM L. TRAVIS
Colonel, USAF
Chief, Intelligence
Division

CHARLES J. POWLEY
Captain, USAF

O Requirements
O Near East
O Central area

INCLS

A US Air Force intelligence report describing the sighting of a circular-shaped craft rising from the sea near Paphos, Cyprus, in May 1952. Witnesses included 'a noted British scientist'. Objects seen entering or leaving the sea have been observed since the last century, at least, and are now referred to as Unidentified Submarine Objects (USOs).

(*US Air Force*)

meteorological office. The Turkish Air Force (Türk Hava Kuvvetleri) was inundated with reports as the sightings continued, and jet fighters were scrambled from the nearby Murtad Air Base. The jets closed to within 12,000 metres, but the UFO always maintained this distance by climbing higher.

The game of cat and mouse continued over several days as and when the UFO returned. On each occasion the object was tracked on radar, and eventually the base commander himself, Ercüment Gökaydin, flew with the interceptors. His report included the following statement:

> Our air force pilots confirmed that this object was not a weather balloon, but were unable to positively identify the object. Our planes reached a height of 35,000 ft. but the object was at a height of at least 50,000 ft. It was oval in shape and a silvery colour. There were no other countries' traffic in the area at the time, or prototypes under test.

The pursuing aircraft were equipped with gun cameras and took film, but none of the frames has been released. One pilot who managed to get closer said the craft appeared to be intelligently controlled, and that it had three round windows like portholes. No explanation was put forward for the sightings, and the object officially remains unidentified.

'I can confirm that film exists of the object, and that the original is still in Turkish hands,' reports investigator Eric Saunders.[44]

US Air Force Jet Disappears During Encounter

On 14 January 1983 a very bright, unidentifiable object appeared in the sky above Adana at around 19.53 hours, and many witnesses stopped their cars to observe it. Soon the UFO was joined by two US Air Force jets from the NATO base at Incirlik.

One of the jets flew in tight circles around the UFO, which dwarfed the fighter in comparison and was described as disc-shaped with a dome underneath. The object accelerated then disappeared over the Mediterranean Sea, with the jets in pursuit. Witnesses claim that only one of the jets returned to base. Although officials admitted to locals that a plane had been lost, they refused to discuss the circumstances. 'I can confirm that Turkish forces were involved in a search-and-rescue mission over the Mediterranean on that date, at the request of the USAF,' states Eric Saunders.[45]

Turkish Airlines Sightings

En route from Istanbul to Ankara on 12 April 1984, a Turkish Airlines
pilot and his co-pilot (who requested anonymity) saw a bright object
falling down from above them at their altitude of 20,000 feet. They
assumed a plane was about to crash, but the object suddenly stopped when
it reached the same flight level as the airliner. The captain contacted air
traffic control, asking if there was any traffic ahead of him. A reply came in
the negative.

The crew reported that the object was no further away than 1,000
metres, and described it as shaped like an elongated diamond (similar to the
UFO seen over south-east London in December 1980 – pp. 53–4), emitting
pulses of bright, coloured light. While the object remained in the same
position relative to the airliner, the captain flashed the plane's landing-
lights. The object responded with such a brilliant flash of light that the pilots
were temporarily blinded. After accompanying the airliner for two minutes
further, the object descended very slowly and disappeared under cloud.[46]

Captain Selahattin Sivri, with twenty-four years of flying experience
for Turkish Airlines, had never experienced anything like the events that
took place during his flight from Zurich to Antalya on 27 October 1989:

We left Zurich at 11.00 p.m. in a Boeing 727. The weather was
clear and we were at an altitude of 11,000 metres. At 12.30 a.m. we
entered Yugoslavian airspace. Suddenly from our left and at a
distance of 2,000 metres we saw a very colourful and bright object.
Both I and my colleague at first thought this was another plane,
but after some time the object became intensely bright and we
began to wonder what it was.

Ten minutes later the object overtook us. We were over the
Belgrade tower and turned on our radio to listen. We felt the
other 'aircraft' was monitoring the radio waves; it was as if there
was other traffic 'keying in' without speaking. The situation grew
stranger as we entered Bulgarian air space. We contacted the
Bulgarian traffic control and waited for the other aircraft to do
likewise. They did not, and our flight engineer Pertev Arikan drew
our attention to the object as it began to split into three: one red,
green, and the other bright white. They now rapidly approached
us and we could see they were egg-shaped and appeared to be
spinning on their axis. The objects were massive – I would say the
size of an apartment block.

I then contacted Istanbul tower to see if they picked up anything on radar. The answer was negative: there was no traffic ahead of us or in the vicinity. I then asked if there was anything approaching them from the west over the Black Sea. Again the answer was negative. It was as if they didn't exist, but we could all see them around us. The three objects were leading us in our path. They again approached each other but remained separate, [then] climbed to a steady altitude of 14,500 metres. As the three objects climbed, the coloured ones became white. As we watched, the three became one again and either accelerated away rapidly or disappeared – I couldn't say.

Captain Sivri told Eric Saunders that the objects gave the impression of spinning, because of a strobe-like effect. No other details of the craft were visible.[47]

Hungary

Some most extraordinary events in Hungary took place at the Tarnaszentmária Army barracks (near Gyöngyös) in October and November of 1989. On 20 October, according to the sworn testimony of an entire Army unit, an eerie noise was heard which increased in volume every twenty seconds. Subsequently, one of the soldiers on guard duty observed three shiny round objects preceded by an exceptionally bright beam of light. After hovering over the barracks, the objects shot off at incredible speed towards the nearby forest and vanished.

Exactly one month later, following a spate of further sightings, soldiers on guard duty noticed a cloud of red mist in the sky with curious flashing lights inside it, followed by a Saturn-shaped UFO, which floated over the barracks and disappeared over the forest. In their affidavit, two of the guards swore that they were illuminated briefly by a powerful beam of light which made them ill. Later that night, conscript Lajos Dioszegi reported seeing 10-foot-tall figures (reminiscent of the September 1989 sightings in Voronezh, Russia) in the forest clearing facing the barracks. 'They were moving as if they were chess pieces,' he stated in his testimony. 'All the animals in the barracks – pigs, sheep and dogs – became frantic, and one of the fear-crazed dogs broke its extremely strong steel chain and ran away from the aliens.'[48,49]

The Tarnaszentmária reports and others were endorsed by Colonel György Keleti, who in a series of articles for a national UFO magazine stated his conviction that we are being visited by extraterrestrials. In an interview for a Hungarian national newspaper in 1994, Keleti – as Minister of Defence – was asked if he feared a UFO invasion. He responded:

> . . . I was a columnist [in Budapest's *Ufomagazin*] and I published UFO cases that were observed and registered within the Hungarian armed forces. I never stated that we were preparing any kind of action against UFO forces; I only pointed out to the public that, as a civilization, we would be unable to defend ourselves here on the Earth . . . Around Szolnok many UFO reports have been received by the Ministry of Defence, which obviously and logically means that [the UFOs] know very well where they have to land and what they have to do. It is remarkable indeed that the Hungarian newspapers – in general, newspapers everywhere – reject the reports of the authorities.[50]

Belgium

The remarkable series of sightings of large, usually triangular-shaped, UFOs reported by over 2,000 witnesses in Belgium – including police officers and airborne pilots of the Royal Belgian Air Force – between 1989 and 1990 – led to an unevaluated report, based on both open and confidential sources, by the US Defense Attaché in Brussels:

> . . . Numerous and various accounts of UFO sightings have surfaced in Belgium over the past few months. The credibility of the observers of the alleged events varies from those who are unsophisticated to those who are well educated and prominently placed.
>   . . .Col [Wilfried] De Brouwer, Chief of Operations for the BAF [Belgian Air Force] . . . noted the large number of reported sightings, particularly in Nov 89 in the Liege area and that the BAF and MOD [Ministry of Defence] are taking the issue seriously. BAF have not been able to explain the phenomena either.

De Brouwer specifically addressed the possibility of the objects being USAF B-2 or F-117 Stealth aircraft which would not appear on Belgian radar, but might be sighted visually if they were operating at low altitude . . . He made it quite clear that no USAF overflight requests had ever been received for this type mission

```
INQUIRE=DOC10D
ITEM NO=00508802
ENVELOPE
CDSN = LGX391   MCN = 90089/26558   TOR = 900901048
RTTCZYUW RUEKJCS5049 0891251-CCCC--RUEALGX.
ZNY CCCCC
HEADER
R 301251Z MAR 90
FM JOINT STAFF WASHINGTON DC
INFO RUEADWD/OCSA WASHINGTON DC
RUENAAA/CNO WASHINGTON DC
RUEAHQA/CSAF WASHINGTON DC
RUEACMC/CMC WASHINGTON DC
RUEDADA/AFIS AMHS BOLLING AFB DC
RUFTAKA/CDR USAINTELCTRE HEIDELBERG GE
RUFGAID/USEUCOM AIDES VAIHINGEN GE
RUETIAQ/MPCFTGEORGEGMEADEMD
RUEAMCC/CMC CC WASHINGTON DC
RUEALGX/SAFE
R 301246Z MAR 90
FM
TO RUEKJCS/DIA WASHDC
INFO RUEKJCS/DIA WASHDC//DAT-7//
RUSNNOA/USCINCEUR VAIHINGEN GE//ECJ2-OC/ECJ2-JIC//
RUFGAID/USEUCOM AIDES VAIHINGEN GE
RHFQAAA/HQUSAFE RAMSTEIN AB GE//INOW/INO//
RHFPAAA/UTAIS RAMSTEIN AB GE//INRMH/INA//
RHDLCNE/CINCUSNAVEUR LONDON UK
RUFHNA/USDELMC BRUSSELS BE
RUFHNA/USMISSION USNATO
RUDOGHA/USNMR SHAPE BE
RUEAIIA/CIA WASHDC
RUFGAID/JICEUR VAIHINGEN GE
RUCBSAA/FICEURLANT NORFOLK VA
RUEKJCS/SECDEF WASHDC
RUEHC/SECSTATE WASHDC
RUEADWW/WHITEHOUSE WASHDC
RUFHBG/AMEMBASSY LUXEMBOURG
RUEATAC/CDRUSAITAC WASHDC
BT
CONTROLS
                        SECTION 01 OF 02          05049


SERIAL: (U) IIR 6 807 0136 90.

BODY
COUNTRY: (U) BELGIUM (BE).

SUBJ: IIR 6 807 0136 90/BELGIUM AND THE UFO ISSUE (U)

WARNING: (U) THIS IS AN INFORMATION REPORT, NOT FINALLY
```

A Defense Intelligence Agency report on the Belgian sightings of 1989–90. (*DIA*)

EVALUATED INTELLIGENCE. REPORT CLASSIFIED

DEPARTMENT OF DEFENSE

DOI: (U) 900326.

REQS:

SOURCE: A- (U) LA DERNIER HEURE, 20 MAR, DAILY FRENCH
LANGUAGE PAPER, CIRC 100,000; B- (U) LE SOIR, 26 MAR,
DAILY FRENCH LANGUAGE PAPER, CIRC 213,000;

SUMMARY: (U) NUMEROUS UFO SIGHTINGS HAVE BEEN MADE IN
BELGIUM SINCE NOV 89. THE CREDIBILITY OF SOME INDIVIDUALS
MAKING THE REPORTS IS GOOD. SOME SIGHTINGS HAVE BEEN
EXPLAINED BY NATURAL/MANMADE PHENOMENA, SOME HAVE NOT.
INVESTIGATION BY THE BAF CONTINUES.

TEXT: 1. (U) NUMEROUS AND VARIOUS ACCOUNTS OF UFO
SIGNTINGS HAVE SURFACED IN BELGIUM OVER THE PAST FEW
MONTHS. THE CREDIBILITY OF THE OBSERVERS OF THE ALLEDGED
EVENTS VARIES FROM THOSE WHO ARE UNSOPHISTICATED TO THOSE
WHO ARE THE WELL EDUCATED AND PROMINENTLY PLACED.

2. (U) SOURCE A CITES MR LEON BRENIG, A 43 YEAR OLD
PROFESSOR AT THE FREE UNIVERSIY OF BRUSSELS (PROMINENT) IN
THE FIELD OF STATISTICS AND PHYSICS. HE CLAIMS TO HAVE
TAKEN PICTURES OF THE PHENOMENA WHICH ARE STILL BEING
DEVELOPED BUT WILL BE PUBLISHED BY THE BELGIAN SOCIETY FOR
THE STUDY OF SPACE PHENOMENA IF THEY ARE OF GOOD QUALITY.

3. (U) MR BRENIG WAS DRIVING ON THE ARDENNES AUTOROUTE IN
THE BEAUFAYS REGION EAST OF LIEGE, SUNDAY, 18 MARCH 1990
AT 2030 HOURS WHEN HE OBSERVED AN AIRBORNE OBJECT
APPROACHING IN HIS DIRECTION FROM THE NORTH. IT WAS IN
THE FORM OF A TRIANGLE ABOUT THE SIZE OF A PING-PONG BALL
AND HAD A YELLOW LIGHT SURROUNDING IT WITH A REDDISH
CENTER VARYING IN INTENSITY. ALTITUDE APPEARED TO BE 500
- 1000 METERS, MOVING AT A SLOW SPEED WITH NO SOUND. IT
DID NOT MOVE OR BEHAVE LIKE AN AIRCRAFT.

4. (U) MR BRENIG CONTACTED A FRIEND VERY NEAR THE AREA
WHO CAME OUT AND TOOK PICTURES OF IT WITH A ZOOM LENS AND
400 ASA FILM. BOTH INSISTED THE OBJECT COULD NOT BE AN
AIRCRAFT OR HOLOGRAMME PROJECTION AS THE SKY WAS CLOUDLESS.

5. (U) THE SOURCE B ARTICLE WHICH DISCUSSES A BELGIAN
TELEVISION INTERVIEW WITH COL WIL ((DEBROUWER)), CHIEF OF

OPERATIONS FOR THE BAF, MOST LIKELY WAS THE RESULT OF A
FOLLOW-ON ACTION TAKEN BY MR BRENIG WHEN HE CONTACTED
LTGEN ((TERRASSON)), COMMANDER, BELGIAN TACTICAL
(OPERATIONAL) COMMAND. GEN TERRASSON CATEGORICALLY
ELIMINATED ANY POSSIBLE BAF AIRCRAFT OR ENGINE TEST
INVOLVEMENT WHICH COL DEBROUWER CONFIRMED DURING THE 25

ADMIN
BT

#5049

NNNN

```
INQUIRE=DOC10D
ITEM NO=00503294
ENVELOPE
CDSN = LGX492   MCN = 90089/26566   TOR = 900891502
RTTCZYUW RUEKJCS5049 0891251-CCCC--RUEALGX.
ZNY CCCCC
HEADER
R 301251Z MAR 90
FM JOINT STAFF WASHINGTON DC
INFO RUEADWD/OCSA WASHINGTON DC
RUENAAA/CNO WASHINGTON DC
RUEAHQA/CSAF WASHINGTON DC
RUEACMC/CMC WASHINGTON DC
RUEDADA/AFIS AMHS BOLLING AFB DC
RUFTAKA/CDR USAINTELCTRE HEIDELBERG GE
RUFGAID/USEUCOM AIDES VAIHINGEN GE
RUETIAQ/MPCFTGEORGEGMEADEMD
RUEAMCC/CMC CC WASHINGTON DC
RUEALGX/SAFE
R 301246Z MAR 90
FM ███████████████████
TO RUEKJCS/DIA WASHDC
INFO RUEKJCS/DIA WASHDC//DAT-7//
RUSNNOA/USCINCEUR VAIHINGEN GE//ECJ2-OC/ECJ2-JIC//
RUFGAID/USEUCOM AIDES VAIHINGEN GE
RHFQAAA/HQUSAFE RAMSTEIN AB GE//INOW/INO//
RHFPAAA/UTAIS RAMSTEIN AB GE//INRMH/INA//
RHDLCNE/CINCUSNAVEUR LONDON UK
RUFHNA/USDELMC BRUSSELS BE
RUFHNA/USMISSION USNATO
RUDOGHA/USNMR SHAPE BE
RUEAIIA/CIA WASHDC
RUFGAID/JICEUR VAIHINGEN GE
RUCBSAA/FICEURLANT NORFOLK VA
RUEKJCS/SECDEF WASHDC
RUEHC/SECSTATE WASHDC
RUEADWW/WHITEHOUSE WASHDC
RUFHBG/AMEMBASSY LUXEMBOURG
RUEATAC/CDRUSAITAC WASHDC
BT
CONTROLS
███████████████████ SECTION 02 OF 02 ██████████ 05049


SERIAL:  (U) IIR 6 807 0136 90.

BODY
COUNTRY: (U) BELGIUM (BE).

SUBJ:  IIR 6 807 0136 90/BELGIUM AND THE UFO ISSUE (U)

MAR TV SHOW.
```

6. (U) DEBROUWER NOTED THE LARGE NUMBER OF REPORTED
SIGHTINGS, PARTICULARLY IN NOV 89 IN THE LIEGE AREA AND
THAT THE BAF AND MOD ARE TAKING THE ISSUE SERIOUSLY. BAF
EXPERTS HAVE NOT BEEN ABLE TO EXPLAIN THE PHENOMENA EITHER.

7. (U) DEBROUWER SPECIFICALLY ADDRESSED THE POSSIBILITY
OF THE OBJECTS BEING USAF B-2 OR F-117 STEALTH AIRCRAFT
WHICH WOULD NOT APPEAR ON BELGIAN RADAR, BUT MIGHT BE
SIGHTED VISUALLY IF THEY WERE OPERATING AT LOW ALTITUDE IN
THE ARDENNES AREA. HE MADE IT QUITE CLEAR THAT NO USAF
OVERFLIGHT REQUESTS HAD EVER BEEN RECEIVED FOR THIS TYPE
MISSION AND THAT THE ALLEDGED OBSERVATIONS DID NOT
CORRESPOND IN ANY WAY TO THE OBSERVABLE CHARACTERISTICS OF
EITHER U.S. AIRCRAFT.

8. (U) MR BRENIG HAS SINCE ASSURED THE COMMUNITY THAT HE
IS PERSONALLY ORGANIZING A NEW UFO OBSERVATION CAMPAIGN
AND SPECIFICALLY REQUESTS THE HELP OF THE BELGIAN MOD.

9. ▆▆▆▆▆▆▆ RELATED A SIMILAR UFO SIGHTING WHICH
APPARENTLY HAPPENED TO A BELGIAN AIR FORCE OFFICER IN THE
SAME AREA NEAR LIEGE DURING NOVEMBER 89. THE OFFICER AD
HIS WIFE WERE ALLEDGEDLY BLINDED BY A HUGE BRIGHT FLYING
OBJECT AS THEY WERE DRIVING ON THE AUTOROUTE. THEY
STOPPED THEIR CAR, BUT WERE SO FRIGHTENED THEY ABANDONED
THE VEHICLE AND RAN INTO THE WOODS. THEY COULD NOT
PROVIDE A DETAILED DESCRIPTION BUT WHATEVER IT WAS
DEFINITELY APPEARED REAL TO THEM. ▆▆▆▆▆▆ UNDERLINED
THEIR CREDIBILITY AS SOLID.

COMMENTS: 1. ▆▆▆▆▆▆▆ COMMENT. HE COULD PROVIDE
VERY LITTLE CONCRETE INFORMAITON EXCEPT TO VERIFY THE
LARGE VOLUME OF SIGHTINGS AND THE SIMILARITY OF SOME
DURING NOV 89.

2. ▆▆▆ THE BAF HAS RULED SOME SIGHTINGS WERE CAUSED BY
INVERSION LAYERS, LAZER BEAMS AND OTHER FORMS OF HIGH
INTENSITY LIGHTING HITTING CLOUDS. BUT A REMARKABLE
NUMBER OCCURRED ON CLEAR NIGHTS WITH NO OTHER EXPLAINABLE
ACTIVITY NEARBY.

3. ▆▆▆ THE BAF IS CONCERNED TO A POINT ABOUT THE UFO
ISSUE AND IS TAKING ACTION TO INVESTIGATE INFORMATION THEY
HAVE. ▆▆▆▆ DOES ADMIT, HOWEVER, THAT HE IS NOT
OPTIMISTIC ABOUT RESOLVING THE PROBLEM.

4. ▆▆▆ FIELD COMMENT. THE USAF DID CONFIRM TO THE BAF
AND BELGIAN MOD THAT NO USAF STEALTH AIRCRAFT WERE
OPERATING IN THE ARDENNES AREA DURING THE PERIODS IN

PAGE:0016

QUESTION. THIS WAS RELEASED TO THE BELGIAN PRESS AND
RECEIVED WIDE DISSEMINATION.

ADMIN
PROJ: (U)
INSTR: (U) US NO.
PREP:
ACQ:
DISSEM: (U) FIELD: AMEMBASSY BRUSSELS (DCM).
WARNING: (U) REPORT CLASSIFIED --

BT

#5049

NNNN

and that the alleged observations did not correspond in any way to the observable characteristics of either U.S. aircraft.

[Deleted] related a similar UFO sighting which apparently happened to a Belgian Air Force officer in the same area during November 89. The officer and his wife were allegedly blinded by a huge bright flying object as they were driving on the autoroute. They stopped their car, but were so frightened they abandoned the vehicle and ran into the woods. They could not provide a detailed description but whatever it was definitely appeared real to them. [Deleted] underlined their credibility as solid . . .

The BAF has ruled some sightings were caused by inversion layers, laser beams and other forms of high intensity lighting hitting clouds. But a remarkable number occurred on clear nights with no other explainable activity nearby.

The BAF is concerned to a point about the UFO issue and is taking action to investigate information . . . [Deleted] does admit, however, that he is not optimistic about resolving the problem . . . The USAF did confirm to the BAF and Belgian MOD that no USAF Stealth aircraft were operating in the Ardennes area during the periods in question.[51]

In a postface to the two-volume book on the UFO wave over Belgium, *Vague d'OVNI sur la Belgique: Un Dossier Exceptionnel*, produced by the Belgian UFO group SOBEPS, Major-General Wilfried De Brouwer (currently Deputy Chief of the Royal Belgian Air Force) commented as follows:

. . . the Air Force has arrived at the conclusion that a certain number of anomalous phenomena has been produced within Belgian airspace. The numerous testimonies of ground observations . . . reinforced by the [Air Force] reports of the night of March 30–31, have led us to face the hypothesis that a certain number of unauthorized aerial activities have taken place. Until now, not a single trace of aggressiveness has been signalled; military [and] civilian air traffic has not been disturbed or threatened . . . .

The day will come undoubtedly when the phenomenon will be observed with technological means of detection and collection that won't leave a single doubt about its origin. This should lift a part of the veil that has covered the [UFO] mystery for a long time; a mystery that continues to the present. But it exists, it is real, and that in itself is an important conclusion.[52]

DIA Attendance at Conferences

Defense Intelligence Agency representatives apparently attend conferences on the paranormal – including UFOs – around the world, and a conference of the Society for Scientific Exploration in Munich in 1992 was the subject of the following report, from which I quote a few brief extracts:

> This report provides information on the program, personalities and parapsychological papers presented at the first European meeting of the Society for Scientific Exploration, which took place 7–8 August 1992 in Munich . . . The expressed aim of the SSE meeting was to promote the exchange of ideas, results and goals among researchers in various fields of anomalies, and inform the public of the discussion among active scientists concerning current controversial issues . . .

The report went on to enumerate the various 'noteworthy' papers presented at the conference, which included the subjects of ball lightning (Alexander Keul) and crop circles (Michael Green), and ended by cross-referencing other DIA reports relating to Chinese parapsychological practitioners, as well as Russian and Hungarian papers on parapsychology presented at Princeton University in June 1992.

This information is hardly of defence interest, one might assume, yet the report was classified SECRET/NOFORN/WNINTEL (i.e. Not releasable to Foreign Nationals/Warning Notice – Intelligence Sources or Methods Involved).[53]

Analysis

From the DIA documents thus far released, it is evident that UFO reporting receives the same level of attention as any other subject or topic on which intelligence is required to be collected. Attaché Intelligence Information Reports (IIRs) are always treated as first-echelon, field-collected raw data made available at theatre and national levels for subsequent refined analysis and 'end-product' reporting; nevertheless, attachés are encouraged to include comments within the reports, normally at the end, to qualify the data in some particular way. At headquarters, this and other raw data are further analysed and blended (a process called 'fusion' in US military jargon) with data and information from other sources and methods of intelligence collection and processing and are subsequently included in serial and final reports. Despite some obviously significant IIRs, the DIA has not released any worthwhile analyses, with the exception of the 1976 Tehran case.

The Director of Central Intelligence (DCI) manages the entire community of intelligence agencies throughout the US Government, as well as being head of the CIA. Admiral Stansfield Turner, DCI during the Carter administration, is scathing about the DIA's analytical product, however, which he describes as 'well below the caliber of the rest of the Intelligence Community'.[54] Admiral Turner also points out that the CIA's analytic work competes with that of the DIA and other intelligence agencies, and leaves us in no doubt that the CIA is superior in this respect.[55] Unlike the CIA, the DIA cannot present its analyses directly to the National Security Council, although the Secretary of Defense can, if he chooses, present DIA estimates that differ from those of the CIA.[56]

Since neither agency is prepared to release its analyses of the mass of UFO reports collated over the years, we are forced to draw our own conclusions from the released documents. But it is evident that their time-span and contents connote a long, continuous, serious and sometimes profound US military interest in UFO activity and technology. How curious, then, that the DIA's official position is that 'This Agency has no requirement for the collection of information pertaining to the subject of UFOs'![57]

It is equally evident from these official documents – as well as from the unofficial reports cited in this chapter and throughout the book – that governments worldwide are reluctant to acknowledge their serious concern with the ubiquitous UFO phenomenon.

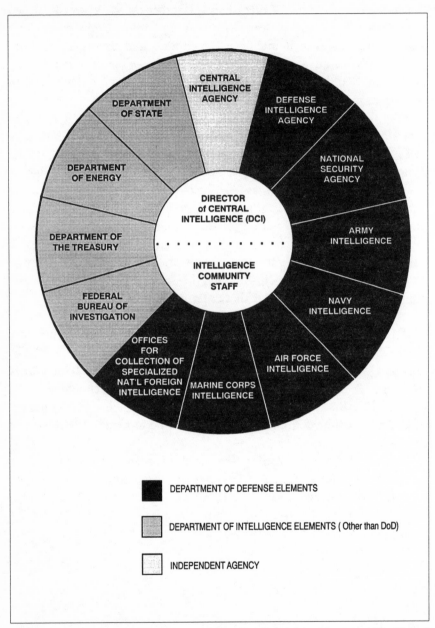

The structure of the US Intelligence Community. (*Tania Long, based on a graphic published by the CIA*)

Part Three

The United States

The Growing Security Threat

IN 1947 'FLYING SAUCERS' – a description coined by the press following pilot Kenneth Arnold's famous sighting of nine crescent-shaped objects over the Cascade Mountains, Washington, on 24 June – began to be seen in ever increasing numbers all over the United States. Reports were being made by qualified observers such as military and civilian pilots, air traffic controllers, and others whose jobs depended on their ability to identify objects in the sky. The intelligence community was alarmed.

Arnold's first sighting[1] was investigated by the Federal Bureau of Investigation and the Army Air Forces. The story is so well-known that I have not included it here, but an FBI agent's comments on the reliability of the report are worth citing:

> It is the personal opinion of the interviewer that [Arnold] actually saw what he states he saw in the attached report. It is also the opinion of the interviewer that [Arnold] would have much more to lose than gain and would have to be very strongly convinced that he actually saw something before he would report such an incident and open himself up for the ridicule that would accompany such a report.[2]

The FBI denied any involvement in UFO investigations until 1976, when Dr Bruce Maccabee, a US Department of the Navy optical physicist, filed a Freedom of Information Act request and obtained about 1,100 pages of documentation on the subject. Only three years earlier, in October 1973, FBI Director Clarence M. Kelley explained to an enquirer that 'the investigation of Unidentified Flying Objects is not and never has been a matter that is within the investigative jurisdiction of the FBI'[3] (see p. 310).

Another early sighting which led to a full-scale official investigation was that of Captain Edward J. Smith and his co-pilot Ralph Stevens, flying a United Airlines DC-3, Flight 105, in the vicinity of Emmet, Idaho, on 4

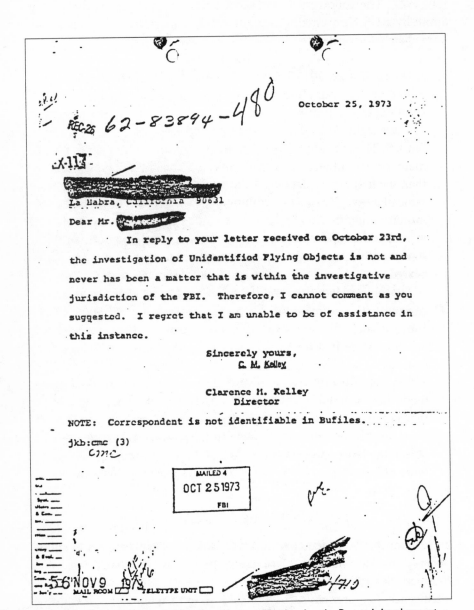

REC26 62-83894-480

October 25, 1973

X-117

La Habra, California 90631

Dear Mr.

In reply to your letter received on October 23rd, the investigation of Unidentified Flying Objects is not and never has been a matter that is within the investigative jurisdiction of the FBI. Therefore, I cannot comment as you suggested. I regret that I am unable to be of assistance in this instance.

                              Sincerely yours,
                              C. M. Kelley

                              Clarence M. Kelley
                              Director

NOTE: Correspondent is not identifiable in Bufiles.

jkb:cmc (3)
    cmc

MAILED 4
OCT 25 1973
FBI

56 NOV 9 1973
MAIL ROOM ☐   TELETYPE UNIT ☐

A 1973 letter from Clarence M. Kelley, Director, FBI, denying the Bureau's involvement in the investigation of UFOs. In 1976 the FBI released 1,100 pages of UFO-related documentation. (*FBI*)

July 1947. The following is extracted from an interview with Captain Smith by a US Navy Intelligence officer a few days later. The report was immediately forwarded to the Director of Naval Intelligence:

> At approximately 2015, the co-pilot called my attention to the first object seen . . . our altitude was approximately 6500, and we were climbing to our proposed cruising altitude of 8000 . . . the object . . . was sighted at approximately 290 degrees, or ten degrees to our left. Then an additional four objects appeared to the left of the main, or first, object. These four objects appeared slightly smaller than the first object sighted, but all of the objects appeared on the same plane . . . They were within our sight for approximately two minutes, then they disappeared . . . one or two minutes later, the second group appeared . . . to the right of the plane . . . [and] stayed within our sight twelve to fifteen minutes, then disappeared . . .
>
> The objects were flat on the base, the top slightly rough in contour. The dimensions appeared the same as a DC-3 approximately five miles from us . . . Actually we have no idea just how large it was since we could not determine its distance from us . . . when first sighted, they were going slow and stayed within sight for quite some time. However, when we lost sight of them, they seemed to disappear practically immediately. I think they either put on a tremendous burst of speed and disappeared from sight, or else they dissipated. Also, it appeared that only one object, the large one, was controlled, and it in turn controlled the other objects.[4]

Air Matériel Command

In September 1947, Lieutenant General Nathan Twining, Commanding General of Air Matériel Command (AMC), sent a memorandum, classified Secret, to Brigadier General George Schulgen, Chief, Air Intelligence Requirements Division at the Pentagon, in response to a request from Air Intelligence concerning 'flying discs'. Twining stated that, in the opinion of AMC, based on a conference of its personnel from the Air Institute of Technology, Intelligence T-2, the Office, Chief Engineering Division, and the Aircraft, Power Plant and Propeller Laboratories of Engineering Division T-3:

7 July 1947

SUBJECT: Report on Flying Saucers

TO: Commanding General
            32d AAF Base Unit
            Bolling Field
            Washington, D.C.

1.   Following are statistics regarding reports by four
witnesses while in flight in two airplanes.

2.   Weather CAVU. Visibility exceptionally good. Scattered altecumulus 6000 feet.

3.   First report; time 1145 hours CST. Alt. of observers
800 feet above the ground. Altitude of saucer 4000 feet MSL.
Observed period – First sighted over Koshkonong, Wisconsin. Flight
was observed from town of Koshkonong to Elkhorn, Wisconsin. This
flight covered twenty-five (25) miles in fifteen (15) seconds,
which is a speed of six thousand (6000) miles per hour.

4.   Second report Time: 1430 hours CST. Altitude of
observers thirty-five hundred feet (3500) MSL. Altitude of saucer
twenty-five hundred feet (2500). Observation period. Observers
at East Troy, Wisconsin, flight observed from Eagle, Wisconsin to
Muskego, Wisconsin. This flight covered twenty-two (22) miles in
twenty (20 seconds, which is a speed of three thousand nine hundred
sixty (3960) miles per hour.

5.   Flight maneuvers: First observation-saucer decended
vertically edgewise through altocumulus clouds, stopped at four
thousand (4000) feet and assumed horizontal position and preceeded
in horizontal flight from a horizontal position for fifteen (15)
seconds covering twenty-five (25) miles and again stopped and
disappeared. Second observation: Observed in horizontal flight in
a horizontal attitude for a period of twenty (20) seconds covering
twenty-two (22) miles. By the time the pilot had removed his
camera from the glove compartment of his plane, the saucer disappeared and again reappeared approximately ten (10) miles farther
along its course after six (6) seconds making its final disappearance.

6.   The first two observers were an instructor and a student,
having just taken off from Elkhorn Airport. The second two observers,
one being Cap't R. J. Southey, Wing Supply Officer and a passenger.

                              John D. Schindler, Jr.
                              Maj. Air Corps, AAF-CAP Liaison Officer

A US Army intelligence report detailing observations of flying saucers observed by airborne
witnesses over Wisconsin in July 1947. (*US Army*)

Form No. 10-814 (Rev 18 Sep 44)   ORS NND.760168 5-4-78   WALJ JAN 47

~~SECRET~~

SAVE

IN REPLY ADDRESS BOTH
COMMUNICATION AND IN-
VELOPS TO COMMANDING
GENERAL, AIR MATERIEL
COMMAND, ATTENTION
FOLLOWING OFFICE SYMBOL:

TSDIN

HEADQUARTERS
AIR MATERIEL COMMAND

TSDIN/HMM/lg/6-4100
WRIGHT FIELD, DAYTON, OHIO

SEP 2 3 1947

SUBJECT: AMC Opinion Concerning "Flying Discs"

TO: Commanding General
Army Air Forces
Washington 25, D. C.
ATTENTION: Brig. General George Schulgen
AC/AS-2

1. As requested by AC/AS-2 there is presented below the considered opinion of this Command concerning the so-called "Flying Discs". This opinion is based on interrogation report data furnished by AC/AS-2 and preliminary studies by personnel of T-2 and Aircraft Laboratory, Engineering Division T-3. This opinion was arrived at in a conference between personnel from the Air Institute of Technology, Intelligence T-2, Office, Chief of Engineering Division, and the Aircraft, Power Plant and Propeller Laboratories of Engineering Division T-3.

2. It is the opinion that:

a. The phenomenon reported is something real and not visionary or fictitious.

b. There are objects probably approximating the shape of a disc, of such appreciable size as to appear to be as large as man-made aircraft.

The Air Matériel Command report by Lieutenant General Nathan Twining to the Commanding General, Army Air Forces, September 1947, originally classified Secret, confirming that 'the phenomenon reported is something real and not visionary or fictitious'.
(*US Air Force*)

   c.   There is a possibility that some of the incidents may be caused by natural phenomena, such as meteors.

   d.   The reported operating characteristics such as extreme rates of climb, maneuverability (particularly in roll), and action which must be considered evasive when sighted or contacted by friendly aircraft and radar, lend belief to the possibility that some of the objects are controlled either manually, automatically or remotely.

   e.   The apparent common description of the objects is as follows:-

     (1) Metallic or light reflecting surface.

SECRET   U-39552

~~SECRET~~

Basic Ltr fr CG, AMC, WF to CG, AAF, Wash. D. C. subj "AMC Opinion Concerning "Flying Discs".

     (2) Absence of trail, except in a few instances when the object apparently was operating under high performance conditions.

     (3) Circular or elliptical in shape, flat on bottom and domed on top.

     (4) Several reports of well kept formation flights varying from three to nine objects.

     (5) Normally no associated sound, except in three instances a substantial rumbling roar was noted.

     (6) Level flight speeds normally above 300 knots are estimated.

   f.   It is possible within the present U. S. knowledge — provided extensive detailed development is undertaken — to construct a piloted aircraft which has the general description of the object in subparagraph (e) above which would be capable of an approximate range of 7000 miles at subsonic speeds.

   g.   Any developments in this country along the lines indicated would be extremely expensive, time consuming and at the considerable expense of current projects and therefore, if directed, should be set up independently of existing projects.

   h.   Due consideration must be given the following:-

     (1) The possibility that these objects are of domestic origin - the product of some high security project not known to AC/AS-2 or this Command.

     (2) The lack of physical evidence in the shape of crash recovered exhibits which would undeniably prove the existence of these objects.

(3) The possibility that some foreign nation has a form
of propulsion possibly nuclear, which is outside of
our domestic knowledge.

3. It is recommended that:

a. Headquarters, Army Air Forces issue a directive assigning
a priority, security classification and Code Name for a detailed study of
this matter to include the preparation of complete sets of all available
and pertinent data which will then be made available to the Army, Navy,
Atomic Energy Commission, JRDB, the Air Force Scientific Advisory Group,
NACA, and the RAND and NEPA projects for comments and recommendations,
with a preliminary report to be forwarded within 15 days of receipt of
the data and a detailed report thereafter every 30 days as the investi-

-2-

SECRET

U-39552

Basic Ltr fr CG, AMC, WF to CG, AAF, Wash. D.C. subj "AMC Opinion Concerning "Flying Discs"

gation develops. A complete interchange of data should be effected.

4. Awaiting a specific directive AMC will continue the investigation within its current resources in order to more closely define the
nature of the phenomenon. Detailed Essential Elements of Information
will be formulated immediately for transmittal thru channels.

N. F. TWINING
Lieutenant General, U.S.A.
Commanding

SECRET

-3-

U-39552

AAG OOO GENERAL "C"

The phenomenon reported is something real and not visionary or
fictitious . . . There are objects probably approximating the shape
of a disc, of such appreciable size as to appear to be as large as
man-made aircraft . . . The reported operating characteristics
such as extreme rates of climb, maneuverability (particularly in
roll), and action which must be considered *evasive* when sighted
or contacted by friendly aircraft and radar, lend belief to the
possibility that some of the objects are controlled either manually,
automatically or remotely.

Twining's report (see pp. 313–15) went on to list common
descriptions of the objects:

(1) Metallic or light reflecting surface.
(2) Absence of trail, except in a few instances when the object
apparently was operating under high performance conditions.
(3) Circular or elliptical in shape, flat on bottom and domed on
top.
(4) Several reports of well kept formation flights varying from
three to nine objects.
(5) Normally no associated sound, except in three instances a
substantial rumbling roar was noted.
(6) Level flight speeds normally above 300 knots are estimated.

The AMC recommended that Army Air Forces Headquarters issue a
directive assigning a priority security classification and code-name for a
detailed study of the discs, including preparation of complete sets of all
available and pertinent data, to be made available to the Army, the Navy,
the Atomic Energy Commission, the Joint Research and Development
Board, the National Advisory Committee on Aeronautics, the Air Force
Scientific Advisory Group, RAND (a West Coast, Air Force-financed
think-tank) and NEPA (Nuclear Energy for Propulsion Applications).[5]
Twining's report stated that there was a 'lack of physical evidence in
the shape of crash recovered exhibits which would undeniably prove the
existence of these objects', although according to numerous military
personnel the debris from at least one UFO was recovered in New Mexico
and flown to AMC Headquarters in July 1947 for examination (see
Chapter 18). So why did Twining cite the lack of physical evidence? As
researcher William Moore explains, if a disc (or discs) had crashed,
Twining would have needed to set up a project to gather as much

information as possible from all over the world. Assuming that access to crashed disc data would have been on a very high 'need-to-know' basis, it would hardly have been appropriate to let those on the other end of the data-collection line know why such data was needed. 'Indeed,' argues Moore, 'it might have been best to maintain that there was no crashed disc in order to allay suspicion.'[6]

There is strong evidence that the Air Intelligence Requirements Division (AIRD), headed by Brigadier General Schulgen, to whom Twining had sent the AMC report, *was* aware of the crashed disc material, and that this information could only have come from Twining's office. An AIRD five-page 'Draft of Collection Memorandum', dated 30 October 1947 and classified Secret at the time, lists the 'current intelligence requirements in the field of Flying Saucer type aircraft', gives much of Twining's AMC data on the phenomenon, and adds some significant and revealing comments: 'While there remains a possibility of Russian manufacture, based upon the perspective thinking and actual accomplishments of the Germans, it is the considered opinion of some elements that the object may in fact represent an interplanetary craft of some kind.'

Listed under 'Requirements' are 'Items of construction (a) Type of material, whether metal, ferrous, non-ferrous, or non-metallic. (b) Composite or sandwich construction utilizing various combinations of metals, metallic foils, plastics, and perhaps balsa wood or similar material. (c) Unusual fabrication methods to achieve extreme light weight and structural stability.' Under 'Power plant' the draft memorandum states: 'Information is needed regarding the propulsion system of the aircraft . . . The presence of an unconventional or unusual type of propulsion system cannot be ruled out and should be considered of great interest.'

Some of this information simply must have come from Twining's office. The reference to 'various combinations of metals, metallic foils, plastics, and perhaps balsa wood or similar material' is particularly significant in that it closely matches Major Jesse Marcel's description of the debris discovered near Corona, 75 miles north-west of Roswell, New Mexico (see Chapter 18).

One former US military scientific and technical intelligence specialist I know, who has studied Schulgen's intelligence-collection tasking order, concludes that it could not have been written in the language it contains unless a drafter (a Lieutenant Colonel Garrett of Schulgen's staff) had already inspected a captured flying saucer.

The Death of Captain Mantell

On 7 January 1948 a flight of four National Guard P-51 Mustang aircraft, led by Captain Thomas Mantell, flying from Marietta, Georgia, to Standiford Field, Kentucky, was requested by the control tower at Godman Air Force Base, Kentucky, to investigate an unidentified flying object in the vicinity of Godman. The official summary describes the incident as follows:

> Three of the ships started to climb toward the object. Pilot Hendricks in NG336 continued on and landed at 1501C [Central Time] at Standiford Field . . . Pilots Hammond, NG737 & Clements NG800, climbed to 22,000 feet with Mantell in NG3869 then continued on to their original destination because of lack of oxygen arriving there at 1540C. Mantell continued climbing toward object. Standiford operations advised Wright Field Service Center at 1750E [Eastern Time] that NG3869 pilot Mantell crashed 2 miles southwest of Franklin, Kentucky at approximately 1645C. Accident fatal to pilot, major damage to aircraft.[7]

While the official explanation was that Mantell had simply been chasing Venus (later changed to a balloon) and had lost consciousness as a result of oxygen starvation, a 1948, Top Secret, joint Air Force and Navy intelligence analysis of UFO incidents, states: 'While it is presumed that this pilot suffered anoxia, resulting in his crash, his last message to the tower was, "It appears to be metallic object . . . tremendous in size . . . directly ahead and slightly above . . . I am trying to close for a better look." '[8]

Request for Interceptor Aircraft

In February 1948 Brigadier General C. P. Cabell, Chief of the Air Intelligence Requirements Division, sent a Secret memo to the Director of Plans and Operations stating that the Commanding General of Air Matériel Command felt that the responsibility assigned to him for collecting and developing information and intelligence on the 'flying discs' should be complemented by a requirement that all Air Force installations in the United States and Alaska 'provide a minimum of one each fighter or interceptor type aircraft, with necessary crews, on a continuous alert basis. These aircraft should be equipped with gun camera, and such armament as deemed advisable, in order to secure photographs necessary to the obtainment of all possible data on any reported and sighted unusual phenomena, of the "flying disc" type, in the atmosphere.'[9]

In his reply to the proposal, the Director of Plans and Operations said that stationing fighter planes at all bases on a continuous alert status was not considered feasible on the grounds that the outlay of aircraft and personnel would be too great: 'proper interception is not possible, except by accident, without complete radar coverage which the Air Force is not capable of providing . . . It is doubtful if fighter aircraft would be able to follow up reports emanating, for the most part, from civilian sources.'[10]

Eastern Airlines Sighting

In the early hours of 25 July 1948 Captain Clarence S. Chiles and co-pilot John B. Whitted, flying an Eastern Airlines DC-3, were approached by an object that seemed to be on a collision course. 'Whatever it was, it flashed down toward us and we veered to the left,' Chiles told investigators. 'It veered to its left and passed us about 700 feet to our right and above us. Then, as if the pilot had seen us and wanted to avoid us, it pulled up with a tremendous burst of flame from the rear and zoomed into the clouds, its prop wash or jet wash rocking our DC-3.'

The pilots reported that the object was 'a wingless aircraft, 100 feet long, cigar-shaped and about twice the diameter of a B-29 with no protruding surfaces'. Captain Chiles said the cabin appeared 'like a pilot compartment, except brighter . . . From the side of the object came an intense, fairly dark blue glow that ran the entire length of the fuselage . . . The exhaust was a red-orange flame, with a lighter color predominant around the edges.'

The sketches drawn by the pilots show that the object had 'windows or openings' in its side. To eliminate the possibility that the pilots had merely seen another plane, Air Force intelligence personnel screened 225 civilian and military flight schedules and found that the only other aircraft in the vicinity was an Air Force C-47, which hardly matches the reported description.[11]

Top Secret USAF Analyses

Less than two weeks after the Eastern Airlines sighting, Air Technical Intelligence Center (ATIC), earlier the T-2 division of Twining's AMC, decided the time had come to make what intelligence jargon refers to as an 'Estimate of the Situation'. Captain Edward Ruppelt, former head of the Air Force Project Blue Book (the USAF's third, and final, official UFO investigation programme), was one of few to see the lengthy Top Secret document, dated 5 August 1948. He confirmed that ATIC concluded that the UFOs were interplanetary in origin. General Hoyt Vandenberg, then Chief of Staff, rejected this conclusion for lack of proof, even after a group from ATIC visited his office at the Pentagon in an attempt to persuade him to change his mind. Some months later, on Vandenberg's instructions, the document was ordered burned.[12] 'The general said it would cause a stampede,' Ruppelt told Major Donald Keyhoe. 'How could we convince the public the aliens weren't hostile when we didn't know it ourselves?'[13]

In 1985 a document that had been classified Top Secret and entitled *Analysis of Flying Object Incidents in the U.S.* was declassified and released, in response to a Freedom of Information request. It is felt by some researchers that this is a watered-down version of the earlier 'Estimate of the Situation'. Dated 10 December 1948, the nineteen-page document does not say that UFOs could be extraterrestrial, but concludes that 'some type of flying objects have been observed, although their identification and origin are not discernible'.[14]

Intrusions over Sensitive Installations

Official concern over sightings in the vicinity of some of the United States' most sensitive installations, such as the Los Alamos Atomic Energy Commission (AEC) facility, led to a deluge of unanswerable questions. In January 1949 Colonel Eustis L. Poland of US Army Intelligence (G-2) sent a memo on behalf of the Commanding General of the 4th Army at Houston, Texas, to the Director, Army Intelligence, at the Pentagon:

> Agencies in New Mexico are greatly concerned over these phenomena. They are of the opinion that some foreign power is making 'sensing shots' with some super-stratosphere device designed to be self-disintegrating . . . Another theory advanced as possibly acceptable lies in the belief that the phenomena are the result of radiological warfare experiments by a foreign power, further, that the rays may be lethal or might be attributed to the cause of the plane crashes that have occurred recently.
>
> Still another belief . . . is that it is highly probable that the

TOP SECRET

ANALYSIS OF FLYING OBJECT INCIDENTS IN THE U. S.

SUMMARY AND CONCLUSIONS

PROBLEM

1. TO EXAMINE pattern of tactics of "Flying Saucers" (hereinafter referred to as flying objects) and to develop conclusions as to the possibility of existence.

FACTS AND DISCUSSION

2. A DETAILED discussion of information bearing on the problem as set forth above is attached as Appendix "A". The main points established therein are summarized below.

3. THE FREQUENCY of reported incidents, the similarity in many of the characteristics attributed to the observed objects and the quality of observers considered as a whole, support the contention that some type of flying object has been observed. Approximately 210 incidents have been reported. Among the observers reporting on such incidents are trained and experienced U.S. Weather Bureau personnel, USAF rated officers, experienced civilian pilots, technicians associated with various research projects and technicians employed by commercial airlines.

4. THE POSSIBILITY that reported observations of flying objects over the U.S. were influenced by previous sightings of unidentified phenomena in Europe, particularly over Scandinavia in 1946, and that the observers reporting such incidents may have been interested in obtaining personal publicity have been considered as possible explanations. However, these possibilities seem to be improbable when certain selected reports such as the one from U.S. Weather Bureau at Richmond are examined. During observations of weather balloons at the Richmond Bureau, one well trained observer has sighted strange metallic disks on three occasions and another observer has sighted a similar object on one occasion. The last observation of unidentified objects was in April, 1947. On all four occasions the weather balloon and the unidentified objects were in view through the theodolite. These observations at the Richmond Bureau occurred several months before publicity on the flying saucers appeared in a U.S. newspaper.

5. DESCRIPTIONS OF the flying objects fall into three configuration categories: (1) disk-shaped (2) rough cigar-shaped (3) balls of fire. Varying conditions of visibility and differences in angles at which the objects may have been viewed introduces a possibility that a single type object may have been observed rather than three different types. This possibility is further substantiated by the fact that in the areas where such objects have been observed the ratio of the three general configurations is approximately the same.

6. THEREFORE, IT appears that some object has been seen; however, the identification of that object cannot be readily accomplished on the basis of information reported on each incident. It is possible that the object, or objects, may have been domestically launched devices such as weather balloons, rockets, experimental flying wing aircraft, or celestial phenomena. It is necessary to obtain information on such domestic activity to confirm or deny this possibility. Depending upon the degree with which this may be accomplished, foreign devices must then be considered as a possibility.

7. THE PATTERN of sightings is definable. Sightings have been most intense throughout the states bordering the Atlantic and Pacific coast lines, and the central states of Ohio and Kentucky. A map showing location of sightings is attached as Appendix "B"

One page from the previously Top Secret 1948 Air Intelligence Report, and (*overleaf*) a page (Secret) detailing official reports from January to October 1948. Note the confirmation for Captain Mantell's last message. (*US Air Force*)

k. On 7 January 1948, a National Guard pilot was killed while attempting to chase an unidentified object up to 30,000 feet. While it is presumed that this pilot suffered anoxia, resulting in his crash, his last message to the tower was, "it appears to be metallic object....of tremendous size....directly ahead and slightly above....I am trying to close for a better book."

l. On 5 April 1948, three trained balloon observers from the Geophysics Laboratory Section, Watson Laboratories, N.J. reported seeing a round, indistinct object in the vicinity of Hollman Air Force Base, New Mexico. It was very high and fast, and appeared to execute violent maneuvers at high speed. The object was under observation for approximately 30 seconds and disappeared suddenly.

m. A yellow or light colored sphere, 25 to 40 feet in diameter was reported by Lt. Comdr. Marcus L. Lowe, USN, just south of Anacostia Naval Air Station, D.C., while he was flying on 30 April 1948. It was moving at a speed of approximately 100 miles per hour at an altitude of about 4,500 feet. Although winds aloft were from the north-northwest, its course was to the north.

n. On 1 July 1948, twelve disks were reported over the Rapid City Air Base by Major Hammer. These disks were oval-shaped, about 100 feet long, flying at a speed estimated to be in excess of 500 mph. Descending from 10,000 feet, these disks made a 30-degree to 40-degree climbing turn accelerating very rapidly until out of sight.

o. On 17 July 1948, a report from Kirtland Air Force Base describes a sighting in the vicinity of San Acacia, New Mexico, of seven unidentified objects flying in a "J" formation at an estimated height of 20,000 feet above the terrain. The formation varied from "J" to "L" to circle after passing the zenith. Flashes from the objects were observed after passing 30 degrees beyond the zenith but there was no smoke or vapor trail. If the reported altitude is correct the speed was estimated at 1,500 miles per hour, according to the report.

p. Other sightings of lights and trails, rather than disks, have been reported, viz:
(1) On 12 September 1947, the pilot and co-pilot of a Pan American aircraft, en route from Midway to Honolulu, saw a blue-white light approaching, changing to twin reddish glows upon withdrawal. The pilot estimated the speed of the light at about 1,000 knots.

(2) On 15 June 1948, Mr. Booneville, territory manager for the B.F. Goodrich Company, observed a reddish glow with a jet exhaust in the vicinity of Miles City, Montana. This glowing light made no sound, traveled about twice the speed of a conventional aircraft and flew from noth to south several times in a wide arc, finally disappearing over the horizon.

q. During the early morning of 25 July 1948, two Eastern Airlines pilots reported having seen a huge flying craft similar to a V-2 pass their aircraft in flight. (See Figs. 7 and 8.) The attached drawings made by these two observers very closely resemble a flying object reported to have been seen on 20 July 1948, by A. D. Otter, chief investigator of Court of Damage Inquiry, and his daughter at Arnham, Netherlands. This object appeared to be a wingless aircraft having two decks. The craft, sighted four times through scattered clouds and unlimited visibility, was traveling at high speed at a high altitude. A sound similar to that made by a V-2 was reported.

r. An object, similar in shape to the one in the preceding incident was reported by an experienced American newspaper reporter about 25 kilometers northeast of Moscow on 3 August 1948. A Russian acquaintance identified it as a rigid airship but the reporter disagrees because it flew at a high, but not excessive speed.

s. On 1 October 1948 at approximately 2030 hours the pilot of a F-51 aircraft, 2nd Lt. George F. Gorman (North Dakota Air National Guard), flying near Fargo, North Dakota, sighted an intermittent white light about 3,000 feet below his 4,500 feet cruising altitude. The pilot pursued the light which appeared to then take evasive tactics. The object or light out-turned, out-speeded, and out-climbed the F-51 in every instance during the attempt to intercept. The pilot lost contact 27

United States may be carrying on some top-secret experiments
. . . It is felt that these incidents are of such great importance,
especially as they are occurring in the vicinity of sensitive
installations, that a scientific board be sent to this locality to
study the situation with a view of arriving at a solution of this
extraordinary phenomen[on] with the least practicable delay.[15]

On 16 February 1949 a secret conference was held at the Los Alamos
National Laboratory to discuss UFO phenomena, in particular the so-
called 'green fireballs' which then were being reported in the area. Among
the scientists and military officials present were the nuclear physicist Dr
Edward Teller and Dr Lincoln LaPaz, an astronomer from the University
of New Mexico, whose expert opinion was called on throughout the
conference. LaPaz was absolutely convinced that the green fireballs were
not conventional fireballs or meteorites. He described his own sighting on
12 December 1948:

This fireball appeared in full intensity instantly – there was no
increase in light . . . Its color, estimated to be somewhere around
wave length 5200 angstroms, was a hue green, such as I had never
observed in meteor falls before. The path was as nearly horizontal
as one could determine by visual observation . . . Just before the
end . . . the green fireball broke into fragments, still bright green.

LaPaz also ruled out other unconventional types of meteors and
fireballs, and left the conference in no doubt that the phenomena were
unexplainable.[16]
On 27 and 28 April 1949, Dr Joseph Kaplan, a member of the Air
Force Scientific Advisory Board (SAB), visited Kirtland Air Force Base's
Office of Special Investigations, as well as the AEC's Sandia Base and Los
Alamos, under orders from Dr Theodore von Karman, Chairman of the
SAB. The purpose of the visits, a previously secret Air Force memorandum
states, was to review the reports of investigations and the circumstances
surrounding the 'unidentified aerial phenomena' that had been observed
in the area, and to make recommendations as to the advisability of a
scientific investigation into the occurrences. Drs Kaplan and LaPaz met
with several security and investigation personnel at Los Alamos on 28
April, so that Kaplan could ascertain the nature of the UFO sightings that
had been reported there by members of the AEC project and AEC
security-service inspectors. He seems to have been impressed, and stated

HEADQUARTERS FOURTH ARMY
Fort Sam Houston, Texas

452.1 AKADB   13 January 1949
/dob

SUBJECT: Unconventional Aircraft (Control No. A-1917).

TO   : Director of Intelligence, GSUSA
        Washington 25, D. C.

1. The inclosed Summary of Information, subject, "Unconventional Aircraft (Control No. A-1917," dated 13 Jan 49, is forwarded for your information and any action deemed necessary.

2. Agencies in New Mexico are greatly concerned over these phenomena. They are of the opinion that some foreign power is making "sensing shots" with some super-stratosphere devise designed to be self-disentergrating. They also believe that when the devise is perfected for accuracy, the disentegrating factor will be eliminated in favor of a warhead.

3. Another theory advanced as possibly acceptable lies in the belief that the phenomena are the result of radiological warfare experiments by a foreign power, further, that the rays may be lethal or might be attributed to the cause of some of the plane crashes that have occurred recently.

4. Still another belief that is advanced is that, it is highly probable that the United States may be carrying on some top-secret experiments.

5. It is felt that these incidents are of such great importance, especially as they are occurring in the vicinity of sensitive installations, that a scientific board be sent to this locality to study the situation with a view of arriving at a solution of this extraordinary phenomena with the least practicable delay.

6. It is further requested that this Headquarters be informed of action taken on this and a previous report in order that reporting agencies may be advised.

FOR THE COMMANDING GENERAL:

1 incl: EUSTIS L. POLAND
  as stated   Colonel, GSC
                                 AC of S, G-2

'... It is felt that these incidents are of such great importance, especially as they are occurring in the vicinity of sensitive installations, that a scientific board be sent to this locality to study the situation with a view of arriving at a solution of this extraordinary phenomenon with the least practicable delay.' A US Army intelligence report. (*US Army*)

that he would immediately submit his report to Dr von Karman: 'Dr Kaplan expressed a great concern, as these occurrences relate to the National Defense of the United States. He advised that he felt that this was of extreme importance and should be investigated scientifically.'[17]

Yet another meeting was convened on 14 October 1949 to discuss the green fireball sightings, attended by representatives of the 4th US Army, the Armed Forces Special Weapons Project, the FBI, the AEC, the Geophysical Research Division of Air Matériel Command and the Air Force Office of Special Investigations (AFOSI), as well as the earlier delegates. 'A logical explanation was not proffered with respect to the origin of the green fireballs,' an AFOSI confidential memo stated. 'It was, however, generally concluded that the phenomena existed and that they should be studied scientifically until these occurrences have been satisfactorily explained. Further, that the continued occurrence of unexplained phenomena of this nature in the vicinity of sensitive installations is cause for concern.'[18]

Of the US Army Intelligence (G-2) representatives present, it is possible that some included members of the Army's then Interplanetary Phenomenon Unit (IPU) of the Scientific and Technical Branch, Counterintelligence Directorate, a UFO investigation group set up in 1947 (or, reportedly, in 1945, by General Douglas MacArthur) and disbanded in the 1950s. Colonel Anthony Gallo Jr, Director of Counterintelligence, informed me that 'the aforementioned Army unit was disestablished during the late 1950's and never reactivated. All records pertaining to this unit were turned over to the US Air Force Office of Special Investigations in conjunction with operation "BLUEBOOK".'[19] AFOSI has not released these records to date. Did the Interplanetary Phenomenon Unit learn disturbing facts that still cannot be revealed?

At weekly conferences of Army, Air Force, FBI and Navy intelligence officers in early 1949, maximum security attached to the UFO problem was reaffirmed, as a contemporary FBI document (see p. 326) reveals: 'the matter of "Unidentified Aircraft" or "Unidentified Aerial Phenomena" otherwise known as "Flying Discs", "Flying Saucers", and "Balls of Fire" . . . is considered top secret by Intelligence Officers of both the Army and the Air Forces'.[20]

Intrusions continued to be reported over nuclear installations and on some occasions led to interception by Air Force jets, as this Army memorandum from Major U. G. Carlan (see p. 327), based on information provided him by Lieutenant Colonel Mildren, reveals:

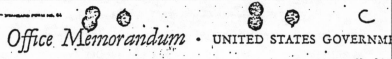

Office Memorandum • UNITED STATES GOVERNM[E]

TO _ DIRECTOR, FBI   DATE: January 31, 194[9]

FROM : SAC, SAN ANTONIO

SUBJECT: PROTECTION OF VITAL INSTALLATIONS
BUREAU FILE # 65-58300

At recent Weekly Intelligence Conferences of G-2, ONI, OSI, and F.B.I., in the Fourth Army Area, Officers of G-2, Fourth Army have discussed the matter of "Unidentified Aircraft" or "Unidentified Aerial Phenomena" otherwise known as "Flying Discs", "Flying Saucers", and "Balls of Fire". This matter is considered top secret by Intelligence Officers of both the Army and the Air Forces.

It is well known that there have been during the past two years reports from the various parts of the country of the sighting of unidentified aerial objects which have been called in newspaper parlance "flying discs" and "flying saucers". The first such sightings were reported from Sweden, and it was thought that the objects, the nature of which was unknown, might have originated in Russia.

In July 1948 an unidentified aircraft was "seen" by an Eastern Airlines Pilot and Co-Pilot and one or more passengers of the Eastern Airlines Plane over Montgomery, Alabama. This aircraft was reported to be of an unconventional type without wings and resembled generally a "rocket ship" of the type depicted in comic strips. It was reported to have had windows; to have been larger than the Eastern Airlines plane, and to have been traveli[ng] at an estimated speed of 2700 miles an hour. It appeared out of a thunder head ahead of the Eastern Airlines plane and immediately disappeared in a cloud narrowly missing a collision with the Eastern Airlines plane. No sound or air disturbance was noted in connection with this appearance.

During the past two months various sightings of unexplained phenomena have been reported in the vicinity of the A.E.C. Installation at Los Alamos, New Mexico, where these phenomena now appear to be concentrated. During December 1948 on the 5th, 6th, 7th, 8th, 11th, 13, 14th, 20th and 28th sightings of unexplained phenomena were made near Los Alamos by Special Agents of the Office of Special Investigation; Airline Pilots; Military Pilots, Los Alamos Security Inspectors, and private citizens. On January 6, 1949, another similar object was sighted in the same area.

 a Meteorologist of some note, has been generally in charge of the observations near Los Alamos, attempting to learn character[is]tics of the unexplained phenomena.

Up to this time little concrete information has been obtained.

JEJ:md
S.-100-7545
K [illegible] El Paso (2)   Little Rock (2)
   Dallas (2)   Oklahoma City (2)   43 [illegible] 18 194[9]

A 1949 FBI document confirming the Top Secret nature of the subject-matter. (*FBI*)

CONFIDENTIAL

MEMORANDUM FOR RECORD:

SUBJECT: Flying Discs *G-3*

The following information was furnished Major Carlan by
Lt Colonel Mildren on 4 August 1950:

Since 30 July 1950 objects, round in form, have been
sighted over the Hanford AEC Plant. These objects reportedly were above 15,000 feet in altitude. Air Force
jets attempted interception with negative results. All
units including the anti-aircraft battalion, radar units,
Air Force fighter squadrons, and the Federal Bureau of
Investigation have been alerted for further observation.
The Atomic Energy Commission states that the investigation is continuing and complete details will be forwarded
later.

U. G. C.

U. G. CARLAN
Major, GSC
Survey Section

DECLASSIFIED
5-79-10
By ___ NARS, Date 4/19/79

CONFIDENTIAL

A US Army intelligence report, 1950. (*US Army*)

Since 30 July 1950 objects, round in form, have been sighted over the Hanford AEC Plant. These objects reportedly were above 15,000 feet in altitude. Air Force jets attempted interceptions with negative results. All units including the anti-aircraft battalion, radar units, Air Force fighter squadrons, and the Federal Bureau of Investigation have been alerted for further observation. The Atomic Energy Commission states that the investigation is continuing and complete details will be forwarded later.[21]

The CIA was equally concerned. A 1952 report, previously classified Secret, referring to 'Sightings of UFOs reported at Los Alamos and Oak Ridge, at a time when the background radiation count had risen inexplicably', concluded with the following: 'Here we run out of even "blue yonder" explanations that might be tenable, and, we are still left with numbers of incredible reports from credible observers.'[22]

In February 1949 Professor George E. Valley, another member of the Air Force Scientific Advisory Board, in offering some possible explanations for the sightings which he proposed in a secret report for Project Sign (the first Air Force UFO study – sometimes called Project Saucer), probably came close to the truth:

If there is an extra-terrestrial civilization which can make such objects as are reported then it is most probable that its development is far in advance of ours. This argument can be supported on probability arguments alone without recourse to astronomical hypotheses.

Such a civilization might observe that on Earth we now have atomic bombs and are fast developing rockets. In view of the past history of mankind, they should be alarmed. We should, therefore, expect at this time above all to behold such visitations.[23]

Army Intelligence on High Alert

On 8 December 1950 the FBI office in Richmond, Virginia, sent the following 'Urgent' cable to the FBI Director:

THIS OFFICE VERY CONFIDENTIALLY ADVISED BY ARMY INTELLIGENCE, RICHMOND, THAT THEY HAVE BEEN PUT ON IMMEDIATE HIGH ALERT FOR ANY DATA WHATSOEVER CONCERNING FLYING SAUCERS. CIC [Counter Intelligence

FBI, RICHMOND   12-8-50   12-09 PM   MEH

DIRECTOR   URGENT

RE FLYING SAUCERS. THIS OFFICE VERY CONFIDENTIALLY ADVISED BY ARMY
INTELLIGENCE, RICHMOND, THAT THEY HAVE BEEN PUT ON IMMEDIATE HIGH
ALERT FOR ANY DATA WHATSOEVER CONCERNING FLYING SAUCERS. CIC HERE
STATES BACKGROUND OF INSTRUCTIONS NOT AVAILABLE FROM AIR FORCE
INTELLIGENCE, WHO ARE NOT AWARE OF REASON FOR ALERT LOCALLY,
BUT ANY INFORMATION WHATSOEVER MUST BE TELEPHONED BY THEM IMMEDIATE
TO AIR FORCE INTELLIGENCE. CIC ADVISES DATA STRICTLY CONFIDENTIAL
AND SHOULD NOT BE DISSEMINATED.

AUERBACH   DEC   1950

RECORDED - 81

END ACK   LA

12-11 PM OK FBI WA NRJ

DEC 19 1950

An FBI message relating to an 'immediate high alert' for data on flying saucers,
December 1950. (*FBI*)

Corps] HERE STATES BACKGROUND OF INSTRUCTIONS NOT
AVAILABLE FROM AIR FORCE INTELLIGENCE, WHO ARE NOT
AWARE OF REASON FOR ALERT LOCALLY, BUT ANY INFORMA-
TION WHATSOEVER MUST BE TELEPHONED BY THEM IMME-
DIATELY TO AIR FORCE INTELLIGENCE. CIC ADVISES DATA
STRICTLY CONFIDENTIAL AND SHOULD NOT BE DISSEMIN-
ATED.

UFOs Encountered by Military Aircraft

One of a number of reports relating to near collisions with unidentified
flying objects was made by Lieutenant Graham Bethune, US Naval
Reserve, co-pilot on Flight 125 from Keflavik, Iceland, to Argentia Naval
Air Station, Newfoundland, on 10 February 1951. 'While flying in the left
seat on a true course of 230 degrees at a position of 49-50 North 50-03
West, I observed a glow of light below the horizon about 1,000 to 1,500
feet above the water,' Bethune stated in the official report (see p. 331). He
continued:

> We both observed its course and motion for about 4 or 5 minutes
> before calling it to the attention of the other crew members . . .
> Suddenly its angle of attack changed, its altitude and size increased
> as though its speed was in excess of 1,000 miles per hour. It closed
> in so fast that the first feeling was we would collide in mid-air. At
> this time its angle changed and the color changed. It then
> [appeared] definitely circular and redish orange on its perimeter.
> It reversed its course and tripled its speed until it was last seen
> disappearing over the horizon. Because of our altitude and
> misleading distance over water it is almost impossible to estimate
> its size, distance and speed. A rough estimate would be at least 300
> feet in diameter, over 1,000 miles per hour in speed and
> approached to within 5 miles of the aircraft.[24]

In 1956, the US Navy reportedly issued orders to its pilots to engage
UFOs in combat if the objects appeared hostile. Operational procedures
for a 'UFO scramble', given by a briefing officer to pilots at Los Alamitos
Naval Air Station in California, were highly classified, and most officers
there refused to discuss the matter when pressed by journalists.[25]

One of numerous US Air Force intelligence reports now released
describes an encounter by Major Ballard and Lieutenant Rogers, of the

CONFIDENTIAL

FLEET LOGISTIC AIR WING, ATLANTIC/CONTINENTAL
AIR TRANSPORT SQUADRON ONE
U. S. NAVAL AIR STATION
PATUXENT RIVER, MARYLAND

10 February 1951

C O N F I D E N T I A L

MEMORANDUM REPORT to Commanding Officer, Air Transport Squadron ONE

Subj: Report of Unusual Sighting on Flight 125/9 February 1951

I, Graham E. BETHUNE, was Co-Pilot on Flight 125 from Keflavik, Iceland
to Naval Air Station, Argentia on the 10th of February 1951. At 0055Z I
signed and observed the following object:

While flying in the left seat at 10,000 feet on a true course
of 230 degrees at a position of 49-50 North 50-03 West, I observed a glow of
light below the horizon about 1,000 to 1,500 feet above the water. Its
bearing was about 2 O'Clock. There was no overcast, there was a thin transparent group of scuds at about 2,000 feet altitude. After examing KINGDON
the object for 40 to 50 seconds I called it to the attention of Lieutenant
KINGDON in the right hand seat. It was under the thin scuds at roughly 30
to 40 miles away. I asked "What is it, a ship lighted up or a city, I know
it can't be a city because we are over 250 miles out." We both observed its
course and motion for about 4 or 5 minutes before calling it to the attention
of the othercrew members. Its first glow was a dull yellow. We were on an
interceping course. Suddenly its angle of attack changed, its altitude and
size increased as though its speed was in excess of 1,000 miles per hour. It
closed in so fast that the first feeling was we would collide in mid air. At
this time its angle changed and the color changed. It then definitely circular
and reddish orange on its primiter It reversed its course and tripled its speed
until it was last seen disappearing over the horizon. Because of our altitude
and misleading distance over water it is almost impossible to estimate its
size, distance and speed. A rough estimate would be at least 300 feet in diameter,
over 1,000 miles per hour in speed and approached within 5 miles of the aircraft.

/s/Graham E. BETHUNE
Lt, U.S. Naval Reserve

ENCLOSURE (4)

A US Navy intelligence report, 1951. (*US Navy*)

AF FORM 112—PART I
APPROVED (JUNE 1940)

(CLASSIFICATION)

COUNTRY	REPORT NO.	(LEAVE BLANK)
U.S.A.	IR-3-51E	

AIR INTELLIGENCE INFORMATION REPORT

SUBJECT

UNIDENTIFIED FLYING OBJECT

AREA REPORTED ON	FROM (Agency)
USA	HQ EADF

DATE OF REPORT	DATE OF INFORMATION	EVALUATION
21 SEPTEMBER 1951	10 SEPTEMBER 1951	B-6

PREPARED BY (Officer)   SOURCE

LT. COL. BRUCE K. BAUMGARDNER   EADF

REFERENCES (Control number, directive, previous report, etc., as applicable)   870904

SUMMARY: (Enter concise summary of report. Give significance in final one-sentence paragraph. List inclosures at lower left. Begin text of report on AF Form 112 Part II.)

On 10 September, Major Ballard and Lt. Rogers were participating in a training flight from Dover AFB, Delaware to Mitchel AFB, New York (Direct), when they spotted an unidentified object over Sandy Hook, New Jersey.

The time was 1135 EDT, and the weather was CAVU. When spotted, the object was at an estimated altitude of 8,000 feet. Flying at 20,000 feet, the pilot immediately made a diving turn in his T-33 and followed and timed the object until it disappeared two minutes later.

Both pilots observed the strange object, which appeared to be the size of an F-86 but much faster (900 + mph), disc-shaped, steady in flight with no visible means of propulsion, and shiny silver in color.

At 1110 EDT a radar station at Ft. Monmouth plotted an unidentified, high speed (above 700 mph) object in approximately the same location.

This headquarters has no information regarding natural phenomena, experimental aircraft or guided missiles that could have caused the observations.

Request USAF evaluation of incident be furnished this headquarters.

BRUCE K. BAUMGARDNER
Lt. Colonel, USAF
Director of Intelligence

INCLS.
1. Rpt. - 1st Lt. W.S. Rogers
2. Rpt. - Maj. E. Ballard
3. Map
4. Rpt. - Ft. Monmouth

A US Air Force intelligence report describing the sighting of a disc-shaped object reported by Major Ballard and Lieutenant Rogers in September 1951. (*US Air Force*)

148th Fighter Interceptor Squadron, on a training flight in a Lockheed
T-33 from Dover Air Force Base, Delaware, on 10 September 1951 (see p.
332). Having observed an unidentified object over Sandy Hook, New
Jersey, the pilots immediately made a diving turn and followed the object
until it disappeared two minutes later:

> Both pilots observed the strange object, which appeared to be the
> size of an F-86 [Sabre] but much faster (900+ mph), disc-shaped,
> steady in flight with no visible means of propulsion, and shining
> silver in color.
>
> At 1100 EDT [Eastern Daylight Time] a radar station at Ft.
> Monmouth plotted an unidentified, high speed (above 700 mph)
> object in approximately the same location.
>
> This headquarters has no information regarding natural
> phenomena, experimental aircraft or guided missiles that could
> have caused the observation.[26]

The July 1952 Flap

A massive build-up of sightings over the United States in 1952,
culminating in July, caused considerable alarm in military intelligence
circles. One such sighting was reported by First Officer William Nash and
Second Officer W. H. Fortenberry, flying in a DC-4 of Pan American
Airways *en route* from New York to San Juan, Puerto Rico, on 14 July.

At 21.12 six glowing discs approached at fantastic speed a mile below
the airliner, in the vicinity of Langley Air Force Base, Virginia. The objects
appeared to be about 100 feet in diameter and were flying in echelon
formation. The leading disc, apparently having sighted the DC-4, slowed
down abruptly, then the next two discs 'wobbled' momentarily, after
which all six UFOs 'flipped up on edge', enabling the pilots to estimate
their thickness at about 15 feet. The objects then accelerated away but
once again lined up in their original position in echelon formation, and a
strange glow around them increased as they performed this manoeuvre.
Two other discs then appeared under the DC-4, glowing brightly as they
joined the six ahead. All the discs suddenly darkened, but glowed again
when eight objects appeared in line. Finally the discs climbed to high
altitude and disappeared, at a speed computed by the pilots to be 200 miles
per minute.[27]

On landing at Miami, the crew were interviewed by agents of the Air
Force Office of Special Investigations. A classified Air Force cable, briefly

describing these events, was distributed to Army and Naval Intelligence, as well as the Armed Forces Security Agency (forerunner of the National Security Agency), the Joint Chiefs of Staff and the CIA.[28]

On the night of 19/20 July UFOs were seen by many witnesses all over Washington, DC, including the crews of several airliners, and were tracked on radar at Andrews Air Force Base as well as the Air Traffic Control Center at Washington National Airport. Sometimes the unidentified targets would hover, cruise along at 100–130 m.p.h., then accelerate to fantastic speeds. But, as Captain Ruppelt drily commented, no one bothered to inform Air Force Intelligence about the sightings, even though jets had been sent aloft to investigate, and the first they got to hear about it was when a headline story appeared the following morning![29]

A week later, on the night of 26 July, UFOs again hovered and described a series of manoeuvres over the nation's capital, and were tracked on radar at Washington National Airport and Andrews Air Force Base.

The following Air Force intelligence report describes these extraordinary events:

> Varying numbers (up to 12 simultaneously) of u/i [unidentified] targets on ARTC [Air Route Traffic Control Center, Washington National Airport] radarscope. Termed by CAA personnel as 'generally, solid returns', similar to a/c [aircraft] return except slower. No definable pattern of maneuver except at very beginning about 2150 EDT, 4 targets in rough line abreast with $1\frac{1}{2}$ mile spacing moved slowly together (giving about a 1″ trace persisting at an estimated speed of less than 100 mph) on heading of 110. At the same time 8 other targets were scattered throughout scope.
>
> ARTC checked Andrews Approach Control by telephone at 2200 EDT and ascertained that they were also picking up u/i targets. U/i returns were picked up intermittently until about 27/0100 EDT, following which weak and sporadic (unsteady) returns were picked up intermittently for another $3\frac{1}{4}$ hours. Washington National Tower radar crew reports only one target positively u/i. This return was termed a 'very good target' which moved across the scope from West to East at about 30 to 40 mph. However, the radar operators stated that there could have been other u/i targets on their scopes, particularly outside their area of a/c control, which they would not have noticed or would have assumed to be

a/c under ARTC Center Control. However, they noticed no other unusual (i.e. very slow or erratic) returns.

ARTC Center controllers also report that a CAA flight inspector, Mr. Bill Schreve, flying a/c #NC-12 reported at 2246 EDT that he had visually spotted 5 objects giving off a light glow ranging from orange to white; his altitude at times was 2200'. Some commercial pilots reported visuals from 'cigarette glow' (red-yellow) to 'a light' (as recorded from their conversations with ARTC controllers).

At 2238 EDT the USAF Command Post was notified of ARTC targets. Command Post notified ADC and KADF at 2245, and 2 F-94's were scrambled from Newcastle at 2300 EDT. ARTC controlled F-94's after arrival in area and vectored them to targets with generally negative results (flew through 'a batch of radar returns' without spotting anything). However, one pilot mentioned seeing 4 lights at one time and a second time as seeing a single light ahead but unable to close whereupon 'went out' (these comments from ARTC controller). One ARTC controller worked a USAF B-25 . . . for about 1 hr 20 mins about 2230 EDT. B-25 was vectored in on numerous targets and commented that each vector took him over a busy highway or intersection.

Maj. Fournet (AFOIN-2A2) and Lt. Holcomb (USN, AFOIN-2C5) arrived at ARTC Center about 27/0015 EDT. Lt. Holcomb observed scopes and reported '7 good, solid targets'. He made a quick check with airport Weather Station and determined that there was a slight temperature inversion (about 1°) from the surface to about 1000'. However, he felt that the scope targets at that time were not the results of this inversion and so advised the Command Post with the suggestion that a second intercept flight be requested. (2nd intercept flight controlled by ARTC, but no strong targets remained when they arrived. They were vectored on dim targets with negative results.) Maj. Fournet and Lt. Holcomb remained in ARTC until 0415, but no additional strong targets were picked up: many dim and unstable targets (assumed due to temperature inversion) were observed throughout the remainder of the period . . .

All ARTC crew members emphatic that most u/i returns were 'solid'. Finally, it was mentioned that u/i returns have been picked up from time to time over the past few months but never before had they appeared in such quantities over such a prolonged period and with such definition as was experienced on the night of 26/27 July 52.[30]

The sightings made headline news around the world, but were explained by the Air Force as having been caused by temperature inversion (when a layer of warm air lies adjacent to a cooler layer, producing optical distortions in the atmosphere). At the overcrowded press conference held at the Pentagon on 29 July 1952, General John Samford, Director of Air Force Intelligence (and later, Director, National Security Agency), was asked by a reporter: 'Is it some very highly secret new weapon that we're working on that's causing these flying saucer reports?', to which Samford replied, perhaps ambiguously: 'We have nothing that has no mass and unlimited power!'[31]

Behind the scenes, a number of intelligence analysts felt that the UFOs might not have a terrestrial origin. An FBI memorandum, written a few days after the Washington sightings, relates to a briefing for FBI officials by one Commander Boyd (presumably on detached duty with the Air Force at the time) of the Current Intelligence Branch, Estimates Division, Air Intelligence, regarding the status of research into the matter. The memo confirms that Boyd

> . . . advised that the objects sighted may possibly be from another planet . . . [but] that at the present time there is nothing to substantiate this theory but the possibility is not being overlooked. He stated that Air Intelligence is fairly certain that these objects are not ships or missiles from another nation in this world. Commander Boyd advised that intense research is being carried out by Air Intelligence, and at the present time when credible reportings of sightings are received, the Air Force is attempting in each instance to set up jet interceptor planes in order to obtain a better view of these objects.[32]

Air Force Jet Attempts to Shoot Down a UFO

It was not just a case of sending Air Force planes aloft to get a closer look, and to film UFOs when possible. Captain Edward Ruppelt, Chief of the Aerial Phenomena Branch at Air Technical Intelligence Center, and former head of the Air Force's Project Blue Book, reported that in one instance in the summer of 1952 an Air Force jet attempted to shoot down a flying saucer.

On a certain morning (no date is given) a radarscope near a certain Air Force base picked up an unknown target that approached at 700 m.p.h., then slowed down to a point north-east of the airfield. Two F-86 Sabre jets were scrambled but at first were unable to locate the target. The second pilot suddenly spotted what at first he took to be a balloon, but a closer view showed that it was definitely saucer-shaped – 'like a doughnut without a hole'. He began chasing the object and got as close as 500 yards away when it began to accelerate. When it was at a range of 1,000 yards (the machine-gun bullets converge at 1,300 yards) he began firing at the target, but it pulled up into a climb and disappeared in seconds.

Ruppelt was given this report by an intelligence officer at the base, who said that he had been ordered to burn all copies, but had saved one.[33]

It is fortunate that the pilot lived to tell the story. Others have not been so lucky. General Benjamin Chidlaw, former Commanding General of Air Defense Command (ADC), told researcher Robert Gardner in 1953: 'We have stacks of reports of flying saucers. We take them seriously when you consider we have lost many men and planes trying to intercept them.'[34]

There are few hints of such disturbing facts in the FOIA-released Air Force intelligence reports. Of course, many reports, especially those classified Top Secret, remain classified on the grounds that their release would compromise national security. But I do have a document that relates to a possible collision with an unidentified object: an 'Emergency' cable sent to the Director of Intelligence at Air Force headquarters, dated 26 June 1953:

FLYING OBJECTS WERE SIGHTED BY PILOTS AT APPROX 2130E 24 JUNE PD TWO JET OUT OF QUONSET POINT HAS [HAD] A MID AIR COLLISION AT 2130E 24 JUNE 53 AIRCRAFT FELL IN FLAMES 15 MILES WEST OF QUONSET POINT MAS PD AMER-ICAN AND EASTERN AIRLINES PILOTS WHO REPORTED FLYING OBJECT WILL SUBMIT ON SIGHTING TO DIR INTELLIGENCE HQ USAF AND TECH INTELLIGENCE CENTER WRIGHT PATTERSON AFB.

Whether the collision *was* related to the UFO interception may never be known, but it is evident that the incident caused considerable consternation, and the distribution list for the emergency cable included the CIA, the Joint Chiefs of Staff, and the National Security Agency (established in 1952).

```
SID A16G                DEPARTMENT OF THE AIR FORCE
                           STAFF MESSAGE DIVISION
HQC188S
                        INCOMING UNCLASSIFIED MESSAGE
        TMB138                                      REC. STF. MSG. DIV.

YTA209                                           Jun 26  15 42 '53
                                                   HQ. USAF
JEDLS4DØ23

EFDØØ2

EMERGENCY JEDUP JEDEN JEPFF JEPHQ JEPRS 555

DE JEDLS 3B

O 261445Z

FM COMDR OLMSTED FLTSV MIDDLETOWN PENN

TO JEPHQ/DIR OF INTEL HQ USAF WASHDC

JEDUP/AIR TECHINTELCEN WRIGHT-PATTERSON AFB OHIO

JEDEN/COMDR ADC ENT AFB COLO

JEPFF/COMDR MATS WASHDC

JEPRS/COMDR HQ FLTSV WASHDC

ATTN ATIAA 2C FLYOBRT SUPPLEMENTAL INFO REF FLYOBRT 24 JUNE

53 PD FLYING OBJECTS WERE SIGHTED BY PILOTS AT APPROX 2130E 24

JUNE PD TWO JET OUT OF QUONSET POINT NAS HAS A MID AIR COLLISION AT

2130E 24 JUN 53 AIRCRAFT FELL IN FLAMES 15 MILES WEST OF QUONSET

POINT NAS PD AMERICAN AND EASTERN AIRLINES PILOTS WHO REPORTED FLYING

OBJECT WILL SUBMITT ON SIGHTING TO DIR INTELLIGENCE HQ USAF AND AIR

TECH INTELLIGENCE CENTER WRIGHT PATTERSON AFB

26 1450Z JUN JEDLS

   ACTION: OIN

   INFO  : OOP, OOP-CP, OAC, ARMY , NAVY, JCS, CIA, NSA

   AF IN :  11479    (26 Jun 53)                      CWS/feh


FORM 0-309d
AF 51
NUS EDITIONS OF THIS FORM MAY BE USED                    U.S. GOVERNMENT PRINTING OFFICE
```

A US Air Force intelligence report, 1953. The distribution list includes the CIA and the
National Security Agency. (*US Air Force*)

Air Force Jet Disappears While Intercepting a UFO

One of the Air Force's most frightening cases that *did* involve an apparent collision with an unidentified object took place later in 1953. On the evening of 23 November an Air Defense Command ground-control intercept (GCI) controller was alerted by the presence of an unidentified and unscheduled target on his radarscope in the vicinity of Soo Locks, Michigan. An F-89C Scorpion jet was immediately scrambled from Kinross Air Force Base, piloted by Lieutenant Felix Moncla Jr and his observer, Lieutenant R. R. Wilson, in the rear seat.

The GCI controller vectored the F-89 to the target, and noted that the UFO changed course as the plane approached at over 500 m.p.h. Nine minutes went by. Gradually the F-89 closed the gap, and the controller advised the men that the target should now be in sight. Suddenly the two blips on the GCI radarscope merged into one, as if they had collided. For a moment a single blip remained on the scope but then disappeared. Marking the position, the controller flashed an emergency message to Search and Rescue. Possibly Moncla and Wilson had managed to bail out in time – possibly not.

After an all-night air/sea rescue search, not a trace of wreckage or the missing men was found. An Air Force press release stated tersely: 'The plane was followed by radar until it merged with an object seventy miles off Keweenaw Point in upper Michigan.' The incident has never been satisfactorily explained.[35,36]

Top Secret Instructions for Reporting Encounters

L. Fletcher Prouty is a distinguished author of several authoritative books on intelligence matters and a retired US Air Force colonel. A pilot in the Second World War, Prouty spent his last nine years of service in the Pentagon as the official focal-point officer, first for the Air Force and then for the entire Defense Department, with the CIA. He also was one of five USAF officers who established the North American Aerospace Defense Command (NORAD). I interviewed him in 1994.

When he was commander of an Air Force heavy transport squadron in Tokyo in 1953–4, Prouty received an intriguing message from the Pentagon:

Our crew was covering nearly half the world, every day, back and forth. And one day I got an official wire from headquarters, Air

Force – a Top Secret wire, for my 'Eyes Only', as commander of the squadron – that if ever any of my crewmen saw something that they did not recognize and could not rationalize – in flight – they were to report to me and I was to get sworn statements and to put those statements in an envelope and to ship them to a certain office in the Pentagon. First of all, that made me think, My God, if this is a false subject or nothing, why is the headquarters of the Air Force insisting that people in my position do that? Commanders in relevant positions got the same order; I've checked that, and we got them all over the world. So I briefed every air flight commander.

One day a crew came in, six to seven months later. They'd been on a flight from Hawaii to Tokyo, that in those days took twenty-four hours, landing at Midway Island [Pacific Ocean] for fuel. And, as I recall, between Midway and Tokyo they saw something. So the commander came in, and he happened to be a very old friend of mine, and he had a twelve-man crew and they were all standing behind him. He said: 'We all saw this thing last night, and it persisted; it stayed there, it went with us, it went off.' So immediately I said: 'I don't want to hear any more. Stop!' I put them in twelve separate rooms in the barracks. I put a military policeman with each one, I put a recorder with each one, and then put copies of the questions into the rooms, and each one had to answer the question *after* they had told their own narrative story. So then I wrapped it all up in a bundle and shipped it to Washington – and never heard another word about it.

Colonel Prouty told me that, in addition to the crew, all sixty passengers observed the large unknown object, which flew close beside the C-54 transport aircraft for over an hour at an altitude of 9,000 feet.[37]

Hundreds of such reports have been made by American military and civilian pilots. I do not insist that every UFO reported is an extraterrestrial spacecraft: some undoubtedly can be explained in terms of meteorological phenomena, balloons, rockets, guided missiles, unmanned aerial vehicles (UAVs), satellite and rocket re-entries, and so on. Pilots are not infallible, but their responsible and qualified status places them in the highest category of witness reliability. Furthermore, they have nothing to gain from filing a UFO report. On the contrary, they have much to lose.

Collision Course

THE UNITED STATES continued to be plagued by sightings of unidentified aerial intruders, and many intelligence reports were forwarded immediately to the Joint Chiefs of Staff, the CIA and the National Security Agency, which gives some indication of the degree of official concern. One such report was made from the ground by a Ground Observer Corps (GOC) witness in San Rafael, California, on 28 August 1953:

> FOURTEEN CIGAR SHAPED OBJECTS WITHOUT WINGS WITH LIGHTS ON THEM IN LOOSE V-FORMATION, ABOUT THE SIZE OF A BI-MOTORED ACFT. NO SOUND OR MEANS OF PROPULSION OBSERVED. ONE OBJECT APPEARED TO BE LEADING THE FORMATION AT AN ESTIMATED SPEED OF 200 MPH . . . OBJECTS WERE FIRST OBSERVED HEADING WEST . . . THROUGH BREAKS IN THE CLOUDS, THEN OBJECTS APPEARED TO TURN AND HEAD NORTH DISAPPEARING BEHIND CLOUDS . . . OBSERVER APPEARED TO BE RELIABLE AND HAS BEEN AN OBSERVER ON DUTY WITH GOC FOR SEV YEARS . . . [1]

Debunker Dr Donald Menzel went to great lengths to explain away all UFO reports in terms of hallucinations, misidentifications and hoaxes. But his debunking statements did not always go down well with those in intelligence circles who were convinced that genuinely anomalous reports existed for which rational explanations were redundant. In a 1953 letter to Major John Samford, Director of Intelligence, US Air Force, and later Director of the National Security Agency (1956–60), Menzel stated: 'I am planning to be in Washington on government business . . . October 22 and 23 . . . From various reports I judge that some of my explanations of flying saucers have been misinterpreted or misunderstood . . . I should be delighted to meet with as many members of ATIC [Air Technical Intelligence Center] as find it convenient to come.'[2] Just what was Menzel's 'government business'?

Physicist Stanton Friedman has discovered that Dr Menzel had been deeply involved in intelligence work throughout his career. In one of several letters to Senator John F. Kennedy in 1960, Menzel wrote:

> I have been associated since 1930 with a small organization that has now grown to the great National Security Agency. I served with them as a naval officer during World War II. I have been a consultant to that activity with Top Secret clearance . . . Because of my length of service, I probably know more about what has gone on in this agency over the years than almost anyone now within it.[3]

A meeting was arranged for Menzel at the Pentagon on 22 October 1953 with representatives of Air Force Headquarters and ATIC. Two months later, an Air Force HQ representative, Colonel George Perry of the Directorate of Intelligence, in a letter to Brigadier General W. M. Burgess, Deputy for Intelligence, Air Defense Command (ADC), made some interesting comments regarding the new responsibilities of ADC as they related to the reporting of sightings:

> In your new function in the Unidentified Flying Object Program, it is our understanding that your 4602nd people will do the 'leg work' so to speak, and furnish ATIC with its findings. For those types that cannot be identified by your Squadron, ATIC will handle an exploratory point of view.
>
> Many times the publicity connected with this program has been somewhat embarrassing, in that we are dealing with a subject, parts of which are not explainable, and the public feeling is that we are holding back information they should know about . . .
>
> As you realize, there is a 10–20% area of unexplained objects in this program . . . we would like to offer you guidance in the publicity angle as it pertains to your activity.
>
> We think it would be well for your 4602nd people in the ZI [Zone of Interior], to discuss a particular sighting with the public or press, anytime the object can be identified. Meaning, if they can verify the object as a balloon, aircraft, helicopter, etc., go ahead and inform interested parties. However, for those times where the object is *not explainable*, it would be well to advise your people to say something on this order, 'The information on this sighting will be analyzed by the Air Technical Intelligence Center at

Dayton, Ohio', and leave it go at that. If your people get into analyzing the 10–20% area to the public, every news media across the country will pick up the story.[4]

Here is further proof that the Air Force hierarchy, embarrassed by the UFO problem, sought to play down the unexplainable sightings. As we shall learn, Colonel Perry's recommendations were approved and adopted as official Air Force policy.

Air Force Regulations for Reporting UFOs

In his letter to Brigadier General Burgess, Colonel Perry alluded to the functions of the 4602nd Air Intelligence Service Squadron (AISS) which, according to Air Force Regulation 200–2 (see pp. 344–7), was comprised of specialists trained for field collection and investigation of matters of air intelligence interest within the so-called Zone of Interior. The squadron's headquarters was at Peterson Field, Colorado, adjacent to Air Defense Command HQ. The 4602nd AISS was highly mobile: flights were attached to air-defence divisions, and detachments were attached to each of the defence forces.

All information on 'UFOB' sightings was to be reported promptly, the method (electrical in most cases) and priority of dispatch to be selected in accordance with the apparent intelligence value of the report. Electrical reports were to be multiple-addressed to the Commander, Air Defense Command; the nearest Air Defense Division; the Commander, Air Technical Intelligence Center; and the Director of Intelligence at Air Force HQ. In some cases such reports were forwarded to the CIA and the NSA, although there is no mention of this in Air Force Regulation (AFR) 200–2 – not surprisingly, since these agencies took care not to publicize their interest in the phenomenon except to those with a 'need to know'. Furthermore, the very existence of the National Security Agency was a closely guarded secret, and remained so for many years.

AFR 200–2, dated 12 August 1954 and signed by General Nathan Twining, Chief of Staff, as well as Colonel K. E. Thiebaud, Air Adjutant General, concluded with the following statement, under the heading 'Release of Facts'.

Headquarters USAF will release summaries of evaluated data which will inform the public on this subject. In response to local enquiries, it is permissible to inform news media representatives

*AFR 200–2
1–5

AIR FORCE REGULATION }
NO. 200–2 }

.DEPARTMENT OF THE AIR FORCE
WASHINGTON, *12 AUGUST 1954*

INTELLIGENCE

Unidentified Flying Objects Reporting (Short Title: UFOB)

1. Purpose and Scope. This Regulation establishes procedures for reporting information and evidence pertaining to unidentified flying objects and sets forth the responsibility of Air Force activities in this regard. It applies to all Air Force activities.

2. Definitions:

a. *Unidentified Flying Objects (UFOB)*—Relates to any airborne object which by performance, aerodynamic characteristics, or unusual features does not conform to any presently known aircraft or missile type, or which cannot be positively identified as a familiar object.

b. *Familiar Objects*—Include balloons, astronomical bodies, birds, and so forth.

3. Objectives. Air Force interest in unidentified flying objects is twofold: First as a possible threat to the security of the United States and its forces, and secondly, to determine technical aspects involved.

a. *Air Defense.* To date, the flying objects reported have imposed no threat to the security of the United States and its Possessions. However, the possibility that new air vehicles, hostile aircraft or missiles may first be regarded as flying objects by the initial observer is real. This requires that sightings be reported rapidly and as completely as information permits.

b. *Technical.* Analysis thus far has failed to provide a satisfactory explanation for a number of sightings reported. The Air Force will continue to collect and analyze reports until all sightings can be satisfactorily explained, bearing in mind that:

    (1) To measure scientific advances, the Air Force must be informed on experimentation and development of new air vehicles.

    (2) The possibility exists that an air vehicle of revolutionary configuration may be developed.

    (3) The reporting of all pertinent factors will have a direct bearing on the success of the technical analysis.

4. Responsibility:

a. *Reporting.* Commanders of Air Force activities will report all information and evidence that may come to their attention, including that received from adjacent commands of the other services and from civilians.

b. *Investigation.* Air Defense Command will conduct all field investigations within the ZI, to determine the identity of any UFOB.

c. *Analysis.* The Air Technical Intelligence Center (ATIC), Wright-Patterson Air Force Base, Ohio, will analyze and evaluate: All information and evidence reported within the ZI after the Air Defense Command has exhausted all efforts to identify the UFOB; and all information and evidence collected in oversea areas.

d. *Cooperation.* All activities will cooperate with Air Defense Command representatives to insure the economical and prompt success of an investigation, including the furnishing of air and ground transportation, when feasible.

5. Guidance. The thoroughness and quality of a report or investigation into incidents of unidentified flying objects are limited only by the resourcefulness and imagination of the person responsible for preparing the report. Guidance set forth below is based on experience and has been found helpful in evaluating incidents:

a. Theodolite measurements of changes of azimuth and elevation and angular size.

b. Interception, identification, or air search

---

*This Regulation supersedes AFR 200–2, 26 August 1953, including Change 200–2A, 2 November 1953.

US Air Force Regulation No. 200–2, setting out official procedures for the reporting of unidentified flying objects, August 1954. (*US Air Force*)

action. These actions may be taken if appropriate and within the scope of existing air defense regulations.

c. Contact with local aircraft control and warning (AC&W) units, ground observation corps (GOC) posts and filter centers, pilots and crews of aircraft aloft at the time and place of sighting whenever feasible, and any other persons or organizations which may have factual data bearing on the UFOB or may be able to offer corroborating evidence, electronic or otherwise.

d. Consultation with military or civilian weather forecasters to obtain data on: Tracks of weather balloons released in the area, since these often are responsible for sightings; and any unusual meteorological activity which may have a bearing on the UFOB.

e. Consultation with astronomers in the area to determine whether any astronomical body or phenomenon would account for or have a bearing on the observation.

f. Contact with military and civilian tower operators, air operations offices, and so forth, to determine whether the sighting could be the result of misidentification of known aircraft.

g. Contact with persons who might have knowledge of experimental aircraft of unusual configuration, rocket and guided missile firings, and so forth, in the area.

6. ZI Collection. The Air Defense Command has a direct interest in the facts pertaining to UFOB's reported within the ZI and has, in the 4602d Air Intelligence Service Squadron (AISS), the capability to investigate these reports. The 4602d AISS is composed of specialists trained for field collection and investigation of matters of air intelligence interest which occur within the ZI. This squadron is highly mobile and deployed throughout the ZI as follows: Flights are attached to air defense divisions, detachments are attached to each of the defense forces, and the squadron headquarters is located at Peterson Field, Colorado, adjacent to Headquarters, Air Defense Command. Air Force activities, therefore, should establish and maintain liaison with the nearest element of this squadron. This can be accomplished by contacting the appropriate echelon of the Air Defense Command as outlined above.

a. All Air Force activities are authorized to conduct such preliminary investigation as may be required for reporting purposes; however, investigations should not be carried beyond this point, unless such action is requested by the 4602d AISS.

b. On occasions—after initial reports are submitted—additional data is required which can be developed more economically by the nearest Air Force activity, such as: narrative statements, sketches, marked maps, charts, and so forth. Under such circumstances, appropriate commanders will be contacted by the 4602d AISS.

c. Direct communication between echelons of the 4602d AISS and Air Force activities is authorized.

7. Reporting. All information relating to UFOB's will be reported promptly. The method (electrical or written) and priority of dispatch will be selected in accordance with the apparent intelligence value of the information. In most instances, reports will be made by electrical means: Information over 24 hours old will be given a "deferred" precedence. Reports over 3 days old will be made by written report prepared on AF Form 112, Air Intelligence Information Report, and AF Form 112a, Supplement to AF Form 112.

a. *Addressees:*

(1) *Electrical Reports.* All electrical reports will be multiple addressed to:

   (a) Commander, Air Defense Command, Ent Air Force Base, Colorado Springs, Colorado.

   (b) Nearest Air Division (Defense). (For ZI only.)

   (c) Commander, Air Technical Intelligence Center, Wright-Patterson Air Force Base, Ohio.

   (d) Director of Intelligence, Headquarters USAF, Washington 25, D. C.

(2) *Written Reports:*

   (a) Within the ZI, reports will be submitted direct to the Air Defense Command. Air Defense Command will reproduce the report and distribute it to interested ZI intelligence agencies. The original report together with notation of the distribution effected then will be forwarded to the Director of Intelligence, Headquarters USAF, Washington 25, D. C.

   (b) Outside the ZI, reports will be submitted direct to Director of Intelligence, Headquarters USAF, Washington 25, D. C. as prescribed in "Intelligence Collection Instructions" (ICI), June 1954.

b. *Short Title.* "UFOB" will appear at the beginning of the text of electrical messages and in the subject of written reports.

c. *Negative Data.* The word "negative"

2

in reply to any numbered item of the report format will indicate that all logical leads were developed without success. The phrase "not applicable" (N/A) will indicate that the question does not apply to the sighting being investigated.

d. *Report Format.* Reports will include the following numbered items:

(1) Description of the object(s):
    (a) Shape.
    (b) Size compared to a known object (use one of the following terms: Head of a pin, pea, dime, nickel, quarter, half dollar, silver dollar, baseball, grapefruit, or basketball) held in the hand at about arms length.
    (c) Color.
    (d) Number.
    (e) Formation, if more than one.
    (f) Any discernible features or details.
    (g) Tail, trail, or exhaust, including size of same compared to size of object(s).
    (h) Sound. If heard, describe sound.
    (i) Other pertinent or unusual features.

(2) Description of course of object(s):
    (a) What first called the attention of observer(s) to the object(s)?
    (b) Angle of elevation and azimuth of the object(s) when first observed.
    (c) Angle of elevation and azimuth of object(s) upon disappearance.
    (d) Description of flight path and maneuvers of object(s).
    (e) Manner of disappearance of object(s).
    (f) Length of time in sight.

(3) Manner of observation:
    (a) Use one or any combination of the following items: Ground-visual, ground-electronic, air-electronic. (If electronic, specify type of radar.)
    (b) Statement as to optical aids (telescopes, binoculars, and so forth) used and description thereof.
    (c) If the sighting is made while airborne, give type aircraft, identification number, altitude, heading, speed, and home station.

(4) Time and date of sighting:
    (a) Zulu time-date group of sighting.
    (b) Light conditions (use one of the following terms): Night, day, dawn, dusk.

(5) Locations of observer(s). Exact latitude and longitude of each observer, or Georef position, or position with reference to a known landmark.

(6) Identifying information of all observer(s):
    (a) Civilian—Name, age, mailing address, occupation.
    (b) Military—Name, grade, organization, duty, and estimate of reliability.

(7) Weather and winds-aloft conditions at time and place of sightings:
    (a) Observer(s) account of weather conditions.
    (b) Report from nearest AWS or U. S. Weather Bureau Office of wind direction and velocity in degrees and knots at surface, 6,000', 10,000', 16,000', 20,000', 30,000', 50,000', and 80,000', if available.
    (c) Ceiling.
    (d) Visibility.
    (e) Amount of cloud cover.
    (f) Thunderstorms in area and quadrant in which located.

(8) Any other unusual activity or condition, meteorological, astronomical, or otherwise, which might account for the sighting.

(9) Interception or identification action taken (such action may be taken whenever feasible, complying with existing air defense directives).

(10) Location of any air traffic in the area at time of sighting.

(11) Position title and comments of the preparing officer, including his preliminary analysis of the possible cause of the sighting(s).

(12) Existence of physical evidence, such as materials and photographs.

e. *Security.* Reports should be unclassified unless inclusion of data required by d above necessitates a higher classification.

8. Evidence. The existence of physical evidence (photographs or materiel) will be promptly reported.

a. *Photographic:*
    (1) *Visual.* The negative and two prints will be forwarded, all original film, including wherever possible both prints and negatives, will be titled or otherwise properly identified as to place, time, and date of the incident

3

(see "Intelligence Collection Instructions" (ICI), June 1954).

(2) *Radar.* Two copies of each print will be forwarded. Prints of radarscope photography will be titled in accordance with AFR 95–7 and forwarded in compliance with AFR 95–6.

b. *Materiel.* Suspected or actual items of materiel which come into possession of any Air Force echelon will be safeguarded in such manner as to prevent any defacing or alteration which might reduce its value for intelligence examination and analysis.

9. Release of Facts. Headquarters USAF will release summaries of evaluated data which will inform the public on this subject. In response to local inquiries, it is permissible to inform news media representatives on UFOB's when the object is positively identified as a familiar object (see paragraph 2b), except that the following type of data warrants protection and should not be revealed: Names of principles, intercept and investigation procedures, and classified radar data. For those objects which are not explainable, only the fact that ATIC will analyze the data is worthly of release, due to the many unknowns involved.

By Order of the Secretary of the Air Force:

Official:

K. E. THIEBAUD
Colonel, USAF
Air Adjutant General

N. F. TWINING
Chief of Staff, United States Air Force

DISTRIBUTON:
S; X:
ONI, Department of the Navy 200
G–2, Department of the Army 10

on UFOB's when the object is positively identified as a familiar object . . . For those objects which are not explainable, only the fact that ATIC will analyze the data is worthy of release, due to the many unknowns involved.

Sightings above Fort Meade

On 7 December 1953, according to Army intelligence records, Private First Class Alfred de Bonise and Sergeant First Class James Conley sighted an unidentified object directly above the Headquarters Battery, 89th AAA Battalion, at Fort George G. Meade, Maryland, where the National Security Agency was later sited.

At 21.30 hours the witnesses' attention was drawn to an object which made a noise that 'resembled the sound of an artillery shell in flight. The sound was not like that of an airplane or a truck. There were no further sounds after the initial whirring noise,' the report states, and adds: 'The object was white and shining "like a star". It appeared to be large, very high, and shaped like a round ashtray. It moved with an erratic motion, eventually fading out of sight in a north-easterly direction. De Bonise and Conley observed the object for about twenty minutes.'[5]

At 22.11 hours on 29 April 1954 an unidentified illuminated object was observed above the Second Army Radio Station, Fort Meade, by the supervising radio operator and two co-workers. Described as round, the colour of the sun, and three or four times the size of a large star, the object appeared out of the sky from the south-west at an undetermined speed. 'The light emitted by the object was blinking on and off as the object moved across the sky in a straight path,' the report states. 'When it got above the Second Army Radio Station it stopped blinking and started to disappear by going straight up and becoming smaller in size.' The entire sighting lasted for seven minutes. Eastern Air Defense Command as well as Army Intelligence were notified.[6]

Army personnel had strict orders not to discuss their sightings with unauthorized parties, as the following order, signed by Colonel Charles L. Odin, Chief of Staff, G-2 (Intelligence), in 1957, reveals: 'Persons involved in sightings will not discuss or disseminate such information to persons or agencies other than their superior officer(s) and other personnel authorized by the Acting Chief of Staff, G-2, this headquarters.'[7]

Mystery Aircraft

In the Prologue I refer to many reports of mysterious, unidentified but conventionally shaped aircraft (in contrast to discs, cigar-like shapes, and so on) seen over Scandinavia and, to a lesser extent, over the US and the United Kingdom in the 1930s. These kind of sightings have continued to be reported over the years. I am convinced that the intelligences responsible for UFOs are able either to construct facsimiles of our own aircraft or to manifest themselves in such a way that we are duped into believing they are conventional aircraft, presumably for purposes of subterfuge.

One Air Force intelligence report that describes an exceptionally well documented sighting of a strange aircraft occurred over Carswell Air Force Base, Texas, at approximately 23.00 on 4 February 1954, in full view of control-tower personnel. The object first was detected by Carswell Ground Control Approach (GCA) Station at a distance of 13 to 15 miles, and showed up as a 1-inch return on the radarscope at a distance of 10 miles. Because the object was approaching the airfield, the GCA operator notified the airdrome officer of the day as well as the control tower.

The object passed directly over the Carswell tower at 3–4,000 feet, observed by all the tower personnel, and was described as having a long fuselage, elliptical wings and a stabilizer, but with no visible means of propulsion. No sound was heard. The aircraft had a very bright light in the nose and tail, and two yellowish lights on the bottom of the fuselage. One observer thought he could see a light on each wing tip. The tower operator kept the object under surveillance with binoculars throughout the observation.

Subsequent investigations revealed that no local aircraft were responsible, and that there was 'no unusual activity, meteorological, astronomical, or otherwise, that could contribute to [the] sighting'. The witnesses (all named) were described as 'completely reliable', and the content of the report as 'probably true'. The Joint Chiefs of Staff, the CIA and the NSA were included in the distribution list (see pp. 350–51).[8]

Near Collisions with Airliners

At midnight on 19 October 1953 an American Airlines DC-6 *en route* to Washington, DC, was buzzed by a UFO over Conowingo Dam, north of Baltimore, Maryland. The object appeared to be heading towards the airliner on a collision course, so Captain J. L. Kidd threw the plane into a

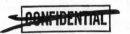

DEPARTMENT OF THE AIR FORCE
STAFF MESSAGE DIVISION

INCOMING CLASSIFIED MESSAGE

CONFIDENTIAL
PRIORITY

PARAPHRASE NOT REQUIRED. NOTIFY
CRYPTOCENTER BEFORE DECLASSIFYING.
NO UNCLASSIFIED REPLY OR REFERENCE
IF THE DTG IS QUOTED.

FROM: COMDR 19 ADIV CARSWELL AFB TEX

TO : CSAF WASH DC FOR: DIR OF INTEL
COMDR ADC ENT AFB COLO
COMDR AIR TECH INTEL CRT WPAFB OHIO
COMDR 8TH AF CARSWELL AFB TEX

NR : 7 DI 1370 UFOB   6 Feb 54   (DTG 061800Z)

(1) Description of the object.

(a) Shape of an acft.

(b) Baseball type was described by cbs as just as large
or larger than B-36.

(c) Dark grey.

(d) 1

(e) NA

(f) Had a long fuselage, eliptical wings, and stabilizer,
and no visible means of propulsion.

(g) Object has tail. Did not leave any trail, nor was
any exhaust visible.

(h) Object emitted no sound. This is predominent phenomena of this rept. Object passed dir over the
Carswell AFB tower at 3000 to 4000 ft and was observed by all tower pers on duty. Not a sound or any
evidence of propulsion was exhibited by object.

CAF IN : 60815   (8 Feb 54)   Page 1 of 5 pages

Incl #1
5p 1c

AFHQ FORM 0-309f
19 JAN 51
PREVIOUS EDITIONS OF THIS FORM MAY BE USED.

CONFIDENTIAL

COPY No.

★ 16—61727—1 U. S. GOVERNMENT PRINTING OFFICE: 1951—O—927444

Two pages from a US Air Force intelligence report describing the sighting of a mysterious
aircraft at Carswell Air Force Base, Texas, in 1954. (*US Air Force*)

DEPARTMENT OF THE AIR FORCE
STAFF MESSAGE DIVISION

INCOMING CLASSIFIED MESSAGE

CONFIDENTIAL

NR :: 7 DI 1370 UFOB fr COMDR 19 ADIV CARSWELL AFB TEX (cont'd)

(1) Object was first detected by the Carswell GCA Sta at a distance of 13 to 15 mi fr Carswell attn was drawn to the object because of the large rtrn presented on the scope. Object when viewed on 10 mi scope gave a rtrn of 1 inch. Obr scanned from 10 degs to 02 degs on search and object retained the same rtrn dur this opn. Because of the unusual rtrn, and because object was approaching directly over the fld the GCA opr notified the Airdrome Off of the Day and the tower. Object had a very bright white light in the nose and tail and two yellowish lights on bottom of fuselage. One observer reported that he thought object also had some type of light on each wg tip, but other two did not substantiate this. One observer kept object under surveillance with binoculars. No cabin or other lights were observed.

(2) Description of course of object.

(a) Unusual radar rtrn recd by GCA site at Carswell.

(b) Not aval. GCA radar could not furn this info.

(c) 05 degrees

(d) Object approached Carswell on a heading of 030 degs fr the SW. Object did not change crse at anytime while under observation. Object passed directly over the Carswell tower and maintained heading of 030 degs until out of sight. Object was watched for an estimat 5 minutes after it passed over tower by pers on duty. The bright white light in the tail estimated that object passed 5 to 6 miles NW of Meacham Fld which is NW of the city of Fort Worth.

CAF IN : 60815 (8 Feb 54) Page 2 of 5 pages

AFHQ FORM 0-309f
19 JAN 51
PREVIOUS EDITIONS OF THIS FORM MAY BE USED.

COPY No.

☆ 16—63737-1 U. S. GOVERNMENT PRINTING OFFICE : 1951—O-927444

dive as the unknown object streaked overhead and disappeared. Several passengers were thrown into the aisle, and Captain Kidd radioed to Washington Airport for ambulances and doctors. The UFO was as large as the DC-6 (length 100 feet, span 117 feet), the crew affirmed. Checks by civil aviation authorities showed that no other aircraft within a 100-mile radius were near the airliner.[9]

An even more serious incident took place on the night of 14 April 1954, when Captain J. M. Schidel of United Airlines Flight 193 was forced to make a sharp climbing turn to avoid colliding with an unknown object over Long Beach, California. One passenger was thrown to the floor, breaking a leg, and a stewardess fractured an ankle. 'It was in sight just two seconds and made no movement to avoid me,' said Schidel. No other known aircraft were in the vicinity at the time.[10]

On 9 March 1957 the Civil Aeronautics Board received a 'flash' message from Miami Air Traffic Control:

DOUGLAS 6A [Pan American Airlines] FLIGHT 257. TO AVOID UNIDENTIFIED FLYING OBJECT TRAVELING EAST TO WEST, PILOT TOOK VIOLENT EVASIVE ACTION. OBJECT APPEARED TO HAVE A BRILLIANT GREENISH-WHITE CENTER WITH AN OUTER RING WHICH REFLECTED THE GLOW FROM THE CENTER . . . ABOVE DESCRIPTION FITS WHAT SEVEN OTHER FLIGHTS SAW . . . MIAMI REPORTS NO MISSILE ACTIVITY . . . ORIGINAL REPORTS OF JET ACTIVITY DISCOUNTED.[11]

The airliner was piloted by Captain Matthew Van Winkle, and the sighting took place at 03.30 hours, 150 miles east of Jacksonville, Florida. Several passengers were injured and the plane was met by ambulances at San Juan, Puerto Rico.[12]

On 17 July 1957, American Airlines Flight 655 *en route* from Dallas to Los Angeles, Captain Edward Bachner at the controls, had a near miss with an object 'at least the size of a B-47', 100 miles east of El Paso, Texas. No known aircraft were in the vicinity at the time.[13] To avoid a head-on collision, Bachner dived his aircraft under the object in such a sharp manoeuvre that many of the eighty-five passengers were thrown from their seats. Ten passengers were injured and several others bruised, causing pandemonium in the cabin. While the flight attendants calmed down the passengers and gave first aid, Captain Bachner radioed the nearest airport and requested an emergency landing. A full report was sent to the Civil Aeronautics Board.[14]

Airline Pilots Affected by Military Regulations

Because of reports like these – and there were many others – airline pilots were subjected to military restrictions contained in a Joint Army–Navy–Air Force Publication (JANAP), drawn up by the Joint Communications–Electronics Committee and promulgated by the Joint Chiefs of Staff, and could thus find themselves liable to a prison term of up to ten years and/or a fine of $10,000 if they discussed their sightings with the media or the public. These restrictions were first imposed during a conference between airline representatives and intelligence officers of the Military Air Transport Service (MATS) in Los Angeles on 17 February 1954.[15] (MATS, now MAC, is the USAF's major command that relates to and conducts liaison with civilian commercial aviation.)

JANAP 146's subject was 'Communication Instructions for Reporting Vital Intelligence Sightings (CIRVIS)'. Unidentified flying objects are listed separately from aircraft and missiles. Under Section III (Security – Military and Civilian), is the following warning:

All persons aware of the contents of a CIRVIS report are governed by the Communications Act of 1934 and amendments thereto, and Espionage Laws. CIRVIS reports contain information affecting the National Defense of the United States within the meaning of the Espionage Laws, 18 U.S. Code, 793 and 794. The unauthorized transmission or revelation of the contents of CIRVIS reports in any manner is prohibited.[16]

Few pilots were affected by this regulation, although the airline companies discouraged public disclosure of sightings, sometimes threatening pilots with their jobs.

A CIRVIS report, transmitted with the second-highest priority, 'Operational Immediate', dated 29 March 1954, gave brief details of a sighting by a United Airlines plane, confirmed by another airliner:

UNIDENTIFIED OBJECT GLOWING BRIGHT GREEN SIGHTED BY UAL-600 FLYING EASTBOUND AT 19 THOUSAND FEET MEAN SEA LEVEL OVER A POINT 12 MILES EAST OF CHEROKEE WYOMING. OBJECT FIRST APPEARED 12 TO 15 DEGREES ABOVE HORIZON AND 100 DEGREES TRUE FROM OBSERVATION POINT AND DISAPPEARED BEHIND CLOUD BANK SLANTING DOWNWARD 30 DEGREES TO LEFT OF VERTICAL. TIME OF OBSERVA-

TION 280125M. DURATION 5 SECONDS . . . CAPTAIN SPERRY,
UAL-600, CONFIRMED BY CO-PILOT, CONFIRMED BY PILOT
N28392 DC3 5 MILES WEST OF SINCLAIR WYOMING AT 13
THOUSAND FEET . . . SAME TIME OF OBSERVATION . . . THIS
MESSAGE HAS BEEN RELAYED TO CIA BY ELECTRICAL MEANS.

As with many UFO-related intelligence reports dating from 1953, the
NSA (as DIRNSA, meaning 'Director, National Security Agency') was on
the distribution list, proving the agency's long-denied involvement with
the UFO phenomenon.

In December 1958, 450 airline pilots signed a petition protesting at the
official policy of debunking sightings, which one pilot described as 'a
lesson in lying, intrigue and the "big brother" attitude carried to the
ultimate extreme'. No fewer than fifty of the pilots had reported sightings,
only to be told by the Air Force that they had been mistaken; at the same
time, the pilots had been warned that they faced up to ten years in prison,
under JANAP 146, if they revealed details of their sightings to the media![17]

Following a sighting by Captain Peter Killian and his crew, as well as
thirty-five passengers aboard an American Airlines DC-6 over Pennsylvania on 24 February 1959, the Air Force issued three separate, contradictory, explanations for the incident, without having interviewed any of
the witnesses. After Killian exposed these contradictions in newspaper
interviews, American Airlines, succumbing to Air Force pressure, told
Killian not to publicize the story any more. A US senator asked Killian if
he would be prepared to testify at a Congressional hearing in Washington.
'Yes, I would,' replied Killian, 'but you would have to subpoena me. Then
I could talk.'[18]

Sighting by Helicopter Pilots

Another CIRVIS report that was sent to the NSA Director is the following,
prioritized 'Emergency' and dated 12 August 1954, from the Flight Service
Center, Maxwell Air Force Base, Alabama, to the Commander, Air Defense
Command at Ent (later Peterson) Air Force Base, Colorado Springs (from
1953 the main receiving-point for UFO reports by the military):

AT 120154Z TOWER OBSERVED AND REPORTED TO BASE
OPERATIONS STRANGE STATIONARY OBJECT VARIABLE IN
BRILLIANCE LOCATED WEST OF TOWER. AFTER INITIAL
SIGHTING . . . IT UNEXPECTEDLY GAINED APPARENT VELO-

CITY AND SPEEDED ACROSS THE SKY IN NNW HEADING WHICH WAS FOLLOWED BY ITS RETURN TO ITS ORIGINAL POSITION IN RELATION TO THE TOWER AND A NOTICEABLE DESCENT AND MOTIONLESS. TOWER IMMEDIATELY NOTIFIED OPERATIONS AND DISPATCHED A LOCAL HELICOPTER NBR ARMY 267 TO OBSERVE THE PHENOMENA. HELICOPTER STATED THAT OBJECT WAS DEFINITELY NOT A STAR . . .

AT 0156Z AIRDROME OFFICER AND DRIVER OBSERVED MYSTERY OBJECT. . . . AT 0205Z TWO MEMBERS OF ALERT CREW OBSERVED OBJECT FROM TOWER. COLUMBUS CAA RADIO ALSO HAS OBJECT IN SIGHT. THE OBJECT THEN BECAME DIMMER AND SHOWING A SLIGHT RED GLOW. AT 0226Z OBJECT STILL STATIONARY. SEVERAL REOCCURRENCE OF VARIABLE BRILLIANCY SHOWN AND NOW BECOMING EXTREMELY DIMMER. 0227Z HELICOPTER 294 RETURNING FROM MISSION SIGHTED OBJECT AND PROCEEDED TOWARD IT. AT 0229Z OBJECT COMPLETELY DISAPPEARED AND . . . 294 LOST SIGHT OF IT. AT 0240Z ARMY OPERATIONS CALLED AND ADVISED THAT PILOT OF HELICOPTERS WISHED TO STRESS FACT THAT OBJECT WAS OF A SAUCER LIKE NATURE, WAS STATIONARY AND AT 2000 FT. AND WOULD BE GLAD TO BE CALLED UPON TO VERIFY ANY STATEMENTS AND ACT AS WITNESSES.

Air Force Special Security Service

The Air Force Special Security Service (now Electronic Security Command), the National Security Agency's Air Force arm, reported several incidents in June 1955 when UFOs were tracked by RB-47 aircraft. The second incident occurred on 4 June, when visual and electronic contact with an unknown aircraft was made in the area of Melville Sound, North West Territories, Canada.

The crew was first alerted to the object when the aircraft's gun warning light flashed intermittently and no. 5 radar registered a contact at 7,000 yards range. Visual contact was then made by the crew chief, who described the unknown aircraft as 'glistening silver metallic'. The object broke off contact to the north with an increase of speed. Although gun-camera films were taken, the report states, they were of such poor quality that no useful information could be gleaned. The radar and visual contacts were maintained for a total of 9 minutes.

On 7 June an RB-47 *en route* to Eilson Air Force Base, Alaska, registered electronic contact with an unknown target south-east of Banks Island at 3,500 yards. 'The [radar] scope return was small and rectangular [which] the pilot interpreted to be a form of jamming. The target warning light went on and off 3 times in as many minutes.'[19]

The Boeing RB-47 was a medium-range reconnaissance aircraft that gathered photographic intelligence (PHOTINT) and electronic intelligence (ELINT) for analysis by the intelligence community, particularly the NSA. It had seven cameras that automatically photographed the ground track, and several crews on board operated equipment that intercepted radio and radar signals for ELINT.

This aircraft, like its successors, engaged in 'stand-off and shallow' penetration sorties from or across potentially hostile borders (in the aforementioned case, the USSR) in order to deliberately trigger radar and radio alerts so that the operating frequencies could be determined and, in time of war, invading bombers could use this information to programme their electronic countermeasures (ECM) equipment to jam or confuse enemy radar.[20] That UFOs are reported to have jammed or confused our radar systems in these cases, and radio communications in others, is sufficient grounds to warrant the close attention of the National Security Agency. As discussed earlier, the Third World War could be triggered by confusing UFOs with hostile aircraft or missiles, so it is small wonder that the NSA has been involved in monitoring UFO reports since 1953 (or even 1952).

Extraordinary Events at Holloman Air Force Base

On a September morning in 1956, a domed, disc-shaped object reportedly landed within the White Sands Proving Grounds, 12 miles west of Holloman Air Force Base, Alamogordo, New Mexico, and 50 yards from US Highway 70. Radios and ignition systems of passing cars went dead as witnesses, including two Air Force colonels, two sergeants, and dozens of base personnel, observed the craft before it took off with a whirring sound. Air Force intelligence officers and CIA experts allegedly arrived from Washington, DC, and all the base personnel were assembled in a hangar, questioned, then sworn to secrecy. A cable from the evaluation team to the Pentagon stated that the object was 'definitely not any type of aircraft under development by the US or any foreign terrestrial power'.

On a summer evening in 1958, a mechanic at Holloman observed a disc-shaped object hovering silently over the tarmac. The craft retracted its

'ball-like landing gear' (similarly described in other cases), and the witness
managed to alert another mechanic in time for them both to see it take off
at high speed. Air Force representatives interrogated the mechanics a few
days later and allegedly showed them a large book which contained over
300 pages of UFO photographs. After identifying the type of craft they had
seen, the witnesses were informed that personnel at the control tower had
observed the same object for a few minutes. Both mechanics were sworn
to secrecy.[21,22]

TV Censorship

On 22 January 1958, CBS Television presented a programme devoted to
UFOs on its *Armstrong Circle Theater* show, and one of those invited to
appear was Major Donald Keyhoe, Director of the civilian organization,
National Investigations Committee on Aerial Phenomena (NICAP).
Keyhoe, a graduate of the US Naval Academy and a former Marine
Corps pilot, had excellent sources of information within military circles,
and had frequently stated on the air – and in his books – that the US
Government was withholding the facts on UFOs to avoid panic.

Several Air Force spokesmen were also scheduled to appear, but
insisted on seeing Keyhoe's script in advance and asked for assurances that
no 'ad libs' would be permitted. Keyhoe was also told that he would be
allotted seven minutes on the programme, whereas the Air Force had been
given twenty-five minutes' air time. When Keyhoe's material was
returned, all the salient points had been deleted on the grounds that the
script was too long, despite the fact that he had carefully timed it. Keyhoe
retained one statement:

> There is an official policy, believed in the best interests of the
> people, not to confirm the existence of UFOs until all the answers
> are known. Captain Edward J. Ruppelt, former chief of Project
> Blue Book, has confirmed the existence of four important
> documents that should be noted. In 1948, in a 'Top Secret'
> estimate, the [Air Technical Intelligence Center] concluded that
> UFOs were interplanetary spaceships. In 1952, an Air Force
> Intelligence analysis of UFO maneuvers brought the same
> conclusion . . . interplanetary. In January 1953 a report by a
> panel of top scientists at the Pentagon reached this conclusion:
> There is strong circumstantial evidence, but no concrete proof
> that UFOs are spaceships.

Keyhoe was told that he could not use this statement. The final show was a farce, bearing little relation to the programme as originally conceived, with the Air Force spokesmen concentrating on some of the sillier stories of contacts with spacemen. By the time Keyhoe appeared with his heavily edited script, little could be done to salvage the situation. In desperation, he suddenly veered from his script on the teleprompter: 'And now I'm going to reveal something that has never been disclosed before . . . for the last six months we have been working with a congressional committee investigating official secrecy about UFOs . . .' But by now the producer had cut the audio off the air and the public never heard Keyhoe's concluding statement: '. . . If all the evidence we have given this committee is made public in open hearings it will absolutely prove that the UFOs are real machines under intelligent control.'

NICAP later obtained a statement from the CBS director of editing, Herbert A. Carlborg, which proves that Major Keyhoe was cut off the air in the interests of national security. 'This program had been carefully screened for security reasons,' he said. 'Therefore, it was the responsibility of this network to ensure performance that was in accordance with predetermined security standards. Any indication that there would be a deviation from the script might lead to a statement that neither this network nor the individuals on the program were authorized to release.'[23]

Congressional Statements

In the late 1950s NICAP revealed some significant statements it had received from prominent members of Congress, of which the following give a clear indication of how seriously the aspect of official secrecy about the subject was treated:

Senator Leverett B. Saltonstall (Massachusetts): 'We must consider the genuine security necessities . . . but I think there are many cases in which more information should be made available to the public.'

Representative Thomas L. Ashley (Ohio): 'I share your concern over the secrecy that continues to shroud our intelligence activities on this subject.'

Representative William H. Ayres (Ohio): 'Congressional investigations have been held and are still being held on the problems of unidentified flying objects . . . Since most of the material presented is classified, the hearings are never printed.'

Representative Walter H. Moeller (Ohio): '[I have] every confidence that the American public would be able to take such information without hysteria. The fear of the unknown is always greater than fear of the known.'

Representative Ralph J. Scott (North Carolina): 'If this information could be presented in such a way as to appeal to reason, and not to emotion, I think it would be a good thing.'[24]

Senator Richard B. Russell, former Chairman of the Senate Armed Services Committee, who had a sighting in the Soviet Union in 1955 (see Chapter 12), was subsequently asked about official secrecy by aviation journalist Tom Towers. 'I have discussed this with the affected agencies of the government,' the Senator replied, 'and they are of the opinion that it is unwise to publicize the matter at this time.'[25]

A Tragic Interception

Physicist Dr Bruce Maccabee has learned of an incident involving an Air Force jet, based in Japan, reportedly scrambled to intercept a UFO in the spring of 1959. The story was related to Maccabee by a former lieutenant colonel who at the time was weather officer at the headquarters of the Fifth Air Force near Tokyo.

According to the officer, four F-106 Delta Dart jets stationed in Okinawa and Masawa, Japan, had been instrumented specially to track and fire on unidentified flying objects. During a visit by the officer to the combat-operations centre at dusk one evening, two F-106s were scrambled to intercept a UFO that had been plotted on radar, south of Masawa. Only one jet took off, however, because the other F-106 had developed an instrument malfunction. 'And so the pilot climbed on out and said he was clear on top,' the officer related:

> And then there were a few minutes or so . . . and then he says he got it in sight. Because there was a general interest in the command centre in what was happening, they put it on a speaker system. I could hear the down-link from the pilot. The radarscope operators had a tie-in with the Masawa operators on the radars, and they were the only ones who could hear the ground link-up, so I could hear only half the conversation . . .
>
> Basically they were vectoring him in, and he said something like 'I've got it in sight', and he described what appeared to be a circular object that was hovering. It was metallic and had a cockpit on top . . . he asked if he should make a firing pass . . . so they called the Pentagon to get authority, and the word came back, yes, make a firing pass . . . So the pilot said, 'Will roll in', and he rolled in and he fired the [missiles] off. Then all of a sudden his voice

went into a high falsetto. It was real strange. He blurted out that he had fired, and they had detonated but did not hit it. They detonated just at the edge of it . . . like an invisible shield. But he said it looked as if none of the shrapnel or anything penetrated through.

And then he says, 'They've turned on some kind of beam, and they're turning . . . They're coming after me'. And then he went into a vertical diving maneuver. And the radar operators started screaming out that it was moving and vectoring towards him, and they started counting out the ranges as it was coming down. The pilot was just breathing heavily and obviously under great stress but controlled, and he said, 'It's moving closer.' And he just kept describing how it kept gaining on him and this beam was coming towards him.

And then the radar operators said, 'Contact.' The two blips matched! And a radar operator said, 'My God, there's no separation . . . The thing has stopped. It's just a single blip hovering, but there's nothing else.' [Subsequently the blip also disappeared.] For four days after that I gave weather briefings every day for a search up there. They never did find anything.[26]

'Serious USAF Business'

On 24 December 1959 the Air Force issued the following warning to every air base commander in the continental United States:

> Unidentified flying objects – sometimes treated lightly by the press and referred to as 'flying saucers' – must be rapidly and accurately identified as serious USAF business in the ZI [Zone of Interior] . . .
>
> The phenomena or actual objects comprising UFOs will tend to increase, with the public more aware of goings on in space but still inclined to some apprehension. Technical and defense considerations will continue to exist in this era.

Rear Admiral Roscoe Hillenkoetter, former Director of the CIA (1947–50) as well as a NICAP committee member (see Chapter 16), said that a copy of the warning, issued by the Inspector General, had been sent to the Senate Science and Astronautics Committee. 'It is time for the truth to be brought out in open congressional hearings,' he said. 'Behind the scenes, high-ranking Air Force officers are soberly concerned about the UFOs. But through official secrecy and ridicule, many citizens are led to believe the unknown flying objects are nonsense.' He also charged that 'to hide the facts, the Air Force has silenced its personnel' through issuance of a regulation.[27]

In April 1959 Major General Donald J. Keirn, Chief of the USAF nuclear engine programme, stated that, although the Air Force had no proof that intelligent beings existed elsewhere, the UFO reports had 'emphasized our innate curiosity . . . It is entirely possible that some of them may have passed through our stage of evolution, and may have already achieved a higher level of social and technological culture than our own.'[28]

In 1962 Major C. R. Hart, an Air Force spokesman at the Pentagon, revealed that UFO investigations and evaluations involved hundreds of Air Force intelligence officers, as well as 'the best scientific brains available in the laboratories of all government agencies, also scientific investigators in commercial laboratories, whenever needed'. Major Hart also disclosed that the chief Air Force scientific consultant, Dr J. Allen Hynek, had conferred with the world's leading scientists regarding the UFO problem. That same year, Lieutenant Colonel Spencer Whedon of the Air Technical Intelligence Center revealed that the Air Force spent an estimated $10,000 on each major sighting investigation.[29]

On 29 October 1962 Defense Department Assistant Secretary Arthur Sylvester admitted that withholding information on UFOs from the public was necessary if the ends justified it, and cited Air Force Regulation 11-7, in which it is stated that sometimes information requested by Congress may not be furnished 'even in confidence'.[30]

A number of Air Force officers opposed official secrecy on UFOs at this time. 'In concealing the evidence of UFO operations the Air Force is making a serious mistake,' said Lieutenant Colonel James McAshan. 'The public should be informed as to the facts.' Major Edwin A. Jerome went further in criticizing 'this inane veil of security classification. I suggest we are several centuries behind the intellects of other planets . . . The national policy should be to educate the public.' Colonel Howard Strand, who had three encounters with UFOs while flying F-94 jets, stressed that 'too many intelligent, competent observers have reported UFOs', and added: 'My conclusion is that this is a reconnaissance by an advanced civilization. I urge a congressional investigation of UFOs and the military secrecy surrounding them.'[31]

Supposing that some UFOs are dangerous, and have been responsible for the deaths of a number of Air Force pilots, as General Benjamin

Chidlaw confirmed, are the authorities not fully justified in their policy of withholding the facts from the public in the interests of national security? This policy may also have been predicated on a suspicion by intelligence analysts that our planet might be viewed acquisitively by beings from elsewhere – a possibility discussed in the final chapter.

Fanciful though this scenario seems, it was accorded a measure of credence by Colonel William C. Odell, Air Force Intelligence, in 1954, when in a script cleared by the USAF but never published, entitled *Planet Earth – Host to Extraterrestrial Life*, he wrote: 'Granted that super-intelligents in another solar system are looking for a suitable planet for a second home, why would Earth be singled out?' Although Colonel Odell's manuscript had been cleared, potential publishers had been put off by Air Force stipulations that Odell was not to be identified as a USAF officer, nor could the clearance by USAF security review be mentioned.[32]

Radiation Effects

On many occasions UFOs have been reported to emit radiation of varying types and strengths, and such cases have led to an official clamp-down. On 6 November 1957 Olden Moore watched a landed UFO for twenty minutes, 30 miles east of Cleveland, Ohio. The following day Moore was questioned by Army representatives as well as by scientists from the Case Institute of Technology. Geiger-counter readings taken from the centre of a 50-feet area registered ten times the normal amount, and about 50 per cent more at the perimeter. Moore claimed that he had spoken to unspecified 'high officials' in Washington and said that he had been sworn to secrecy.[33]

A former Navy pilot who saw three oval-shaped UFOs while flying from Hobbs to Albuquerque, New Mexico, on 13 August 1959, allegedly was warned by an Air Force major at Kirtland Air Force Base that he might become ill after the incident. The UFOs had caused the pilot's Magnesyn compass to revolve, following the bearing of the 8-feet-diameter objects as they circled his Cessna 170. The pilot said that he had been ordered not to discuss the case with anyone (hence anonymity), except for his wife, who had to be prepared in the event he became ill. The Air Force said it would look after him if this happened within six months, but, since nothing further was reported about this case as far as I am aware, presumably the pilot was unaffected.[34]

On 21 December 1964 Horace Burns encountered an object resembling an inverted spinning-top about 125 feet in diameter near Staunton, Virginia. The object, which remained on the ground for sixty to ninety seconds, caused the engine of his car to cut out. Radiation readings taken by Professor Ernest Gehman registered 60,000 counts per minute, confirmed by two other engineers present. It was concluded that the radiation was of the alpha type, not the more dangerous gamma type. On 12 January 1965 two Air Force sergeants from Wright-Patterson Air Force Base went to the site and checked it with a Model 2586 Beta–Gamma Survey Meter. Checks were made at over eight spots and, although rain and snow had fallen in the area since the landing, a high reading was picked up by one of the men, which fact he immediately attempted to suppress. Two weeks later the official report was released, denying that there had been a landing of a UFO or traces of radioactivity.[35,36]

UFO Destroys Atlas Missile

An astonishing case was revealed in 1982 by a former first lieutenant in the Air Force, Dr Robert Jacobs, now a university professor in a department of journalism and broadcasting. Dr Jacobs states that in September 1964, when he was Officer-in-Charge of Photo-optical Instrumentation in the 1369th Photographic Squadron at Vandenberg Air Force Base, California, a UFO was responsible for the destruction of an Atlas missile during a test firing. He stated that this event was recorded by a 35mm movie camera attached to a high-powered telescope at the tracking-site near Anderson Peak, Big Sur, 124 miles from Vandenburg.

The Atlas test flight was part of the Nike–Zeus project to develop an anti-missile missile weapon. As the rocket lifted off from Vandenburg, the telescope locked on to it by radar and the camera rolled. 'As the nosecone package approached T plus 400 seconds, sufficient angle of view had been established that we were literally locked down with the whole inflight package centered in the frame,' reported Dr Jacobs. 'No one on the site was watching the screen by this point. Our mission to provide the engineers with a side look at three stages of powered flight had been accomplished and we were a very happy bunch, congratulating each other and letting the film run . . .'

Jacobs took the exposed cans of film to the photographic processing laboratory at Vandenberg AFB. A couple of days later he was ordered to report to Major Florenz J. Mansmann, chief science officer of the unit. 'When I arrived,' said Jacobs, 'I found a movie projector set up in the office and a group of people waiting. Among these I recall two men in plain suits who spoke little and watched me intently as the lights were dimmed and the film played . . .' He continued:

I was quite amazed and very pleased with the quality, especially at the distance involved, as we could make out quite plainly the separated nosecone, the radar experiment and the dummy warhead all sailing along beautifully about 60 miles straight up from planet Earth and some 300 to 500 nautical miles down range. As we neared the end of the camera run, Major Mansmann said, 'Watch carefully now, Lieutenant Jacobs.'

At that point the most remarkable vision of my life came on the screen. Another object *flew into the frame* from left to right. It approached the warhead package and *maneuvered around it*. That is, this 'thing' flew a relative polar orbit around our warhead package which was itself heading toward the South Pacific at some 18,000 miles an hour! As the new object circumnavigated our hardware, it emitted four distinct, bright flashes of light at approximately the four cardinal compass points of its orbit. These flashes were so intense that each 'strike' caused the I.O. [Image Orthicon] tube to 'bloom' or form a halo around the spot.

Following this remarkable aerial display, the object departed the frame in the same direction from which it had come. The shape of the object was that of a classic 'flying saucer'. In the middle of the top half of the object was a dome. From that dome, or just beneath it, seemed to issue a beam of light which caused the flashes described. Subsequently the warhead malfunctioned and tumbled out of suborbit hundreds of miles short of its target. This unidentified flying 'thing' had apparently 'shot down' an American dummy atomic warhead!

They switched on the office lights again, and I found myself confronted by three very intense faces. Speaking very quietly, Major Mansmann then said: 'Lieutenant, just what the hell *was* that?' I replied that I had no idea. Then we ran the film through several more times, and I was permitted to examine it with a magnifying glass. Then Mansmann again asked me what I thought, and I answered that in my opinion it was a UFO. Major Mansmann smiled and said: 'You are to say nothing about this footage. As far as you and I are concerned, it never happened! Right?' . . . The film was turned over to the two men in plain clothes from Washington, who I believe were CIA agents. The film hasn't been heard of since. Major Mansmann added: 'I don't have to remind you, of course, of the seriousness of a security breach . . .'

When this story finally broke, Dr Mansmann (later a research consultant at Stanford University) was besieged with requests for information, and for his version of the incident. 'My respect and admiration for him was vindicated as he categorically verified my account,' wrote Dr Jacobs.

> The Air Force has alternately denied that I was ever an officer, that I was ever stationed at Vandenberg, that I was OIC of Photo-optical Instrumentation in the 1369th Photographic Squadron, that there was a tracking site at or near Big Sur, that an Atlas-F, or for that matter, any other missile was launched on or about the date or dates I reported . . . We have been able to verify through [Freedom of Information] requests and my military records everything except the specific launch and the fact of its having been filmed.

Dr Jacobs did manage to trace an official unclassified Air Force Operations Analysis Staff Study by Kingston A. George, dated 13 October 1964, which refers to eleven launches having been made from Vandenberg between 31 August and 30 September 1964 and confirms that one 'powered-flight anomaly was observed' and that a missile malfunctioned during this period.[37,38]

Californian Contact

Stories of encounters with the occupants of UFOs are invariably greeted with a barrage of ridicule, particularly if the witnesses claim to have met beings similar to ourselves in appearance. Having made an intensive study of many such cases over a period of more than three decades, I am absolutely convinced that some of the claimants have had real, objective, experiences. The case of Sid Padrick, which took place in California four months after the Atlas-missile incident, deserves our attention, not least because the witness claims he was asked by the Air Force not to discuss certain details.

Forty-five-year-old Sid Padrick, a TV and radio technician as well as a private pilot with 600 flying hours experience, served in the Air Force during the Second World War and at the time of the incident was serving in the Air Force Reserve. At 02.00 on 30 January 1965, as he was taking a customary late-night walk, Padrick claimed to have encountered a landed UFO near his home at Manreso Beach (the Air Force report says La Selva

Beach), near Watsonville, 75 miles south of San Francisco. He saw the shadowy outline of an unlit craft some 75 feet in diameter and 30 feet high 'like two real thick saucers inverted' approach him and come to rest just above the ground. He panicked, began to run, then heard a voice coming from the craft: '*Do not be frightened, we are not hostile,*' it said. Padrick ran further. The voice repeated the phrase, then added: '*We mean you no harm,*' and invited him on board.

As he cautiously approached the craft, a door opened and he went inside, finding himself in a small compartment about 6 by 7 feet. Another door slid open and he entered, to be met by a man.

The Aliens

'He was no different than me in basic appearance, had clean-cut features, and wore a type of flying suit that covered the body fully,' said Padrick. On board were another seven men, similar in appearance, and one woman, described as extremely pretty. They were all about 5 feet 8 inches to 5 feet 9 inches tall.

> By our own standards I would say they all looked between 20 and 25 years old, very young, pert, energetic and intelligent looking. Their features were similar to ours. There was only one feature I noticed that would differ from us greatly, and that was that their faces came to a point, much more than ours. They had sharp chins and noses. Their skin was somewhat of an 'Armenian' colour. Their eyes were all very dark . . . there was nothing unusual about them – their brightness, depth or luminescence.
>
> All the men appeared to have very short auburn hair, but it looked as though it had never been cut – it looked like a natural growth. The lady had long hair and it was pushed down inside her clothing . . . Their fingers were a little longer than mine. The hands were very clean – the fingernails looked as if somebody had just given them a manicure.
>
> All of them were wearing two-piece suits – slip-on type – light bluish-white in colour. They had no buttons or zippers that I could see. The bottom section actually included the shoes – it looked like boots which continued on up to the waistline, without any break around the ankles, just like a child's snow-suit . . . There was a large band in the middle, and large cuffs, and a large collar that came down with a 'V' neck. The collar had a very pretty

design on it . . . and the neck piece – right around the neck – had a braid of some kind on it . . . They had soles and heels . . . I could hear them walking on the rubbery-like floor.

The first man Padrick saw acted as spokesman, explaining that he was the only one on board who spoke English.

He had no accent whatsoever. It was just as plain and just as perfectly-spoken English as anyone had ever spoken on this Earth. I believe they can adapt themselves to whatever condition they are working under.

Every question I asked him, he would pause for about 25 or 30 seconds before he would answer, regardless of how minor it was. Perhaps he was getting instructions mentally – in what response to give. I think if the crew communicated with each other, it was through mental telepathy, because I could see nothing that would indicate communication otherwise.

Inside the Craft

Each of the rooms that was occupied had instrument panels on the walls, with the crew members concentrating on the instruments. 'They merely glanced around at me when I entered their room, then turned back to their work, as if they were unconcerned,' said Padrick.

Some rooms had four or five instruments, others had 15 or 20, but they were of a similar type in each room. They were nothing like ours. I didn't get close to any of the walls that had the movable instruments on them, because when I started to advance in the first room he held out his hand for me not to advance and I didn't, either. He didn't say why and I didn't ask. I saw markings on some of the instruments; something like a tape moving along, with little tiny dots and dashes on it – like our teletype tapes, except they were going from left to right . . . I wouldn't classify it as a code, like our CW [continuous wave]. There were no screens, such as our oscilloscopes. They had meters, but I could not see dials on them. He said they lit up only when in use.

Padrick was shown an oblong lens, which he took to be part of a viewing system, with a magnified three-dimensional effect. On it he saw an object which he was told was a 'navigation craft' that looked like a 'blimp'.

> This was 2.45 or 3.00 in the morning, and the object was in sunlight, so it had to be pretty far out – I imagine 1,000 miles out, or better. I didn't see any markings or portholes in it . . . he told me that the power source [of the craft he was in] was transferred to them from the other craft, and that it did all the navigation and manipulation through space.
>
> He told me they don't measure time and distance as we know it but rather in terms of light. When I asked him how fast they travelled through space, he answered that their speed was limited only by the speed at which they could transfer their energy source.

Outside the Craft

After a while the spaceman told Padrick that they had travelled some distance and were now parked in a deserted area, which on subsequent investigation turned out to be near Leggett, California, 175 miles north-west of Watsonville.

> After we had landed on the hillside, he told me to step out so that I could come back to the place later – to know this was real and not dreamed. I stepped out alone and walked around the outside of the ship.
>
> I felt the hull. It seemed very hard but not metallic: I never felt anything like it before. The closest thing to it I ever felt on this Earth would be a windshield – plexiglass. It had a very fine finish, a highly polished finish. He didn't tell me that touching this craft would do me harm, and I had no bad effects from it – none whatever. I was outside for not more than three minutes. I got down and looked at the legs it was on and I tried to find markings on it: I didn't find a mark on it anyplace.

Origin and Purpose

Padrick asked where the craft and its people came from, and received a somewhat cryptic reply. 'He told me they were from a planet in back of a planet which we observe – but we do not observe them. He did not say we couldn't observe them – he merely said we didn't observe them . . . I think their planet is in our solar system.'

Padrick was shown a photo of a city on the visitors' planet:

Every building in that picture was rounded off, half-moon shaped. I saw windows in the buildings. I cannot say the picture looked like anything I had ever seen before, because the buildings were spaced differently – offset from each other. It looked like they put one about 50 feet from another and the next one 150 feet. There appeared to be roads in the distance and there was foliage in the foreground – trees and bush too.

The spaceman described his Utopian society to Padrick: '*As you know it, we have no sickness, we have no crimes, we have no police force. We have no schools – our young are taught at an early age to do a job, which they do very well. Because of our long life expectancy we have a very strict birth control. We have no money. We live as one.*'

Padrick asked what the purpose of the visit was. The man replied: '*Observation only.*' Padrick explained:

I don't think it meant for them to observe us, I think it was for *me* to observe *them* . . . because he did not ask me at any time my name, my age, how many teeth I had, how many members of my family: he didn't ask me one thing about myself, and this leads me to believe that they know about us already, and he came for us to observe them . . . They did say they would come for further observations . . . I think they are observing people, mostly. There was no mention of earthquakes, fault-lines, or of anything government-wise, or political-wise, or anything that would affect our future [except that] they gave me the impression that they will pick up more people in future.

A Spiritual Experience

Sid Padrick was taken into what was referred to by the visitors as a 'consultation room'. The colour effect in this room defied description. '*Would you like to pay your respects to the Supreme Deity?*' he was asked.

When he said that I almost fainted. I didn't even know how to accept it. I said to him, 'We have one, but we call it God. Are we talking about the same thing?' He replied, '*There is only one.*' . . . So I knelt and did my usual prayer . . . Until that night I had never felt the presence of the Supreme Being – but I did feel Him that night.

It's obvious that they are on a very high scientific level, but their relation with the Supreme Being means a lot more to them than their technical and scientific ability and knowledge. I would say that their religion and their science are all in one.

Padrick was taken back to where he had been picked up two hours earlier, then stepped out of the craft and walked home.

The Air Force Investigation

Sid Padrick reported his experience to the Air Force, and was grilled for three hours by a team headed by Major Damon B. Reeder from Hamilton Air Force Base (Headquarters, Western Air Defense Force, near Sacramento):

> . . . they tried to frighten me. They said, 'Mr Padrick, you are a real lucky person . . . these craft that come down here are real hostile, and you had no business even approaching them.' I disagreed with them, because when this craft came down, they did not want to frighten me . . . they did not *tell* me to go aboard their craft, they *invited* me aboard.

The Air Force investigators allegedly told Padrick that there had been two instances where hostility had been involved: one the Mantell case, and the other an incident when an aircraft completely vanished from a radar screen (in fact there have been more such incidents, as we have learned). Padrick claimed the Air Force informed him that there was more than one group of UFOs visiting Earth, and that there were friendly as well as hostile craft, from more than one source.

> There were certain details they [the Air Force] asked me not to talk about publicly, but I think in telling it that everything should be disclosed. I can see no reason for anything being held back. They didn't want me to say that the space people had no money. They didn't want me to disclose the type and shape of the craft because that would indicate that the Air Force is not doing its

duty. I told them I could see no reason for that, either . . . They didn't want me to divulge their means of communication and where they got their power from. Also, the man's name – they told me I should never repeat that because it didn't mean anything. The spaceman had said: '*You may call me Xeno.*' He didn't say it *was* his name. [Xeno means 'stranger' or 'foreigner' in Greek.][39,40,41]

The official Air Force report, signed by Major Reeder (base operations officer, Hamilton AFB) and forwarded to the Foreign Technology Division at Wright-Patterson AFB, includes further details of Padrick's alleged conversation with the spaceman, from which I cite the following:

(1) Q. How did you evade our radar? A. The hull of our space craft absorbs energy and will not allow a reflection or harmful penetration . . .
(4) Q. Are you human? A. Yes, we are human, but not your type . . .
(13) Q. How did you pick me for this experience? A. We did not pick you. It was your choice. You are the first person ever to come aboard this ship. We have invited many before but they were frightened away.
(14) Q. If I were a scientist could I have learned more? A. No . . .

Major Reeder reported that Padrick 'appears to be of above average intelligence with an excellent vocabulary and command of the English language. He is a glib talker . . . It is my opinion that this is not a valid UFO contact but rather an attempt on Mr Padrick's part to get the Air Force involved in order to lend his story some authenticity and credibility.'[42]

I disagree. Although I never met the late Sid Padrick (he disappeared from the scene in the late 1960s, having become tired of being harassed), I have listened to every inflection of his voice in the recorded interview on which this account is based, and he comes across as truthful. Under a barrage of cross-questioning by civilian investigators at the time, his answers were always clear, precise and without guile, and he was always quick to appreciate the humorous aspects of the incredible situation in which he found himself.

The Silencers

Mysterious men dressed in Air Force uniform or bearing impressive credentials from government agencies, who intimidate witnesses and sometimes confiscate evidence from them, have now become inextricably enmeshed in UFO lore. In 1967 even the Air Force was obliged to acknowledge that such incidents took place, but denied any involvement. 'These men are not connected with the Air Force,' said Colonel George Freeman, Pentagon spokesman for Project Blue Book.

After highway inspector Rex Heflin took four Polaroid photographs of a low-flying UFO near Santa Ana, California, on 3 August 1965, he was visited at his home by a man claiming to represent 'North American Air Defense Command G-2' (possibly the USAF Aerospace Intelligence Division), who demanded the prints. They were never returned. Heflin had previously loaned the photos to the El Toro Marine Station and had received them back safely, so he assumed that NORAD (or whoever) would do likewise.

Major General M. Magee, NORAD's Chief of Staff, later told Representative James B. Utt (Republican, California): 'For your information NORAD does not have the responsibility for the evaluation of UFOs and therefore would not knowingly be in the business of collecting UFO pictures for evaluation.' (Yet Air Defense Command, as NORAD's predecessor, clearly had that responsibility.)

Police officers and other witnesses to a UFO sighting at Wanaque, New Jersey, in 1966, were assembled by a man wearing an Air Force uniform who told them they hadn't seen anything and should not discuss the matter any further. 'We checked with the local Air Force base,' said Colonel Freeman, 'and discovered that no one connected with the Air Force had visited Wanaque on the date in question. Whoever he was, he wasn't from the Air Force.'

In April 1966 a man claiming to represent 'a government agency so secret that he couldn't give its name' grilled two twelve-year-old boys for two hours about a disc-shaped object that had pursued them at ground level.

'We haven't been able to find out anything about these men,' said Colonel Freeman. 'By posing as Air Force officers and government agents they are committing a federal offence.'[43,44] (Though not if they actually are officials!) Perhaps Colonel Freeman, genuinely unaware of government involvement in these incidents, was telling the truth. Owing to compartmentalization of intelligence he may not have had a 'need to know' about the investigations, nor would he necessarily have known which agency was involved. And if he did, it would hardly have been in the Government's best interests to admit as much. The Air Force Office of Special Investigations (AFOSI), with a long, continuous history of involvement in clandestine UFO investigations, could well have been responsible, in my opinion.

NORAD

The North American Aerospace Defense Command (formerly US Air Defense Command) is responsible for protecting the North American continent from attack by enemy missiles or aircraft. While the vast majority of the 25,000 observations each day that are recorded by NORAD's Space Detection and Tracking System (SPADATS) and the Naval Space Surveillance System (NAVSPASUR) turn out to be readily identifiable, a certain percentage are classed as 'uncorrelated observations', of which there have been approximately 10 million since the early 1960s. Assuming that the majority of these, too, can be explained, we are still left with thousands of possibly bona-fide UFO reports. NORAD has released a number of documents under provisions of the Freedom of Information Act which detail some incidents, such as the intrusions over Strategic Air Command bases – including nuclear missile bases – in Maine, Michigan, Montana, North Dakota and Canada, in 1975 (see Chapter 10), but many more are being withheld. When Citizens Against UFO Secrecy (CAUS) filed a FOIA request for this data in NORAD files, it was quoted a search fee of over $155,000![45] More recently, CAUS acquired a document relating to NORAD's Unknown Track Reporting System (NUTR) which states that 7,000 trackings of unknown objects had been recorded since 1971, but nearly all these are exempt from disclosure in the interests of national security. Eventually CAUS was supplied with five examples – classified 'NORAD SECRET' – under provisions of the FOIA, but these are almost completely censored.[46]

The respected researcher Raymond Fowler, who once served in the USAF Security Service (the Air Force's cryptologic major command), has revealed details of a NORAD-related incident that occurred on 5 March 1967. NORAD radar tracked an uncorrelated target descending over the Minuteman missile site at Minot AFB (91st Strategic Missile Wing), North Dakota. Strike teams were notified immediately and sighted a metallic disc-shaped UFO with bright flashing lights moving slowly over the site. Three armed trucks chased the intruder until it stopped and hovered at

500 feet. The teams had orders to capture the UFO undamaged if it landed, but it then began circling over a launch-control facility. F-106 jets were about to be scrambled when the UFO climbed vertically and disappeared at high speed.[47] Fowler has received confirmation from undisclosed sources that there have been other instances when UFOs have hovered directly over nuclear-missile sites.

In the spring of 1966 the command and status consoles at a launch-control centre in Great Falls, Montana, indicated that a fault existed in each of the ten missiles simultaneously. The missile crew checked the faults electronically and discovered that a 'no-go fault condition' existed in the guidance and control systems, which meant in effect that none of the missiles could have been launched. Above-ground personnel had reported seeing UFOs at the precise moment the failures were detected. An identical incident occurred during the week of 20 March 1967, Fowler reports, when radar at Malstrom Air Force Base, Montana, confirmed the presence of a UFO at the same time that ten missiles became inoperative.[48]

If these events actually took place – and I see no reason to doubt that they did, given the documented cases of intrusions by UFOs over missile sites in 1975 – then we must consider the possibility that in the event of a full-scale nuclear alert our intercontinental ballistic missiles could be rendered impotent by UFOs. This is a comforting thought, with profound implications for the survival of humanity, though there is an additional possibility that the UFO intelligences are merely demonstrating that we have no adequate defence against *them*.

Police Chief Photographs 'Spaceman'

In October 1973 the United States (and other countries) were inundated with sightings of UFOs, leading to a revival of public and media interest in the subject. One of the more interesting reports for me is the encounter of Police Chief Jeff Greenhaw (in fact, the only policeman) in the small town of Falkville, Alabama, on 17 October.

Shortly before 22.00, Greenhaw was at home when a woman telephoned him to report that an object with flashing lights appeared to be landing in a field west of the town. Because there had been a spate of sightings in south Morgan County, Greenhaw grabbed his Polaroid camera and drove to the remote area. Two miles from town he encountered a 6-foot-tall, metallic-suited, humanoid being standing in the middle of the road. 'I got out of my car and said, "Howdy, stranger,"' reported Greenhaw. 'He didn't say a word. I reached back, picked up my

Polaroid camera, and started taking pictures of him.' The policeman took four photographs, then got back into his car and turned on the revolving blue light(s), at which point the being turned and started running down the road.

'I jumped into my car and took after him,' said Greenhaw, 'but couldn't catch up with him in a patrol car. He was running faster than any human I ever saw.' The patrol car was doing 30–40 m.p.h. before going into a spin on the gravel road. The being had vanished by this time. It moved like a robot and ran in huge paces, Greenhaw said.

A hoax? Perhaps. Yet after Jeff Greenhaw related his experience on NBC-TV news he began receiving threatening phone calls. Within two weeks of the incident his car engine blew up, his wife left him, and an arsonist set fire to his house trailer, destroying the original photographic prints (fortunately, copies had been made). To add insult to injury, Greenhaw was forced to resign as police chief. 'So now I've lost my car, my wife, and my job. And I guess I'll just have to go wherever I can to find another job,' he said.[49,50,51] Hoaxers seldom go that far.

Army Helicopter in Near Collision

On 18 October 1973 four Army Reserve crewmen in a Bell Huey helicopter had an alarming close encounter with a UFO in the vicinity of Mansfield, Ohio. The pilot in command was Captain Lawrence J. Coyne, and the other airmen were Crew Chief Robert Yanacsek, Co-pilot Arrigo Jezzi and Staff Sergeant John Healey. The Army disposition form, signed by the four witnesses (see p. 379), records the incident as follows:

> Army helicopter 68-15444 was returning from Columbus, Ohio, to Cleveland, Ohio, and at 2305 hours east, southeast of Mansfield Airport in the vicinity of Mansfield, Ohio, while flying at an altitude of 2500 feet and on a heading of 030 degrees, SSG Yanacsek observed a red light on the east horizon, 90 degrees to the flight path of the helicopter.
>
> Approximately 30 seconds later, SSG Yanacsek indicated the object was converging on the helicopter at the same altitude at an airspeed in excess of 600 knots and on a midair collision heading. CPT Coyne observed the converging object, took over the controls of the aircraft and initiated a power descent from 2500 feet to 1700 feet to avoid impact with the object.
>
> A radio call was initiated to Mansfield Tower who acknowl-

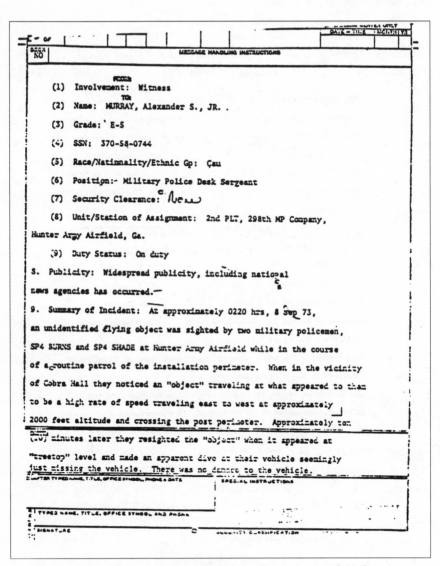

A 'Serious Incident Report' relating to a sighting at Hunter Army Airfield, Georgia, on 8 September 1973. (*US Army*)

The "object" again reappeared at another location and came to
a hover for approximately fifteen (15) minutes in front of them.
The unidentified object appeared to have brilliantly flashing
lights, blue, white, and amber in color. They then returned to
the main post area and were "followed" by the unidentified object
50 to 100 feet away at tree top level until it finally veered off
and visual contact was lost. The "object" made no noise. The
alleged UFO was described as round or oval in shape and between
35 and 75 feet across. SGT Murray and SP4 Burns reported that
at approximately 0430 hrs, 9 Sep 73, while sitting in their
vehicle at the end of the airfield at Hunter Army Airfield,
Ga., they observed what they first believed to be the red
light of an aircraft some distance away. The light then moved
rapidly and disappeared into the woods.

10. Remarks: The above information is based upon information
furnished by the above witnesses.

11.)Commander reporting to HQDA: Frank L. Dietrich, Colonel,
Infantry, Commanding, HCS, Ft Stewart, JFt Stewart, Ga.

12. Prot. mark. excl. from auto. term. (Para 13, AR 340-16).

edged the helicopter and was asked by CPT Coyne if there were
any high performance aircraft flying in the vicinity of Mansfield
Airport, however there was no response received from the tower.
The crew expected impact from the object; instead, the object was
observed to hesitate momentarily over the helicopter and then
slowly continued on a westerly course accelerating at a high rate of
speed, clear west of Mansfield Airport then turn 45 degree heading
to the Northwest.

CPT Coyne indicated the altimeter read a 100 fpm [feet per
minute] climb and read 3500 feet with the collective in the full
down position. The aircraft was returned to 2500 feet by CPT
Coyne and flown back to Cleveland, Ohio. The Flight plan was
closed and the FAA Flight Service Station notified of the
incident.[52]

'From a speed of 600 miles an hour, it abruptly slowed down to our
exact speed of 100 miles an hour and hovered above us,' reported Captain
Coyne. Co-pilot Jezzi described the object as 'cigar-shaped, metallic grey,
with a dome on top', and Staff Sergeant Healey added that it was 'about 60
feet long, without any portholes or intake openings that we could see. At
first it was just showing a red light in the nose. Then a green spotlight at
the back swept around and shone into our cabin.'[53]

The radio returned to normal ten minutes after the incident, having
gone completely dead on both UHF and VHF frequencies just after Coyne
had established contact with Mansfield control tower. Some witnesses on
the ground reported seeing the helicopter as well as an object 'like a blimp'
and 'as big as a school bus' hovering above the helicopter. When the
UFO's green light appeared it was described by the witnesses as 'like rays
coming down . . . The helicopter, the trees, the road . . . everything turned
green'.[54]

Intrusions at Kirtland Air Force Base

According to official documents released under provisions of the Freedom
of Information Act, there were a number of intrusions by unidentified
flying objects in the vicinity of nuclear-weapons storage areas at Kirtland
Air Force Base, Albuquerque, New Mexico, in August 1980. The sightings
were associated with radar jamming and blackout, as these Air Force
Office of Special Investigations complaint forms reveal:

DISPOSITION FORM

For use of this form, see AR 340-15; the proponent agency is The Adjutant General's Office.

ERENCE OR OFFICE SYMBOL	SUBJECT
· 4	Near Midair Collision with UFO Report

Commander 83D USARCOM ATTN: AHRCCO Columbus Support Facility Columbus, Ohio 43215	FROM Flight Operations Off DATE 23 Nov 73 CAT 1 USAR Flight Facility Cleveland Hopkins Airport Cleveland, Ohio 44135

1. On 18 October 1973 at 2305 hours in the vicinity of Mansfield, Ohio, Army Helicopter 68-15444 assigned to Cleveland USARFFAC encountered a near midair collision with a unidentified flying object. Four crewmembers assigned to the Cleveland USARFFAC for flying proficiency were on AFTP status when this incident occurred. The flight crew assigned was CPT Lawrence J. Coyne, Pilot in Command, 1LT Arrigo Jezzi, Copilot, SSG Robert Yanacsek, Crew Chief, SSG John Healey, Flight Medic. All the above personnel are members of the 316th MED DET(HEL AMB), a tenant reserve unit of the Cleveland USARFFAC.

2. The reported incident happened as follows: Army Helicopter 68-15444 was returning from Columbus, Ohio to Cleveland, Ohio and at 2305 hours east, south east of Mansfield Airport in the vicinity of Mansfield, Ohio while flying at an altitude of 2500 feet and on a heading of 030 degrees, SSG Yanacsek observed a red light on the east horizon, 90 degrees to the flight path of the helicopter. Approximately 30 seconds later, SSG Yanacsek indicated the object was converging on the helicopter at the same altitude at a airspeed in excess of 600 knots and on a midair collision heading. Cpt Coyne observed the converging object, took over the controls of the aircraft and initiated a power descent from 2500 feet to 1700 feet to avoid impact with the object. A radio call was initiated to Mansfield Tower who acknowledged the helicopter and was asked by CPT Coyne if there were any high performance aircraft flying in the vicinity of Mansfield Airport however there was no response received from the tower. The crew expected impact from the object instead, the object was observed to hesitate momentarily over the helicopter and then slowly continued on a westerly course accelerating at a high rate of speed, clear west of Mansfield Airport then turn 45 degree heading to the Northwest. Cpt Coyne indicated the altimeter read a 1000 fpm climb and read 3500 feet with the collective in the full down position. The aircraft was returned to 2500 feet by CPT Coyne and flown back to Cleveland, Ohio. The Flight plan was closed and the FAA Flight Service Station notified of the incident. The FSS told CPT Coyne to report the incident to the FAA GADO office a Cleveland Hopkins Airport MR. Porter, 83d USARCOM was notified of the incident at 1530 hours on 19 Oct 73.

3. This report has been read and attested to by the crewmembers of the aircraft with signatures acknowledgeing this report.

FORM 2496 - REPLACES DD FORM 96, EXISTING SUPPLIES OF WHICH WILL BE ISSUED AND USED UNTIL 1 FEB 63 UNLESS SOONER EXHAUSTED. ☆U.S. GPO: 1972-473-003 P.O. 1

A disposition form describing the near collision with an unidentified flying object reported by four Army Reserve helicopter crewmen in the vicinity of Mansfield, Ohio, in October 1973. (*US Army*)

N M C C
THE NATIONAL MILITARY COMMAND CENTER
WASHINGTON, D.C. 20301

THE JOINT STAFF

21 January 1976
0630 EST

MEMORANDUM FOR RECORD

Subject: Report of UFO - Cannon AFB NM

Reference: AFOC Phonecon 2105S EST Jan 76

The following information was received from the Air Force
Operations Center at 0555 EST:

"Two UFOs are reported near the flight line at Cannon AFB,
New Mexico. Security Police observing them reported the UFOs
to be 25 yards in diameter, gold or silver in color with blue
light on top, hole in the middle and red light on bottom. Air
Force is checking with radar. Additionally, checking weather
inversion data."

J.B. MORIN
Rear Admiral, USN
Deputy Director for
Operations, NMCC

A National Military Command Center memorandum relating to a sighting at Cannon Air
Force Base, New Mexico, in January 1976. (*US Defense Department*)

On 13 August 80, 1960 COMMSq Maintenance Officer reported Radar Approach Control equipment and scanner radar inoperative due to high frequency jamming from an unknown cause. Total blackout of entire radar approach system to include Albuquerque Airport was in effect between 1630–2215 hrs. Radar Approach Control backup systems also were inoperative . . . Defense Nuclear Agency Radio Frequency Monitors determined, by vector analysis, the interference was being sent from an area . . . located NW of Coyote Canyon Test area. It was first thought that Sandia Laboratory, which utilizes the test range was responsible. However . . . no tests were being conducted in the canyon area . . . [55]

On 2 Sept 80, SOURCE [Major Ernest E. Edwards] related on 8 Aug 80, three Security Policemen assigned to 1608 SPS, KAFB, NM, on duty inside the Manzano Weapons Storage Area sighted an unidentified light in the air that traveled from North to South over the Coyote Canyon area of the Department of Defense Restricted Test Range . . . The Security Policemen identified as: SSGT STEPHEN FERENZ, Area Supervisor, AIC MARTIN I. RIST and AMN ANTHONY D. FRAZIER, were later interviewed separately by SOURCE . . . At approximately 2350 hrs., while on duty in Charlie Sector, East Side of Manzano, the three observed a very bright light in the sky approximately 3 miles North-North East of their position. The light traveled with great speed and stopped suddenly in the sky over Coyote Canyon. The three first thought the object was a helicopter, however, after observing the strange aerial maneuvers (stop and go), they felt a helicopter couldn't have performed such skills. The light landed in the Coyote Canyon area. Sometime later, [the] three witnessed the light take off and leave proceeding straight up at a high speed and disappear . . .

On 11 Aug 80, RUSS CURTIS, Sandia Security, advised that on 9 Aug 80, a Sandia Security Guard, (who wishes his name not to be divulged for fear of harassment), related the following: At approximately 0020 hrs., he was driving East on the Coyote Canyon access road on a routine building check of an alarmed structure. As he approached the structure he observed a bright light near the ground behind the structure. He also observed an object he first thought was a helicopter. But after driving closer, he observed a round disk shaped object. He attempted to radio for a back up patrol but his radio would not work. As he approached the object on foot armed with a shotgun, the object took off in a vertical direction at a high rate of speed . . .

SOURCE advised on 22 Aug 80, three other security policemen observed the same aerial phenomena described by the first three. Again the object landed in Coyote Canyon. They did not see the object take off . . . Coyote Canyon is part of a large restricted test range used by the Air Force Weapons Laboratory, Sandia Laboratories, Defense Nuclear Agency and the Department of Energy . . .

. . . another Security Guard observed an object land near an alarmed structure sometime during the first week of August, but did not report it until just recently for fear of harassment . . . The two alarmed structures located within the area contain HQ CR 44 [nuclear] material.[56]

In July 1989, during a research trip to Albuquerque, Major Ernest Edwards, who had been in charge of security at the Manzano Nuclear Weapons Storage Area at the time of the 1980 sightings, confirmed the contents of these reports and pointed out to me in person where they had taken place.

Witnesses Severely Harmed by UFO – But was it One of Ours?

The further our technology advances, the harder it may become to differentiate between true UFOs and new types of aircraft, spacecraft and unmanned aerial vehicles (UAVs). Researchers are still debating the origin of an unknown aerial device that was seen by three witnesses on the night of 29 December 1980 near Huffman, a suburb of Houston, Texas.

The witnesses, Betty Cash, her friend Vickie Landrum and the latter's seven-year-old grandson Colby were driving toward Dayton, Texas, when at about 21.00 hours a fiery object was seen high in the sky. It quickly descended to tree-top level above the road and hovered in front of them no more than about 135 feet away. Flames were shooting down from the object. The witnesses stopped the car, got out, and watched, although they were all very frightened – particularly Colby, who pleaded with the others to get back inside the car. This they did, though Betty Cash spent more time outside than the others. Mrs Landrum – convinced that the end of the world had arrived – began praying.

	COMPLAINT FORM	Hq 1 V O S

ADMINISTRATIVE DATA

TITLE	DATE	TIME
KIRTLAND AFB, NM, 8 Aug - 3 Sep 80, Alleged Sigthings of Unidentified Aerial Lights in Restricted Test Range.	2 - 9 Sept 80	1200

PLACE

AFOSI Det 1700, Kirtland AFB, NM

HOW RECEIVED

X IN PERSON	TELEPHONICALLY	IN WRITING

SOURCE AND EVALUATION

MAJOR ERNEST E. EDWARDS

RESIDENCE OR BUSINESS ADDRESS	PHONE
Commander, 1608 SPS, Manzano Kirtland AFB, NM	4-7516

CR 44 APPLIES

II   SUMMARY OF INFORMATION

REMARKS

1. On 2 Sept 80, SOURCE related on 8 Aug 80, three Security Policemen assigned to 1608 SPS, KAFB, NM, on duty inside the Manzano Weapons Storage Area sighted an unidentified light in the air that traveled from North to South over the Coyote Canyon area of the Department of Defense Restricted Test Range on KAFB, NM. The Security Policemen identified as: SSGT STEPHEN FERENZ, Area Supervisor, AIC MARTIN W. RIST and AMN ANTHONY D. FRAZIER, were later interviewed separately by SOURCE and all three related the same statement; At approximately 2350hrs., while on duty in Charlie Sector, East Side of Manzano, the three observed a very bright light in the sky approximately 3 miles North-North East of their position. The light traveled with great speed and stopped suddenly in the sky over Coyote Canyon. The three first thought the object was a helicopter, however, after observing the strange aerial maneuvers (stop and go), they felt a helicopter couldn't have performed such skills. The light landed in the Coyote Canyon area. Sometime later, three witnessed the light take off and leave proceeding straight up at a highg speed and disappear.

2. Central Security Control (CSC) inside Manzano, contacted Sandia Security, who conducts frequent building checks on two alarmed structures in the area. They advised that a patrol was already in the area and would investigate.

3. On 11 Aug 80, RUSS CURTIS, Sandia Security, advised that on 9 Aug 80, a Sandia Security Guard, (who wishes his name not be divulged for fear of harassment), related the following: At approximately 0020hrs., he was driving East on the Coyote Canyon access road on a routine building check of an alarmed structure . As he approached the structure he observed a bright light near the ground behind the structure. He also observed an object he first thought was a helicopter. But after driving closer, he observed a round disk shaped object. He attempted to radio for a back up patrol but his radio would not work. As he approached the object on foot armed with a shotgun, the object took off in a vertical direction at a high rate of speed. The guard was a former helicopter mechanic in the U.S. Army and stated the object he observed was not a helicopter.

4. SOURCE advised on 22 Aug 80, three other security policemen observed the same

DATE FORWARDED HQ AFOSI	AFOSI FORM 88 ATTACHED	YES	NO
Hq 1 V O S 10 Aug 80			

DATE	TYPED OR PRINTED NAME OF SPECIAL AGENT	SIGNATURE
3 Sept 80	RICHARD C. DOTY, SA	Richard C. Doty

DISTRICT FILE NO	DCII RESULTS
8017 93-c/29	NEGATIVE ✓ POSITIVE (See Attached)

AFOSI FORM 1 JUN 76   PREVIOUS EDITION WILL BE USED

A US Air Force Office of Special Investigations complaint form describing the intrusions by unidentified flying objects over sensitive nuclear storage areas at Kirtland Air Force Base, Albuquerque, New Mexico, in August 1980. (*US Air Force*)

CONTINUED FROM COMPLAL FORM 1, DTD 9 Sept 80

aerial phenomena described by the first three. Again the object landed in Coyote Canyon. They did not see the object take off.

5. Coyote Canyon is part of a large   restricted test range used by the Air Force Weapons Laboratory, Sandia Laboratories, Defense Nuclear Agency and the Department of Energy. The range was formerly patrolled by Sandia Security, however, they only conduct building checks there now.

6. On 10 Aug 80, a New Mexico State Patrolman sighted a aerial object land in the Manzano's between Belen and Albuquerque, NM. The Patrolman reported the sighting to the Kirtland AFB Command Post, who later referred the patrolman to the AFOSI Dist 17. AFOSI Dist 17 advised the patrolman to make a report through his own agency. On 11 Aug 80, the Kirtland Public Information office advised the patrolman the USAF no longer investigates such sightings unless they occurs on an USAF base.

7. WRITER contacted all the agencies who utilized the test range and it was learned no aerial tests are conducted in the Coyote Canyon area. Only ground tests are conducted.

8. On 8 Sept 80, WRITER learned from Sandia Security that another Security Guard observed a object land near an alarmed structure sometime during the first week of August, but did not report it until just recently for fear of harassment.

9. The two alarmed structures located within the area contains HQ CR 44 material.

The object was described by Cash as an extremely bright light with no distinct shape, but Landrum thought it was oblong with a rounded top and a pointed lower half. Colby is certain that it was diamond-shaped. The bursts of flame coincided with sounds 'like a flame thrower', and a 'roaring' as well as a 'beeping' noise lasted throughout the encounter. The car was so hot that Cash was unable to touch the door with her bare hand.

The witnesses followed the object in the car and noticed that about twenty-three twin-rotor helicopters (later identified as Chinooks) appeared to be escorting the fiery object, but never getting closer than about three-quarters of a mile. After stopping three more times to watch the spectacle, Cash drove the others home and arrived at her own house at 21.50. Then horrific physical symptoms became apparent.

Betty Cash reported a blinding headache, pains in her neck, and nodules on her head and scalp that burst, seeping clear fluid. Her eyes swelled shut, she was unable to see properly, and she suffered from nausea, vomiting and diarrhoea. Four days later she was admitted as a burn victim to Parkway General Hospital, Houston. Various specialists were called in, but none was able properly to diagnose her complaints. A week after leaving hospital Cash had to return, still suffering from headaches, nausea, swelling and loss of appetite. Even more alarming, her hair began falling out, leaving a temporary bald patch. By the end of February 1981 Cash's medical bill had risen to $10,000. Finally, she developed breast cancer and had to have a mastectomy, although this may be coincidental.

The other witnesses, who spent less time outside the car, were irradiated to a lesser degree. Vickie Landrum suffered from inflammation of the eyes and temporary loss of some hair, and developed line-like indentations across her fingernails. Colby suffered from 'sunburn' on his face as well as eye inflammation.[57]

There is no question that the three witnesses were subjected to varying degrees of radiation emitting from a vehicle of unknown origin. But whose was it? The presence of helicopters escorting the object suggests that it was an experimental device that had malfunctioned, the main purpose of the helicopters being to ensure that in the event of a forced landing the area could be sealed off immediately by troops. I have heard several rumours from normally reliable sources that the device was either a nuclear-powered experimental space shuttle or a 'lighting device' that had got into difficulties. The device apparently has an auxiliary conventional rocket propulsion unit. Intriguing but less reliable rumours suggest that the object was a nuclear-powered device on a test flight as part of 'Project Snowbird' – supposedly established in 1972 to test-fly a recovered alien vehicle. In 1988 the rumour was reinforced when an intelligence officer claimed that 'the craft was an alien craft piloted by military aircraft pilots'.[58]

Betty Cash and Vickie Landrum are in no doubt that the craft was American, and sued the US Government for $20 million damages. I kept in touch with Peter Gersten (their lawyer) as the case dragged on in the US District Court, Houston. In August 1986 the case was dismissed on the grounds that no such object was owned, operated, or in the inventory of the Air Force, the Army, the Navy or NASA (experts from each were represented in court). But, as the principal investigator of the case, John Schuessler, emphasizes, hardly any attention was paid to the evidence regarding the twenty-three helicopters (there were additional witnesses). 'Judge Ross Sterling considered the expert testimony to be sufficient reason to dismiss the case,' he says. 'That means he will not meet Betty Cash, Vickie and Colby Landrum, and he will not hear the evidence they wanted their attorneys to present.'[59]

Close Encounters of the Third Kind – a Reality

During a talk given to the Tulsa, Oklahoma, Astronomy Club in 1982, former Air Force intelligence officer Steve Lewis revealed that the twelve years he spent investigating UFOs for the military both in the US *and* abroad convinced him that intelligent extraterrestrial beings are visiting Earth. Apologizing for being unable to be more specific owing to strict orders from the Air Force not to divulge specific details about his UFO research from 1965 to 1977 (including a period with Project Blue Book), Lewis stated that only a fraction of information accumulated by the military has been released. He admitted that, although the majority of sightings have a mundane explanation, the bona-fide reports are often associated with a common feature of very bright, blinding lights. The Air Force believes that the light may be related to an advanced propulsion system, enabling UFOs to travel at the speed of light, Lewis said.

'That movie *Close Encounters of the Third Kind* is more realistic than you'd believe,' he told the audience. 'You can believe that or not.'

Pressed to reveal what had convinced him that UFOs are extra-terrestrial spacecraft rather than top-secret military devices, Lewis commented: 'The records, the information I saw while in my job. I no longer rule out what the possibilities might be.'[60]

Central Intelligence

THE CENTRAL INTELLIGENCE AGENCY was formed, with much help from Britain's Secret Intelligence Service, out of the Office of Strategic Services and the Central Intelligence Group in 1947. Officially the CIA employs a staff of about 11,000 (down from 15,000 in the late 1970s), of whom 40 per cent are women, but this figure does not take into account its foreign agents nor the thousands of contracted personnel; nor does it include subsidiary staff from other branches of the US Government.

The CIA is divided into four directorates, each directorate containing many different offices and services. The *Directorate of Operations* oversees foreign intelligence (espionage) as well as counter-intelligence, and includes the Covert Action Staff (disinformation and propaganda). The *Directorate of Science and Technology* monitors scientific and technical developments in foreign countries, and includes the Foreign Broadcast Information Service and the National Photographic Interpretation Center. The *Directorate of Intelligence* is largely responsible for the analysis (and production) of intelligence, with offices of analysis for numerous foreign countries. It also includes the Office of Scientific and Weapons Research, the Office of Imagery Analysis, and the Office of Global Issues. The *Directorate of Administration* is responsible for personnel, training, finance, medical service, security, logistics and communications.[1]

Above these four directorates is the *National Intelligence Council* (formerly the Intelligence Resources Advisory Committee), which co-ordinates the various methods of intelligence-gathering according to the priorities assigned to the requests that are presented to it. At the same level of authority are the National Intelligence Officers who prepare the National Intelligence Estimates which go to the National Security Council and sometimes to the President.[2,3]

According to Todd Zechel, a former employee of the National Security Agency, all four directorates of the CIA have been engaged in collecting, analysing and suppressing UFO data since 1948. Zechel claims that the National Photographic Interpretation Center has been analysing all UFO photographic data, and the Office of Scientific Intelligence (as it used to be called) has been analysing worldwide UFO data since its inception, including non-photographic cases, physical evidence and secondary analysis of photographic cases.

Zechel further claims that domestic reports were collected by the CIA from the Air Force and from other intelligence agencies such as the NSA and the Defense Intelligence Agency. Domestic reports have been collected from the CIA's Domestic Collection Division offices in cities throughout the United States, he maintains. Foreign reports were collected by the National Foreign Assessment Center via the Foreign Broadcast Information Service, the Office of Current Intelligence and the Office of Operations, as these departments were called in the 1970s.

Zechel also makes the disturbing claim that agents of the CIA's Directorate of Operations have interrogated UFO witnesses and that agents of the Domestic Collection Division have been involved in harassing, intimidating and silencing witnesses.[4] Is there evidence for these claims, made by Zechel in 1977?

The CIA and the Freedom of Information Act

It is due largely to the efforts of Todd Zechel, together with William Spaulding of Ground Saucer Watch (GSW), an Arizona-based UFO research organization, that almost 1,000 pages of CIA UFO-related documents were released under the Freedom of Information Act in 1978, following months of legal battles. Henry Rothblatt and Peter Gersten, two New York lawyers who acted on GSW's behalf, had sued the CIA in 1977 under the FOIA in a successful attempt to force the Agency to release its files on UFOs. On 20 December 1978 a press release announcing 'CIA Releases UFO Documents' was distributed to the news media in Washington, DC. It had been prepared by Citizens Against UFO Secrecy, an organization founded a few months previously by Mr Zechel.[5]

It is believed that there are over 10,000 pages of classified UFO documents at the CIA's headquarters in Langley, Virginia, yet the Agency then admitted to withholding only fifty-seven documents. In 1980 Peter Gersten told me that, based on references in the released documents, it was clear the CIA had failed to disclose the existence of 200 or more documents. Perhaps this can be explained by the fact that in 1980 the House of Representatives passed the Foreign Affairs Committee Bill, which effectively exempted the CIA from the majority of requirements flooding into it under the FOIA[6] (though, out of nine exemptions to

FOIA, not one pertains to UFO records). When researchers such as myself request certain UFO records from the CIA, the NSA, the DIA and other agencies, we are often told that they are exempt from release due to national security or that 'records cannot be released because they have been destroyed'.

The Released Documents

The CIA's public position on UFOs, before release of the documents, is summed up in a letter it wrote to Bill Spaulding, dated 26 March 1976:

> In order that you may be aware of the true facts concerning the involvement of the CIA in the investigation of the UFO phenomena, let me give you the following brief history. Late in 1952, the National Security Council levied upon the CIA the requirement to determine if the existence of UFOs would create a danger to the security of the United States. The Office of Scientific Intelligence established the Intelligence Advisory Committee to study the matter. That committee made the recommendations [in] the Robertson Panel Report. At no time prior to the formation of the Robertson Panel and subsequent to this issuance of the panel's report [January 1953], has the CIA engaged in the study of UFO phenomena. The Robertson Panel Report is the summation of the Agency's interest and involvement in this matter.

The released documents, copies of most of which are in my files, unambiguously show that the CIA's interest in UFOs pre-dates the National Security Council directive to set up the Robertson Panel. It was in fact the CIA that urged the NSC to conduct the investigation, as is evident from the following extracts taken from a four-page Secret memorandum (see pp. 391–4) to the Director of Central Intelligence, General Walter Bedell Smith, from H. Marshall Chadwell, Assistant Director of Scientific Intelligence, dated 24 September 1952:

> 1. Recently an inquiry was conducted by the Office of Scientific Intelligence to determine whether there are national security implications in the problem of 'unidentified flying objects', i.e., flying saucers; whether adequate study and research is currently being directed to this problem in its relation to such national

security implications; and what further investigation and research should be instituted, by whom, and under what aegis.

2. It was found that the only unit of Government currently studying the problem is the Directorate of Intelligence, USAF, which has charged the Air Technical Intelligence Center (ATIC) with the responsibility for investigating the reports of sightings . . . A world-wide reporting system has been instituted and major Air Force bases have been ordered to make interceptions of unidentified flying objects . . .

3. Since 1947, ATIC has received approximately 1500 *official* reports of sightings . . . During 1952 alone, *official* reports totaled 250. Of the 1500 reports, Air Force carries 20 percent as *unexplained* and of those received from January through July 1952 it carries 28 percent *unexplained* . . .

6. . . . public concern with the phenomena . . . indicates that a fair proportion of our population is mentally conditioned to the acceptance of the incredible. In this fact lies the potential for the touching-off of mass hysteria and panic . . .

8. . . . In order to minimize risk of panic, a national policy should be established as to what should be told the public regarding the phenomena . . .

11. I consider this problem to be of such importance that it should be brought to the attention of the National Security Council in order that a community-wide coordinated effort toward its solution may be initiated.

Although Marshall Chadwell states in paragraph 2 that 'the only unit of Government currently studying the problem is the Directorate of Intelligence, USAF', the CIA (and the FBI) had been closely monitoring the phenomenon since 1947, as the documents show. According to investigative journalist Warren Smith, the Office of Strategic Services (OSS), headed by Major General William ('Wild Bill') Donovan, was taking an interest in UFOs before it was subsumed into the newly created CIA in 1947. The 'foo-fighters' were being sighted in increasing numbers during the latter stages of the Second World War, and the OSS was at first convinced that they were German pilotless probes. Investigation by OSS agents in Europe proved otherwise, and Donovan and his staff decided that the foo-fighters were unusual but harmless phenomena.

Shortly after pilot Kenneth Arnold's famous sighting on 24 June 1947, Smith was told, the OSS met at the prestigious Brooks Club in New York

Declassified by O 53375
date 2 0 APR 1911

MEMORANDUM FOR: Director of Central Intelligence

THROUGH : Deputy Director (Intelligence)

SUBJECT : Flying Saucers

1. Recently an inquiry was conducted by the Office of Scientific Intelligence to determine whether there are national security implications in the problem of "unidentified flying objects," i.e., flying saucers; whether adequate study and research is currently being directed to this problem in its relation to such national security implications; and what further investigation and research should be instituted, by whom, and under what aegis.

2. It was found that the only unit of Government currently studying the problem is the Directorate of Intelligence, USAF, which has charged the Air Technical Intelligence Center (ATIC) with responsibility for investigating the reports of sightings. At ATIC there is a group of three officers and two secretaries to which come, through official channels, all reports of sightings. This group conducts investigation of the reports, consulting as required with other Air Force and civilian technical personnel. A world-wide reporting system has been instituted and major Air Force Bases have been ordered to make interceptions of unidentified flying objects. The research is being conducted on a case basis and is designed to provide a satisfactory explanation of each individual sighting. ATIC has concluded an arrangement with Battelle Memorial Institute for the latter to establish a machine indexing system for official reports of sightings.

3. Since 1947, ATIC has received approximately 1500 official reports of sightings plus an enormous volume of letters, phone calls, and press reports. During July 1952 alone, official reports totaled 250. Of the 1500 reports, Air Force carries 20 percent as unexplained and of those received from January through July 1952 it carries 28 percent unexplained.

4. In its inquiry into this problem, a team from CIA's Office of Scientific Intelligence consulted with a representative of Air Force Special Studies Group; discussed the problem with those in charge of the Air Force Project at Wright-Patterson Air Force Base; reviewed a considerable volume of intelligence reports; checked the Soviet press and broadcast indices; and conferred with three CIA consultants, who have broad knowledge of the technical areas concerned.

A Secret memorandum from the Assistant Director, Scientific Intelligence, to the Director of Central Intelligence, 1952. (*CIA*)

5. It was found that tho ATIC study is probably valid if the purpose is limited to a case-by-case explanation. However, that study does not solve the more fundamental aspects of the problem. These aspects are to determine definitely the nature of the various phenomena which are causing these sightings, and to discover means by which these causes, and their visual or electronic effects, may be identified immediately. The CIA consultants stated that those solutions would probably be found on the margins or just beyond the frontiers of our present knowledge in the fields of atmospheric, ionospheric, and extraterrestrial phenomena, with the added possibility that the present disposal of nuclear waste products might also be a factor. They recommended that a study group be formed to perform three functions:

    a. analyze and systematize the factors which constitute the fundamental problem;

    b. determine the fields of fundamental science which must be investigated in order to reach an understanding of the phenomena involved; and

    c. make recommendations for the initiation of appropriate research.

Dr. Julius A. Stratton, Vice President of the Massachusetts Institute of Technology, has indicated to CIA that such a group could be constituted at that Institute. Similarly, Project Lincoln, the Air Force's air defense project at MIT, could be charged with some of these responsibilities.

6. The flying saucer situation contains two elements of danger which, in a situation of international tension, have national security implications. These are:

    a. Psychological - With world-wide sightings reported, it was found that, up to the time of the investigation, there had been in the Soviet press no report or comment, even satirical, on flying saucers, though Gromyko had made one humorous mention of the subject. With a State-controlled press, this could result only from an official policy decision. The question, therefore, arises as to whether or not these sightings:

    (1) could be controlled,

    (2) could be predicted, and

    (3) could be used from a psychological warfare point of view, either offensively or defensively.

Unclassified

The public concern with the phenomena, which is reflected both
in the United States press and in the pressure of inquiry upon the
Air Force, indicates that a fair proportion of our population
is mentally conditioned to the acceptance of the incredible.
In this fact lies the potential for the touching-off of mass
hysteria and panic.

    b. <u>Air Vulnerability</u> – The United States Air Warning System
will undoubtedly always depend upon a combination of radar screening and visual observation. The U.S.S.R. is credited with the
present capability of delivering an air attack against the
United States, yet at any given moment now, there may be
current a dozen <u>official</u> unidentified sightings plus many
unofficial ones. At any moment of attack, we are now in a
position where we cannot, on an instant basis, distinguish
hardware from phantom, and as tension mounts we will run the
increasing risk of false alerts and the even greater danger
of falsely identifying the real as phantom.

    7. Both of these problems are primarily operational in nature
but each contains readily apparent intelligence factors.

    8. From an operational point of view, three actions are
required:

    a. Immediate steps should be taken to improve identification
of both visual and electronic phantom so that, in the event of
an attack, instant and positive identification of enemy planes
or missiles can be made.

    b. A study should be instituted to determine what, if any,
utilization could be made of these phenomena by United States
psychological warfare planners and what, if any, defenses should
be planned in anticipation of Soviet attempts to utilize them.

    c. In order to minimize risk of panic, a national policy
should be established as to what should be told the public
regarding the phenomena.

    9. Other intelligence problems which require determination
are:

    a. The present level of Soviet knowledge regarding
these phenomena.

    b. Possible Soviet intentions and capabilities to
utilize these phenomena to the detriment of United States
security interests.

SECRET

   c. The reasons for silence in the Soviet press regarding flying saucers.

10. Additional research, differing in character and emphasis from that presently being performed by Air Force, will be required to meet the specific needs of both operations and intelligence. Intelligence responsibilities in this field as regards both collection and analysis can be discharged with maximum effectiveness only after much more is known regarding the exact nature of these phenomena.

11. I consider this problem to be of such importance that it should be brought to the attention of the National Security Council in order that a community-wide coordinated effort towards its solution may be initiated.

                      H. MARSHALL CHADWELL
                      Assistant Director
                      Scientific Intelligence

and organized a funded effort to establish the truth about the flying discs. At first it was believed that the Russians were responsible, assisted by captured German scientists, but certain characteristics of the reports negated this theory. The OSS was concerned that such sightings could cause panic, and that phone lines and military communication channels would be swamped. The flying saucers had to be debunked. Psychological warfare and propaganda were brought to bear, using hoaxes, false sightings and wild reports. Articles ridiculing flying saucers were planted in national newspapers and magazines.[7] The practice of deception, denial and cover-up regarding US Government involvement in UFO intelligence and exploitation continues to the present time. A CIA memorandum, dated 31 March 1949 and classified 'Secret' from one H. L. Bowers to a Dr Machle, subject 'Notes and Comments on "Unidentified Flying Objects" – Project Sign' (the first official US Air Force study), concluded:

> Studies on the various possibilities have been made by Dr. Langmuir of GE, Dr. Valley of MIT, Dr. Lipp of Project Rand, Dr. Hynek of Ohio State and Aero Medical Lab.
>
> That the objects are from outer space or are an advanced aircraft of a foreign power is a possibility, but the above group have concluded that it is highly improbable.
>
> In discussion of this subject with Mr. Deyarmond at Wright Patterson Air Force Base, he seemed to think, and I agree, that the 'flying discs' will turn out to be another 'sea-serpent'. However, since there is even a remote possibility that they may be interplanetary or foreign aircraft, it is necessary to investigate each sighting.

Evidence that the CIA was monitoring the UFO phenomenon for several years before the Robertson Panel in 1953 is contained in several documents. One, caveated 'Eyes Only', is a memorandum from Ralph L. Clark, Acting Assistant Director for the Office of Scientific Intelligence, to the Deputy Director of Intelligence, dated 29 July 1952:

> In the past several weeks a number of radar and visual sightings of unidentified aerial objects have been reported. Although this office has maintained a continuing review of such reported sightings during the past three years, a special study group has been formed to review this subject to date. O/CI [Office of Central

Intelligence] will participate in this study with O/SI [Office of Scientific Intelligence] and a report should be ready by 15 August.

Another document, a Secret memorandum written on 1 August 1952, was from Edward Tauss, then Acting Chief of the Weapons and Equipment Division of the Office of Scientific Intelligence, to the Deputy Assistant Director of the OSI. Although expressing scepticism about the reliability of even the unexplained reports, Tauss nevertheless adds:

. . . so long as a series of reports remains 'unexplainable' (interplanetary aspects and alien origin not being thoroughly excluded from consideration) caution requires that intelligence continue coverage of the subject . . . It is recommended that CIA surveillance of subject matter, in coordination with proper authorities of primarily operational concern at ATIC, be continued. It is strongly urged, however, that no indication of CIA interest or concern reach the press or public, in view of their probable alarmist tendencies to accept such interest as 'confirmatory' of the soundness of 'unpublished facts' in the hands of the U.S. Government.

The CIA special study group was established in August 1952, and the documents relating to the briefing – classified 'Secret' at the time – make interesting reading. The first is dated 14 August:

During the past weeks, with the phenomenal increase in the number of Flying Saucer reports there has been a tremendous stimulation of both public and official interest in the subject. Requests for information have poured in on the Air Force, including an official query from the White House . . .

At this point, OSI felt that it would be timely to make an evaluation of the Air Force study, its methodology and coverage, the relation of its conclusions to various theories which have been propounded, and to try to reach some conclusion as to the intelligence implications of the problem – if any. In view of the wide interest within the Agency, this briefing has been arranged so that we could report on the survey. It must be mentioned that outside knowledge of Agency interest in Flying Saucers carries the risk of making the problem even more serious in the public mind than it already is, which we and the Air Force agree must be avoided.

The report adds that 'we have reviewed our own intelligence, going back to the Swedish sightings of 1946', and lists the various types of UFO reported to the Air Force:

> Grouped broadly as visual, radar, and combined visual and radar, ATIC has two major visual classes – first, spherical or elliptical objects, usually of bright metallic luster, some small (2 or 3 feet across), most estimated at 100 foot diameter and a few 1000 feet wide. There are variants in this group, such as torpedos, triangulars, pencils, even mattress-shapes. These are all daylight reportings.
>
> The second visual group, all night reporting, consists of lights and various luminosities, such as green, flaming-red or blue-white fire balls, moving points of light, and luminous streamers.
>
> Both categories are reported as single objects, in non-symmetrical groups and in formations of various numbers.
>
> Reported characteristics include three general levels of speed: hovering; moderate, as with a conventional aircraft; and stupendous, up to 18,000 miles per hour in the White Sands Incident. Violent maneuvering was reported in somewhat less than 10%. Accelerations have been given as high as 20 g's. With few exceptions, there has been a complete absence of sound or vapor trail. Evasion upon approach is common.
>
> Radars have shown many unidentified 'blips' but there is no reported instance of complete tracking in and out of the maximum drum, and no report of a track from station to station. The blip, in almost every case, passed through the center of the scope.

Various instances of radar/visual sightings are cited, including one that 'occurred a few days ago at Wright Field and has not yet been fully analyzed. Two F-94's with camera guns were vectored in on a blip. Both pilots sighted an object and one locked on with his AI [airborne intercept] equipment. Reaching his maximum allowable altitude, he triggered his camera and the negative shows "an object".'

The CIA reviewed the likelihood that the UFOs were US weapons, and concluded that the hypothesis was untenable:

> This has been denied officially at the highest level of government and to make certain we queried Dr. Whitman, Chairman of the

Research and Development Board. On a Top Secret basis, he, too, denies it. However, in view of the Manhattan District early super security [relating to the first atom bomb], two factors might be mentioned which tend to confirm his denials – first, the official action of alerting all Air Force commands to intercept, and second, the unbelievable risk aspect of such flights in established airlanes.

The CIA also ruled out the possibility that UFOs were Soviet secret weapons. 'Though we know that the Russians have done work on elliptical and delta wing principles,' the report states, 'we have absolutely no intelligence of such a technological advance as would be indicated here in either design or energy source. Further, there seems to be no logical reason for the security risk which would be involved and there has been no indication of a reconnaissance pattern.'

The extraterrestrial hypothesis was then reviewed by the CIA/OSI special study group:

Even though we might admit that intelligent life may exist elsewhere and that space travel is possible, there is no shred of evidence to support this theory at present. There have been no astronomical observations in confirmation – no slightest indication of the orbitting which would probably be necessary – and no tracking. However, it might be noted that Comdr. McLaughlin (of the White Sands report), a number of General Mills balloon people and many others are reported to be convinced of this theory.

Although the group stated that there was not a shred of evidence to support the extraterrestrial hypothesis, at least one crashed disc was recovered in New Mexico in July 1947. However, absurd though this may seem, there is now so much substantive evidence that I have reviewed it in Chapter 18. Why was the CIA not informed about it? In my view, the explanation is simple. Owing to strict compartmentalization of intelligence – restricting the Agency's extremely sensitive information (ESI) to those with a 'need to know' – the facts about the New Mexico discs (and possibly others) were restricted to those with more sensitive accesses than those of the group, and the *full* facts were further restricted to the small and highly secret group, headed by Dr Vannevar Bush, referred to by Wilbert Smith in a Top Secret Canadian Government document (see pp.

181–3). One of the alleged members was Rear Admiral Roscoe Hillen-koetter, the CIA's first director (1947–50), whose statements attesting to the reality and non-terrestrial origin of UFOs appear later in this chapter.

As to the group's statement that there had been no astronomical observations or evidence of orbiting that would tend to support the extraterrestrial hypothesis, there is an interesting story related by journalist Warren Smith in this connection. Smith allegedly was told by a CIA informant that in 1953 the US Air Force developed a sophisticated radar tracking-system which detected huge unidentified objects orbiting at 100 to 500 miles above the Earth on thirteen different occasions that year. This alarming information was relayed to the Department of Defense and the CIA, and a tracking-station was set up at the White Sands Proving Grounds, New Mexico, under the direction of the eminent astronomer Dr Clyde Tombaugh, the discoverer of Pluto in 1930 and a person who witnessed several UFOs in the late 1940s. In an article published in February 1954 for the Astronomical Society of the Pacific, Tombaugh confirmed that such a tracking-system existed, but stated that the project was sponsored by the Army Ordnance Research Department to keep an accurate check on 'natural phenomena' in space.[8]

Finally, there is the 1952 CIA comment on the fourth major theory, then held by the Air Force, that, given adequate data, the sightings could be explained on the basis of either misinterpretation of known objects or of as yet poorly understood natural phenomena. This theory was endorsed in a lengthy briefing by a certain Mr Eng, who nevertheless concluded: '. . . sightings of UFOs reported at Los Alamos and Oak Ridge, at a time when the background radiation count had risen inexplicably. Here we run out of even "blue yonder" explanations that might be tenable, and we still are left with numbers of incredible reports from credible observers.'

Another review of the CIA/OSI study group's findings is to be found in a sanitized copy of a six-page document dated 19 August 1952, originally classified 'Secret'. The CIA was puzzled not to have found 'one report or comment, even satirical, in the Russian press. This could result only from an official policy decision and of course raises the question of *why* and of whether or not these sightings could be used from a psychological warfare point of view either offensively or defensively.' The document continues:

> Air Force is aware of this and had investigated a number of the civilian groups that have sprung up to follow the subject. One – the Civilian Saucer Committee in California has substantial funds,

MEMORANDUM TO: The Executive Secretary
National Security Council

SUBJECT: Unidentified Flying Objects (Flying Saucers)

1. The Central Intelligence Agency has reviewed the current situation concerning unidentified flying objects which have caused extensive speculation in the press and have been the subject of concern to Government organizations. The Air Force, within the limitations of manpower which could be devoted to the subject, has thus far carried the full responsibility for investigating and analyzing individual reports of sightings. Since 1947, approximately 2000 official reports of sightings have been received and, of these, about 20% are as yet unexplained.

2. It is my view that this situation has possible implications for our national security which transcend the interests of a single service. A broader, coordinated effort should be initiated to develop a firm scientific understanding of the several phenomena which apparently are involved in these reports, and to assure ourselves that the incidents will not hamper our present efforts in the Cold War or confuse our early warning system in case of an attack.

3. I therefore recommend that this Agency and the agencies of the Department of Defense be directed to formulate and carry out a program of intelligence and research activities required to solve the problem of instant positive identification of unidentified flying objects. A draft of an appropriate directive is attached.

Walter B. Smith
Director

Enclosure

Declassified by _____
Date _____

'It is my view that this situation has possible implications for our national security which transcend the interest of a single service. A broader, coordinated effort should be initiated to develop a firm scientific understanding of the several phenomena which apparently are involved in these reports . . .' Walter B. Smith, Director of Central Intelligence, to the Executive Secretary of the National Security Council (previously classified Secret), 1952.

(CIA)

NATIONAL SECURITY COUNCIL DIRECTIVE

SUBJECT: Unidentified flying objects.

Pursuant to the provisions of Section 102 of the National Security Act of 1947 and for the purposes annunciated in Paragraphs d and e thereof, the National Security Council hereby authorizes and directs that:

1. The Director of Central Intelligence shall formulate and carry out a program of intelligence and research activities as required to solve the problem of instant positive identification of unidentified flying objects.

2. Upon call of the Director of Central Intelligence, Government departments and agencies shall provide assistance in this program of intelligence and research to the extent of their capacity provided, however, that the DCI shall avoid duplication of activities presently directed toward the solution of this problem.

3. This effort shall be coordinated with the military services and the Research and Development Board of the Department of Defense, with the Psychological Strategy Board and other Governmental agencies as appropriate.

4. The Director of Central Intelligence shall disseminate information concerning the program of intelligence and research activities in this field to the various departments and agencies which have authorized interest therein.

Declassified by ____
date _____

strongly influences the editorial policy of a number of newspapers and has leaders whose connections may be questionable. Air Force is watching this organization because of its power to touch off mass hysteria and panic. Perhaps we, from an intelligence point of view, should watch for any indication of Russian efforts to capitalize upon this present American credulity.

Of even greater moment is the second danger. Our air warning system will undoubtedly always depend upon a combination of radar scanning and visual observation. We give Russia the capability of delivering an air attack against us, yet at any given moment now, there may be current a dozen *official* unidentified sightings plus many unofficial. At the moment of attack, how will we, on an instant basis, distinguish hardware from phantom? The answer of course [deleted] is that until far greater knowledge is achieved of the causes back of the sightings – the little understood phenomena [deleted] has described – we will run the increasing risk of false alerts and the even greater danger of tabbing the real as false.

The CIA continued to be haunted by the spectre of the Third World War being triggered by UFOs mistaken as Soviet missiles or aircraft. The Office of Scientific Intelligence would continue to monitor Russian research and development in the scientific fields involved, the report concluded.

A few days later, evidence of Russia's first mention of the subject was cited in a Secret memorandum from George G. Carey, Assistant Director for Operations, to the Deputy Director of Intelligence, dated 22 August 1952. The second paragraph states:

FBID [Foreign Broadcasts Information Division] has one broadcast on this subject, dated 10 June 1951, which is quoted below:
Summary – In what appears to be Moscow's first mention of Flying Saucers 'Listener's Mailbag' answers questions on the subject to the effect that 'The Chief of Nuclear Physics in the US Naval Research Bureau' explained them recently as used for stratospheric studies. US Government circles knew all along of the harmless nature of these objects, but if they refrained from denying 'false reports, the purpose behind such tactics was to fan war hysteria in the country'.

On 2 December 1952 H. Marshall Chadwell, Assistant Director of Scientific Intelligence, sent a Secret memorandum to the CIA Director, discussing the preparation of the National Security Council directive referred to earlier. Paragraph 4 makes particularly interesting reading:

Recent reports reaching CIA indicated that further action was desirable and another briefing by the cognizant A-2 [Air Force Intelligence] and ATIC [Air Technical Intelligence Center] personnel was held on 25 November. At this time, the reports of incidents convince us that there is something going on that must have immediate attention . . . Sightings of unexplained objects at great altitudes and traveling at high speeds in the vicinity of major U.S. defense installations are of such nature that they are not attributable to natural phenomena or known types of aerial vehicles.

The Robertson Panel Report

Evidently, by the end of 1952 the situation became so worrying for the CIA that a panel of scientists was convened by the Office of Scientific Intelligence, and secret meetings were held at the Pentagon from 14 to 17 January 1953. Although sanitized copies had been available to certain officials outside the CIA for a number of years, the Robertson Panel Report (sometimes referred to as the Durant Report) was not completely declassified until 1975. To this day there are those who believe that the report has not been released in its entirety. I wrote to the CIA in 1975 requesting a copy (under the FOIA), and it arrived a few months later.

Members of the Scientific Advisory Panel were Dr H. P. Robertson (Chairman), whose speciality was physics and weapons systems; Dr Luis Alvarez (physics and radar); Dr Lloyd V. Berkner (geophysics); Dr Samuel Goudsmit (atomic structure and statistical problems), and Dr Thornton Page (astronomy and astrophysics). The associate members were Dr J. Allen Hynek (astronomy) and Frederick C. Durant (missiles and rockets).

Interviewees were Brigadier William H. Garland, Commanding General of Air Technical Intelligence Center; Dr H. Marshall Chadwell, Assistant Director of the CIA/OSI; Ralph L. Clark, Deputy Assistant Director CIA/OSI; Lieutenant Colonel F. C. Oder and D. B. Stevenson, OSI staff members; Philip G. Strong, Chief, Operations Staff, OSI; Stephen T. Possony, Acting Chief, Special Study Group, Directorate of Air Force Intelligence; Colonels William A. Adams and Wesley S. Smith, also of Air

Force Intelligence; Major Dewey Fournet, Headquarters, Air Force Intelligence Monitor of the UFO Project; Captain Edward J. Ruppelt, Chief, Aerial Phenomena Branch, ATIC; Lieutenant R. S. Neasham and Henry Woo of the US Navy Photo Interpretation Laboratory, and Albert M. Chop, the Air Force press officer handling UFO enquiries.

After twelve hours of meetings, during which the panel was shown movie films of UFOs, case histories of sightings prepared by the ATIC, and intelligence reports relating to the Soviet Union's interest in US sightings, as well as numerous charts depicting, for example, frequency and geographic location of sightings, the panel came up with a largely sceptical view of the UFO situation. In Part IV of the report, headed 'Comments and Suggestions of Panel', it was concluded that 'reasonable explanations could be suggested for most sightings . . . by deduction and scientific method it could be induced (given additional data) that other cases might be explained in a similar manner'.

The panel also concluded unanimously that 'there was no evidence of a direct threat to national security in the objects sighted' and that 'the absence of any "hardware" resulting from unexplained UFO sightings lends a "will-of-the-wisp" nature to the ATIC problem. The results of their investigation, to date, strongly indicate that no evidence of hostile act or danger exists.' The panel found no evidence that any of the unexplained objects sighted could be extraterrestrial in origin, but nevertheless noted that:

> Mr. Fournet, in his presentation, showed how he had eliminated each of the known and probable causes of sightings leaving him 'extra-terrestrial' as the only one remaining in many cases. Fournet's background as an aeronautical engineer and technical intelligence officer (Project Officer, BLUEBOOK for 15 months) could not be slighted. However, the Panel could not accept any of the cases sighted [sic] by him because they were raw, unevaluated reports . . . Dr. Page noted that present astronomical knowledge of the solar system makes the existence of intelligent beings . . . elsewhere than on the earth extremely unlikely, and the concentration of their attention by any controllable means confined to any one continent of the earth quite preposterous.

The panel members were in agreement with the opinion of OSI that, although there was no evidence of direct threat from the sightings, related dangers might result from the following: '(a) Misidentification of actual enemy artifacts by defense personnel. (b) Overloading of emergency reporting channels with "false" information . . . (c) Subjectivity of public to mass hysteria and greater vulnerability to possible enemy psychological warfare.'

One of the panel's recommendations was that a policy of debunking UFO reports should be instigated:

The 'debunking' aim would result in reduction in public interest in 'flying saucers' which today evokes a strong psychological reaction. This education could be accomplished by mass media such [as] television, motion pictures, and popular articles. Basis of such education would be actual case histories which had been puzzling at first but later explained. As is the case of conjuring tricks, there is much less stimulation if the 'secret' is known. Such a program should tend to reduce the current gullibility of the public and consequently their susceptibility to clever hostile propaganda. The panel noted that the general absence of Russian propaganda based on a subject with so many obvious possibilities for exploitation might indicate a possible Russian official policy.

The panel discussed the various insidious methods that could be implemented to execute such a programme: 'It was felt strongly that psychologists familiar with mass psychology should advise on the nature and extent of the program,' the report states, and three specific psychologists were suggested as consultants. Documentary films and cartoons (Walt Disney Inc. being recommended for the latter) were proposed, and 'It was believed that business clubs, high schools, colleges, and television stations would all be pleased to cooperate in the showing of documentary type motion pictures if prepared in an interesting manner. The use of true cases showing first the "mystery" and then the "explanation" would be forceful.' Dr Allen Hynek suggested that amateur astronomers in the US might be a potential source of enthusiastic talent to 'spread the gospel'.

Another sinister recommendation of the panel was that civilian UFO groups should be watched 'because of their potentially great influence on mass thinking if widespread sightings should occur. The apparent irresponsibility and the possible use of such groups for subversive purposes should be kept in mind.'

The panel concluded that 'the continued emphasis on the reporting of these phenomena does, in these parlous times, result in a threat to the orderly functioning of the protective organs of the body politic', and recommended:

a. That the national security agencies take immediate steps to strip the Unidentified Flying Objects of the special status they have been given and the aura of mystery they have unfortunately acquired;
b. That the national security agencies institute policies on intelligence, training, and public education designed to prepare the material defenses and the morale of the country to recognize most promptly and to react most effectively to true indications of hostile intent or action.

We suggest that these aims may be achieved by an integrated program designed to reassure the public of the total lack of evidence of inimical forces behind the phenomena, to train personnel to recognize and reject false indications quickly and effectively, and to strengthen regular channels for the evaluation of and prompt reaction to true indications of hostile measures.

An Air Force Intelligence colonel present at the meetings complained afterwards that the CIA merely wanted to bury the subject. 'We had over a hundred of the strongest verified reports,' he told Major Donald Keyhoe:

The agents bypassed the best ones. The scientists saw just fifteen cases, and the CIA men tried to pick holes in them. Fournet had sightings by top military and airline pilots – even scientists. The agents made it seem as if the witnesses were dopes, so the scientists brushed off the whole Fournet report . . . I know those CIA agents were only following orders, but once or twice I nearly blew up.[9]

Dr Allen Hynek, the Air Force's astronomical consultant on UFOs for Project Blue Book both before and after the Robertson Panel, also expressed criticism. 'I was an associate member of that panel,' he stated, 'but was not invited to participate in all the sessions. I was dissatisfied even then with what seemed to me a most cursory examination of the data and the set minds implied by the Panel's lack of curiosity and desire to delve deeper into the subject.'[10] Dissatisfied he may have been, but Hynek apparently offered his cooperation with the CIA in the debunking programme, as the report shows.

Captain Edward J. Ruppelt, Chief of the ATIC's Aerial Phenomena

Branch, said that the CIA ordered the Air Force to debunk sightings and discredit witnesses. 'We're ordered to hide sightings when possible,' he told Major Keyhoe, 'but if a strong report does get out we have to publish a fast explanation – make up something to kill the report in a hurry, and also ridicule the witness, especially if we can't find a plausible answer. We even have to discredit our own pilots.'[11]

Dr David R. Saunders, who was on the University of Colorado UFO Committee (see later in this chapter) before resigning in disgust at its bias against the subject, believes that the Robertson Panel Report, as released, is no more than a cover story, 'conceived and executed for the dual purposes of confusing foreign intelligence and reassuring the cadre of our own establishment. There is ample precedent for the use of such double and triple layers of security in connection with really important projects. For example, the mere existence of the Manhattan Project was a secret, but the nature and importance of that project was an even bigger secret.'[12]

UFOs – 'Maximum Security'

In 1952 George Adamski claimed to have met an extraterrestrial in the Californian desert, witnessed from a distance by six friends who subsequently signed affidavits to this effect. Adamski's initial experiences were described in *Flying Saucers Have Landed*, a book he co-authored with Desmond Leslie, which became a worldwide best-seller.[13] In his second book, *Inside the Space Ships*, published in 1955, Adamski described further encounters with extraterrestrials.[14] That year, researcher Thomas Eickhoff made an attempt to bring Adamski to federal court so that Adamski could prove, by testimony of two scientists who he claimed had witnessed one of his alleged trips into space, that he really had been on board a space ship. This would give the Government the opportunity to press the case, Eickhoff reasoned, and thereby, when Adamski was (presumably) unable to produce the scientists, they could prosecute him for 'an act of fraud committed by illegal use of the U.S. mail system'.

My lawyer [said Eickhoff] suggested a letter of enquiry to be sent to a certain agency in Washington [the CIA] . . . and called me to his office. He had received the answer which also included instructions for all parties concerned to deny any connections with the statement [which] came from a Mr. [Allen Dulles] of a certain top agency in Washington. Said [Dulles]: 'Yes, I did have a case for Federal Court.' However [he said], by use of the injunction if necessary he would prevent anyone from testifying in court concerning this book because maximum security exists concerning the subject of UFOs.[15]

Allen Welsh Dulles was Director of the CIA from 1953 to 1961. Following a FOIA request to the Agency in 1984, I was sent a copy of a letter from Dulles to the Honourable Gordon H. Scherer, House of Representatives, Washington, DC, dated 4 October 1955:

The questions which Mr. Eickhoff had raised in his letter to you are largely outside of the jurisdiction of this Agency. Section 102(d) of the National Security Act of 1947 provides that the CIA shall have no police, subpoena, law-enforcement powers, or internal security functions. Insofar as Mr. Eickhoff appears interested in pursuing the problem of mail fraud in connection with George Adamski's book entitled 'Inside The Space Ships', it would appear to be a problem of law-enforcement, from which we are specifically barred by statute.

CIA, as a matter of policy, does not comment on the truth or falsity of material contained in books or other published statements, and therefore it is not in a position to comment on Mr. Adamski's book or the authenticity of the pictures which it contains.

The subject matter of Mr. Adamski's book would appear to be more in the jurisdiction of the Department of Defense and the National Science Foundation.

The CIA was unable to locate any further documents pertaining to Adamski. Possibly more exist, possibly not, but certainly the FBI had an extensive file on him, and these documents have now been released and are in my possession. (Adamski's remarkable film of an aerial vehicle taken in 1965 will be discussed in the following chapter.)

Developments in the Office of Scientific Intelligence

On 9 February 1956 a 'Memorandum for the Record' was written by the Chief of the CIA Office of Scientific Intelligence Applied Science Division, W. E. Lexow, confirming that the ASD had now assumed responsibility within OSI for 'Non-Conventional Types of Air Vehicles'. Files would be maintained in ASD on 'incoming raw reports where, *in our judgement*, the subject matter may provide information bearing on *foreign* weapons' system research or development'. Reports in this category were to be forwarded to the 'Fundamental Science Area' for review, and those which did not fit would be forwarded to the FSA for retention or destruction, and reports 'which fit under none of the above will be destroyed'. The memorandum continued (Reference 2):

e. A chronological file of all OSI correspondence and action taken in connection with the United States U.F.O. program will be maintained by ASD.

f. A file of unfinished intelligence reports published by members of the United States intelligence community on U.F.O. will be maintained in ASD.

The Applied Science Division was anxious to avoid the accumulation of reports 'which experience and Reference 2 have shown cannot be analyzed in a manner useful to OSI in carrying out its mission . . . It has been recommended that the raw intelligence and the obsolete finished reports on UFO now filed in Electronics Division will be destroyed.'

In early November 1957, according to researcher Brad Sparks, Congress secretly pressed the CIA for an evaluation of a nationwide UFO 'flap' then in progress. The OSI issued instructions to the Office of Operations' Contact Division to have its field offices collect UFO data for the ensuing one-week period.[16]

The Socorro Landing

During the late afternoon of 24 April 1964 a landed UFO complete with two occupants was reported by Sergeant Lonnie Zamora of the Socorro, New Mexico, Police Department. The case was investigated at the time by the Air Force and the FBI. Dr Allen Hynek also had a hand in the investigations, as did other investigators such as Ray Stanford, who wrote a book detailing his findings.[17] The following is a synopsis of an undated CIA document cited in *Clear Intent*, the ground-breaking book on UFOs and the US intelligence community by Lawrence Fawcett and Barry Greenwood.

Sergeant Zamora was chasing a speeding car on US Highway 85 outside the town of Socorro when he heard a roar and saw flames in an area where a dynamite shack was known to be located. Abandoning the car chase, he headed to the area in search of the cause of the noise and flames. Eventually he came across what he thought was an upturned car and two relatively small humanoid occupants, both dressed in coveralls. Zamora radioed police headquarters and reported that he was going to investigate what he believed to be an automobile accident. Proceeding up the road to a point where he could observe the object, which was in a gully, Zamora stopped the car, got out, and headed towards the object. The CIA report (abbreviated by Fawcett and Greenwood) continues:

> The object was on girderlike legs, white . . . and egg-shaped or oval. As he approached the object there were some noises and flame and smoke began to come from the bottom of the vehicle. The noise increased from low pitch to high pitch, was different from that of a jet or helo [helicopter] and not like anything Sgt. Zamora had ever heard. The flame was blue like a welders torch, turning to orange or yellow at the ends. Thinking that the object was going to explode he became frightened . . . He turned, ran back to get behind the police car, bumping his leg and losing his glasses on the way. He crouched down, shielding his eyes with his arm while the noise continued for another 10 seconds. At this time the noise stopped and he looked up. The object had risen to a point about 15–20 ft. above the ground and the flame had ceased to come from the object. The object had a red marking about 1 ft. or maybe 18 inches in height, shaped like a crescent with a vertical arrow and horizontal line underneath. The object hovered in this spot for several seconds and then flew off in a SW direction following the center of the gully. It cleared the dynamite shack by not more than 3 ft. He watched the object disappear in the distance over a point on Highway 85 about 6 miles from where he was standing. The object took about 3 minutes to travel that far. Disappearance was by fading in the distance and at no time did he observe the object rise more than 20 ft. off the ground.

Zamora had kept radio contact with police headquarters while proceeding to the location. Because the state police used the same radio frequency, his call was monitored by one Sergeant Chavez. Zamora attempted to direct Chavez to the location, but the latter took the wrong road and missed the sighting. When he reached Zamora, three minutes after the object had disappeared, he found that 'Sgt. Zamora was pale and upset at what he had witnessed.' Chavez proceeded to the landing-site. 'Here he found the marks and burns,' the CIA report states. 'Smoke appeared to be coming from a bush which was burned but no flames or coals were visible . . . The marks were fresh and no other marks were in the area. Diagonals of the four impressions intersect in a perpendicular and the major distance seems to be approximately 13 ft. Sgt. Chavez secured the area and contacted local military authorities.'[18]

While there is no official confirmation for the incident, an article subsequently appeared in a classified CIA publication, *Studies in Intelligence*, in which Major Hector Quintanella, head of Project Blue Book at the time, referred to the Socorro case at some length. For some reason, Quintanella avoided any reference to the humanoids (who had hastily boarded their craft when Zamora arrived on the scene) but quoted excerpts from Zamora's own report (which I have further abbreviated), including his description of the object's departure:

> . . . It appeared about directly over the place where it rose from. I was still running . . . [then] about 50 feet from car I ducked down, just over edge of hill . . . I stopped because I did not hear the roar. I was scared of the roar, and I had planned to continue running down the hill. I turned around toward the object and at the same time put my head toward ground, covering my face with my arms . . . When the roar stopped, heard a sharp tone whine [which] lasted maybe a second. Then there was complete silence about the object. That's when I lifted up my head and saw the object going away from me . . . It appeared to go in straight line and at same height . . . The object seemed to lift up slowly, and to get small in the distance very fast. It disappeared as it went over the mountain. It had no flame whatsoever as it was traveling over the ground, and no smoke or noise . . .

'During the course of the investigation and immediately thereafter,' Major Quintanella wrote, 'everything that was humanly possible to verify was checked.' Enquiries at Air Force bases and local airfields, the White Sands Missile Range, the Pentagon, the White House Command Post, as well as with companies engaged in lunar vehicle research, failed to yield a conventional explanation.

'There is no doubt that Lonnie Zamora saw an object which left quite an impression on him,' Quintanella concluded. 'There is also no question about Zamora's reliability. He is a serious officer, a pillar of his church, and a man well versed in recognizing airborne vehicles in his area. He is puzzled by what he saw, and frankly, so are we. This is the best documented case on record.'[19]

The University of Colorado UFO Project

In 1966 the US Air Force contracted with the University of Colorado to make a scientific study of UFOs, headed by physicist Dr Edward Condon. On 20 February 1967 Dr Condon, together with Dr Richard Low, Dr David Saunders, Dr William Price and Dr Rachford, visited the CIA's National Photographic Interpretation Center (NPIC) to familiarize themselves with 'selected photographic analysis capabilities of NPIC'. The following brief extract from a CIA memo dated 23 February 1967 shows how wary the Agency was of allowing Condon's team to reveal the CIA's 'unofficial' interest in the controversial UFO problem:

> Any work performed by NPIC to assist Dr. Condon in his investigation will not be identified as work accomplished by the CIA. Dr. Condon was advised by Mr. Lundahl [NPIC's Director] to make no reference to CIA in regard to this work effort. Dr. Condon stated that if he felt it necessary to obtain an official CIA comment he would make a separate distinct entry into CIA not related to contacts he has with NPIC.[20]

Rumours that the CIA was responsible for the biased negative conclusions of Dr Condon have abounded since his committee's 965-page *Scientific Study of Unidentified Flying Objects* was published in 1969.[21] These conclusions were widely publicized. That 30 per cent of the 117 cases investigated resisted an adequate explanation is seldom mentioned. There can be no denying that Condon and some key members of his committee deliberately set out to convey to the public an image of scientific impartiality, while systematically debunking the subject, as has been shown in a leaked memorandum from Low to Condon, and in Dr David Saunders's book on the inside story of the infamous UFO study.[22]

When Dr Condon was in the process of finalizing the committee's deliberations, he asked UFO researcher Dr James Harder what he would do if he were responsible for a project report that might reflect a conclusion that UFOs were a manifestation of extraterrestrial intelligence. Harder's reaction was:

> I said that I thought there would be other issues than the scientific ones, notably international repercussions and national security. He smiled the smile of a man who sees his own opinions reflected in the opinions of others and said that he had given the matter

much thought, and had decided that if the answer was to be a positive finding of ETH [extraterrrestrial hypothesis], he would not make the finding public, but would take the report, in his briefcase, to the President's Science Adviser, and have the decision made in Washington.[23]

The CIA and NICAP

The most vociferous civilian UFO research organization opposing US Government secrecy in the 1950s and 1960s was the National Investigations Committee on Aerial Phenomena (NICAP), founded by former Navy physicist Thomas Townsend Brown in 1956, then headed for many years by Major Donald Keyhoe, US Marine Corps (Retired). NICAP's board of governors at one time included former Director of the CIA, Rear Admiral Roscoe Hillenkoetter, who had been the Pacific Fleet's chief intelligence officer in the Second World War. While on the NICAP board he made a number of extraordinary statements attesting to the reality and seriousness of the UFO phenomenon. He was convinced that UFOs were unknown objects operating under intelligent control and that 'the Air Force is still censoring UFO sightings. Hundreds of authentic reports by veteran pilots and other technically trained observers have been ridiculed or explained away as mistakes, delusions or hoaxes . . . It is imperative that we learn where the UFOs come from and what their purpose is. The public has a right to know.'

In a signed statement, dated 22 August 1960, sent to Congress, Hillenkoetter wrote:

It is time for the truth to be brought out . . . Behind the scenes high-ranking Air Force officers are soberly concerned about the UFOs. But through official secrecy and ridicule, many citizens are led to believe the unknown flying objects are nonsense . . . I urge immediate Congressional action to reduce the dangers from secrecy about Unidentified Flying Objects . . . Two dangers are steadily increasing:

1. The risk of accidental war from mistaking UFO formations for a Soviet surprise attack.

2. The danger that the Soviet Government may, in a critical moment, *falsely* claim the UFOs as secret Russian weapons against which our defences are helpless.[24]

In 1962 Hillenkoetter suddenly resigned from NICAP. 'In my opinion, NICAP's investigation has gone as far as possible,' he wrote in his letter of resignation. 'I know the UFOs are not U.S. or Soviet devices. All we can do now is wait for some action by the UFOs. The Air Force cannot do any more under the circumstances. It has been a difficult assignment for them, and I believe we should not continue to criticize their investigations.'[25] Keyhoe was convinced that Hillenkoetter had been pressurized 'at a very high level' to resign. Whatever the truth, it was a severe blow to NICAP's prestige. Keyhoe was bitterly disappointed.

Another former CIA official on the board of NICAP was Colonel Joseph J. Bryan III, founder and first chief of the CIA's Psychological Warfare Staff, and former Special Assistant to the Secretary of the Air Force as well as aviation adviser to NATO. In a letter to Keyhoe, Colonel Bryan outlined his evaluation of the UFO problem.

> I am aware that hundreds of military and airline pilots, airport personnel, astronomers, missile trackers and other competent observers have reported sightings of UFOs. I am also aware that many of these UFOs have been reported maneuvering in formation, and that many were simultaneously tracked by radar. It is my opinion that:
>
> The UFOs reported by competent observers are devices under intelligent control. Their speeds, maneuvers and other technical evidence prove them superior to any known aircraft or space devices now produced on earth. These UFOs are interplanetary devices systematically observing the earth, either manned or under remote control, or both.
>
> Information on UFOs, including sighting reports, has been and is still being officially withheld. This policy is dangerous, especially since mistaken identification of UFOs as a secret Russian attack might accidentally set off war. Unless this policy is changed, a Congressional investigation should be held to reduce or eliminate this and other dangers.[26]

This statement was made in 1960, shortly after Bryan joined NICAP. Keyhoe was unaware of Bryan's involvement with the CIA, a fact which did not emerge until 1977, when Bryan admitted to having been a former covert official for the Agency, and asked that this not be made public since 'it might embarrass CIA'. He denied any association with the CIA during the period he served on the board of NICAP.[27]

General Nathan Twining, who as Commanding General of Air Matériel
Command in September 1947 signed a report testifying to the reality of the
UFO phenomenon. (*Popperfoto*)

General George Marshall, US Army Chief of Staff during the Second World War, who reportedly confirmed that the US authorities had retrieved several alien craft and bodies. (*Imperial War Museum*)

'It is my view that this [UFO] situation has possible implications for our national security which transcend the interests of a single service.' General Walter Bedell Smith, Director of Central Intelligence (1950–53), in a memorandum to the National Security Council. (*CIA*)

Douglas MacArthur, General of the US Army, who is believed to have
established the Army's Interplanetary Phenomenon Unit in 1945, and who
in 1955 said that the nations of the world would in the future have to unite
to make a common front against a threat from other planets.
(*Imperial War Museum*)

Right: Leonard Stringfield (1920–94), the former US Air Force intelligence officer and UFO researcher who was the world's leading specialist on cases dealing with recoveries of alien vehicles and occupants. (*Author*)

Below: Part of Roswell Air Force Base, New Mexico. (*Author*)

Congressman Steven Schiff, who instructed the Congress's General Accounting Office to search for official records pertaining to the recovery of unusual materials near Roswell in July 1947. (*Author*)

Major Donald Keyhoe on CBS TV in January 1958, when he was cut off the air in the middle of making a statement testifying that 'UFOs are real machines under intelligent control'. (*CBS*)

'In the firm belief that the American public deserves a better explanation than that thus far given by the Air Force, I strongly recommend that there be a committee investigation of the UFO phenomenon.' Former President Gerald Ford in a letter he sent as a Congressman to the Chairman of the Armed Services Committee, 28 March 1966. (*Popperfoto*)

NASA test pilot Joseph Walker beside the rocket-powered X-15 plane following a record-breaking flight in October 1961. Walker revealed that it was one of his tasks to look for UFOs during his flights in the X-15 and in April 1962 he succeeded in filming some. (*NASA*)

Former astronaut Gordon Cooper, who as a US Air Force pilot chased flying discs over Germany and who confirms that a disc-shaped vehicle landed and was filmed at Edwards Air Force Base, California, in the late 1950s. (*Popperfoto*)

One of two photographs of a craft seen by Stephen Darbishire and his cousin
Adrian Myers, in Coniston, Cumbria, February 1954. (*Stephen Darbishire*)

'Behind the scenes high-ranking Air Force officers are soberly concerned about the UFOs. But through official secrecy and ridicule, many citizens are led to believe the unknown flying objects are nonsense.' Rear Admiral Roscoe Hillenkoetter, Director of Central Intelligence (1947–50). (*CIA*)

Above: Meeting at the United Nations in July 1978 to discuss the need for UN support for UFO studies. Left to right: Gordon Cooper, Jacques Vallée, Claude Poher, J. Allen Hynek, Prime Minister of Grenada Sir Eric Gairy, UN Secretary General Kurt Waldheim and (*near right*) David Saunders and Leonard Stringfield. (*UN/Saw Lwin*)

Left: 'It is my conclusion that UFOs do exist, are very real, and are spaceships from another or more than one solar system.' Professor Hermann Oberth, the great pioneer of space travel. (*Author*)

ve: A light-enhanced frame from the 8mm movie film taken by George nski in the presence of Madeleine Rodeffer and other witnesses at Silver g, Maryland, in February 1965. Note the apparent distortion in this and er frames, believed to be caused by a gravity field associated with the propulsion of the craft. (*Madeleine Rodeffer*)

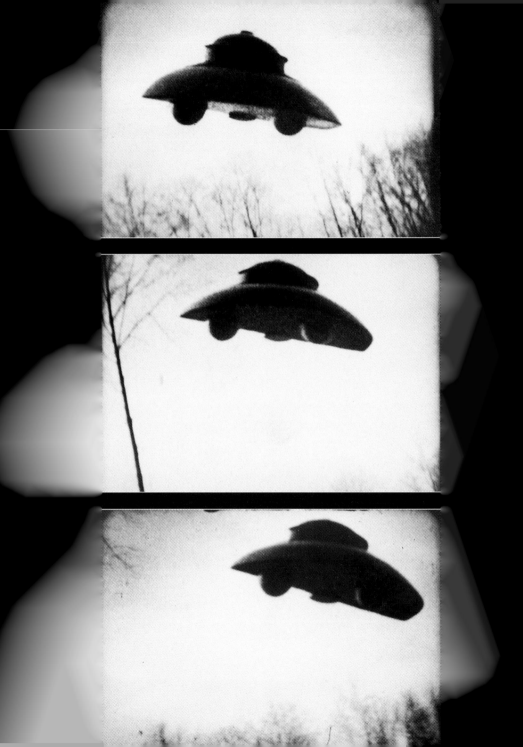

Right: George Adamski (1891–1965). Although some of Adamski's claims relating to his contacts with extraterrestrials may be ludicrous, his photos and films of UFOs – such as those depicted here – are less easy to dismiss.

Below: One of four telescopic photos taken by Adamski at Palomar Gardens, California, in March 1951, showing what he claimed were 'scout craft' leaving a large 'mother ship'. (*George Adamski Foundation*)

Left: Madeleine Rodeffer, outside her home, two years after Adamski's film was taken. (*Author*)

Below: Presidents Ronald Reagan and Mikhail Gorbachev at the Geneva Summit, 1985. 'The US President said that if the Earth faced an invasion by extraterrestrials,' reported Gorbachev, 'the United States and the Soviet Union would join forces to repel such an invasion . . .' (*Associated Press/Topham*)

Infiltration

According to Todd Zechel, a number of covert CIA officers worked themselves into key positions with NICAP. One was Count Nicolas de Rochefort, who had been a member of the CIA's Psychological Warfare Staff, and who became Vice-Chairman of NICAP in the year it was founded. Another was Bernard J. Carvalho, who had been a go-between for such secretly owned companies as Fairway Corporation, a charter airline used by CIA executives. Carvalho was appointed Chairman of NICAP's membership subcommittee at one time.

Zechel further claims that an undated CIA document, anonymously written, indicates familiarity with G. Stuart Nixon, former assistant to NICAP's President, John L. Acuff, and states that in the late 1960s and early 1970s the NICAP daily logs show that Nixon had frequent meetings with several past and present CIA employees. The CIA officials allegedly included Arthur Lundahl, then Director of the CIA's National Photographic Interpretation Center; Frederick Durant, former CIA Office of Scientific Intelligence missile expert and author of the Robertson Panel Report; and Dr Charles Sheldon, a CIA consultant.

Zechel believes that Major Keyhoe was deliberately ousted by the CIA infiltrators in 1969, after which a former head of the Society of Photographic Scientists and Engineers (with putative CIA affiliations), John Acuff, took over as President. 'Maybe it's a coincidence that the founder of the CIA's Psychological Warfare Staff [was] on the board [of NICAP] for nearly twenty years,' wrote Zechel:

Maybe it's another coincidence that Charles Lombard, a former CIA covert employee . . . would seek out a retired CIA executive to run the organization (i.e. after Jack Acuff was replaced by *retired* CIA agent, Alan N. Hall in 1979!) . . . The timing couldn't have been better, in any case. Keyhoe, after all, was beginning to focus on the CIA in 1969, instead of his tunnel-visioned attacks on the Air Force . . .[28]

One documented link between NICAP and the CIA is a letter to researcher Larry Bryant, dated 19 September 1973, from John Maury of the CIA's Legislative Council, which refers to the Agency's contact with Richard H. Hall in 1965.

In January 1965, the Agency made an inquiry into the research being conducted on UFO sightings and contacted Mr. Hall, then Acting Director of the National Investigations Committee on Aerial Phenomena. Mr. Hall explained how his organization operated and loaned the Agency several of its publications which were reviewed and returned. No excerpts were made from the publications, nor did the Agency come to any conclusions on the substance therein. There was no further contact with Mr. Hall or any other representative of his organization, and the Agency had no further interest in the subject of UFOs.

This would seem to argue against CIA infiltration of NICAP. Why would Hall need to explain 'how his organization operated' if the CIA had infiltrated it since 1956? If John Maury was telling the truth, we have to assume that either the lengthy list of NICAP officials with established CIA connections was entirely coincidental – that they joined NICAP out of a purely personal interest – or that Maury was unaware of the true purpose of the meeting with Hall, and knew nothing of the CIA/NICAP background. It is also possible, of course, that Maury was dissembling: the CIA, after all, is of necessity not in the habit of revealing its actions and motives!

A CIA memorandum dated 25 January 1965, with the names of the writer and recipient blacked out ('To Chief, Contact Division, Attention [deleted] from Chief [deleted]') throws further light on the meeting with Hall. It begins: 'This confirms [deleted] conversation 19 January 1965, at which time various samples and reports on UFO sightings procured from NICAP were given to [deleted] for transmittal to OSI. The information was desired by OSI to assist them in the preparation of a paper for [deleted] on UFOs.' There follows a description of NICAP's investigative procedures, with particular reference to Air Force reports:

> A printed form, prepared by the Air Force for NICAP's use, is utilized during the interview . . . It was our understanding that copies of these reports go directly to various Air Force bases. There apparently is a strong feeling on the part of NICAP officials, i.e. Kehoe [sic] and Hall, that the Air Force tends to downgrade the importance of UFO sightings because they (the Air Force) do not care to have too much made of the sightings by the US press. We were told by Mr. Hall that there have been instances where the Air Force has attempted to intimidate witnesses and get them to sign false statements relative to UFO sightings.

A detailed description of NICAP's investigation into radar trackings of UFOs at Patuxent Naval Air Station in December 1964 follows, as well as a sighting report 'within the last week or 10 days' at Constitution Avenue, Washington, DC. According to researcher Brad Sparks, former CIA Director John McCone asked the Office of Scientific Intelligence for an evaluation of the Washington-area wave of sightings at that time – probably, Sparks believes, as a result of the privately expressed concerns of Congressmen. The OSI instructed the CIA's local Contact Division office to approach NICAP for a brief résumé of those sightings. After consultation with the Air Force, the OSI informed McCone of its negative conclusions.[29]

The memo concludes: '[deleted] informed us that she is requesting a security clearance on Mr. Hall predicated upon biographic information provided by [deleted].' Richard Hall has thus far been unable to obtain the CIA's classified files relating to the latter. 'By what right does the CIA maintain a "dossier" on me that I am not allowed to see?' he argues. 'Why, and for what purpose did the CIA run a security clearance or background check on me without my knowledge or consent?'[30]

It is evident that the CIA had become interested in NICAP's activities by 1965 – if not earlier – and an undated CIA memorandum from the early 1970s gives a highly detailed run-down on NICAP's organization and the impressive credentials of its advisory group, and furthermore confirms that ex-CIA personnel were included therein:

> This board relies heavily on both a loosely structured advisory group and a fairly well placed network of investigators. The advisory group is made up of experts in many disciplines including physics, astronomy, anthropology, medicine and psychology. This group also includes some ex-CIA and Defense Intelligence types who advise on investigative techniques and NICAP/Government relations . . .
>
> The system of investigators is a good one . . . As of a few months ago some 35 investigators were located throughout the country, with NICAP in the process of establishing even more. A breakdown of their backgrounds looked like the following: 7 PhDs, 2 MAs or MS, 23 BAs or BS, 1 AA and 2 with college training but no degrees. Occupationally they included 4 physical scientists, 13 engineers, 3 college profs, 13 specialists, including doctor, technician, computer programmer and businessman. Five of the 35 are pilots . . .

It is my belief – shared by some other investigators – that the CIA had become concerned by the enormous influence over public opinion that NICAP undoubtedly wielded at the time. No other organization before or since has so consistently and effectively challenged official attempts to debunk the subject of UFOs. It is hardly surprising that NICAP's influence dwindled significantly from 1970 onward, although other factors may have contributed to this, such as Dr Condon's widely publicized negative conclusions in the *Scientific Study of Unidentified Flying Objects*. Serious problems with management ensued, and NICAP eventually became so ineffective that it was dissolved; its files were taken over in 1973 by Dr Allen Hynek's newly formed Center for UFO Studies (CUFOS).

Lawrence Fawcett and Barry Greenwood offer their opinion – which I share – that the CIA needed to infiltrate NICAP for the following reasons: '(1) To gather intelligence through NICAP's investigators networks. (2) To identify and plug leaks from government sources . . . (3) To monitor other hostile intelligence agencies (NICAP received several overtures from the Soviet KGB).' Fawcett and Greenwood further speculate that, after NICAP's mismanagement, its effectiveness as a CIA front was diminished, and the Agency allowed it to be taken over by CUFOS. They stop short of suggesting that CUFOS itself may have been infiltrated or influenced by the CIA, but nevertheless theorize that this could happen to any prominent UFO group if it became too effective.[31]

It will be recalled that one of the recommendations of the CIA Robertson Panel Report was that civilian UFO groups should be watched, 'because of their potentially great influence on mass thinking if widespread sightings should occur'. With his worldwide knowledge of UFO groups, Dr Hynek would have been invaluable to the CIA as a consultant, and there is a possibility that he may have acted in this capacity ever since he sat on the Robertson Panel in 1953.

Surveillance

Another group which may have come in for CIA surveillance is the former Aerial Phenomena Research Organization (APRO), founded in 1952 by Jim and Coral Lorenzen. In the Robertson Panel Report, APRO was one of two civilian groups to be singled out for monitoring.

One of APRO's earliest supporters was a man who helped with donations and suggestions for the organization. He also claimed to have a background in intelligence work. A letter from him to the Lorenzens in February 1953 had apparently been used as a platen for what looked like an intelligence report on Coral, inadvertently impressed into the paper. The report listed her previous residences and followed with impressions of her personal character.

On other occasions various salesmen turned up at the Lorenzens' home yet showed little interest in promoting their business, preferring instead to engage the couple in conversation. There is no proof that the CIA was involved, though the Lorenzens did establish that at one time they were monitored by the local Air Force Office of Special Investigations. Apparently the AFOSI dossier was favourable, in that neither of them was prevented from obtaining the high-level security clearances that their work in the Air Force entailed at the time.[32]

In 1974 Dr Hynek visited APRO's headquarters in Tucson, Arizona, and tried to persuade the board of directors to give him a list of APRO's field investigators, together with their addresses and telephone numbers.[33] Hynek's motives may well have been innocent, and perhaps we should give him the benefit of the doubt, particularly since he died in April 1986. Yet certain questions remain unanswered.

Dr Robert Creegan, formerly an APRO consultant in social sciences, has also voiced suspicions about Hynek's involvement in the UFO scene. 'Professor Hynek was never asked to be a member of either the Robertson Panel in 1953, nor the Condon Commission, 1966–69. Yet he was able to sit in on at least some of the meetings of both,' he wrote in 1985. 'He made no evident criticism of the evasiveness of the conclusions in either case. As a matter of fact, the astronomer has been able to attend many or most UFO conferences in the US and abroad, and has gone to the locales of major flaps. Obviously funds were adequate . . .'[34]

I do not know if Dr Hynek actually was employed as a CIA consultant subsequent to the Robertson Panel, but it seems evident that he was in an ideal position to perform such a function, with worldwide contacts at official and unofficial levels. Many fellow researchers in a number of countries agree with me that, while Hynek was always interested in gathering information, he seemed reluctant to give out much in return. At the same time, it has to be said that his contribution in putting across this controversial subject to the sceptical scientific fraternity was immense, and for this we owe him a debt of gratitude.

My own experiences of possible surveillance have also been circumstantial. On several occasions in the United States, my hotel rooms have been entered by persons unknown while I was absent: on the first occasion (in the early 1970s) an important research notebook was taken, while expensive photographic equipment lay untouched. I recall that a US Government 'pool' car had been parked outside. In March 1976 I wrote to the CIA Freedom of Information and Privacy Co-ordinator, Gene F. Wilson, thanking him for sending me a copy of the Robertson Panel Report and adding that I was on the point of embarking on a tour of the United States with the London Symphony Orchestra, with a scheduled visit to Washington, DC, between 19 and 23 March. On the last day, my photograph was taken in the lobby of the Statler-Hilton Hotel by a man with a large-format camera and a flashgun. Before I had a chance to approach him, he made a hasty exit. It may have been coincidental, of course, but it led to a suspicion that the CIA could have been responsible, since I had deliberately informed Wilson of my impending visit just to see if any such thing as did happen would.

In 1985 I filed a request under the Privacy Act to review a copy of my possible file with the Agency, and later provided it with a notarized statement attesting to my identity, in accordance with CIA Privacy Regulations. Under the Privacy Act an individual is supposed to be able to see a copy of his or her file (if one exists) so that amendments can be made to any inaccuracies contained therein. In the mid-1970s the Agency's main file index in the Directorate of Operations allegedly contained about 7.5 million names and about 750,000 individual personality files. For collection of intelligence from domestic sources the CIA reputedly had another index, containing about 150,000 names as well as about 50,000 files on 'active' sources, while the Office of Security was said to have about 900,000 files mostly relating to individuals, including 75 members of Congress, in addition to records of approximately 500,000 people who had visited CIA installations.[35] It was not altogether out of the question, I surmised, that in view of my correspondence with the Agency over a ten-year period, and more than a passing interest in its involvement with UFO research, a file on me would exist. I was wrong – apparently.

Nearly a year after my initial FOIA request was filed I received a letter from Lee Strickland, Information and Privacy Co-ordinator, which stated in part: 'Our processing included a search for records in existence as of and through the date of our acceptance letter . . . No records responsive to your request were located . . . We appreciate the patience and understanding during the period required to process this request.' The search costs, consisting of two on-line computer searches, a quarter-hour's professional time, and an hour of clerical search time, amounted to a relatively modest fee.[36]

Missing Evidence

Cases involving missing films, photographs and hardware associated with UFO sightings are plentiful, but it is hard to prove that the CIA is responsible. Nevertheless, federal and military intelligence agencies have definitely 'borrowed' or taken material which has never been returned, as I have mentioned elsewhere in this book.

Todd Zechel claims that photographic evidence found missing from the Air Force Project Blue Book files eventually found its way to the CIA's Office of Scientific Intelligence in the 1950s, and specifies a number of movie films taken at White Sands Proving Grounds, New Mexico: a cinétheodolite film taken by a camera tracking-station on 27 April 1950; another such film taken by two camera stations on 29 May 1950, allegedly showing two huge UFOs travelling at 2,000 m.p.h.; and a 35mm film taken by a military pilot on 14 July 1951. Zechel also specifies an 8mm movie film taken at Port Moresby, New Guinea, on 31 August 1953 (see p. 153), and a reconnaissance photograph taken by a pilot of an RB-29 aircraft on 24 May 1954 near Dayton, Ohio.[37]

Yet another case cited by Zechel relates to a 16mm movie film taken by Ralph C. Mayher, a Marine Corps photographer, on 29 July 1952 at Miami, Florida. Mayher had the film processed immediately and submitted it to the Marine Air Station. Some frames were released to the local press and were published, but within days Mayher was visited by Air Force and CIA investigators, who reportedly told him to keep quiet about the incident. On 31 July the film was given to the Air Force for analysis; it has not been seen since. (The few frames given to the press were returned.) In June 1975 William Spaulding of Ground Saucer Watch wrote to the CIA asking for information about the film, and a lengthy correspondence ensued. Spaulding was unsuccessful in obtaining the data he wanted, but he did manage to learn from the CIA memoranda released to him that some of the information on the Mayher film was still classified.[38,39]

The CIA memoranda in my files contain no reference to the Agency's having examined the film, but it is evident that five stills were studied, and a memo dated 7 November 1957 states that 'the original negatives are in Air Force hands'. Another memo, dated 12 December 1957, adds that the 'five photographs of flying saucers which were obtained from [deleted]' were returned, and that '[deleted] asked if it would be possible for us to submit to him any evaluations which might have been made on these photographs and I replied that it was very doubtful but that I would pass on the request to headquarters'. Back came the reply on 20 December 1957:

We did not receive evaluations of photography which source submitted. For your information only, the material was reviewed at a 'high level' and returned to us without comments . . . The subject of UFO was under the review of CIA for a limited time only. This was caused by a request from 'the hill' [Capitol Hill] which stemmed from all of the publicity given to recent UFO sightings. We assume that the request has been satisfied because the case has been closed and the subject dropped by CIA . . .

No evidence of the actual film having been reviewed or confiscated is contained in the released documents. Probably the writers were unaware of the complete picture – their comments on the CIA's involvement in UFO research betray ignorance – or else the Air Force retained the film. The evidence is arbitrary, but the film has not been returned.

Freelance journalist Warren Smith relates a rather sinister encounter with alleged CIA officers in the 1970s, when he was coerced into handing over a piece of metal that he had acquired from a farmer who had discovered some fragments after witnessing a UFO hovering over his orchard in Wisconsin. Word got around about the incident, and the farmer reported being subsequently visited by a 'fertilizer salesman' who seemed more interested in learning about the samples than in selling fertilizer. The farmer informed the 'salesman' that he had given one of the pieces to Smith. The salesman told the farmer that he was staying in a motel and suggested that it might be the same one as Smith. When Smith learned of this he tied the piece of metal to the inside of his motel room's television set at the Holiday Inn, Madison, as a precaution.

'Within one day, I was the most popular person in Madison, particularly when I was out,' said Smith. 'I asked the maids and motel maintenance man to watch my room during my absence. Two men with a room key were moving in as soon as I left. One maid had the courage to enter the room on the pretense of checking it for cleanliness. She excused herself when she saw the two men going through my suitcase.'

When Smith visited the farmer again he learned that two men in Air Force uniforms had persuaded him to part with his metal fragment, citing 'national security, a danger to the world, and the government's desire to have that fragment of metal' as the reasons. On Smith's return to the motel the two men were waiting in his room – one stretched out on the bed and the other sitting at the desk. After an exchange of false pleasantries one of the men said: 'You have something we want. A farmer gave you a piece of metal the other day. Our job is to pick it up.'

Smith prevaricated for as long as possible, pretending that he had sent the metal to someone else, but the men began to threaten him, warning him that he should think of his wife, children and career. Smith asked for identification. 'Name the agency and we'll produce it,' they replied. 'Would you like Air Force, FBI or maybe NORAD?' Smith finally agreed to give them the piece of metal on condition that they answered a few questions, and the conversation was continued over coffee at the motel restaurant. The men refused to answer questions, of course, but before leaving they revealed that 'UFOs involve more than you or any civilian can realize. They're the most important thing and perhaps the greatest hazard that mankind has ever faced.'

As the men drove off, Smith memorized the car licence number and eventually discovered – with the aid of friends who had access to law-enforcement channels – that the unissued licence plate had been given to a Chicago man with close links to the CIA. Or so Smith claims.[40] It is difficult to know how much credence should be given to the story. Smith neglects to mention the date or the name of the farmer he spoke to, so it is difficult to check the facts. However, I did discuss the alleged incident with the researcher and author Brad Steiger, whom Smith called on the phone immediately following the incident. (Steiger had previously tried contacting Smith at the motel, only to be told that he was not registered there.) Brad told me that, whereas Smith was inclined to exaggerate his stories on occasions and to indulge in practical jokes, in this particular instance he sounded genuinely frightened by the experience he had just undergone.

Warren Smith further claims to have acquired a great deal of knowledge regarding the CIA's involvement in UFO research from an Agency source (in the 1970s), although he freely admits that he might have been fed false information. According to Smith's informant, the CIA maintains a worldwide surveillance on the UFO situation. Foreign journals dealing with the subject, for example, are sent to the agency's foreign-translation departments and, when translated, are fed into computers. The data is cross-indexed and can easily be retrieved,' said Smith.

If someone wants to know how many sightings of low-level flying saucers have been reported in a specific nation, or world-wide, the computer will provide a summary . . . I have obtained data from the computer on several different occasions. It is always quite precise. I'm still a little dubious about the 'help' given by my informant. But it has always proven to be factual.[41]

Disinformation

Miles Copeland, a former CIA organizer and intelligence officer, related an interesting story to me involving the Agency's attempt on one occasion to use fictional UFO sightings to spread disinformation. The purpose, in this case, was to 'dazzle' and 'intoxicate' the Chinese, who had themselves on several occasions fooled the CIA into sending teams to a desert in Sinkiang province, west China, to search for non-existent underground 'atomic energies'.

The exercise took place in the early 1960s, Copeland told me, and involved launching fictional UFO sighting reports from many different areas. The project was headed by Desmond Fitzgerald of the Special Affairs Staff (who made a name for himself by inventing hare-brained schemes for assassinating Fidel Castro). The UFO exercise was 'just to keep the Chinese off-balance and make them think we were doing things we weren't,' Copeland explained:

> The project got the desired results, as I remember, except that it somehow got picked up by a lot of religious nuts in Iowa and Nebraska or somewhere who took it seriously enough to add an extra chapter to their version of the New Testament!
>
> I wouldn't attribute too much Machiavellian thinking behind it, because in those days the CIA was just doing all sorts of things . . . characterized by a lot of rich guys who read too many John Buchan books and were just horsing around![42]

Copeland said that he couldn't recall anything else about the CIA's involvement with UFOs, but this is hardly surprising, since, as he himself acknowledged:

> Regardless of the trust placed in any employee, he is allowed to know only what he needs to know in order to carry out his job. Moreover, these agencies are so organized that their secrets are tightly compartmentalized. Even the Director of the Central Intelligence Agency is 'protected' by need-to-know regulations which keep from him all information that is not essential to his job – and this would be almost all of the detailed information held in his organization.[43]

Declining CIA Interest?

A series of released CIA Domestic Collection Division memoranda written in 1976 give the impression that the Agency was no longer actively engaged in UFO research at this time, although one memo, dated 14 April, confirms that the Agency still retained experts on the subject: 'Source seeks guidance from CIA UFO experts as to material in his report that should remain classified.' A 26 April memo confirms that the CIA was continuing to monitor the subject, but not on an official basis:

> It does not seem that the government has any formal program in progress for the identification/solution of the UFO phenomena. Dr. [deleted] feels that the efforts of independent researchers, [deleted], are vital for further progress in this area. At the present time, there are offices and personnel within the agency who are monitoring the UFO phenomena, but again, this is not currently on an official basis. Dr. [deleted] feels that the best approach would be to keep in touch with and in fact develop reporting channels in this area to keep the agency/community informed of any new developments. In particular, any information which might indicate a threat potential would be of interest, as would specific indications of foreign developments or applications of UFO research . . . We wish to stress again, that there does not now appear to be any special program of UFOs within the intelligence community.

Another CIA/DCD memo written a month later (27 May 1976) states:

> Our source felt that [deleted] work might be of interest to the US Government and that it should be evaluated by the Agency. The source also felt that it could be analyzed outside the context of its UFO connection if necessary to remove it from a controversial subject.
>
> As before we are faced with the problem of having UFO related data which is deemed potentially important for the US by our S&T [Science & Technology] sources, evaluated. As you are aware, at this time there is no channel or working group to which we can turn for this type of analysis and dissemination. Thus, if it is acceptable to you we will continue to periodically advise you or your designee of any new or potentially important FI [Foreign

Intelligence] developments which might arise from current independent scientific research on the UFO phenomena.

Finally, a CIA/DCD memo dated 14 July 1976 sheds further light on the CIA's apparent attitude to the subject at the time:

At a recent meeting to evaluate some material from [deleted], you mentioned a personal interest in the UFO phenomena. As you may recall, I mentiond my own interest in the subject as well as the fact that DCD had been receiving UFO related material from many of our S&T sources who are presently conducting related research. These scientists include some who have been associated with the Agency for years and whose credentials remove them from the 'nut' variety.

The attached material came to my attention through these sources and it appears to have some legitimate FI or community interest potential.

The [deleted] work being carried out by Dr. [deleted] should, in the view of our S&T sources, be evaluated by the Agency or community.

In view of the expertise associated with your office, as well your own interest in the subject, I felt you might like to see the material.

These Domestic Collection Division memoranda appear to indicate the CIA's declining involvement in UFO research, although it is evident that the Agency continued to monitor the subject. Since intelligence is highly compartmentalized, the probability exists that the writers of the DCD memos did not have access to all the information on the subject obtained by the Directorate of Science and Technology, nor other divisions of the Agency. It is also probable that the DCD officers were unaware of any hypothetical above Top Secret research being conducted within the CIA and other intelligence agencies.

From further CIA documents released under the Freedom of Information Act, as well as from more recent documents released by other agencies, such as the Defense Intelligence Agency, it is evident that the CIA continues to monitor the subject, since these other agencies apparently have orders to forward details to the CIA.

In 1983 I wrote to the CIA's Information and Privacy Co-ordinator, Larry R. Strawderman, asking the following questions: Is the CIA still involved in the study of UFO reports? How many – or what percentage – of those reports remain unexplained? Of those unexplained reports, has the Agency found any evidence of extraterrestrial activity, in the sense that intelligently controlled vehicles are operating in our atmosphere? I received the following reply:

> There is no organized Central Intelligence Agency effort to do research in connection with the UFO phenomena, nor has there been an organized effort to collect intelligence on UFOs since the 1950s. Since then there have been sporadic instances of correspondence dealing with the subject and the receipt of various kinds of reports of UFO sightings.
>
> The Agency interest lies in its forewarning responsibility. This interest is principally in the possibility of a hostile power developing new weapon systems which might exhibit phenomena that some might categorize as an UFO.
>
> Under the Freedom of Information Act the only role of my office is to provide Agency records that can be described so that they can be located and reviewed for declassification and release to the public. In view of this, and in view of the fact that this Agency terminated active participation in any investigation into the UFO phenomena many years ago, I regret that I am unable to address the other questions posed in your letter.[44]

Brian Freemantle, author of *CIA*,[45] has confirmed to me that, according to his information, the Agency's involvement in the UFO question was mainly in the early 1950s, and that it has substantially diminished since then. Freemantle considered including a chapter in his book on the Agency's interest in UFOs, but he was unable to obtain enough information. 'The problem was that the CIA's enquiries were conducted largely by their Scientific and Technical division, with whom I had no contacts,' he explained to me.

> As you will be aware, intelligence agencies are strictly compart-mented and people who assisted me did not have access to divisions other than their own. I was told at one stage, however, that the Agency contracted out some of their research through Stanford University, in Palo Alto, California. And that the concentration of enquiries, both in the early 1950s and subsequently, has come under the umbrella of Air Force

intelligence and the National Security Agency – through its electronic expertise – rather than the CIA itself.[46]

Todd Zechel maintains that the NSA has always played a subordinate role to the CIA in this respect, and whatever data it gathered was passed on to the CIA, where it was analysed by the Office of Scientific Intelligence, with the NSA kept in ignorance of the conclusions. Admiral Stansfield Turner, former Director of Central Intelligence (DCI), confirms that the NSA is essentially subservient to the DCI, but that there have been occasions when it has performed its own analysis and failed to turn over the material to the CIA. States Turner:

> The NSA is mandated to collect intelligence, not to analyze it. It must do enough analysis about what it has collected to decide what it should collect next . . . this level of analysis is called 'processing'. Processing is regularly stretched by the NSA into full-scale analysis . . . Although the NSA has excellent analysts to do its processing, it does not have the range of analytic talent needed for responsible analysis, nor all of the relevant data from the other collecting agencies needed for a comprehensive job . . . and is less likely to take account of photographic or human intelligence.

Professional rivalry seems to have caused considerable problems between the two agencies, Turner reports.[47]

To what extent this rivalry has caused problems with regard to analysis of the UFO question I do not know, and my comments to Admiral Turner on the matter were not touched on during our correspondence. I also asked the Admiral: (a) if he was briefed on the subject following his appointment as DCI; (b) whether it was possible that some highly secret information had been withheld from him during his tenure; and (c) if he was aware of the top-secret 'Majestic-12' group, reportedly established under President Truman in 1947 following the retrieval of crashed alien material that year (see Chapter 18). In his friendly and helpful replies, the former DCI pointed out that he was not specially briefed on the subject, but in due course he did look at what information the Agency had. He believed that I was drawing unwarranted conclusions from the available data. Anytime there is a UFO sighting, he explained, the intelligence agencies must take an interest. Regarding information still being withheld, the Admiral emphasized that it was only comparatively recently – under the Freedom of Information Act – that hitherto secret information has been declassified and released to the public. There was also not the slightest evidence to support the theory that sensitive information had been withheld from him.

Admiral Turner emphasized an important and perfectly understandable point: there is a genuine concern that anything written in intelligence channels which gives any credence whatsoever to UFOs may be highly distorted when released to the public.[48] He refrained from commenting in any way on the putative Majestic-12 group.

The CIA Cover-Up

In 1979 Victor Marchetti, former executive assistant to the Deputy Director and special assistant to the Executive Director of the CIA, stated that during his time in the Agency UFOs were not normally discussed, because the subject came under the area of 'very sensitive activities'. Marchetti said that, although from 'high levels' in the Agency he had heard rumours that 'little gray men' whose craft had crashed were being kept by the Air Force at the Foreign Technology Division, Wright-Patterson Air Force Base, he had not seen any conclusive evidence for the reality of UFOs. He conceded, however, that the CIA's attempts to debunk the phenomenon have all the classic hallmarks of a cover-up.

Marchetti believes that the released CIA/UFO information tells us perhaps more than the Government thinks. From the very beginning, in 1947, the CIA has closely monitored UFO reports on a worldwide basis. Although most of the FOIA documents indicate only a routine interest in the problem, which was handled largely by the Foreign Broadcast Information Service, Foreign Documents Division, and the Domestic Contact Service – all innocuous, non-clandestine units – they also disclose, by inference, a standing requirement of the Directorate of Science and Technology for gathering UFO data. This, says Marchetti, in turn, indicates other collection units, such as the Clandestine Services, the CIA's directorate which was given the task of providing information from all over the world on the UFO phenomenon. 'However,' he adds, 'few such reports were released – and that implies a cover-up!'

Marchetti's theory is that we have indeed been visited – perhaps even contacted – by extraterrestrial beings, and the US Government, in collusion with the other national powers of the Earth, is determined to keep this information from the general public.[49]

Aerospace Intelligence

THE NATIONAL AERONAUTICS and Space Administration, established in 1958, co-ordinates and directs aeronautical and space research programmes in the United States. Although officially a civilian agency, NASA collaborates with the CIA, the Department of Defense, the National Reconnaissance Office, the National Security Agency and other agencies. Many of its personnel have high security clearances.

During a lecture at the Second National Conference on the Peaceful Uses of Space Research in Seattle, Washington, on 11 May 1962, NASA pilot Joseph A. Walker said that it was one of his appointed tasks to detect unidentified objects during his flights in the rocket-powered X-15 aircraft. He referred to UFOs he had filmed during his record-breaking 50-mile-high flight a few weeks previously.[1] Former Air Force intelligence officer and UFO researcher Leonard Stringfield was given further details about the incident by a NASA test engineer who had worked on the X-15 programme at Edwards Air Force Base, California.

On 30 April 1962 two disc-shaped objects overtook Walker's X-15 as it was flying at 3,400 m.p.h. at an altitude of approximately 200,000 feet, climbing at an angle of about 30 degrees. 'Two UFOs just passed overhead,' Walker reported, according to the engineer, who was in the Flight Research Center (FRC) control room at the time. No other details were supplied by the pilot. The aft fuselage cameras on the X-15 caught the UFOs on film, which was later seen by the engineer during the post-flight debriefing. The film clearly showed two white or silver disc-shaped aircraft flying in tight formation, rapidly overtaking the X-15 from behind and passing overhead, possibly 100–200 feet above the plane.[2]

Walker revealed that it was the second occasion on which he had filmed UFOs in flight. 'I don't feel like speculating about them,' he said during the Seattle conference. 'All I know is what appeared on the film which was developed after the flight.'[3]

Britain's *Flying Saucer Review* magazine cabled NASA headquarters requesting further information and copies of stills from the film taken by Walker. 'Objects recently reported by NASA pilot Joe Walker have now been identified as ice flaking off the X-15 aircraft,' NASA responded. 'Analysis of additional film cameras mounted on top the X-15 led to identification of the previously unidentifiable objects . . . No still photos are available.'[4]

On 17 July 1962 Major Robert White piloted an X-15 to its maximum altitude of 314,000 feet when, according to Stringfield's source, White reported to NASA FRC Control that 'several' UFOs were flying in formation with him and were 'like the colour of paper'. Twenty other control-room personnel overheard the communication.[5] According to *Time* magazine, Major White is reported to have said excitedly over his radio: 'There *are* things out there. There absolutely is!'[6]

'Two years ago,' a NASA scientist said in 1967, 'most of us regarded UFOs as a branch of witchcraft, one of the foibles of modern man. But so many reputable people have expressed interest in confidence to NASA, that I would not be in the least surprised to see the space agency begin work on a UFO study contract within the next twelve months.'[7]

One of those who expressed interest was Dr Allen Hynek, who wanted NASA to use its superlative space-tracking network to monitor and document the entry of unidentified objects into the Earth's atmosphere. The problem then, as now, is that UFO sightings tracked by NASA remain exempt from public disclosure because they are classified. Yet there have been leaks.

In April 1964 two radar technicians at Cape Kennedy revealed that they had observed UFOs in pursuit of an unmanned Gemini space capsule. In January 1961 it was reliably reported that the Cape's automatic tracking gear locked on to a mysterious object which was apparently following a Polaris missile over the South Atlantic.[8]

A 1967 NASA management instruction established procedures for handling reports of sightings of objects such as 'fragments or component parts of space vehicles known or alleged by an observer to have impacted upon the earth's surface as a result of safety destruct action, failure in flight, or re-entry into the earth's atmosphere', and also covers reports of sightings of objects not related to space vehicles' – a rather euphemistic way of putting it. The instruction continues: 'It is KSC [Kennedy Space Center] policy to respond to reported sightings of space vehicle fragments and unidentified flying objects as promptly as possible . . . Under no circumstances will the origin of the object be discussed with the observer or person making the call.'[9]

KMI 8610. 4
June 28, 1967

    b.   Unidentified Flying Object: An unidentified object observed
in the atmosphere.

5.   <u>PROCEDURES FOR HANDLING REPORTS OF SIGHTINGS</u>

    a.   <u>KSC telephone operators</u> will refer all telephone calls
coming into the KSC switchboard from persons reporting
sightings, as defined herein, to the KSC Scheduling Branch,
Test Support Management Office, telephone 867-3013.

    b.   <u>Persons other than telephone operators</u> receiving initial
reports of sightings will, if possible, transfer the call to the
KSC Scheduling Branch. If the call cannot be transferred,
the following information should be obtained from the caller
and immediately transmitted to the KSC Scheduling Branch:

        (1)   Name, address, and telephone number of the observer
and any other information needed to establish the identity
of the observer for possible immediate follow-up
contact.

        (2)   Description of the object sighted, i.e., shape, size,
color, etc.

        (3)   Location of the object: state, city, etc.

    NOTE: Under no circumstances will the origin of the object be
discussed with the observer or person making the call.

    c.   <u>The KSC Scheduling Branch</u>, in response to a report of a
sighting, will:

        (1)   Contact military bases nearest the sighting to enlist
their aid in determining the validity of the sighting.

        (2)   Contact the KSC Security Office who will in turn contact
municipal and State police nearest the sighting to enlist
their aid in determining the validity of the sighting.

        (3)   Consult with the Public Information Branch, Public
Affairs Office, on reported sightings that may be of
public interest.

2

Two pages from a NASA management instruction relating mostly to the processing of
reports of unidentified flying objects. Issued by Kurt Debus, Director, John F. Kennedy Space
Center, June 1967. (*NASA*)

KMI 8610. 4
June 28, 1967

    (4)   Refer all inquiries from news media to the Public Information Branch.

    (5)   Consult with the Senior Scientist, KSC, on all sightings reported.

    (6)   Call in unidentified flying object reports to the Patrick Air Force Base Command Post, telephone 494-7001.

  d.   All written communications received from persons or activities reporting a sighting will be immediately transmitted to the Senior Scientist, KSC.

6.   RESPONSIBILITIES

    a.   Test Support Management Office will be responsible for:

        (1)   Developing and maintaining a capability for receiving, screening, and processing reports of sightings, as defined in paragraph 4, on a 24-hour-day, 7-day-week basis.

        (2)   Ensuring close liaison with the Senior Scientist, KSC, and the Public Affairs Office on matters pertaining to this Instruction.

        (3)   Coordinating with the Senior Scientist, KSC, as soon as possible after a reported sighting to determine the action to be taken.

    b.   The KSC Scheduling Branch, Test Support Management Office, will be responsible for maintaining a 24-hour-day, 7-day-week capability for receiving, screening, and processing reports of sightings, in accordance with paragraph 5c.

    c.   The Senior Scientist, KSC, will be responsible for:

        (1)   The overall monitoring of the space vehicle fragment sighting program at KSC.

3

A 1978 NASA information sheet gives the agency's official policy on the subject:

> NASA is the focal point for answering public inquiries to the White House relating to UFOs. NASA is not engaged in a research program involving these phenomena, nor is any other government agency. Reports of unidentified objects entering United States air space are of interest to the military as a regular part of defense surveillance. Beyond that, the U.S. Air Force no longer investigates reports of UFO sightings.[10]

In 1978 Citizens Against UFO Secrecy (CAUS) filed a request for information relating to a NASA report entitled *UFO Study Considerations*, previously prepared in association with the CIA. In his response, Miles Waggoner of NASA's Public Information Services Branch denied CIA involvement. 'There were no formal meetings or any correspondence with the CIA,' he stated. Following another enquiry by CAUS, NASA's Associate Administrator for External Relations, Kenneth Chapman, explained that the NASA report had been prepared solely by NASA employees but that the CIA had been consulted by telephone to determine 'whether they were aware of any tangible or physical UFO evidence that could be analyzed; the CIA responded that they were aware of no such evidence, either classified or unclassified'.[11]

NASA's statement in the 1978 information sheet that it was not engaged in a research programme involving UFOs (it had issued instructions for the reporting of sightings, at least), 'nor is any other government agency', is demonstrably false, as is its denial of Air Force investigations.

President Carter Seeks to Reopen Investigations

During his presidential election campaign in 1976, Governor Jimmy Carter revealed that he and others had seen a UFO at Leary, Georgia, in 1969 before giving a speech at the local Lions Club. 'It was the darndest thing I've ever seen,' he told reporters. 'It was big, it was very bright, it changed colours, and it was about the size of the moon. We watched it for ten minutes, but none of us could figure out what it was. One thing's for sure; I'll never make fun of people who say they've seen unidentified objects in the sky.'[12]

Carter's sighting has been ridiculed by sceptics such as Philip Klass

NASA

National Aeronautics and
Space Administration

INFORMATION SHEET

Number 78-1

Prepared by:

LFF-3/Public Services Branch
Office of External Relations
NASA Headquarters
Washington, DC 20546

UNIDENTIFIED FLYING OBJECTS

The information contained here has been compiled to respond to queries on Unidentified Flying Objects directed to the White House as well as NASA.

NASA is the focal point for answering public inquiries to the White House relating to UFOs. NASA is not engaged in a research program involving these phenomena, nor is any other government agency.

Reports of unidentified objects entering United States airspace are of interest to the military as a regular part of defense surveillance. Beyond that, the U.S. Air Force no longer investigates reports of UFO sightings.

February 1, 1978

A 1978 NASA information sheet perpetuating the myth that no government agency is engaged in UFO research. (*NASA*)

NATIONAL INVESTIGATIONS COMMITTEE ON AERIAL PHENOMENA (NICAP)®
3535 University Blvd. West
301-949-1267   Kensington, Maryland 20795

REPORT ON UNIDENTIFIED FLYING OBJECT(S)

This form includes questions asked by the United States Air Force and by other Armed Forces' investigating agencies, and additional questions to which answers are needed for full evaluation by NICAP.

After all the information has been fully studied, the conclusion of our Evaluation Panel will be published by NICAP in its regularly issued magazine or in another publication. Please try to answer as many questions as possible. Should you need additional room, please use another sheet of paper. Please print or typewrite. Your assistance is of great value and is genuinely appreciated. Thank you.

1. Name **Jimmy Carter**   Place of Employment

    Address **State Capitol Atlanta**   Occupation **Governor**
                                      Date of birth
                                      Education
                                      Special Training **Graduate**
    Telephone **(404) 656-1776**   Military Service **Nuclear Physics**
                                                 U.S. Navy

2. Date of Observation **October 1969**   Time   AM   PM   Time Zone
                                                       7:15   **EST**

3. Locality of Observation **Leary, Georgia**

4. How long did you see the object?_____ Hours **10-12** Minutes_____ Seconds

5. Please describe weather conditions and the type of sky; i.e., bright daylight, nighttime, dusk, etc. **Shortly after dark.**

6. Position of the Sun or Moon in relation to the object and to you. **Not in sight.**

7. If seen at night, twilight, or dawn, were the stars or moon visible? **Stars.**

8. Were there more than one object? **No.**   If so, please tell how many, and draw a sketch of what you saw, indicating direction of movement, if any.

9. Please describe the object(s) in detail. For instance, did it (they) appear solid, or only as a source of light; was it revolving, etc.? Please use additional sheets of paper, if necessary.

10. Was the object(s) brighter than the background of the sky? **Yes.**

11. If so, compare the brightness with the Sun, Moon, headlights, etc. **At one time, as bright as the moon.**

12. Did the object(s) —   (Please elaborate, if you can give details.)

    a. Appear to stand still at any time? **yes**   f. Drop anything?
    b. Suddenly speed up and rush away at any time?   g. Change brightness? **yes**
    c. Break up into parts or explode?   h. Change shape? **size**
    d. Give off smoke?   i. Change color? **yes**
    e. Leave any visible trail?

Seemed to move toward us from a distance, stopped-moved partially away—returned, then departed. Bluish at first, then reddish, luminous, not solid.

13. Did object(s) at any time pass in front of, or behind of, anything? If so, please elaborate giving distance, size, etc, if possible. **no.**

14. Was there any wind? **no.**   If so, please give direction and speed.

15. Did you observe the object(s) through an optical instrument or other aid, windshield, windowpane, storm window, screening, etc? What? **no.**

16. Did the object(s) have any sound? **no**   What kind?   How loud?

17. Please tell if the object(s) was (were) —

    a. Fuzzy or blurred.   b. Like a bright star.   c. Sharply outlined. **X**

President Carter's report of a UFO sighting he witnessed while Governor of Georgia in 1969.
(*NICAP*)

18. Was the object — . . .   **a.** Self-luminous? x   **b.** Dull finish?   **c.** Reflecting?   **d.** Transparent?

19. Did the object(s) rise or fall while in motion? came close, moved away-came close then moved away.

20. Tell the apparent size of the object(s) when compared with the following held at arm's length:

    a. Pinhead   **c.** Dime   **e.** Half dollar   **g.** Orange   **i.** Larger
    b. Pea   **d.** Nickel   **f.** Silver dollar   **h.** Grapefruit

Or, if easier, give apparent size in inches on a ruler held at arm's length. About the same as moon, maybe a littl smaller. Varied from brighter/larger than planet to apparent size of moon.

21. How did you happen to notice the object(s)? 10-12 men all watched it. Brightness attracted us.

22. Where were you and what were you doing at the time? Outdoors waiting for a meeting to begin at 7:30pm

23. How did the object(s) disappear from view? Moved to distance then disappeared

24. Compare the speed of the object(s) with a piston or jet aircraft at the same apparent altitude. Not pertinent

25. Were there any conventional aircraft in the location at the time or immediately afterwards? If so, please elaborate. no.

26. Please estimate the distance of the object(s). Difficult. Maybe 300-1000 yards.

27. What was the elevation of the object(s) in the sky? Please mark on this hemisphere sketch.
About 30° above horizon.

28. Names and addresses of other witnesses, if any.

Ten members of Leary Georgia Lions Club

29. What do you think you saw?

    a. Extraterrestrial device?   **e.** Satellite?
    b. UFO?   **f.** Hoax?
    c. Planet or star?   **g.** Other? (Please specify).
    d. Aircraft?

30. Please describe your feelings and reactions during the sighting. Were you calm, nervous, frightened, apprehensive, awed, etc.? If you wish your answer to this question to remain confidential, please indicate with a check mark. (Use a separate sheet if necessary)

31. Please draw a map of the locality of the observation showing North; your position; the direction from which the object(s) appeared and dis appeared from view; the direction of its course over the area; roads, towns, villages, railroads, and other landmarks within a mile.

Appeared from West--About 30° up.

32. Is there an airport, military, governmental, or research installation in the area? No

33. Have you seen other objects of an unidentified nature? If so, please describe these observations, using a separate sheet of paper. No

34. Please enclose photographs, motion pictures, news clippings, notes of radio or television programs (include time, station and date, if possible) regarding this or similar observations, or any other background material. We will return the material to you if requested. Non

35. Were you interrogated by Air Force investigators? By any other federal, state, county, or local officials? If so, please state the name and rank or title of the agent, his office, and details as to where and when the questioning took place.

Were you asked or told not to reveal or discuss the incident? If so, were any reasons or official orders mentioned? Please elaborate carefully. No.

36. We should like permission to quote your name in connection with this report. This action will encourage other responsible citizens to repo similar observations to NICAP. However, if you prefer, we will keep your name confidential. Please note your choice by checking the pro per statement below. In any case, please fill in all parts of the form, for our own confidential files. Thank you for your cooperation.

You may use my name.   (x)   Please keep my name confidential.   ( )

37. Date of filling out this report   Signature:

9-18-73

Jimmy Carter

and Robert Sheaffer. While there appear to be legitimate grounds for disputing the date of the incident, Sheaffer's verdict that the UFO was nothing more exotic than the planet Venus is not tenable.[13] As a graduate of nuclear physics who served on US Navy nuclear submarines, Carter would not have been fooled by anything so prosaic as Venus, and in any case he described the UFO as being about the same size as the Moon. 'If I become President,' Carter vowed, 'I'll make every piece of information this country has about UFO sightings available to the public and the scientists.'[14]

Although President Carter did what he could to fulfil his election pledge, he was thwarted, and it is clear that NASA had a hand in blocking his attempts to reopen investigations. When Carter's science adviser, Dr Frank Press, wrote to NASA administrator Dr Robert Frosch in February 1977 suggesting that NASA should become the 'focal point for the UFO question',[15] Dr Frosch replied that although he was prepared to continue responding to public enquiries, he proposed that 'NASA take no steps to establish a research activity in this area or to convene a symposium on this subject'.

In a letter from Colonel Charles Senn, Chief of the Air Force Community Relations Division, to Lieutenant General Duward Crow of NASA, Colonel Senn made the following astonishing statement: 'I sincerely hope you are successful in preventing a reopening of UFO investigations.'[16] It is clear that NASA, as well as the Air Force, the CIA and the National Security Agency, was anxious to ensure that the President's election pledge remained unfulfilled.

Dr James McDonald

Dr James McDonald, senior physicist at the Institute of Atmospheric Physics and a professor in the Department of Meteorology at the University of Arizona, who committed suicide in unusual circumstances in 1971, tried unsuccessfully to persuade NASA to take on primary responsibility for UFO investigations.

'Curiously, I have said this both in NASA and fairly widely reported public discussions before scientific colleagues, yet the response from NASA has been nil,' McDonald reported in 1967:

> Even attempting to get a small group within NASA to undertake a study group approach to the available published effort seems to have generated no response. I realize, of course, that there may be

DEPARTMENT OF THE AIR FORCE
WASHINGTON D C 20330

OFFICE OF THE SECRETARY

1 SEP 1977

Lieutenant General Duward L. Crow, USAF (Ret)
National Aeronautics and Space Administration
400 Maryland Avenue
Washington, D. C. 20546

Dear General Crow:

Inclosed are the UFO Fact Sheet and standard response
to UFO public inquiries you requested.

I sincerely hope you are successful in preventing a
reopening of UFO investigations.

Sincerely,

CHARLES H. SENN, Colonel, USAF
Chief, Community Relations Division
Office of Information

Attachments

Action Copy to _AOA_
I to Copy to _FW_
 _AB, AC,_
A 35481 _S.F.L, W, C_
 _AE_
Rec'd in NASA _9-2-77_

Date _NbNE._

For

_A 39611_

A letter from Colonel Charles Senn, US Air Force Office of Information, to Lieutenant
General Duward Crow, NASA, September 1977 (*US Air Force*)

semi-political considerations that make it awkward for NASA to fish in these waters at present, but if this is what is holding up serious scientific attention to the UFO problem at NASA this is all the more reason Congress had better take a good hard look at the problem and reshuffle the deck . . . I have learned from a number of unquotable sources that the Air Force has long wished to get rid of the burden of the troublesome UFO problem and has twice tried to 'peddle' it to NASA – without success.[17]

While McDonald recognized that there were 'semi-political considerations' affecting NASA's reluctance to become publicly involved in UFO investigations, he perhaps failed to perceive that UFOs are more an intelligence problem than a scientific one. He was simply unaware of the true extent of the intelligence community's involvement.

During Congressional hearings on UFOs before the House Committee on Science and Astronautics in July 1968, Dr McDonald felt it his duty to report that the great north-east-America power blackout of 9 November 1965 may have been caused by UFO activity. 'There were reports all over New England in the midst of that blackout,' he stated:

It is rather puzzling that the pulse of current that tripped the relay on the Ontario Hydro Commission Plant has never been identified . . . Just how a UFO could trigger such an outage on a large power network is however not clear. But this is a disturbing series of coincidences that I think warrant much more attention than they have so far received.[18]

Dr Hermann Oberth

A great pioneer in astronautics was the late Dr Hermann Oberth, whom I had the honour of meeting in 1972. In 1955 Oberth was invited by Dr Wernher von Braun to go to the United States, where he worked on rockets with the Army Ballistic Missile Agency, and later with NASA at the George C. Marshall Space Flight Center. Oberth's statements on the UFO question were unequivocal, and he reaffirmed to me that he was convinced that UFOs are extraterrestrial in origin. In the following, he elaborated on his hypothesis for UFO propulsion:

. . . today we cannot produce machines that fly as UFOs do. They are flying by means of artificial fields of gravity. This would explain the sudden changes of direction [and] the piling up of these discs into a cylindrical or cigar-shaped mothership upon leaving the earth, because in this fashion only one field of gravity would be required for all discs.

They produce high-tension electric charges in order to push the air out of their path . . . and strong magnetic fields to influence the ionized air at higher altitudes [which] would explain their luminosity . . . Secondly, it would explain the noiselessness of UFO flight. Finally, this assumption also explains the strong electrical and magnetic effects sometimes, but not always, observed in the vicinity of UFOs.[19]

Earlier, Dr Oberth hinted that there had been actual contact with the occupants of UFOs at a scientific level. 'We cannot take the credit for our record advancement in certain scientific fields alone; we have been helped,' he is quoted as having said. When asked by whom, he replied: 'The people of other worlds.'[20] There are persistent rumours that the United States has even test-flown a few advanced vehicles, based on information allegedly acquired as a result of contact with extraterrestrials and the study of grounded alien craft – reports to which I have devoted several chapters in my book *Alien Liaison*.

The Silver Spring Film

In the previous chapter I alluded briefly to George Adamski, who claimed to have had numerous encounters with extraterrestrials, including trips into space. Adamski also was the first to claim that contact had been established at a restricted level in the scientific community, and that extraterrestrials had provided assistance with the space programme, as confirmed by Dr Oberth. These claims generally have been dismissed – the very name of Adamski is guaranteed to provoke ridicule – yet my own intensive investigations over several decades have led to the conviction that, even if some of his claims are nonsensical, others are legitimate. One such is the controversial 8mm colour movie film taken by Adamski (two months before his death) in the presence of Madeleine Rodeffer and three other unnamed witnesses outside Rodeffer's home in Silver Spring, Maryland, in February 1965. I have been taken to task for endorsing the authenticity of this 'obviously fake' film taken by a 'proven charlatan', but I have yet to see any convincing evidence that it actually *was* faked.

Sometime between 15.00 and 16.00 on 26 February 1965, an

unidentified craft of the famous type photographed by Adamski in 1952 (and others subsequently) described a series of manoeuvres over Rodeffer's front yard, retracting and lowering one of its three pods and making a gentle humming and swishing sound as it did so. Adamski began filming the craft with Rodeffer's 8mm camera. 'It looked blackish-brown or greyish-brown at times,' Rodeffer told me in 1967, 'but when it came in close it looked greenish and blueish, and it looked aluminum: it depended on which way it was tilting. Then at one point it actually stood absolutely still between the bottom of the steps and the driveway.' The craft then disappeared from view, but reappeared above the roof and described manoeuvres once more before finally disappearing vertically. Rodeffer told me that she could make out human-like figures at the portholes, but details were obscured.

When the film was developed the following week, something was evidently wrong with many of the frames and it was apparent that it had been interfered with. Obviously faked frames had been spliced into the original by person or persons unknown, apparently.

Fortunately, enough frames showing the craft as they remembered it survived out of the 25 feet that had been taken, and these were analysed by William T. Sherwood, an optical physicist who was formerly a senior project development engineer for the Eastman-Kodak Company in Rochester, New York. I spent many hours discussing the film with Sherwood, and in 1968 he provided me, in the form of a letter, with a brief technical summary of his evaluations as they related to the prints he made from the original film:

> It's hard to capture the nuances of the original film. None of the movie duplicates are good: too much contrast. The outlines look 'peculiar' due to distortions, I believe, caused by the 'forcefield'. The glow beneath the flange is, I think, significant. Incidentally, the tree [near the top of which the craft manoeuvred] is very high (90 ft?). Roughly, the geometry of imagery is this:

$$\frac{\text{object size}}{\text{image size}} \simeq \frac{\text{distance}}{\text{focal length}} \quad \text{or} \quad \frac{27\text{ft}}{2.7\text{mm}} \simeq \frac{90\text{ft}}{9\text{mm}}$$

In 1977 Bill Sherwood sent me further details of his evaluations:

> The camera was a Bell & Howell Animation Autoload Standard 8, Model 315, with a f1.8 lens, 9–29mm, used in the 9mm position

. . . As you can measure, the image on the film (original) is about 2.7mm maximum. So for a 90ft distant object, [the diameter] would be about 27 feet . . . It was a large tree, and the limb that the saucer seems to 'touch' could have been about that distance from the camera . . . but unfortunately I could not find a single frame where the saucer could clearly be said to be *behind* the limb. So it is not conclusive as for distance, and therefore for size . . . In some of the frames of the original, portholes are seen.

In reply to my query as to whether it was possible to authenticate the film unequivocally, Sherwood said there is no absolutely foolproof way of assessing whether a photo is 'real' or not. One must just take everything into account, including as much as one can learn about the person involved, and then make an educated assessment. In the final analysis, he said, it comes down to this question: 'Is this the kind of person whom I can imagine going to all the trouble and expense of simulating what only a well-equipped studio with a large budget could begin to approximate, and defending it through the years with no apparent gain and much inconvenience?'

One of the peculiarities of the film is that the outlines of the craft look distorted at times (see plate section). Bill Sherwood believes this is due to a powerful gravitational field that produces optical distortions – an opinion that is shared by Leonard Cramp, author of a book which discusses UFO propulsion technology and its effects.[21] Cramp is an aeronautical engineer and designer who has worked for De Havilland, Napier, Saunders-Roe and Westland Aircraft companies. (At Napier he patented the invention of an Induction Mixed-Fluid Ramjet.) Like Bill Sherwood and myself, he is in no doubt that the film is authentic.

Two years after it had been taken, on 27 February 1967, the film was shown to twenty-two NASA officials at the Goddard Space Flight Center, Greenbelt, Maryland. Discussion afterwards lasted for an hour and a half. In reply to my later queries, NASA scientist Paul D. Lowman Jr, of the Geophysics Branch at Goddard, stated that, according to one of those present, Herbert A. Tiedemann, everyone considered the Silver Spring film to be a fake. Dr Lowman, who had helped set up the meeting but was unable to attend, offered the following comments on the colour photos from the film that I sent him:

First, it is not possible to make any precise determination of the object's size from the relationship (which is basically correct) quoted by Mr. Sherwood. Given any three of these quantities, one can calculate the fourth. The focal length and image size are obviously known, but not the distance, which can only be roughly estimated. The equation can be no better than its most inexact quantity, and one might as well just estimate the size of the object directly. My own strong impression is that these frames show a small object, perhaps up to 2 or 3 feet across, a short distance from the camera. Judging from the photo of Mrs. Rodeffer's house, a 27 foot UFO would have occupied most of the cleared area in the front yard, and from such a short distance would have been a very large photographic object.[22]

Although Bill Sherwood readily concedes that his estimate of the precise distance from the camera is arbitrary, he is sure that it is reasonably accurate, and my own tests at the site show that, with the camera lens set on wide angle (as it was at the time), an object of this approximate size and distance would appear exactly as it does on the film. That either Adamski or Rodeffer (or both) could have faked the film using a small model, and then have the audacity to show it to NASA, seems far-fetched. Moreover, to produce the distortion effects as well as the lowering and retracting of one of the pods with a small model is out of the question. As a photographer experienced in working with both movie and still cameras, I am able to speak with some experience on this matter.

Following the death of Adamski, Madeleine Rodeffer experienced a great deal of ridicule and harassment, and nearly all copies of the 'faked' film have been stolen – in the United States and elsewhere.

Two photographs of an identical craft were taken by young Stephen Darbishire in the presence of his cousin Adrian Myers in Coniston, England, in February 1954 (see plate section) – one of which (rarely reproduced, owing to its poor quality) shows a peculiar distortion effect similar to that observed in the Adamski/Rodeffer movie. For the benefit of those who contend that Darbishire had faked the pictures and recanted later, the following statement from a letter he wrote to me is illuminating:

When I said that I had seen a UFO I was laughed at, attacked, and surrounded by strange people . . . In desperation I remember I refuted the statement and said it was a fake. I was counter-attacked, accused of working with the 'Dark Powers' . . . or patronizingly 'understood' for following orders from some secret government department. There was something. It happened a long time ago, and I do not wish to be drawn into the labyrinth again. Unfortunately the negatives were stolen and all the prints gone . . .[23]

The Astronauts

In the early 1970s the well-known conductor, pianist and composer André Previn kindly arranged several meetings for me in Britain and the United States with his friend Scott Carpenter, a former US Navy test pilot, intelligence officer and pioneer astronaut. Reputedly, Carpenter had seen UFOs and photographed one of them during his flight in the Mercury 7 capsule on 24 May 1962. Carpenter vehemently denied this, and poured scorn on other reports of sightings by fellow astronauts. I noticed that he appeared to be ill at ease when discussing the subject, especially when I produced documentary evidence for official concern.

I asked Carpenter several times for the facts on the photograph he took from space. According to a commentator on BBC Television in 1973, Carpenter had been withdrawn from duties as an astronaut for wasting time taking pictures of 'sunrise'. I thought this unlikely, especially since André Previn told me that Carpenter had not been allowed in space again owing to a slight heart murmur. The released photograph showed what some have interpreted as a UFO; others as a lens flare, ice crystals, or the fabric-and-aluminium balloon that was deployed at one stage. I wanted the facts.

When I reminded Scott Carpenter of my request a year later, he replied that he resented my 'continuing implication that I am lying and/or withholding truths from you. Your blindly stubborn belief in Flying Saucers makes interesting talk for a while, but your inability to rationally consider any thought that runs counter to yours makes further discussion of no interest – indeed unpleasant in prospect – to me . . . Let's do be friends, Tim, but let's talk about such things as music . . . where maybe both of us can learn something.'[24]

I do not know what Scott Carpenter photographed, but I find it puzzling that he was unwilling to discuss the matter with me. Nevertheless, in November he kindly wrote on my behalf to astronauts Gordon Cooper, Dick Gordon, James Lovell and James McDivitt, asking about reports attributed to them. James Lovell responded as follows:

I have to honestly say that during my four flights into space, I have not seen or heard any phenomena that I could not explain . . . I don't believe any of us in the space program believe that there are such things as UFOs . . . However, most of us believe that there must be a star like our sun that also has a planetary system [which] must support intelligent life as we know it . . .[25]

But according to the transcript of Lovell's flight on Gemini 7, an anomalous object was encountered:

SPACECRAFT: Bogey at 10 o'clock high.
CAPCOM: This is Houston. Say again 7.
SPACECRAFT: Said we have a bogey at 10 o'clock high.
CAPCOM: Gemini 7, is that the booster or is that an actual sighting?
SPACECRAFT: We have several, looks like debris up here. Actual sighting.
CAPCOM: Estimate distance or size?
SPACECRAFT: We also have the booster in sight . . .[26]

Franklin Roach, of the University of Colorado UFO study set up by the Air Force in 1966, concluded that in addition to the booster rocket travelling in an orbit similar to that of the spacecraft, 'there was another bright object [the "bogey"] together with many illuminated particles. It might be conjectured,' he said, 'that the bogey and particles were fragments from the launching of Gemini 7, but this is impossible if they were traveling in a polar orbit as they appeared to be doing.'[27]

James McDivitt confirmed to me (via Scott Carpenter) that, although he did see an unidentified object during the Gemini 4 flight on 4 June 1965, he does not believe it was anomalous:

During Gemini 4, while we were in drifting flight, I noticed an object out the front window of the spacecraft. It appeared to be cylindrical in shape with a high fineness ratio. From one end protruded a long, cylindrical pole with the approximate fineness of pencil. I had no idea what the size was or what the distance to the object was. It could have been very small and very near or very large and very far away.

I attempted to take a photograph of this object with each of the two cameras we had on board. Since this object was only in my view for a short time, I did not have time to properly adjust the cameras and I just took the picture with whatever settings the camera had at that time. The object appeared to be relatively close and I went through the trouble of turning on the control system in case I needed to take any evasive actions.

The spacecraft was in drifting flight and when the sun shone on the duty window, the object disappeared from view. I was unable to relocate it, since the attitude reference in the spacecraft was also disabled, and I did not know which way to maneuver to find it.

After landing, the film from Gemini 4 was flown back to Houston immediately, whereas Ed White and I stayed on the aircraft carrier for three days. During this period of time a film technician at NASA evaluated the photographs and selected what he thought was the photograph of this particular object. Unfortunately, what he selected was a photograph of sunspots [flares] on the window and had nothing whatsoever to do with the object that I had seen. The photograph was released before I returned and had a chance to point out the error in the selection. I, subsequently, went through the photographs myself and was unable to find any photograph like the object I had seen. Apparently, the camera settings were not appropriate for the pictures.

I do not feel that there was anything strange or exotic about this particular object. Rather, only that I could not identify it. In a combination of both Gemini 4 and Apollo 9 I saw numerous satellites, some of which we identified and some of which we didn't . . . I have seen a lot of objects that I could not identify, but I have yet to see one that could be identified as a spaceship from some other planet. I do not say that there aren't any, only that I haven't seen any. I hope this helps Tim.[28]

UFO sceptic James Oberg of NASA told me that he believes the object was merely the second stage of the Titan rocket which launched Gemini 4 into space. If this is the case, the only puzzle remaining is McDivitt's apparent failure to identify his own rocket! Moreover, McDivitt (who retired from the military with the rank of brigadier general) is emphatic that, although the object may not have been anomalous, it remains unidentified. 'It turned out when we looked at the records that there weren't any upper stages or rockets anywhere near me,' he emphasized during a television interview in 1974. 'So, no, it could not have been. It wasn't a Russian one. It wasn't any other country's because we know where they all are.'[29]

Neither Gordon Cooper nor Dick Gordon replied to Carpenter's letter, it seems. Yet Cooper's interest in UFOs was one of the reasons that inspired him to become an astronaut. 'I . . . had the idea that there might be some interesting forms of life out in space for us to discover and get acquainted with,' he wrote in 1962. 'As far as I am concerned there have been far too many unexplained examples of unidentified objects sighted around this earth . . . the fact that many experienced pilots had reported strange sights . . . did heighten my curiosity about space . . . This was one of several reasons, then, why I wanted to become an Astronaut.'[30]

In 1967, U Thant, former Secretary-General of the United Nations, reportedly confided to friends that, next to the Vietnam War, he considered UFOs to be the most important problem facing the UN.[31] In 1978 two debates on the subject were held at the UN. The first of these, a meeting of the Special Political Committee of the United Nations General Assembly, was attended by Gordon Cooper. Later that year, a letter from Cooper was read at a UN debate on UFOs held in the General Assembly:

> . . . I believe that these extra-terrestrial vehicles and their crews are visiting this planet from other planets, which obviously are a little more technically advanced than we are here on earth. I feel that we need to have a top level, coordinated program to scientifically collect and analyze data from all over the earth concerning any type of encounter, and to determine how best to interface with these visitors in a friendly fashion. We may first have to show them that we have learned to resolve our problems by peaceful means, rather than warfare, before we are accepted as fully qualified universal team members . . .
>
> Also, I did have occasion in 1951 to have two days of observation of many flights of them, of different sizes, flying in fighter formation, generally from east to west over Europe. They were at a higher altitude than we could reach with our jet fighters at that time.

Cooper pointed out that most astronauts were very reluctant even to discuss UFOs, 'due to the great numbers of people who have indiscriminately sold fake stories and forged documents abusing their names and reputations without hesitation. Those few astronauts who have continued to have a participation in the UFO field have had to do so very cautiously.' He added: 'There are several of us who do believe in UFOs and who have had occasion to see a UFO on the ground, or from an airplane. There was only one occasion from space which may have been a UFO.'[32]

Gordon Cooper did not elaborate on these cases in his letter, but in an interview with Lee Spiegel, a decade later, he disclosed a remarkable incident which had occurred at Edwards Air Force Base, California, in 1957 or 1958, when he was project manager of the Flight Test Center. A flying disc hovered over the dry lake, 'then it slowly came down and sat on the lake bed for a few minutes'. A camera team filmed the entire incident. 'There were varied estimates by the cameramen on what the actual size of the object was,' said Cooper, 'but they all agreed that it was at least the size of a vehicle that would carry normal-sized people in it.' Although Cooper did not witness the sighting, he did study the film. 'It was a typical circular-shaped UFO. Not too many people saw it, because it took off at quite a sharp angle and just climbed out of sight.'[33]

In a video-recorded interview in 1994, Cooper gave some more details. The camera crew was filming the installation of a precision landing-system on the dry lake bed – using both movie and still film – when the incident occurred:

> They came running in to tell me that this UFO – this saucer – had come right over them, put down three [landing] gear, and landed about 50 yards from them. And as they proceeded to go on over to get a closer shot of it, it lifted up, put the gear in the well, and disappeared at a rapid rate of speed.
>
> And so I had to follow my directions as a military [person]: I had to look up the regulations on who I was to call or to report this, which I did. They ordered me to immediately have the films developed, put them in a pouch, and send them by the commanding general's airplane to Washington, which I did. That was the last I've ever heard of the films.[34]

Gordon Cooper has confirmed the accuracy of this report for me.

In November 1979 the Swiss researcher Lou Zinsstag and I received an unofficial invitation to visit the Lyndon B. Johnson Space Center in Houston. The invitation came from Alan Holt, a physicist and aerospace engineer whose main work at that time centred on the development of the astronaut and flight-controller training programmes associated with the Spacelab. He also was engaged in theoretical research into advanced types of propulsion for spacecraft (see *Alien Liaison*), and was involved in an unofficial NASA UFO study group called Project VISIT (Vehicle Internal Systems Investigative Team). I asked about photographs and films of UFOs allegedly taken by astronauts, and was simply told that the National Security Agency screens *all* films before releasing them to NASA.

Former Director of the National Security Agency and Deputy Director of the CIA Lew Allen was appointed head of NASA's Jet Propulsion Laboratory (JPL) in June 1982. JPL runs NASA's unmanned planetary space programme, whose phenomenal achievements included the landing on Mars by the Viking probes and, more recently, the Voyagers which transmitted such spectacular pictures of Jupiter, Saturn and Uranus. Allen had also been the USAF Chief of Staff, and as one of the pioneers of aerial espionage served as Deputy Director for Advanced Plans in the Directorate of Special Projects of America's spy-satellite intelligence agency, the National Reconnaissance Office, and later Director of the NRO's Office of Space Systems.[35] The NRO liaises closely with the CIA, the NSA and of course NASA.

In an interview in 1986 Lew Allen stated that up to a third of JPL's work was funded by the Department of Defense, but gave details of various fascinating civilian projects. 'One of the most exciting of these future programs, called Cassini,' he said, 'is an investigation of Saturn's moon Titan. Its atmosphere was too dense for the Voyagers to give us any clues about what lies beneath. The Cassini mission . . . would probe this atmosphere . . . we've concluded that it is very similar to what the earth's must have been at the earliest stages of its evolution.'[36]

Maurice Chatelain, a former NASA communications specialist, claims that all the Apollo and Gemini flights were followed at a distance and sometimes quite closely by space vehicles of extraterrestrial origin, but Mission Control ordered absolute secrecy. Chatelain believes that some UFOs may come from our own solar system – specifically Titan.[37]

During a BBC radio interview in 1972, astronaut Edgar Mitchell, the lunar-module pilot on Apollo 14, was asked by a listener if NASA had made any provisions for encountering extraterrestrials on the Moon or nearby planets. He replied in the affirmative. When the interviewer intervened and suggested that, if and when we ultimately come into contact with other civilizations, it would only be via radio-astronomy, Mitchell emphatically disagreed, making a point of recommending Dr Allen Hynek's book *The UFO Experience*,[38] which contradicted official policy on the subject.[39]

I wrote to Dr Mitchell and asked him to elaborate on this and another statement he made on the programme, to the effect that there had been no concealment of UFO sightings either in transit or on the Moon, and that such information was open to all. Mitchell's assistant, Harry Jones, replied: 'Dr. Mitchell asked me to write and tell you that to his knowledge there have been no unexplained UFO sightings. All unexplained sightings have subsequently been explained. Dr. Mitchell personally attests that there has never been any lid of secrecy placed on any NASA astronaut that he is aware of.'[40] Although puzzled by this contradictory reply, I did not pursue the matter further.

The subject of UFOs cropped up during an Oprah Winfrey show in 1991, which featured some of the Apollo astronauts. Dr Mitchell, following the rather negative comments of his former colleagues, rejoined: 'I do believe that there is a lot more known about extraterrestrial investigation than is available to the public right now [and] has been for a long time.' Pressed by Winfrey, Mitchell added: 'It's a long, long story. It goes back to World War II when all of that happened, and [it is] highly classified stuff.'

I wrote to Dr Mitchell and asked if he was prepared to elaborate on this intriguing statement. 'I really have little that I can add to what I have already said, for frankly I know very little,' he replied. 'My own assessment after years of sceptical observation is that the evidence has become so consistent and overwhelming that it can hardly be ignored. This being the case it will sooner or later break open and we will all be pleased to know the results.'[41]

'I'm one of those guys who has never seen a UFO,' said Eugene Cernan, commander of Apollo 17, at a press conference in 1973. 'But I've been asked, and I've said publicly I thought they were somebody else, some other civilization.'[42]

In 1979 former Mercury astronaut Donald 'Deke' Slayton revealed in an interview with Paul Levy that he had seen a UFO while test-flying an aircraft in 1951:

I was testing a P-51 fighter in Minneapolis when I spotted this object. I was at about 10,000 feet on a nice, bright, sunny afternoon. I thought the object was a kite, then realized that no kite is gonna fly that high. As I got closer it looked like a weather balloon, gray and about three feet in diameter. But as soon as I got behind the darn thing it didn't look like a balloon anymore. It looked like a saucer, a disc. About that same time, I realized that it was suddenly going away from me – and there I was, running at about 300 miles an hour. I tracked it for a little way, and then all of a sudden the damn thing just took off. It pulled about a 45-degree climbing turn and accelerated and just flat disappeared.

A couple of days later I was having a beer with my commanding officer, and I thought, 'What the hell, I'd better mention something to him about it.' I did, and he told me to get on down to intelligence and give them a report. I did, and I never heard anything more on it.[43]

Did Apollo 11 Encounter UFOs on the Moon?

According to unofficially confirmed reports, both Neil Armstrong and Edwin 'Buzz' Aldrin saw UFOs shortly after that historic landing on the Moon in Apollo 11 on 21 July 1969. I recall hearing one of the astronauts refer to a 'light' in or near a crater during the live televised transmission (which I watched in Chicago), followed by a request from Mission Control for further information. Nothing more was heard.

In 1979 Maurice Chatelain, the former NASA communications specialist, confirmed that Armstrong had indeed reported seeing two UFOs on the rim of a crater. 'The encounter was common knowledge in NASA,' he revealed, 'but nobody has talked about it until now.'

Reportedly, Soviet scientists were the first to confirm the incident. 'According to our information, the encounter was reported immediately after the landing of the module,' said Dr Vladimir Azhazha, a physicist and Professor of Mathematics at Moscow University. 'Neil Armstrong relayed the message to Mission Control that two large, mysterious objects were watching them after having landed near the moon module. But his message was never heard by the public – because NASA censored it.' According to another Soviet scientist, Dr Aleksandr Kazantsev, Buzz Aldrin took colour movie film of the UFOs from inside the module, and continued filming them after he and Armstrong went outside. Dr Azhazha claims that the UFOs departed just minutes after the astronauts came out on to the lunar surface.

Maurice Chatelain confirmed that Apollo 11's radio transmissions were interrupted on several occasions in order to hide the news from the public. NASA chief spokesman John McLeaish denied that the agency censored any voice transmissions from Apollo 11, but admitted that a slight delay in transmission took place, due simply to processing through electronic equipment.[44]

Before dismissing Chatelain's sensational claims, it is worth noting his impressive background in the aerospace industry and the space programme. His first job after moving from France was as an electronics engineer with Convair, specializing in telecommunications, telemetry and radar. In 1959 he was in charge of an electromagnetic research group, developing new radar and telecommunications systems for Ryan. One of his eleven patents was an automatic radar landing-system that ignited retro rockets at a given altitude, used in the Ranger and Surveyor flights to the Moon. Later, at North American Aviation, Chatelain was offered the job of designing and building the Apollo communication and data-processing system.[45]

Chatelain also claims that 'all Apollo and Gemini flights were followed, both at a distance and sometimes also quite closely, by space vehicles of extraterrestrial origin – flying saucers, or UFOs . . . if you want to call them by that name. Every time it occurred, the astronauts informed Mission Control, who then ordered absolute silence.' He goes on:

> I think that Walter Schirra aboard Mercury 8 was the first of the astronauts to use the code name 'Santa Claus' to indicate the presence of flying saucers next to space capsules. However, his announcements were barely noticed by the general public. It was a little different when James Lovell on board the Apollo 8 command module came out from behind the moon and said for everybody to hear: 'We have been informed that Santa Claus does exist!' Even though this happened on Christmas Day 1968, many people sensed a hidden meaning in those words . . .[46]

I asked Dr Paul Lowman of NASA's Goddard Space Flight Center what he thought about the Apollo 11 story. He replied:

> Most of the radio communications from the Apollo crew on the surface were relayed in real time to earth. I am continually amazed by people who claim that we have concealed the discovery of extraterrestrial activity on the Moon. The confirmed detection of extraterrestrial life, even if only by radio, will be the greatest scientific discovery of all time, and I speak without exaggeration. The idea that a civilian agency such as NASA, operating in the glare of publicity, could hide such a discovery is absurd, even if it wanted to. One would have to swear to secrecy not only the dozen astronauts who landed on the moon but also the hundreds of engineers, technicians, and secretaries directly involved in the missions and the communication links.[47]

Not all communications between the astronauts and ground control are public, as NASA itself admits. John McLeaish, Chief of Public Information at the Manned Spacecraft Center (now the Lyndon B. Johnson Space Center) in Houston, explained to me in 1970 that, although there is no separate radio frequency used by the astronauts for private conversations with Mission Control, private conversations – 'usually to discuss medical problems' – are rerouted:

> When the astronauts request a private conversation, or when a private conversation is deemed necessary by officials on the ground, it is transmitted on the same S-band radio frequencies as are normally used but it is routed through different audio circuits on the ground; and unlike other air-to-ground conversations with the spacecraft, it is not released to the general public.[48]

Rumours persist about the Apollo 11 story. In 1988 Major (Ret.) Colman VonKeviczky, a New York-based researcher, was informed by an associate of Neil Armstrong that three objects were reportedly seen and photographed at close quarters by the Apollo crew as their craft was about a quarter of the way to the Moon. VonKeviczky's source makes some more, rather unbelievable, claims: that the shadows of alien beings were seen on board, and that, while the Eagle lander made its approach for landing, three (not two, as usually reported) such objects were already on the lunar surface, and that aliens alighted from them. Armstrong allegedly disobeyed orders by Houston not to step out of the module, for which he was forced out of the space programme.[49]

A friend of mine who formerly served in a branch of British military intelligence has provided me with possible corroboration for some of the claims surrounding the Apollo 11 story. I am not permitted to reveal the name of my source, nor the location and date of the following conversation that was overheard and subsequently confirmed by my friend, which inevitably will lay me open to charges of fabricating the story or being the victim of a hoax. Yet the story must be told.

According to my friend, whose hotel room at a NASA symposium in Europe adjoined that of Neil Armstrong, a certain professor (name known to me) was engaged in earnest conversation with Armstrong in the latter's room. Part of the conversation (paraphrased) went as follows:

PROFESSOR: What really happened out there with Apollo 11?
ARMSTRONG: It was incredible . . . of course, we had always

known there was a possibility . . . the fact is, we were warned off. There was never any question then of a space station or a moon city.

PROFESSOR: How do you mean, 'warned off'?

ARMSTRONG: I can't go into details, except to say that their ships were far superior to ours both in size and technology – boy, were they big! . . . and menacing . . . No, there is no question of a space station.

PROFESSOR: But NASA had other missions after Apollo 11?

ARMSTRONG: Naturally – NASA was committed at that time, and couldn't risk a panic on earth . . . but it really was a quick scoop and back again . . .

Later, when my friend confronted Armstrong, the latter confirmed that the story was true but refused to go into further detail, beyond admitting that the CIA was behind the cover-up.

What does Neil Armstrong have to say about the matter officially? In reply to my enquiry he simply stated: 'Your "reliable sources" are unreliable. There were no objects reported, found, or seen on Apollo 11 or any other Apollo flight other than of natural origin. All observations on all Apollo flights were fully reported to the public.'[50]

As a postscript to the Apollo 11 story, there is a tantalizing report by the Spanish pilot José Antonio Silva. At a conference in Victoria, Spain, Silva reportedly claimed as follows: 'During one of the Moon landings [not specified] I had the opportunity in [NASA's] Spanish ground [relay] station at Fresdenillas to follow how one of the astronauts . . . reported the arrival of some beings or objects which, according to the Americans, were seen the day before on the Moon's surface.' The director of the ground station allegedly ordered Silva out of the control room, and forbade him to tell the press what he had overheard.[51]

Physical Evidence?

According to information supplied to science journalist Andreas von Rétyi by a qualified and credible source, NASA may be in possession of physical evidence relating to extraterrestrial materials.

In 1974 'Dr Cris' (pseudonym), a Polish biophysicist and engineer contracted to NASA, was a member of an international team including English, French and Italian scientists which was given some odd metallic-and plastic-like material to analyse. The material supposedly originated from the Soviet Union or another potentially hostile foreign power. Precise details were not given to the team, Dr Cris told von Rétyi, but the team's task over the ensuing months was to research this foreign material to further NASA's own technology.

The outer part of the metallic material was very smooth and shiny, whereas the areas where the material had fractured were matt. The team was allowed to use only tiny samples taken from the separately tagged material. Under analysis with an electron microscope, small pyramid structures in the nanometre range (i.e. one thousand millionth, or 10^{-9} metre), showing a kind of 'super-reflectivity', were revealed. Allegedly, the metallurgical experts found alloys that could only have been made in conditions of weightlessness. Other tests showed traces of unusual Kapton- and Kevlar-type synthetics. Because the materials appeared to have been made in the early 1950s or even earlier, the scientists became suspicious of their origin. 'The main thing', explained Dr Cris, 'is that these "foamed" metals – material like Kevlar – had not existed at that time, and Kapton was unknown. The metal foil had been produced in a similar way as nowadays "glass-metal" is produced; a production procedure unknown at that time.' The melting point of the metal samples was above 2,000 °C, and it was not affected by tests using helium–neon and ruby lasers. Furthermore, the foil seemed to possess a 'memory', such as current memory metals, but to a factor of 10^3 or better. (Several witnesses to the Roswell, New Mexico, incident of July 1947 described some of the recovered metal foil as being impervious to bending or folding, in that it always returned to its original shape.) When the scientists had completed their analysis, the materials were returned to an unnamed facility.

In 1977 the team met again, when a certain NASA official decided to leave the agency because so many programmes were being cancelled owing to lack of funds. The official, also a physicist, organized a small, semi-official 'insider' party at the Jet Propulsion Laboratory, Pasadena, California. At this party, attended by Dr Cris, the official informed his guests that they might be interested in seeing some special 'equipment', and, after much trepidation as to whether or not he should do so, he led them to a restricted area in one of the buildings at the JPL facility. There, three floors below ground level, the team of five scientists entered a secured room, protected by a heavy steel door with two seals. The English scientist broke the upper seal, and the Swiss the lower one. 'The craziest thing was, they actually did it and opened the door!' said Dr Cris. The room, about 8–10 metres in length and over 4 metres wide, seemed to serve principally to exhibit certain items.

'The first thing we saw was two small, shiny plexiglass containers,' continued the biophysicist. 'In one of the two was a hip bone, a bit broken at the bottom. It looked like a child's hip bone, but the form was different . . . ' The structure, shape and colour were somewhat different – that is, not typical yellowish-white but light greyish-white, the cavity for the bone marrow was much smaller, and the structures where the muscles would have been attached were formed differently.

> In the second container we saw the fragment of a skull; maybe one-third or forty percent of it. The segment included the eye socket and part of the right half of the skull. This head was about as big as that of an elderly child. It looked human-like, but derived neither from a child nor from an ape. The colour was different from that of the hip bone – it appeared lighter. I don't know if some parts of the bone had been damaged by fire; in any case, the colour was not the same . . . part of the skull protecting the brain was much thinner than a human's skull. There was even a short, small explanation: *From the first and second incidents in New Mexico.* We took our American friend aside and asked him what this meant. 'That's highly secret,' he replied. 'We are not really allowed to talk about that.'

In addition, three of the five scientists were surprised to recognize the materials from which they had analysed samples in 1974. 'These objects were about half a year in our laboratory,' said Dr Cris:

> The material was probably presented to us to test us; to what extent we would agree, or even find out new things about it. These samples [evidently] had been investigated umpteen times by several teams of scientists in order to gain further insight . . .
>
> In 1947 [Dr Cris learned later] there had been altogether at least two spaceships, with at least three crew, that crashed. It was reported that one member of the second crew had survived. I don't know anything specific about his fate. The first three beings were totally charred, whereas the other two corpses were mostly preserved; for example, the skull, skin and bones. There were also parts of clothing found. As I learned from biologists, their blood is similar to ours but not the same, and it shows a totally different reaction toward oxygen; so inside the spaceship they must breathe a mixture of helium and oxygen, since nitrogen, for whatever reasons, is really not good for them.

Is the whole story a fabrication? Andreas von Rétyi remains open to this possibility, but stresses the credibility of his source. 'In lengthy personal conversations with Dr Cris, I have been able to convince myself of his great knowledge and insights,' he affirms. 'This doesn't prove anything, but his explanations seem logical. Besides, he is unquestionably in a position where he doesn't need to draw attention to himself by making up such a story. He doesn't want any publicity and makes no profit from his statements.'[52,53]

Dr Cris was unable to ascertain the whereabouts of other materials relating to the New Mexico crashes. These incidents, known collectively as 'The Roswell Incident', are the subject of the next chapter.

The Roswell Incident

ONE OF THE MOST CONTENTIOUS aspects of the many-faceted UFO enigma is the allegation that a number of flying saucers, together with their occupants, have crash-landed, and have been recovered by the military forces, acting in great secrecy. Such claims generally are dismissed for lack of proof, yet evidence in some cases is compelling.

One series of incidents that seems indisputable – in the sense that several hundred witnesses have testified to it – is among the most thoroughly documented cases on record. Numerous TV documentaries and a film have now appeared as well as several books describing investigations into the so-called Roswell Incident (by William Moore and Charles Berlitz; Stanton Friedman and Don Berliner; Kevin Randle and Donald Schmitt; and Karl Pflock). The following is a necessarily abbreviated account of a complex case which seems to have involved three separate crash sites in New Mexico. One was at Corona; the precise locations of the other two are still in dispute.

The Corona Debris

During a violent thunderstorm in the first week of July 1947, an unusual aerial vehicle crashed on the J. B. Foster Ranch, south-east of Corona and about 75 miles north-west of Roswell, New Mexico. Early the next morning, ranch manager William 'Mac' Brazel discovered a large amount of unusual debris scattered over a wide area. A few days later, Brazel drove into Roswell and alerted Sheriff George Wilcox, who in turn contacted Roswell Army Air Field, home of the élite 509th Bomb Group, the world's first atomic-bomb unit.

Major Jesse Marcel, the bomb group's intelligence officer, together with Captain Sheridan Cavitt, a Counter Intelligence Corps officer, accompanied Mac Brazel to the site, where a quantity of wreckage was eventually recovered. Marcel testified that he found an area measuring about three-quarters of a mile long by 200 to 300 feet wide, strewn with a large amount of extremely lightweight, strong material.

RAAF Captures Flying Saucer On Ranch in Roswell Region

No Details of Flying Disk Are Revealed

Roswell Hardware Man and Wife Report Disk Seen

The intelligence office of the 509th Bombardment group at Roswell Army Air Field announced at noon today, that the field has come into possession of a flying saucer.

According to information released by the department, over authority of Maj. J. A. Marcel, intelligence officer, the disk was recovered on a ranch in the Roswell vicinity, after an unidentified rancher had notified Sheriff Geo. Wilcox, here, that he had found the instrument on his premises.

Major Marcel and a detail from his department went to the ranch and recovered the disk, it was stated.

After the intelligence office here had inspected the instrument it was flown to "higher headquarters."

The intelligence office stated that no details of the saucer's construction or its appearance had been revealed.

Mr. and Mrs. Dan Wilmot apparently were the only persons in Roswell who have seen what they thought was a flying disk.

They were sitting on their porch at 105 South Penn. last Wednesday night at about ten minutes before ten o'clock when a large glowing object zoomed out of the sky from the southeast, going in a northwesterly direction at a high rate of speed.

Wilmot called Mrs. Wilmot's attention to it and both ran down into the yard to watch. It was in sight less than a minute, perhaps 40 or 50 seconds. Wilmot estimated.

Wilmot said that it appeared to him to be about 1,500 feet high and going fast. He estimated between 400 and 500 miles per hour.

In appearance it looked oval in shape like two inverted saucers, faced mouth to mouth, or like two old type washbowls placed together in the same fashion. The entire body glowed as though light were showing through from inside, though not like it would be if a light were merely underneath.

From where he stood Wilmot said that the object looked to be about 5 feet in size, and making allowance for the distance it was from town he figured that it must have been 15 or 20 feet in diameter, though this was just a guess.

Wilmot said that he heard no sound but that Mrs. Wilmot said she heard a swishing sound for a very short time.

The object came into view from the southeast and disappeared over the treetops in the general vicinity of six-mile hill.

Wilmot, who is one of the most respected and reliable citizens in town, kept the story to himself, hoping that someone else would come out and tell about having seen one, but finally today decided that he would go ahead and tell about seeing it. The announcement that the RAAF was in possession of one came only a few minutes after he had decided to release the details of what he had seen.

—o—

Part of the front-page story from the *Roswell Daily Record* (8 July 1947) describing some of the early events associated with the Roswell incident. (*Roswell Daily Record*)

'We found some . . . small bits of metal, but mostly we found some material that's hard to describe,' Marcel told journalist Bob Pratt in 1979. 'I'd never seen anything like that, and I still don't know what it was . . . I lit a cigarette lighter to some of this stuff, and it didn't burn.' There were also 'small, solid members that you could not bend or break, but it didn't look like metal. It looked more like wood. They varied in size . . . perhaps three-eighths of an inch by one quarter of an inch thick . . . None of them were very long.' The largest of these was about 3 feet long, but weightless. 'You couldn't even tell you had it in your hands – just like you handle balsa wood.' Marcel also described having seen unusual two-colour 'hieroglyphics' on some of the pieces, as well as parchment-like material which, again, did not burn.[1]

In another interview in 1979, Marcel described how later he tried unsuccessfully to bend or dent a piece of extremely light and thin metal which was about 2 feet long and a foot wide. 'I tried to bend the stuff [but] it wouldn't bend,' he said. 'We even tried making a dent in it with a sixteen-pound sledge hammer. And there was still no dent in it . . . It was possible to flex this stuff back and forth, even to wrinkle it, but you could not put a crease in it that would stay . . . I would almost have to describe it as a metal with plastic properties.'[2] Marcel was convinced that the material had nothing to do with a weather balloon or radar target.

The area near Corona was sealed off by the military, and a wide search was initiated to recover the remaining debris. An official press statement was released at the Roswell base, authorized by Colonel William Blanchard, Commander of the 509th Bomb Group. 'I had a call from Colonel Blanchard, and he told me to report to his office,' said Walter Haut, base press officer at the time, during an interview with me. 'He gave me the basic facts that he wanted put into the news release . . . that we had in our possession a flying saucer. A rancher had brought parts of it in to the Sheriff's office, and the material was flown to General Ramey, who was Commanding General of the Eighth Air Force.'[3]

Major Marcel was ordered to load the debris on a B-29 (one of several aircraft said to have been involved in transporting the materials from Roswell Army Air Field) and fly it to Wright Field (now Wright-Patterson Air Force Base) at Dayton, Ohio, for examination. On arrival at an intermediate stop at Fort Worth Army Air Field (later Carswell Air Force Base), Texas (headquarters of the Eighth Air Force), General Roger Ramey took charge. He ordered Marcel and others on the plane not to talk to reporters. A second press statement then was issued which stated that the wreckage was nothing more than the remains of a weather balloon and its attached tinfoil radar target, which were prominently displayed at the press conference. Meanwhile, the *real* wreckage arrived at Wright Field under armed guard; Marcel returned to Roswell, and Brazel was held incommunicado by the military for nearly a week while the crash site was stripped of every scrap of debris.

A news leak via press wire from Albuquerque describing this fantastic story was interrupted and the radio station in question, and another, were warned not to continue the broadcast: 'ATTENTION ALBUQUERQUE: CEASE TRANSMISSION. REPEAT. CEASE TRANSMISSION. NATIONAL SECURITY ITEM. DO NOT TRANSMIT. STAND BY . . .'[4]

Project Mogul

It has been suggested that at least *some* of the wreckage found near Corona could have come from a Top Secret project to develop a means of detecting and monitoring Soviet nuclear weapons – code-named Project Mogul – which conducted its operations from Alamogordo Army Air Field, New Mexico, in June and July 1947, using high-altitude balloon arrays and attached instrument packages. Flight 7, for instance, which lifted off on 2 July – when the unidentified aircraft is reported as having crashed near Corona – incorporated twenty meteorological balloons (to support the various devices attached). The array measured about 450 feet from top to bottom. All that was recovered at the landing-site – 31 miles east of Alamogordo in the Sacramento Mountains – was 'one balloon neck'. On 3 July, another array of balloons (Flight 8) – made of then new polyethylene material – touched down about 20 miles west-north-west of the Alamogordo base and last was seen dragging north across the desert. Nothing ever was recovered.[5] Although there is no proof that these balloons (and others in the Mogul series) came down in the Corona area, it is certainly possible that one of them – or at least some of the materials – did.

In his book *Roswell in Perspective*, Karl Pflock, a former CIA officer whose background in government included a position as Deputy Assistant Secretary of Defense (Deputy Director) for Operational Test and Evaluation, states his belief that one or more of these balloon arrays was responsible for the debris found near Corona (a conclusion shared by the Air Force in its 1994 report, to be discussed later). More recent research suggests that Mogul Flight 4, launched on 4 June 1947, was the one most likely to have come down in the vicinity of Corona. (Pflock remains open-minded, however, to the probability that alien or unusual bodies were recovered elsewhere.) He correlates descriptions of the unknown debris with the known materials used in the Mogul arrays, including the testimony of Dr Jesse Marcel Jr (Major Marcel's son) who handled some of the Corona wreckage collected by his father. In an affidavit, Jesse Jr reported that the debris included:

> . . . a brittle, brownish-black plastic-like material, like Bakelite; and there were fragments of what appeared to be I-beams. On the inner surface of the I-beam, there appeared to be a type of writing [of] a purple-violet hue, and it had an embossed appearance. The figures were composed of curved, geometric shapes. It had no resemblance to Russian, Japanese or any other foreign language. It resembled hieroglyphics, but it had no animal-like characters.[6]

As Pflock points out, materials used in the construction of Project Mogul's instrument packages included aluminium foil laminated on to a tough white or brown paper or tough aluminium-coated paper, struts of hardened balsa wood, Bakelite, and clear or whitish sticky tape, about 2 inches wide, with 'pink and purple flower-like figures on it'.[7] Mac Brazel's daughter, Bessie, who helped her father collect some of the debris on their ranch, recalls that:

> The debris looked like pieces of a large balloon which had burst . . . Most of it was a kind of double-sided material, foil-like on one side and rubbery-like on the other . . . the foil more silvery than the rubber. Sticks, like kite sticks, were attached to some of the pieces with a whitish tape . . . about two or three inches wide and had flower-like designs on it . . .[8]

It is evident from the foregoing that at least *some* of the wreckage recovered on Mac Brazel's ranch may have been of man-made origin, though it is impossible to reconcile this explanation with all the facts. Major Marcel, it should be noted, was familiar with balloon debris and was convinced that the material *he* handled was unfamiliar, in that it was impossible to dent or burn, and that, no matter what was done to it, the foil-like metal always returned to its original shape. Such materials hardly relate to Mogul.

Currently the State Surgeon of Montana and a colonel with the Montana Air National Guard (flying helicopters), Jesse Jr disputes the contention that the debris he handled was from a Mogul balloon or instrument package. 'The Mogul device apparently was a lot of metal foil with white paper backing to strengthen it,' he said in 1995. 'The material I saw was metal foil, but did not have the white paper backing.' Lieutenant McAndrew – the Air Force's principal researcher for the 1994 report, who interviewed Dr Marcel after the Air Force had prepared its report, also said that the debris included tape with flowery figures written across it. 'Well, I didn't see any tape,' said Dr Marcel. 'And there was supposed to be some balsa wood struts with the Mogul device, but I didn't see any balsa wood. I saw metal struts, not balsa wood struts, and the writing I saw was on the metal strut itself, not on tape.'[9]

Containment Strategy

Numerous military and civilian personnel have testified that an elaborate deception operation followed the recovery of the Corona wreckage. It is hard to believe that this was initiated solely to avoid compromising the classified Mogul project.

Thomas Jefferson DuBose was Chief of Staff to Major General Roger Ramey at Fort Worth Army Air Field during the Roswell incident. A colonel at the time, he retired from the Air Force in 1959 with the rank of brigadier general. In an interview with Billy Cox (whom I know to be reliable), DuBose confirmed that a 'containment strategy' was ordered by Major General Clements McMullen, Deputy Commander, Strategic Air Command. 'Knowing General McMullen,' said DuBose, '[the cover-up] was an effort to get it off the front pages, to keep people from thinking about it. I couldn't blame him for that.'

On the evening of 6 July 1947, after a stopover in Fort Worth and by order of McMullen, the debris was flown to Washington, according to DuBose. '[Some of] this stuff, this junk, this whatever you want to call it, came in a mail pouch,' he recalled:

> I didn't look at it, I wasn't supposed to. McMullen told me to send it to him immediately, and for me not to say anything about it to anyone, to forget about it, and that was an order. I sealed it personally with a lead seal and handcuffed it to the wrist of [Colonel] Al Clark, which is a rather unusual step, and he delivered it to McMullen. Later, after the whole thing was over, I asked Clements what happened to it, and he said he sent it out to Wright Field so they could analyze it . . .

Following the press release issued by Walter Haut, the Roswell Army Air Field was deluged with calls. 'It was getting ridiculous,' said DuBose:

There was a host of people descending on our headquarters [at Forth Worth] seeking information from Ramey, badgering him for information we didn't have. I didn't know what it was. Blanchard didn't know. Ramey didn't know – we were in a real bind. McMullen said, Look, why don't you come up with something, anything you can use to get the press off our back? So we came up with this weather balloon story. Somebody got one and we ran it up a couple of hundred feet and dropped it to make it look like it crashed, and that's what we used. Now I imagine, privately, some people felt bad about doing things that way. But it worked. The story stuck.

There were also other reasons for the containment strategy. 'You have to understand what was happening in this country at the time, things that had never happened before in the history of man,' DuBose explained to Billy Cox. 'We had just gone through a world war. We had seen the firebombing of great cities, atomic bombs, destruction on an unprecedented scale. Then came this flying saucer business. It was just too much for the public to have to deal with.'[10]

Top-Secret Studies

Brigadier General Arthur Exon (retired) is a former pilot with over 300 hours of combat during the Second World War. After the war he was assigned to Air Matériel Command HQ at Wright Field (later Wright-Patterson Air Force Base), and became commander of the base in 1964. In interviews with Kevin Randle and Don Schmitt, authors of two books on the Roswell incident, Exon confirmed that the peculiar fragments from New Mexico were secretly flown to Wright Field, and that laboratory chiefs established a special projects unit to study them. As a lieutenant colonel at the time, Exon says that he handled some of the wreckage. Various scientific tests were carried out, including 'chemical analysis, stress tests, compression tests, flexing', he told Randle and Schmitt:

It was brought into our material evaluation labs . . . [Some of it] could be easily ripped or changed . . . there were other parts of it that were very thin but awfully strong and couldn't be dented with heavy hammers . . . It was flexible to a degree . . . some of it was flimsy and was tougher than hell and other[s] almost like foil but strong . . . The metal and material was unknown to anyone I talked to. Whatever they found, I never heard what the results were. A couple of guys thought it might be Russian but the overall consensus was that the pieces were from space.

Exon surmised that some remnants were still stored at Wright-Patterson Air Force Base, most probably at the Foreign Technology Division (now the National Air Intelligence Center).[11] Interestingly, I have learned from a confidential source that even some recovered fabric was subjected to a process of analysis known as 'reverse engineering', in an endeavour to discover the composition of unknown materials contained therein.

An unauthenticated 'Top Secret/Eyes Only' memorandum (see p. 467) leaked to the researcher Timothy Cooper may shed further light on the initial studies of the recovered materials. Purportedly written by Rear Admiral Roscoe Hillenkoetter, Director of Central Intelligence, and sent to the Joint Intelligence Committee, the memo states:

> Currently, the core material is being secured at the Naval Research Laboratory hangar facilities at the White Sands Proving Ground, the Sandia Base facilities (Armed Forces Special Weapons Project), Alamogordo AAF and the Aero Medical Research facilities at Randolph Field, Texas . . . The research scientists at the Air Forces Research and Development Center, Wright Field, are utilizing their test facilities and a new biological laboratory in an on-going study program . . .[12]

Majestic-12

In December 1984 Hollywood TV producer Jaime Shandera received in the post a package from an anonymous source containing an undeveloped roll of 35mm film. When developed, the frames showed eight pages of an alleged preliminary briefing-paper prepared on 18 November 1952 for President-elect Eisenhower by Rear Admiral Roscoe Hillenkoetter, the former CIA Director, and a 24 September 1947 memo from President Truman to Secretary of Defense James Forrestal, supposedly authorizing 'Operation Majestic Twelve'. The briefing-paper, classified 'TOP SECRET/ MAJIC/EYES ONLY', summarized what the alleged Majestic-12 committee

CENTRAL INTELLIGENCE GROUP
2430 E Street, N. W.
Washington 25, D. C.

19 SEP 1947

MEMORANDUM FOR THE MILITARY ASSESSMENT OF THE JOINT INTELLIGENCE
COMMITTEE

SUBJECT: Examination of Unidentified Disc-like Aircraft near Military
           Installations in the State of New Mexico: A Preliminary Report

1.   Pursuant to the recent world events and domestic security
problems within the Atomic Energy Commission, the intelligence reports
of so-called "Flying Saucers" and the intrusion of unknown aircraft over
the most secret defense installations, a classified intelligence project
is warranted. The National Security Act of 1947 established a Central
Intelligence Agency under the National Security Council. When the
Director of Central Intelligence assumes his official responsibilities,
the National Intelligence Authority is abolished the files pertaining to
unidentified aircraft sightings, intelligence personnel and funds of the
Central Intelligence Group will be transferred to the Agency.

2.   The recovery of unidentified planform aircraft in the state of
New Mexico on 6 July 1947, ten miles northwest of Oscura Peak, and a debris
field 75 miles northwest of the Army's 509th Atomic Bomb Group, Roswell
Army Air Field, is confirmed. A subsequent capture of another similar cra
30 miles east of the Army's Alamogordo Army Air Field on 5 July 1947, has
convinced the Army Air Forces S-2, Army G-2 and Navy ONI, that the craft
and wreckage are not of US manufacture.

3.   Until a clear directive from the President is issued, there can
be no co-ordinated scientific examination of the objects in question.
Currently, the core material is being secured at the Naval Research
Laboratory hanger facilities at the White Sands Proving Ground, the Sandia
Base facilities (Armed Forces Special Weapons Project), Alamogordo AAF and
the Aero Medical Research facilities at Randolph Field, Texas.

4.   The research scientists at the Air Forces Research and Development Center, Wright Field, are utilizing their test facilities and a new
biological laboratory in an on-going study program. The offices of the
JRDB, FBI and the State Department are assisting the Joint Intelligence
Committee in acquiring any intelligence from MI5 and MI6 on possible Sovie
long-range reconnaissance aircraft/missile research and development tests.

/s/

R. H. HILLENKOETTER
Rear   Admiral, USN
Director of   Central Intelligence

TOP SECRET/EYES ONLY

An unauthenticated 'Top Secret/Eyes Only' memorandum from Rear Admiral Roscoe
Hillenkoetter, Director of Central Intelligence, relating to unidentified discs recovered by the
military in New Mexico in July 1947. The handwritten note seems to read: 'Joint Chiefs
concern'. (*Timothy Cooper*)

had learned about the UFO problem up to 1952, including details about the Roswell recovery.

In early 1987 I received a copy of the documents from an intelligence source in the United States, and these were published for the first time in my book *Above Top Secret* later that year. Some valid objections to the authenticity of the documents have been made over the years,[13] not least that the signature of Truman almost certainly was 'lifted' from a known-to-be-authentic document. And surely General Eisenhower, as Army Chief of Staff in 1947, would already have been given *some* details of the Roswell incident, at least. These and other apparent inconsistencies are discussed in exhaustive studies by Stanton Friedman[14] and by William Moore and Jaime Shandera,[15] who suggest that, even if the documents are bogus (which I believe to be the case), some of the details contained therein are factual: it is evident that whoever produced the documents had inside knowledge. For this reason, I regard the MJ-12 briefing-paper as 'positive disinformation'.

I have been criticized for publishing an 'obviously fraudulent' document. Still, it has to be said that at least one intelligence expert shared my original belief that the MJ-12 papers *seemed* authentic. In a letter to aerospace engineer Lee Graham, Richard M. Bissell Jr, a former CIA Deputy Director of Plans who had been on President Truman's White House staff, wrote that, although he had no knowledge of Majestic-12, the Eisenhower briefing-document 'certainly *looks* authentic', and added: 'On the basis of the material you have sent me I personally have little doubt that it is authentic.'[16] Later he changed his opinion, explaining in a letter to sceptic Philip Klass that initially he had been 'unaware that the authenticity of the material had been seriously questioned'.[17]

Yet even if both documents are bogus, several scientific and intelligence personnel have confirmed that a committee known as Majestic-12 (Majic-12 or MJ-12) did indeed exist, and that it dealt with the recovery of extraterrestrial craft. British-born Dr Eric A. Walker, for example, who died in 1995, was a Harvard graduate whose former posts included Executive Secretary of the Research and Development Board, Chairman of the National Science Foundation's Committee for Engineering, Chairman of the Institute for Defense Analysis, and President of Pennsylvania State University. In a recorded telephone conversation with researcher William Steinman, Dr Walker confirmed that he had attended meetings at Wright-Patterson Air Force Base (around 1949–50) concerning the military recovery of flying saucers and bodies of occupants.

'Did you ever hear of the MJ-12 group?' asked Steinman. 'Yes, I know of MJ-12. I have known of them for forty years,' replied Dr Walker. 'You are delving into an area that you can do absolutely nothing about,' he added. 'Why don't you just leave it alone and drop it?'[18]

French researcher Jean Sider reports that he too has obtained confirmation for the existence of MJ-12. 'One comes first-hand from a retired American scientist, the other second-hand from a friend, himself an official, who received the information from a high-ranking military officer still on active duty.'[19]

The briefing-document names the alleged twelve original members of the MJ-12 panel, as follows:

Dr Lloyd Berkner: a scientist who was Executive Secretary of the Joint Research and Development Board in 1946 (under Dr Vannevar Bush). He headed a special committee to direct a study that led to the establishment of the Weapons Systems Evaluation Group, and was also a member of the CIA's 'Robertson Panel', a scientific advisory panel on UFOs requested by the White House and sponsored by the CIA in 1953 (see Chapter 16).

Dr Detlev Bronk: an internationally known physiologist and biophysicist who was Chairman of the National Research Council and a member of the Medical Advisory Board of the Atomic Energy Commission. With Dr Edward Condon, Director of the National Bureau of Standards (who later headed the Air Force-sponsored UFO project at the University of Colorado), Bronk became a member of the Scientific Advisory Committee of the Brookhaven National Laboratory.

Dr Vannevar Bush: recognized as one of America's leading scientists, he organized the National Defense Research Council in 1941 and the Office of Scientific Research and Development in 1943, which led to the establishment of the Manhattan Project to develop the first atomic bomb. After the war Dr Bush became head of the Joint Research and Development Board. As the Canadian Government scientist Wilbert Smith noted in a Top Secret memorandum (Chapter 10), Dr Bush headed a 'small group' set up to investigate UFOs, which matter 'is the most highly classified subject in the United States Government, rating higher even than the H-bomb'. Could this 'small group' have been 'Majestic 12'? If so, Bush's background in co-ordinating top-secret intelligence research projects – and his concern with the compartmentalization of classified information – would have made him the ideal choice to head the group. In 1949, for instance, the US Intelligence Board, the co-ordinating body of all US Government intelligence agencies, commissioned Bush to recommend methods of linking all the intelligence bureaucracies, a move initiated by James Forrestal – coincidentally another alleged member of MJ-12.

James Forrestal: served as Secretary of the Navy before becoming Secretary of Defense in July 1947 (the time of the Roswell incident) – a position held until a mental breakdown led to his resignation in March 1949. He committed suicide at Bethesda Naval Hospital in May 1949. The MJ-12 briefing paper names General Walter Bedell Smith (see below) as his successor.

Gordon Gray: Assistant Secretary of the Army at the time MJ-12 was supposedly established, he became Secretary of the Army in 1949. In 1949 he was also appointed as Special Assistant to President Truman on National Security Affairs, and in 1951 directed the CIA's Psychological Strategy Board. (The latter is referred to in a 1952 directive to the National Security Council from CIA Director Walter Bedell Smith – see p. 401.) He was also adviser on national security matters to President Eisenhower in the last two years of his term of office, and was a chairman of the highly secret '54/12 Group' or 'Special Group' formed in the early years of the Eisenhower administration.[20]

Rear Admiral Roscoe Hillenkoetter: the third Director of Central Intelligence, from 1947 to 1950, and the first Director of the CIA, which was established in the same month as the supposed MJ-12 group – September 1947. Hillenkoetter was one of the first intelligence chiefs to make public his conviction that UFOs are real, and that 'through official secrecy and ridicule, many citizens are led to believe the unknown flying objects are nonsense' (Chapter 16). Hillenkoetter was also on the board of directors of the National Investigations Committee on Aerial Phenomena, and was therefore in an excellent position to monitor the activities of this influential civilian group.

Dr Jerome Hunsaker: a brilliant aircraft designer who headed the Departments of Mechanical and Aeronautical Engineering at the Massachusetts Institute of Technology, he was Chairman of the National Advisory Committee for Aeronautics. His opinion on the materials recovered at Roswell would have been invaluable.

Dr Donald Menzel: Director of the Harvard College Observatory, he is chiefly remembered for his dismissive statements and books on UFOs, *all* of which, he insisted, could be explained in mundane terms. The name of Menzel on the MJ-12 list came as a complete surprise, until Stanton Friedman learned that he had been a top-class expert in code-breaking (holding a Top Secret Ultra security clearance), had a lengthy association with the National Security Agency and its predecessor Navy group, and furthermore had been a consultant to several US Presidents on national security affairs![21]

General Robert Montague: base commander at the Atomic Energy Commission installation at Sandia Base, Albuquerque, New Mexico, from July 1947 to February 1951.

Rear Admiral Sidney Souers: the first Director of Central Intelligence (January–June 1946), who in September 1947 (when MJ-12 was allegedly set up) became Executive Secretary of the National Security Council. Following his resignation in 1959 Souers was retained as a special consultant to the Executive on security matters.

General Nathan Twining: an outstanding commander of bombing operations in both the European and Pacific theatres during the Second World War. In 1945 he was appointed Commanding-General of Air Matériel Command, based at Wright Field (Wright-Patterson Air Force Base). A declassified document reveals that in September 1947 Twining presented the conclusions of AMC that 'the phenomenon reported is something real' (see Chapter 14). Significantly, Twining suddenly cancelled a planned trip to the West Coast on 8 July 1947, the day of the first press release announcing the recovery of a crashed disc near Roswell, 'due to a very important and sudden matter'. Researcher William Moore has learned that while reporters were told that Twining was out of the office, 'probably in Washington DC', he had in fact made a sudden trip to New Mexico, where he remained until 10 July.[22]

The remaining member of the alleged MJ-12 panel was General Hoyt Vandenberg. Following a distinguished career in the Army Air Forces, he became the second Director of Central Intelligence in 1946, a position he held until May 1947. In August 1948, when a Top Secret 'Estimate of the Situation' by the Air Technical Intelligence Center offered its opinion that UFOs were interplanetary, Vandenberg – Air Force Chief of Staff at the time – ordered the document to be burned (Chapter 14).

The Bodies

The most controversial and confusing aspect of the Roswell case centres around the claim by a number of military and civilian witnesses that not only were there *three* crash sites, but that alien bodies were discovered at two of them, and controversy surrounds the precise location of these sites. In the unauthenticated Top Secret memorandum cited earlier (not to be confused with the MJ-12 briefing-paper), Rear Admiral Hillenkoetter allegedly stated that:

The recovery of unidentified planform aircraft in the state of New Mexico on 6 July 1947, ten miles northwest of Oscura Peak, and a debris field 75 miles northwest of the Army's 509th Atomic Bomb Group, Roswell Army Air Field, is confirmed. A subsequent capture of another similar craft 30 miles east of the Army's Alamogordo Army Air Field on 5 July 1947, has convinced the Army Air Forces S-2, Army G-2 and Navy ONI, that the craft and wreckage are not of US manufacture.

No reference is made in this document to the recovery of alien bodies, possibly because – assuming the document to be genuine – such information would have been restricted to those with an appropriate Top Secret-based compartmented access.

Major Jesse Marcel was quite certain that no bodies were among the debris he collected near Corona, and that whatever the object was it must have exploded above ground. In a recorded interview with Randle and Schmitt, Brigadier General Arthur Exon testified that in November 1947 he personally flew over two crash sites. At the second site – reported by Schmitt and Randle to be about 35 miles north-north-west of Roswell Army Air Field, based on dubious testimony (and not corroborated by Exon) – the main body of the craft apparently had come to rest. 'They did say there were bodies,' said Exon. 'They were all found, apparently, outside the craft itself but were in fairly good condition. In other words, they weren't broken up a lot.'[23]

Interestingly, although professing no knowledge of a 'Majestic-12' group, Exon stated that, following the incident, a highly secret committee – which he referred to as the 'Unholy Thirteen' – was set up under President Truman and controlled all access to the wreckage, bodies and all information thereon and, later, to all classified UFO reports. The committee members, he is quoted as having told Randle and Schmitt, included General Carl Spaatz, first US Air Force Chief of Staff; James Forrestal, then Secretary of War; and probably the Director of the CIA, Rear Admiral Hillenkoetter.[24] (General Exon has subsequently pointed out that he only suggested these names as possibilities.)

Stanton Friedman, who has devoted many years to studying the Majestic-12 affair, is convinced that the briefing-document contains significant information – not least, regarding the Roswell incident. According to the document, during the recovery of the debris 75 miles north-west of Roswell:

. . . aerial reconnaissance discovered that four small human-like beings had apparently ejected from the craft at some point before it exploded. These had fallen to earth about two miles east of the wreckage site. All four were dead and badly decomposed due to action by predators and exposure to the elements during the approximately one week time period which had elapsed before their discovery. A special scientific team took charge of removing these bodies for study . . .

The briefing-paper goes on:

A covert effort organized by Gen. Twining and Dr. Bush acting on the direct orders of the President, resulted in a preliminary consensus . . . that the disc was most likely a short range reconnaissance craft. This conclusion was based for the most part on the craft's size and the apparent lack of any identifiable provisioning . . . A similar analysis of the four dead occupants was arranged by Dr. Bronk. It was the tentative conclusion of this group . . . that although these creatures are human-like in appearance, the biological and evolutionary processes responsible for their development has [sic] apparently been quite different from those observed or postulated in homo-sapiens. Dr. Bronk's team has suggested the term 'Extra-terrestrial Biological Entities', or 'EBEs', be adopted as the standard term of reference for these creatures until such time as a more definitive designation can be agreed upon.

Although not mentioned in the spurious MJ-12 briefing-paper, there was reportedly another crash site in an area west of Socorro, New Mexico, in the Plains of San Agustin, where witnesses allegedly discovered not only a damaged metallic disc resting on the flat desert ground, but also dead bodies – and possibly a survivor. The location of this site remains in dispute. If the unauthenticated memorandum from Hillenkoetter of 19 September 1947, for example, is anything to go by, the second recovery of an 'unidentified planform aircraft' (in addition to the wreckage site 75 miles north-west of Roswell) occurred 10 miles north-west of Oscura Peak, 35 miles *south-east* of Socorro. This would place it within the White Sands Proving Ground, but nowhere near the Plains of San Agustin. According to Hillenkoetter's report, the first recovery took place 30 miles east of Alamogordo Army Air Field, over 100 miles south-east of Socorro – again, nowhere near the Plains.

An early witness on the scene was Grady L. 'Barney' Barnett, a civil engineer with the US Soil Conservation Service who was on a military assignment at the time, working from Magdalena. He told his friends LaVerne and Jean Maltais that in the late 1940s (the July 1947 date later established by Stanton Friedman) he had encountered a metallic, disc-shaped 'aircraft' in the desert. While he was examining it, a small group of people arrived who said they were part of an archaeological research team from the University of Pennsylvania.

According to the Maltaises, Barnett recalled that the bodies apparently had fallen out of the craft, which had split open on impact. The disc seemed to be made of a metal that looked like dirty stainless steel. When Barnett approached for a closer look, he noticed dead bodies inside and outside the vehicle – the ones outside thrown out by the impact. They were like humans but they were not humans, he reported. The heads were round and larger in proportion to their bodies, hairless, and the eyes small and oddly spaced. Their clothing seemed to be one-piece and grey in colour, without zippers, belts or buttons. Military personnel approached and cordoned off the area. 'We were told to leave the area and not to talk to anyone whatever about what we had seen . . . that it was our patriotic duty to remain silent,' Barnett told the Maltaises.[25] In his affidavit, included in a briefing for the Congressional Staff prepared by Fred Whiting and the Fund for UFO Research, LaVerne Maltais stated as follows:

> . . . Around 1950, Mr. Barnett told me that several years before, during a field trip in New Mexico, he discovered a crashed disc-shaped craft with the bodies of strange beings on the ground. He was absolutely convinced that the craft was from outer space.
>
> The beings he described were similar – but not identical – to humans. They were 3½ to 4 feet tall; slim and hairless, with large pear-shaped heads. They had four fingers on each hand. They were dressed in tight-fitting, metallic suits. All of them were dead.
>
> Mr. Barnett said that at the time of his discovery, he was joined by four or five people on an archeology dig.
>
> Shortly afterward, military personnel arrived and escorted them from the area. They told him to keep quiet about the incident, that it was in the national interest for them to get out of there.
>
> Mr. Barnett was a man of great personal integrity who would never tell a lie.[26]

At least three other local people told Stanton Friedman about their recollections of a flying saucer having crashed 'out in the Plains' at the time: one confirmed that it had been brought out at night by the military, through Magdalena.[27] And in the 1960s William D. Leed III, then a Colonel with the US Army Reserve Signal Corps, who had a strong interest in UFOs, went to visit Barnett, at the suggestion of a fellow officer. In his affidavit, included in the Fund for UFO Research's Congressional briefing, Leed stated:

> . . . In early September of 1964 or 1965, I visited Mr. Barnett at his home in Roswell, N.M., and identified myself as a member of the military whose interest was purely personal and not official. I talked with him for about 15 minutes. He told me of coming upon a 'flying saucer' in the desert more than 10 years before and inspecting it. He said he touched it and found it not to be hot. It had a very smooth surface. He said it was about 12 feet across and saucer-shaped. He walked around it but was unable to enter it.
>
> He said that, two-to-three days later, the area was swarming with people from the U.S. Army Air Forces who removed the 'saucer'.
>
> Mr. Barnett told me he was subsequently interviewed for many hours on at least three occasions by men from several different levels of government, was told to 'shut up', and was threatened, and felt threatened by them . . .[28]

Another, more controversial witness to the alleged Plains of San Agustin incident is Gerald Anderson, who claims to have been present at the crash site (near Horse Springs) when he was six years old, together with his father, brother, uncle and cousin. He confirms that five college students and their professor (Dr Buskirk) subsequently arrived on the scene, and insists that one of the three alien creatures survived the crash. Anderson has provided a great deal of intriguing information, published in Stanton Friedman's and Don Berliner's book *Crash at Corona*.[29] Although Schmitt and Randle reject the Anderson story outright, Friedman and Berliner present some evidence for its authenticity.

The Plains of San Agustin are about 150 miles west of the Corona site. Was the disc allegedly recovered near Horse Springs another craft that had also come to grief independently, or had it collided with the disc supposedly recovered closer to Roswell? Randle and Schmitt have satisfied themselves that the archaeological research team was present at a site 35 miles north-north-west of Roswell (their preferred location for the recovery of bodies) – not the Plains of San Agustin[30] – but Friedman and Berliner dispute this. And it has to be said that the testimony of Frank Kaufmann, who provided the location of this site, is extremely dubious, as Karl Pflock shows convincingly.[31]

Among those assigned to guarding one of the crash sites and, later, removing the bodies to the Roswell base was Sergeant Melvin Brown, who years later told his family about the incident. 'They had to form a ring around whatever it was they had to cover, and everything was put on trucks,' said Beverley Bean, one of Brown's daughters, when I interviewed the family:

> They were told not to look and to take no notice, and were sworn to secrecy. I can remember my dad saying he couldn't understand why they wanted refrigerated trucks. And him and another guy had to sit on the back of the truck to take this stuff to a hangar. They were packed in ice. And he lifted up the tarpaulin and looked in, and he saw three (or possibly two) dead bodies.
>
> He told us they were nothing to be scared of. They were friendly-looking and had nice faces. They looked Asian, he said, but had larger heads and no hair. They looked a yellowy colour. He was frightened a bit, because he knew he shouldn't be doing it, so he only had a quick glimpse.[32]

According to other witnesses, the initial autopsies were carried out at Roswell Army Air Field. Glenn Dennis, a mortician with the Ballard Funeral Home, who did contract work at the base (including ambulance work), is one of many who have signed affidavits for a Congressional inquiry, testifying to the recovery of alien wreckage and bodies. For me, his testimony is reliable and convincing.

One afternoon in July 1947 Dennis was asked by the base mortuary officer about the availability of small, hermetically sealed coffins, in case they might be needed 'in future'. Less than an hour later the officer called again, asking Dennis to describe the chemical preparation for bodies that had been lying in the desert for a period of time and what effect such procedures would have on the bodies' chemical compounds, blood and tissues.

Dennis explained that the chemicals he used were mainly strong solutions of formaldehyde and water, and that the procedure would probably alter the bodily chemical composition. 'I offered to come out to the base to assist with any problem he might have,' Dennis stated, 'but he reiterated that the information was for future use.'

Just over an hour later Dennis received a request to transport a serviceman who had been injured in an unrelated incident. He drove an ambulance to the back of the base infirmary and parked alongside another ambulance. 'The door was open and inside I saw some wreckage,' he reports in his affidavit. 'There were several pieces . . . about three feet in length [which] resembled stainless steel with a purple hue, as if it had been exposed to high temperature. There was some strange-looking writing on the material resembling Egyptian hieroglyphics. Also two MPs [military policemen] were present.'

After checking in the serviceman, Dennis proceeded to the staff lounge, intending to look for a nurse – a second lieutenant – with whom he was romantically involved.

> I saw her coming out of one of the examining rooms with a cloth over her mouth. She said, 'My gosh, get out of here or you're going to be in a lot of trouble.' She went into another door where a captain stood. He asked me who I was and what I was doing here. I told him, and he instructed me to stay there. I said, 'It looks like you've got a crash; would you like me to get ready?' He told me to stay right there. The two MPs came and began to escort me out of the infirmary. They said they had orders to follow me out to the funeral home.

Another captain then advised Dennis that he had seen nothing, that there had been no crash, and that if he said anything he could get into a lot of trouble. 'Hey look, mister,' said Dennis, 'I'm a civilian and you can't do a damn thing to me.' 'Yes we can,' replied the captain, 'somebody will be picking your bones out of the sand.'

The following day, Dennis tried to contact the nurse, who later called back and agreed to meet him. 'Before I talk to you,' she insisted, 'you have to give me your sacred oath that you will never mention my name.' Dennis gave his word, and she told him an extraordinary story.

The nurse said she had been asked by two doctors to take notes while they performed a preliminary autopsy on three small bodies, $3\frac{1}{2}$ to 4 feet in height. There was a terrible smell, and it was the most gruesome sight she had ever seen. Two of the bodies were mangled and dismembered, but one was fairly intact. Their heads were disproportionately large for their bodies, and the skulls were flexible. Their eyes were deeply set, their noses concave with two small orifices, and the mouths consisted of a fine slit, with what the doctors described as heavy cartilage instead of teeth. The ears were merely small orifices with flaps. They had no hair, and the skin was very darkened – perhaps from exposure to the sun. The arms were long and slender, with four fingers on the hand which appeared to have small suction cups at each tip. The nurse said that she and the doctors became ill, and the air conditioning had to be turned off in case the smell permeated the hospital. Eventually the autopsy had to be moved to an aircraft hangar.'[33]

Glenn Dennis reports that the nurse (recently named as Naomi Maria Seiff) was transferred to England, and later he learned that apparently she had been killed in a plane crash during a training mission. No evidence for such a crash has been forthcoming.

Oliver Wendell Henderson, stationed at Roswell Army Air Field during the time of the New Mexico crash/retrievals, is yet another witness who has provided testimony. 'Pappy' Henderson, who held a Top Secret clearance, ran the 'Green Hornet Airline', which involved flying C-54 and C-47 military transport aircraft, carrying VIPs, scientists and materials from Roswell to the Pacific, during the atom-bomb tests. After seeing an article about the Roswell incident in a newspaper in 1980 or 1981, Henderson told his wife to read the article. 'It's a true story,' he said. 'I'm the pilot who flew the wreckage of the UFO to Dayton, Ohio. I guess now that they're putting it in the papers, I can tell you about this.'

According to an affidavit by Sappho Henderson, her husband described the beings as small, with large heads for their size. 'He said the material that their suits were made of was different from anything he had ever seen. He said they looked strange. I believe he mentioned that the bodies had been packed in dry ice to preserve them.'[34]

Congressional Inquiry

In March 1993, armed with numerous affidavits, US Congressman Steven Schiff (First Congressional District, New Mexico) decided to initiate official inquiries into the Roswell incident. Schiff, who has a background in law and serves as a lieutenant colonel in the New Mexico Air National Guard, began with a letter to Defense Secretary Les Aspin, requesting a written report and a full briefing by Pentagon officials on the nature of the debris recovered outside Roswell in July 1947 and an explanation for the Government's actions. There was no response.

A second request resulted in a reply from the Defense Department's congressional liaison office, referring the Congressman to the National Archives, on the grounds that all Air Force records from Project Blue Book were stored there. But no files on Roswell could be found in Blue Book records.

'I thought this would be a routine request handled in a routine way,' said Congressman Schiff during an interview in his office with Lawrence Moore and me for a British documentary in 1994. 'I felt that the response I got was not routine – to just be referred to another agency without even an offer of assistance . . . That simple bit of courtesy is something frankly I would have expected from a Government agency. And I don't recall any such similar response where basically the request was just blown off.'[35]

In October 1993 Schiff decided to take up the matter with the Comptroller General, Charles Bowsher, head of the General Accounting Office (GAO), the investigative arm of Congress. Within a few days Schiff's office received a call from the GAO investigator (a specialist in military and intelligence matters) who had been assigned to the case.

The GAO investigation ran into difficulties at its outset. Colonel Larry Shockley, Director for Plans and Operations in the Secretary of Defense's congressional liaison office, reportedly told the GAO investigator who indicated an interest in the Roswell case that 'You've got no business getting into that.'[36]

'My own inclination is not toward an extraterrestrial explanation,' Schiff told us in 1994:

There remains every possibility that this was a weather balloon accompanied by a public-relations fiasco. If it's not a weather balloon, I would look for something maybe being tested at White Sands Missile Range, which is nearby, for an explanation. But clearly a lot of questions have been raised – questions which suggest that, even if one does not believe in extraterrestrial visitation, this wasn't a weather balloon. From the statements of witnesses that I've seen and read, a number of individuals described that whatever it was that was recovered . . . the materials were under armed guard. And I think it's logical to say that weather balloons aren't normally flown in special planes under armed guard.

To Congressman Schiff the overall issue is not exactly what the device was but the US Government's accounting for what it was. 'I think everybody has a right to go to their Government and to see documents, unless there is a clear and immediate and present security reason why they may not be permitted to do so,' he says.[37]

The Air Force Report

In September 1994 – perhaps to pre-empt the GAO's findings, which were made available to Congressman Schiff's office in July 1995 – the Air Force issued a twenty-three-page *Report of Air Force Research Regarding the 'Roswell Incident'*. The report concluded that a Project Mogul balloon array and instrument package were most probably responsible for the tales of a crashed flying saucer:

> The Air Force research did not locate or develop any information that the 'Roswell Incident' was a UFO event. All available official materials, although they do not directly address Roswell *per se*, indicate that the most likely source of the wreckage recovered from the Brazel Ranch was from one of the Project Mogul balloon trains . . . Additionally, it seems that there was over-reaction by Colonel Blanchard and Major Marcel, in originally reporting that a 'flying disc' had been recovered when, at that time, nobody for sure knew what the term even meant since it had only been in use for a couple of weeks.
>
> Likewise, there was no indication in official records from the period that there was heightened military operational or security activity which should have been generated if this was, in fact, the first recovery of material and/or persons from another world. The post-War US Military (or today's for that matter) did not have the capability to rapidly identify, recover, coordinate, cover-up, and quickly minimize public scrutiny of such an event. The claim that they did so without leaving even a little bit of a suspicious paper trail for 47 years is incredible . . .

Aside from the fact that key military records from the period have been destroyed illegally (see later) – thus sabotaging the chances of uncovering a paper trail – it is curious that the Air Force investigation failed to interview most of the dozens of still-surviving military and civilian witnesses (e.g. Brigadier General Arthur Exon or Glenn Dennis). Perhaps anticipating criticism for this neglect, the Air Force report commented:

Lastly, persons who have come forward and provided their names and made claims, may have, in good faith but in the 'fog of time', misinterpreted past events. The review of Air Force records did not locate even one piece of evidence to indicate that the Air Force has had any part in an 'alien' body recovery operation or continuing cover-up . . .

Most interestingly, as this report was being written, [Karl] Pflock published his own report [and] concluded from his research that the Brazel Ranch debris originally reported as a 'flying disc' was probably debris from a Mogul balloon; however, there was a simultaneous incident that occurred not far away, that caused an alien craft to crash and that the [Army Air Forces] subsequently recovered three alien bodies therefrom. Air Force research did not locate any information to corroborate that this incredible incident occurred, however . . .

It is recommended that this document serve as the final Air Force report related to the Roswell matter, for the GAO, or any other inquiries.[38]

Although the Air Force report was released by the USAF's Public Affairs Media Relations Division, its author was Colonel Richard Weaver, Director, Security and Special Program Oversight, of the Air Force Office of Special Investigations – an agency whose work involves counter-intelligence operations and deception, and which has a long record of deep involvement in the UFO problem.

Colonel Weaver's mid-1994 report draws unusual and prominent attention to its author's high-level organization within the Office of the Secretary of the Air Force, i.e. the department's secretariat. Weaver's office reports to the Secretary through but one intermediary, the Secretary of the Air Force Administrative Assistant (SAF/AA). Colonel Weaver was the SAF/AA deputy for security and investigative programs (SAF/AAZ), and the report itself says this. SAF/AAZ is, therefore, a very high-level organization within the entire Department of the Air Force that includes the Air Force as a military service. SAF/AAZ also is peculiar in that the secretariats of the other two military departments (Army and Navy) do not have organizations similar or equivalent to SAF/AAZ.

Located in Room 5D972 of the Pentagon, one floor above the office of the Secretary, SAF/AAZ's office is next door to the office of the Air Force's Scientific Advisory Board (SAB), which reports directly to the Secretary and to the Chief of Staff, US Air Force. The SAB first held a meeting to discuss the UFO problem in 1948 (see Chapter 14). Variously, during the period 1946 to 1964, five persons with other connections to the UFO question served on the SAB: Dr Detlev Bronk; Lieutenant General James Doolittle; Dr H. P. Robertson; Dr George E. Valley Jr, and Dr Theodore von Karman.

The personnel complement of SAF/AAZ is interesting. In addition to Colonel Weaver (replaced later in 1994 by Lieutenant Colonel Eric Patterson), members include an executive assistant, an assistant for special programmes and oversight (likely the Special Access Programs, or 'SAPs', mentioned in the report); two security officers (one civilian employee and one NCO); two administrative assistants (an NCO and an airman); and two special planners (both USAF officers). In Air Force parlance, the term 'special plans' is a euphemism for deception as well as for 'perception management' plans and operations (not to be confused with psychological operations (PSYOP)).

Special planners plan and monitor for effectiveness Air Force deception operations that ordinarily support combat and other wartime operations. Typically, special plans provide diversionary, misleading and false manoeuvres, equipment and information, with the aim of distracting and confusing enemy commanders and their intelligence staffs during warfare operations. Perception management is an extension of deception on a broader or strategic scale, perhaps not always limited to warfare.

According to the position descriptions of the special planners in SAF/AAZ, apparently one plans while the other assesses effects and results. The other two military service secretariats do not appear to employ special planners.

In a report which debunks UFO research in general and that about the Roswell incidents in particular, it is curious that SAF/AAZ should draw new, unprecedented attention to itself among UFO researchers. On page 11, the report states, in effect, that if a UFO Special Access Program office were to exist in the Air Force, SAF/AAZ would be that office and that, looking within itself, it finds nothing of the kind. It would be hard to imagine a more self-serving statement vis-à-vis the Congressional investigation of the Roswell incident. The Weaver report seems, regrettably, poorly contrived and defensively crafted to foil the outcome of the General Accounting Office's investigation.

The General Accounting Office Report

In late July 1995 the GAO delivered its report to Congressman Steve Schiff's office. Rather than quoting from the actual report,[39] I here reproduce part of the press release issued from Schiff's office in Washington, DC, dated 28 July 1995, which encapsulates the GAO's findings:

> Congressman Steve Schiff today released the General Accounting Office (GAO) report detailing results of a records audit related to events surrounding a crash in 1947, near Roswell, New Mexico, and the military response.
>
> The 20-page report is the result of constituent information requests to Congressman Schiff and the difficulty he had getting answers from the Department of Defense in the now 48-year-old controversy.
>
> Schiff said important documents, which may have shed more light on what happened at Roswell, are missing. 'The GAO report states that the outgoing messages from Roswell Army Air Field (RAAF) for this period of time were destroyed without proper authority.' Schiff pointed out that these messages would have shown how military officials in Roswell were explaining to their superiors exactly what happened.
>
> 'It is my understanding that these outgoing messages were permanent records, which should never have been destroyed. The GAO could not identify who destroyed the messages, or why.' But Schiff pointed out that the GAO estimates that the messages were destroyed over 40 years ago, making further inquiry about their destruction impractical . . .

The Roswell incident is unique in that so many have come forward with corroborative evidence, yet it is not an isolated case. Although the majority of military and civilian personnel reporting the incidents described in the following chapter have declined to have their names published, their testimony is equally deserving of our consideration.

Down to Earth

IT WAS THE COLUMNIST Frank Scully who first alerted the world to sensational stories of recovered flying saucers and little men in his best-selling book *Behind the Flying Saucers*, published in 1950. Scully claimed that up to that time there had been four such recoveries (though, curiously, the Roswell events are not mentioned in his book). The claims have been widely dismissed by many UFO researchers as a hoax perpetrated on Scully.

While it is certainly true that two of Scully's informants had shady backgrounds, and that some of the facts provided to him had been distorted – intentionally or not – there is evidence in abundance that the stories are not without substance. One point invariably overlooked is that the mysterious 'Dr Gee', Scully's principal source of information, was in fact a composite character of eight scientists, each of whom supplied him with various details, 'Dr Gee' being merely a literary device as well as a means of protecting his sources.[1]

Paradise Valley

One of Scully's stories relates to the recovery of a crashed disc in Paradise Valley, north of Phoenix, Arizona, in 1947. According to Scully's informants the craft was 36 feet in diameter, and two humanoid bodies were retrieved – one sitting inside and the other halfway out of the 'hatch'.

In 1987 I spoke with former businessman and private pilot Selman E. Graves, who witnessed what he believes was part of the recovery operation with two friends during a hunting trip on a Saturday morning in early October 1947. The incident took place at Cave Creek, Graves told me, in the north-west section of Paradise Valley, on property owned by his friend Walt Salyer, whose son was Graves's brother-in-law.

Graves arrived at the house with four others, expecting to be met by Salyer who was to join them on the hunting trip.

When we arrived that morning [Graves told me], Salyer and his wife were away. He'd been living in the basement and had just completed an upstairs section, so we made ourselves at home. He came back about twenty minutes later and was kind of distressed to find us there, which was unlike him . . . He told us that we couldn't go due west of there, that it wasn't a good time to hunt there, and that the Air Force had restricted the area; that if we fired our guns in that direction we could hit someone, and so forth.

We told him we were interested in going to the Go John Mine, at right angles to what was the Cave Creek Road. This place today is called Carefree – it didn't exist then – and Cave Creek was just a couple of small shacky homes.

Graves and two others from the hunting party went ahead on horseback, leaving Salyer and two other men at the house. 'We said we'd meet them at the River Road, which was just at right angles, and his property sat on the corner there,' Graves recalled.

There were some mine shafts, what you might call an out-cropping, and a small hill, and we went up there and the three of us could look back and see everything that was taking place. From this vantage point you could see Salyer's house and I could see the corral very clearly, and his water tank, and so you had perspective there as to size. And there was a large – I can best describe it as a large aluminium dome-shaped thing there, which was roughly the size of the house – it was measured to be 36 feet in diameter.

We could see that there were pitched buildings – tents – and men moving about. We at that time didn't have any idea what we were looking at. We thought it might have been an observatory dome, except why would they have it down there on that piece of ground?

We didn't leave there until probably about 10–10.30 at night, so we were actually around there a good twelve hours.

The three men later met up with the others at Salyer's house. 'The others had bypassed us on the road and went up to the Go John Mine. We never went to the mine at all,' Graves explained.

Selman Graves told me that he thought little about the incident until he read Scully's book years later, and was astonished to learn of the

Paradise Valley recovery. Later he met Silas Newton, one of Scully's more dubious informants, who provided further information. 'Supposedly there were a couple of small humanoids – about $4\frac{1}{2}$ feet tall – that were reported to have been there,' said Graves:

> What I tied that in with was Salyer's great anxiety about our going near the deep freeze! It was abnormal . . . I expect that probably what happened was that Salyer (an ex-military man) was the first one to see this object and notify the authorities. If you want to make a conjecture, perhaps they thought, 'Jeepers! What are we going to do with these bodies? How are we going to keep them?'
>
> My brother-in-law said that he saw afterwards a 'vehicle' and wondered if it was part of what we had viewed – not knowing what it was – and this military flatbed truck going from the Cave Creek Road south, which at that time would have been the most logical way for them to get out of there. It seems to me that it would have had to have been something to do with the military or Air Force . . . There wasn't anything else so I presume that that was actually sections [of the object] being trucked out.

Cover-Up

The lengths to which the Government (or federal authorities) went to literally cover-up the landing-site are quite remarkable. Selman Graves told me:

> Right after the war they made a topographical map of that area in little quarter quadrangles, and they showed the site on it . . . In that short span of time they made another quadrangle and you couldn't get hold any more of the original one. They changed the location of Cave Creek Road: they moved the thing east and you wouldn't even know there had ever been another road there now unless you were really familiar and had really studied around. Also, there were some changes to the new River Road and the grading of it.
>
> The federal Government sponsored a project through the state . . . subsequently the state came in and told the county area of what was going to be Carefree that they had to locate some satisfactory spot for refuse disposal . . . and what they did was take the site of the landing and dig it up with a bulldozer!

Selman Graves, who struck me as being totally genuine, told me that he witnessed the bulldozing operations years later. 'I went in to observe what was taking place,' he said:

The ditches were somewhat helter-skelter. They were not doing a methodical digging, burning, burying – in other words, digging a new excavation – but just mucking up everything, destroying, and so on. While I was watching it a fellow, rather well-groomed for a bulldozer operator, stopped the machine, got off, and came over and asked if he could help me. I said: 'Well, I'm just interested in what you're doing. I find it rather interesting because for what you're supposed to be doing you're not really using a system that would go with it.' 'Oh, of course we are,' he said. 'No you're not,' I said. 'Look at what you're doing here. How long has this been going on anyway?' 'Oh,' he said, 'something like eight years.' 'That's a long time,' I said. 'It doesn't look like that sort of an operation.' 'Oh yes,' he said: 'It's the way we're doing it.'

I said: 'You're sure about that time? It can't have been that long.' 'Oh no,' he said: 'I'm quite sure.' I said: 'Isn't that odd? I was here about a year ago and there was nothing going on here. I guess you're mistaken.' He laughed and said: 'That's right. I guess you're right. I'm mistaken.'

Then he became more talkative, and told me that he'd done this operation for them in a place over on the Arizona/California border between Kingman and Barstow . . .

The latter site was the scene of a recovery operation in May 1953, described later.

The Aztec Case

According to Frank Scully's informants, a disc which had landed near Farmington, in the vicinity of Aztec, New Mexico, in 1948, was 99.99 feet in diameter, its exterior made of a light metal resembling aluminium but so durable that no amount of heat (up to 10,000 °F was applied) or diamond-tipped drilling had the slightest effect. The disc apparently incorporated large rings of metal which revolved around a central, stabilized cabin, using an unfamiliar gear ratio. There were no rivets, bolts, screws or signs of welding. Investigators were eventually able to gain entry, Scully was told, because of a fracture in one of the portholes, which they enlarged, revealing a knob inside the cabin which when pushed (with a pole) caused a hidden 'door' to open.

Sixteen (!) small humanoids, ranging in height from 36 to 42 inches, were supposedly found dead inside the cabin, their bodies charred to a dark brown colour. Scully was told that the craft was undamaged, having landed under its own propulsion. The craft eventually was dismantled, the investigators having discovered that it was manufactured in segments which fitted in grooves and were pinned together around the base. The complete cabin section, measuring 18 feet in diameter, was lifted out of the base of the saucer, around which was a gear that fitted a gear on the cabin. These segments, together with the bodies, were then transported to Wright Field (Wright-Patterson Air Force Base). Some of the bodies were later dissected and examined by the Air Force.

Scully actually examined some of the objects recovered from the disc, including a 'tubeless radio, some gears' and other items, and claimed that, even after more than 150 tests, the metal of the gears could not be identified.[2]

This, then, is another of the incredible stories of recovered discs related to Scully, who stood by its authenticity for the rest of his life and never revealed the names of most of his sources, despite large cash inducements. But is there any truth to it?

Leonard Stringfield, a former Air Force intelligence officer who died in 1994, was the world's leading specialist on what he called 'Retrievals of the Third Kind'. Captain V. A. Postlethwait (USAF), on detached service with Army G-2 (Intelligence) in 1948, told Stringfield that he was cleared to see a Top Secret cable describing the crash of a saucer-shaped craft 100 feet in diameter and 30 feet high, with one porthole broken, causing suffocation of the five occupants (not sixteen, as reported to Scully), who had turned blue as a result. The bodies were about 4 feet tall with relatively large heads, Postlethwait recollected. The metallic skin of the saucer was too tough to penetrate, though as thin as newspaper. The incident was said to have occurred near White Sands, New Mexico, however, which is over 200 miles from Aztec.[3] Aside from this and other discrepancies, there are some intriguing parallels with the Aztec case. I am tempted to wonder if Postlethwait was mistaken about the date. If this is the case, the cable he saw might have referred to the craft allegedly recovered near the White Sands Proving Ground in July 1947, described in the unauthenticated document supposedly written by Rear Admiral Hillenkoetter (see Chapter 18).

Leonard Stringfield also spoke with Dr Robert Spencer Carr, a retired

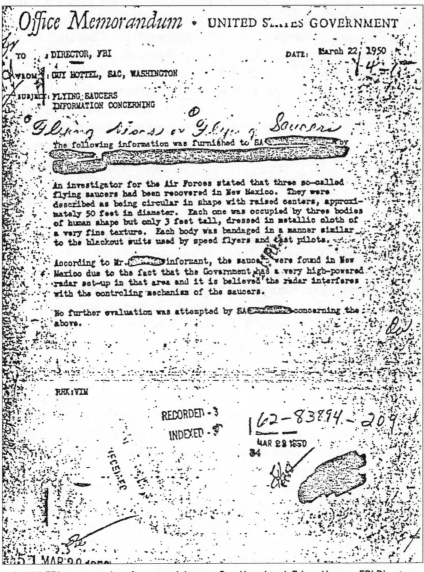

Office Memorandum • UNITED STATES GOVERNMENT

TO : DIRECTOR, FBI

DATE: March 22, 1950

FROM : GUY HOTTEL, SAC, WASHINGTON

SUBJECT: FLYING SAUCERS
INFORMATION CONCERNING

Flying Disss or Flying Saucers

The following information was furnished to SA _____ by

An investigator for the Air Forces stated that three so-called flying saucers had been recovered in New Mexico. They were described as being circular in shape with raised centers, approximately 50 feet in diameter. Each one was occupied by three bodies of human shape but only 3 feet tall, dressed in metallic cloth of a very fine texture. Each body was bandaged in a manner similar to the blackout suits used by speed flyers and test pilots.

According to Mr. _____ informant, the saucers were found in New Mexico due to the fact that the Government has a very high-powered radar set-up in that area and it is believed the radar interferes with the controling mechanism of the saucers.

No further evaluation was attempted by SA _____ concerning the above.

RHK:VIM

RECORDED - 3
INDEXED - 3

162-83894 - 209

MAR 28 1950
34

A 1950 FBI memorandum from special agent Guy Hottel to J. Edgar Hoover, FBI Director, describing information supplied to another special agent by an informant claiming knowledge of flying discs recovered in New Mexico. (*FBI*)

University of South Florida professor who claimed to have testimonial evidence from five sources, including a nurse and a high-ranking Air Force officer who participated in the recovery of a crashed UFO and occupants in 1948 – presumed to be the one at Aztec. In 1982 Stringfield asked Carr to disclose the name of his principal source, on the premiss that their ages afforded them little time in their search for the truth.

'When Professor Carr named his source,' said Stringfield, 'I sat back dumbfounded. I knew his name well in research, and recalled some of his comments on UFOs while he served as an Air Force officer . . . "Please, Len," pleaded Carr, "keep the name to yourself; please spare me any trouble as long as I live . . . My key witness participated in the 1948 retrieval and saw alien bodies on location." '[4]

According to William Steinman, who together with Wendelle Stevens has published the results of his extensive investigations into this case in their book *UFO Crash at Aztec*, two of Carr's sources were aeronautical engineers who provided important information regarding the saucer's construction and propulsion. A source now named is Arthur Bray (not to be confused with the Canadian researcher), a security guard involved with the recovery project. Carr also interviewed a woman whose father was present during the recovery. Information pertaining to the flying saucers must be suppressed, he told his daughter. 'If news of this vehicle's water-driven engine got out to the whole scientific community, that would be the end of the oil industry.'[5] The comment is of course pure hearsay, but if there is any truth in it a further possible reason for the cover-up is brought to light.

Other investigators remain sceptical. William Moore is certain that the story, as related to Scully, is a hoax. He was unable, for example, to find any local residents to back it up. George Bowra, owner of the local Aztec newspaper for many years, reportedly spoke to over 100 cowboys, Indians, ranchers and lawmen and never found a single person who could recall either the saucer recovery or subsequent military movements.[6] Steinman claims, however, to have traced at least four people who knew where the crash site was located (12 miles north-east of Aztec), one of whom, 'V.A.', recalled that sometime between 1948 and 1950 a huge disc-shaped flying object with a dome on top skimmed about 100 feet above the ground not far from him. The witness pointed out to Steinman a cliff jutting above the Animas River. 'That thing, or flying saucer, tried hard to clear that cliff, but it hit the very corner up there, shooting sparks and rocks in every direction,' he claims. 'Finally, it made a right-angle turn in mid-air and headed straight north [in the direction of the alleged crash site at Hart

Canyon]. That's the last I saw of it. I ran into the house and called the military in Albuquerque. I never heard from them about it.'[7]

In 1994 a new witness came forward with some supporting information for the Aztec story. The witness – given the pseudonym 'Alfred' by investigator Glenn Campbell – had worked as a technical photographer at the nuclear test site in Nevada from 1961 to 1964 and was assigned to the late Otto Krause, a German physicist who came to the US after the Second World War. Alfred claims that Krause – who was project physicist for some of the nuclear tests – confirmed that he knew of two saucers which had crashed:

> We got talking one night at a card game and I was telling Otto about growing up in Farmington and seeing those UFOs when I was a kid [on 17 March 1950, when most of the town's population witnessed literally hundreds of flying saucers in the sky] . . . and he laughed and said 'Yeah', that he was at White Sands at that time. He had been assigned down there . . . Otto said that one had crashed in Roswell and one had crashed at Aztec. He said they were both brought to White Sands and put in a hangar there. The aliens he never saw. He talked to people that had seen the bodies and evidently one [from the Roswell incident] supposedly lived, and they took him out to Area 51.

Krause reportedly stated that 'a small-bodied creature' had survived the Roswell crash.

Questioned closely about Krause's comment regarding Area 51 (a test site which was not operational as such until the early 1950s), Alfred explained:

> Well, he said they eventually brought him out to the test site . . . I don't recall he said exactly Area 51, [but] that's the only area they would have brought him, because the military controls Area 51 . . . Otto said it took them a long time to get into the thing and figure out how it worked. That was what was the classified part of the UFO – the mechanism that powered it. That was more classified than the atomic bomb . . .

According to Otto Krause, the propulsion or navigation of the craft was based on magnetic principles (as claimed by Scully's sources), which were explained to Alfred in simplified terms, owing to the highly sensitive nature of this aspect of the project. Less believable is Krause's allegation that by 1962 numbers of US-built saucers, based on these principles, were capable of flight, and Alfred himself claims to have seen several of these during his tenure at the Nevada Test Site.[8] Yet, however unbelievable, an increasing number of witnesses have come forward over the years who maintain that such discs have indeed been test-flown.

Area 51 at Groom Dry Lake (also called 'Dreamland') has been America's most secret installation since the early 1950s, where many spy planes (such as the U-2, SR-71, and the Aurora aircraft) as well as stealth aircraft (such as the F-117A) were test-flown. There is also allegedly a super-secret site – S-4 – at Papoose Dry Lake in the Nevada Test Site, 10 to 15 miles south of Groom Lake. Both sites have been mentioned in connection with recovered alien vehicles, and three chapters in my book *Alien Liaison* are devoted to this aspect of the subject. Mike Hunt, for example, who held an Atomic Energy Commission 'Q' clearance and an inter-agency Top Secret clearance, claims to have seen a disc-shaped aircraft on the ground at Area 51 during the early 1960s, and to have been present during take-offs and landings (though he was not allowed to observe these). Hunt believed that a highly secret programme connected with the discs – known as Project Red Light – was in operation at Area 51 at the time.

Engineer Robert Lazar claims to have been employed at S-4 for a few months in 1988–9. He insists he saw a total of nine discs, worked on the propulsion system of one of them, and witnessed a test flight at close quarters there. Despite Lazar's dubious background and lack of credentials, there is a considerable body of evidence indicating that his story could be essentially true.[9]

When I spoke with Alfred in 1995, I asked him if he knew anything more about the Aztec incident. It is claimed, for example, that a story appeared in the local newspaper, though no one yet has been able to find it. (As mentioned earlier, local newspaper owner George Bowra, for example, is reported to have discovered no evidence for the crash at all.) Alfred insists that such a story did appear:

> We used to go riding with a horse . . . What came out in the paper about the crash at Aztec was [that it happened] right out in a canyon where we had ridden. And then we rode back out there trying to see if we could see anything – this was probably a couple of weeks after the newspaper story – and the next day it came out in the newspaper that this was all a big hoax, that nothing had

(~~CONFIDENTIAL~~ (

HEADQUARTERS FIFTH ARMY
INTELLIGENCE DIVISION
OFFICE OF AC of S, G-2

6 October 1950
(Date)
Chicago 15, Illinois
(Place)

SUBJECT: Purchase Offer of Flying Saucer Photographs

Summary of Information:

    1. The Fifth Army Regional Office in Denver, Colorado, reported the following information: On 30 September the Regional Office received a call from CID, Denver, reporting that an ————— ————— Melwyn Hotel, Denver, said that when he was at the Edelweiss Bar a man named ————— offered him $1500 for photographs he had taken of a flying saucer. ————— said he photographed this saucer which had crashed near Aztec, New Mexico. ————— said that "army officials" had attempted to take the photographs of the crashed saucer away from him but that he had given them another roll of film. He said that ————— in some way had found out about the photographs and offered him $1500 for the photographs.

    2. On 2 October ————— was interviewed at the Fifth Army Regional Office in Denver. He then denied any knowledge of the flying saucer episode. The Regional Office commented that in spite of his denials his manner indicated that he had some knowledge of the incident or may have taken pictures of it. His appearance did not give the impression of one who was either mentally unbalanced or was seeking attention. He stuck persistently to his story of being drunk when he made the call to CID.

    3. ————— said that ————— was from "The Baltimore Sun."

	Evaluation	
	—of source	—of information
Previous Distribution:	x Reliable	
	Credible	
	Questionable	
Distribution:	Undetermined	
AC of S, G-2, Wash	Unknown	x
FBI, Chgo		
CHI OSI		
PCRM 62		
1947		

~~CONFIDENTIAL~~

A US Army intelligence report relating to the disc reportedly recovered near Aztec, New Mexico, in 1948. (*US Army*)

crashed . . . And then, when I worked with Otto at the test site, I'd
called my mom to go to the *Daily Times* and get me a copy of that
paper for that issue, because I wanted to show it to Otto. And she
went there, but the issue didn't exist – it conveniently
disappeared. We never did go to check with the library, or check
[again] with the Aztec newspaper.

It has been suggested that Alfred merely had read a review of Scully's
book. 'I said all this before Glenn [Campbell] told me about the book,' he
insisted. 'I'd no idea there'd been a book about it.'

According to Otto Krause, there were no survivors from the craft
which crashed near Aztec (as reported to Scully). 'All the bodies inside
were dead,' Alfred told me. The craft itself was 'pretty much intact', with
the exception of a very small hole in one of the portholes. 'The one at
Aztec is the one they gained the technology from . . .'[10]

Further information on what seems almost certainly to have been the
Aztec crash has been provided by a former military officer to the reliable
researcher, Chuck Oldham. While stationed at a certain base, the officer's
special security clearance enabled him to gain access to a restricted library,
where, on one occasion, he studied a file describing the retrieval of an alien
craft and its dead occupants. A photograph of a 'perfectly intact, circular
shaped craft', which had been retrieved before 1950 somewhere near
Farmington, was included with the report. The craft, with a diameter of
about 30 feet (at variance with the other reports) and made of a material
which resembled brushed aluminium, was so light that two men could lift
or move it.

It was stated in the report that on the cabin part of the craft there were
portholes which were not made of any type of glass, the officer informed
Oldham, though he was unable to discern these in the photograph. One
porthole had a small puncture. 'That was the only defect discovered on the
entire ship,' said the officer:

Our people tried diamond drills, an acetylene torch – everything
they could come up with on the porthole where this opening was
located, but nothing would break through it . . . It was concluded
that they would somehow have to gain access through this hole
and they eventually did, because a door popped open: it appeared
from a place where there were no obvious seams or other
indications of a door.

Referring to the opening and closing of this door, the report said that it was 'almost as if the material of the craft had liquefied and then solidified again', leaving no clue as to the door's location.

The aliens found inside were described as beings like us, but smaller. Two of the bodies were badly charred, though the clothing – one-piece flight suits woven with a type of fabric with a tensile strength of 800 lb/in^2 – was unaffected.

No reference to the craft's propulsion system was made in the report, other than that technology utilizing magnetic or gravitational fields was involved. 'They use the natural magnetic lines of a planet and a gravity field to move their ships from one place to another,' the officer explained to Chuck Oldham. 'That's how they are able to make near right-angle turns.' It was speculated that the aliens were able to cross greater distances of space within a much shorter time than we thought possible. The report further speculated that this craft (and others) had come to grief due to 'magnetic faults' located in the areas where the crashes had occurred.[11]

Corroboration

The most convincing evidence that Scully's claims are fundamentally sound has been provided by the Canadian Government engineer Wilbert Smith, who in a 1950 Top Secret document stated that the subject of flying saucers was classified higher than the hydrogen bomb, and that 'their modus operandi is unknown but concentrated effort is being made by a small group headed by Dr Vannevar Bush' (see pp. 180–83). Smith's informant was the scientist Dr Robert Sarbacher, a consultant to the US Government's Research and Development Board. In his handwritten notes made after a meeting with Sarbacher, Smith recorded the following, dated 15 September 1950:

SMITH: . . . I have read Scully's book on the saucers and would like to know how much of it is true.
SARBACHER: The facts reported in the book are substantially correct.
SMITH: Then the saucers do exist?
SARBACHER: Yes: they exist.
SMITH: Do they operate as Scully suggests on magnetic principles?
SARBACHER: We have not been able to duplicate their performance.
SMITH: Do they come from some other planet?

SARBACHER: All we know is, we didn't make them, and it's pretty certain they didn't originate on Earth.

SMITH: I understand the whole subject is classified.

SARBACHER: Yes, it is classified two points higher even than the H-bomb. In fact it is the most highly classified subject in the US Government at the present time.

SMITH: May I ask the reason for classification?

SARBACHER: You may ask, but I can't tell you.[12]

Interviewed by Bill Moore in 1979, Mrs Frank Scully maintained that the basic story behind her husband's book was factual. She also referred to a revealing comment made to her and her husband in 1953 by Captain Edward Ruppelt, who had recently retired as head of the Air Force's Project Blue Book. 'Confidentially,' said Ruppelt, 'of all the books that have been published about flying saucers, your book was the one that gave us the most headaches because it was the closest to the truth.'[13]

Recovery in Arizona

Raymond Fowler, formerly with the USAF Security Service and one of America's most respected UFO researchers, is convinced by a particular UFO recovery story which was related to him in person by a highly reputable witness with impeccable credentials who claims to have participated in the analysis of a recovered disc in May 1953. The witness, given the pseudonym 'Fritz Werner' by Fowler (real name known to me), held a number of engineering and management positions at Wright-Patterson Air Force Base from 1949 to 1960, during which period he worked in the Office of Special Studies. As a designer of aircraft landing-gear, he headed a branch of the Aircraft Laboratory at Wright Air Development Center. His subsequent numerous positions have included that of senior project engineer for the Curtiss-Wright Corporation (Curtiss Division), and aerospace programs manager for the Raytheon Company (Equipments Division).

During a special assignment for the Air Force on contract to the Atomic Energy Commission's 'Operation Upshot-Knothole' in Nevada in May 1953, Werner, whose job at the time involved measuring the effects of blast on various types of building following nuclear tests, received a phone call one evening from Dr Ed Doll, the test director, informing him that he would be required for a special job the following day.

Werner reported for duty and was driven to Indian Springs Air Force

Base, near the proving ground, where he was joined by about fifteen other specialists. 'We were told to leave all valuables in the custody of the military police,' Werner recalled.

We were then put on a military plane and flown to Phoenix, Arizona. We were not allowed to fraternize. There, we were put on a bus with other personnel, who were already there. But the windows were blacked out so that we couldn't see where we were going. We rode for an estimated four hours. I think we were in the area of Kingman, Arizona, which is north west of Phoenix and not too far from the atomic proving ground in Nevada.

During the bus trip Werner and the others were told that a highly secret Air Force vehicle had crashed, and were instructed to investigate the accident in terms of their own special expertise. On arrival at the site the personnel were escorted to an area where two floodlights illuminated the 'aircraft'. In his sworn statement, made in the presence of Raymond Fowler, Werner describes the scene as follows:

I . . . do solemnly swear that during a special assignment with the U.S. Air Force on May 21, 1953, I assisted in the investigation of a crashed unknown object in the vicinity of Kingman, Arizona.

The object was constructed of an unfamiliar metal which resembled brushed aluminum. It had impacted 20 inches into the sand without any sign of structural damage. It was oval and about 30 feet in diameter. An entranceway hatch had been vertically lowered and opened. It was about $3\frac{1}{2}$ feet high and $1\frac{1}{2}$ feet wide. I was able to talk briefly with someone on the team who did look inside only briefly. He saw 2 swivel seats, an oval cabin, and a lot of instruments and displays.

A tent pitched near the object sheltered the dead remains of the only occupant of the craft. It was about 4 feet tall, dark brown complexion and had 2 eyes, 2 nostrils, 2 ears, and a small round mouth. It was clothed in a silvery metallic suit and wore a skull cap of the same type of material. It wore no face covering or helmet.

Werner's job was to find out how fast the vehicle's forward and vertical velocities had been, by determining the angle and depth of impact into the sand.

As soon as each of the specialists had completed his job he was interviewed on tape then escorted back to the bus. 'After we all returned to the bus,' Werner stated, 'the Air Force colonel who was in charge had us raise our right hands and take an oath not to reveal what we had experienced. I was instructed to write my report in longhand and not to type or reproduce it.' Werner told Fowler that he sympathized with the cover-up. The Air Force believed that UFOs were interplanetary, he said, but did not know where they came from, and were anxious to avoid panic.[14]

Leonard Stringfield learned further details about the incident from Fritz Werner. Regarding the alien body, for instance, he said it was very slender, with disproportionately long arms. 'Since it's been 27 years, details like this are pretty foggy and I may even be influenced by other descriptions I've seen or heard in the interim,' he wrote to Stringfield in 1980. 'In short, I don't really remember any earlobes; eyes, I didn't see; head shape was oval; don't recall that there was a nose, *per se* . . .' Werner said that he and the other specialists were checked for radiation and other possibly harmful effects, but none had been found.[15]

According to investigators Jeff Young and Paul Chetham, who were the first to interview Fritz Werner, in 1971, Werner claimed to have later made contact with extraterrestrials.[16] Interestingly, a new source has recently testified that communications were established with the being(s) associated with the craft recovered near Kingman (see Chapter 20).

Further possible verification for what I assume, perhaps incorrectly, to be the Kingman case was given to Leonard Stringfield in 1977 by a pilot in the Air National Guard, who claims to have accidentally witnessed three (not one, as reported by Werner) humanoid bodies at Wright-Patterson Air Force Base, recovered from a UFO crash site in Arizona in 1953. According to the pilot, the bodies were 4 feet tall and typical of other described specimens, crated individually in small, hastily constructed wooden boxes.

> While the lids were being temporarily opened by the overseeing officer [wrote Stringfield], the pilot also got a glimpse of a plastic liner separating the body from a bed of dry ice, probably to prevent epidermis damage. They were not human or simian, he stressed, as he had observed them from a distance of 12 feet under strong hangar lights. Later that night, while billeted in the same barracks with officers of the flight crew who had transported the secret cargo, he got confirmation of the UFO crash and other details of the retrieval operation.[17]

*

If there were only a few of these incredible stories it would be easy to dismiss them as straightforward hoaxes, delusions or disinformation by the intelligence community in order to discredit the subject. But there are *dozens* of cases, and Leonard Stringfield was convinced, as I am, that many are authentic. Until his death, Stringfield was the most outspoken champion of the retrieval cases, and even though he steadfastly refused to disclose the names of his sources – a prerequisite to being given information – he once received anonymous death threats warning him not to discuss the matter publicly.

Alien Bodies at Wright-Patterson Air Force Base

In his book *Preuves Scientifiques OVNI* (Monaco, 1981), Jean-Charles Fumoux relates how Leon B. Visse, an expert on histones (proteins connected with cellular genetic material), was invited in 1959 to a military compound at Wright-Patterson Air Force Base, where he was asked to perform an experiment on the historic weight of particular cells. In the first experiment Visse found an inordinately low historic weight – far lower than in human cells. Either he was mistaken or there had to be a complete revision of genetic theories, he reasoned. But Visse obtained the same results when he repeated the experiment, so he asked if he could look at the organism from which the cells came. To his astonishment, Visse was taken into a special room where the corpses of two humanoids lay.

The bodies were very tall – a little over 7 feet – and from their terrible injuries they appeared to have been in an accident, although the heads were intact, Fumoux relates, and continues: 'the forehead high and broad. Very long blond hair. The eyes were stretched towards the temples which gave them an Asiatic look. The nose and mouth were small. The lips were thin, perfectly delineated. Despite slight differences in their facial appearances, the two humanoids looked like twins.' The bodies had been preserved in formalin but remained perfectly white, apparently lacking the [melanin] granules which cause normal human beings to tan in strong sunlight. The eyes were very light blue and looked no different from normal, Visse reported. The hands were human-like but slender, while their feet were absolutely flat, with small toes.

Dr Jean Gille of the French National Centre for Scientific Research (CNRS) eventually tracked down Leon Visse, who promptly denied that he had been personally involved in the case. Nevertheless, he admitted there was some truth to the story. Only a highly qualified biologist could have come up with such a story, he told Dr Gille. It had been alleged, for example, that the aliens' bodies exhibited a far more developed lymphatic system than normal, and Visse explained that, hypothetically, hyperdevelopment of the lymphatic system might be a normal attribute of extraterrestrial beings.

Another of the alleged witnesses, Professor André Lwoff, also denied involvement and said he had never heard of Visse. So what are we to make of this extraordinary story? A straightforward hoax? Dr Gille summarized his feelings about Visse in a letter to Leonard Stringfield:

> I have no definite opinion if he was the right man or not . . . Visse had indeed knowledge about covert operations . . . it seemed to me – but it could have been my imagination – that he was accustomed to military ways of thinking and behaviour . . . Visse was absolutely unmoved by the Fumoux story when I told him . . . he didn't show any surprise, he was not shocked at all by the odd subject . . . In short, I believe Fumoux knew *something* about alien/retrieval affairs. But what he knew was certainly distorted.

Dr Gille concluded that either Visse or Fumoux, or both, knew the truth about the Wright-Patterson incident but had subsequently covered it up with disinformation. Two further points are worth noting. Visse had allegedly been sworn to secrecy for ten years by the Americans, and it was precisely ten years later (in 1969) that he revealed the story for the first time, according to Fumoux. Fumoux himself had been in the French Air Force and had ties with the intelligence community.[18] Was the story a way of bringing out the truth – albeit in a distorted form – or simply a hoax from beginning to end? Like so many apocryphal accounts of alien retrievals, we shall simply have to suspend judgement until the day arrives when the authorities decide to reveal the facts.

Guarded Disc at Wright-Patterson Air Force Base

Thanks to researcher Tommy Blann, Leonard Stringfield was able to contact a former US Navy test pilot (subsequently a commercial pilot) – identified as 'P.J.' – who together with other Navy pilots inadvertently came across a saucer-shaped 'aircraft' guarded at Wright-Patterson Air Force Base in 1962. In April of that year, while temporarily attached to the 354th TAC (Tactical Air Command) Fighter Wing as an exchange pilot, the 352nd Tactical Fighter Squadron was sent to Wright-Patterson Air Force Base on a hurricane evacuation from Myrtle Beach, South Carolina.

As flight commander of the 'B' flight Bluebirds, it was P.J.'s custom to keep his men physically and mentally fit by organizing a programme of running, touch football or handball.

On the first day, as P.J. led his flight crew of five on a running exercise through the base, the group came across an extraordinary sight, P.J. related to Stringfield:

As we crossed two baseball fields we approached the first hangar which, without hesitating, we guessed was the Special Services Hangar. We busted through both doors on a full sprint to look for the equipment room [to] check out for gear. Once inside, we were stunned by dead silence and [were] approached by an air police sentry with a sub-machine gun.

Standing about eight feet away was a strange-looking object. It was about 12–15 feet long and eight feet deep and resembled two plates stuck together . . . It was suspended off the ground by two engine test stands. There were no markings or insignia, but most noticeable, it was without rivets. The object was roped off and eight guards stood parade rest around it.

The guard challenged by saying: 'I don't think you're supposed to be here, Sir.' I replied in the affirmative and we turned about face . . . Once outside, we had reassured each other that the good old U.S. had developed, or had all along, flying saucers in service.

On our return to Myrtle Beach AFB . . . a week later, I was requested to report to the Brigadier General of the Combat Wing . . . He informed me that I had broken security. He only asked one question – 'What did you see?' My reply was 'Nothing!' His answer was, 'You have the right answer to the question', and I was dismissed . . .

Having a Top Secret clearance enabled me to gain valuable information that otherwise would be impossible to obtain . . . for a brief 30 seconds [we saw] a disc-shaped object of metallic color . . . I cannot confirm anything other than it was there.

P.J. was puzzled by the relative lack of security. 'It wasn't even located in the test facility of Wright-Patterson AFB,' he said. 'It was near the flight line having just arrived or awaiting deployment. That is just my guess.'[19]

Another Recovery in New Mexico

Tommy Blann has interviewed an Air Force colonel who claims to have been present during the recovery of a crashed disc and humanoid occupants in northern New Mexico in the summer of 1962. According to Colonel 'X', the craft looked like two saucers end-on-end, was of a dull aluminium colour, had a dark section around the centre, and was about 30 feet in diameter and 12 feet high. Blann was told that there was no noticeable landing-gear and that the craft had apparently skidded on impact, digging up a small trench. The colonel said that a team of eight men were at the site, wearing jump suits and gas masks, and that each had a specific task to perform. Only preliminary analysis is conducted at retrieval sites, the Colonel stated, and he went on to describe the scene further:

> There were two bodies recovered from the craft and they were put in a large unmarked silver van and whisked off. I did not get a good look at the bodies; however, they looked small and were dressed in silver, skin-tight flight suits. They were taken to Holloman AFB as well as the craft, and then sections of the craft were sent to various research labs, including Los Alamos Laboratories. I believe the bodies were also taken to Los Alamos and samples sent to other locations.

Colonel 'X' revealed that underground installations, as well as isolated areas of military reservations, have squadrons of unmarked helicopters with sophisticated instrumentation which are dispatched to monitor areas of UFO activity or to airlift UFOs out of the vicinity in the event of a malfunction.

Tommy Blann asked the Colonel about the many rumours that crashed discs and bodies were sent to Wright-Patterson Air Force Base. 'In the earlier years,' he replied, 'they had taken some bodies to this base, but later it depended on where they were found. They had a hell of a time setting up procedures for this operation, as well as getting craft out of the area without it being observed. Usually this was done at nighttime.' The Colonel told Blann he believed that in more recent years the bodies were flown outside the US to a secret naval installation on an island in the Pacific.[20]

The reference to special squadrons of helicopters is intriguing and has been substantiated on various occasions – most significantly, perhaps, in the case of Betty Cash and Vickie and Colby Landrum, who saw about twenty-three helicopters 'escorting' an unidentified flying object near Huffman, Texas, on 29 December 1980 (see p. 382).

Senator Goldwater Confirms Withheld UFO Material

In Chapter 13 I refer to Captain Bruce Cathie's claim that a secret UFO research centre is permanently manned at Wright-Patterson Air Force Base. Leonard Stringfield uncovered some additional evidence to support this claim, having spoken with an intelligence officer (J.K.), who stated:

> Since 1948, secret information concerning UFO activity involving the US military has been contained in a computer center at Wright-Patterson AFB. At this base, a master computer file is maintained with duplicate support backup files secreted at other military installations . . . Get the complete 'Dump File', both the master and the support backup files, and you've got all the hidden UFO data.

J.K. also claims to have seen on one occasion nine deceased alien bodies at the base, preserved in deep-freeze conditions under a thick glass enclosure. The area was under heavy guard, and J.K. was told at the time (1966) that thirty bodies in total were held there. He did not see any alien craft but was told that some were stored at the base and elsewhere, including Langley AFB, Virginia, and McDill AFB, Florida.[21]

From another source Stringfield learned that the bodies at Wright-Patterson were stored in 1953 in Building 18-F, 3rd Floor, and then at Langley AFB.[22] Senator Barry Goldwater, former Chairman of the Senate Intelligence Committee, visited Wright-Patterson hoping to get permission from General Curtis LeMay to examine the UFO evidence stored there, but was refused. Copies of letters from Goldwater to various researchers (in my files) are worth quoting here. In a letter to Shlomo Arnon on 28 March 1975, he wrote:

> The subject of UFOs is one that has interested me for some long time. About ten or twelve years ago I made an effort to find out what was in the building at Wright-Patterson Air Force Base where the information is stored that has been collected by the Air Force, and I was understandably denied this request. It is still classified above Top Secret. I have, however, heard that there is a

plan under way to release some, if not all, of this material in the near future. I'm just as anxious to see this material as you are, and I hope we will not have to wait too much longer.

On 11 April 1979 Goldwater wrote to the aerospace engineer and UFO researcher Lee Graham. 'It is true I was denied access to a facility at Wright-Patterson,' he confirmed. 'Because I never got in, I can't tell you what was inside. We both know about the rumours.' The room the Senator tried to visit is called the 'Blue Room', and according to my information it contains UFO artefacts, but no craft or bodies. In another letter to Lee Graham, dated 19 October 1981, Goldwater wrote:

> First, let me tell you that I have long ago given up acquiring access to the so-called blue room at Wright-Patterson, as I have had one long string of denials from chief after chief, so I have given up . . . I don't know of anyone who has access to the blue room, nor am I aware of its contents and I am not aware of anything having been relocated . . . To tell you the truth, Mr. Graham, this thing has gotten so highly classified, even though I will admit there is a lot of it that has been released, it is just impossible to get anything on it.

Alien Bodies and Craft Examined at Secret Base in Arizona

One of the most fascinating stories relating to recovered alien craft and humanoid occupants was related by a former military intelligence officer to the psychiatrist and researcher Dr Berthold Schwarz in the early 1980s. Dr Schwarz graduated from Dartmouth College and Dartmouth Medical School and received his MD from the College of Medicine, New York University; he is a diplomat of the American Board of Psychiatry and Neurology, as well as a fellow of the American Board of Psychiatry and Neurology. Because I know him to be objective in his analyses of UFO cases and witnesses, I am including the following account, first published in his book *UFO Dynamics*.

The intelligence officer (who is now a successful private citizen) received many commendations for his courage under fire during the Vietnam War, and has written a number of authoritative monographs on security matters as well as being fluent in several Oriental languages. 'The officer's credentials seem as impeccable as his need for anonymity,' Schwarz reports:

BARRY GOLDWATER
ARIZONA

COMMITTEES:
AERONAUTICAL AND SPACE SCIENCES
ARMED SERVICES
PREPAREDNESS INVESTIGATING SUBCOMMITTEE
TACTICAL AIR POWER SUBCOMMITTEE
NATIONAL STOCKPILE AND NAVAL PETROLEUM
RESERVES SUBCOMMITTEE

United States Senate
WASHINGTON, D.C. 20510

March 28, 1975

Mr. Shlomo Arnon
U.C.L.A. Experimental College
308 Westwood Plaza
Los Angeles, California 90024

Dear Mr. Arnon:

The subject of UFOs is one that has interested me
for some long time. About ten or twelve years ago
I made an effort to find out what was in the building
at Wright Patterson Air Force Base where the information
is stored that has been collected by the Air Force, and
I was understandably denied this request. It is
still classified above Top Secret. I have, however,
heard that there is a plan under way to release some,
if not all, of this material in the near future. I'm
just as anxious to see this material as you are, and I
hope we will not have to wait too much longer.

Sincerely,

Barry Goldwater

A letter from Senator Barry Goldwater confirming that information about UFOs is classified
above 'Top Secret'. (*Shlomo Arnon*)

Interviews of some people who know him well and who are known to myself vouchsafe for his honesty and excellent work record . . . The officer spoke in a clear, direct manner, but it was obvious that he did not enjoy discussing his experiences. It was as if he was relieved to tell me what happened, and then he wanted to have nothing further to do with the subject.

The witness claims that while serving with a military intelligence unit in the 1970s he met a fellow intelligence officer who invited him to see some recovered alien bodies at a secret base in Arizona. As he told Schwarz:

I doubt if I could ever find that place again. There was a highway above ground that went over the base, and after a turn at the entrance, we went underground. We violated every security code in the book. Because of this and the fact that I had a Top Secret clearance at the time I wondered if this was a set-up – that they wanted to put a man with combat experience in this spot and see what he does – to sow the seeds of doubt. It was too obvious. We used a staff car and not a private one. We entered a vaulted area. Now, this was on a weekend, and the security amazed me because it was so lax.

When we got in I observed five humanoid figures . . . Remember, I doubted what I saw. They were very, very white. There were no ears; no nostrils. There were only openings: a very small mouth and their eyes were large. There was no facial hair, no head hair, no pubic hair. They were nude. I think the tallest one could have been about 3½ feet – maybe a little bit taller. As I recall there were three males and two females. The heads were large – not totally out of proportion – but large . . . it wasn't exaggerated, in other words. Slender fingers; slender legs. There was a small bone structure.

'Did you see any genitals?' asked Dr Schwarz. 'I don't remember seeing that in the men or the female organs in the women . . . I don't remember seeing breasts on the women,' the officer responded. So how could he tell that some of them were women? He replied that his friend had told him so (the sex presumably having been determined during autopsy).

When I saw the smallest female in the group I could see clear suture marks. My friend said there had been an autopsy and that from a study of her brain it was estimated that she was 200 years old. The smallest woman had a complete autopsy, opened with a Y incision . . . There was no bruising on the body. There were no signs of injuries to any of the bodies . . . He told me they were vegetarians. The teeth were smooth, flat and very small.

Dr Schwarz questioned the witness more closely about the alien anatomy:

SCHWARZ: How about the eyes . . . ?
OFFICER: Oh, that was interesting. They were tear-shaped with the slant going to the outside.
SCHWARZ: Wrap-around?
OFFICER: No, no . . . They were large, open.
SCHWARZ: Did they have lids? Could you tell?
OFFICER: No, I could not tell.
SCHWARZ: Eyebrows? Or anything like that?
OFFICER: No brows. Two openings for the nostrils and the same for the ears. They were delicate. They looked as if you touched them they would break. No signs of wrinkling on them either.
SCHWARZ: How could you make the guess that the lady was more than 200 years old?
OFFICER: This is what I asked him. He said from the count of the ridges on the brain. I never heard of that before.
SCHWARZ: Approximately when did this happen?
OFFICER: In the middle '70s. But they had this [craft and bodies] from several years before . . .

Apparently the craft had been tracked on radar as it came down to Earth, the location pinpointed by triangulation. 'When [the military] got out there they found a small hole,' said the witness (which suggests that the craft may have been the one recovered near Aztec, New Mexico). 'Evidently a meteorite had hit this craft, causing rapid decompression, and the people died from that.' The officer saw parts of this craft at the secret base in Arizona, including seats. 'The seats were a dull bronze metal – not cold to the touch. I left my fingerprints all over . . . They still have the craft, but where, I don't know.'

A Craft Stored at the Base

The intelligence officer claims to have seen a complete, recovered craft, which had come to grief in Nevada and was found half-buried in sand, yet completely undamaged (in some respects similar to the one described by Fritz Werner near Kingman, Arizona, which is close to the Nevada border).

> From the bottom it was almost flat. It was almost 20 feet across – almost – because I walked it. There was a slight dome, but with a gradual rise. It was dull silver, but it was not paint. Inside the craft no cloth, but dull brown material like a coating over it . . . There was a chair in front of a screen. It looked like a screen. It might have been for some navigational purpose. He wouldn't tell me about it.
>
> There were instruments off to the side. Anyway, there were other slots to the side, and a big piece of metal moved – a computer-like appearance. There were switches and lights. I saw symbols. The screen looked like a TV – circular, no grid marks. You could put your hand in it. It was more than seven feet high, as I judged it when I walked in and therefore I would guess about four feet round. I didn't ask about the symbols, triangles, circles, rectangles, odd shapes.
>
> The cabin wasn't dull, it was bright. Everything was flush, nothing standing out. There were levers by the seats – stuff I can't describe. There were no holes or rivets. A [container] came out of the wall and part of the food was there. They must have been vegetarians. The aisle was very narrow with thick black cloth over it. There were no screws, weld marks or rivets – smooth as if it were painted, but it wasn't painted. It was not metal, yet it was firm, not cloth or plastic or fibreglass . . . They knew how to open and close the doors. This guy had been handling it for some time.

A Hoax?

It is tempting to dismiss the intelligence officer's story as a hoax, yet Dr Schwarz is convinced that nothing would be gained by the officer's deceiving him. The witness himself constantly expressed doubts – as indeed would anyone who found themselves in a similar situation. 'Now that I look back on it, I doubt what I saw,' he said:

I find it difficult to believe . . . I figure that the deal in Arizona was a 'sow-and-seed' to sow the disbeliever among the crowds. It is really a damn good maneuver when you think about it, because it comes from a man with good credentials, who was spewing forth madness. So, if you look at it in that light, yes, it does make sense now.

Dr Schwarz is equally convinced that the intelligence officer's story is not the product of a deranged mind:

As far as I am aware he has experienced no previous emotional instability, use of psychoactive or psychedelic drugs, or contact with noxious chemicals in line of duty . . . My cursory psychiatric examination of this person revealed no evidence for overt psychopathology, and if what he is saying is apocryphal or untrue, one would have to ask what his motive would be in view of his failure to receive any monetary gain or prestige from his story. If his account is part of a ruse on his part, or if he is consciously or surreptitiously being used by organizations for purposes not clear at this time, this would be an extraordinarily expensive operation, and many would have been fooled for no ostensible reason.

Harassment

Following these extraordinary experiences at the secret Arizona base, the officer's family was visited by fellow intelligence personnel. 'I get the feeling that some of my brother spooks did the usual follow-up,' he related to Schwarz:

Although I had the rank, I did not have the 'need to know'. They never said a thing, but they just sort of asked – my family was getting used to this. My Dad is a good officer. Although he has seen and taken a lot in his career, he was effectively shook. He was visited by three nondescript individuals in a nondescript car with credentials that were not authenticated . . . not FBI . . . They wouldn't attract open attention by their clothing or conversation. Dad never saw their eyes . . . they wore sunglasses . . . They asked questions about my career . . . They would come and ask questions in my neighborhood and then get out, leaving everybody upset. My family would get calls from Washington.

Now that I am married and because my wife's relatives are in Eastern Europe, I lost my Top Secret clearance, and I don't have the access that I used to have.[23]

There was further harassment, Bert Schwarz related to me:

Shortly after he told me his story with much sweat, he was visited by two 'Mutt and Jeff' characters in dark suits who said they were from the government, flashed appropriate credentials and then proceeded to tell him everything that he had told me, plus that which he didn't tell me for obvious reasons. Shortly afterwards, his double-locked, steel door apartment was broken into and various war medals, snapshots, negatives and other memorabilia were taken . . . It is a rather involved and sticky situation, as you might surmise.[24]

Dr Schwarz remains convinced by the officer's sincerity and integrity, and has kept in touch with him from time to time, 'but, as you might imagine,' he remarked to me, 'he is tight-lipped about what he had told me. Once he did say, however, that he probably should have said nothing.'

Further Confirmation for the Recoveries

However unbelievable the stories of recovered UFOs and their occupants may be, there has been confirmation from reliable sources that a number of such incidents have actually taken place. The late Dr Robert Sarbacher, a former consultant to the Research and Development Board and President and Chairman of the Board of the Washington Institute of Technology, sent a letter to William Steinman in 1983 which clearly acknowledges this fact:

. . . Relating to my own experience regarding recovered flying saucers, I had no association with any of the people involved in the recovery and have no knowledge regarding the dates of the recoveries . . . Regarding verification that persons you list were involved, I can only say this: John von Neuman was definitely involved. Dr. Vannevar Bush was definitely involved, and I think Dr. Robert Oppenheimer also.

My association with the Research and Development Board under Doctor Compton during the Eisenhower administration was rather limited so that although I had been invited to participate in several discussions associated with the reported recoveries, I could not personally attend the meetings. I am sure that they would have asked Dr. von Braun, and the others that you listed were probably asked and may or may not have attended. This is all I know for sure . . .

About the only thing I remember at this time is that certain materials reported to have come from flying saucer crashes were extremely light and very tough. I am sure our laboratories analyzed them very carefully.

There were reports that instruments or people operating these machines were also of very light weight, sufficient to withstand the tremendous deceleration and acceleration associated with their machinery. I remember in talking with some of the people at the office that I got the impression these 'aliens' were constructed like certain insects we have observed on earth wherein because of the low mass the inertial forces involved would be quite low.

I still do not know why the high order of classification has been given and why the denial of the existence of these devices.[25]

General George C. Marshall, US Army Chief of Staff in the Second World War and Secretary of State from 1947 to 1949, has also reportedly confirmed that the authorities have recovered alien craft and their occupants. In 1951 General Marshall spoke with Dr Rolf Alexander, following sightings of UFOs at Mexico City Airport when many films and photographs allegedly were taken while newsmen awaited the arrival of the General.

Marshall later revealed to Dr Alexander that the UFOs were from another planet and that they were friendly; their hovering over defence establishments and airports was taken to mean that they could blow us all to bits if they had any evil intent. Marshall stated that they were undoubtedly trying to work out a method of remaining alive in our atmosphere before landing and establishing friendly communications, and that the US authorities were convinced that Earth had nothing to fear from them.

Questioned about landings, Marshall admitted that contact with the men in the craft had been established, and that on three occasions there had been landings which had proved disastrous for the occupants. On each of these occasions, he said, breathing the heavily oxygenated atmosphere of Earth had literally incinerated the visitors from within and burned them to a crisp. (This may be true in some cases – but not all.)

WASHINGTON INSTITUTE OF TECHNOLOGY

· OCEANOGRAPHIC AND PHYSICAL SCIENCES ·

DR. ROBERT I. SARBACHER
PRESIDENT AND CHAIRMAN OF BOARD

November 29, 1983

*Answer
from Dr. Sarbach
Received 12-5-83
Wm Steinman*

Mr. William Steinman
15043 Rosalita Drive
La Mirada, California 90638

Dear Mr. Steinman:

I am sorry I have taken so long in answering your letters. However, I have moved my office and have had to make a number of extended trips.

To answer your last question in your letter of October 14, 1983, there is no particular reason I feel I shouldn't or couldn't answer any or all of your questions. I am delighted to answer all of them to the best of my ability.

You listed some of your questions in your letter of September 12th. I will attempt to answer them as you had listed them.

1. Relating to my own experience regarding recovered flying saucers, I had no association with any of the people involved in the recovery and have no knowledge regarding the dates of the recoveries. If I had I would send it to you.

2. Regarding verification that persons you list were involved, I can only say this:

John von Neuman was definitely involved. Dr. Vannever Bush was definitely involved, and I think Dr. Robert Oppenheimer also.

My association with the Research and Development Board under Doctor Compton during the Eisenhower administration was rather limited so that although I had been invited to participate in several discussions associated withthe reported recoveries, I could not personally attend the meetings. I am sure thatthey would have asked Dr. von Braun, and the others that you listed were probably asked and may or may not have attended. This is all I know for sure.

500 BRAZILIAN AVENUE   PALM BEACH, FLORIDA 33480   305-833-1116

A letter from the late Dr Robert Sarbacher confirming the recovery of alien craft and bodies. (*William Steinman*)

Mr. William Steinman
November 29, 1983 – Page 2

3.   I did receive some official reports when I was
in my office at the Pentagon but all of these were left
there as at the time we were never supposed to take them
out of the office.

4.   I do not recall receiving any photographs such
as you request so I am not in a position to answer.

5.   I have to make the same reply as on No. 4.

I recall the interview with Dr. Brenner of the Canadian
Embassy. I think the answers I gave him were the ones you
listed. Naturally, I was more familiar with the subject
matter under discussion, at that time. Actually, I would
have been able to give more specific answers had I attended the meetings concerning the subject. You must understand
that I took this assignment as a private contribution. We
were called "dollar-a-year men." My first responsibility
was the maintenance of my own business activity so that my
participation was limited.

About the only thing I remember at this time is that certain
materials reported to have come from flying saucer crashes
were extremely light and very tough. I am sure our
laboratories analyzed them very carefully.

There were reports that instruments or people operating
these machines were also of very light weight, sufficient
to withstand the tremendous deceleration and acceleration
associated with their machinery. I remember in talking
with some of the people at the office that I got the
impression these "aliens" were constructed like certain
insects we have observed on earth, wherein because of the
low mass the inertial forces involved in operation of
these instruments would be quite low.

I still do not know why the high order of classification has
been given and why the denial of the existence of these
devices.

I am sorry it has taken me so long to reply but I suggest
you get in touch with the others who may be directly involved
in this program.

Sincerely yours,

Dr. Robert I. Sarbacher

P. S.   It occurs to me that Dr. Bush's name is inccorrect
as you have it. Please check the spelling.

and as I spell it.

Asked by Dr Alexander why such emphasis had been put on denying the existence of UFOs and censoring reports, Marshall replied that the US wanted its people to concentrate on the real menace – Communism – and not be distracted by the visitors from space. He went on to say that the famous Orson Welles pre-war broadcast of H. G. Wells's science-fiction story *The War of the Worlds* had demonstrated what reaction might be expected were the true facts generally known: a welter of hysterical nonsense and a complete disorientation from the tasks in hand. Rumours and speculation would create an atmosphere that the propagandists of the Kremlin would be certain to exploit, he said.[26]

Rolf Alexander graduated in medicine at Prague and went on to other European universities where he did postgraduate work in analytical psychology, neurology and biochemistry. I do not know how accurately he reported his meeting with General Marshall, but I do know that he refused to allow Marshall's name to be associated with the news release at the time, and it was not revealed until his own death as well as that of Marshall.

Years later Dr Alexander made a comment as relevant today as it was then. 'The trouble is,' he wrote, 'UFOs, alas, are no longer news unless we can manage to land one and have it photographed, and its crew interviewed by the press. This may not be impossible, but no-one has managed it yet.'[27]

Beyond Top Secret

The National Security Agency

FOUNDED IN 1952 UNDER President Truman, America's vast National Security Agency has grown into the world's largest eavesdropping empire, with an estimated annual budget ten years ago of $2 billion. An agency so secret that at one time its acronym was referred to humorously as standing for 'No Such Agency' or 'Never Say Anything', the NSA is based in 1,000 acres at Fort George Meade, Maryland, with its own power station, television station and studio, and a total (in 1982) of 50,000 personnel.[1] This figure includes the many staffs of the US military services' and Department of Defense civilian 'listening posts' in the US, in several foreign countries, in large US Navy ships, in USAF aircraft, and so forth. Less than half this total number are cryptologic (code-making and -breaking) and other (for example, logistic) specialists assigned to the Fort Meade headquarters. The military services' cryptologic organizations comprise the so-called Central Security Service, tasked and managed but not commanded by the NSA.

Depending on the degree of intelligence interest, in the uncertain aftermath of the Cold War, the NSA's headquarters is organized in from ten to fifteen major groups. Three or four such groups are 'target country'/ area-focused, and one to three others are directed at providing technical 'exploitation' in support of the target groups. Two or three groups are policy and administrative organizations. Three or four groups provide common services pertaining across the Agency – for example, logistics, research and development, telecommunications and 'watchkeeping'. There is one very large group for information security (INFOSEC): this group plans, administers and controls all US Government (including military) communications and computer-systems security processes and procedures, and specifies the US Government's systems security standards.

Of the half-dozen or fewer so-called 'intelligence disciplines' (that is, the major sources of raw intelligence), the NSA is the sole US Government authority and executive for the collection and reporting of signals intelligence (SIGINT): it treats all other disciplines or source categories as 'collateral' – for example, human intelligence (HUMINT) and imagery intelligence (IMINT) (the latter acquired by reconnaissance aircraft and satellites) – until the point where finished SIGINT and related judgements are blended with other intelligence in inter-agency studies and reports, such as National Intelligence Estimates (NIE).

The CIA, the Defense Intelligence Agency (by means of its all-service defence-attaché programme, discussed earlier), and elements of the military services' intelligence organizations are the providers and producers of HUMINT as well as of IMINT (via the National Photographic Interpretation Center (NPIC)) – the latter recently augmented by the Central Imagery Office (CIO) that eventually will merge with the National Reconnaissance Office (NRO) at its new headquarters in Chantilly, Virginia.

The customers of the NSA's finished SIGINT reports are, in one way or another, all US Government departments, agencies and uniformed services having various national security responsibilities. Contrary to a widely held belief, the NSA scrupulously avoids (officially, at least) intercepting or processing any communications, even though of foreign origin, related to US persons, corporations and private entities, and it does not provide SIGINT support of any US local or state law-enforcement or investigation agency. (For those interested, I thoroughly recommend the NSA's National Cryptologic Museum, operated by the Agency's education and training group and housed in the Fort Meade facility, which is open to the public.)

Like the other federal agencies that have consistently and routinely collected and reported UFO-related intelligence – probably since 1942 but certainly since 1947 – the NSA also is tasked to collect and report SIGINT about, for instance, the reactions of foreign air forces and air-defence forces to UFO incursions. Until the 1980s, however, few outside the intelligence community had the slightest hint of NSA involvement with the UFO subject. When Robert Todd wrote to the NSA in 1976 requesting information on its role in UFO research, he received a blunt reply: '. . . please be advised that NSA does not have *any* interest in UFOs in *any* manner'.[2]

Thanks to Citizens Against UFO Secrecy (CAUS), eighteen documents on UFOs originating with the NSA were admitted during litigation against the CIA. Lawyer Peter Gersten filed a request under provisions of the Freedom of Information Act for their release, but was informed that the documents were 'exempt from disclosure', under 5 US Code, Section 552 (b)(1), in the interests of national security. After another unsuccessful attempt under the FOIA to obtain the documents, Gersten eventually succeeded in securing the release of two documents in January 1980. The NSA admitted that other documents on UFOs were being withheld, and that a further seventy-nine documents were being referred to other originating agencies for review.[3] Later that year NSA representative Eugene Yeates admitted in a court hearing that the NSA had found a total of 239 documents on UFOs that were relevant to the FOIA request.

Following another refusal to release more documents, Peter Gersten filed suit against the NSA on behalf of CAUS in the District Court, Washington, DC, in the spring of 1980 to obtain the 135 documents then admitted to being withheld by the agency. Judge Gesell studied a twenty-one-page NSA affidavit *in camera* and ruled that the Agency was fully justified in withholding the documents in their entirety:

> The bulk of the material withheld consists of communications intelligence reports, which defendant asserts are protected by Exemptions 1 and 3 of the Freedom of Information Act . . . The Court first carefully reviewed the public affidavit of National Security Agency official Eugene Yeates and then, after receiving plaintiff's opposition, examined personally a top secret affidavit from Yeates, submitted by defendant *in camera* . . . On the basis of these affidavits, the Court finds that the claimed exemptions have been properly and conscientiously applied.
>
> The communications intelligence reports clearly relate to the most sensitive activities of the defendant . . .
>
> Throughout the Court's review of this material, the Court has been aware of the public interest in the issue of UFOs and the need to balance that interest against the agency's need for secrecy. The *in camera* affidavit presents factual considerations which aided the Court in determining that the public interest in disclosure is far outweighed by the sensitive nature of the materials and the obvious effect on national security their release may well entail . . . The case is dismissed.[4]

The affidavit (sections of which are reproduced on pp. 000–0) was itself stamped 'Top Secret Umbra'. 'Umbra' is not a level of classification *per se*, but rather just the communications intelligence category-three (COMINT CAT III) code-word associated with Top Secret material. 'Top Secret' refers to 'information or material the unauthorized disclosure of which reasonably could be expected to cause exceptionally grave damage to the national security'.[5] The additional caveat (e.g. 'Umbra') restricts access still further to those with a 'ticket' to the right 'compartment' – a need to know about that particular intelligence matter: in the NSA, this is known as Sensitive Compartmented Information (SCI), defined by the US Army as 'Information and material that requires special controls for restricting handling within compartmented intelligence systems and for which compartmentation is established.' A Special Access Program (SAP) is defined as 'Any program imposing need-to-know or access controls beyond those normally required for access to Confidential, Secret, or Top Secret information. Such a program includes, but is not limited to, special clearance, adjudication, or investigative requirements; special designation of officials authorized to determine need-to-know; or special lists of persons determined to have a need-to-know.'[6]

According to several intelligence sources with whom I have spoken, access to sensitive information can be *further* restricted within the 'compartment' when necessary. A former high-ranking British defence chief told me that he was once privy to above Top Secret information (*not* UFO-related) that only about fifty people had access to. In this case the 'compartment' list included neither the Minister of Defence nor the Prime Minister. If you want to keep a secret, the fewer people who know about it, the better.

As stated, the NSA's COMINT reports 'clearly relate to the most sensitive activities of the defendant'. While not denying its involvement in UFO intelligence collection, the NSA maintains that the principal reason for non-disclosure is that the documents would reveal the means whereby it obtained the COMINT and SIGINT information in the first place; and in this respect I believe the NSA is neither duplicitous nor dissembling. According to the affidavit (which the NSA sent me, in censored form):

> In processing the plaintiff's FOIA request, a total of two hundred and thirty-nine documents were located in NSA files. Seventy-nine of these documents originated with other government agencies and have been referred by NSA to those agencies for their direct response to the plaintiff . . . One document . . . is an account by a person assigned to NSA of his attendance at a UFO symposium and it cannot fairly be said to be a record of the kind sought by the plaintiff. Another document . . . was recently declassified and released to plaintiff. Two additional non-COMINT records have been released . . . with the exempted material deleted . . .

TOP SECRET

UNITED STATES DISTRICT COURT
FOR THE DISTRICT OF COLUMBIA

CITIZENS AGAINST UNIDENTIFIED)
FLYING OBJECTS SECRECY,)
)
Plaintiff,)
)
v.) Civil Action No.
) 80-1562
NATIONAL SECURITY AGENCY,)
)
Defendant.)
_____)

IN CAMERA
AFFIDAVIT OF EUGENE F. YEATES

County of Anne Arundel)
) ss:
State of Maryland)

Eugene F. Yeates, being duly sworn, deposes and says:

1. (U) I am the Chief, Office of Policy, of the National Security Agency (NSA). As Chief, Office of Policy, I am responsible for processing all initial requests made pursuant to the Freedom of Information Act (FOIA) for NSA records. The statements herein are based upon personal knowledge, upon my personal review of information available to me in my official capacity, and upon conclusions reached in accordance therewith.

2. (U) This affidavit supplements my unclassified affidavit executed on September 30, 1980 regarding all documents which have been located by NSA pursuant to plaintiff's FOIA request but which have been withheld wholly or in part by NSA. I submit this affidavit in camera for the purpose of stating facts, which cannot be publicly disclosed, that are the basis for exempting the records from release to the plaintiff.

3. (S) At the beginning of each paragraph of this affidavit, the letter or letters within parentheses designate(s) the degree of sensitivity of information the paragraph contains.

TOP SECRET

Three pages from the twenty-one-page Top Secret Umbra affidavit giving the National Security Agency's reasons for withholding many of its documents dealing with UFOs. Most of the released document is censored. (*NSA*)

The letters "U", "C", "S" and "TS" indicate respectively that
the information is unclassified or is classified CONFIDENTIAL,
SECRET or TOP SECRET.

THE RELEVANT DOCUMENTS

4.   In processing the plaintiff's FOIA request, a
total of two hundred and thirty-nine documents were located
in NSA files. Seventy-nine of these documents originated with
other government agencies and have been referred by NSA to
those agencies for their direct response to the plaintiff.
One document, which I addressed in paragraph 20c of my public
affidavit, was erroneously treated as part of the subject matter
of plaintiff's FOIA request. It is an account by a person

2

The remaining one hundred and fifty-six records being withheld are communications intelligence (COMINT) reports which
were produced between 1958 and 1979. For purposes of my
discussion here, these records are organized into three groups
based upon the source of the report.

The following thirteen pages of the affidavit are almost completely
blacked out. The only information we are given by Eugene Yeates, NSA's
Chief of Policy, is as follows:

> As I have stated in my open affidavit, when alerted to the extent of
> NSA's capability, and if given information from which inferences
> could be drawn as to the processing methods used, foreign
> intelligence services would be able to evade or defeat portions of
> NSA's present foreign intelligence efforts . . . The disclosure of
> other records at issue here, would result in the loss of the
> intelligence information . . . The value of intelligence data
> collected from these sources is obvious.

In the final two pages of the affidavit we are told that:

> . . . the one hundred and fifty-six [deleted] reports relating to
> COMINT activities at issue here are based on intercepted
> communications of foreign governments or SIGINT operations
> and, thus, remain properly classified. In conducting this review I
> have weighed the significant need for openness in government
> against the likelihood of damage to our national security at this
> time and have determined that each record should continue to be
> classified. No meaningful portion can be segregated from the
> records without revealing classified information about the
> intercepted communications underlying the COMINT reports.[7]

Of 502 lines in the affidavit, 412 are totally or partially deleted. An
appeal to the US Court of Appeals in October 1981 led nowhere. As
researcher William Moore remarked:

> In a brief decision issued barely a week after the oral arguments
> were presented (normal time for such decisions is about two
> months), the panel . . . upheld the lower court's position virtually
> without comment. All three judges, along with US defense

attorney Cheryl M. Long (but not plaintiff attorney Gersten) had been granted special security clearances to enable them to view the same NSA classified affidavit which had been presented to Judge Gesell a year earlier.[8]

Peter Gersten filed a petition in 1982 to have the US Supreme Court hear the case of *CAUS* v. *NSA*. The eighty-four-page petition argued against the NSA's 'sweeping classifications of all UFO data', but in March 1982 the Supreme Court upheld the earlier ruling of the District Court. As well it might. The NSA was not necessarily refusing to provide UFO intelligence that it has; rather it was refusing to reveal the specific foreign sources of that SIGINT. Many have jumped to the conclusion that the censored information contained in the NSA affidavit *per se* relates to sensational accounts of recovered alien craft and bodies, and so on. This is not the case. I have been informed by a reliable source, who has reviewed the uncensored document, that the withheld data relate solely to 'methods and sources' by which and from whom the data were obtained.

The Central Security Service

All my Freedom of Information requests to the NSA have been dealt with by the Central Security Service (CSS), the Agency's 'inner sanctum'. Created in 1972 under President Nixon, the CSS is, according to James Bamford, author of *The Puzzle Palace*, the 'eyes and ears of America's cryptological establishment. They are the soldiers, sailors, Marines and airmen who sit in long rows with earphones, turning dials, activating tape recorders, and tapping out messages on six-ply, multicolored carbon paper. Before NSA can attach a code or read a message, it first must be able to capture and record the elusive signal. Such is the job of the Central Security Service . . .'[9]

As I have already pointed out, the NSA has been receiving UFO reports from the military since 1953. Why? Because it needs to gather as much information as possible (*not* relating exclusively to UFOs) on a twenty-four-hour basis for its main client, the Department of Defense. The NSA has now improved its eavesdropping capability to the extent that it can monitor virtually any communication transmitted from anywhere in the world – and beyond. Coded and scrambled messages, broadcasts, telex, satellite transmissions, and even commercial and private telephone calls and faxes are monitored when deemed necessary – though officially only those of foreign origin. Thus the NSA, together with other similar agencies, is in a position to know almost anything of intelligence significance that is transmitted electronically.

The NSA/CIA Link

While working with the NSA in 1964, Todd Zechel saw messages transmitted from the Air Force Special Security Service (an NSA/USAF subsidiary) to the CIA's Special Security Office (the organization within the CIA that controls the distribution of SIGINT). The transmissions were radar plottings of a UFO flying in an erratic manner near the border of a certain country; they had been picked up by a reconnaissance plane during a tracking mission.

Zechel assumes that the CIA had issued instructions to the NSA to report on all UFOs it tracked. 'The fact that the messages were being routed to the CIA station certainly indicates a prior arrangement to do so,' he believes. 'I think it would be safe to assume that the CIA – which worked closely with Air Force Special Security anyway – had instructed the unit to keep them informed of any sightings.'

Zechel relates that it did not come as a surprise to any of those with whom he worked at the NSA that UFOs existed or that the CIA had an interest in them. 'In fact,' he says, 'most of the personnel I worked with were convinced of the reality of UFOs, and many had had personal experiences with these puzzling craft during the course of their jobs.' He states that, although certain personnel in the NSA know a great deal about the UFO phenomenon and have encountered much in the way of photographic and radar intelligence (PHOTINT and RADINT), the NSA is for the most part kept ignorant of the subsequent analysis. 'NSA has always been in a subordinate role to the CIA,' he claims, 'and whatever data it did gather was passed on to the CIA. Therefore, the analysis of the data was performed by CIA personnel; specifically, the CIA's Office of Scientific Intelligence, with NSA being kept ignorant of the conclusions.'[10]

While it may be true that the majority of NSA personnel are kept ignorant, the same cannot be said of the NSA hierarchy. In 1989 Admiral Bobby Ray Inman, whose former posts include that of Director of the NSA as well as Deputy Director of the CIA and Director of Naval Intelligence, was asked by investigator Bob Oechsler, during a recorded telephone conversation on behalf of Admiral Lord Hill-Norton and myself: 'Do you anticipate that any of the recovered vehicles would ever become available for technological research – outside of the military circles?' 'I honestly don't know,' responded Admiral Inman. 'Ten years ago the answer would have been no. Whether as time has evolved they are beginning to become more open on it, there's a possibility . . .' Inman referred Oechsler to Rear Admiral Sumner Shapiro, former Director of Naval Intelligence, as well as the then Deputy Director for Science and Technology at the CIA, Everett Hineman, for further information.[11]

'UFO Hypothesis and Survival Questions'

In 1983 I wrote to the NSA's Director of Policy, James Devine, asking if he was prepared to admit that the Agency still monitored the UFO situation and to reveal what conclusions had been arrived at. On the one hand, I said, we are told that the vast majority of sightings can be explained and that there is no evidence that any of the unexplained reports constitute a defence threat, while on the other hand documents released under the FOIA show that many sightings relate to high-performance structured vehicles, reports of which are treated extremely seriously at a high level.

'I appreciate your frustration in attempting to obtain information on such a complex topic,' Mr Devine replied. 'Unfortunately, however, I have nothing further to add to the information in Mr Yeates' affidavit.'[12]

I had not expected, of course, that the NSA would let me know its conclusions on the matter. But one of the handful of documents it released on the subject addresses the problem of 'human survival implications' relating to UFO phenomena. The document, entitled *UFO Hypothesis and Survival Questions*, was sent to me by the NSA in 1984. It was originally classified, the NSA's Deputy Director of Policy, Frederick Berghoff, explained, 'because certain portions tangentially discussed protected activities pertaining to the NSA/CSS. Most of the remaining portions of the document reflected open-source information on UFOs. The text of this document is being released to you in its entirety. The deletions reflect classification markings which are no longer applicable as well as the name of an NSA/CSS employee.'

The 1968 seven-page NSA article discusses the various hypotheses, which I summarize below:

HOAXES	. . . Rarely have men of science, while acting within their own professional capacities, perpetrated hoaxes. The fact that UFO phenomenon [*sic*] have been witnessed all over the world from ancient times, and by considerable numbers of reputable scientists in recent times, indicates rather strongly that UFOs are not all hoaxes . . .
HALLUCINATIONS	. . . a considerable number of instances exist in which there are groups of people and a radar or radars seeing the same thing at the same time; sometimes a person and a guncamera confirm each other's testimony . . .

The sum of such evidence seems to argue strongly against all UFOs being hallucinations . . .

NATURAL PHENOMENA   If this hypothesis is correct the capability of air warning systems to correctly diagnose an attack situation is open to serious question . . . Many UFOs have been reported by trained observers to behave like high speed, high performance, high altitude rockets or aircraft. The apparent solidity and craft-like shape of the objects have often been subject to radar confirmation . . .

Sometimes the phenomena appear to defy radar detection and to cause massive electromagnetic interference . . .

SECRET EARTH   . . . Undoubtedly, *all UFOs* should be carefully scrutinized to ferret-out such
PROJECTS   enemy (or 'friendly') projects. Otherwise a nation faces the very strong possibility of being intimidated by a new secret 'doomsday' weapon.

EXTRATERRESTRIAL   If 'they' discover you it is an old but hardly invalid rule of thumb, 'they' are
INTELLIGENCE   your technological superiors . . . Human history has shown us time and again the tragic results of a confrontation between a technologically superior civilization and a technologically inferior people . . .

Although the well-informed NSA author delves deeply into the problems associated with confrontation between a technologically advanced society and an inferior one on Earth, there is no conclusion as to whether or not UFOs could be extraterrestrial in origin.

The NSA also sent me a heavily censored three-page monograph and appendix on UFOs by the same writer. 'We wish to emphasize', Mr Berghoff wrote, 'that these draft documents were never published, formally issued, acted upon, or responded to by any government official or agency. Moreover, they are not NSA/CSS reports and in no way reflect an official NSA/CSS position concerning UFOs. They are subject to the provisions of the FOIA only because they have been retained by this Agency for historical reference purposes.'[13]

Why No Leaks?

One of the main objections to the cover-up hypothesis is that there have been no leaks of information from intelligence sources regarding the subject of UFOs, and that it is next to impossible to keep anything secret for long in Washington. The fact is that there *have* been numerous leaks by those claiming association with or employment by various intelligence agencies, as well as positive statements by various intelligence chiefs, many of which are alluded to in this book.

Todd Zechel argues persuasively that secrets *can* be kept, and cites an instance during his service with the Army Security Agency when a Soviet rocket and space capsule were recovered, partially intact (probably relating to Project Moon Dust, at the time a programme of the US Air Force

System Command's Foreign Technology Division, the primary function of the project being to recover foreign space debris). 'All told, several hundred persons were involved in the operation,' he wrote in 1985:

> Most were intelligence personnel with very high security clearances. Over a period of time, one supposes, as many as 1000 persons have had access to the secret. Yet to this day not one word about the operation has leaked out anywhere – except for what is revealed here. Obviously, the event did not have the same transcendental impact as the recovery of a crashed flying saucer, but it does provide a model of a similar big secret that was kept. And it does demonstrate that properly motivated and cleared personnel can keep a lid on something of sensational value.[14]

Reasons for Secrecy

Although throughout this book I have enumerated various reasons for the cover-up of UFO information, it might be appropriate in this final chapter to review the opinions of various experts as well as to offer my own assessment of the situation.

Protection of Defence Intelligence

Since the early 1940s it must have become evident to defence intelligence chiefs that intelligently controlled objects of unknown origin and purpose were operating in our atmosphere. Even as early as 1942, when mysterious objects appeared over Los Angeles, General George Marshall, as Army Chief of Staff, was unable to account for the incident in conventional terms.

By July 1947, when sightings proliferated throughout the United States, and several discs crashed in New Mexico, it must have become obvious that the 'flying saucers' were of extraterrestrial origin. A public admission to this effect undoubtedly would have generated disquiet – particularly since the alien agenda was unknown. 'We had just gone through a world war,' explained General DuBose during the interview in which he confirmed the cover-up following the Roswell incident. 'We had seen the firebombing of great cities, atomic bombs, destruction on an unprecedented scale. Then came this flying saucer business. It was just too much for the public to have to deal with.' In addition, the military needed to learn as much as possible about the construction and propulsion of the craft, in case another nation (particularly the Soviet Union) might acquire this knowledge first; hence another valid reason for absolute secrecy attached to the investigations. We know from the testimony of Dr Robert Sarbacher that the stories of recovered discs are factual, that the subject was classified higher than the hydrogen bomb at the time, that a small group, headed by Dr Vannevar Bush, was established in order to learn as much as possible about the 'modus operandi' of the saucers, and that only those with a need to know were kept informed of the findings.

Nuclear physicist Stanton Friedman, who has been involved in many highly classified projects in the nuclear industry, is equally certain that a main reason for secrecy about UFOs is the defence intelligence aspect:

> From a government and military viewpoint, the most significant aspect of visits to planet Earth by technologically sophisticated vehicles is the potential for military utilization by earth-based groups of that technology. Surely the first government to be able to duplicate that hyper-maneuverable high speed flight of flying saucers will use that capability for the delivery of nuclear and other weapons . . . for defense and attack purposes. In the real world of the late 20th century these potential information gains from the careful scientific investigation of flying saucers – in the air or captured – greatly overshadow any philosophical, religious or humanitarian concerns of the general public. One need only note that collectively the countries of planet Earth spend about 400 billion dollars [1979] on military items each year. Is it really any wonder that governments do not want to reveal whatever sophisticated scientific data they have about flying saucers?[15]

Former Air Force pilot Lieutenant Colonel Donald Ware shares this view. He believes that by 1947 (following the New Mexico incidents) the top military authorities had concluded that some UFOs were extraterrestrial. They would then have realized, he says, 'that if our adversaries acquired the technology represented by these vehicles before we did, our security would be severely threatened. Information on such technology must receive the most extreme protection.'[16]

Although there have been at least forty accounts of UFOs alleged to have been recovered throughout the US and elsewhere, the evidence suggests that it took a long time before we could even begin to comprehend the alien technology. As Stanton Friedman puts it:

You might have handed Thomas Edison one of today's pocket calculators forty years ago, and there's no way in the world he could have figured out how it worked. So if they have significantly advanced technology, it's going to take a lot of effort for us. Even if we figure out how it works, that doesn't mean we can duplicate it. It's like knowing about A-bombs; without the fissionable material, you can't build them, no matter how much you know about them. So it's a multiprong problem, and one that I don't expect the people working in secret would talk about in public. Because he who is able to duplicate flying saucers in quantity is going to rule this planet.[17]

There is also the very real possibility that alien technology could be used for new types of weaponry – again, a compelling reason for withholding data.

Military and Political Embarrassment

No government can be happy to admit that alien vehicles invading our airspace can come and go as they please, and that our defence against them is inadequate. There is evidence in abundance that *some* UFOs are dangerous and that both civilian and military personnel have been injured or even killed. That some UFOs have been responsible for the disappearance and even destruction of our aircraft is not something that could be admitted comfortably. Throughout this book I have documented several such alarming incidents, as well as quoting General Benjamin Chidlaw's privately expressed statement in 1953 that 'we have lost many men and planes trying to intercept them'. As head of Air Defense Command at the time, he presumably knew what he was talking about. I have also learned via a former high-ranking general that further incidents have occurred.

Nobody likes to look silly. Fear of ridicule is a very compelling reason for politicians to debunk the subject, especially if they do not have access to all the facts. British Air Minister George Ward expressed this point perfectly in 1954. While publicly debunking UFO reports as 'balloons' in the House of Commons, he admitted privately: '. . . until I've got a saucer on the ground in Hyde Park and can charge the public sixpence a go to enter, it must be balloons, otherwise the Government would fall and I'd lose my job!'

Ward explained that, if he admitted the existence of UFOs without evidence that the general public could actually touch, the public would consider that the Government had gone barmy. This was an honest admission by an Air Minister who was fully convinced of the reality of UFOs, and it tells me that Her Majesty's Government at the time had not been fully appraised of the true situation by those few in American intelligence circles who were fully aware that actual alien craft already had been recovered. The Americans evidently were less than enthusiastic about allowing the British to exhibit a flying saucer in Hyde Park! (Interestingly, however, there are rumours that a small group within the US intelligence community has been considering the worldwide exhibition of an alien craft, as revealed in *Alien Liaison*.)

Few politicians – in Britain, the United States, and worldwide – have any inside knowledge of the subject of UFOs, which is why their repeated pronouncements debunking all the reports are so convincing. And those few who have troubled to study the matter, or who have been privy to top-secret information, may be so bewildered and even alarmed by the awesome complexity of the phenomenon that they would rather say nothing at all. 'You don't know the half of it,' was all former CIA Director George Bush could say when asked by a campaign-committee member about UFO secrecy during his first presidential election campaign.[18]

Politicians, furthermore, are unlikely to speak out on such a controversial topic without a mandate from the electorate. Relatively few people write to their elected representatives about UFOs, although I am pleased to report that an increasing number are doing so.

Society in Upheaval?

Public reaction to an admission by a major government that some UFOs are extraterrestrial would be predicated on how much we are told, and this must present our leaders with an awesome dilemma. Such an admission would lead to a deluge of questions, some of which simply cannot be answered without disclosing vital defence interests, alarming cases of missing aircraft, abductions, animal mutilations, and cases so bizarre that they may remain beyond our comprehension for centuries to come. In these respects I am fully in sympathy with the current official policy. 'From an intelligence point of view,' remarks Dr James Harder, 'the UFO phenomenon must be truly awesome – the worst of science fiction come to life . . . However, over the years, the intelligence agencies must have come to the realization that the strangers from space are nothing exactly new – that evidence from the past indicates that we are experiencing only an intensification of what may have been going on for centuries.'[19]

The effects on the economic and political front are equally deserving of consideration. 'Every nation is concerned about the effects on worldwide economies and political power structures if the world were to be in touch with aliens with a different technology,' Stanton Friedman believes. 'Is the oil in the ground now worthless? . . . Would the big-shots of today be deposed tomorrow? The best policy is to hope that the aliens go away or that the contacts and shakings up of earthly society happen during the next administration's reign.'[20]

Victor Marchetti, former executive assistant to the Deputy Director and special assistant to the Executive Director of the CIA, theorizes that:

> The purpose of the international conspiracy is to maintain stability among the nations of the world and for them, in turn, to retain institutional control over their respective populations. Thus, for these governments to admit that there are beings from outer space . . . with mentalities and technological capabilities obviously far superior to ours, could, once fully perceived by the average person, erode the foundations of the Earth's traditional power structure. Political and legal systems, religions, economic and social institutions could all soon become meaningless in the mind of the public. The national oligarchical establishments, even civilization as we now know it, could collapse into anarchy. Such extreme conclusions are not necessarily valid, but they probably accurately reflect the fears of the 'ruling classes' of the major nations, whose leaders (particularly those in the intelligence business) have always advocated excessive government secrecy as being necessary to preserve 'national security'.[21]

A Worst-Case Scenario

In the 1970s, journalist Warren Smith claimed to have acquired a great deal of information about the CIA's conclusions regarding the UFO phenomenon. The information reads like something straight out of *The Invaders* (the vintage television science-fiction series), but it is interesting none the less. According to Smith's CIA informant, UFOs represent an advanced technology from another planet, which in many respects is similar to Earth. The problem is that its sun is dying and this planet has begun to cool. 'The aliens have decided their only way to survive is to migrate to another world that would have an environment similar to their own planet,' Smith was supposedly told. 'Our planet represents the one opportunity for their civilization to endure. The problem for mankind is that we're living here.' Smith's source went on to explain that – not surprisingly – it would be impossible for our civilization to absorb immigrants from another planet. 'The social turmoil would be beyond comprehension. The economic chaos that would come about would destroy the foundations of our lives.'

The CIA ostensibly has obtained data showing that the UFOs have conducted a systematic plan of surveillance, beginning with collecting plant and animal specimens, then establishing contact at random with humans. 'Currently, they are embarked on a biological study of people to determine how we differ,' Smith's informant volunteered. 'They're determining whether our two races can interbreed and, if so, what the mutant will look like, its genetic composition, and so forth . . . We also know they've tested our defenses to see if we can withstand an invasion. Therefore, at some time in the future, we expect UFOs to become increasingly hostile.'

Smith wanted to know if the world's governments were aware of this alarming situation. 'Some are,' he was told. 'Others are on a need to know basis. We've maintained secrecy because the truth might destroy us.' Why then was Smith given this information? 'It doesn't have the official stamp,' came the reply. 'You're not the only person who is receiving information. A slow, gradual release of the facts will prevent panic.'

Smith asked about the wilder tales of alien encounters. 'Some of those come from our government attempting to confuse the facts,' replied the informant. 'Many of the reports are being created by the aliens to achieve the same ends. The past several years has produced some incredibly wild contactee reports. We believe the extraterrestrials are testing our ability to withstand psychological warfare. To date, the people selected haven't done too well in that respect.'

The CIA officer added that he expected an increase in bizarre contactee cases such as those where witnesses have been approached by UFOs and then had their memories erased. (Since this conversation took place in the early 1970s there has indeed been a proliferation of such cases.) 'We know there's a purpose behind their actions and the end result may not be for the betterment of humanity,' he said.

'Can we believe the CIA story?' asks Warren Smith. 'Or is this another of the agency's efforts to confuse the facts in ufology?'[22]

A Satellite Government?

It has become increasingly evident to me that the above-Top Secret facts about this multi-faceted subject are restricted to a relatively small group of individuals within the military and scientific intelligence community – a group which, in the US at least, operates outside the normal and legal parameters of government.

In July 1991 Dr Jesse Marcel Jr (whose father, Major Jesse Marcel, had shown him debris from the Roswell crash) was invited to a meeting with an official from the National Security Council. The meeting took place in a secure room in the US Capitol Building (Senate, Room S-128) in Washington, DC. 'He locked the door in back of us, and I thought, gee, I'm in real trouble now,' Dr Marcel reported. 'We walked into this room, and on the table was a book about Roswell. And as we sat down, he pointed to the book and he says, "This is not fiction."'

It has been suggested that those in the know are concerned about the reaction of the public and religious authorities to revelations regarding the link between the UFO phenomenon and religion (one hypothesis being that *homo sapiens* is genetically linked with extraterrestrials). It is interesting that the NSC official asked Dr Marcel if the knowledge that there are extraterrestrial beings had changed his life:

> And I said, well, as far as religion goes, I still am religious. It didn't bother my feelings there . . . His main thrust was to see if I had ever had any threats. Now, I've gotten some crank calls, but none of which had any threat content . . . He said that . . . reading between the lines, there is an arm of the government that is keeping [UFOs] under wraps. And it's his job or mission to try to determine who is doing this . . . he says money is being spent to keep a story covered up . . . the money is being spent illegally . . . there is a 'black' or clandestine arm of the government that is doing this. And I guess that he wanted to find out if I knew of any threats to help maybe backtrack . . . where they came from . . . He did leave me his name, number, everything, in case I ever did get any threatening calls, because he wanted to know about that immediately. And I said, the only thing I was worried about is that I have a Top Secret security [clearance] with the military right now. And he said, 'Don't worry about that' . . . if anybody said anything about that, 'You tell me, and I'll fix it.'[23]

Dr Marcel has confirmed the accuracy of this report for me.[24] Furthermore, I had meetings with the same official in the early 1990s, one in London and several in Washington, DC, thanks to an introduction from Whitley Strieber (who describes his own meetings in his book *Breakthrough*[25]). Though the official did not identify himself as being a representative of or associated with the National Security Council, his work in the US Senate does involve international and national security policies and the appropriations thereof, and he possesses all the requisite security clearances and budget authority over the entire range of national intelligence and Special Access Programs in the intelligence community, Department of Defense, and other relevant Executive branch agencies. I put him in contact with various individuals who I hoped would be able to assist him with his official enquiries.

In 1994 a retired seventy-year-old engineer came forward claiming to have worked for a secret government programme from the mid-1950s until his retirement in the late 1980s. Using the pseudonym 'Jarod 2' (pronounced Jay-rod), the witness informed investigator Glenn Campbell that he had worked on the mechanical design for the avionics of simulators for US-built reproductions of alien vehicles.

Equally controversially, Jarod claims that four aliens had survived a crash in Arizona in 1953 (see Chapter 19), and that communications were eventually established. Originally secured at an unnamed medical facility (possibly Los Alamos National Laboratories), the aliens were transferred to a facility in the Nevada Test Site, and a 'liaison' with the visitors began.

> To protect what was found at the disc crash sites in New Mexico and Arizona [Jarod reports], those in charge at the time scrambled for a position and a decision as to whom in the government would carry the responsibility. This included security, material, personnel, documents, and military and civilian intelligence. It was not decided until the Eisenhower administration in the early part of 1953. A group was formed by the President, and the chairman of the group was Vice President Richard Nixon. Around June of 1953, the final decision was made to set up a 'satellite government'. This separate government would interface with the US Government for support only.

Personnel involved in any part of the disc retrievals were reassigned to this satellite government. Additionally, new security requirements were established and new clearances assigned. 'Think what you would do to maintain a level of secrecy of something inherently totally bizarre in nature,' Jarod explained. 'Nixon did it right by establishing the satellite government. This provided cover for the visitors plus a totally new concept for protecting all information relating to this subject . . .'

Although Jarod has gradually released the information at his own initiative, it has always been with the permission of his former employers. Could this lend further credence to Senator Barry Goldwater's remark that 'there is a plan under way to release some, if not all, of this material in the near future'? 'Some topics have been nixed and others approved,' reported Glenn Campbell in 1995, 'and what [Jarod] has told us so far appears to be only a small part of what he knows.'

But is it all a hoax or disinformation? 'What makes Jarod different for us is that we know him personally,' says Campbell (whom I know to be objective and reliable). 'We have talked with him many times over the past six months, and we see in his words and behaviour all the nuances of reality . . .'[26]

Why No Open Contact?

Why, journalists ask me, don't aliens land on the White House lawn, hold a televised press conference, and establish proper diplomatic relations with us instead of carrying on in such an elusive manner? One reason might be that long-term observation of our belligerent, disunited and perhaps relatively primitive planet would have convinced the visitors that landing openly might not be in their best interests. Asked in Detroit what reaction the visitors from space would receive if they landed openly, the majority of those polled said that a friendly reception could be expected. 'I'd welcome them,' said one. 'They couldn't be any stranger than what's walking around Detroit.' Others were less optimistic. 'If they landed in Detroit they'd probably get mugged,' said one, while another was positively discouraging: 'I'd teach them to stay on their own planet. We've got enough people on welfare without supporting a bunch of Martians.'[27]

It is my conviction that we are being visited by several different groups of extraterrestrials, and that, while some may not be well-disposed towards us, others are benevolent. All seem to share a common 'foreign policy' of avoiding open contact with Earth, which to me seems entirely logical. From my own investigations throughout the world, however, I am convinced that selective contacts have been made with possibly thousands of individuals. The visitors have no need to establish open contact, nor do they want the majority of us to know what they are doing here. It is probable, in my view, that the cover-up is sustained to a certain extent by the aliens themselves.

Where do They Come From and Why are They Here?

There are many hypotheses for the origin of UFOs other than the extraterrestrial one: secret aircraft and spacecraft, natural phenomena, a secret civilization based on Earth, time-travellers from our own future (which is good news since it presupposes that we have a future!), denizens of other dimensions, or psychological 'projections'. Regarding the latter, a miasma of psychological and sociological hypotheses has been proposed to account for the UFO phenomenon. None of these theories comes anywhere near explaining *all* the facts. The extraterrestrial hypothesis may not fulfil this requirement, but it is the only one that explains *most* of the facts.

There are about 200 billion stars in our galaxy alone. Many of these stars are likely to have planets around them, on some of which life may have evolved to the extent that space travel and colonization are commonplace.

Since I do not know where the visitors come from, I can only speculate as to their origin. But I have been informed by reliable sources that some of them have established bases within our solar system – even here on Earth. Neither do I know why they are here, although I can think of numerous possible reasons for their visits. From a tourist's point of view, for example, Earth offers some spectacular attractions. But a vested interest in Earth and its resources – unique in the solar system – is another, more probable, reason. 'We are not here for entirely philanthropic purposes,' my most reliable source was told.

I believe that Man's progress on planet Earth has been monitored by beings whose technological and mental resources make ours look primitive and theirs 'supernatural' by comparison. The fact that some of the visitors are similar to us physiologically suggests that we share a genetic link. Could it be that some of them have had a hand in our evolution?

Now that our technology has reached the stage where we are endangering the planet and expanding our exploration of space, surveillance has intensified. Is it mere coincidence that the modern wave of sightings began during the Second World War as we began developing nuclear weapons and rockets? Is it also coincidental that UFOs have exhibited so much interest in our nuclear-missile sites and have demonstrated their ability to paralyse launching systems?

Are We Entitled to the Truth?

It is as well at this stage to remind ourselves of the official position on the subject as set out by the US Government. From 1947 to 1969 a total of 12,618 sightings was reported to Project Blue Book, the USAF fact sheet sent to me in 1986 states. Of these, 701 remain unidentified. The conclusions of Project Blue Book were as follows:

(1) No UFO reported, investigated, and evaluated by the Air Force has ever given any indication of threat to our national security; (2) there has been no evidence submitted to or discovered by the Air Force that sightings categorized as 'unidentified' represent technological developments or principles beyond the range of present-day scientific knowledge; and (3) there has been no evidence indicating that sightings categorized as 'unidentified' are extraterrestrial vehicles . . . Since Project Blue Book was closed [1969], nothing has happened to indicate that the Air Force ought to resume investigating UFOs.[28]

All these statements are demonstrably false. For instance, reports of UFOs affecting national security were not routed to Project Blue Book and are therefore not included in the 75,000 pages of Blue Book records now stored at the National Archives Building in Washington, DC. Nor have we yet been permitted to review the records, or even to learn the official existence, of the Air Force's Project Fang, which according to information supplied to me by William Birkholz, a former Blue Book non-commissioned officer who later served as an analyst with the Foreign Technology Division at Wright-Patterson Air Force Base, was believed to be a separate project, concurrent with Projects Sign, Grudge, and Blue Book, that dealt only with UFO events in countries foreign to the United States.[29]

In its various fact sheets issued over the years, the Air Force has disingenuously failed to acknowledge the significant percentage of sightings which remain unidentified. The USAF-sponsored study at the University of Colorado, headed by the late Dr Edward Condon, for example, found that 30 per cent of the 117 cases studied resisted an adequate explanation.[30] As a UFO subcommittee of the American Institute of Aeronautics and Astronautics remarked: 'The opposite conclusions [to Condon's negative statements] could have been drawn from the content of the report, namely that a phenomenon with such a high ratio of unexplained cases should arouse sufficient scientific curiosity to continue its study.'[31]

Furthermore, Air Force official policy statements contradict the Air Force's own findings. Project Blue Book Special Report No. 14 contains far more UFO sighting reports than any other official compilation, and tables show clearly that, of the sightings reported in the 'Excellent' category of witness reliability, 33.3 per cent remained 'Unknown', as distinct from those reports categorized as 'Insufficient Information'.[32] As Stanton Friedman observes:

> Project Blue Book Special Report No. 14 was never publicly distributed by the Air Force either when it was completed in 1955 or anytime later . . . An accompanying summary of the study somehow managed to avoid including any of the massive amount of factual data in the report. No one questioned the totally false statements by Secretary of the Air Force Donald Quarles, who said, 'On the basis of this report we believe that no objects such as those popularly described as flying saucers have overflown the United States. Even the unknown 3% could have been identified as conventional phenomena or illusions if more complete observational data had been available.'[33]

Although a few UFO reports affecting but apparently not compromising national security can be found among the 1,800 pages of USAF Intelligence documents released in 1985–6, many Top Secret reports remain exempt from disclosure, according to the records.[34] Likewise, the CIA, the DIA, the NSA and other agencies are withholding Top Secret and additionally compartmented information pertaining to UFOs that would compromise national security if released, and it is evident that what *has* been released represents only the tip of the iceberg.

The policy statement that 'nothing has happened to indicate that the Air Force ought to resume investigating UFOs' is disproven by the released documents indicating continued investigations by the Air Force Office of Special Investigations. That no sightings 'represent technological developments or principles beyond the range of present-day scientific knowledge' is sheer nonsense, given the wealth of documentary evidence from unimpeachable sources testifying to the contrary. Even if the testimonial evidence is arbitrary, what about the many confiscated or withheld photographs and films showing UFOs as structured objects, to say nothing of the retrieved craft and occupants?

We have learned to live – albeit uneasily – with the threat of nuclear annihilation hanging over us like the proverbial sword of Damocles. Surely nothing that governments are concealing about UFOs can compare with this prospect? As the great psychologist Dr Carl Jung commented in a letter to Major Donald Keyhoe:

> If it is true that the [Air Force] or the Government withholds telltale facts, then one can only say that this is the most unpsychological and stupid policy one could invent. Nothing helps rumours and panics more than ignorance. It is self-evident that the public ought to be told the truth, because ultimately it will come to the light of day. There can be hardly any greater shock than the H-bomb and yet everyone knows of it without fainting.[35]

Some politicians and military officials have hinted at the potential threat posed by a confrontation with alien forces. In Chapter 12 I alluded to the private discussion between Mikhail Gorbachev and Ronald Reagan during the Geneva summit conference in 1985. 'The US President said that if the Earth faced an invasion by extraterrestrials,' Gorbachev revealed, 'the United States and the Soviet Union would join forces to repel such an invasion . . .' President Reagan (who witnessed a UFO from the air in 1974, leading to his interest in the subject)[36] referred to this discussion on at least three public occasions, hypothesizing the benefits of international co-operation in the event of an extraterrestrial threat. Of these statements, the following seems particularly significant:

'In our obsession with antagonisms of the moment, we often forget how much unites all the members of humanity,' said Reagan, towards the end of a speech given before the 42nd General Assembly of the United Nations on 21 September 1987. 'Perhaps we need some outside, universal threat to make us recognize this common bond. I occasionally think how quickly our differences worldwide would vanish if we were facing an alien threat from outside this world. And yet, I ask, is not an alien force already among us?' The President then seemed to retreat from this last provocative statement by posing another, unrelated, question: 'What could be more alien to the universal aspirations of our peoples than war and the threat of war?'[37]

In conversation with Mayor Achille Lauro of Naples in 1955, Douglas MacArthur, General of the Army, who is believed to have established the Army's Interplanetary Phenomenon Unit in 1945, was quoted as having said that the politics of the future would be cosmic, or interplanetary in scope. 'He believes,' Mayor Lauro elaborated, 'that because of the developments of science all the countries on earth will have to unite to survive and to make a common front against attack from other planets.'[38] And in 1962, during an address to the United States Military Academy at West Point, General MacArthur made another intriguing statement:

> You now face a new world, a world of change. The thrust into outer space . . . marks a beginning of another epoch in the long story of mankind . . . We deal now, not with things of this world alone, but with the illimitable distances and as yet unfathomed mysteries of the universe . . . of ultimate conflict between a united human race and the sinister forces of some other planetary galaxy . . .[39]

Yet even if certain matters affecting national, international and perhaps interplanetary security simply cannot be revealed, we are entitled to know *some* of the truth at least. The dilemma, which I recognize as a complex and difficult one, is: How much is 'some'? One authority in a position to know the facts – as known at the time – was former CIA Director Rear Admiral Roscoe Hillenkoetter, who was unequivocal in his condemnation of official policy. 'The public has a right to know,' he declared in 1960. 'It is time for the truth to be brought out in open Congressional hearings . . . through official secrecy and ridicule, many citizens are led to believe the unknown flying objects are nonsense.'[40]

Thirty-five years later, we are still being misled. Until we wake up to the fact that information of quite unprecedented and profound significance is being withheld from us, we shall continue to remain in ignorance.

References

Introduction

1. Letter to the author from H. Chapman Pincher, 4 October 1981.
2. *Hansard* (House of Lords), Vol. 397, No. 23, January 1979, p. 1310.

Prologue

1. Keel, John A.: 'Mystery Aeroplanes of the 1930s', Part I, *Flying Saucer Review*, FSR Publications Ltd, PO Box 162, High Wycombe, Bucks. HP13 5DZ, England, Vol. 16, No. 3, 1970, pp. 10–13.
2. *New York Times*, 3 February 1934.
3. Keel, John A.: 'Mystery Aeroplanes of the 1930s', Part II, *Flying Saucer Review*, Vol. 16, No. 4, 1970, pp. 9–14.
4. Braenne, Ole Jonny: 'The Norwegian "Ghost Fliers" of 1933–37', *The INFO Journal*, Summer 1995, pp. 6–11.
5. Collins, Paul T.: 'The UFOs of 1942', *Exploring the Unknown*, No. 48, September 1968.
6. *Los Angeles Examiner*, 27 February 1942.
7. Letter from John E. Seidel, published in *Air & Space*, February/March 1990, p. 8.
8. Letter to the author from G. J. Carpenter Jr, 4 July 1988.
9. *Los Angeles Examiner*, 27 February 1942.
10. Clark, Jerome, and Farish, Lucius: 'The Mysterious Foo Fighters of WWII', *UFO Report*, Vol. 2, No. 3, 1975, pp. 44–7, 64–6.
11. *Just Cause*, PO Box 218, Coventry, Connecticut 06238, No. 32, June 1992.
12. Files of the National Investigations Committee on Aerial Phenomena (NICAP); Lore, Gordon, and Deneault, Harold: *Mysteries of the Skies*, Robert Hale, London, 1969, p. 127.
13. *Just Cause*, No. 32, June 1992.
14. Stringfield, Leonard H.: *Situation Red, The UFO Siege!*, Doubleday & Co., Inc., New York, 1977, pp. 9–10.
15. Gross, Loren E.: 'Ghost Rockets of 1946', *The Encyclopedia of UFOs*

(edited by Ronald D. Story), New English Library, London, 1980, pp. 147–49.

16. *Intelligence Review*, US Air Force, No. 47, 9 January 1947, pp. 17–20.
17. Flammonde, Paris: *UFO Exist!*, G. P. Putnam's Sons, New York, 1976, pp. 127–34.
18. *New York Times*, 23 August 1946.
19. Jones, Professor R. V.: 'The Natural Philosophy of Flying Saucers', *Physics Bulletin*, Vol. 19, July 1968, pp. 225–30.
20. *New York Times*, 11 October 1946.
21. *Daily Telegraph*, London, 6 September 1946.
22. *Sydney Sun*, 25 February 1967. The 'foreign officials' cited by Santorini are identified as being from the Pentagon.
23. Fowler, Raymond E.: *UFOs: Interplanetary Visitors*, Exposition Press, New York, 1974, pp. 105–6.
24. *Sydney Sun*, 25 February 1967.

Chapter 1: Defence Intelligence

1. Letter to the author from Simon Weeden, Defence Secretariat 8, Ministry of Defence, 28 November 1980.
2. Prime Minister's Personal Minute to the Secretary of State for Air (Serial No. M. 412/52), 28 July 1952.
3. Memo to the Prime Minister from the Secretary of State for Air, Air Ministry, Whitehall, 9 August 1952.
4. *Analysis of Flying Object Incidents in the U.S.*, Air Intelligence Report No. 100-203-79, Directorate of Intelligence and Office of Naval Intelligence, 10 December 1948.
5. Twining, Lieutenant General N. F.: *A.M.C. Opinion Concerning 'Flying Discs'*, HQ Air Matériel Command, to Commanding General, Army Air Forces, 23 September 1947.
6. Memorandum from H. Marshall Chadwell, Assistant Director of Scientific Intelligence, to the Director of Central Intelligence, CIA, September 1952.
7. *Sunday Dispatch*, London, 21 September 1952.
8. Ruppelt, Captain Edward J.: *The Report on Unidentified Flying Objects*, Doubleday, New York, 1956, p. 196.
9. Ibid., p. 130.
10. *Sunday Dispatch*, London, 28 September 1952.
11. Ibid., 7 December 1952.

12. Pitt, John: 'Tell us please, Mr Birch!', *Flying Saucer Review*, Vol. 2, No. 5, 1956, pp. 10–13.

13. Letter to Nicholas Redfern from the Public Record Office, Kew, 21 September 1990.

14. Letter to Ralph Noyes from Group Captain Harold B. Collins, 26 January 1985.

15. Keyhoe, Major Donald E.: *Aliens from Space: The Real Story of Unidentified Flying Objects*, Panther Books, London, 1975, p. 27.

16. Girvan, Waveney: *Flying Saucers and Common Sense*, Frederick Muller, London, 1955, pp. 106–14.

17. *The Times*, London, 25 November 1954.

18. Memo from Flight Lieutenant C. P. B. Russell, for Senior Air Staff Officer, Headquarters No. 11 Group, 16 December 1953.

19. Interview with the author, 10 October 1985.

20. *Sunday Dispatch*, London, 7 November 1954.

21. Ibid., 28 March 1954.

22. Letter to the author from Major the Hon. Andrew Wigram, Buckingham Palace, 10 December 1985.

23. Leslie, Desmond: 'Politicians and the UFO', *Flying Saucer Review*, Vol. 9, No. 3, 1963, pp. 8–10.

24. *Sunday Dispatch*, London, 11 July 1954.

25. Ziegler, Philip: *Mountbatten: The Official Biography*, Collins, London, 1985, p. 493.

26. Leslie, Desmond: 'Did Flying Saucers Land at Broadlands?', *Flying Saucer Review*, Vol. 26, No. 5, 1980, pp. 2–4.

27. Ziegler: op. cit., p. 494.

Chapter 2: Flying Saucers – Top Secret

1. Dempster, Derek: Editorial, *Flying Saucer Review*, Vol. 1, No. 2, 1955.

2. *Los Angeles Examiner*, 23 May 1955.

3. Rehn, K. Gösta: *UFOs Here and Now!*, Abelard-Schuman, London, 1974, pp. 38–40.

4. Letter from F. H. C. Wimbledon, *Flying Saucer Review*, Vol. 24, No. 1, 1978, p. 31.

5. *Sunday Times*, London, 9 April 1978.

6. Thayer, Gordon D.: 'Optical and Radar Analyses of Field Cases', *Scientific Study of Unidentified Flying Objects*, Bantam Books, New York, 1969, p. 164. See also pp. 248–56, and McDonald, Dr James E.: 'UFOs over Lakenheath in 1956', *Flying Saucer Review*, Vol. 16, No. 2,

1970, pp. 9–17, 29. The best synopsis of this case is by Thayer in *The Encyclopedia of UFOs*, ed. Ronald D. Story, New English Library, London, 1980, pp. 200–202.

7. Bowen, Charles: 'The Hazards of Television', *Flying Saucer Review*, Vol. 18, No. 2, 1972, pp. 18–19.

8. Interview with the author, 21 August 1985.

9. Letter to the author from N. G. Pope, Secretariat (Air Staff) 2a, Ministry of Defence, London, 13 January 1994.

10. *Sunday Dispatch*, London, 7 April 1957.

11. 'Unidentified Objects at West Freugh', Deputy Directorate of Intelligence (Technical), 30 April 1957, Public Record Office reference AIR 20/9321.

12. *Reynolds News*, 15 June 1957.

13. Interview with the author, March 1985.

14. 'UFO Cuts out Radio of an Airliner over Kent', *Flying Saucer Review*, Vol. 3, No. 6, 1957, p. 2.

15. 'UFO Over a British A-Bomber Base', *Flying Saucer Review*, Vol. 4, No. 1, 1958, p. 6.

16. *Flying Saucer Review*, Vol. 4, No. 4, 1958, p. 5.

17. Letter to the author from A. Mathewson, Defence Secretariat 8, Ministry of Defence, London, 20 September 1984.

18. *Flying Saucer Review*, Vol. 4, No. 5, 1958, back page.

19. Ibid., Vol. 5, No. 1, 1959, p. 2.

20. Ibid., Vol. 5, No. 2, 1959, p. 2

21. Ibid., Vol. 5, No. 3, 1959, p. 10.

22. The order forbidding aircrews to discuss their sightings publicly was issued by the Air Ministry on 25 January 1954, according to Harold T. Wilkins in his book *Flying Saucers Uncensored*, Arco Publishers, London, 1956, p. 118.

23. Leslie, Desmond: 'Politicians and the UFO', *Flying Saucer Review*, Vol. 9, No. 3, 1963, pp. 8–10.

Chapter 3: A Matter of National Security

1. Muirfield, Roger: 'Silence in the Press: A Glimpse behind the Scenes', *Flying Saucer Review*, Vol. 6, No. 3, 1960, pp. 16–19.

2. Girvan, Waveney: Editorial, *Flying Saucer Review*, Vol. 6, No. 5, 1960, pp. 1–2.

3. 'Security Procedures in the Public Service', *First Radcliffe Committee Report*, Her Majesty's Stationery Office, London, April 1962.

4. Good, Timothy: *Above Top Secret: The Worldwide UFO Cover-Up*, Sidgwick & Jackson, London, 1987.

5. Editorial, *Heywood Advertiser*, 1 June 1989.

6. Redfern, Nicholas: *A Covert Agenda: UFO Secrecy Exposed* [provisional title].

7. *Hansard* (House of Commons), 15 July 1964.

8. *Daily Telegraph*, London, 20 July 1966.

9. Letter to the author from the Rt. Hon. Lord Wilson of Rievaulx, 1 January 1985.

10. Letter to the author from the Rt. Hon. Edward Heath MP, 12 February 1982.

11. *Camberley News*, 15 March 1963.

12. Letter to the author from Graham Sheppard, 11 May 1995.

13. Ibid.

14. Letter from Graham Sheppard to the Editor, *Sunday Telegraph*, 9 July 1991, published in *The UFO Report 1992*, ed. Timothy Good, Sidgwick & Jackson, London, 1991.

15. Chapman, Robert: *Unidentified Flying Objects*, Robert Barker, London, 1969, pp. 42–4.

16. Letter to the author from Peter Hucker, Secretariat (Air Staff) 2, Ministry of Defence, London, 22 August 1985.

17. Letter to the author from Peter Hucker, Ministry of Defence, London, 30 May 1986.

18. Brooks, Angus: 'Remarkable Sighting near Dorset Coast', *Flying Saucer Review*, Vol. 14, No. 1, 1968, pp. 3–5.

19. Chapman: op. cit., pp. 25–35.

20. *Daily Express*, London, 7 November 1967.

21. Falla, Geoffrey: *Vehicle Interference Project*, British UFO Research Association, 1979.

22. *Hansard* (House of Commons), 8 November 1967.

23. Ibid., 22 November 1967.

24. Ibid., 22 January 1968.

25. Ibid., 11 June 1968.

26. *Flying Saucers – and the People Who See Them*, BBC Television, 9 May 1968.

27. Stanway, Roger H., and Pace, Antony R.: *Flying Saucer Report: UFOs Unidentified, Undeniable*, privately published (revised edition), 1972.

28. Ibid., pp. 62–5.

29. Ibid., appendices 1 and 2.

30. Letter to the author, 8 October 1986.

31. Interview with the author, 23 October 1986.
32. Interview with the author, 8 December 1986.
33. Bowen, Charles: Editorial, *Flying Saucer Review*, Vol. 23, No. 1, 1977, pp. 1–2.
34. Letter to the author from Simon Weeden, Defence Secretariat 8, Ministry of Defence, London, 18 November 1981.
35. *Daily Mirror*, London, 18 August 1978.
36. *Middlesex Chronicle*, 15 September 1978.
37. Birdsall, Graham, and Birdsall, Mark: 'Landing and Possible Traces near Leeds', *Northern Ufology*, No. 62, July 1979.
38. British UFO Research Association (Yorkshire branch) report forms.
39. *Yorkshire Post*, 24 February 1979.
40. Interview with the author, 27 July 1986.
41. *Hansard* (House of Lords), Vol. 397, No. 23, 18 January 1979.

Chapter 4: No Defence Significance?

1. Birdsall, Graham: 'Radar Tracks UFO Over RAF Woodbridge', *UFO Magazine*, May/June 1995, pp. 44–5.
2. 'Unidentified Flying Objects', *The Manual of Air Traffic Services*, Part I (CAP 493), 14 November 1991, ed. M. R. Sutton, Safety Regulation Group, Civil Aviation Authority, Gatwick Airport South.
3. Letter to the author from Simon Weeden, Defence Secretariat 8, Ministry of Defence, London, 25 March 1981.
4. Letter to Robert Todd from Col. Peter W. Bent, Commander, Headquarters, 513th Combat Support Group (USAFE), 14 June 1983.
5. Butler, Brenda, Street, Dot, and Randles, Jenny: *Sky Crash: A Cosmic Conspiracy*, Neville Spearman, Sudbury, Suffolk, 1984, p. 34. Rev. edn., Grafton Books, London, 1986.
6. Ibid. (1984), p. 102.
7. *Omni*, Vol. 5, No. 6, 1983.
8. Butler, Street and Randles: op. cit., p. 167.
9. Ibid., pp. 7–10, 90–1.
10. Ibid., p. 27.
11. Letter to Nicholas Redfern from Squadron Leader E. E. Webster, Royal Air Force, Eastern Radar, Watton, Norfolk, 16 January 1989.
12. Lecture by Charles Halt organized by Harry Harris and Quest International, Centenary House, Leeds, 31 July 1994.
13. Randles, Jenny: *From Out of the Blue: The Incredible UFO Cover-Up at*

Bentwaters NATO Air Base, Global Communications, Box 753, New Brunswick, New Jersey 08903, 1991, pp. 8–10, 14–19, 121.

14. Huneeus, Antonio: 'Bentwaters, Part III: The Testimony of John Burroughs', *Fate*, September 1993, pp. 70–71.

15. Ibid., p. 71.

16. *Strange But True?*, London Weekend Television, 9 December 1994.

17. Randles, Jenny, and Hough, Peter: *Strange But True?*, LWT Productions Ltd, published by Judy Piatkus Ltd, London, 1994, pp. 134–5.

18. Lecture by Charles Halt, Centenary House, Leeds, 31 July 1994.

19. Recorded interview, supplied to the author by Ray Boeche.

20. Lecture by Charles Halt, Centenary House, Leeds, 31 July 1994.

21. From Ray Boeche's research notes, supplied to the author.

22. Interview with the author, London, 21 October 1993.

23. Warren, Larry, and Robbins, Peter: *Left at East Gate* [provisional title].

24. Randles, Jenny: 'Military Contact alleged at Air Base', *Flying Saucer Review*, Vol. 26, No. 6, 1980 (published 1981), p. iii.

25. Randles, Jenny: 'The Rendlesham Forest Mystery', *Flying Saucer Review*, Vol. 27, No. 6, 1981 (published 1982), pp. 4–8.

26. Beabey, Keith: 'UFO Lands in Suffolk – and That's Official', *News of the World*, 2 October 1983.

27. *Daily Telegraph*, London, 17 October 1983.

28. *Hansard* (House of Commons), 24 October 1983.

29. Letter to Ralph Noyes from Brian M. Webster, Defence Secretariat 8, Ministry of Defence, London, 20 March 1984.

30. Letter to Ralph Noyes from Peter M. Hucker, Ministry of Defence, London, 15 May 1985.

31. A copy of the Halt tape is available from Quest Publications International Ltd, 1st Floor, 66 Boroughgate, Otley, Near Leeds, LS21 1AE.

32. Grant, John: 'Recording of UFO Sighting "not hoax"', *East Anglian Daily Times*, 25 October 1984.

33. Noyes, Ralph: *A Secret Property*, Quartet Books, London, 1985, pp. 182–3.

34. Letter to Admiral of the Fleet the Lord Hill-Norton from Lord Trefgarne, Parliamentary Under-Secretary of State for the Armed Forces, Ministry of Defence, London, 19 June 1985.

35. Letter from Lord Hill-Norton to Lord Trefgarne, 24 June 1985.

36. Interview with the author, 6 October 1986.

37. *Strange But True?*, London Weekend Television, 9 December 1994.

38. Interview with the author, 28 August 1995.

39. Notes by Mark Birdsall, provided to the author.
40. *Strange But True?*, London Weekend Television, 9 December 1994.

Chapter 5: The Security Threat

1. Grant, Patricia B.: 'A Very Personal Encounter "Somewhere in Sussex"', *Flying Saucer Review*, Vol. 25, No. 2, 1979, pp. 18–25; plus Pat Grant's voluminous file on the case.
2. Interview with the author, 13 July 1986.
3. Randles, Jenny: *The Pennine UFO Mystery*, Granada, London, 1983, pp. 122–35, 147–68.
4. *Central Weekend*, Central Television, Birmingham, 5 September 1986.
5. *Plymouth Evening Herald*, 28 October 1981.
6. Boyd, Bob: *UFOs over Plymouth*, Plymouth UFO Research Group, 40 Albert Road, Stoke, Plymouth, PL2 1AE, 1982.
7. *Hansard* (House of Lords), 4 March 1982.
8. *Out of Court*, BBC Television, 10 March 1982.
9. *Hansard* (House of Lords), 7 April 1982.
10. George Adamski was the first witness to report a central column in an extraterrestrial craft, described in his book *Inside the Space Ships*, Neville Spearman, London, 1956.
11. Collins, Debbie: 'Alf's "Close Encounter"', *Aldershot News*, 14 October 1983.
12. Fowler, Omar: 'A Landing and Close Encounter near Aldershot', *Flying Saucer Review*, Vol. 29, No. 2, 1983 (published December 1983), pp. 3–5.
13. 'UFO Expert says: Alf is Telling the Truth', *Aldershot News*, 25 November 1983.
14. Collins, John: 'Top UFO Expert Confirms Man's Astounding Claim', *National Enquirer* (US), 17 July 1984.
15. Letter to the author from Peter M. Hucker, Secretariat (Air Staff) 2a, Ministry of Defence, London, 30 May 1986.
16. *Hansard* (House of Commons), 9 March 1984.
17. Ibid., 14 March 1984.
18. *Lancashire Evening Telegraph*, 1 May 1984.
19. *Central Intelligence Machinery*, Her Majesty's Stationery Office, London, 1993.
20. Ibid.
21. Letter from James Rusbridger, *Daily Telegraph*, London, 13 December 1986.

22. Interview with the author, 18 March 1985.
23. Interview by the author with Peter Hucker, 18 March 1985.
24. Interviews by the author with David Ross of Secretariat (Air Staff) 2a, Ministry of Defence, 23 October and 8 December 1986. Other branches of the Defence Intelligence Staff which have been involved in UFO investigations include DI10, DI61E, and DI65B, according to Public Record Office papers released to Nicholas Redfern, published in his book *A Covert Agenda* [provisional title].
25. Letter to the author from Ralph Noyes, 28 April 1985.
26. Interview with the author, 23 June 1995. For further details, see Redfern: op. cit.
27. Letter to the author from M. R. Sutton, Editor, *Manual of Air Traffic Services* Part 1, Safety Regulation Group, Civil Aviation Authority, Gatwick Airport South, 12 October 1994.
28. Letter to the author from Miss K. Philpott, Secretariat (Air Staff) 2a, Ministry of Defence, London, 11 January 1996.
29. Good, Timothy: *Alien Liaison: The Ultimate Secret*, Century, London, 1991, pp. 13–14.
30. Pope, Nick: *Open Skies, Closed Minds*, Simon & Schuster, London, 1996.
31. Interview with the author, 7 June 1995.
32. Commercial Air Transport Airmiss Reports (January–April 1995), Joint Airmiss Working Group, Civil Aviation Authority, January 1996.
33. Sheppard, Captain Graham: *Safety Implications of UFO Close Approaches*: Briefing Notes prepared for the Joint Airmiss Working Group, 20 February 1995.
34. Letter to the author from Dr Robert F. Creegan, State University of New York at Albany, 15 August 1985.
35. Creegan, Robert F.: 'Signs of Panic', *APRO Bulletin*, Aerial Phenomena Research Organization, Vol. 32, No. 3, 1984, p. 7.

Chapter 6: France

1. *Sunday Dispatch*, London, 3 October 1954.
2. 'French Minister Speaks on UFOs': text of the radio interview given on France-Inter, translated by Gordon Creighton, *Flying Saucer Review*, Vol. 20, No. 2, 1974, pp. 3–4.
3. Michel, Aimé: *Flying Saucers and the Straight-Line Mystery*, Criterion Books, New York, 1958, pp. 44–6.
4. *Flying Saucer Review*, Vol. 28, No. 5, 1982, pp. 15–16.

5. Ibid., Vol. 2, No. 2, 1956, p. 3.

6. Michel: op. cit., pp. 5–7.

7. *Sud-Ouest*, Bordeaux, 17 February 1965.

8. Michel, Aimé: 'The Valensole Affair', *Flying Saucer Review*, Vol. 11, No. 6, 1965, pp. 7–9.

9. Michel, Aimé, and Bowen, Charles: *The Encyclopedia of UFOs*, ed. Ronald D. Story, New English Library, London, 1980, p. 377.

10. Bourret, Jean-Claude: *The Crack in the Universe*, Neville Spearman, Jersey, pp. 98–106, translated by Gordon Creighton from the original book, *La Nouvelle Vague des Soucoupes Volantes*, France-Empire, Paris, 1974.

11. Gille, Dr Jean F.: 'The Bankruptcy of the French UFO Research Body, GEPAN', *Flying Saucer Review*, Vol. 28, No. 5, 1982, p. 15.

12. Creighton, Gordon: 'The Gendarmerie and UFOs', *Flying Saucer Review*, Vol. 17, No. 5, 1971, pp. 27–8, quoting *La Revue d'Etudes et d'Information de la Gendarmerie Nationale*, No. 87, Premier Trimestre, 1971.

13. Sachs, Margaret: *The UFO Encyclopedia*, Perigee Books, G. P. Putnam's Sons, New York, 1980, pp. 132–3.

14. Commentary by Gordon Creighton in Gille: op. cit., p. 17.

15. Lagarde, Fernand: 'A Warning to All', *Flying Saucer Review*, Vol. 28, No. 1, 1982, p. 2.

16. Interview with the author, 6 November 1984.

17. Guérin, Dr Pierre: 'Are the Reasons for the Cover-Up *Solely* Scientific?', *Flying Saucer Review*, Vol. 28, No. 6, 1982, pp. 2–8.

18. GEPAN: *Note Technique No. 16, Enquête 81/01, Analyse d'une Trace*, Toulouse, 1 March 1983. (English translation published in the *MUFON UFO Journal*, March 1984.)

19. Velasco, Jean-Jacques: 'Report on the Analysis of Anomalous Physical Traces: The 1981 Trans-en-Provence UFO Case', *Journal of Scientific Exploration*, Vol. 4, No. 1, 1990.

20. GEPAN: Ibid.

21. Roussel, Robert: *Les Vérités Chassées de l'Enquête Officielle*, Albin Michel, 1994; quoted in Huneeus, Antonio: 'The French Government UFO Dossier', *Fate*, October 1994.

22. Velasco, Jean-Jacques: 'Action of Electromagnetic Fields in the Microwave Range on Vegetation'; paper presented at a meeting of the Society for Scientific Exploration, Glasgow, August 1994.

23. Paskov, David: 'Flying saucer has the boffins baffled', *Daily Express*, London, 24 July 1983.

24. Creighton, Gordon: 'Another French Report on GEPAN', *Flying Saucer Review*, Vol. 30, No. 3, 1984, p. 27.
25. Baker, Sherry: 'UFO Update', *Omni*, Vol. 8, No. 4, 1986, p. 83.
26. SOS OVNI, Boîte Postale 324, 13611 Aix-en-Provence Cédex 1, France.
27. Eberhart, George M.: 'The European Parliament', *International UFO Reporter*, J. Allen Hynek Center for UFO Studies, Vol. 19, No. 2, March/April 1994, p. 19.
28. Letter to the author from Colonel Claude Rossello, Attaché de l'Air, Ambassade de France, London, 30 October 1986.
29. Letter to the author from Colonel Rossello, 18 November 1986.
30. Chassin, General L. M.: 'Success is in Sight', *Flying Saucer Review*, Vol. 7, No. 6, 1961, pp. 3–5.

Chapter 7: Italy

1. Perego, Dr Alberto: 'The Great Cross above the Vatican', *Flying Saucer Review Case Histories*, No. 15, June 1973, pp. 3–6.
2. *Veneto Notte*, 19 November 1973, cited in *Flying Saucer Review*, Vol. 20, No. 5, 1973, p. iii.
3. Chiumiento, Antonio: 'UFO Alert at a NATO Base in Italy', *Flying Saucer Review*, Vol. 30, No. 2, 1984, pp. 2–5.
4. Creighton, Gordon: 'A Problem for the Italian Minister of Defence?', *Flying Saucer Review*, Vol. 24, No. 1, 1978, pp. 26–7.
5. Pinotti, Roberto: 'The Italian Ministry of Defence and UFOs', *Flying Saucer Review*, Vol. 24, No. 6, 1978, pp. 14–15, 18.
6. Verga, Maurizio: 'Two Entity Reports in Italy', *Flying Saucer Review*, Vol. 24, No. 6, 1978, pp. 24–5, quoting *La Sicilia*, 6 July 1978.
7. Guerrini, Remo: 'Secret UFO Report', *Epoca*, No. 1802, 19 April 1985.
8. Chiumiento, Antonio: 'An Italian Pilot's Sighting: And Another Italian Government Cover-up?', *Flying Saucer Review*, Vol. 33, No. 1, 1988, pp. 1–4.
9. *UFO: Rivista di Informazione Ufologica*, No. 13, December 1993 (Centro Italiano Studi Ufologici, Casella Postale 82, 10100 Torino).
10. *Oggetti Volanti Non Identificati (O.V.N.I.): Rilevazione Statistische (1979–1990)*, Air Force General Staff (2nd Department), published in *UFO: Rivista di Informazione Ufologica*, No. 13, December 1993, pp. 9–12.
11. Ibid., p. 12.
12. Svahn, Clas and Liljegren, Anders: 'Close Encounters with Unknown

Missiles', *International UFO Reporter*, Vol. 19, No. 4, July/August 1994, pp. 13–14.

13. *Sunday Times*, London, 5 May 1991.

14. Ward, Stephen: 'Inquiry into pilot's sighting of missile', *Independent*, London, 6 May 1991.

15. Evans, Michael: 'UFO blamed for air-miss with jet', *The Times*, London, 6 May 1991.

16. *L'Indipendente*, 30 June 1993.

17. The Caponi family was interviewed by Giancarlo Magalli on *I Fatti Vostri*, RAI-DUE, 5 November 1993.

18. Interview with the author, 4 February 1994.

19. Eberhart, George M.: 'The European Parliament', *International UFO Reporter*, Vol. 19, No. 2, March/April 1994, p. 19.

20. *Report of the Committee on Energy, Research and Technology on the Proposal to Set Up a European Centre for Sightings of Unidentified Flying Objects*, European Parliament session documents (English edition), 2 December 1993.

21. Interview with Tullio Reggi by Paolo Toselli, *UFO: Rivista di Informazione Ufologica*, No. 14, July 1994, pp. 10–11, translated by Luciano Iorio.

Chapter 8: Portugal and Spain

1. Ferreira, Captain José Lemos: 'Air Force Pilots Spend 40 Minutes with Saucers', *Flying Saucer Review*, Vol. 4, No. 3, 1958, pp. 2–3.

2. Benítez, Juan José: 'Encuentros en Montaña Roja', *Colección Varia*, Plaza y Janes SA, Esplugues de Llobregat, Barcelona, 1981, pp. 79–84.

3. Department of Defense Intelligence Information Report, US Embassy, Madrid, 22 August 1974.

4. Creighton, Gordon: 'UFO Lands on Spanish Air Force Target Range', *Flying Saucer Review*, Vol. 24, No. 5, 1978, pp. 17–18.

5. *Guardian*, London, 9 January 1975.

6. Creighton, Gordon: 'The Spanish Government Opens its Files', *Flying Saucer Review*, Vol. 23, No. 3, 1977, p. 3.

7. Benítez, Juan José: 'Release of Further Official Spanish Documents on UFOs', *Flying Saucer Review*, Vol. 25, No. 2, 1979, pp. 24–8.

8. *ABC*, Seville, 29 June 1976, quoted in *Flying Saucer Review*, Vol. 22, No. 3, 1976, p. 2.

9. Smith, Dr Willy: 'Unknown Intruder over Portugal', *International UFO Reporter*, Vol. 10, No. 6, November–December 1985, pp. 6–8.

10. Letter to the author from Eugénio Lisboa, Cultural Counsellor, Portuguese Embassy, London, 14 January 1987.

11. Benítez, Juan José: 'Jetliner "Intercepted" by UFO near Valencia', *Flying Saucer Review*, Vol. 25, No. 5, 1979, pp. 13–15.

12. Crivillén, J. Plana: 'The Official Study of the UFO Phenomenon in Spain', *Flying Saucer Review*, Vol. 33, No. 3, 1988, pp. 16–17.

13. Crivillén, J. Plana: 'Encounters in Spanish Air-Space between Aircraft and UFOs', *Flying Saucer Review*, Vol. 34, No. 1, 1989, p. 22; quoting from *'Incidente en Manises'* by J. J. Benítez, published in the *Colección Realismo Fantastico*, Plaza y Janes SA, Esplugues de Llobregat, Barcelona, 1982, and *'Fuera de Control'* by Andreas Faber-Kaiser, published in *Colección Documento*, Planeta SA, Barcelona, 1984.

14. Letter to the author from Vicente-Juan Ballester Olmos, 21 November 1995.

15. Ballester Olmos, Vicente-Juan: 'UFO Declassification in Spain – Military UFO Files Available to the Public: A Balance'; paper presented to the Eighth BUFORA International UFO Congress, Sheffield Hallam University, 19–20 August 1995, published by Information Management, 47d Roland Gardens, London, SW7 3PG.

16. Ballester Olmos, Vicente-Juan: 'Spanish Air Force UFO Files: The Secrets End', *MUFON 1993 International Symposium Proceedings*, edited by Dennis Stacy, Mutual UFO Network, 1993, pp. 140–41. See also *Expedientes Insólitos: El Fenómeno OVNI y Los Archivos de Defensa* by Vicente-Juan Ballester Olmos, published by Temas de Hoy, Madrid, 1995, available from the author: Apartado de Correos 12140, 46080 Valencia, Spain.

17. Fernandes, Joaquim: 'First Scientific UFO Symposium held in Portugal', *MUFON UFO Journal*, No. 311, March 1994, p. 7.

18. *ABC*, Seville, 29 June 1976.

Chapter 9: Australia and New Zealand

1. Letter to the author from W. A. Smither, Defence Public Relations, Department of Defence (Air Force Office), Canberra, 30 August 1982.

2. Department of Defence pro-forma statement, RAAF Public Relations Office.

3. Norman, Paul B.: 'Countdown to Reality', *Flying Saucer Review*, Vol. 31, No. 2, 1986, pp. 13–22.

4. Ibid., p. 14.

5. *Flying Saucer Review*, Vol. 4, No. 3, 1958, p. 6.

6. Norman: op. cit., p. 14.

7. Chalker, W.: 'Australian A.F. UFO Report Files', *APRO Bulletin*, Vol. 30, No. 10, 1982, pp. 5–7.

8. Holledge, James: *Flying Saucers over Australia*, Horwitz Publications, Sydney, 1965, p. 31.

9. Holledge: op. cit., pp. 22–4.

10. Seers, Stan, and Lasich, William: 'North Queensland UFO Saga 1966', *Flying Saucer Review*, Vol. 15, No. 3, 1969, pp. 2–5.

11. Dutton, T. W. S.: 'The Ion Engine and the UFOs', *Australasian Engineer*, Sydney, October 1970.

12. Chalker, W.: 'Australian A.F. UFO Report Files' (Part II), *APRO Bulletin*, Vol. 30, No. 11, 1982, p. 6.

13. Zachary, Ted [Todd Zechel]: 'The CIA Has Proof that UFOs Exist!', *UFO Report*, New York, August 1977.

14. Llewelyn, Ken: *Flight into The Ages*, Felspin Pty Ltd, 16/2 Forest Road, Warriewood, NSW 2102, 1991, pp. 137–9.

15. Chalker, W.: 'Australian A.F. UFO Report Files' (Part I), *APRO Bulletin*, Vol. 30, No. 10, 1982, p. 7.

16. Letter to the author from Wing Commander S. D. White for Chief of Staff, Air Staff, Ministry of Defence Headquarters, Wellington, New Zealand, 6 September 1985.

17. Chalker, W.: 'The North West Cape Incident: UFOs and Nuclear Alert in Australia', *International UFO Reporter*, Center for UFO Studies, January/February 1986, pp. 9–12.

18. Seers, Stan: *UFOs – the Case for Scientific Myopia*, Vantage Press, New York, 1983, pp. 7–11.

19. Letter to the author from Colin A. Phillips, UFO Research Queensland (PO Box 222, 50 Albert Street, Brisbane, Queensland 4002), 1 September 1985.

20. Chalker, W.: 'The UFO Connection: Addendum', *Flying Saucer Review*, Vol. 31, No. 5, 1986, p. 20.

21. Chalker, W.: 'Australian A.F. UFO Report Files' (Part II), pp. 4–5.

22. Holledge: op. cit., p. 89.

23. Hervey, Michael: *UFOs over the Southern Hemisphere*, Horwitz Publications, Sydney, 1969, pp. 18–19.

24. Chalker: 'Australian A.F. UFO Report Files' (Part II), p. 5.

25. Letter to M. L. Roberts, Queensland Flying Saucer Research Bureau (now UFO Research Queensland), from John Meskell, Criminal Investigation Branch, Townsville, 28 July 1965. (A copy of the original is in the author's possession, supplied by Colin Phillips.)

26. Letter to Peter E. Norris, Commonwealth Aerial Phenomena Investigation Organization, from Squadron Leader R. J. Wheeler, Directorate of Air Force Intelligence, 18 August 1965, supplied to the author by Colin Phillips.

27. Letter to Peter Norris from D. S. Graham, for Director-General of Civil Aviation, 3 November 1965.

28. Seers: op. cit., p. 92.

29. Hynek, J. Allen: *The UFO Experience: A Scientific Enquiry*, Abelard-Schuman, London, 1972, p. 15.

30. Hopkins, Budd: *Missing Time: A Documented Study of UFO Abductions*, Richard Marek, New York, 1981, p. 253.

31. Letter to the author from Bruce Cathie, 19 March 1986.

32. Cathie, B. L., and Temm, P. N.: *Harmonic 695: The UFO and Anti-Gravity*, A. H. & A. W. Reed, New Zealand and Australia, 1971, p. 68.

33. Letter to the author from Bruce Cathie, 17 April 1986.

34. Deyo, Stan: *The Cosmic Conspiracy*, West Australian Texas Trading, PO Box 70, Morley, WA 6062, 1978, pp. 28–9.

35. Norman, Paul B.: 'Motherships over Australia', *Flying Saucer Review*, Vol. 24, No. 5, 1978, pp. 9–13.

36. Norman, Paul B.: 'Countdown to Reality', *Flying Saucer Review*, Vol. 31, No. 2, 1986, p. 17.

37. Bolotin, Professor H. H.: 'UFOs – Do They Come From Outer Space?', 1977 (article supplied to the author by the Department of Defence, Air Force Office).

38. Chalker, W.: 'The UFO Connection: Startling Implications for Australia's North West Cape, and for Australia's Security', *Flying Saucer Review*, Vol. 31, No. 5, 1986, pp. 13–21.

39. *Aircraft Accident Investigation Summary Report*, Department of Transport, Ref. No. V116/783/1047, 27 April 1982.

40. Chalker, W.: 'The Missing Cessna and the UFO', *Flying Saucer Review*, Vol. 24, No. 5, 1978, pp. 3–5.

41. Norman, Paul B.: 'Countdown to Reality', p. 17.

42. *Melbourne Herald*, 9 December 1980.

43. Letter to the author from Guido Valentich, September 1985.

44. Letter to the author from William Chalker, 13 September 1985.

45. Chalker, W.: 'Vanished? – The Valentich Affair Re-examined', *Flying Saucer Review*, Vol. 30, No. 2, 1984, pp. 6–12.

46. Haines, Richard F.: *Melbourne Episode: Case Study of a Missing Pilot*, LDA Press, PO Box 880, Los Altos, California 94023-0880, 1987.

47. Chalker, W.: 'Vanished? – The Valentich Affair Re-examined'.

48. Ibid.
49. Ibid.
50. Letter to the author from Guido Valentich, September 1985.
51. Chalker, W.: 'The Valentich–Bass Strait Affair', *The Encyclopedia of UFOs*, ed. Ronald D. Story, New English Library, London, 1980, pp. 379–80.
52. Norman, Paul B.: Article in *The Australian UFO Bulletin*, March 1991, Victorian UFO Research Society, PO Box 43, Moorabbin, Victoria 3189.
53. Chalker, W.: 'The UFO Connection: Startling Implications for Australia's North West Cape, and for Australia's Security', *Flying Saucer Review*, Vol. 31, No. 5, 1986, p. 18.

Chapter 10: Canada

1. Bray, Arthur: *The UFO Connection*, Jupiter Publishing, PO Box 5528, Station 'F', Ottawa, Ontario, K2C 3M1, 1979, pp. 57–66.
2. Letter to Wilfred Daniels, signed on behalf of F. G. Nixon, Director, Telecommunications and Electronics Branch, Department of Transport, 29 April 1964, published in *Flying Saucer Review*, Vol. 10, No. 4, 1964, p. 29.
3. Bray: op. cit., p. 186.
4. Ibid., p. 188.
5. Ibid., pp. 147–52.
6. Ibid., pp. 153–9.
7. Ibid., pp. 62–3.
8. Ibid., pp. 63–6.
9. Ibid., pp. 66–9.
10. Ibid., pp. 70, 191.
11. Edwards, Frank: *Flying Saucers – Serious Business*, Lyle Stuart, New York, 1966, pp. 87–8.
12. Ibid., p. 86.
13. *The Canadian Magazine/Star Weekly*, 4 January 1969.
14. Howard, James: 'The BOAC Labrador Sighting of 1954', *Flying Saucer Review*, Vol. 27, No. 6, 1981, pp. 2–3.
15. Kanon, Gregory M.: 'UFOs and the Canadian Government – Part I', *Canadian UFO Report*, Vol. 3, No. 6, 1975, pp. 21–3.
16. Kanon, Gregory M.: 'UFOs and the Canadian Government – Part II', *Canadian UFO Report*, Vol. 3, No. 7, 1976, pp. 17–18.
17. *Canadian–United States Communications Instructions for Reporting*

Vital Intelligence Sightings (CIRVIS/MERINT) JANAP 146(E), The Joint Chiefs of Staff, Washington, DC 20301, 31 March 1966.

18. *Sun*, Vancouver, 12 January 1985.
19. Kanon, Gregory M.: 'UFOs and the Canadian Government – Part II', pp. 17–18.
20. *Sun*, Vancouver, 12 January 1985.
21. Kanon, Gregory M.: 'UFOs and the Canadian Government – Part II', pp. 17–18.
22. Letter to an enquirer (name deleted) from Brigadier General L. A. Bourgeois, Director, General Information, Department of National Defence, Ottawa, 24 October 1962.
23. Bray: op. cit., p. 56.
24. *Toronto Star*, 10 October 1968.
25. Bray, Arthur: 'Government Cover-up Exposed', *Canadian UFO Report*, Vol. 3, No. 2, 1974, p. 74.
26. Magor, John: *Our UFO Visitors*, Hancock House, Saanichton, BC, Canada, and Seattle, Washington, USA, 1977, p. 74.
27. Letter from John Pushie, *Journal UFO*, Vol. 2, No. 4, 1981, pp. 13–15.
28. *Sun*, Vancouver, 26 April 1976.
29. *Journal UFO*, Vol. 2, No. 2, 1981, p. 11.
30. Rutkowski, Chris: 'The Falcon Lake Incident', Parts I–III, *Flying Saucer Review*, Vol. 27, Nos. 1, 2, and 3, 1981.
31. Cannon, Brian: 'Strange Case of Falcon Lake – Part II', *Canadian UFO Report*, Vol. 1, No. 2, 1969.
32. Lorenzen, Jim and Coral: *UFOs over the Americas*, Signet Books, New York, 1968, p. 41.
33. Rutkowski: op. cit.
34. Letter from Graham Conway, *Flying Saucer Review*, Vol. 29, No. 2, 1983, p. 28.
35. Kanon, Gregory M.: 'UFOs and the Canadian Government – Part I', p. 21.
36. Bray: *The UFO Connection*, p. 45.
37. Kanon, Gregory M.: 'Something's Up Here with Us!', *Canadian UFO Report*, Vol. 4, No. 6, 1978, pp. 3–4.
38. Bray: *The UFO Connection*, p. 45.
39. Kanon: 'Something's Up Here with Us!'
40. Bray: *The UFO Connection*, p. 45.
41. Smith, Wilbert B.: 'Official Reticence', *Flying Saucer Review*, Vol. 6, No. 3, 1960, pp. 30–31, iv.

42. Smith, Wilbert B.: 'Why I Believe in the Reality of the Spacecraft', *Flying Saucer Review*, Vol. 4, No. 6, 1958, pp. 8–11.
43. Letter to Ronald Caswell from Wilbert Smith, 23 February 1959.

Chapter 11: China

1. Heng, Sheng-Yen: 'UFOs – an Unsolved World Puzzle', *People's Daily*, 13 November 1978.
2. *Guang Ming Daily*, 12 May 1980.
3. Stevens, Wendelle C., and Dong, Paul: *UFOs over Modern China*, UFO Photo Archives, PO Box 17206, Tucson, Arizona 85710, 1983, p. 22.
4. Associated Press, 14 July 1947.
5. Stevens and Dong: op. cit., p. 33.
6. Ibid., pp. 44–5.
7. Ibid., p. 45.
8. Ibid., pp. 48–9.
9. Ibid., pp. 49–50.
10. Ibid., pp. 61–3.
11. Ibid., pp. 93–4.
12. Lee, Anthony: 'UFO Reports from China (2)', *Flying Saucer Review*, Vol. 28, No. 4, 1982, pp. 23–4.
13. Stevens and Dong: op. cit., pp. 119–20.
14. Ibid., p. 132.
15. Ibid., pp. 140–41.
16. Ibid., p. 146.
17. Dong: op. cit., p. 18. Report edited for the author by Leslie Banks, DFC, AFC.
18. Stevens and Dong: op. cit., pp. 216–18.
19. Ibid., p. 202.
20. Ibid., pp. 219–20.
21. Ibid., pp. 243–5.
22. *People's Daily*, 28 July and 9 August 1985.
23. *Sunday Express*, London, 25 August 1985.
24. *Liberation Daily*, 30 August 1987.
25. New China News Agency, 28 August 1987.
26. Dong, Paul: 'Army Personnel chased by a UFO, 1990', *The UFO Report 1991*, ed. Timothy Good, Sidgwick & Jackson, London, 1990, pp. 129–30.
27. Dong, Paul: 'The Chinese Scene 1990–91', *The UFO Report 1992*, ed. Timothy Good, Sidgwick & Jackson, London, 1991, pp. 56–7. Article

also supplied to the author by Professor Xie Chu, editor-in-chief of *Aerospace Knowledge*, published by the Chinese Society of Aeronautics & Astronautics, 100083 Beijing, People's Republic of China.

28. *Cheng Du Evening News*, 20 May 1991, quoted by Dong: ibid., p. 57.
29. Letter to the author from Zhang Laigui, Air Attaché, Embassy of the People's Republic of China, London, 25 January 1986.
30. *China Daily*, 27 August 1985.
31. 'China bids for first world UFO conference', *Asian Times*, London, 14 June 1992.
32. Poole, Teresa: 'Close encounters of an intimate kind', *Independent*, London, 17 March 1995.

Chapter 12: The Soviet Union

1. Menzel, Donald H.: *Flying Saucers*, Harvard University Press, Cambridge, Massachusetts, 1953.
2. Zigel, Professor F. Y.: 'Mysteries of the 20th Century: UFOs – What Are They?', ed. B. P. Konstaninov, Vice-President of the USSR Academy of Sciences, *Smena*, Moscow, 7 April 1967.
3. Interview with Professor V. Burdakov, Russian Academy of Sciences, published in *Rabochaya Tribuna*, 13 August 1991.
4. Brill, Joe: 'UFOs Behind the Iron Curtain', *Skylook*, No. 87, February 1975, Mutual UFO Network, pp. 14–15.
5. Gunston, Bill: *Aircraft of the Soviet Union: The Encyclopaedia of Soviet Aircraft Since 1917*, Osprey Publishing, 1983.
6. Letter to the author from V. Bashkirov, Director of the M. V. Frunze Central House of Aviation and Space, Moscow, 22 January 1986.
7. Gindilis, L. M., Menkov, D. A., and Petrovskaya, I. G.: *Observations of Anomalous Atmospheric Phenomena in the USSR: Statistical Analysis*, USSR Academy of Sciences Institute of Space Research Report, PR 473, 1979, pp. 1–74. Translation published as 'NASA Technical Memorandum No. 75665', available from the J. Allen Hynek Center for UFO Studies.
8. Letter to the author from Dr L. M. Gindilis, Sternberg State Astronomical Institute, Moscow, 20 February 1986.
9. Air Intelligence Information Report No. IR 193–55, 13 October 1955.
10. Greenwood, Barry; 'Can We Trust Official Files?', *Just Cause*, No. 35, March 1993, citing a volume of *UFOs: A History*, by Loren Gross (available from Arcturus Books, 1443 S.E. Port St. Lucie Blvd., Port St. Lucie, Florida 34952).

11. See, for example, W. A. Harbinson: *Projekt UFO: The Case for Man-Made Flying Saucers*, Boxtree, London, 1995.

12. There is no doubt, however, that man-made flying saucers have been successfully flown in more recent years, as mentioned in Part Three.

13. Zigel, Dr Felix: 'Unidentified Flying Objects', *Soviet Life*, London, March 1968.

14. Fenoglio, Alberto: 'Oltre il Cielo', *Missile e Razzi*, No. 105, 1–15 June 1962.

15. 'UFOs over Russia', *Flying Saucers*, No. 47, Palmer Publications, Amherst, Wisconsin, May 1966, pp. 6–10.

16. Ibid.

17. Gindilis, Menkov, and Petrovskaya: op. cit.

18. Fenoglio: op. cit.

19. Vyatkin, Lev: 'My Encounter with a UFO', *Aura-Z*, PO Box 224, Moscow 117463, Vol. 1, No. 1, March 1993, pp. 21–3. *Aura-Z* is also available from OVNI Presence, B.P. 57, 13244 Marseille-La Pleine Cedex 01, France.

20. Saunders, David R., and Harkins, R. Roger: *UFOs? Yes!*, Signet Books, New York, 1968, p. 134.

21. *Flying Saucer Review*, Vol. 3, No. 3, 1957, p. 3.

22. Marchetti, Victor: 'How the CIA Views the UFO Phenomenon', *Second Look*, Washington, DC, Vol. 1, No. 7, May 1979, pp. 2–5.

23. Hobana, Ion, and Weverbergh, Julien: *UFOs from Behind the Iron Curtain*, Souvenir Press, London, 1974, p. 25; *Flying Saucer Review*, Vol. 13, No. 6, 1967, p. 2. At the inaugural meeting of the committee, those present also included Professor Heinrich Ludwig; Doctors of Science Nikolai Zhirov and Igor Bestuzhev-Lada; chief of Soviet polar aviation Valentin Akkuratov; Generals Leonid Reino, Georgi Uger and Georgi Zevalkin; twice Hero of the Soviet Union Grigori Sivkov MSc.; Heroes of the Soviet Union docent Yekaterina Ryabova and Natalia Kravtsova.

24. Creighton, Gordon: 'Dr Felix Zigel and the Development of Ufology in Russia – Part I', *Flying Saucer Review*, Vol. 27, No. 3, 1981, p. 9.

25. Ibid. Hobana and Weverbergh report that Stolyarov, not Zigel, made the concluding statement.

26. Brill, Joe: 'UFOs behind the Iron Curtain', *Skylook*, No. 86, Mutual UFO Network, January 1975.

27. *Daily Telegraph*, London, 1 June 1984.

28. Defense Intelligence Agency report, 19 January 1968.

29. Hobana and Weverbergh: op. cit., p. 26.

30. *New York Times*, 10 December 1967.
31. Defense Intelligence Agency report, 19 January 1968.
32. *Phénomènes Spatiaux*, No. 15, January 1968.
33. *Pravda*, Moscow, 29 February 1968.
34. Gindilis, Menkov and Petrovskaya: op. cit.
35. Creighton: op. cit., p. 10.
36. Hunter, Harriot: 'Official UFO Study Programs in Foreign Countries', *Scientific Study of Unidentified Flying Objects*, ed. Dr Edward U. Condon, Bantam Books, New York, 1969, p. 555.
37. Brill: op. cit., p. 14.
38. *Network First: UFO*, produced (with Livia Russell), written and directed by Lawrence Moore; chief consultant Timothy Good: Central Productions for Central Television, 10 January 1995.
39. Gresh, Bryan: 'Soviet UFO Secrets', *MUFON UFO Journal*, No. 306, October 1993, p. 4.
40. Interview with Lawrence Moore and Livia Russell, Moscow, March 1994.
41. Vallee, Jacques, in collaboration with Martine Castello: *UFO Chronicles of the Soviet Union: A Cosmic Samizdat*, Ballantine Books, New York, 1992, pp. 28–30.
42. *Nedelya*, No. 3, 1979.
43. *Tekhnika Molodezhi*, No. 3, 1979.
44. Schnee, Nikita: 'Ufology in the USSR', *Flying Saucer Review*, Vol. 27, No. 1, 1981, pp. 8–13.
45. *Gente*, 31 July and 7 August 1981.
46. Creighton, Gordon: 'Naughty Henry Gris says it again! Soviet Space Centre knocked out by UFOs', *Flying Saucer Review*, Vol. 28, No. 6, 1983, pp. 27–8.
47. *Guardian*, London, 7 January 1983.
48. *The Times*, London, 30 May 1984.
49. Chulkov, Lev: 'UFO and Politics: Several Episodes in the 40-Year History of Soviet Ufology', *Aura-Z*, Vol. 1, No. 1, March 1993, pp. 8–9.
50. Vostrukhin, V.: 'At 4:10 precisely . . . We report in detail', *Trud*, 30 January 1985, translated by Gordon Creighton, *Flying Saucer Review*, Vol. 30, No. 5, 1985, pp. 14–16.
51. Chulkov: op. cit., p. 9.
52. Ibid., citing *Vozdushny Transport*, 25 February 1989.
53. *Krasnaya Zvezda*, 13 April 1985, cited in *Japan Times*, 16 April 1985.

54. 'Classification: "Secret" from the KGB Archives', *Aura-Z*, Vol. 1, No. 1, 1993, p. 13.
55. Hiscock, John: 'KGB signs up for Hollywood', *Sunday Telegraph*, 5 April 1992.
56. KGB file: 'Communication on Observation of Anomalous Event in the District of Kapustin Yar (28 July 1989)', translated by Dimitri Ossipov. Excerpts from this file, selected by Dr Vladimir Zamoroka, are published in *Aura-Z*, Vol. 1, No. 1, March 1993, pp. 19–20.
57. Vallee and Castello: op. cit., pp. 40–61.
58. *Moscow News*, 22 October 1989.
59. Haines, Richard: 'A Scientific Research Trip to the Soviet Union', *The UFO Report 1992*, ed. Timothy Good, Sidgwick & Jackson, London, 1991, pp. 61–2, 63.
60. Good, Timothy: *Alien Liaison: The Ultimate Secret*, Century, London, 1991, pp. 7–10.
61. *Rabochaya Tribuna*, Moscow, 19 April 1990.
62. Foreign Press Note, published by the CIA's Foreign Broadcast Information Service, 2 January 1991.
63. *Sovietskaya Molodezhi*, 4 May 1990.
64. *Pravda*, 27 April 1990.
65. Ibid., 11 October 1990.
66. *Trud*, 5 October 1990.
67. *Literaturnaya Gazeta*, 7 November 1990.
68. Lebedev, Nikolai: 'The Soviet Scene 1990', *The UFO Report 1992*, ed. Timothy Good, Sidgwick & Jackson, London, 1991, pp. 73–7.
69. *Sovietskaya Molodezhi*, 2 November 1990.
70. *Rabochaya Tribuna*, 16 October 1990.
71. Alexandrov, V.: *L'Ours et la Baleine*, Stock, Paris, 1958, cited by Jacques Vallee in *Anatomy of a Phenomenon: Unidentified Objects in Space – A Scientific Appraisal*, Neville Spearman, London, 1966, p. 114.
72. *Daily Telegraph*, London, 5 December 1985.
73. Speech at the Grand Kremlin Palace, Moscow, 16 February 1987, published in *Soviet Life* (supplement), May 1987, p. 7A.

Chapter 13: Defence Intelligence around the World

1. *I Kathimerini*, Athens, 9 July 1952, translated and published in Central Intelligence Agency Report No. OO-W-23682.
2. Marchetti, Victor, and Marks, John D.: *The CIA and the Cult of Intelligence*, Coronet Books, London, 1976, p. 117.

3. Department of Defense Intelligence Information Report No. 1-817-0057-65, 13 September 1965.

4. *Informe Oficial O.V.N.I.*, Summary S# A.02778-DTO, OVNI, Captain Sanchez Moreno, Naval Air Station Comandante Espora, published in 1979 by Major (Ret.) Colman VonKeviczky, ICUFON, 35–40 75th Street, Suite 4G, Jackson Heights, New York, NY 11372.

5. Department of Defense Intelligence Information Report No. 1-804-0123-68, 9 August 1968.

6. ASI, Buenos Aires, 21 April 1964.

7. Uriondo, Oscar A.: 'UFOs over the Andes: Official Gendarmeria reports revealed', *Flying Saucer Review*, Vol. 28, No. 4, 1982, pp. 11–13.

8. Agence France-Presse, 1 August 1995.

9. De Vedia, Mariano, and Arenes, Carolina: 'A reporter from La Nación was in the plane when a UFO was seen over Bariloche', *La Nación*, Buenos Aires, 2 August 1995, translated by Jane Thomas Guma and published in *Flying Saucer Review*, Vol. 40, No. 3, 1995, pp. 20–21.

10. Flight Report (undated) by Captain Oswaldo Sanviti, Compañia de Aviacion 'Faucett' S.A., Hotel Bolivar, Lima.

11. Department of Defense Intelligence Information Report No. 6-876-0146-80, received by the Joint Chiefs of Staff Message Center on 3 June 1980.

12. *O Cruzeiro*, Rio de Janeiro, 11 December 1954.

13. *O Globo*, Rio de Janeiro, 28 February 1958.

14. Letter from Colonel João Glaser, IV COMAR, Força Aérea Brasileira, 28 November 1984, to the Centro Brasileiro de Pesquisas de Discos Voadores (CBPDV – Caixa Postal 2182, R. Bezerra de Menezes 68, 79008-970 Campo Grande (MS), Brazil.

15. Bemelmans, Hans: 'Reports from Ibiuna', *Flying Saucer Review*, Vol. 16, No. 1, 1970, pp. 15–19.

16. Creighton, Gordon: 'Brazil: Censorship of UFO Reports', *Flying Saucer Review*, Vol. 19, No. 6, 1973, p. 29.

17. Fontes, Olavo T., MD: 'UAO Sightings over Trindade', *APRO Bulletin*, January, March, May 1960.

18. Letter to Coral Lorenzen from Dr Olavo Fontes, 27 February 1958.

19. Department of Defense Intelligence Information Report No. 1-809-0112-67, March 1967.

20. Smith, Dr Willy: 'UFO Chase in Brazil (May 1986)', *Flying Saucer Review*, Vol. 32, No. 1, 1987, pp. 6–8. Because of conflicting accounts in the Brazilian press, some details in this case are likely to be inaccurate. My copy of the report in *O Globo* of 24 May 1986, for

example, states that it was Lieutenant Kleber Caldas Marinho who was followed by thirteen radar targets, not Captain Viriato.

21. Letter to Yusuke J. Matsumura from Air Marshal Roesmin Nurjadin, Commander-in-Chief, Indonesian Air Force, Djakarta, 5 May 1967.

22. Letter from Air Commodore J. Salutun, Indonesian Air Force, Member of Parliament, Secretary of the National Aerospace Council of the Republic of Indonesia, published in *UFO News*, Vol. 6, No. 1, 1974, CBA International, Yokohama, Japan.

23. Received by Stanton T. Friedman, 27 October 1977.

24. Sparks, Brad: 'FBI Interrogates UFO Researcher: Government May Confiscate Documents', *APRO Bulletin*, Vol. 27, No. 1, July 1978.

25. Vallee, Jacques, with Castello, Martine: *UFO Chronicles of the Soviet Union: A Cosmic Samizdat*, copyright © 1992 by Jacques Vallee, Ballantine Books, a division of Random House Inc., New York, pp. 82–5.

26. Girvan, Waveney: *Flying Saucers and Common Sense*, Frederick Muller, London, 1955, p. 119.

27. *Flying Saucer Review*, Vol. 1, No. 3, 1955, p. 23.

28. *The Herald*, Harare, 2 August 1985.

29. *The Times*, London, 3 August 1985.

30. Letter to the author from Air Commodore David R. Thorne, Director General Operations, Headquarters, Air Force of Zimbabwe, Harare, 24 October 1985.

31. Letter to the author from Mrs J. Clark, Information Officer, Embassy of Japan, London, 26 November 1986.

32. Interview with General Kanshi Ishikawa, former Chief of Staff, Air Self-Defence Force, when he was Commander of the 2nd Air Wing, Chitose Air Base, published in *UFO News*, Vol. 6, No. 1, p. 123.

33. Letter from Colonel Fujio Hayashi, Commander, Air Transport Wing, Irima Air Squadron, JASDF, *UFO News*, op. cit., p. 123.

34. Draper, Richard [Robert Dorr]: 'Japan's Secret UFO Probe', *UFO Report*, Vol. 5, No. 4, New York, 1978, pp. 26–9, 51.

35. *Guardian*, London, 3 January 1987.

36. *Sunday Mirror*, London, 4 January 1987.

37. *The Times*, London, 6 January 1987.

38. Report by Ronald E. Mickle, Department of Transportation, Federal Aviation Administration, Air Transportation Security, 17 November 1986.

39. *Time*, 18 September 1989.

40. Letter from Prime Minister Toshiki Kaifu to Mayor Shiotani of Hakui City, Ishikawa Prefecture, 24 June 1990.

41. Department of Defense Intelligence Information Report No. 6-846-0139-76, September 1976.

42. *Sightings*, Paramount Pictures, 5555 Melrose Avenue, Mae West 146, Hollywood, California 90038-3197.

43. Department of Defense Intelligence Information Report No. 6-846-0392-78, 19 July 1978.

44. Saunders, Eric: *UFO Cases from Turkey*, available from the author at 209 Silverdale Road, Earley, Reading, RG6 7NY, UK.

45. Ibid.

46. Ibid.

47. Ibid.

48. Ronay, Gabriel: 'Baffling rise in close encounters of the Hungarian kind', *The Times*, London, 19 April 1990.

49. Ronay, Gabriel: 'Hungarians are spaced out by extra-terrestrial sightings', *Scotland on Sunday*, 13 November 1994.

50. *Nepszava* (The People's Voice), Budapest, 18 August 1994.

51. Department of Defense Intelligence Information Report No. 6-807-0136-90, March 1990.

52. De Brouwer, Wilfried: Postface in *Vague d'OVNI sur la Belgique: Un Dossier Exceptionnel*, Société Belge D'Etude des Phénomènes Spatiaux (SOBEPS), Avenue Paul Janson 74, B-1070 Brussels, 1991.

53. Department of Defense Intelligence Information Report No. 2-760-0268-92, September 1992.

54. Turner, Stansfield: *Secrecy and Democracy: The CIA in Transition*, Sidgwick & Jackson, London, 1986, p. 276.

55. Ibid., p. 34.

56. Kennedy, Colonel William V.: *The Intelligence War*, Salamander Books, London, 1983, p. 39.

57. Letter to Clifford E. Stone from Robert C. Hardzog, Freedom of Information and Privacy Act Staff, Defense Intelligence Agency, 1 May 1991.

Chapter 14: The Growing Security Threat

1. Kenneth Arnold had another sighting on 29 July 1947, when twenty to twenty-five small, brass-coloured objects came within 400 yards of his plane as he was flying over La Grande Valley, Oregon. The movie film he took revealed only a few of the objects, and no detail could be made

out. (Arnold, Kenneth, and Palmer, Ray: *The Coming of the Saucers*, Amherst Press, Wisconsin, 1952, pp. 25–7.)

2. Memorandum to the Officer-in-Charge from Frank M. Brown, Special Agent, FBI, 16 July 1947.

3. Letter from Clarence M. Kelley, Director, FBI, 25 October 1973.

4. Interview with Captain E. J. Smith by the District Intelligence Officer, 13th Naval District, Seattle, 9 July 1947.

5. Memorandum to the Commanding General, Army Air Forces, from Lieutenant General Nathan F. Twining, Air Matériel Command, 23 September 1947.

6. Moore, William L.: *Crashed UFOs: Evidence in the Search for Proof*, William L. Moore Publications and Research, 4219 W. Olive Street, Suite 247, Burbank, California 91505, 1985.

7. Report of Aircraft Accident, signed by Major Armond E. Matthews, Wright Field Service Center, Dayton, Ohio, 9 January 1948.

8. *Analysis of Flying Object Incidents in the U.S.*, Air Intelligence Division Study No. 203, Directorate of Intelligence and Office of Naval Intelligence, Washington, DC, 10 December 1948, Appendix (classified Secret), p. 12.

9. Memorandum from Brigadier General C. P. Cabell, USAF, Chief, Air Intelligence Requirements Division, Headquarters, Army Air Forces, 12 February 1948.

10. Memorandum from Major General S. E. Anderson, USAF, Director of Plans and Operations, 3 March 1948.

11. Arnold, Kenneth, and Palmer, Ray: *The Coming of the Saucers*, Amherst Press, Wisconsin, 1952, pp. 90–91.

12. Ruppelt, Edward J.: *The Report on Unidentified Flying Objects*, Doubleday, New York, 1956, pp. 41, 45.

13. Keyhoe, Major Donald E.: *Aliens from Space: The Real Story of Unidentified Flying Objects*, Panther Books, St Albans, UK, 1975, p. 27.

14. *Analysis of Flying Object Incidents in the U.S.*, Summary and Conclusions (classified Top Secret), p. 2.

15. Memorandum from Colonel Eustis L. Poland, for the Commanding General, Headquarters Fourth Army, Fort Sam, Houston, Texas, to the Director of Intelligence, GSUSA, Washington, DC, 13 January 1949.

16. 'Report of Trip to Los Alamos, New Mexico, 16 February 1949' by Commander Richard S. Mandelkorn, US Navy, Research and Development Division, Sandia Base, Albuquerque, 18 February 1949.

17. Memorandum (Secret) from Lieutenant Colonel Doyle Rees, USAF, District Commander, 17th District Office of Special Investigations,

Kirtland AFB, Albuquerque, New Mexico, to the Director of Special Investigations, Office of the Inspector General USAF, Washington 25, DC, 12 May 1949.

18. Memorandum from Lieutenant Colonel Doyle Rees, USAF, to Brigadier General Joseph F. Carroll, Director of Special Investigations, 25 May 1950.

19. Letter to the author from Colonel Anthony Gallo Jr, Colonel, General Staff, Director of Counterintelligence, Department of the Army, Washington, DC, 12 March 1987.

20. FBI memorandum from the Special Agent in Charge, San Antonio, Texas, to the FBI Director (J. Edgar Hoover), 31 January 1949.

21. Memorandum (Confidential) from Major U. G. Carlan, General Staff Corps, Survey Section, US Army (undated).

22. CIA draft report, 15 August 1952.

23. USAF Project Sign Report No. F-TR-2274-1A, February 1949.

24. Memorandum report (Confidential) by Lieutenant Graham E. Bethune, US Naval Reserve, Fleet Logistic Air Wing, Air Transport Squadron One, US Naval Air Station, Patuxent River, Maryland, to Commanding Officer, 10 February 1951.

25. *News Tribune*, Fullerton, California, 26 June 1956.

26. Air Intelligence Information Report No. IR-3-51E, prepared by Lieutenant Colonel Bruce K. Baumgardner, USAF, Director of Intelligence, 21 September 1951.

27. Keyhoe, Major Donald E.: *Flying Saucers from Outer Space*, Henry Holt, New York, 1953, pp. 124–6.

28. Outgoing classified message, Department of the Air Force Staff Message Division, Headquarters USAF, AFOIN-2A3, 16 July 1952.

29. Ruppelt: op. cit., p. 158.

30. US Air Force document entitled: 'Washington, D.C. – Night of 26/27 July 52 (Partially witnessed by Maj. Fournet and Lt. Holcomb, AFOIN-2C5; remainder as reported to them).'

31. Davidson, Dr Leon: *Flying Saucers: An Analysis of the Air Force Project Blue Book Special Report No. 14*, Saucerian Publications, Clarksburg, Virginia, 4th edn, January 1971, p. 48.

32. FBI memorandum from V. P. Keay to A. H. Belmont, 29 July 1952.

33. Ruppelt: op. cit., pp. 2–5.

34. Stringfield, Leonard H.: *Inside Saucer Post – 3-0 Blue*, Civilian Research, Interplanetary Flying Objects, Cincinnati, Ohio, 1957, p. 91.

35. Keyhoe, Major Donald E.: *The Flying Saucer Conspiracy*, Hutchinson, London, 1957, pp. 11–19.

36. Flammonde, Paris: *UFO Exist!*, G. P. Putnam's Sons, New York, 1976, pp. 279–81.
37. Interview with the author, 16 February 1994.

Chapter 15: Collision Course

1. Classified message from Hamilton AFB, California, to Headquarters, USAF, 31 August 1953.
2. Letter from Dr Donald H. Menzel, Harvard College Observatory, to Major John A. Samford, Air Technical Intelligence Center, Dayton, Ohio, 16 October 1953.
3. Letter from Dr Donald Menzel to Senator John F. Kennedy, 3 November 1960.
4. Letter from Colonel George Perry, Directorate of Intelligence, to Brigadier General W. M. Burgess, Deputy for Intelligence, Air Defense Command, Ent AFB, Colorado, 23 December 1953.
5. US Army Intelligence report from Lieutenant Colonel W. Miller, Director, Counterintelligence Division, to the Assistant Chief of Staff, G-2, Washington 25, DC, 10 December 1953.
6. Report filed by Irvin Kabus, 890th CIC Det., 30 April 1954.
7. US Army Order 30-13, 31 January 1957.
8. Classified message from the Commander, 19th Air Division, Carswell AFB, to the Directorate of Intelligence; Commander, Air Defense Command; Commander, Air Technical Intelligence Center; Commander, 8th Air Force, Carswell AFB, 8 February 1954.
9. Keyhoe, Major Donald E.: *The Flying Saucer Conspiracy*, Hutchinson, London, 1957, pp. 48–9.
10. Keyhoe: op. cit., p. 103.
11. Keyhoe, Major Donald E.: *Aliens from Space: The Real Story of Unidentified Flying Objects*, Panther Books, St Albans, UK, 1975, p. 186.
12. Edwards, Frank: *Flying Saucers – Serious Business*, Lyle Stuart, New York, 1966, pp. 69–70.
13. Lorenzen, Coral and Jim: *UFOs: The Whole Story*, Signet, New York, 1969, p. 79.
14. Keyhoe: *Aliens from Space*, pp. 185–6.
15. Fowler, Raymond E.: *Casebook of a UFO Investigator*, Prentice-Hall, Englewood Cliffs, New Jersey, 1981, pp. 182–3.
16. JANAP 146(c), Joint Chiefs of Staff, Joint Communications, Electronics Committee, Washington, DC, 10 March 1954.

17. *Newark Star Ledger*, 22 December 1958.

18. Maney, Professor Charles A.: 'The New UFO Policy of the US Air Force', *Flying Saucer Review*, Vol. 6, No. 5, 1960, pp. 6–9.

19. Memo and reports from the Air Force Special Security Office, Headquarters, Northeast Air Command, APO 862, New York, 18 July 1955.

20. Yost, Graham: *Spy-Tech*, Harrap, London, 1985, p. 17.

21. Branch, David, and Klinn, Robert E.,: 'White Sands Sightings Kept Secret', *Santa Ana Register*, California, 15 November 1972, p. C-2, cited in *Beyond Earth: Man's Contact with UFOs*, by Ralph Blum with Judy Blum, Corgi Books, London, 1974, pp. 102–3.

22. 'Cover Up Exposed', *Santa Ana Register*, 23 November 1972, p. A-11, cited in Blum and Blum: op. cit.

23. Flammonde, Paris: *The Age of Flying Saucers*, Hawthorn Books, New York, 1971, pp. 114–16.

24. *Flying Saucer Review*, Vol. 5, No. 6, 1959, pp. 27–8.

25. Keyhoe: *Aliens from Space*, pp. 89–90.

26. Maccabee, Bruce: 'Hiding the Hardware', *International UFO Reporter*, Vol. 16, No. 5, September/October 1991, pp. 8–9.

27. *New York Sunday Times*, 28 February 1960.

28. UPI, Washington, DC, 14 April 1962.

29. *NICAP Bulletin*, National Investigations Committee on Aerial Phenomena, August 1962.

30. Keyhoe; *Aliens from Space*, pp. 103–4.

31. Ibid., p. 228.

32. Ibid., pp. 152–3.

33. Maney: op. cit., p. 8.

34. *The UFO Investigator*, NICAP, March/April 1965.

35. *Flying Saucer Review*, Vol. 11, No. 3, 1965, pp. 3–4.

36. *Fate*, July 1966.

37. Jacobs, Bob, Ph.D.: 'Deliberate Deception: The Big Sur UFO Filming', *MUFON UFO Journal*, No. 249, January 1989, pp. 3–8.

38. Crain, T. Scott, Jr.: 'UFO Intercepts Rocket', *MUFON UFO Journal*, No. 225, January 1987, pp. 5–6.

39. Lecture by Sid Padrick at Reno, Nevada, 10 July 1966.

40. *The Little Listening Post*, Washington, DC, Vol. 12, No. 3, 1965.

41. Clark, Jerome: 'Two New Contact Claims', *Flying Saucer Review*, Vol. 11, No. 3, 1965, pp. 20–22.

42. Report by Major Damon B. Reeder, Base Operations Officer, Headquarters, Hamilton AFB and 78th Combat Support Group, California

94935, 10 February 1965, forwarded to the Foreign Technology Division, Wright-Patterson AFB.

43. Faulkner, Alex: 'Mystery Men in Flying Saucer Probe', *Sunday Telegraph*, London, 29 January 1967.

44. Rankow, Ralph: 'The Heflin Photographs', *Flying Saucer Review*, Vol. 14, No. 1, 1968, pp. 21–4.

45. Fawcett, Lawrence, and Greenwood, Barry J.: *Clear Intent: The Government Coverup of the UFO Experience*, Prentice-Hall, Englewood Cliffs, New Jersey, 1984, pp. 9–11.

46. Good, Timothy: *Alien Liaison: The Ultimate Secret*, Century, London, 1991, pp. 206–7, 233.

47. Fowler: op. cit., p. 187.

48. Ibid., pp. 186–7.

49. *Birmingham News*, Alabama, 19 October 1973.

50. *Decatur Daily*, Alabama, 16 November 1973.

51. Smith, Warren: 'Invasion of the UFO Space Men', *Saga*, Vol. 49, No. 1, October 1974, pp. 35, 48.

52. 'Near Collision with UFO Report', Army Disposition Form, Flight Operations Office, USAR Flight Facility, Cleveland Hopkins Airport, Cleveland, Ohio 44135, 23 November 1973.

53. *National Enquirer*, 13 December 1973.

54. Zeidman, Jennie: 'Coyne (Mansfield, Ohio) Helicopter Incident', *The Encyclopedia of UFOs*, ed. Ronald D. Story, New English Library, London, 1980, pp. 93–5.

55. Complaint Form, Air Force Office of Special Investigations (AFOSI) District 17, Kirtland AFB, Albuquerque, New Mexico, 14 August 1980.

56. Complaint Form, AFOSI Det 1700, Kirtland AFB, 2–9 September 1980 (source and evaluation by Major Ernest E. Edwards).

57. 'Burns Follow UFO Incident', *APRO Bulletin*, Vol. 29, No. 8, 1981, pp. 1–4.

58. Good: op. cit., p. 127.

59. Schuessler, John: 'Cash–Landrum Case Closed?', *MUFON UFO Journal*, No. 222, October 1986, pp. 12–17.

60. *APRO Bulletin*, Vol. 30, No. 7, 1982, p. 5.

Chapter 16: Central Intelligence

1. Ranelagh, John: *The Agency: The Rise and Decline of the CIA*, Weidenfeld & Nicolson, London, 1986.

2. Yost, Graham: *Spy-Tech*, Harrap, London, 1985, pp. 6–7.

3. Marchetti, Victor, and Marks, John D.: *The CIA and the Cult of Intelligence*, Coronet Books, London, 1976, pp. 96–7.

4. Zachary, Ted [Todd Zechel]: 'The CIA Has Proof that UFOs Exist!', *UFO Report*, New York, August 1977.

5. Klass, Philip J.: *UFOs: The Public Deceived*, Prometheus Books, Buffalo, NY, 1983, p. 10.

6. Freemantle, Brian: *CIA*, Futura, London, 1983, p. 73.

7. Smith, Warren: *UFO Trek*, Zebra Books, New York, 1976, pp. 221–3.

8. Ibid., pp. 224–5.

9. Keyhoe, Major Donald E.: *Aliens from Space*, Panther Books, St Albans, 1975, p. 86.

10. Slate, B. Ann, and Druffel, Ann: 'UFOs and the CIA Cover-Up', *UFO Report*, Vol. 2, No. 4, New York, 1975, p. 20.

11. Keyhoe: op. cit., p. 87.

12. Saunders, Dr David R., and Harkins, R. Roger: *UFOs? Yes!: Where the Condon Committee Went Wrong*, Signet, New York, 1968, p. 105.

13. Leslie, Desmond, and Adamski, George: *Flying Saucers Have Landed*, Werner Laurie, London, 1953.

14. Adamski, George: *Inside the Space Ships*, Arco/Spearman, London, 1956.

15. Stringfield, Leonard: *Inside Saucer Post – 3-0 Blue*, Civilian Research, Interplanetary Flying Objects, Cincinnati, Ohio, 1957, pp. 41–2.

16. Sparks, Brad C.: 'CIA Involvement', *The Encyclopedia of UFOs*, ed. Ronald D. Story, New English Library, London, 1980, p. 73.

17. Stanford, Ray: *Socorro 'Saucer' in a Pentagon Pantry*, Blueapple Books, Austin, Texas, 1976.

18. Fawcett, Larry, and Greenwood, Barry J.: *Clear Intent: The Government Coverup of the UFO Experience*, Prentice-Hall, Englewood Cliffs, New Jersey, 1984, pp. 139–40.

19. Quintanilla, Hector, Jr.: 'The Investigation of UFOs', *Studies in Intelligence*, Central Intelligence Agency, Fall 1966.

20. Fawcett and Greenwood: op. cit., pp. 141–2.

21. Condon, Dr Edward U. (ed.): *Scientific Study of Unidentified Flying Objects*, Bantam Books, New York, 1969.

22. Saunders and Harkins: op. cit.

23. Harder, Dr James: 'UFO Secrecy: The International Dimension', *APRO Bulletin*, Vol. 32, No. 4, 1984, pp. 6–7.

24. Keyhoe: op. cit., p. 103.

25. Ibid., p. 102.

26. Edwards, Frank: *Flying Saucers – Here and Now!*, Lyle Stuart, New York, 1967, pp. 42–3.
27. Fowler, Raymond E.: *Casebook of a UFO Investigator*, Prentice-Hall, Englewood Cliffs, New Jersey, 1981, p. 60.
28. Zechel, W. Todd: 'NI-CIA-AP or NICAP?', *Just Cause*, January 1979, pp. 5–8.
29. Sparks: op. cit.
30. Hall, Richard: *UFO Magazine*, Vol. 10, No. 1, January/February 1995, p. 13.
31. Fawcett and Greenwood: op. cit., pp. 207–8.
32. Lorenzen, Coral and Jim: *UFOs Over the Americas*, Signet, New York, 1968, pp. 187–90.
33. Lorenzen, Coral: 'Hynek: UFO Movement Basically Amateurs', *APRO Bulletin*, Vol. 33, No. 2, 1986, p. 7.
34. Creegan, Dr Robert F.: 'Beyond Hynek', *APRO Bulletin*, Vol. 32, No. 9, 1984, pp. 6–7.
35. *Report to the President by the Commission on CIA Activities within the United States* (Rockefeller Commission), US Government Printing Office, Washington, DC, June 1975, p. 249.
36. Letter to the author from Lee S. Strickland, Information and Privacy Co-ordinator, Central Intelligence Agency, 29 July 1986.
37. Zachary, Ted [Todd Zechel]: 'The CIA Has Proof that UFOs Exist!', *UFO Report*, New York, August 1977.
38. Stringfield, Leonard: *Situation Red: The UFO Siege*, Doubleday, New York, 1977, p. 154.
39. Spaulding, William: 'UFOs: The Case for a Cover Up', *The Unexplained*, Vol. 5, No. 53, Orbis, London, 1981, p. 1044.
40. Smith: op. cit., pp. 210–19.
41. Ibid., pp. 220–28.
42. Interview with the author, 22 January 1986.
43. Copeland, Miles: *The Real Spy World*, Sphere, London, 1978, p. 26.
44. Letter to the author from Larry R. Strawderman, Information and Privacy Co-ordinator, Central Intelligence Agency, 29 November 1983.
45. Freemantle, Brian: *CIA*, Futura, London, 1983.
46. Letter to the author from Brian Freemantle, 9 September 1985.
47. Turner, Admiral Stansfield: *Secrecy and Democracy: The CIA in Transition*, Sidgwick & Jackson, London, 1986, pp. 227–8, 235.
48. Letters to the author from Admiral Stansfield Turner, 18 June and 15 July 1986.

49. Marchetti, Victor: 'How the CIA Views the UFO Phenomenon', *Second Look*, Vol. 1, No. 7, Washington, DC, May 1979, pp. 2–7.

Chapter 17: Aerospace Intelligence

1. *Le Matin*, Paris, 13 May 1962.
2. Stringfield, Leonard: 'Roswell & the X-15: UFO Basics', *MUFON UFO Journal*, No. 259, November 1989, pp. 6–7.
3. *Le Matin*, op. cit.
4. Letter to *Flying Saucer Review* from NASA, 22 May 1962.
5. Stringfield: op. cit.
6. *Time*, 27 July 1962.
7. *Evening Standard*, London, 8 February 1967.
8. Ibid.
9. NASA Management Instruction from Dr Kurt Debus, Director, John F. Kennedy Space Center, 28 June 1967.
10. NASA Information Sheet, NASA Headquarters, Washington, DC 20546, 1 February 1978.
11. Fawcett, Lawrence, and Greenwood, Barry J.: *Clear Intent: The Government's Coverup of the UFO Experience*, Prentice-Hall, Englewood Cliffs, New Jersey, 1984, p. 193.
12. Ball, Ian: 'Flying saucer seen by down-to-earth Carter', *Daily Telegraph*, London, 2 June 1976.
13. Sheaffer, Robert: *The UFO Verdict: Examining the Evidence*, Prometheus Books, Buffalo, New York, 1981, pp. 4–12.
14. Ball: op. cit.
15. Letter from Dr Frank Press, Executive Office of the President, Office of Science and Technology Policy, Washington, DC 20500, 21 July 1977.
16. Letter to Lieutenant General Duward Crow, NASA, from Colonel Charles Senn, Chief, Air Force Community Relations Division, 1 September 1977.
17. Speech by Dr James McDonald to the American Society of Newspaper Editors, Washington, DC, 22 April 1967.
18. Fuller, John G.: *Aliens in the Skies: The Scientific Rebuttal to the Condon Committee Report*, G. P. Putnam's Sons, New York, 1969, p. 87.
19. Sigma, Rho: 'Dr Hermann Oberth looks at UFOs', *Fate*, December 1968, pp. 45–8.
20. Collyns, Robin: *Did Spacemen Colonise the Earth?*, Pelham Books, London, 1974, p. 236.

21. Cramp, Leonard G.: *Piece for a Jig-Saw*, Somerton Publishing Co., Cowes, Isle of Wight, UK, 1966.

22. Letters to the author from Dr Paul D. Lowman Jr, Geophysics Branch, Laboratory for Earth Sciences, NASA, Goddard Space Flight Center, Greenbelt, Maryland 20771, 17 May 1984 and 12 January 1987.

23. Letter to the author from Stephen Darbishire, 9 August 1986.

24. Letter to the author from Scott Carpenter, 30 November 1974.

25. Letter to Scott Carpenter from James A. Lovell, Deputy Director, Science and Applications, NASA, Manned Spacecraft Center, Houston, Texas 77058, 12 December 1972.

26. Roach, Franklin E.: 'Visual Observations Made by Astronauts', *Scientific Study of Unidentified Flying Objects*, ed. Dr Edward U. Condon, Bantam Books, New York, 1969, pp. 207–8.

27. Ibid.

28. Letter to Scott Carpenter from James A. McDivitt, Senior Vice-President, Power Consumers Company, Jackson, Michigan 49201, 27 November 1972.

29. *Today*, NBC-TV, 12 April 1974.

30. *We Seven*, by the Mercury astronauts, Simon & Schuster, New York, 1962, pp. 62–3.

31. Pearson, D., and Anderson, J.: 'U Thant and UFOs', *New York Post*, 27 June 1967.

32. Letter to Ambassador Griffith, Mission of Grenada to the United Nations, New York, from L. Gordon Cooper, Col. USAF (Ret.), 9 November 1978.

33. Beckley, Timothy Green: *MJ-12 and the Riddle of Hangar 18*, Inner Light Publications, PO Box 753, New Brunswick, New Jersey 08903, 1989, pp. 13–14.

34. Video-recording made in 1994 by Michael Hesemann, ETCON, Worringer Strasse 1, D-4000 Düsseldorf 1, Germany.

35. Bamford, James: *The Puzzle Palace*, Sidgwick & Jackson, London, 1983, pp. 192–3.

36. *Omni*, Vol. 8, No. 4, 1986.

37. Berlitz, Charles: *Doomsday 1999 AD*, Doubleday, New York, 1981, pp. 206–7.

38. Hynek, Dr J. Allen: *The UFO Experience: A Scientific Inquiry*, Abelard-Schuman, London, 1972.

39. 'Moondrive Special', BBC Radio 4, 11 December 1972.

40. Letter to the author from Harry Jones, executive assistant to Edgar

D. Mitchell & Associates Inc., Houston, Texas 77017, 6 February 1973.

41. Letter to the author from Edgar D. Mitchell, Sc.D, 21 April 1992.

42. Chriss, Nicholas: 'Cernan Says Other Earths Exist', *Los Angeles Times*, 6 January 1973.

43. Levy, Paul F.: 'Ex-Astronaut: Why I Believe There's Intelligent Life in Space', *National Enquirer*, 23 October 1979.

44. Faucher, Eric; Goodstein, Ellen; and Gris, Henry: 'Alien UFOs Watched Our First Astronauts on Moon', *National Enquirer*, 11 September 1979.

45. Chatelain, Maurice: *Our Ancestors Came from Outer Space*, Pan Books, London, 1980, p. 25.

46. Ibid.

47. Letter to the author from Paul D. Lowman Jr, NASA, Goddard Space Flight Center, 17 May 1984.

48. Letter to the author from John McLeaish, Chief, Public Information, Public Affairs Office, NASA, Manned Spacecraft Center, Houston, Texas 77058, 20 May 1970.

49. Letter to Major (Ret.) Colman VonKeviczky, 24 May 1988.

50. Letter to the author from Neil A. Armstrong, 29 December 1986.

51. *Niewe Gazet*, Antwerp, Belgium, 20 January 1984.

52. Von Rétyi, Andreas: *Das Alien Imperium: UFO-Geheimnisse der USA*, Langen Müller, Munich, 1995. (The extracts quoted from lengthy interviews with 'Dr Cris' by Andreas von Rétyi were translated by Dorothee Walter.)

53. Various letters to the author from Andreas von Rétyi, August/ September 1995.

Chapter 18: The Roswell Incident

1. Interview with Jesse A. Marcel Sr by Bob Pratt, 8 December 1979, published in Karl T. Pflock: *Roswell in Perspective*, Fund for UFO Research Inc., PO Box 277, Mount Rainier, Maryland 20712, 1994, pp. 119–26.

2. Berlitz, Charles, and Moore, William: *The Roswell Incident*, Granada, London, 1980, pp. 68–9.

3. Interview with the author, Roswell, 1 June 1993.

4. Moore, William L.: *Crashed UFOs: Evidence in the Search for Proof*, William L. Moore Publications and Research, 4219 W. Olive Street, Suite 247, Burbank, California 91505, 1985, p. 46.

5. Pflock: op. cit., pp. 84–5.
6. Affidavit by Jesse A. Marcel Jr, M.D., 6 May 1991, published in Pflock: op. cit., p. 162.
7. Pflock: op. cit., p. 88.
8. Affidavit by Bessie Brazel Schreiber, published in Pflock: op. cit., p. 169.
9. Interview with Dr Jesse Marcel Jr by Vicki Cooper Ecker (ed.): *UFO magazine*, PO Box 1053, Sunland, California 91041-1053, Vol. 10, No. 2, March/April 1995, pp. 14–15.
10. Cox, Billy: 'Crash at Roswell: UFO Cover-up?', *Florida Today*, Melbourne, Florida, 24 November 1991.
11. Randle, Kevin D., and Schmitt, Donald R.: *UFO Crash at Roswell*, Avon Books, New York, 1991, pp. 108–11.
12. Alleged memorandum to the Joint Intelligence Committee from R. H. Hillenkoetter, Rear Admiral, USN, Director of Central Intelligence, Central Intelligence Group, Washington 25, DC, 19 September 1947.
13. See, for example, 'New Evidence of MJ-12 Hoax', by Philip J. Klass, *The Skeptical Inquirer*, Vol. 14, No. 2, Winter 1989, pp. 135–40, and 'The Crashed Saucer Forgeries', *International UFO Reporter*, Vol. 15, No. 2, March–April 1990.
14. Friedman, Stanton T.: *Final Report on Operation Majestic 12*, Fund for UFO Research, 1990.
15. Moore, William L., and Shandera, Jaime H.: *The MJ-12 Documents: An Analytic Report*, William L. Moore Publications and Research, 1990.
16. Letter to Lee M. Graham from Richard M. Bissell Jr, 30 July 1987.
17. Letter to Philip J. Klass from Richard M. Bissell Jr, 29 September 1987.
18. Cameron, Grant, and Crain, T. Scott Jr.: *UFOs, MJ-12 and the Government: A Report on Government Involvement in UFO Crash Retrievals*, MUFON, 103 Oldtowne Road, Seguin, Texas 78155-4099, 1991, pp. 8–10.
19. Ibid., pp. 12–13.
20. Wise, David, and Ross, Thomas B.: *The Invisible Government*, Bantam Books, New York, 1965, p. 278.
21. Friedman: op. cit., pp. 13–22.
22. Letter from Lt. Gen. Nathan Twining to J. E. Schaefer, Boeing Airplane Company, 17 July 1947. Additional quotes supplied by William Moore in *Phil Klass & The Roswell Incident: The Sceptics Deceived*, William L. Moore Publications and Research, 1986.
23. Randle, Kevin D., and Schmitt, Donald R.: *The Truth About the UFO Crash at Roswell*, M. Evans, New York, 1994, pp. 62–3.
24. Randle and Schmitt: *UFO Crash at Roswell*, pp. 231–3.

25. Berlitz and Moore: op. cit., pp. 57–63.
26. *The Roswell Events*: Congressional Staff briefing prepared by Fred Whiting and the Fund for UFO Research Inc., PO Box 277, Mount Rainier, Maryland 20712, 1993.
27. Friedman, Stanton T., and Berliner, Don: *Crash at Corona: The U.S. Military Retrieval and Cover-up of a UFO*, Paragon House, New York, p. 88.
28. *The Roswell Events*.
29. Friedman and Berliner: op. cit., pp. 89–97.
30. Randle and Schmitt: *UFO Crash at Roswell*.
31. Pflock: op. cit., pp. 41–53.
32. Interviews with the author, January–March 1988.
33. Affidavit by Glenn Dennis, 7 August 1991, published in Pflock: op. cit., pp. 149–52.
34. Affidavit by Sappho Henderson, 9 July 1991, published in Pflock: op. cit., p. 157.
35. *Network First: UFO*, Central Productions for Central Television, 10 January 1995.
36. Interview with Fred Whiting of the Fund for UFO Research, *Network First: UFO*.
37. *Network First: UFO*.
38. *Report of Air Force Research Regarding the 'Roswell Incident'*, July 1994, released by US Air Force Public Affairs Media Relations Division, 8 September 1994.
39. *Government Records: Results of A Search for Records Concerning the 1947 Crash Near Roswell, New Mexico*, document number GAO/NSIAD-95-187, US General Accounting Office, PO Box 6015, Gaithersburg, Maryland 20884-6015.

Chapter 19: Down to Earth

1. Scully, Frank: *In Armour Bright*, Chilton, 1963, p. 199.
2. Scully, Frank: *Behind the Flying Saucers*, Henry Holt, New York, 1950, pp. 128–37.
3. Stringfield, Leonard H.: *UFO Crash/Retrievals: Amassing the Evidence*, Status Report III, published by the author, 4412 Grove Avenue, Cincinnati, Ohio 45227, 1982, p. 10.
4. Ibid., p. 33.
5. Steinman, William S., and Stevens, Wendelle C.: *UFO Crash at Aztec: A*

Well Kept Secret, UFO Photo Archives, PO Box 17206. Tucson, Arizona 85710, 1987, p. 199.

6. Moore, William L.: *Crashed UFOs: Evidence in the Search for Proof*, William L. Moore Publications and Research, 4219 W. Olive Street, Suite 247, Burbank, California 91505, 1985, pp. 23–4.

7. Steinman and Stevens: op. cit., p. 258.

8. *The Groom Lake Desert Rat*, PO Box 448, Rachel, Nevada 89001, Issue 23, 17 March 1995, pp. 1–5.

9. Good, Timothy: *Alien Liaison: The Ultimate Secret*, Century/Arrow, London, 1991/1992. The updated American edition, *Alien Contact: Top-Secret UFO Files Revealed*, published by William Morrow, New York, 1993, contains additional information relating to the claims of Robert Lazar.

10. Interview with the author, 17 May 1995.

11. Report by Chuck Oldham, published by Leonard Stringfield in his *UFO Crash/Retrievals: The Inner Sanctum*, Status Report VI, 1991, pp. 40–44.

12. Wilbert Smith's handwritten notes were obtained from his widow by Arthur Bray.

13. Berlitz, Charles, and Moore, William: *The Roswell Incident*, Granada, London, 1980, p. 51.

14. Stringfield, Leonard H.: 'Retrievals of the Third Kind – Part I', *Flying Saucer Review*, Vol. 25, No. 4, 1979, p. 43, and Fritz Werner's affidavit (copy in the author's files).

15. Stringfield, Leonard H.: *UFO Crash/Retrievals: Amassing the Evidence*, Status Report III, 1982, p. 43.

16. Randle, Kevin D.: *A History of UFO Crashes*, Avon, New York, 1995, p. 59.

17. Stringfield, Leonard H.: 'UFO Crash/Retrievals: The Concept of Proof', *Flying Saucer Review*, Vol. 37, No. 4, 1992, p. 12; originally published in *For the People*, USA, April 1990.

18. Stringfield: *UFO Crash/Retrievals: Amassing the Evidence*, pp. 27–30.

19. Ibid., pp. 12–13.

20. Ibid., pp. 24–5.

21. Stringfield, Leonard H.: 'The UFO Crash/Retrieval Syndrome Status Report II: New Sources, New Data, Part I', *Flying Saucer Review*, Vol. 28, No. 2, 1982, pp. 6–7.

22. Stringfield, Leonard H.: 'The UFO Crash/Retrieval Syndrome Status Report II', *Flying Saucer Review*, Vol. 28, No. 4, 1982, p. 6.

23. Schwarz, Berthold Eric, MD: *UFO Dynamics: Psychiatric and Psychic*

Dimensions of the UFO Syndrome, Book II, Rainbow Books/Betty Wright, PO Box 1069, Moore Haven, Florida 33471, 1983, pp. 536–45.

24. Letter to the author from Berthold Schwarz MD, 10 October 1983.
25. Letter to William S. Steinman from Dr Robert I. Sarbacher, Washington Institute of Technology (Oceanographic and Physical Sciences), Palm Beach, Florida 33480, 29 November 1983.
26. *Flying Saucer Review*, Vol. 2, No. 1, 1956, p. 2.
27. *Flying Saucer Review*, Vol. 11, No. 2, 1965, pp. 8–9.

Chapter 20: Beyond Top Secret

1. Bamford, James: *The Puzzle Palace*, Sidgwick & Jackson, London, 1983.
2. Letter to Robert Todd from the NSA's information officer, 20 February 1976.
3. Fawcett, Lawrence, and Greenwood, Barry J.: *Clear Intent: The Government Coverup of the UFO Experience*, Prentice-Hall, Englewood Cliffs, New Jersey, 1984, pp. 181–2.
4. Memorandum Opinion and Order Granting Motion for Summary Judgement in the US District Court, District of Columbia: *Citizens Against UFO Secrecy* (Plaintiff) v. *National Security Agency* (Defendant), 18 November 1980.
5. Department of the Army Information Security Program, Army Regulation (AR) 380-5, quoted in Clifford E. Stone: *UFOs: Let The Evidence Speak For Itself*, Image Colors Graphic California, 1991, p. 68.
6. Ibid., p. 67.
7. *In-camera* affidavit of Eugene F. Yeates (NSA), US District Court of the District of Columbia, 9 October 1980.
8. Moore, William L.: 'CAUS v/s NSA Lawsuit goes to US Supreme Court', *APRO Bulletin*, Vol. 30, No. 1, 1982, pp. 2–3.
9. Bamford: op. cit., pp. 155–6.
10. Zachary, Ted [Todd Zechel]: 'The CIA Has Proof that UFOs Exist!', *UFO Report*, New York, August 1977.
11. Good, Timothy: *Alien Liaison: The Ultimate Secret*, Century/Arrow, London, 1991/1992. For a complete transcript of the recorded conversation with Admiral B. R. Inman, see *Alien Update*, ed. Timothy Good, Arrow, London, 1993/Avon Books, New York, 1995.
12. Letter to the author from James J. Devine, Director of Policy, National Security Agency, Central Security Service, Fort George G. Meade, Maryland 20755, 4 November 1983.
13. Letter to the author from Frederick J. Berghoff, Deputy Director of

Policy, National Security Agency, Central Security Service, 21 June 1984.

14. Letter from Todd Zechel, *International UFO Reporter*, Center for UFO Studies, November/December 1985, pp. 17–19.

15. Friedman, Stanton T.: 'The Case for the Extraterrestrial Origin of Flying Saucers', *1979 MUFON UFO Symposium Proceedings*, p. 215.

16. Ware, Donald: 'Security Policy', *MUFON UFO Journal*, No. 212, December 1985, pp. 7, 18.

17. Friedman, Stanton T.: 'Flying Saucers are Real', *Worlds Beyond*, ed. Larry Geis and Fabrice Florin, with Peter Beren and Aidan Kelly, And/ Or Press, PO Box 2246, Berkeley, California 94702, p. 221.

18. Andrus, Walter H. Jr: 'UFOLOGY: The Emergence of a New Science', *MUFON UFO Journal*, No. 295, November 1992, p. 3.

19. Harder, Professor James A.: 'UFO Secrecy – the International Dimension', *APRO Bulletin*, Vol. 32, No. 4, 1984, pp. 6–7.

20. Friedman, Stanton T.: 'A Scientific Approach to Flying Saucer Behavior', Joint Symposium sponsored by the Los Angeles and Orange County sections of the American Institute of Aeronautics & Astronautics and the Los Angeles section of the World Future Society, Los Angeles, 27 September 1975.

21. Marchetti, Victor: 'How the CIA Views the UFO Phenomenon', *Second Look*, Vol. 1, No. 7, Washington, DC, May 1979, pp. 2–7.

22. Smith, Warren: *UFO Trek*, Zebra Books, New York, 1976, pp. 220–28.

23. Remarks made by Jesse Marcel Jr., MD, Midwest Conference on UFO Research, Springfield, Missouri, 7–19 September 1992, transcribed by Robert J. Durant.

24. Letter to the author from Jesse Marcel Jr, 8 August 1995.

25. Strieber, Whitley: *Breakthrough: The Next Step*, HarperCollins, New York, 1995, pp. 249–50.

26. Campbell, Glenn: 'The Story of "Jarod"', *The Groom Lake Desert Rat*, PO Box 448, Rachel, Nevada 89001, Issue 24, 4 April 1995, pp. 1–3.

27. *The Free Press*, Detroit, Michigan, August 1971.

28. *UFOs and Project Blue Book*, Fact Sheet, United States Air Force, Public Affairs Division, Wright-Patterson AFB, Ohio 45433, January 1985.

29. Letter to the author from William L. Birkholz, 1 February 1995.

30. Condon, Dr Edward U. (ed.), *Scientific Study of Unidentified Flying Objects*, Bantam Books, New York, 1969.

31. *Aeronautics & Astronautics*, Vol. 8, No. 11, November 1970, p. 49.

32. Project Blue Book Special Report No. 14 (Analysis of Reports of Unidentified Aerial Objects), Project No. 10073, Air Technical

Intelligence Center, Wright-Patterson Air Force Base, Ohio, 5 May 1955.

33. Friedman, Stanton T.: 'The Case for the ET Origin of UFOs', *MUFON Symposium Proceedings*, July 1979, p. 213.

34. National Archives and Records Administration withdrawal notices.

35. Letter to Major Donald E. Keyhoe from C. G. Jung, 16 August 1958.

36. Good: op. cit.

37. Huneeus, J. Antonio: 'Science Frontiers', *New York City Tribune*, 12 May 1988, and the UN verbatim record.

38. 'MacArthur Greets Mayor of Naples', *New York Times*, 8 October 1955.

39. 'Duty, Honor, Country': address by General Douglas MacArthur upon his acceptance of the Sylvanus Thayer Award at the United States Military Academy, West Point, New York, 12 May 1962, published by Armed Forces Information and Education, Department of Defense, US Government Printing Office, 1962.

40. Statement to the US Congress by Rear Admiral R. H. Hillenkoetter, 22 August 1960, cited in Major Donald E. Keyhoe: *Aliens from Space*, Panther Books, London, 1975, p. 103.

Appendix

Some British and American UFO Journals

Flying Saucer Review
FSR Publications Ltd, PO Box 162,
High Wycombe, Bucks, HP13 5DZ, UK

Journal of UFO Studies
The J. Allen Hynek Center for UFO Studies,
2457 W. Peterson Avenue, Chicago, Illinois 60659, USA
(N.B. Scientific papers only)

MUFON UFO Journal
The Mutual UFO Network, 103 Oldtowne Road,
Seguin, Texas 78155-4099, USA

UFO
PO Box 1053, Sunland, California 91041-1053, USA

UFO Magazine
Quest Publications International Ltd,
1st Floor, 66 Boroughgate, Otley near Leeds,
LS21 1AE, UK

For details of UFO magazines available in other countries, as well as addresses of other UFO organizations, please consult the Reference section.

Index